ANCIENT SPARTA

PLATE 1.—DEDICATION TO ORTHIA BY A BOAGOS WITH IRON
SICKLE PRESERVED (see pp. 88, 95, 254 f.).

ANCIENT SPARTA

A RE-EXAMINATION OF THE EVIDENCE

BY

K. M. T. CHRIMES, M.A. (Oxon.)

ὅπῃ ἂν ὁ λόγος ὥσπερ πνεῦμα φέρῃ, ταύτῃ ἰτέον

MANCHESTER
UNIVERSITY PRESS

First published by Manchester University Press 1949
Reprinted 1952
Special edition for Sandpiper Books Ltd, 1999

Published by Manchester University Press
Oxford Road, Manchester M13 9NR
http://www.man.ac.uk/mup

British Library Cataloguing-in-Publication Data
A catalogue record for this book is available from the British Library

05 04 03 02 01 00 99   7 6 5 4 3

ISBN 0 7190 5741 8

Printed in Great Britain by
Bookcraft (Bath) Ltd, Midsomer Norton

INTRODUCTION

No student of ancient Greece could be satisfied with the present state of our knowledge about Sparta. A city which undoubtedly had more influence upon Greek history than any other except Athens chose to hide from the world at that period the true nature of its own institutions, but at the same time allowed it to be known that these institutions were what would now be called 'totalitarian' in character, utterly opposed to any theory of the state acceptable to other Greeks. Whether Sparta really was unique, and how, if so, this came about, are questions which cannot be answered from the evidence directly relating to the pre-Hellenistic period. But in the present century a very large body of new material has become available through the excavations at Sparta conducted by the British School at Athens, and in particular through the labours of Kolbe and Woodward upon the epigraphical part of this material. These inscriptions, since they relate to the Hellenistic and Roman periods, have not hitherto received much attention from historians whose main interest lies with Sparta in the time of its political importance. But a closer study of them does in fact reveal so many obvious survivals from an early period that it has seemed desirable to make a study of later Sparta, based mainly upon the epigraphical evidence, the starting-point for a fresh examination of the evidence about the earlier period. It is for this reason that a chronological arrangement has not in the main been followed. Of the two main sections into which the material has been divided, Part I relates to the later and Part II to the earlier Sparta, the object in view throughout being to trace constitutional and social survivals back to their roots in the past. Each separate chapter in fact depends in large measure on what precedes it, and the writer asks that it should be borne continually in mind that although many different explanations may be possible of any one section of the material viewed in isolation, the only solution which can be regarded as satisfactory must be that which accounts for all the ascertainable facts. To strive for that ideal is after all the duty of the historian.

From these preliminary observations it will be seen that the work is not intended as a complete history of Sparta ; it is in fact little concerned with political history except in the obscure period linking the age of independence with Roman times. The investigations contained in it lead to a number of conclusions which are opposed to widely accepted views, conclusions which are in the main the following : (1) the Spartan *agoge* was not the work of any lawgiver, but a spontaneous growth from conditions of society in a very remote period ; (2) the institutions of that primitive period were feudal in character ; (3) there were never at any time five Spartan tribes, or five villages, which could account for the number of the ephors ; (4) the ephors originated in the Homeric period as assistants to the king and to the *phylobasileis* ; (5) the doubling of the monarchy is to be associated with the Lycurgan reforms, and with the substitution of a unified state for the earlier feudal system.

A word must be said in explanation of the Appendices, which deal with special questions of detail incident to the main enquiry. They are included with the rest of the work in the belief that each contributes something to the main thesis, and Appendix IV in particular is indispensable as evidence for the organisation of the training ' herds ' and of the whole social and political system in the Roman period. Appendix V (*The Hereditary Priesthoods*) also provides one of the main links between Roman and early Greek times.

Consistency in the spelling of technical and proper names, a problem which has baffled all my predecessors in the field of Greek and Roman history, presents particular difficulties in a work dealing with both the Greek and the Roman periods, and with individuals who bore both Greek and

Roman names at once, and I am conscious that I have failed to achieve it. Names of common occurrence in earlier works have for the most part been given in their Latin form ; unfamiliar personal and technical names have been retained in their Greek spelling.

I wish to record my grateful thanks to those who have read my manuscript or have helped me in other ways to prepare the work for the Press, and especially to Sir John L. Myres, to whom I am indebted for reading the whole and for many valuable criticisms ; to my husband, Professor Donald Atkinson, for unfailing encouragement and for great assistance in the compilation of the indices ; and to Miss Phyllis Corner, for typing the manuscript.

The book appears under the auspices of the Tout Memorial Publications Fund Committee, to whom my especial thanks are due. I have also to thank the Trustees of the Council of the Society for the Promotion of Hellenic Studies, the Trustees of the late Sir Arthur Evans, and Messrs. Macmillan and Co., for courteous permission to reproduce illustrations from books published by them. Plates 1–3, 7 and 9 are taken either in whole or in part from illustrations in *Artemis Orthia* (edited by R. M. Dawkins, 1929), Plates 4 and 5 from Sir Arthur Evans' *Palace of Minos* (1921–1936).

Since no map suitable for my purpose existed, the map at the end of the book is based on the evidence of the Ordnance Survey map of Greece (1 : 1,000,000), Provisional Edition, North J 34 (Athenai), 1915 ; the *Admiralty Handbook of Greece* (1 : 1,000,000), 1920 ; *Inscriptiones Graecae*, vol. V, i., 1913, and the *Journal of Hellenic Studies*, vol. XV, Plate 1.

The work was completed for press in 1944 and since that time only minor alterations have been possible. Works published abroad during the war period were thus inaccessible to me.

KATHLEEN CHRIMES ATKINSON

University College, Leicester

July 1948

CONTENTS

PART I

SPARTA IN THE HELLENISTIC AND ROMAN PERIODS

PART II

THE EARLIER SPARTA

LIST OF PLATES

LIST OF ABBREVIATIONS
AND EDITIONS

Admiralty Handbook. Handbook of Greece, compiled by the Geographical section of the Naval Intelligence Division, Naval Staff, Admiralty, Vol. I, ed. 1, 1920.

A.J.A. American Journal of Archæology.

Artemis Orthia. The Sanctuary of Artemis Orthia at Sparta, ed. Dawkins, 1929 ; published by the Council of the Society for the Promotion of Hellenic Studies : Supplementary Paper No. 5.

A.O. (followed by a number) refers to the inscriptions of Chapter X of *Artemis Orthia* (*cf.* above).

Beloch, Gr. Gesch. Griechische Geschichte, 2 Auflage, 1912–1927.

Bluemner, Technologie. Technologie u. Terminologie der Gewerbe u. Künste der Griechen u. Römern, ed. 2 1912.

B.M.C. (Pelop., etc.). Catalogue of the Greek Coins in the British Museum ; (Peloponnesus, by P. Gardner, 1887, etc.).

B.S.A. Annual of the British School at Athens.

Busolt-Swoboda. Busolt, Griechische Staats- und Rechtsaltertümer, ed. 3, bearbeitet von H. Swoboda, in Iwan Müllers Handbuch des Altertumswissenschaft, vol. IV, i. 1, Griechische Staatskunde, 1 Hälfte (1920) ; 2 Hälfte (1926).

C.A.H. Cambridge Ancient History, 1923–39.

Cauer, Delectus². Delectus Inscriptionum Graecarum propter dialectum memorabilium, ed. 2, 1883.

C.I.G. Boeckh, Corpus Inscriptionum Graecarum, 4 vols., 1827–1877.

C.I.L. Corpus Inscriptionum Latinarum.

Clinton, F. H. Fasti Hellenici, 3 vols., 1834.

Dar-Sagl. Daremberg et Saglio, Dictionnaire des Antiquités grecques et romaines, 5 vols., 1881–1919.

Diehl. Anthologia Lyrica, Teubner, vol. 1, ed. 2, 1933 ; vol. 2, ed. 1, 1925.

Eckhel. Doctrina Numorum Veterum, ed. 2, 1839.

F. Gr. Hist. Jacoby, Die Fragmente der Griechischen Historiker (2 Teil, Bd. iii, 1929).

F.H.G. Müller, Fragmenta Historicorum Graecorum, 5 vols., 1841–70.

H.N.² Head Historia Numorum, ed. 2, 1911.

I.G. Inscriptiones Graecae, ed. 1 (vol. V, i. Inscriptiones Laconiae et Messeniae, ed. Kolbe, 1913).

Inscr. Iur. Gr. Dareste, Haussoullier, Reinach, Recueil des Inscriptions Juridiques grecques, 2 vols., 1891–1904.

I.L.S. Dessau, Inscriptiones Latinae Selectae, 3 vols., 1892–1916.

Jahrb. Inst. Jahrbuch des deutschen archäologischen Instituts.

J.H.S. Journal of Hellenic Studies.

J.R.S. Journal of Roman Studies.

Kahrstedt, Sparta. Griechische Staatsrecht, Bd. I, Sparta und seine Symmachie, etc., 1922.

Kornemann, Neue Dokumente. Neue Dokumente zum lakonischen Kaiserkult, 1929.

L.—S. Liddell and Scott, Greek Lexicon ed., Stuart Jones (1925–40).

M.A.L. Monumenti Antichi, publicati a cura della Reale Accademia dei Lincei, 1889–

Müller, Dorians. Müller, The History and Antiquities of the Doric Race, ed. 2 (1839).

Pfuhl, Malerei und Zeichnung. Malerei und Zeichnung der Griechen, 3 vols., 1923.

Pfuhl, Meisterwerke. Meisterwerke griechischer Zeichnung und Malerei, 1924.

Philol. Philologus, Zeitschrift für das klassische Alterthum, Göttingen.

P.I.R. Prosopographia Imperii Romani, ed. 1897/8 : ed. 2, partes 1 and 2, 1933–6. Klebs, etc.

P. of M. Sir Arthur Evans, The Palace of Minos, 4 vols. and Index, 1921–1936.

Poralla. Prosopographie der Lakedaemonier bis auf die Zeit Alexanders des Grossen, Diss., Breslau, 1913.

P.W. Paulys Real-Encyclopädie der classischen Altertumswissenschaft, neue Bearbeitung von Wissowa und Kroll.

Roscher. Ausführliches Lexikon der griechischen und römischen Mythologie, 1884.

S.G.D.I. Collitz-Bechtel, Sammlung der griechischen Dialektinschriften, 4 vols, 1884–86.

Sitz. Berl. Akad. Sitzungsberichte der Kgl. Preussischen Akademie der Wissenschaften zu Berlin.

Sparta Catalogue. Tod and Wace, A Catalogue of the Sparta Museum, 1906.

*   *   *   *   *   *   *   *   *   *

Aristotle, Politics. References are to Opera ed. Bekker, vol. X, 1837.

Hesiod, Works and Days. References are to Opera, ed. Teubner, 1878.

Philostratus, Vita Apollonii. References are to Opera, ed. Kayser (Zürich), 1844.

Pindar, Carmina. References are to Pindar, ed. Donaldson, 1868 (cited by heavy type numbers).

Pliny, Naturalis Historia. References are to N.H., ed. Detlefsen, 1866 (cited by small marginal sections).

Polybius, Histories. References are to Opera ed. Hultsch (Berlin), 1867–1872.

Strabo. References are to Geographica, ed. Teubner (cited by the pages of Casaubon's edition).

PART I

SPARTA IN THE HELLENISTIC AND ROMAN PERIODS

CHAPTER I

RELATIONS WITH THE ACHAEAN LEAGUE AND WITH ROME

THUCYDIDES tells us that he is unable to give a detailed account of the Spartan military organisation because the facts of their constitution are kept secret : [1] Strabo refuses to describe the Spartan constitution and its vicissitudes because they are so well known.[2] These two extreme points of view reflect not merely the personal judgment of the two writers, but a real change, and may well serve as an excuse for beginning a history of Spartan political institutions by examining them as they existed in the Roman period. At least from the time of the annexation of Achaea, Sparta held few secrets for the Romans, and what there was to learn from present contact with Laconia could be supplemented from several books which had been written upon the antiquities and existing institutions of Sparta during the Hellenistic period, when political reasons for secrecy existed no longer. Many foreign philosophers had been attracted to Sparta during this period by the reputed superiority of her political institutions to those of all other Greek states, and the result was a spate of *Constitutions of Sparta*, especially in the third century B.C.[3] Moreover,

[1] Thuc. V, 68 : διὰ τῆς πολιτείας τὸ κρυπτόν.

[2] Strabo, VIII, 365 : περὶ δὲ τῆς Λακώνων πολιτείας καὶ τῶν γενομένων παρ' αὐτοῖς μεταβολῶν τὰ μὲν πολλὰ παρείη τις ἂν διὰ τὸ γνώριμον.

[3] Apart from Aristotle's allusion to works on Sparta by ' Thibron and others ' (*Pol.* VII, 14. 17), Λακεδαιμονίων Πολιτεῖαι or Λακωνικά are ascribed to Dioscorides, a pupil of Isocrates, to Dicaearchus of Messene, a pupil of Aristotle, to Persaeus of Citium, a Stoic philosopher who flourished about 260 B.C., to Sphaerus the Borysthenite who wrote

excavations at Sparta have yielded a mass of inscriptions of the period of the Principate, and it is one of the main purposes of this book to examine these, and to decide what light they throw upon the most secretive state of the pre-Roman period.

In Strabo's time Sparta was a *civitas libera et immunis*,[1] and as such enjoyed its own laws and exemption from Roman interference. But the question arises whether it was not already a totally changed Sparta to which Rome gave this privileged status. It is impossible to accept Cicero's sweeping statement that Sparta in his time, alone among ancient states, had preserved her customs and laws unchanged for over seven hundred years.[2] Obvious facts give Cicero the lie at once ; for example, the traditional dual kingship disappeared with the reign of Cleomenes III (*c.* 235–221 B.C.), and there were no more kings at all after the murder of Nabis (192 B.C.) during a war with the Achaean League. More credence has naturally been accorded to Polybius (himself the source of the opinions of most of the later ancient writers on the history of Greece in the Hellenistic period) who speaks of ' the complete destruction of the ancient constitution ' by Cleomenes III, of its ' restoration ' by Antigonus Doson, and of its subsequent final destruction by a whole series of Spartan ' tyrants ', with Nabis as the last and worst.[3] On these matters, according to Polybius, the possibility of controversy is excluded ; the facts from the time of the Cleomenic War onwards are too well known.[4]

But a doubt remains ; for this is a subject on which

soon after the middle of the third century B.C., to a certain Molpis of whom nothing more is known, also to the Spartans Hippasus and Pausanias of unknown date, and to the Spartan Nicocles who is thought to have been tutor of the Emperor Julian. Plutarch (*Agesilaus*, 19) also mentions Λακωνικαὶ 'Αναγραφαί which seem to have been official records of the descent of members of the two royal houses.

[1] Strabo, *loc. cit.* : ἔμειναν ἐλεύθεροι, πλὴν τῶν φιλικῶν λειτουργιῶν ἄλλο συντελοῦντες οὐδέν. The ' friendly assistance ' could be called for by Rome in virtue of a long-standing *amicitia et societas*, on which see below, p. 25, n. 3.

[2] Cic. *Pro Flacco*, 26. 63 : *Adsunt Lacedaemonii . . . qui soli toto orbe terrarum septingentis iam annis amplius unis moribus et nunquam mutatis legibus vivunt*. Cicero may be thinking only of Spartan social organisation, but even so his statement needs modification.

[3] Polyb. IV, 81 ; *cf.* Joseph, *contra Apionem*, II, 31. [4] Polyb. *ibid.*

Polybius, deeply involved as he was by tradition, birth, and personal choice in the imperialist policy of the Achaean League,[1] is not likely to have an unbiassed opinion. How could he have, when the source of his information for the period before 220 B.C. was Aratus,[2] and when in addition Aratus was his ideal of all that a statesman should be ? [3] For Sparta from the first was the state which presented the greatest obstacle to Achaean domination in the Peloponnese, the goal which Aratus made it his life-work to attain. No sooner did Aratus ' free ' Corinth (spring 242) [4] than the youthful Agis IV at Sparta, up to this moment an ally of the Achaeans,[5] but perceiving Achaean occupation of Corinth to be a more dangerous threat to Greek liberties than occupation by a Macedonian garrison, made haste to occupy Pellene (near Sicyon).[6] Aratus promptly dislodged him, but Agis was killed himself soon afterwards in an internal revolution at Sparta, and Aratus preferred to postpone further hostilities with Sparta until the cities of the northern Peloponnese were securely under Achaean control. A far more serious obstacle to Achaean ambitions arose in Cleomenes III (235–221 B.C.). The very name of the ' Cleomenic War ', so-called by Aratus in his history of his own times, proves the part which this king played in postponing the day of final Achaean domination in the Peloponnese, and in forcing Aratus even then to accept subsidies from Ptolemy,[7] and to make the Macedonians partners in his final victory. It may well be imagined how these facts rankled, not only with Aratus, but also with his successors in control of Achaean policy. Thus Polybius was doubly biassed, both by his admiration for Aratus as a historian,[8] and by his whole-hearted acceptance of the foreign policy which Aratus had initiated.

[1] Polybius was the son of Lycortas, whose indebtedness to the policy of Aratus, and responsibility for the later prosperity of the Achaean League, he refers to in II, 40.

[2] *Ibid*. I, 3 ; II, 40 ; IV, 2.   [3] *Ibid*. II, 40 ; V, 12 ; VII, 13 f.

[4] For the date see Appendix II, p. 431.

[5] In the Aetolian expedition of Aratus' first strategia ; *cf.* Plut. *Agis*, 13 ; *Arat*. 16 ; Paus. II, 8, 4, and for the date, Appendix II, p. 431.

[6] Paus. II, 8, 5 ; VII, 7, 3.   [7] Plut. *Cleom.* 19.

[8] *Cf.* Polyb. II, 40 : τῶν μέντοι γε Ἀράτῳ διῳκημένων καὶ νῦν καὶ μετὰ ταῦτα πάλιν ἐπικεφαλαιούμενοι μνησθησόμεθα, διὰ τὸ καὶ λίαν ἀληθινοὺς καὶ σαφεῖς ἐκεῖνον περὶ τῶν ἰδίων συντεταχέναι πράξεων ὑπομνηματισμούς.

There is not indeed any reason to doubt the substantial accuracy of the mere facts recorded by Aratus in his *Commentaries* ; for he seems to have been ready enough to admit even his own defeats and some errors of judgment. But even his admirer Polybius admits that reasons of policy sometimes obliged him to practise in his writings a certain economy, and even deliberate misrepresentation, of the truth.[1] It does not, however, appear to occur to Polybius that Aratus may have pursued precisely this method in his account of the policy and character of Cleomenes, for since it was the main aim of Aratus to create a new Peloponnesian League under Achaean domination by adopting the ancient Spartan battle-cry of τυράννων κατάλυσις, Aratus must of necessity represent Cleomenes as one more tyrant ripe for extermination. The general character of the literary evidence therefore leaves scope to the modern historian for interpreting the facts.

Unfortunately the Spartan side of the question found a dangerous champion (contemporary with Aratus) in the historian Phylarchus, and Polybius, by a scathing exposure of the inaccuracies of this writer, and his love of dramatisation,[2] not to speak of his obvious antagonism to Aratus and the Achaean League, has succeeded in entirely discrediting the anti-Achaean version. Similarly, Plutarch accuses Phylarchus of writing like an advocate in the courts, too eager to defend his client at all costs.[3] It thus appears that not only political bias on the part of the ancient historians, but literary convention also, tended to obscure the real condition of Sparta at this period.

It is Phylarchus who has left us, through the mediation of Plutarch, the only account which has survived of the internal condition of Sparta at the beginning of its long conflict with the Achaean League. Plutarch's life of Agis IV is conspicuous for all the faults for which Phylarchus is criticised, and therefore cannot itself be accepted without criticism. Moreover it is distorted in perspective as a result of Plutarch's notion that Agis IV and Cleomenes III at Sparta correspond in their internal policy to the Gracchi at Rome.[4] In consequence, the *Life of Agis* is confined to

[1] Polyb. II, 47, *ad fin.*   [2] *Ibid.* II, 56.
[3] Plut. *Arat.* 38.   [4] Plut. *Agis*, 2.

a romantic and idealistic account of the young king's attempted economic reforms, whereas there are some indications that he distinguished himself far more in the military sphere, in operations against the Achaean League.[1]

The supposed resemblance to Tiberius Gracchus rests upon an abortive scheme for redistribution of the land, proposed by Agis in 243 B.C.,[2] before he had yet reached his twentieth year.[3] To increase the number of Spartan citizens, Agis is said to have proposed to redistribute all the land within the area limited by Pellene, Taygetus, Malea and Sellasia.[4] The 4,500 land-lots so created were to be taken up by Spartan citizens, the required number being made up by the inclusion of Perioikoi and even complete foreigners (ξένοι) of military age.[5] For the reconstituted citizen body of 4,500, membership of a *Syssition* and adoption of the strict Lycurgan régime were once more to be compulsory ; the 4,500 were to be divided into fifteen *Syssitia*, each with a membership of 400 or 200.[6]

Agis is said to have been moved to propose these reforms because the existing social organisations no longer corresponded with the traditional Lycurgan regime ; there was great inequality of wealth, and the austere mode of life adopted by Agis himself was in great contrast with that of the majority of noble Spartans.[7] These statements may well be true, but it is unnecessary to suppose on that account that the internal condition of Sparta had still further decayed since the fourth century, when Aristotle passed exactly the same criticisms on the revised Spartan land laws. These laws, according to Aristotle, were responsible for a large part of Laconia coming under the control of heiresses, and for the rapid decline in numbers of the citizen population.[8]

The accounts of Plutarch (Phylarchus) and of Aristotle are in fact so similar as to arouse the suspicion that the

---

[1] Droysen, *Gesch. d. Hellenismus*, II, pp. 379 f. ; *cf.* Paus. VII, 7. 3.

[2] Droysen (II, p. 381) puts the first proposal of the scheme soon after the liberation of Corinth by Aratus.

[3] *Cf.* Plut. *Agis*, 4 : μηδέπω γεγονὼς εἰκοστὸν ἔτος.

[4] Plut. *Agis*, 8. On the interpretation of this passage see, further, Appendix I (pp. 429 f.).   [5] Plut. *loc. cit.*

[6] Plut. *ibid.* Note that this division, which sounds plausible at first reading, is mathematically impossible, and therefore the passage gives no clue to the normal number in a *Syssition*.

[7] Plut. *Agis*, 4.   [8] Arist. *Pol.* II, 9. 15 ; *cf.* Plut. *Agis*, 7.

corroborative detail in the later account is either invented later, or derived from Ephorus as the common source of both. Plutarch traces the condition of affairs in the reign of Agis IV to the passing of the Rhetra of the Ephor Epitadeus, of which the main provision was the establishment of freedom of gift and bequest of property, including land.[1] Plutarch does not assign a precise date to this law, but a date before Leuctra is clearly implied by his ensuing statement that the diminution of citizen lot-holders consequent upon this law went on until ' not more than 700 Spartiatae were left '.[2] Xenophon gives the same number for the Spartiatae at the battle of Leuctra.[3] When Aristotle seeks to account for the passing of land at Sparta into the hands of a few, two-fifths of their number being heiresses,[4] he says, ὠνεῖσθαι μὲν γὰρ ἢ πωλεῖν τὴν ὑπαρχοῦσαν ἐποίησεν (sc. ὁ νόμος) οὐ καλόν, ὀρθῶς ποιήσας, διδόναι δὲ καὶ καταλείπειν ἐξουσίαν ἔδωκε τοῖς βουλομένοις,[5] with the result that at the time of the Theban invasion ' they were not even a thousand in number '.[6] The verbal correspondence in the two accounts of the law itself, as well as the general correspondence in sense, makes it clear that Plutarch and Aristotle are both referring to the same law and passing the same criticisms upon it. It would therefore appear that Plutarch's source Phylarchus lacked direct information about the internal condition of Sparta in the time of Agis IV, and merely adopted a stock criticism from a much earlier period, embroidering it with references to the vast wealth of two Spartan women in particular, the mother and grandmother of Agis himself.[7]

Nothing in Plutarch's (Phylarchus') account would suggest that there had been any further change in the laws or constitution since the passing of the Rhetra of Epitadeus. The mere fact that Agis proposed to fill up the numbers of the citizen body by means of a cancellation of

[1] Plut. Agis, 5 : ἐξεῖναι τὸν οἶκον αὐτοῦ καὶ τὸν κλῆρον ᾧ τις ἐθέλοι καὶ ζῶντα δοῦναι καὶ καταλιπεῖν διατιθέμενον.
[2] Ibid.   [3] Xen. Hell. VI, 4. 15.
[4] Arist. Pol. II, 9. 15.   [5] Ibid. II, 9. 14.
[6] Ibid. II, 9. 16. For the time referred to cf. II, 9. 10. The ' single blow ' referred to in II, 9. 16 is obviously the battle of Leuctra. This indication of a date some considerable time before Leuctra disposes of Cary's suggestion of c. 350 B.C. for the Rhetra of Epitadeus (cf. Class. Quart. 1926, pp. 186 f.).   [7] Plut. Agis, 4, 6.

debts, redistribution of the land, and creation of new *Syssitia*, shows that the possession of a land-lot, enabling the holder to pay his contribution to a *Syssition*, was still the indispensable condition of full citizenship, as it had been under the old Lycurgan regime.[1] In his work on the Spartan constitution written in the reign of Cleomenes III, Sphaerus the Borysthenite described the ancient procedure at meals in the *Syssitia* as if it was still in force in his own time.[2] Some extremely archaic laws were invoked by Agis IV for the purpose of deposing the other king Leonidas, who set his face against the scheme—a law forbidding any of the Heraclidae to marry a foreign wife, another forbidding any Spartan to settle abroad, and finally a law which permitted the Ephors every nine years to watch the sky for unfavourable omens and to depose whichever of the two kings was found to be transgressing the laws.[3] For a very long period, according to Suidas, a work by Dicaearchus of Messene on the Spartan constitution was read annually by the Ephors to the young Spartans who had just reached the age of manhood.[4] This implies that the old organs of government were still in force at the time of the proposed reforms of Agis IV. Legislation was effected through the proposal of a Rhetra by one of the Ephors to the Gerontes,[5] who then placed it before the Apella if a majority in favour was first reached in the Gerusia.[6] The two kings were still members of the Gerusia,[7] as in early times. Personal example, not legislation, was all that was needed for the restoration of the austere traditional way of life.[8]

In short, the reforms of Agis were not intended to restore the ancient constitution and laws, but simply to create a larger citizen body for military purposes. This is evident from the stipulation that all new citizens admitted to the ranks of the 4,500 should be men of the right age and physique for active military service.[9] But the proposed

---

[1] *Cf.* Chap. VI, p. 245.   [2] *Cf.* Athen. IV, 141c. ff. ; Plut. *Cleom.* 11.

[3] Plut. *Agis*, 11.

[4] *Cf.* F.H.G. II, p. 241, fr. 21.   Dicaearchus was a pupil of Aristotle.

[5] Plut. *Agis*, 8.   [6] *Ibid.* 11.

[7] Hence the necessity for deposing Leonidas in order to get the Rhetra passed (Plut. *Agis*, 11).

[8] The traditional system of education was in existence at the time of the invasion of Pyrrhus (272 B.C.) ; *cf.* Plut. *Pyrrhus*, 26.

[9] Plut. *Agis*, 8.

reforms ended less than two years later (241 B.C.) with the
trial and execution of Agis himself,[1] and the attempt to
make Sparta a military power capable of withstanding the
Achaean League had failed.

The renewal of this task was taken up by Cleomenes III
(235–221 B.C.),[2] the son of Agis' obstructive colleague
Leonidas. Cleomenes had many advantages which Agis had
lacked—he was older when he began to reign, he had a more
forceful personality,[3] greater military ability, and an easily
controlled colleague on the throne. He had become step-
father and guardian to Eurydamidas, the infant heir of
Agis, immediately upon the latter's death, to satisfy his own
father's desire to enrich his family.[4] Eurydamidas nomin-
ally succeeded Agis as king,[5] but died while still a child,[6]
soon after Cleomenes' accession, and was succeeded by his
paternal uncle Archidamus. But Archidamus had not been
long on the throne before he thought it prudent to go into
voluntary exile in Messenia. According to Polybius, the
reason was fear of his colleague,[7] but there may have been
some deeper political motive for putting Cleomenes in a
position apparently closely resembling that of the numerous
' tyrants ' who at this time were being rapidly expelled from
northern Peloponnesian towns by Aratus,[8] for the greater
power and glory of the Achaean League.

---

[1] Plut. *Agis*, 19.

[2] Cleomenes was king for sixteen years (Plut. *Cleom.* 38). This period
may have been reckoned either to his flight from Sparta in 222 or 221 B.C.
(on this point *cf*. Appendix II, p. 434) or to his death at Alexandria nearly
three years later (*cf*. Polyb. IV, 35). The latter interpretation seems the
more probable, giving late 235 or early 234 as the date of his accession.

[3] *Cf*. Polybius' description (V, 39) : ἀνὴρ γενόμενος καὶ πρὸς τὰς ὁμιλίας
ἐπιδέξιος καὶ πρὸς πραγμάτων οἰκονομίαν εὐφυής, καὶ συλλήβδην ἡγεμονικὸς
καὶ βασιλικὸς τῇ φύσει; and the description of Pausanias (II, 9. 1), ἅτε
δὲ ὄντι αὐτῷ Παυσανίου θερμοτέρῳ καὶ οὐ φιλοψύχῳ ταχὺ τὰ πάντα ὑπὸ φρονή-
ματος καὶ τόλμης κατείργαστο.   [4] Plut. *Cleom.* 1.

[5] Paus. II, 9. 1. This statement, in a source hostile to Cleomenes,
renders improbable Tarn's suggestion (*cf*. C.A.H. VII, p. 752) that after
the execution of Agis Leonidas ruled unconstitutionally for six years
without a colleague.

[6] Pausanias (*ibid*.) says that he was murdered by Cleomenes, but this
seems unlikely in view of Cleomenes' great affection for his wife, the child's
mother (Plut. *Cleom.* 1, 22).   [7] Polyb. V, 37.

[8] Plut. *Arat.* 25–30, and for the date, C.A.H. VII, pp. 745 f. During
the Cleomenic War Cleomenes was generally believed to favour the setting
up of ' tyrannies ' in the towns seeking escape from Achaean control
(*cf*. Plut. *Arat.* 40 : ἰδίων ἐπιθυμίᾳ δυναστειῶν).

Sparta was certainly in direct danger from the League from the very beginning of Cleomenes' reign, but was saved from immediate attack by the personal jealousy between the two Achaean Strategoi. It was Lydiades who first openly advocated war on Sparta, in 235-4,[1] while Aratus was determined to reserve the military glory for himself.[2] Cleomenes actually made the first move about five years later, by occupying Belbina [3] near the sources of the Eurotas, which was at that time under the control of Megalopolis, and controlled the approaches into Laconia from the north. During the eight years' war with the Achaean League (the ' Cleomenic War ') which followed, Cleomenes inflicted defeat after defeat upon the Achaeans. By the end of 223 almost the whole of the Peloponnese, including the key-town of Corinth, was in his hands,[4] Aratus was shut up in Sicyon, and the Achaean League only escaped final disaster by calling in Macedonian assistance. A predominantly Achaean literary tradition recompenses Cleomenes in the manner which we should expect.

But even in his own city Cleomenes at first met with apathy and even opposition in his anti-Achaean crusade. This was reflected in the attitude of successive boards of Ephors during the first few years of war, for after the initial authorisation of the attack on Belbina,[5] the Ephors, who still had their traditional powers of controlling war-supplies and even the actual levying of troops,[6] continually impeded the efforts of Cleomenes.[7] But in view of the fact that the Ephors were still annual officials popularly elected, we may infer that the fundamental reason for this hostility to Cleomenes' policy was lack of enthusiasm for the war among the citizen soldiers, this in turn being in part accounted for by a decline in the spirit of patriotism (a tendency general in the Peloponnese at this time) [8] and in part by the

---

[1] Plut. *Arat.* 30 (for the date of the first strategia of Lydiades, see Appendix II, p. 431).   [2] Plut. *ibid.* ; *Cleom.* 3.

[3] Plut. *Cleom.* 4 (in a Strategia of Aratus preceding the Strategia of Aristomachus). For the date, see Appendix II, pp. 431 f.

[4] On the difficult question of the chronology of the Cleomenic War see Appendix II, pp. 431 f.

[5] Plut. *ibid.*   [6] *Cf.* Part II, p. 408.

[7] *Cf.* Plut. *Cleom.* 7, *init.* 27 (cited below, p. 14, n. 6).

[8] This is clear from the ease with which towns changed sides in the Cleomenic War and earlier. A concrete example appears in the apathy

consciousness of inferior equipment as compared with the Achaean armies, which were equipped in Macedonian fashion.

Hostilities had already been in progress, in somewhat desultory fashion, for about two years, when, probably in the first half of 228 B.C.,[1] Cleomenes felt himself driven to consider the extreme step of reforming the constitution and reducing the powers of the Ephors, this being an indispensable preliminary to army reforms. As he intended to justify his revolution on the ground that it was a return to the Lycurgan constitution, it was clearly expedient for him to begin by restoring the double kingship, and Archidamus was accordingly invited to return, only to meet his end in mysterious circumstances soon afterwards. Polybius, with his strong pro-Achaean bias, naturally has no hesitation in saying that he was murdered by order of Cleomenes,[2] but the inexpedient timing of the murder from Cleomenes' point of view suggests that Phylarchus is more likely to be right in maintaining that Archidamus was murdered by the same party as had brought about his brother's death.[3]

It was at this point that the most unconstitutional act of Cleomenes' reign occurred, the election of his own brother Euclidas to succeed Archidamus,[4] although Archidamus left two young sons,[5] and there was thus no excuse for this unprecedented concentration of the kingship in the control of the Agiad house. In assessing the character and policy of Cleomenes himself, it should, however, be noted that this unconstitutional step was taken before Cleomenes attempted any general reform of the constitution, and while he was still professing to be under the control of the Ephors, whose collaboration was necessary to carry through the election of the new king.[6] It is, therefore, rather an indica-

of the Argives during the Achaean attack on their city in 237 (Plut. *Arat.* 27).

[1] For the chronology see Appendix II, p. 433.

[2] Polyb. V, 37.   [3] *Cf.* Plut. *Cleom.* 5.

[4] Paus. II, 9. 1. Pausanias is inaccurate in saying that Euclidas directly succeeded Eurydamidas, the son of Agis. For relationships in the Spartan royal houses, see Tables in Appendix VIII.

[5] *Cf.* Polyb. IV, 35. That both were young boys follows from the fact that their father was the younger brother of Agis IV, who was born *c.* 262 B.C. ; *cf.* above, p. 5.

[6] *Cf.* Paus. II, 9. 1.

tion of the corruptibility of the Ephors than of the tyrannical disposition of Cleomenes himself, who may well have thought that the existing war with the Achaean League made it essential that both Spartan kings should be able to fulfil in person their chief function of acting as commanders in the field ; or again his new ally Ptolemy Euergetes [1] may have demanded the change as a guarantee against divided policy. The history of Sparta in the past provided many instances in which the state had been weakened in a crisis by the existence of a regency in one of the royal houses.

Further considerable successes in the war with the Achaean League followed. After a resounding victory over the Achaeans in the territory of Megalopolis (summer, 228), in which Lydiades the former tyrant of Megalopolis was killed,[2] Cleomenes felt himself strong enough to carry through the projected internal reforms, cn the model of those proposed earlier by Agis IV (autumn, 228 B.C.).[3] The ease with which the *coup* was effected [4] is explained by the careful preparations which had been made for it, and by no means gives the impression of a sudden unpremeditated bid for tyrannical power. Nor can external pressure have interfered with the consolidation of the reforms, for the most probable reconstruction of the chronology of the war with the Achaean League shows a lull of over two years after the defeat of Aratus and Lydiades,[5] and restored confidence in Sparta during the interval was shown by Mantinea and Tegea joining Cleomenes without a battle. It was Cleomenes himself who reopened hostilities in the Strategia of Hyperbatas, when the full forces of the Achaean League were defeated at Dyme,[6] and a temporary peace was concluded which, according to Pausanias, was immediately afterwards broken by Cleomenes.[7] After this

[1] *Cf.* Polyb. II, 51. Euergetes had been allied with the Achaeans at the beginning of the war.

[2] *Cf.* Polyb. II, 51 ; Plut. *Cleom.* 6 ; *Aratus* 37. The mention of this fact by the two main authorities serves to fix the chronological relation of their accounts, of which that of Plutarch gives the fuller account of the constitutional reforms.

[3] On the date, see Appendix II, p. 433.

[4] Plut. *Cleom.* 8, 10. It was necessary to exile only eighty citizens (*ibid.* 10), and the only blood shed was that of the Ephors.

[5] *Cf.* Appendix II, p. 432.

[6] Polyb. II, 51 ; Plut. *Cleom.* 14 ; *Arat.* 39 ; Paus. VII, 7. 3.

[7] Paus. VII, 7. 3, 4.

12 ANCIENT SPARTA

victory one Peloponnesian city after another came over to
the Spartan side—Polybius mentions Caphyae, Pellene,
Pheneus, Argos, Phlius, Cleonae, Epidaurus, Hermione,
Troezen and Corinth,[1] and Plutarch further adds Penteleum.[2]
Sicyon stood a siege, which had to be raised by Cleomenes
when Antigonus and the Macedonian army began their
determined advance which was to end eventually, after
some reversals of fortune,[3] in the complete defeat of
Cleomenes at Sellasia, probably in 221.[4]

The internal reforms of Cleomenes had therefore been
in existence for about six and a half years at the time of
his defeat, and their nature was such that they could not
readily be overthrown by a victor who withdrew from
Sparta after only two days,[5] leaving the city in enjoyment
of its ancient laws and 'traditional constitution' (πάτριον
πολίτευμα).[6] Leaving aside for the moment the question
whether Cleomenes had overthrown this constitution, as
his detractors on the Achaean side maintained,[7] or had
revived and fortified it as Cleomenes himself declared,[8]
it is clear that some of his more conspicuous changes must
have survived the effects of the short-lived Macedonian
intervention. This applies particularly to the emancipation of 6,000 Helots,[9] and to the redistribution of the land.

The land redistribution was modelled on the scheme
of Agis IV, but provided for a privileged citizen body of
only 4,000 [10] instead of 4,500 and involved no attempt to

[1] Polyb. II, 52 ; cf. Plut. Cleom. 17–19.
[2] Plut. Arat. 39 ; Cleom. 17.
[3] Notably the capture of Megalopolis by Cleomenes (Polyb. II, 55 ;
Plut. Cleom. 23, 24).
[4] For the reasons for preferring this date for Sellasia rather than 222,
which is accepted by Beloch and Tarn, see Appendix II, pp. 433 f.
[5] Plut. Cleom. 30.
[6] Polyb. II, 70 ; V, 9 ; cf. Paus. II, 9. 2 ; Plut. Cleom. 30, and the
inscription on a statue-base from Geronthrae : βασιλέος ᾿Αντιγόνου Σωτῆρος
(I.G. V, i, 1122).
[7] Polyb. II, 47 : τοῦ μὲν Κλεομένους τό τε πάτριον πολίτευμα καταλύσαντος,
κ.τ.λ. ; cf. Paus. II, 9. 1 ; VIII, 27. 16.
[8] Plut. Cleom. 10.   [9] Ibid. 23.
[10] Ibid. 11 : ἀναπληρώσας δὲ τὸ πολίτευμα τοῖς χαριεστάτοις τῶν περιοίκων
ὁπλίτας τετρακισχιλίους ἐποίησε. For the meaning of πολίτευμα here, see
further below, pp. 16 f. The passage in Plutarch offers no support for
the view that the 4,000 were all new citizens drawn from the Perioikoi,
as maintained by Jouguet (Macedonian Imperialism, 1929, p. 238) and
by Cary (A History of the Greek World, 326–146 B.C., p. 157).

redistribute the land of the Perioikoi. Cleomenes' own political opponents, men who were in exile at the time, received a share like the rest in the general allocation of land, with a promise of reinstatement when peace was restored.[1] It may be supposed that one of the ' signal benefits ' conferred by Antigonus upon individual Spartans [2] was to implement this promise after Cleomenes' flight to Egypt, and to leave the rest of the 4,000, or their heirs if they had been killed at Sellasia, in possession of their κλῆροι.

Was this redistribution of the land in fact in accordance with the πάτριος πολιτεία, the traditional Lycurgan constitution which Cleomenes was proposing to uphold or restore ? Many modern critics have denied the claim, and indeed have suggested that Cleomenes, like Agis before him, was appealing to a mere philosophers' fancy about Sparta, the legend of one-time equality, to bolster up a scheme which was wholly subversive and was now being introduced into Sparta for the first time.[3] But this interpretation is based upon a misconception, as may be demonstrated by comparison of Cleomenes' reorganisation with schemes in force in other Greek constitutions from the late fifth century onwards. The 4,000 lot-holders did not represent the whole number of Spartan citizens in Cleomenes' constitution, but only a privileged section of them. This is proved by Plutarch's statement that 6,000 ' Lacedaemonians ' (meaning in this case Spartan citizens) fought in the battle of Sellasia.[4] Some of these additional citizens were no doubt ex-Helots from among the 6,000 of that class who received the franchise shortly before Sellasia,

---

[1] Plut. *Cleom.* 23. [2] *Cf.* Polyb. V, 9.

[3] *Cf.* Andreades, *History of Greek Public Finance* (English edition, 1933), p. 46, where references to other authorities are given ; also Cary, *op. cit.* pp. 155 f. ; Ollier, *Le Mirage Spartiate* (1933), p. 5.

[4] Plut. *Cleom.* 28 : ἀποθανεῖν δὲ καὶ τῶν ξένων πολλοὺς λέγουσι καὶ Λακεδαιμονίους ἅπαντας πλὴν διακοσίων, ἑξακισχιλίους ὄντας. According to the normal usage, Λακεδαιμονίους might well include Perioikoi (*cf.* Hampl, *Hermes*, 72, 1937, pp. 1 ff.), but the more precise account of the disposition of the troops at Sellasia given by Polybius (II, 65) shows that it cannot bear this meaning here. According to Polybius, Euclidas was in command of τοὺς περιοίκους συμμάχους, *i.e.* the Perioikoi, while Cleomenes himself τὸν Ὄλυμπον κατεῖχε μετὰ Λακεδαιμονίων καὶ τῶν μισθοφόρων. The passage of Plutarch cited above clearly refers to the contingent on Olympus, *i.e.* Spartans and mercenaries, since immediately before this he has already mentioned the destruction of troops under Euclidas on the other hill. The 6,000 must accordingly be supposed to be Spartans.

and therefore a few years after the redistribution of the
land, on payment of five minas each.[1] But the rest cannot
be simply accounted for by the 4,000, for Polybius' account
of the battle distinguishes, among the Spartan contingent
who fought with Cleomenes,[2] between those armed with
the *sarissa* (*i.e.* the heavy-armed), the εὔζωνοι (light-armed)
and the ἱππεῖς.[3] The εὔζωνοι must be regarded as a less-
privileged political class, the ἱππεῖς (after as before Cleomenes'
reforms) as a social and political *élite*. This interpretation
is suggested by what is known of earlier Greek oligarchical
constitutions, and will find its confirmation in the social
divisions of Sparta in a later period.[4]

The most significant distinction between the 4,000 and the
rest, which justified the preferential treatment for the 4,000 in
the matter of land redistribution, was that they were liable
for service in a new corps of more heavily armed hoplites,
equipped to fight the Macedonians with Macedonian weapons,
including the *sarissa*.[5] Since all branches of the Spartan
citizen army continued to be unpaid and to be liable to
provide their own equipment,[6] and since the cost of the
Macedonian type of equipment was very much heavier than
that of the ordinary hoplite,[7] it was necessary to secure
additional means to those upon whom the duty was now
imposed of equipping themselves in the new fashion. The
rest of the citizens, probably those with the inferior status
of *Neodamodeis*,[8] continued to be equipped as ordinary

---

[1] *Cf.* below, p. 15, n. 1.   [2] *Cf.* above, p. 13, n. 4.
[3] Polyb. II, 69 (*cf. ibid.* 65, 67).   [4] See pp. 102 f.
[5] Plut. *Cleom.* 11 : καὶ διδάξας αὐτοὺς ἀντὶ δόρατος χρῆσθαι σαρίσῃ
δι᾽ ἀμφοτέρων καὶ τὴν ἀσπίδα φορεῖν δι᾽ ὀχάνης, μὴ διὰ πόρπακος κ.τ.λ. For
the part played by these troops in the battle of Sellasia, *cf.* Polyb. II, 69 ;
Plut. *Cleom.* 28. They were again used in the battle of Mantinea in 207
(Polyb. XI. 15).
[6] *Cf.* Plut. *Cleom.* 27 : ὁ Ἀντίγονος . . . κατήθλει τὸν Κλεομένη γλίσχρως
καὶ μόλις πορίζοντα τοῖς ξένοις μισθὸν καὶ τροφὴν τοῖς πολίταις. This means
that the citizen army received only an allowance of food during the actual
campaign. The special measures taken to furnish with equipment the
2,000 enfranchised Helots (*cf.* below, p. 15, n. 1) shows that the citizen
soldiers normally furnished their own equipment, as was the usual practice
in Greek states.
[7] The ordinary equipment of the heavy-armed Macedonian hoplite
in the third century B.C. cost a talent, but might cost as much as 2 talents
(Plut. *Demetr.* 21) ; the equipment of Cleomenes' corps of ex-Helots corresponding to the Macedonian *Leukaspides* cost only a quarter of a talent
per man (*cf.* p. 15, n. 1) though even these were armed in Macedonian
fashion.   [8] On this class see below, pp. 39 f.

hoplites, with the exception of 2,000 enfranchised Helots who in the last phase of the war were specially equipped in Macedonian fashion out of public funds, the money being obtained by the charge of five minas each for the enfranchisement of the 6,000 Helots.[1]

Another significant distinction between Cleomenes' 4,000 and the rest of the citizens is that they were all of military age and physically fit for service. This fact is not indeed explicitly stated in regard to Cleomenes' reform, but it is so stated in regard to the projected scheme of Agis IV,[2] upon which that of Cleomenes was obviously based. Plutarch and the modern writers who base their criticisms of Cleomenes upon him, are therefore quite wrong in supposing that Cleomenes was aiming at the establishment of universal equality.[3] They have doubtless been led to this belief by recalling passages in the fourth-century writers in which the same interpretation is put upon the institutions of Lycurgan Sparta.[4] It is clear that in reality Cleomenes' redistribution of land affected only a part of all the available land in Laconia, for it would be fantastic to suppose that all those above or below military age, or unfit for service, as well as all women, were dispossessed in order to provide for the 4,000. The distinction between State land and private land had existed in earlier times, and no doubt Cleomenes limited his redistribution to the γῆ πολιτική,[5] as the Gracchi were later to limit theirs to the Roman *Ager Publicus*. At all events it is clear that there was nothing idealistic about the scheme, and that its

---

[1] Plut. *Cleom.* 23 : τῶν μὲν εἰλώτων τοὺς πέντε μνᾶς Ἀττικὰς καταβαλόντας ἐλευθέρους ἐποίει καὶ τάλαντα πεντακόσια συνέλεξε, δισχιλίους δὲ προσκαθοπλίσας Μακεδονικῶς ἀντίταγμα τοῖς παρ' Ἀντιγόνου λευκάσπισιν, κ.τ.λ.

[2] Plut. *Agis*, 8 : ἀναπληρωθῆναι δὲ τούτους ἔκ τε περιοίκων καὶ ξένων, ὅσοι τροφῆς μετεσχηκότες ἐλευθερίου καὶ χαρίεντες ἄλλως τοῖς σώμασι καὶ καθ' ἡλικίαν ἀκμάζοντες εἶεν.

[3] *Cf.* Plut. *Cleom.* 10 (the land to be the common possession of all) ; *ibid.* 11 (all the citizens gave up their private property) ; *ibid.* 18 (ἐν τῇ τῶν κτημάτων ἐξισώσει).

[4] *Cf.* Polyb. VI. 45 : τῆς μὲν δὴ Λακεδαιμονίων πολιτείας ἴδιον εἶναι φασί (sc. Ephorus, Xenophon, Callisthenes and Plato) πρῶτον μὲν τὰ περὶ τὰς ἐγγείους κτήσεις, ὧν οὐδενὶ μέτεστι πλεῖον, ἀλλὰ πάντας τοὺς πολίτας ἴσον ἔχειν δεῖ τῆς πολιτικῆς χώρας. Plutarch (Lycurg. 8) follows the same tradition : συνέπεισε (ὁ Λυκοῦργος) τὴν χώραν ἅπασαν εἰς μέσον θέντας ἐξ ἀρχῆς ἀναδάσασθαι καὶ ζῆν μετ' ἀλλήλων ἅπαντας ὁμαλεῖς καὶ ἰσοκλήρους τοῖς βίοις γενομένους.

[5] *Cf.* Part II, p. 286.

main purpose was neither economic nor political, but military. It was carried out in order to bring the Spartan army up to date, at a time when Cleomenes already had reason to expect that Aratus would call in the assistance of Macedon.

But although the policy with regard to the Four Thousand was dictated by purely military considerations, the change brought Sparta into line with other Greek constitutions of approximately the same period by establishing a specially privileged πολίτευμα within a much larger citizen body (πολῖται). The Athenian constitution of the Five Thousand set up in 411, and the constitutions of the towns of the Boeotian confederacy in the early fourth century,[1] belong to the same general type of moderate oligarchy, but the most interesting parallel is the Constitution of Cyrene set up under the influence of the reigning Ptolemy about 308 B.C., not only because detailed epigraphic evidence exists in this case,[2] but because most of the other institutions of Cyrene are directly derived from Sparta. It is perhaps worth noting that at the time of his reform Cleomenes also was relying upon Egyptian support,[3] and may have received advice about his political and military reorganisation from Ptolemy Euergetes.

The main purpose of the revision of the Cyrene constitution would appear from the internal evidence of the document concerning it to have been to secure a more efficient organisation for war conditions ;[4] the institutions of Spartan origin which had existed previously were changed as little as possible. The constitution draws a distinction between the whole body of πολῖται, namely those living within the boundaries of the state who were the children of Cyrenean fathers or of colonists from Cyrene,[5] and a privileged body, theoretically 10,000 in number, who in

---

[1] Cf. Hellenica Oxyrhynchia, 11.

[2] Cf. Taeger, Verfassungsdiagramm von Kyrene, Hermes, 64 (1929), pp. 432 ff.

[3] Cf. above, p. 11.

[4] Cf. l. 34 of the inscription (referred to above, n. 2) : πρασσόντων δὲ οἱ μὲγ γέροντες ἃ οἱ γέροντες ἐπ' εἰρήνης ἔπρασσον ; it is also significant that one of the changes made is the substitution of five generals for the previous twelve (ll. 27, 73 ff.).

[5] Or those admitted on the personal recommendation of Ptolemy himself (ibid. ll. 5, 7).

addition to the qualification just mentioned possessed real property to the value of twenty Alexandrian minae and were not less than thirty years of age. The Ten Thousand alone were eligible for certain offices,[1] perhaps for all offices, though this is not directly stated in the written constitution.[2] It was the Ten Thousand who filled up by election vacancies in the Gerusia,[3] and it seems to be implied that they monopolised the right of election to all elective offices, though no clear statement is made in the inscription about this, doubtless because it is already implied in the statement that the Ten Thousand are to take over the functions previously exercised by the Thousand.[4] The probable explanation of this great increase in number is that a συμπολιτεία extending over the whole of the territory once colonised by Cyrene—an area which later was to become the Roman province of Cyrene—was now taking the place of the old city-state of Cyrene, the constitution of which had to be modified accordingly. One of the changes made concerned the nature of the property qualification for membership of the πολίτευμα,[5] but the principle of selecting a privileged πολίτευμα on the basis of a property qualification remained unchanged, as also did the functions assigned to this body. These functions may be summed up in the words of Aristotle, an approximate contemporary : ' πολιτεία and πολίτευμα are words which mean the same, but the πολίτευμα is the governing body in the state '.[6] Those outside the πολίτευμα, but still citizens, were citizens only in respect of their private rights under the same system of law. Such was the constitution of the old Spartan colony of Cyrene, which still testified to its Spartan origin by its Gerusia and Ephors [7]

---

[1] Cf. ibid. ll. 44 f., μὴ συνπορευέσθω μυριακὰς ἀρχάς, and l. 12 f., τιμητῆρας δὲ αἱρείσθων οἱ γέροντες ἐκ τῶν μυρίων.

[2] It is, however, stated that the generals, who in time of peace may only be elected from men above fifty, in time of war must be elected ἐκ παντὸς τοῦ πολιτεύματος (ibid. l. 28).

[3] Ibid. ll. 21 f.   [4] Ibid. l. 35.

[5] Ibid. ll. 15 f.: τῶι δὲ πρώτωι ἔτει πολιτευέσθωσαν ἐκ τῶν πρότερον τιμημάτων. It is possible that this was not merely a change of amount : the earlier qualification may have been based on ownership of land, as the small number of the Thousand suggests.

[6] Arist. Pol. III, 7. 1 : πολιτεία μὲν καὶ πολίτευμα σημαίνει ταὐτόν, πολίτευμα δ'ἐστὶ τὸ κύριον τῶν πόλεων.

[7] Hermes, ibid. ll. 20 f., 33 f. The Nomophylakes (l. 32) are also probably a Spartan element ; cf. chap. IV, p. 155.

2

in the time of Aristotle. It will be recognised to be strikingly similar to that of Sparta as reorganised by Cleomenes III.[1]

But there was one important difference. The privileged πολίτευμα in Cleomenes' reorganisation was almost certainly composed of men of military age, whereas there was no upper age-limit for membership of the πολίτευμα of Cyrene. In this respect the Spartan constitution under Cleomenes was a return to a much earlier stage of Greek political evolution, though it belongs to a type of which the contemporary existence is recognised by Aristotle, who draws a distinction between πολιτεῖαι ἐκ τῶν ὁπλιτευόντων and πολιτεῖαι καὶ ἐκ τῶν ὡπλιτευκότων.[2] The second type, which also included men who had formerly served as soldiers but were now beyond military age, is exemplified in the constitutions of the Boeotian towns in the late fifth and early fourth century, and in the constitution of Cyrene in Aristotle's time ; it is probably the normal type of moderate oligarchy in the period of developed Greek political institutions. The type of oligarchy in which only men still of military age were included in the πολίτευμα is regarded by Aristotle [3] as the oldest of all types of Greek constitution next to absolute monarchy, though he points out that the evolution of the hoplite army to take the place of the cavalry of early times has involved a certain democratisation in the πολιτεύματα of such oligarchical states ; [4] at first only those who could equip themselves as cavalry were eligible, later, all those who could equip themselves as hoplites. It is therefore possible that Cleomenes was reviving the constitution of Sparta as it had existed before the collapse of the old economic system,[5] in fact the ' constitution of Lycurgus '. This, however, is a matter which needs more detailed discussion in the light of what is known about the earlier constitution of Sparta.[6] A much more recent example of a πολιτεία ἐκ τῶν ὁπλιτευόντων appears to be furnished by

[1] The Ephors and the other traditional organs of government survived under Cleomenes. See further below, pp. 19 f.

[2] Arist. Pol. IV, 13. 9.

[3] Ibid. IV, 13. 10.   [4] Ibid. IV, 13. 11.

[5] Cf. above, pp. 5 f.

[6] See further, pp. 350 f., 424 f. It is significant that the Apella in 397 B.C. contained ' over 4,000 ' (Xen. Hell. III, iii, 5), including, of course, those above military age.

the Athenian ' Five Thousand ' of 411 B.C.,[1] but it is more likely that this designedly temporary constitution, adopted expressly to further present military needs and to beat Sparta, was modelled on that of Sparta than that later Greek oligarchies, including that of Cleomenes III, were modelled on the Athenian ' Five Thousand '.

The unfavourable tradition has allowed it to be supposed that Cleomenes suppressed the other traditional elements of the Spartan constitution,[2] and this view has been echoed by modern writers on Cleomenes. But Polybius offers no specific support for his general condemnation except to say that Cleomenes ' turned the constitutional monarchy into a tyranny ', a matter in which, as we have seen, Cleomenes may not have been a free agent, and which in any case involved no change in the traditional form of the constitution. There were still two kings, even if they were brothers. The absence of more detailed criticism from so determined an adversary as Polybius in itself renders suspect the statement of Pausanias that Cleomenes abolished the Gerusia in favour of a new board of Patronomoi.[3] He may be right about the institution of Patronomoi, since there is no evidence for these magistrates before Cleomenes' reforms and there is evidence for them later ;[4] but apart from the silence of Polybius, the fact that Cleomenes thought it necessary to have another king appointed, even if it had to be his own brother, shows that he desired to respect the traditional forms of the constitution, and to that extent supports Plutarch's account (presumably derived from Phylarchus) of the reasons which Cleomenes himself gave for the changes he was making. According to Plutarch,[5] Cleomenes said that he proposed to strip the Ephors of their improperly acquired powers, and to reduce them, to their original

---

[1] This aspect of the constitution of the 5,000 does not seem to have attracted the attention of historians, who tend to assume that the property qualification was the significant change ; cf. however, Thuc. VIII, 65. 3 : οὔτε μεθεκτέον τῶν πραγμάτων πλείοσιν ἢ πεντακισχιλίοις, καὶ τούτοις οἳ ἂν μάλιστα τοῖς τε χρήμασι καὶ τοῖς σώμασιν ὠφελεῖν οἷοί τε ὦσιν. The words καὶ τοῖς σώμασιν are significant ; cf. also ibid. 97. 1 : εἶναι δὲ αὐτῶν ὁπόσοι καὶ ὅπλα παρέχονται, Ath. Pol. 33. 1.

[2] Cf. above, p. 12, n. 7.

[3] Paus. II, 9. 1 : τὸ κράτος τῆς γερουσίας καταλύσας πατρονόμους τῷ λόγῳ κατέστησεν ἀντ' αὐτῶν.

[4] Cf. pp. 143 f.   [5] Cleom. 10.

position of subservience to the kings ; he argued in defence
of this decision that Lycurgus, whose intentions he was
professing to follow, had not instituted Ephors at all, but
had put the government in the hands of the Gerusia and the
kings. But there is yet another reason for thinking that
Cleomenes left the Gerusia in existence ; its later composition and organisation reveals a change which cannot well
be supposed to have occurred at any later time, and which
was almost certainly introduced by Cleomenes.[1]

With regard to the Ephors, it seems to have been
commonly assumed, on the evidence of the passage of
Plutarch which has just been cited, that Cleomenes abolished
the office.[2] Yet the passage in question offers no support
for this view, and quotes Cleomenes as saying that it was
best for the Ephorate to remain, if only the Ephors themselves would observe moderation.[3] This was a proviso which
Cleomenes himself could easily make sure was kept, once his
Four Thousand were safely established with their new land-
lots, and the only obstacle to the immediate carrying out
of this reform was the existing board of Ephors, who were
hostile to it, and a comparatively small number of other
political opponents. The Ephors in office were accordingly
murdered, with the exception of one who escaped by taking
refuge in a temple,[4] and eighty political opponents were
driven into exile.[5] Since there are other instances in Spartan
history of assassination of the existing board of Ephors
without abolition of the office,[6] it is strange that Cleomenes'
action should have been regarded as proof that he abolished
the office. Moreover, the position of the Ephors in later
times is found to be modified in the direction of Cleomenes'
desires,[7] and it therefore seems probable that the Ephorate
in the πάτριον πολίτευμα, as restored by Antigonus after
Sellasia, was that magistracy as Cleomenes left it.

To sum up the part played by Cleomenes in remodelling
the Spartan constitution for the future : Antigonus allowed
the reformed Gerusia of Cleomenes, his reformed Ephorate,

---

[1] Cf. pp. 138 f., 147 f.   [2] Cf. Kolbe, I.G. V, i, p. 22.
[3] Plut. Cleom. 10 : μετριάζοντας μὲν οὖν αὐτούς, ἔφη, κρεῖττον ἦν ὑπομένενι,
ἐξουσίᾳ δὲ ἐπιθέτῳ τὴν πάτριον καταλύοντας ἀρχήν . . . οὐκ ἀνεκτόν.
[4] Plut. Cleom. 8.   [5] Ibid. 10.
[6] E.g. in 219 B.C. and again in 218 (Polyb. IV, 35 ; IV, 81).
[7] Cf. pp. 155 ff.

and the board of Patronomoi to be perpetuated ; with the redistribution of land he could scarcely interfere after the lapse of over six years ; and the result was described as the restoration of the πάτριον πολίτευμα. The importance of Cleomenes' reforms as a guide to the nature of the earlier constitution can therefore scarcely be over-estimated.

But the pro-Achaean tradition has handed down an account of the next thirty years in Spartan history which gives the impression that in this period internal conditions rapidly deteriorated until no remnant of the old traditions or constitution remained. According to Polybius' version, the Achaeans had let the Macedonians into the Peloponnese once more merely to safeguard the liberties of the Peloponnesian states, Sparta herself among the rest ; [1] and it was the Spartans themselves who ungratefully threw away the liberty conferred upon them, by persisting in the foreign policy of Cleomenes,[2] and by putting themselves under the control of a series of oppressive tyrants, Lycurgus, Machanidas, and finally Nabis, who was overthrown by the Romans. There is no alternative tradition to set against this, for Livy and Plutarch also reflect the Achaean point of view. But certain incidental pieces of information given by these writers themselves would lead us to suppose that they have not done justice to the Spartan side of the matter.

The Peloponnesian states in general knew what value to set upon their new ' liberty ' when a Macedonian governor was set up for the whole country.[3] It may easily be shown that Sparta was not placed in any specially favoured position.

To begin with, it appears that part of the so-called ' liberation ' of Sparta consisted in depriving her of a considerable amount of territory. Sparta had already lost Cynuria to Argos by the Macedonian settlement of 338 B.C.,[4] but still kept the towns of the Perioikoi.[5] Now all the coast towns of the Perioikoi north of and including Zarax were handed over to Argos, and since Leucae was also

---

[1] Cf. Polyb. IV, 16.

[2] Cf. ibid. 35 : συνέθεντο δὲ πρὸς τοὺς Αἰτώλους τὴν συμμαχίαν. ἐποίουν δὲ ταῦτα διά τε τὴν πρὸς 'Αχαιοὺς ἀπέχθειαν, καὶ τὴν πρὸς τοὺς Μακεδόνας ἀχαριστίαν . . . οὐχ ἥκιστα δὲ διὰ Κλεομένην, καὶ τὴν πρὸς ἐκεῖνον εὐνοίαν.

[3] Polyb. IV, 87.   [4] Cf. Kolbe, I.G. V, i, introd., p. vii.

[5] Cf. Paus. II, 20. 1, and below, p. 57, n. 3. Zarax was presumably threatening revolt when it was attacked by Sparta about 273 B.C. (Paus. III, 24. 1 For the date, cf. Plut. Pyrrhus, 26).

included in the ceded territory it would appear that it was
not only the coastal strip which was affected.[1] Similarly,
the regions on the west of the upper Eurotas valley
(Belbinatis and Aegytis) were handed over to Megalopolis,[2]
and the much-disputed Ager Dentheliatis, containing the
ancient shrine of Diana Limnatis in the upper valley of the
river Choerios, was definitely restored to Messenia.[3] It
is clear that all those Spartans whose spirit was not crushed
by the defeat at Sellasia must have been anxious to recover
this lost territory on the first opportunity, and their attitude
sufficiently explains the election as king in 219 of Lycurgus,
who was prepared to come forward as a military leader, and
who actually did recover a great deal of the ceded territory.[4]

Again, although Polybius maintains that Antigonus
left Sparta absolutely free and independent and mistress
of her own constitution, he mentions incidentally in another
connection that Antigonus established a Boeotian governor
in the city.[5] It was no doubt this governor who secured
that the Ephors in the next two years after Sellasia should
be pro-Macedonian and pro-Achaean, and since Polybius
has nothing further to say of his rule it seems likely that
he was expelled at the time of the first revolution against
Macedonian and Achaean domination, in 220 B.C. In this
year secret negotiations were opened with the Aetolians,[6]
with whom Sparta had been in alliance under Cleomenes,
and immediately afterwards one of the Ephors, of known
Macedonian sympathies, was murdered by order of the
rest, together with several political supporters.[7] The young
king, Philip, decided to overlook the incident, and contented himself with sending envoys to warn the Spartans
to be loyal to their friendship with Macedon,[8] but the
realisation that he was preparing to turn his forces against
the Aetolians [9] only served to encourage the nationalistic
party in the following year (219) to secure a powerful
ally while they could. All five Ephors were accordingly

[1] Cf. Polyb. IV, 36 ό: δὲ Λυκοῦργος . . . ἐνέβαλεν εἰς τὴν Ἀργείαν,
ἀφυλάκτως διακειμένων . . . τῶν Ἀργείων διὰ τὴν προυπάρχουσαν κατάστασιν.
καὶ Πολίχναν μὲν καὶ Πρασίας καὶ Λεύκας καὶ Κύφαντα προσπεσών, ἄφω
κατέσχε. Γλυμπεῦσι δὲ καὶ Ζάρακι προσπεσών, ἀπέσπασε. On the location
of Leucae, see I.G. V, i, p. 194.
[2] Polyb. II, 54.   [3] Cf. Kolbe, Ath. Mitt. XXIX (1904), p. 376.
[4] Cf. above, n. 1.   [5] Polyb. XX, 5.   [6] Ibid. IV, 16.
[7] Ibid. 22.   [8] Ibid. 24.   [9] Ibid. 25f.

murdered, others of the pro-Aetolian party were elected, and the renewal of alliance with the Aetolian League was confirmed.[1]

The news of Cleomenes' death in Egypt about this time removed any hesitation there had been until now over the desirability of electing new kings, and the election was forthwith carried through (winter 219–18).[2] One king, Agesipolis, was the direct heir in the house to which Cleomenes had belonged, but as he was still a child, his uncle Cleomenes was appointed as his guardian.[3] The other king, Lycurgus, is said by Polybius not to have been even distantly related to either royal house, but to have bought his throne by a bribe of five talents distributed among the Ephors.[4] The malice of rival claimants, one of whom soon afterwards raised a plot against Lycurgus,[5] combined with the natural prejudice of Polybius against a successful Spartan military leader, is probably enough to account for this story. The very name of Lycurgus is against it, for he almost certainly owed his name to his having been born at the time of the great nationalist and antiquarian revival under Agis IV, and probably among the relatives of the king himself, since these had been the most enthusiastic in his support from the first.[6]

Like many prominent Greeks, Lycurgus advertised his public policy in the name which he gave to his son Pelops, who was probably born after his accession to the throne.[7] Lycurgus was determined to win back Spartan hegemony in the Peloponnese, recovering for his own son the heritage of the mythical Pelops. In this ambition he had some considerable measure of success, in spite of severe set-backs at the beginning of his reign. Twice in the first year of

---

[1] Polyb. XX, 35.   [2] On the date, see Appendix II, p. 434.

[3] Polyb. IV, 35 ; cf. Livy XXXIV, 26 : *Princeps erat exulum Agesipolis, cuius iure gentis regnum Lacedaemone erat, pulsus infans ab Lycurgo tyranno post mortem Cleomenis, qui primus tyrannus Lacedaemone fuit.* Livy seems to have been guilty of confusing the guardian of Agesipolis with Cleomenes III, and may be supposed to mean that Agesipolis was driven out after his guardian's death.

[4] Polyb. IV, 35.   [5] *Ibid.* 81.   [6] *Cf.* Plut. *Agis.* 9.

[7] Pelops is described as παῖδα τὴν ἡλικίαν ὄντα in or soon after 207 (Diod. XXVII, 1) which makes it highly probable that he was born after his father's accession. But the name Pelops itself confirms this conclusion, for it is too remarkable to have been given without a political purpose, or before the father was already in a position to direct policy.

his short reign he was forced to flee for his life, the first time when a rival claimant to the throne attempted a revolution which failed,[1] the second time when Lycurgus was himself accused of plotting revolution, probably in connection with an invasion of Laconia by Philip V in 218.[2] He was recalled on this occasion by the Ephors of 217, when they discovered the suspicions which had been entertained against him to be unfounded. Busolt has drawn from these events the conclusion that Lycurgus was a mere weak tool in the hands of the Ephors,[3] but similar misfortunes had overtaken Cleomenes I and other Spartan kings in the past who were far from weak. Lycurgus in fact spent his second enforced absence in Aetolia, arranging for a combined attack with the Aetolians upon the Messenians, who had enthusiastically supported Philip in his recent invasion of Laconia.[4] The combined attack upon Messenia was carried out immediately upon Lycurgus' return, in 217, but failed in its main purpose owing to Aetolian inefficiency.[5] But three years later Philip is found invading not Laconia, but Messenia,[6] a proof that the Messenians had changed sides in the interval. They were to continue in alliance with Sparta, except for a period of enforced Achaean occupation,[7] until 195 ; so that the policy of Lycurgus was responsible for a notable strengthening of Sparta's position in the western Peloponnese. Of his purely military achievements the most notable was perhaps the recovery from Argos of Polichna, Prasiae, Leucae and Cyphanta,[8] thus driving the Argives out of most of the territory of the Perioikoi which they had occupied after Sellasia. But everything recorded of him goes to show that he was an extremely capable military leader, and the absence of further information about him after 217, in the pro-Achaean sources at least, gives no ground for suspecting that Sparta was further humbled or deprived of her liberties by the Achaeans or by Macedonia in the interval.

One decisive change in the constitution had, however, taken place. Cleomenes III had already realised that the

[1] Polyb. IV, 81.   [2] Ibid. V, 29, 91 ; cf. V, 18–24.
[3] Busolt, Die Griechische Altertümer (1892), p. 116.
[4] Polyb. V, 20.   [5] Ibid. 92.   [6] Ibid. VIII, 10.
[7] See below, pp. 30 f.   [8] Cf. above, p. 22, n. 1.

traditional dual kingship, held by representatives of two different houses with different traditions and prejudices, was fatal to the chance of success against constant threat from without. Lycurgus took the first opportunity of ridding himself of Agesipolis by driving him into exile,[1] and this was the final end of dual kingship. The monarchy thus created passed on the death of Lycurgus, which occurred some time before 211 B.C., to his son Pelops, but as Pelops was still a child, the effective government was carried on by his guardian [2] Machanidas.

It was in the regency of Machanidas that a decisive new step was taken in Spartan foreign policy, the alliance with Rome. A powerful new enemy of Macedon was a potential ally not to be overlooked. Spartan hopes in this direction must have risen as soon as Philip V concluded his alliance with Carthage, and when the Romans themselves made an offer of alliance to the Spartans immediately after concluding an alliance with the Aetolians,[3] the chance must have been eagerly seized. Sparta herself was already the long-standing ally of the Aetolians ; the date of her alliance with Rome was probably 211 B.C.[4]

[1] Cf. above, p. 23, n. 3. Agesipolis met his death about 183 B.C., while still in exile (Polyb. XXIII, 6).

[2] According to the probable hypcthesis of Wolters, Ath. Mitt. XXII, 1897, p. 144. That his position was constitutional is indicated by the continued commemoration of his name in that of a public building at Sparta ; cf. B.S.A. XXVII, p. 228.

[3] Livy, XXVI, 24 : igitur conscriptae condiciones, quibus in amicitiam societatemque populi Romani venirent (Aetoli); additumque, ut si placeret vellentque, eodem iure amicitiae Elei, Lacedaemoniique . . . essent. These overtures were actually made (cf. Polyb. IX, 28 ff.), and the consequence was the alliance between Rome and Sparta referred to by Flamininus in 195 B.C. ; cf. Livy, XXXIV, 32 : amicitia et societas nobis nulla tecum (i.e. with Nabis) sed cum Pelope, rege Lacedaemoniorum iusto ac legitimo, facta est.

[4] The date of the Aetolian alliance with Rome was either 212 or 211 (cf. C.A.H. VIII, p. 124), and the Roman alliance with Sparta followed immediately (cf. preceding note). But some historians find a difficulty in the words of Nabis in 195 (cf. Livy, XXXIV, 31) : cum ipse respexi, eum esse spero cui et publice, sicut ceteris Lacedaemoniis, vobiscum vetustissimum foedus sit: et meo nomine privatim amicitia ac societas, nuper Philippi bello renovata. Since an alliance concluded in 211 could scarcely be described as vetustissimum foedus sixteen years later, Holleaux rejects the evidence for the alliance in the reign of Pelops altogether, and thinks that an alliance with Nabis in 197 (on which see below, pp. 28 f.) was the first to be concluded between Rome and Sparta (see his Rome, la Grèce et les monarchies héllénistiques, Bibliothèque des Ecoles d'Athènes et de Rome,

From the point of view of Rome, Sparta could render valuable assistance merely by furthering her own interests in the Peloponnese, since the Macedonian king had already found it necessary more than once to make descents into Laconia, and it was in the interests of Rome that his attention should be distracted as much as possible from the Adriatic.

During the few years of his rule, before his death in battle at Mantinea in 207 against the Achaeans under Philopoemen,[1] Machanidas gave the Romans valuable aid in precisely this manner by perpetually harassing Philip's ally in the Peloponnese. Few details are recorded, but there is a note of exasperation, not unnatural in an Achaean writer under the circumstances, in Polybius' remark that after their victory at Mantinea the Achaeans were at last free to invade and ravage Laconian territory.[2] Shortly before this very battle, the army of Machanidas had been on the Argive frontier not far from Argos itself, threatening invasion,[3] and was only forced to retire by a rapid descent upon the Peloponnese by Philip himself, who penetrated as far as the Argive Heraeum.[4] Livy has a story that Philip was coming to forestall a surprise attack by Machanidas upon the Eleans when they were preparing to celebrate the Olympic festival [5]—a most unlikely tale in view of the fact that Elis had long been the faithful ally of Sparta, and continued to be so for long afterwards [6]— and no doubt a rumour deliberately started with the

vol. cxxiv, 1921, pp. 258 f.). But the evidence for the alliance of 211 is too good to be dismissed in this fashion. A possible explanation of the description *vetustissimum foedus* is that the Romans either believed, or (as is more likely) professed to believe in order to have some reputable excuse for interference in Peloponnesian affairs, that the alliance of 211 was a renewal of an alliance concluded at the time of the embassy sent to enquire into the laws and institutions of famous Greek states before the publication of the Twelve Tables (*cf.* Livy, III, 31 *fin.*).

[1] For descriptions of the battle, see Polyb. XI, 11–18 ; Plut. *Philop.* 10 ; Paus. VIII, 50. 2, 3. All these accounts are evidently derived from the same source, the two later ones being independent of Polybius, as is shown by their anecdote about the line from the *Persae* of Timotheus, a story which does not occur in Polybius. But there can be no doubt that the source is Achaean, and older than Polybius.

[2] Polyb. XI, 18 : καὶ πολλῷ χρόνῳ οὐ δυνάμενοι τοὺς πολεμίους ἐκ τῆς οἰκείας ἀπώσασθαι, τότε πᾶσαν ἀδεῶς ἐπορθοῦν τὴν Λακωνικήν.

[3] Livy, XXVIII, 5 ; *cf.* Polyb. X, 41.

[4] Livy. XXVIII, 7.   [5] *Ibid.*

[6] *Cf.* Polyb. IV, 5, 84 ; V, 2 ; V, 30 ; IX, 30 ; XVI, 13.

intention of helping the Macedonian and Achaean cause. The pro-Achaean sources naturally represent Machanidas as the arch-enemy of all free Greek states,[1] and the rumour about Elis was in keeping with the general propaganda to this effect. In reality his defeat at Mantinea, especially in view of the heavy losses sustained by the Spartan army,[2] was a much more real threat to the liberties of the Peloponnesian Greeks.

But fortunately another gifted military leader now arose in Nabis the son of Demaratus, whose father's name indicates his descent from one of the royal families.[3] He is said to have removed Pelops (who was still a boy) from his path by murdering him,[4] which may or may not be true, in view of the many exaggerated and distorted stories which were told about his reign. At all events it seems probable that he began his reign as the guardian of Pelops. He assumed himself the title of βασιλεύς,[5] and was recognised as such outside Sparta at Delos at least.[6] The Achaean sources call him consistently ' tyrannus ', which is only to be expected in view of the fact that he was the most formidable, because the nearest, of the enemies of the Achaean League from the beginning of his reign. The Romans gave him the title of king from his accession until after the defeat of Philip at Cynoscephalae,[7] their later appellation of ' tyrant ' denoting the changed attitude to a former ally who, according to his own account at least,[8] had not changed in either policy or character in the interval. At the

---

[1] Cf. Plut. Philop. 10 : ἀπὸ πολλῆς καὶ μεγάλης δυνάμεως ἐπιβουλεύοντα πᾶσι Πελοποννησίοις.

[2] Polyb. XI, 18, says that not less than 4,000 ' Lacedaemonians ' were killed and even more taken prisoner. Perioikoi were certainly included in this number, which would be impossibly large if it referred only to Spartan citizens.

[3] Cf. Homolle, Bull. Hell. XX (1896), pp. 505 f. On the earlier history of this branch of the Eurypontid house in exile in the Troad, cf. Herod. VI, 67 f. ; Xen. Hell. III, i, 6 ; Paus. III, 7. 8. Homolle argues convincingly from the evidence of inscriptions of Delos that a direct ancestor of Nabis, of this family, again became domiciled at Sparta in the late fourth century, B.C. [4] Diod. XXVII, 1.

[5] I.G. V, i, 885 a-c (wall-tiles inscribed βαίλεῖ Νάβι ; βαίλέος Νάβιος).

[6] Ditt. Syll.[3] 584 (grant of the privileges of a Proxenos to ' king Nabis ' at Delos).

[7] Livy, XXXIV, 31 : tum me regem adpellari a vobis memini; nunc (195) tyrannum vocari video.

[8] See his general apologia in Livy, loc. cit.

beginning of his reign he had concluded a new alliance with Rome,[1] presumably a renewal of the one concluded in 211 under Machanidas. His assistance was renewed in the Second Macedonian War, but the Romans treated him scurvily when in 199 they received into alliance the deadly enemy of Sparta, the Achaeans, who were now despairing of the success of their present ally Philip.[2]

In 197 it appeared likely that Nabis was going to turn the tables on Rome, for he agreed to a treaty of alliance with Philip, sealed by a promise of marriage between his own sons and Philip's daughters, in return for an undertaking on his part to occupy with a garrison Argos, where Philip was no longer able to maintain himself.[3] If Philip won the war with Rome, Nabis was to restore the city to him ; if Philip lost, Nabis was to keep it.[4] It anyone was betrayed on this occasion it was not the Romans but Philip. No sooner was Nabis in effective control of Argos than he re-opened negotiations with Flamininus,[5] and took all possible steps to ensure that Philip should lose the war, even agreeing to a four months' truce (he still refused a peace) with the Achaean League, and furnishing a contingent of 600 Cretan archers to the Romans.

The affair of Argos, and the continued control of the city by Nabis, was made the chief reason for their declaration of war upon him by Rome in 195. But although many of the circumstances of the occupation are obscure, and although it does not seem likely that Nabis was telling the truth when he claimed that the Argives themselves had called him to their assistance,[6] it is at all events clear

[1] For the date, *cf.* Ehrenberg, P. W., *s.v. Nabis* (1935), who rejects the dating proposed by Holleaux (*cf.* above, p. 25, n. 4). It appears certain from Livy, XXIX, 12 (*foederi adscripti . . . ab Romanis . . . Nabis Lacedaemoniorum tyrannus, Elei, Messenii, Athenienses*), that Nabis was already allied with Rome when peace was concluded with Philip in 205, and therefore he had presumably been allied with Rome since the beginning of his reign two years earlier. The renewal alluded to in Livy, XXXIV, 31 (*cf.* above, p. 25, n. 4) must be that of 197, on which see further below.

[2] *Cf.* C.A.H. VIII, pp. 170 f.   [3] *Cf.* Livy, XXXII, 38.

[4] *Ibid.: optimum ratus Nabidi eam . . . velut fiduciariam dare, ut victori sibi restitueret; si quid adversi accidisset, ipse haberet.*

[5] *Ibid.* 39 *init.*

[6] *Id.* XXXIV, 31 : *ipsis vocantibus et tradentibus urbem eam accepi.* But *cf.* XXXII, 38 : *ut frequenti contione non adspernantes modo, sed abominatos etiam nomen tyranni audivit,* and *ibid.* 40, *init.*

that Flamininus acquiesced in Nabis' control of Argos when he renewed the alliance with him in 197,[1] and that he thereby committed the Roman government to confirm Nabis in possession of Argos after Philip's defeat, in accordance with the terms which Nabis had himself made with Philip. A difficulty was that the Achaean League, also in alliance with Rome, also claimed Argos.[2] There was the further difficulty that after the defeat of Philip the senate had decided on the general policy of ' freeing Greece ', and with this the occupation of Argos by Nabis was certainly not compatible. At first the peace commissioners seem to have shelved the issue ; the first extravagant demand for freedom and autonomy for ' all Greek cities both in Europe and in Asia '[3] was modified in Flamininus' famous declaration at the Isthmian Games of 196 into a demand for freedom for all states which had been directly under Macedonian control, and all these states were north of the Isthmus.[4]

But the more sweeping claim had struck the popular imagination : the herald at the games was reported as having proclaimed the liberation of *all* Greek cities ;[5] and in order to sustain their prestige the Romans found themselves committed to the side of the Achaean League, which had for so long been professing to uphold the cause of freedom in the Peloponnese, against Nabis in the war which in any case was bound to come between the Achaean League and Sparta.[6]

[1] *Cf.* Livy, XXXIV, 31 : *ut vobis mitterem ad bellum auxilia, non ut Argis praesidium deducerem pepigistis.*   [2] *Cf.* Polyb. XVIII, 2.

[3] Livy, XXXIII, 30 : *Omnes Graecorum civitates quae in Europa quaeque in Asia essent libertatem et suas leges haberent.*   Polyb. XVIII, 44, adds that the towns under Philip's direct control were first to be surrendered to Rome.

[4] *Ibid.* 32 : *Senatus Romanus et T. Quinctius imperator, Philippo rege Macedonibusque devictis, liberos, immunes, suis legibus esse iubet Corinthios, Phocenses, Locrensesque omnes, et insulam Euboeam, et Magnetas, Thessalos, Achaeos Phthiotas.* (A translation of Polyb. XVIII, 46, *ad fin.*, who also includes the Perrhaebians).

[5] *Ibid.* 33 : *una voce praeconis liberatos omnes Graeciae atque Asiae urbes.* (A translation of Polyb. XVIII, 46, *ad fin.*) Acting on this assumption, Gytheum established a cult of Flamininus (Kornemann, *Neue Dokumente*, 1929, p. 8, l. 11).

[6] As shown by the refusal of Nabis in 197 to conclude any more than a four months' truce with the League, and by his immediate mobilisation of all the financial and military resources of Argos (Livy, XXXII, 38, 40) ; *cf.* I.G. IV, 497 : ἐπειδὴ ἀπαχθέντων ἐφήβων τῶν Μυκανέων ὑπὸ Νάβιος ἐς Λακεδαίμονα, κ.τ.λ.

It is certain that the Achaean League itself had no intention of granting universal autonomy in the Peloponnese, and was in fact making claims upon the territorial possessions of other allies of Rome at that very time.[1] Indeed the Romans themselves appear to have thought that the Spartan occupation of Argos did not provide a clear case against Nabis, for they also began a campaign of denunciation against the character of his rule in Sparta itself (although there is no reason to think that this had changed since the early part of his reign), and somewhat later yet another charge against him was discovered and put forward—an attack which he was said to have made on Messene in 201. It seems worth while to expose the unscrupulous nature of this accusation, since it affords yet another proof that neither the Achaean nor the Roman tradition about Nabis is to be taken—as so far nearly all historians seem to have taken it—at its face value.[2]

One ally of Rome at least was deceived by the accusation about Messene. Eumenes of Pergamum recorded on his dedication of spoils from the campaign of 195 in Laconia that the war had been against ' the subjugator of the Argives and of the Messenians '.[3] The Messenians were not, however, subject to Sparta when the war against Nabis began or during its course, but in alliance with the other allies of Rome against her.[4] Neither were they left subject to Sparta after the alleged attack of Nabis in 201,[5] for Plutarch, who gives the fullest account of this affair which has been preserved,[6] says that it ended in the flight of Nabis from Messene and the ' liberation ' of the town by Philopoemen.[7] How long it remained in this ' liberated ' condition is not clear, for Philopoemen had no official position at the time,

---

[1] Cf Polyb. XVIII, 42 : γενομένης δὲ ἀντιρρήσεως . . . διὰ τὸ κατὰ πρόσωπον Ἠλείους μὲν ἀμφισβητεῖν τοῖς Ἀχαιοῖς ὑπὲρ τῆς Τριφυλίας, Μεσσηνίους δ'ὑπὲρ Ἀσίνης καὶ Πύλου, συμμάχους τότε Ῥωμαίων ὑπάρχοντας, κ τ.λ.

[2] Ehrenberg (P.W. s.v. Nabis) points out that the Achaean account was certainly biassed against Nabis, but omits to notice that the Romans had similar reasons for misrepresentation. The version usually given of the affair of Messene will be found in C.A.H. VIII, p. 147.

[3] Inschr. v. Pergamon, 60 : ἐκ τῆς στρατείας . . . ἣν ἐστρατεύσατο . . . ἐπὶ Νάβιν τὸν Λάκωνα τὸν καταστρεψάμενον Ἀργείους καὶ Μεσσηνίους.

[4] Cf. above, n. 1.   [5] For the date, cf. C.A.H. ibid.

[6] Cf. also Polyb. XVI, 13, 16, 17 ; Paus. IV, 29. 10.

[7] Plut. Philop. 12, ad fin.: καὶ διέφυγε, Μεσσήνη δ'ἐλευθέρωτο. Paus. loc. cit., says : καὶ ὁ μὲν Σπαρτιάτης τύραννος ἀπῆλθεν ὑπόσπονδος.

and was acting against the decision of the Strategos of the League.[1] But Pausanias agrees with Plutarch that the occupation by Nabis had lasted less than a single night,[2] and until that night Messene had certainly been in alliance both with Rome [3] and Sparta.[4] On the other hand the Achaean League was in alliance with Philip at the time, and until two years later, so that the original indignation of the Romans at the affair must have been directed not against Nabis, their own ally, but against Philopoemen. Moreover, Plutarch's account implies that the question of sending an Achaean force to occupy Messene had been brought up in the League council *before* the supposed attack by Nabis took place, and that the Strategos Lysippus had advised against it.[5] Nabis is said to have maintained a formidable intelligence service in Arcadia,[6] and so probably got wind of this. The most likely explanation of his action at Messene is therefore that he had warned the inhabitants of a possible Achaean coup, and had been called in with a small garrison himself as a precautionary measure. But he had not expected the surprise attack of Philopoemen on the same night as his own arrival, and so was forced to withdraw, leaving the Achaeans in possession. Later on, when the Romans were preparing war on Nabis, they conveniently forgot that at the time of the Messene affair Philopoemen had represented the enemy, and spoke only of the attack by Nabis on an ally of themselves,[7] while the Achaeans stressed the treachery of an attack by Nabis upon an ally of his own [8]—whom in fact he was not attacking but supporting.

[1] Plut. *loc. cit.*
[2] Ref. in notes 6 and 7 above, p. 30.
[3] *Cf.* below, n. 7.
[4] *Cf.* below, n. 8.
[5] Plut. *Philop.* 12.

[6] On the occasion of a raid by Philopoemen into Laconia in 200, the Achaean general was forced to all kinds of subterfuges in organising his attack διὰ τὸ πλῆθος τῶν ὠτακουστῶν καὶ κατασκόπων τοῦ τυράννου (Polyb. XVI, 37).

[7] Livy, XXXIV, 32 : *nam et Messenen, uno atque eodem iure foederis quo et Lacedaemonem in amicitiam nostram acceptam* (*cf.* above, p. 25, n. 3) *socius ipse sociam nobis urbem vi et armis cepisti.*

[8] Polyb. XVI, 13 : (ὁ Νάβις) σύμμαχος ὑπαρχὼν Αἰτωλοῖς, Ἠλείοις, Μεσσηνίοις, καὶ πᾶσι τούτοις ὀφείλων καὶ κατὰ τοὺς ὅρκους καὶ κατὰ τὰς συνθήκας βοηθεῖν, εἴ τις ἐπ' αὐτοὺς ἴοι, παρ' οὐδὲν ποιησάμενος τὰς προειρημένας πίστεις ἐπεβάλετο παρασπονδῆσαι τὴν τῶν Μεσσηνίων πόλιν. He refers to the affair again in XVI, 16, as a παρασπόνδημα.

These misrepresentations of the facts in the alleged seizure of Messene and of Argos should prepare us for further misrepresentation when the Achaean and Roman writers come to discuss the character of Nabis himself and of his rule in Sparta and the rest of Laconia. When their accusations are examined, they are in fact seen to be composed partly of the usual stock-in-trade of abuse against ' tyrants ', partly of facts true in themselves but utilised for propaganda purposes. It is, for example, true that Nabis employed a large force of mercenaries in addition to his citizen army. So did the Achaean League, and so did all Hellenistic states both at this period and before the time of Nabis. Both Sparta and the Achaean League had long made use of Cretans in particular.[1] But Polybius asks us to believe that only in the army of Nabis were the low types to be found ; his mercenary army was deliberately composed of ' murderers, armed gangsters, footpads, and burglars from all parts of the world, to whom their own country was closed on account of their crimes '.[2] Having given the impression that there were vast numbers of these men, Polybius somewhat weakens his effect by going on to say that they formed the personal bodyguard of Nabis himself.[3] But it is not so much the discrepancy of numbers which creates suspicion as the unmistakable echo of Plato, whose typical tyrants compose their bodyguard of precisely the same classes of ruffians as those described by Polybius.[4] Nor are Aristotle's accusations against tyrants overlooked,[5]

---

[1] *Cf.* Polyb. V, 36 ; XIII, 6 ; XXXIII, 16 ; Livy, XXXV, 28, 29.

[2] Polyb. XIII, 6 : οὗτοι δ'ἦσαν ἀνδροφόνοι καὶ παρασχισταί, λωποδύται, τοιχωρύχοι. καθόλου γὰρ τοῦτο τὸ γένος ἠθροίζετο πρὸς αὐτὸν ἐπιμελῶς ἐκ τῆς οἰκουμένης, οἷς ἄβατος ἦν ἡ θρέψασα δι'ἀσεβείαν καὶ παρανομίαν. Diod. XXVII, 1, echoes Polybius in similar terms.

[3] *Ibid.* : ὧν προστάτην καὶ βασιλέα αὐτὸν ἀναδείξας, καὶ χρώμενος δορυ-φόροις καὶ σωματοφύλαξι τούτοις, δῆλον ὅτι ἔμελλε. πολυχρόνιον ἔχειν τὴν ἐπ'ἀσεβείᾳ φήμην καὶ δυναστείαν. Holleaux seeks to avoid the contra-diction implied in Polybius by a modern parallel, and speaks of Nabis forming ' a *Red Guard* of Cretans and mercenaries recruited from among the adventurers of all Greece ' (C.A.H. VIII, p. 147).

[4] *Cf.* Plato, *Rep.* IX, 575B f. The δορυφόροι of the typical tyrant begin by breaking into houses, robbing lonely pedestrians at night, robbing temples, until finally οὔτε τινὸς φόνου δεινοῦ ἀφέξεται οὔτε βρώματος οὔτ' ἔργου. Temple robbers are included in Diodorus' version (referred to above, n. 2) and are specially mentioned among the employees of Nabis in Polyb. XIII, 8.

[5] *Pol.* V, 11. 4–10, 32.

and Polybius duly accuses Nabis of oppression and expulsion of the aristocracy, of maintaining a spy system, of rapacity in collecting funds, and of emancipation of the slaves—or rather, in the case of Nabis, of Helots. In all these strictures there seems to be a small grain of truth in a large quantity of propaganda.

With regard to the expulsion of Spartan nobles, Nabis is said not to have been content merely to drive them out and to confiscate their property, but employed his gangs of hired desperadoes to seek them out wherever they sought refuge throughout the Peloponnese, and to kill them by one means or another until nearly all of them were destroyed.[1] Yet when Flamininus invaded Laconia in 195 his army was accompanied, according to Livy, by ' immense numbers ' of Spartan exiles driven out by the tyrants,[2] and even if Livy also is exaggerating, there were certainly considerable numbers of Spartan exiles available to return after the overthrow of Nabis, since the question of their return was one of the chief problems which exercised the Roman government with regard to Sparta in the succeeding period.[3] The cruelty and persistence of Nabis in seeking out and destroying all exiles from Sparta must therefore have been much exaggerated by Polybius.

Nabis himself admitted that he had liberated Helots and had distributed lands to landless citizens,[4] but pointed out that, in the first place, he had already done this when the Romans renewed their alliance with him in 197,[5] and that, in the second place, it was in accordance with the long-established practice of Sparta to do so,[6] even if the Romans regarded it as revolutionary. This claim was undoubtedly true, and may be substantiated not only by the more recent instances in the reign of Cleomenes III and later, but by the liberation of Helots on several occasions

[1] Polyb. XIII, 7 : καὶ δὴ τῷ τοιούτῳ τρόπῳ τοὺς μὲν πλείστους αὐτῶν ἠφάνισε.

[2] Livy, XXXIV, 26 : *Lacedaemoniorum exules permulti, tyrannorum iniuria pulsi.*

[3] *Cf.* below, pp. 44 f.

[4] Livy, XXXIV, 31 : *Ceterum nomen tyranni et facta me premunt, quod servos ad libertatem voco, quod in agros inopem plebem deduco.*

[5] *Cf.* above, pp. 28 f.

[6] Livy, *ibid.*: *sed si nunc ea fecissem, non dico, quid in eo vos laesissem . . . sed illud, nae more atque instituto maiorum fecisse.*

3

in the Peloponnesian War, and by the rapid growth of the class of *Neodamodeis*.[1] To the Romans such a practice was unthinkable, and therefore appeared to be subversive ; but from the Spartan point of view the Roman method of allowing private persons to create new citizens by manumission must have seemed far more shocking. Nabis is said to have pointed out to Flamininus the unreasonableness of judging Spartan internal policy by Roman standards,[2] but the warning, though obvious, has not been sufficiently heeded by modern scholars who tend to fall into the same trap. It is certainly a mistake, for example, to represent Nabis as a socialist reformer and as having introduced communism into Sparta.[3] Nabis had a perfect right to claim that he was acting in this respect ' *tamquam aemulus Lycurgi* '.[4]

Flamininus himself apparently realised that there was no real ground for attacking Nabis on the score of liberating Helots, for he is said by Livy to have assigned much more importance to the absence of any free assembly either at Sparta or at Argos under Spartan rule.[5] But this accusation is even more *ad captandum* than the last. The Spartan Apella had never, at any time in Spartan history, enjoyed the right of discussion or had the final voice in deciding policy.[6] In this respect it was neither more nor less free than the Roman Assemblies with respect to the Senate at the very time when Flamininus was speaking. The history of the popular Assembly at Argos is much more obscure, but we may safely assume that it was no less free under Spartan rule than it had been under Macedonian rule, with a Macedonian garrison in occupation. Nor in fact had the Romans any intention of setting up free public assemblies everywhere in Greece, as their later policy showed : their only intention for the present was to overthrow an embarrassingly powerful ruler, and as a means

[1] See further below, pp. 39 f.

[2] Livy, XXXIV, 31 : *nolite ad vestros leges et instituta exigere ea quae Lacedaemone fiunt.*

[3] This is the view expressed by Holleaux (C.A.H. VIII, p. 147) ; *cf.* also Tarn (C.A.H. VII, p. 757).

[4] Livy, *loc. cit.*

[5] *Ibid.; Exhibe liberam contionem vel Argis, vel Lacedaemone, si audire iuvat vera dominationis impotentissimae crimina.*

[6] *Cf.* below, Appendix VI, pp. 482 f.

to that end, to blacken his reputation in the eyes of the world.

As far as posterity is concerned, it must be admitted that Roman propaganda has been remarkably successful. The story of the instrument of torture, made in the likeness of his wife Apega, which Nabis used to extract money from his victims,[1] sounds too fantastic to impose on the credulity of any but the most ignorant, but it has contributed to the general legend none the less, and it is now difficult to escape from the impression that Nabis was a mere robber chief and a monster of cruelty. And yet he was honoured at Delos with all the privileges of a ' Proxenos and Bene- factor ' on account of ' his public services to the state and temple and his private services to individual Delians whenever they sought his help '.[2] Since the same formula is found in other Delian Proxenia decrees of the period,[3] relating to private persons, there is no justification for supposing the one relating to Nabis to imply that he was terrorising the Aegean with a pirate fleet at the time, and that the Delians conferred honours upon him with a view to injuring their enemies the Romans.[4] The decree testifies rather to normal peaceful relations and civilised transactions between Sparta under Nabis and the islands of the Aegean. As for the pirate fleet, the only evidence that Nabis main- tained one is the accusation made by Flamininus during the Roman invasion of Laconia in 195 ; *bellum adversus nos gerens mare circa Maleam infestum navibus piraticis fecisti . . . tutiorque Macedoniae ora, quam promontorium Maleae commeatus ad exercitus nostros portantibus navibus fuit.*[5] To the twentieth-century reader this complaint on the part of the Romans will scarcely seem justified, and the sympathy will go rather to Nabis in his attempt to deprive the invaders of supplies.

The behaviour of Nabis' own subjects in Laconia, Perioikoi as well as Spartans, during the Roman invasion

[1] *Cf.* Polyb. XIII, 7.
[2] Ditt. *Syll.*[3] 584 : ἐπειδὴ βασιλεὺς Νάβις Δαμαράτου Λακεδαιμόνιος ἀνὴρ ἀγαθὸς ὢν διατελεῖ περί τε τὸ ἱερὸν καὶ τὸν δῆμον τὸν Δηλίων καὶ χρείας παρέχεται καὶ κοινῆι τῆι πόλει καὶ ἰδίαι τοῖς ἐντυγχάνουσιν αὐτῶι τῶν πολιτῶν, εἰς ἃ ἄν τις αὐτὸν παρακαλεῖ. κ.τ.λ.
[3] *Cf. ibid.* no. 500.   [4] *Cf.* Dittenberger, *ibid.* no. 584, n. 2.
[5] Livy, XXXIV, 32.

supposedly undertaken for their liberation, does not bear out the contention that Nabis was an oppressive tyrant. The force which the Romans collected against them was overwhelming, and yet nearly all were determined to resist. The Romans indeed spread abroad afterwards the idea that the Perioikoi had hastened to join the Romans,[1] but this is not the impression which Livy's account of the actual invasion conveys. The towns of the Perioikoi on the coast are said to have joined the Romans *partim voluntate, partim vi et metu*,[2] and in most cases they were compelled to submit by the appearance of the considerable Roman fleet.[3] But Gytheum at least stood a siege by land and sea which might have ended successfully for the defenders had not Flamininus been able to throw in another four thousand picked troops at the crucial moment.[4]

The main army of Nabis, which included among its best troops Perioikoi,[5] with one voice refused to submit to the terms of a truce proposed by Flamininus [6] even though by that time the whole of Laconia had been laid waste [7] and there was nothing left for them to do except to defend the city itself. This loyalty on the part of the subjects of Nabis shows that the Achaean Strategos was not overstepping the bounds of possibility in suggesting at this moment that Nabis should follow the example of other despotic rulers in the Peloponnese, that he should lay down his power and live to a safe and honoured old age in the state over which he had ruled as a tyrant.[8] But the suggestion reveals the utter baselessness of the charges brought against Nabis by the Achaeans and the Romans.

The war with Rome in 195 left Nabis still in control at Sparta, but he was forced to give up Argos, some towns which he had occupied in Crete [9] and all the coast towns

---

[1] *Cf.* Strabo, VIII, 366 : ἐπειδὴ 'Ρωμαίοις προσέθεντο πρῶτοι οἱ Περίοικοι, τυραννουμένης τῆς Σπάρτης. The word προσέθεντο implies that the Perioikoi joined the Romans of their own free will.

[2] Livy, XXXIV, 29.

[3] *Ibid.; ingens multitudo navalium sociorum, e tribus contracta classibus.*

[4] Livy, *ibid.*

[5] *Ibid.* 36 : *iuventutem praeterea civitatium earum* (*i.e.* of the towns of the Perioikoi) *supplementum longe optimi generis militum habebat.*

[6] *Ibid.* 37 : *prope una voce omnes ' Nihil respondere, bellum geri ', iusserunt.*

[7] *Ibid.* 28 ; *cf.* 34 : *nihil iam praeter nudum solum ager hostium habebat.*

[8] *Ibid.* 33.   [9] *Ibid.* 35.

of the Perioikoi, these last being placed under the ' protection ' of the Achaean League.[1] He was also forced to give up his fleet and all prisoners of war, and to pay an indemnity of 400 talents in annual instalments over a period of eight years.

In the war which broke out three years later between Nabis (now seeking to recover Gytheum) and the Achaean League the Romans were obviously anxious, in view of the imminent war with Syria, not to interfere ; [2] the senate would evidently have preferred that Nabis should remain independent to counterbalance the power of the League. This plan was upset by the treachery of the Aetolians, who organised the assassination of Nabis,[3] and so made it possible for the Achaean League to assert its complete domination of Sparta, which was forced to become a member of the League.[4] There were no more kings of Sparta after 192 B.C., and with this date there begins a new period in the history of the city, which was no longer an independent sovereign state.

According to Ehrenberg, Nabis was the last Spartan great leader, but was also responsible for the final destruction of all the institutions which had made Sparta what she was in the past.[5] This conclusion has been shown to rest in general upon the distorted version of the facts which has come down to us through Achaean and Roman sources. But there is one matter in particular which merits further investigation, the policy of Nabis with regard to the Helots. The literary sources imply a wholesale liberation of them,[6] and apart from Strabo's reference to their disappearance at the beginning of the Roman period,[7] there appears to be no further evidence for the existence of this class throughout the whole of the later history of Sparta. This certainly suggests that Nabis changed the whole character of the

---

[1] Livy, XXXV, 13.   [2] Cf. ibid. 20, ad fin., 23, 25.   [3] Ibid. 35.
[4] Ibid. 37 :   Philopoemen . . . societati Achaeorum Lacedaemonios adiunxit.   [5] P.W. s.v. Nabis.
[6] Cf. Polyb. XVI, 13 : ἐκβαλὼν τοὺς πολίτας ἠλευθέρωσε τοὺς δούλους, καὶ συνῴκισε ταῖς τῶν δεσποτῶν γυναιξὶ καὶ θυγατράσιν.
[7] According to Strabo, VIII, 5. 4 (365), the Helot system lasted until the Roman period (μεχρὶ τῆς 'Ρωμαίων ἐπικρατείας), i.e. presumably until 146 B.C. This may mean that the system was then legally abolished : it seems doubtful whether in fact any Helots remained after the reign of Nabis.

Spartan citizen body and that his claim to be the upholder of the Lycurgan régime had no justification in fact.

But it is evident from Livy's account (although Livy himself appears to be unaware of this) that the position of the Helots in general had already changed considerably before the time of Nabis, as compared with their status in the time of Thucydides. Livy's definition of Helots, given in connection with the Roman invasion of 195 B.C., is *iam inde antiquitus castellani agreste genus*.[1] It happens that a Roman inscription of precisely this period has survived which shows exactly what Livy's source—presumably here Roman—must have meant by this technical term *castellani*. The inscription records an edict of L. Aemilius Paullus as *imperator* (between 191 and 189 B.C.), which decrees that slaves from Hasta occupying a certain *turris Lascutana* in southern Spain shall be free, and shall have *possessio* during the pleasure of the Senate and Roman people of the territory and the *oppidum* which they occupy at the time of the edict.[2] These liberated slaves are clearly the garrison of the fortress,[3] and in view of their holdings of land in the vicinity, might appropriately be described in exactly the same terms as Livy's Helots, as *castellani, agreste genus*. The Laconian Helots of the period were also obliged to serve as soldiers, as appears from Livy's inclusion of them in the ' tyrant's ' army of native troops : [4] they were not merely resident as agricultural labourers at the *castella* in question but were actively employed in their defence.

Although Livy says that the Helots in the reign of Nabis

---

[1] Livy, XXXIV, 27.

[2] I.L.S. 15 : *L. Aimilius L. f. inpeirator decreivit, utei quei Hastensium servei in turri Lascutana habitarent, leiberei essent; agrum oppidumqu, quod ea tempestate posedisent, item possidere habereque iousit, dum populus senatusque Romanus vellet. Act. in castreis a.d. XII, k. Febr.*

[3] If they had been employed as slaves in the fort, they would not have been occupying land (as the edict implies that they had) before the decree itself was issued. Moreover, the *turris* was not in the territory of Hasta, which appears from Pliny (N.H. III, 11–15) to have been in a different conventus from Lascuta. Whole or part of the population of Hasta, among them slaves whose emancipation was recognised by the edict, had therefore been transplanted by the Romans to Lascuta to serve as its garrison.

[4] *Cf.* Livy, XXXIV, 27 : *decem milia popularium cum castellanis agrestibus in armis habuit.* This force represented the native Laconian troops as opposed to the mercenaries.

had been in this position from ancient times (*iam inde antiquitus*) the contrast between these *castellani* and the Helots of the fifth century B.C. is most marked. The earlier Helots were serfs with no measure of freedom whatever, attached to the hereditary estates of individual Spartans,[1] whereas the *castellani* mentioned by Livy would appear to have been free men, though presumably not free to leave the *castella* to which they were attached, for otherwise they could scarcely have still retained the name of Helots. It seems probable that their position was very much like that of the *castellani* on the frontiers of the later Roman empire, in a position intermediate between liberty and serfdom.[2] But although this was a status quite unlike that of the earlier Helots, there are indications that the system itself was not a recent innovation at Sparta, but was already in existence in the fifth century B.C.

At Lepreon in 421, and at Oion in the Sciritis in 369, the Spartans planted settlers with the status of *Neodamodeis* to act as a garrison.[3] In the case of Lepreon at least, some of these colonists were ex-Helots who had shortly before been emancipated as a reward for their services in Thrace under Brasidas, and had been given permission to live where they liked.[4] The settlement at Lepreon therefore marked the conferment upon these ex-Helots, in return for their services as garrison soldiers, of a further privilege beyond mere emancipation, which privilege evidently consisted in the grant of land and in the grant of some form of citizenship, as implied by the name *Neodamodeis*.[5] That the citizenship of this class was of an inferior kind is clear from the discontent which they harboured against the class of Equals,[6] and it seems probable that their disability consisted in the hereditary obligation to remain as garrison soldiers on the land which had been given to them or to their ancestors. This hypothesis would explain both the

[1] *Cf.* pp. 301 f.
[2] *Cf.* Rostovtzeff, *Social and Economic History of the Roman Empire* (1926), p. 608, n. 49; also Stein, *Geschichte des Spätrömischen Reiches*, I (1928), p. 22, on the *gentiles* and *laeti*.
[3] Thuc. V, 34; Xen. *Hell.* VI, 5. 24.
[4] Thuc. *ibid.*: ἐψηφίσαντο τοὺς μὲν μετὰ Βρασίδου Εἵλωτας μαχεσαμένους ἐλευθέρους εἶναι καὶ οἰκεῖν ὅπου ἂν βούλωνται.
[5] See further, Appendix VI, p. 480.
[6] *Cf.* Xen. *Hell.* III, iii, 6, on the conspiracy of Cinadon.

desire of the *Neodamodeis* in the fourth century to ' eat
the Spartiates raw '[1] and the emergence in the second
century B.C. of a class who correspond in other respects
to the earlier *Neodamodeis*, but are once again called Helots
by Livy and by other writers following the same tradition.
Pausanias, for example, speaks of the sale into slavery by
Philopoemen, after his second descent upon Sparta in 189
B.C., of 3,000 ' Helots ' ;[2] but the same persons are referred
to by Plutarch as ' those who had been declared citizens
by the tyrants '.[3] Livy, referring to the same incident,
cites a decree of the Achaean League Council ordering that
Helots freed by the tyrants (*quae servitia tyranni liber-
assent*) should leave Laconia before a certain date on pain
of re-enslavement.[4] In translating the term used in the
Achaean decree to describe this class of persons, Livy uses
the expression *Lacedaemoniis adscripti*, which implies that
the Helots in question had been not merely emancipated
but had been given some form of citizenship.[5] The conclusion seems to follow that the term used in the decree
itself was *Neodamodeis*, especially as the persons in question
had not left the country on their liberation but had settled
down there and were unwilling to leave. In any case,
later writers appear not to realise the difference, and to
describe as Helots those who were in fact *Neodamodeis*.
The liberation of 6,000 ' Helots ' by Cleomenes III, recorded
by Plutarch,[6] is probably another instance of this confusion, since the condition of liberation was the payment
of five Attic minas, a considerable sum in itself and surely
impossible to acquire for any Helot under the true meaning
of the name. The 6,000 may well have been *Neodamodeis*
who had received land in return for acting as garrison troops.
The same misunderstanding appears in Strabo, who says
that the Helots were something like public slaves (τρόπον
τινα δημοσίους δούλους), and that the Spartans assigned
them to special settlements (κατοικίας τινὰς αὐτοῖς ἀπο-
δέξαντες) and laid special obligations upon them (λειτουργίας
ἰδίας).[7] His use of the same word in other parts of his

---

[1] *Cf.* Xen. *Hell.* III, iii, 6, on the conspiracy of Cinadon.
[2] Paus. VIII, 51, 3.   [3] Plut. *Philop.* 16.   [4] Livy, XXXVIII, 34.
[5] *Cf.* Livy, *ibid.* The meaning of *Lacedaemoniis adscripti* for a Roman
writer of this period is well illustrated by Cic. *Pro Archia*, 4.
[6] *Cf.* above, p. 15, n. 1.   [7] Strabo, VIII, 5. 4 (365).

work makes it clear that Strabo means by κατοικίαι not barracks in which serfs were kept, but colonial settlements.[1] Λειτουργίαι would also be a word inappropriate to describe the menial tasks of the enslaved Helots, but appropriate to the obligation to defend the *castella* which devolved upon the *Neodamodeis*. And finally, the earlier Helots were in no sense public slaves, but were owned by individual Spartans.[2] It therefore seems certain that Strabo's description properly applies to the enfranchised Helots given the status of *Neodamodeis ;* though it must also be supposed that in the last period of Spartan independence the *Neodamodeis* had sunk into a position in which they were by no means wholly free ; hence the confusion among the ancient writers on the subject.

In assessing the general condition of Sparta at the beginning of the period of Achaean domination, factors of the highest importance are the disappearance of the Helots (theoretically postponed until the Roman annexation of Achaea,[3] but in fact already nearly complete before the reign of Nabis) and the deliberate expulsion of the large class of *Neodamodeis* by the Achaean League. The removal of the *Neodamodeis* deprived Laconia at one blow of about half its defenders,[4] not counting the Perioikoi who had already been separated from the rest of Laconia. No longer could Sparta be described as *validissimam urbem viris armisque*, as it had been in 195,[5] and no doubt the military weakening of Sparta was the main purpose of the provision about the *Neodamodeis* in the Achaean decree. The rest, the full citizens, could easily be cowed into subjection after their heavy loss of men in the invasion of 192 B.C.,[6] especially with the pro-Achaean exiles recalled,[7]

---

[1] *Cf.* Strabo, V, 4. 8 (246 *ad fin.*), and *ibid.* 11 (249), where Heraclea, Suessula, Atella, Nola, Nuceria, Acerrae, Abella and ' other even smaller κατοικίαι ' are mentioned.

[2] *Cf.* below, pp. 301 f. Pausanias (III, 20. 6) makes the same mistake as Strabo and calls the Helots Λακεδαιμονίων δοῦλοι τοῦ κοινοῦ.

[3] *Cf.* above, p. 37, n. 7.

[4] *Cf.* above, p. 38, n. 4, and pp. 12 ff., on the size of the full-citizen army of Cleomenes III.

[5] Livy, XXXIV, 33.

[6] *Cf.* Livy, XXXV, 30 : *ita multi caesi captique sunt, ut vix quarta pars de toto exercitu evaserit.*

[7] *Cf.* Livy, XXXVIII, 34 : *nihil . . . aegrius passi sunt, quam exsules reduci.*

and the leaders of the nationalist party driven into exile.
But the change in the economic situation was even more
serious. These *castellani agrestes* must have formed the
backbone of Laconian agriculture at this period, for their
numbers were large,[1] and to judge from the ability of 6,000
to pay five minae each in the reign of Cleomenes for their
complete emancipation, they were comparatively wealthy.
In the reign of Nabis Laconian agriculture was still flourishing in spite of many recent devastations of the countryside :
the district round Amyclae was in the first half of the second
century B.C. exceedingly rich in forest and corn.[2] In the
late third century B.C., according to Polybius, the region
round Helos was even more conspicuous than Amyclae
for its crops.[3] Many references in all periods to choice
agricultural produce in Laconia [4] show that the deliberate
policy of economic isolation which Sparta had adopted in
the period of her greatness had at least the effect of encouraging the cultivation of Laconia itself. But even
before the expulsion of the *castellani agrestes* Sparta was
unable to maintain her population without importing
necessities by sea : hence, as Livy tells us,[5] the ill-fated
attack on Las in 189 B.C., which precipitated another
Achaean invasion.

This particular grievance imposed by the Achaean
League, the lack of ports, was not remedied until Augustus
made grants to Sparta of some isolated ports in Messenia
and the island of Cythera.[6] It would appear that Augustus
also stimulated the export of animal skins and perhaps of

---

[1] *Cf.* above, p. 38, n. 4, and Livy, XXXVIII, 34, who remarks of
the enfranchised Helots driven out by the Achaean League *ea magna
multitudo erat.*

[2] Polyb. V, 19 : τόπος ἐστὶ τῆς Λακωνικῆς καλλιδενδρότατος καὶ
καλλικαρπότατος.

[3] *Cf. ibid.*: ἥτις ἐστὶν ὡς πρὸς μέρος θεωρουμένη πλείστη καὶ καλλίστη
χώρα τῆς Λακωνικῆς. ὅθεν ἀφεὶς τὰς προνομὰς . . . τὸν τόπον τοῦτον πάντα
κατεπυρπόλει, καὶ διέφθειρε τοὺς ἐν αὐτῷ καρπούς.

[4] *E.g.* wine (Alcman *ap.* Athen. I, 31c) ; fine wheat (*siligo :* Pliny,
N.H. XVIII, 92) ; ἑσπερίδων μῆλα (Aristocrates *ap.* Athen. III, 82c) ; early
figs (Pliny, N.H. XVI, 113, says that the Laconian kind sometimes bore
two crops) ; gourds (*ibid.* XIX, 68) ; lettuces (*ibid.* XIX, 124).

[5] *Cf.* Livy, XXXVIII, 30 : *ut aliqua liberum ad mare haberent aditum,
si quando Romam aliove quo mitterent legatos, simulque ut emporium et
receptaculum peregrinis mercibus ad necessarios usus esset, nocte adorti
vicum maritimum nomine Lan improviso occupavere.*

[6] See below, p. 56.

other products of the Taygetus region.[1] But in the interval, which was one of economic insecurity for the whole East Mediterranean area, the internal prosperity of Sparta, additionally hampered by lack of agricultural labourers, inevitably suffered decay. The age-old traditions of a military aristocracy are hard to break, and must have made it difficult for the country to adapt itself to new economic opportunities when they came at last ; [2] and Sparta in the Roman period presents, in fact, the rather pathetic spectacle of a museum city, clinging tenaciously to all its ancient institutions for the sake of attracting tourists. Such was the lasting legacy of Philopoemen.

On the other hand, the constitutional changes which Achaean rule brought to Sparta were short-lived. The first of these was introduced about three years after the murder of Nabis, in punishment for an ill-timed revolt ; the last of them was overthrown nine years later, in 179, through the agency of the pro-Roman Callicrates at the beginning of his year as Strategos of the Achaean League.[3] But in considering the extent and actual duration of these constitutional changes, we are faced at the outset with two different versions in our ancient sources, giving rise to a difference of opinion in modern times. Livy takes the view that in the spring of 188 the whole of the traditional constitution at Sparta was overthrown by Philopoemen,[4] and this has been accepted by various modern authorities.[5] Their interpretation would imply that there was ample time, in the nine years which followed, for the final obliteration of all the traditional Spartan

---

[1] See below, pp. 74, 79 f.   [2] *Cf.* below, pp. 79 f.
[3] Ditt. *Syll.*[3] 634. See further below, p. 50.
[4] *Cf.* Livy, XXXVIII, 34 : *Lycurgi leges moresque abrogarent. Achaeorum adsuescerent legibus institutisque.* This passage, in which all the other terms imposed by the Achaean League in 188 are summarised, serves Livy as the foundation for all his later allusions to the same settlement, *e.g.* XXXIX, 33 (Spartan complaint in 184), *ademptas, quibus ad eam diem civitas stetisset, Lycurgi leges; ibid.* 36 (Roman protests on the same occasion), *muros dirutos . . . leges vetustissimas abrogatas, inclitamque per gentes Lycurgi disciplinam sublatam; ibid.* 37 (reply of Lycortas), *Quod ad leges ademptas attinet, ego antiquas Lacedaemoniis leges tyrannos ademisse arbitror; nos non suas ademisse, quas non habebant, sed nostras leges dedisse.*
[5] *Cf.* Busolt-Swoboda, *Griech Staatsk.* (1926), pp. 733 f. ; Kolbe, I.G. V, i, 4, n.

institutions. But the supposition that the whole constitution was overthrown in 188 may be shown to rest
on unsatisfactory premises. For in the first place, Livy's
statement may be shown not to concur with the view of
Polybius ; in the second place, the overthrow of the traditional constitution would have been quite incompatible
with the return to power of the ' old exiles '. These represented the old aristocracy driven out by Nabis and his
predecessors, and members of the ancient royal families,
who had been among the exiles, were prominent in politics
at Sparta in the years following their restoration in 188.[1]
It would be idle to deny that Sparta was effectually domin-
ated by the Achaean League during the whole of the nine
years in question ; this was the burden of all the complaints
made to Rome from the Spartan side at that time. But
that this was done through substituting an Achaean constitution and Achaean laws for those of Lycurgus is for
the reasons just mentioned (in spite of Livy) most unlikely.

The question of the ancient evidence resolves itself into
this. What did Polybius say about the matter ? For of
our literary sources, Polybius, Livy, Plutarch and Pausanias,
the last three can be shown to be directly dependent on the
first, and in view of his close association with the events
under consideration, and the frankness of his admissions
with regard to the policy of the Achaean League, the
authority of Polybius must here be regarded as final. His
history of this particular period has unfortunately been preserved only in excerpts, but enough has survived to show
close correspondence between his original account and those
of Pausanias, Plutarch and Livy [2] (the last-named repre-

[1] *Cf.* Livy, XXXIV, 26 (195 B.C.) : *Princeps erat exulum Agesipolis
cuius iure gentis regnum Lacedaemone erat.* In 183 B.C., after a second
expulsion, the same Agesipolis and Arcesilaus were killed by pirates on
an embassy to Rome (Polyb. XXIII, 6). In the interval Areus and
Alcibiades (both formerly ' old exiles ') had been leading men at Sparta
(Paus. VII, 9. 2 ; *cf.* Livy, XXXIX, 35 ; Polyb. XXII, 15). Areus
bears the same name as two Spartan kings of the previous century.

[2] The interdependence of the four sources may easily be seen by comparing Polyb. XXII, 15, 16 with Livy, XXXIX, 33 ; Livy, XXXIX,
35–37 with Paus. VII, 9. 3–5 ; Paus. VII, 9. 5–7 with Polyb. XXIII, 4 ;
Polyb. XXIII, 12 (an excerpt dealing with the last expedition and death
of Philopoemen) with Livy, XXXIX, 49, 50 ; Plut. *Philop.* 18–2 ; Paus.
VIII, 51. 5–8. In XXXIX, 52 Livy quotes Polybius for statements about
the year 183 (after Philopoemen's death) which show that the original

senting an obviously extended version, with much imaginary reconstruction of speeches). Polybius' own account (as preserved) of the settlement of Sparta in 188 speaks of the expulsion of the democratic party, the destruction of the walls, the subordination of Spartan policy to the general decrees of the Achaean League Council (a disability shared by all members of the Achaean League) and, lastly, the complaint that Sparta in particular (as distinguished apparently from other states which were members of the League) was deprived of free speech through the necessity of being subservient τοῖς ἀεὶ καθισταμένοις ἄρχουσι.[1] Even if this ambiguous expression meant annual Achaean governors sent to Sparta, this would not necessarily imply the overthrow of the existing constitution and laws and the substitution of what Livy calls ' Achaean laws and institutions '.[2] But in fact it is unthinkable that an Achaean governor of Sparta would have permitted the constant sending of Spartan embassies to Rome (contrary to the policy and indeed to the whole constitution of the Achaean League)[3] which was so marked a feature of this period. Polybius must rather be interpreted as referring here to the Strategoi of the Achaean League, Philopoemen and others, who did in fact intervene personally in the internal affairs of Sparta.[4] The excerpt says nothing of the ancient constitution and laws.

Of the other three literary sources, Livy is the only one who mentions the abolition of the Lycurgan constitution. Plutarch and Pausanias are silent on the subject in describing Philopoemen's treatment of Sparta. Apart from this discrepancy, Plutarch gives exactly the same information as Livy, and in words which, allowing for the differences of the two languages, are, as will be seen presently, practically

account of Polybius was very much fuller than the surviving excerpts would suggest. Plut. (*Philop.* 21) reveals his source in mentioning that Polybius carried the urn at Philopoemen's funeral. Livy testifies to his direct dependence on Polybius in XXXIII, 10, where he calls him *non incertum auctorem cum omnium Romanarum rerum, tum praecipue in Graecia gestarum;* cf. also Livy, XXXIV, 50 ; XXXVI, 19 ; XXXIX, 52.

[1] Polyb. XXII, 16.   [2] *Cf.* above, p. 43, n. 4.
[3] *Cf.* Paus. VII, 9. 4 ; 12. 5.
[4] Plut. *Philop.* 16. The statement in Plut. *Compar. Philop. et Titi*, 1, that Philopoemen διέφθειρε τὴν πολιτείαν may be explained by the observation in *Philop.* 16 that the abolition of the Lycurgan ἀγωγή meant in fact the changing of the whole πολιτεία.

identical. It can scarcely be doubted that the two accounts are derived from a single source, which, according to Livy's version, appears to be a decree of the Achaean League Council. The account of Pausanias is very much shorter, but so far as it goes, it is in exact agreement with that of Plutarch. Both the Greek writers give quite a different flavour to Livy's words, *Lycurgi leges moresque abrogarent; Achaeorum adsuescerent legibus institutisque.* Plutarch's version is ἄνειλε γὰρ καὶ διέφθειρε τὴν Λυκούργειαν ἀγωγὴν ἀναγκάσας τοὺς παῖδας αὐτῶν καὶ τοὺς ἐφήβους τὴν Ἀχαϊκὴν ἀντὶ τῆς πατρίου παιδείας μεταβαλεῖν.[1] Pausanias says καὶ τοῖς ἐφήβοις προεῖπε μὴ τὰ ἐκ τῶν νόμων τῶν Λυκούργου μελετᾶν, ἐφήβοις δὲ τοῖς Ἀχαιῶν κατὰ ταῦτὰ ἀσκεῖσθαι.[2] Both clearly limit the substitution of Achaean for Spartan laws to the Spartan Ephebic organisation, and in view of the obvious derivation of all three sources from the common Greek one, which must be Polybius' version of the decree of the Achaean League Council, it is permissible to conclude that Livy has misunderstood the meaning of the expression Λυκούργειος ἀγωγή, or some similar phrase, supposing it to refer to the whole traditional constitution and laws instead of merely to the system of Ephebic training.

It is true that the suppression of the famous *agoge*, had it been permanent or even of long duration, would have been as effective in destroying the whole character of the traditional Sparta as the abolition of the constitution itself. Livy and Plutarch both imply that this was so ;[3] only after analysing the *agoge* in detail shall we be in a position to realise how essential its preservation was. In the event, only three or four year-classes can have been seriously affected by the abolition, for the *agoge* was permanently restored by order of Rome not later than 179,[4] and possibly

---

[1] Paus. VIII, 51. 3 ; *cf.* VII, 8. 5 : τά τε οὖν τείχη τῆς Σπάρτης οἱ Ἀχαιοὶ καθεῖλον καὶ τὰ ἐς μελέτην τοῖς ἐφήβοις ἐκ τῶν Λυκούργου νόμων καταλύσαντες ἐπέταξαν τοῖς Ἀχαιῶν ἐφήβοις τὰ αὐτὰ ἐπιτηδεύειν.

[2] *Cf.* preceding note.

[3] For Plutarch, *cf.* above, p. 45, n. 4. For Livy, *cf.* XXXVIII, 34 : *nulla tamen res tanto erat damno, quam disciplina Lycurgi, cui per septingentos annos adsueverant, sublata.* Both authors are probably (as usual for the period) echoing the view of Polybius, who was in a better position to realise the implications of Philopoemen's policy towards Sparta.

[4] For the fact, *cf.* Plut. *Philop.* 16 ; Paus. VIII, 51. 3. For the date, see further below.

about four years earlier. Those who had been young enough at the time of the abolition not to have profited much from the traditional training would still be young enough to profit by an intensive course when it was restored, and of an age to be enthusiastic about the re-introduction of a semi-military regime, such as the *agoge* was.[1]

The actual date of the restoration of the *agoge* is not stated by our literary sources, but may be deduced from the political developments. In 184 it had not yet been restored, in spite of frequent requests from Rome to the League, both that this should be done and that the democratic exiles driven out by Philopoemen should be restored.[2] A year later the democratic exiles actually were restored, against the will of the League.[3] At the same time the walls of Sparta were rebuilt,[4] and the League was required to extend certain special privileges to Sparta while continuing to count the city among its members. Independent Spartan embassies might now be sent to Rome, and the League Council was no longer to have the right of trying Spartans on a criminal charge, such cases being destined in future for a neutral court.[5] Since the Roman commissioners who made all these changes were obviously aiming at the removal of all Spartan grievances, it is possible that the *agoge* was at least temporarily restored at this time.

But the newly-restored democrats were discontented with the régime under which they now found themselves, and before the end of the same year had driven out the aristocratic party (the ' old exiles ').[6] The new government at first announced its independence of the League,[7] but whether the constitution was also overthrown at this

---

[1] See further below, pp. 86 f.

[2] Livy, XXXIX, 36 ; Polyb. XXII, 16.

[3] Livy, XXXIX, 48 ; Paus. VII, 9. 5.

[4] Paus. *ibid*. The majority of the tile-stamps from the walls (I.G. V, i, 886 ff.) presumably belong to this and immediately following years.

[5] Paus. *ibid*. For the meaning of ξενικὰ δικαστήρια in this context *cf*. the Roman refusal to arbitrate for Sparta in a matter of disputed territory (Paus. VII, 12. 4, 148 B.C.).

[6] Polyb. XXIII, 5 ; *cf*. *ibid*. 9, 17. The date of the expulsion was before the death of Philopoemen in 183, for which *cf*. Livy, XXXIX, 50.

[7] *Cf*. Polyb. XXIII, 17. A request for re-admission to the League was made later, and was granted in 181 (*ibid*. 18. For the date, *cf*. Livy, XL, 20).

time is not clear. Two Spartan Proxenia-decrees which appear from their lettering to belong to about this period include in their prescript the words ἔδοξε τῷ δάμῳ without any reference to Gerusia or Ephors.[1] Similarly, a letter to the Spartans from an Illyrian town, approximately dated by its lettering, is addressed simply Λακεδαιμονίων δήμωι.[2] But the formula of address in letters from other states to Sparta varies considerably in other periods,[3] and does not necessarily represent the technically correct form ; nor in the absence of any other Spartan Proxenia-decrees whatever can we be sure that the formula adopted in the two under consideration does not merely reflect the procedure appropriate to such applications at Sparta in all periods. One thing is certain ; if these three inscriptions do in fact reflect a change of government, they must belong to the period 183–179 B.C., not to 188–179 B.C. as is sometimes supposed.[4] A stray piece of information preserved by Polybius does, however, suggest a doubt. In 181, when a socialist agitator called Chaeron, one of the former democratic exiles, started a haphazard programme of confiscating private property and redistributing both this and public funds to the poor, an attempt to frustrate him was made by the appointment of δοκιμαστῆρες τῶν κοινῶν κατὰ τοὺς νόμους.[5] This implies that these public auditors were not a part of the normal machinery of government, but that their occasional appointment was in accordance with the constitution. But this further suggests that the constitution then theoretically in force was the one which had existed before the recent exile of the aristocratic party.

[1] I.G. V, i, 4, 5. The application was made ἐπί τε τὰς συναρχίας καὶ τὸν δᾶμον. The probable meaning of συναρχίαι here is either the Gerusia alone (see further, pp. 148 f.) or the Gerusia together with the Ephors and their σύναρχοι (I.G. v. i, Index, IV, s.v. σύναρχοι).

[2] Ibid. 28.

[3] Cf. ibid. 8, 9, 30 (Λακεδαιμονίων ἐφροις καὶ τᾶι πόλει). These all appear to belong to the second and first centuries B.C., and correspond to the formula employed in the Spartan letter to Delphi of 29 B.C. (I.G. V, i, 1566 (p. xxi) : Λακεδαιμονίων ἔφοροι καὶ ἀ πόλις) ; cf. also I.G. IX, 2. 518 (of uncertain date). But Joseph. Antiq. XIII, 5. 8, referring to c. 145 B.C., has ἐφόροις καὶ γερουσίᾳ καὶ δήμῳ . . . χαίρειν ; I.G. V, i, 17 (of Flavian date or later) has Λακεδαιμονίων βουλῆι καὶ τῶι [δήμωι].

[4] Cf. Kolbe (following Swoboda), I.G. V, i, 4, n.

[5] Polyb. XXIV, 7. (Perhaps identical with the Damosiomastai of the inscriptions. Cf. p. 138, n. 1.)

It is also far from clear that the ' new exiles ' who had been restored in 183 were as a class in favour of a more democratic government than had existed previously. In fact Polybius' account of one of the numerous Spartan embassies to Rome suggests the contrary. In 185 or 184 four different parties sent delegates, of which two groups represented the now-restored ' old exiles ', a third, led by Serippus, wanted to restore exactly the state of affairs which had existed during the early period of Sparta's membership of the Achaean League [1] (*i.e.* from 192 to 188),[2] and the fourth, led by Chaeron, the future demagogue, represented those still in exile at the time of the embassy. These last agreed with Serippus about the constitution.[3] In other words, they demanded their own restoration and the reversal of all that Philopoemen had done in 188— they wanted, namely, the banishment of the ' old exiles ', rebuilding of the walls, restoration of the *agoge*, in short, to get back the traditional constitution but to be rid of the extremists of the aristocratic faction. It is therefore probable that this last party, on securing its restoration and all or most of its other demands,[4] restored in its entirety the internal state of affairs which existed from 192 to 188. This would mean that the Lycurgan constitution continued. But admittedly the point cannot at present be proved.

Whether a more democratic constitution was in fact introduced or not during the second exile of the aristocratic faction, it does not appear that it took a very strong hold. A sign of the weakness of the new government is that it was after all unable to maintain itself without submitting to the Achaean League, in return for a solemn undertaking from the League Council that the ' old exiles ' should never be allowed to return to Sparta.[5] No sooner had this step been taken than the Strategos of the League intervened in person to suppress the internal disorders started by the agitator Chaeron, who was himself thrown into prison.[6] In the meantime the Roman government in disgust had

---

[1] *Cf.* Polyb. XXIII, 4 : Σήριππος δὲ ἐπρέσβευε περὶ τοῦ μένειν τὴν ὑποκειμένην κατάστασιν, ἣν ἔχοντές ποτε συνεπολιτεύοντο μετὰ τῶν Ἀχαιῶν.

[2] *Cf.* above, p. 37.

[3] Polyb. *ibid.* : κάθοδον αὐτοῖς ἀξιοῦντες συγχωρηθῆναι, καὶ τὴν πολιτείαν τοιαύτην (*sc.* as that indicated by Serippus). [4] *Cf.* above, p. 47.

[5] Polyb. XXIII, 17 ; XXIV, 11. [6] *Ibid.* XXIV, 7 ; *cf.* above, p. 48.

4

washed its hands of the new Sparta,[1] which was thus left
friendless and unprotected at the mercy of the Achaean
League. As the pro-Roman Strategos Callicrates pointed
out to the Senate, it was only necessary for Rome to show
a little firmness in 179 for complete loyalty to Rome to be
restored at Sparta as everywhere else in Greece.[2] The
recall of the aristocratic ' old exiles ' was now insisted
upon,[3] and a reconciliation duly took place, as testified
by the inscription on the statue of Callicrates which the
restored exiles set up at Olympia.[4]

From now onwards the constitution and internal policy
of Sparta remained as previously established by Rome four
years earlier, in 183, at that time without conspicuous
success. If the *agoge* had not already been restored, it
was certainly restored in 179, and then the whole constitution went back to where Cleomenes III and Nabis had left
it. Livy speaks of Sparta as *disciplina institutisque memor-*
abilem in 168,[5] and an incidental allusion to the characteristic Spartan manner of cutting the hair and beard, and
fashion of dress, implies that in the sphere of social customs
all the details of the Lycurgan régime were still being
strictly observed twenty years later.[6]

In the constitutional sphere, the essentially oligarchical
character of the government during this period is indicated
by the very small number (twenty-four) of those whom
the Achaean League wished to see exiled in order to bring
Sparta once more under its control. In 150 B.C., twenty-
four prominent Spartans whose names had been indicated
by the Achaean Strategos were persuaded by a Spartan
criminal court to go into voluntary exile for the time being,
in the expectation of their speedy restoration by the
Romans.[7] The description of these twenty-four as πρω-

---

[1] *Cf.* Polyb. XXIII, 17 : 'Ρωμαίους μὲν ἀποτρίβεσθαι τὴν πρότερον αὐτοῖς
δοθεῖσαν ἐπιτροπὴν ὑπὲρ τῆς πόλεως ταύτης. ἀποκέκρισθαι γὰρ αὐτοὺς νῦν,
μηδὲν εἶναι τῶν κατὰ Λακεδαίμονα πραγμάτων εἰς αὐτούς.

[2] *Ibid.* XXIV, 11.   [3] *Ibid.* 12.

[4] Ditt. *Syll.*[3] 634 : Λακεδαιμονίων οἱ φυγόντες ὑπὸ τῶν τυράνν[ων]
Καλλικράτη Θεοξένου Λεοντήσιον καταγαγόντα εἰς τὰν πατρίδα καὶ διαλύσαντα
ποτὶ τοὺς πολίτας καὶ εἰς τὰν ἐξ ἀρχᾶς ἐ[οῦσαν] φιλ[ίαν ἀποκ]αταστάσαντα.

[5] Livy, XLV, 28.

[6] *Cf.* Paus. VII, 14. 2. The date (148 B.C.) follows from the sequence
of the Strategoi of the League mentioned by Paus. VII, 12–15.

[7] *Cf.* Paus. VII, 12. 7 f.

τεύοντες τὰ πάντα ἐν Σπάρτῃ implies that the last con-stitutional settlement in 179 had restored the old aristo-cratic party to political power.[1] The same conclusion results from the study of the names of the members of the Spartan aristocracy under the Principate. Many of them were demonstrably descended from the ancient royal families.[2]

It was not long after the flight of the twenty-four Spartans to Rome [3] that a Roman proconsul, then Mummius as consul, were sent to put an end once for all to the tyranny exercised by the Achaean League. Sparta was rewarded [4] for the part she had played in resisting Achaean aggression by force of arms when resistance must have seemed hope-less ; [5] it is therefore inconceivable that at the same time she was punished by an infraction of her former autonomy, when the constitutions of the Greek cities in general were revised by Rome as a part of the initial organisation of the new province Achaea (146 B.C.). And indeed Sparta already possessed, as has been shown in the preceding account, a constitution of precisely the form which Rome was anxious to make universal in Achaea, namely a non-democratic organisation in which office-holding depended upon a property qualification.[6] For the admission of new citizens, apparently without property qualification, in the period between Cleomenes' reforms (228 B.C.) and the last general settlement of 179 B.C. in no wise altered the general principle that the constitution (apart perhaps from the periods when the aristocratic faction was in exile) was ἀπὸ τιμημάτων, based on a property qualification for office. As in the late fourth-century constitution of Cyrene, we must imagine at Sparta in her final period, as a *civitas libera et immunis* under Roman protection, a clear distinction between the citizens in general (πολῖται) and the privileged section who alone had the right to hold office. This

---

[1] *Cf.* above, p. 44, n. 1.   [2] See further below, p. 113.
[3] *Cf.* Paus. VII, 12. 8 ff.
[4] By the infliction of a fine of 200 talents upon the cities on the Achaean side, to be paid to Sparta (Paus. VII, 16. 10).
[5] *Cf.* Paus. VII, 12. 6 ; 13. 7 (ἐχόντων δὲ αὐτῶν ἐς τε τὴν πᾶσαν πολέμου παρασκευὴν καὶ οὐχ ἥκιστα τοῖς χρήμασιν ἀσθενῶς).
[6] *Cf.* Paus. VII, 16. 9 : (Mummius) δημοκρατίας μὲν κατέπαυε, καθίστατο δὲ ἀπὸ τιμημάτων τὰς ἀρχάς.

distinction will be revealed more clearly through the detailed study of the later inscriptions.[1]

For the period after 146 B.C. we are left without consecutive literary evidence for the internal condition of Sparta ; its sudden cessation in the later authorities in itself proves the dependence of the later authorities upon Polybius,[2] and therewith the general reliability of the evidence for Spartan affairs in the period from Cleomenes III to the Roman annexation of Achaea. From this date onwards we are dependent for the history of Sparta upon scattered and rare allusions in literary writers, and upon the study of the inscriptions from Sparta itself.

In approaching the study of the later Spartan inscriptions the preceding study of the period 235–146 B.C. enables us to start from certain definite premises. Sparta still claimed to be essentially ' Lycurgan ' in laws and customs, and Cicero's observation that it had been the same for seven hundred years [3] turns out on further examination to be far less preposterous than would appear at first sight. There is therefore no initial objection to regarding the later Spartan inscriptions as potential material to assist in the reconstruction of a more detailed picture of pre-Hellenistic Sparta than has hitherto been possible. The Roman emperors were in general anxious to leave Sparta alone, being well aware that nothing could be more conducive to the quiescence of a large area of the Peloponnese [4] than the preservation of an intensely conservative and unambitious Sparta, a state by long tradition without a personal head. The generally accepted view that Augustus permitted despotic government to arise at Sparta under C. Julius Eurykles, and that after an interval of free government under Tiberius, Eurykles' son Lakon was reinstated in his father's princedom by Claudius, involves the supposition that these two emperors departed from the usual policy of the Principate towards Sparta. But in point of fact the whole of the evidence for the position of the family of Eurykles needs further investigation before the current

[1] See below, pp. 113 f.
[2] Whose history was planned to end with the year 146 B.C.
[3] *Cf.* above, p. 2, n. 2.
[4] On the extent of Spartan territory under the Principate, see Chap. II.

view can be finally accepted.[1] And in any case the inscriptions capable of throwing light on the earlier condition of Sparta belong with very few exceptions to the period after Claudius, by which time free republican government was certainly restored.

In connection with the appointment of his friend Maximus to investigate the internal affairs of the *civitates liberae* in Achaea, Pliny indeed speaks of Sparta, as also of Athens, as enjoying no more than the shadow and the mere name of real liberty.[2] This was no doubt strictly true so far as external relations were concerned, but in the internal affairs of the *civitates liberae* the Roman government had certainly not interfered before this time, as Pliny himself implies by his injunctions to Maximus to observe the most scrupulous consideration and tact in dealing with so delicate a matter. Towards all their existing institutions, political, social and religious, he must exercise the greatest respect, remembering that he is being sent *ad homines maxime homines, ad liberos maxime liberos.* The later policy of Trajan and his successors towards the free Greek cities in general shows indeed that the purpose of this investigation was primarily to remedy or prevent financial disorganisation ; there is no reason to think that in the case of Sparta it involved any interference with the constitution or with social institutions. The city was apparently satisfied with its treatment under Trajan, since in A.D. 115 it set up a statue of the emperor with a bronze inscription, in which Maximus (having then held his position in Achaea for a number of years) was mentioned, apparently as having licensed this expenditure from the city's revenues.[3]

The only certain instances of interference by the Imperial government in the affairs of Sparta concern the

---

[1] See Chap. V.

[2] Pliny, *Ep.* VIII, 24 : *reliquam umbram et residuum libertatis nomen.*

[3] *Cf.* I.G. V, i, 380, with its fragmentary end : [- -τὸ ἀνάλωμα π]οιη[σαμέν]ων ἐκ τῶν τῆς πόλεως [πρ]ο[σόδων - - -] γυμνασίου καὶ [- - οντ]ος Κυντι[λί]ου Μαξίμου κατὰ τὸ ψήφισμα τὸ τῆς πόλεως βουλ - - - -. (Perhaps should be restored καὶ [κελεύσαντ]ος Κυυιλίου Μαξίμου ?) The identification of the ' Maximus ' mentioned by Pliny, *loc. cit.*, and Epictetus, *Diss.* 3. 7, with Sex. Quinctilius Valerius Maximus is accepted in P.I.R. (1898) *s.v.*, but without reference to the inscription here cited. The inscription was apparently found in Cythera which belonged to Sparta at the time (*cf.* below, p. 56, n. 4).

practice of exposing unwanted or weakly children, and their status if afterwards rescued and brought up by strangers. Exposure of children was not uncommon under the Principate in all the Greek-speaking provinces, but was evidently more than usually frequent at Sparta, since all three Flavian emperors addressed letters to the Spartans upon the subject.[1] It may be supposed that the reason for the custom being more prevalent at Sparta than elsewhere was that it had been a recognised and necessary part of the Lycurgan régime.[2] It is, however, clear that the Flavian emperors did not enforce any change in this matter at Sparta, since the institution was condoned by the rescripts of Domitian to the governors of two provinces,[3] of which one (though both are unfortunately left unnamed in Pliny) can be shown to have been Achaea.[4]

According to Philostratus, a letter was addressed to the Spartans by Nero, accusing them of presuming unduly upon the privileges implied in their status of *civitas libera*.[5] The complaint had apparently been forwarded by a governor of Achaea, and may well have referred to this same matter of exposing children, since the Spartans, with the help of the sophist Apollonius of Tyana, are said to have drafted a non-committal reply, and, as we have seen, the Flavian emperors more than once had occasion to complain to Sparta of this practice.

Another imperial letter, the author of which cannot with certainty be identified,[6] clearly illustrates the principle that

---

[1] Pliny, *Ep.* X, 65.   [2] *Cf.* Plut. *Lycurg.* 16.
[3] *Cf.* Pliny, *Ep.* X, 66.
[4] Since (1) Domitian and his immediate predecessors had all concerned themselves with this question at Sparta. (2) The practice was openly continued in Achaea later. I.G. V, 1, 1208 (early third century), records a woman's bequest of her θρεπτοί to the town of Gytheum. (3) From the small number of Greek-speaking provinces to which Domitian's rescripts on this subject are likely to have referred Bithynia-Pontus was excluded (*cf.* Pliny, *Ep.* X, 66, Trajan's reply).
[5] Philostr. *Vit. Apoll.* 173: ἐπιστολὴ ἐκ βασιλέως . . . ἐπίπληξιν ἐς τὸ κοινὸν αὐτῶν φέρουσα, ὡς ὑπὲρ τὴν ἐλευθερίαν ὑβριζόντων.
[6] I.G. V, i, 21. Reasons are given elsewhere (p. 59) for attributing the letter on historical grounds to Vespasian. Fraenkel's suggestion of a second-century date presumably rests on the lettering, but this seems rather to favour the first century, to judge from its close resemblance on the one hand to V, i, 48 (assigned by Tod and Kolbe to first century B.C.), on the other hand to *ibid.* 1432, of which Kolbe says *litterae valde apicatae I a. vel potius p. Chr. n. saec.*, and to *ibid.* 97, which is *c.* A.D. 100.

complete autonomy for Sparta must be safeguarded. It limits the right of Spartan citizens (*i.e.* those possessing in addition Roman citizenship ?) to appeal to the emperor to criminal cases and to civil suits in which more than 1,000 denarii are involved, and in any case makes the appeal subject to the permission of οἱ σύνεδροι (probably the Gerusia).[1] While throwing an interesting side-light on judicial administration under the Principate, the letter also stresses the main principle to be observed, for the emperor declares himself determined to frustrate the schemes of any traitors at Sparta who may seek to prevent public or private business being conducted in accordance with (Spartan) laws.[2] The criterion for Sparta is to be τὸ πάτριον ἔθος.[3]

The chapters which follow will for the most part be devoted to showing with what faithfulness the Spartans under the Principate did in fact make ancestral custom their guide, in the organisation of society, in their constitution, in their cults and festivals. But in order to gain some idea of the resources and the general character of Sparta in this period, it will first be necessary to examine the extent of Spartan territory.

[1] The word σύνεδροι does not otherwise occur in Spartan inscriptions, and is not likely to be technically accurate here, in view of the wide variety in its use elsewhere (*cf.* Ditt. *Syll.*³, Index *s.v.*). It is at all events less appropriate to the Ephors than to the Gerusia (*cf.* the Jewish *Sanhedrim*). For the traditional competence of the Gerusia in criminal cases, *cf.* Arist. *Pol.* III, i, 10 ; Plut. Lycurg, 26. A Roman *consilium* is obviously not in question in I.G. V, i, 21, in view of the words διακρινέτωσαν . . . [οἱ σύνε]δροι τῷ πατρίῳ ἔθει (l. 12).

[2] *Loc. cit.*, col. ii, l. 2 f. : οὔτε ἀφορμὴν ταύτην (οἴομαι δεῖν) γείνεσθαι τοῖς συκοφαντοῦσιν ὡς τά τε δημόσια καὶ ἰδιωτικὰ μὴ τελεῖσθαι κατὰ τοὺς νόμους.

[3] *Cf.* above, n. 1.

CHAPTER II

SPARTAN TERRITORY UNDER THE PRINCIPATE [1]

§ 1. *The Frontiers*

WE can trace fairly exactly the boundaries of Spartan territory under the Principate. Outside them lay all the towns, formerly those of the Spartan Perioikoi, which were now organised as a separate state in the League of Free Laconians.[2] Pausanias enumerates the eighteen towns which comprised this league in his time, namely Gytheum, Teuthrone, Las, Pyrrhicus, Caenepolis (the old Taenarum), Oetylus, Leuctra, Thalamae, Alagonia, Gerenia, Asopus, Acriae, Boeae, Zarax, Epidaurus Limera, Brasiae (or Prasiae), Geronthrae, Marios.[3] Thus in the region south of the latitude of Sparta Spartan territory was now practically limited to the Eurotas valley ; the exceptions to this were the island of Cythera, and Cardamyle on the east coast of the Messenian Gulf, both of which possessions were given to Sparta by Augustus.[4] In Messenia itself, near the head of the Messenian Gulf, Sparta also acquired from Augustus the isolated possession of Thuria, and still retained it in Pausanias' time.[5] In spite of its geographical position and its inclusion by Pausanias in the list of eighteen Free Laconian towns, Thalamae, near the east coast of the Messenian Gulf between Leuctra and Oetylus, is also known

[1] See map at end of volume.

[2] On this League see, further, the Appendix to this chapter (App. III).

[3] Paus. III, 21. 7. For details of the composition of this League before Pausanias' time see Appendix III.

[4] The grant of Cythera (*cf.* Dio Cass. LIV, 7. 2, referring to 21 B.C.) finds confirmation in the appearance of a Spartan Κυθηροδίκας (a title revived from antiquity, *cf.* Thuc. IV, 53. 2) in the first half of the second century A.D. (B.S.A. XXVII, pp. 228, 232). For the grant of Cardamyle, *cf.* Paus. III, 26. 7.

[5] Paus. IV, 31. 1. Continued dependence on Sparta is indicated by the letters ΛΛ on the bronze coinage issued at Thuria under Septimius Severus and Caracalla.

from its inscriptions to have been a Spartan possession in the time of Hadrian.[1]

(a) The Southern Frontier

The possession by Sparta of Cardamyle, and (for a time at least) of Thalamae raises the question how far Spartan territory extended into the Free Laconian region to the south-west of Sparta. In the south, Spartan territory stopped just short of the coast at Gytheum, which was Free Laconian ; Aegiae (only three and a half miles from Gytheum) was Spartan.[2] In view of this it would be natural for Augustus, when he gave Cardamyle to Sparta, to carry the boundary north-westward from Aegiae to the coast at Cardamyle. Direct confirmation of this hypothesis is lacking, but there is no evidence against it,[3] and general probability in its favour. For Cardamyle possessed an excellent natural harbour which would serve to compensate for the loss of Gytheum, over which Sparta had exercised some definite control until it received from Augustus complete independence.[4] But now that Sparta no longer controlled any port in the Laconian Gulf, Cardamyle would

---

[1] I.G. V, 1. 1314, 1315. See further, pp. 59 f.

[2] Cf. Paus. III, 21. 5, 6. The absence of Aegiae (called by Paus. ibid. πόλισμα) from the list of Eleutherolaconian towns (ibid. 7) confirms the view that Pausanias intends to imply that it was Spartan. On the other hand Croceae, which was not Spartan (see below, p. 73), is also excluded from the list of Eleutherolaconian towns; the explanation is probably that it was a mere κώμη (Paus. III, 21. 4) not a πόλις.

[3] The statement in Paus. VIII, 1. 1, that the territory of the ' Lacedaemonian Perioikoi' extends (present tense) without a break along the coast from the borders of Argos to the borders of Messenia is certainly taken from an earlier authority and applies literally to the ' Perioikoi' in the period before 195 B.C., not to the ' Eleutherolaconians'. This is clear from Pausanias' further observation that the Messenian border was in the vicinity of ' Methone and Pylos ', for the towns on the west side of the Messenian Gulf, which no doubt continued to be Perioikoi under Sparta until 195 B.C., were certainly not included in the Free League of the Principate. This passage in Pausanias does not therefore constitute any objection to the view that Cardamyle, although it was on the coast, was not cut off from Sparta by any intervening Free Laconian territory.

[4] Strabo (VIII, 5. 2, 363) calls Gytheum τὸ τῆς Σπάρτης ἐπίνειον, referring apparently to his own time ; cf. Paus. III, 21. 6 : οὓς (sc. Gytheum and other Eleutherolaconian towns) βασιλεὺς Αὔγουστος δουλείας ἀφῆκε Λακεδαιμονίων τῶν ἐν Σπάρτῃ κατηκόους ὄντας. On the meaning of this subjection before the reign of Augustus see further, Appendix III, pp. 435 f.

have been quite useless to her unless it could be approached directly by land, and a pass exists across Taygetus which would make such access from Sparta easy.[1] Moreover, there is some reason to think, in spite of a certain amount of confusion on the subject in the ancient authors, that the older town of Cardamyle, built on a steep hill about a mile from the sea, was removed in the early Principate, under Spartan occupation, to the site round the harbour which the modern town now occupies. Ancient foundations and terra-cottas are said to have been found under the modern town,[2] and archaeology may eventually settle the matter finally. It would appear that the ancient hill-town referred to both by Pausanias and by Pliny was certainly already deserted in the time of the elder Pliny, and probably before the middle of the reign of Augustus.[3] This implies that the development of the port followed soon after the acquisition of Cardamyle by Sparta. An anecdote in Philostratus relating to a young Spartan of Nero's reign, still under the authority of the Ephors, who engaged in commerce by sea,[4] points in the same direction, for Cardamyle was the only port available to Sparta at this period,[5] with the possible exception of a little harbour at the mouth of the Pamisus, about eight miles to the south of it,[6] which would raise the same problem of access to Sparta as Cardamyle itself. This second and smaller harbour evidently lay in the territory of Thalamae (Koutephari), which Pausanias enumerates among the Free Laconian towns,

[1] *Cf. Admiralty Handbook*, route 75, mile 16¼, route 68, mile 18½. The road descends into the valley of the Eurotas about 10 miles south of Sparta.

[2] *Cf.* Forster, B.S.A. X (1903–4), p. 163 (a general description of the site and its harbour).

[3] *Cf.* Pliny, N.H. IV, 16 : *et intus Sparta, Therapne, atque ubi fuere Cardamyle, Pitane, Anthea.* This information seems to come from Agrippa's survey (before 12 B.C.), and so renders out-of-date the references of Strabo (VIII, 360) and Pausanias (III, 26. 7), both of whom speak as if the hill-town was still in existence. Strabo reveals confusion by observing (VIII, 360) that Cardamyle, as contrasted with Pherae, which he says was five stades from the sea, was ἐπ' αὐτῇ ; for the hill-town of Cardamyle was rather over a mile from the sea (Forster, *ibid.;* Paus. III, 26. 7 gives the distance as eight stades).

[4] *Cf.* p. 161.

[5] Pherae, at the head of the Messenian Gulf, was not given by Augustus to Sparta but became a member of the League of Free Laconians (Paus. IV. 30. 2 is thus rightly interpreted by Kolbe, *Ath. Mitt.* XXIX, p. 376).

[6] *Cf. Admiralty Handbook*, route 75, mile 22½.

but which is known from inscriptions to have belonged to Sparta in Hadrian's reign.[1] It presumably ceased to be included in Spartan territory about the time when Pausanias was writing, for in another passage he seems to imply that it still belonged to Sparta.[2] When it first became attached to Sparta is not known. Its inclusion would give Sparta a fertile strip of coast and a very productive region round the Bardounia river further inland,[3] and it is tempting to suggest that the grant of land to Sparta mentioned in the letter of a first-century emperor to the Spartan government [4] refers to this region, and that it was Vespasian who made the grant at the time when he ordered the survey of the western boundary of Spartan territory which was completed before the end of his reign.[5] The interest which the author of the imperial letter takes in the question of precisely how the territory is to be administered for revenue purposes, and the recommendation of a method which is likely to bring the highest return,[6] is certainly characteristic of Vespasian. It is also to be considered that loss of independence by Thalamae would seem less of a hardship at a time when numerous other towns of Achaea, injudiciously liberated by Nero, were losing theirs ; and it is perhaps not fantastic to suggest that Vespasian's temperament naturally inclined him to be

---

[1] *Cf.* I.G. V, i, 1314, 1315.

[2] *Cf.* Paus. III, 26. 3. It is possible that the Spartans were deprived of it as a punishment for the νεωτερισμοί which occurred at Sparta about the middle of the second century (see Appendix IV, § 8, n. D, p. 469), but in any case it is known that there was a quarrel between Sparta and the Free Laconians in the reign of Pius (I.G. V, i, 37). The oracular shrine of Pasiphae at Thalamae had been exploited for revolutionary purposes both in the reign of Agis IV (*cf.* Plut. *Agis*, 9) and in that of Cleomenes III (Plut. *Cleom.* 7). On the oracle in question see further, pp. 404 f. It was still consulted in Pausanias' time (Paus. III, 26. 1).

[3] *Cf. Admiralty Handbook*, route 75, p. 502. The boundary is likely to have followed the route across the hills from the vicinity of Thalamae to the vicinity of Aegiae (in Spartan territory under the Principate). *Cf.* the observations on Vespasian's survey, p. 61.

[4] I.G. V, i, 21 On the epigraphic indications of the date of this letter see p. 54, n. 6.

[5] See further, pp 61 ff.

[6] I.G. V, i, 21 (col. 1) ; πότερον πραθῆναι ἢ μισθοῦσθαι καὶ [π]ό[τερον σύμπαντας - - - -τ]ους ἀγροὺς ἢ κατὰ μέρος, παραινῶι[- - - - - - προσ]όδους μέμνημαι πολλῶ μείζονας [- - - -]ν καὶ δεδωρημένον ὑμῖν ἀιτ[η]σιν [- - - προσόδ]ους ἔσεσθαι, εἰ ἑτέρα μίσθωσις γένοι[το - - - - π]οεῖν ὑμᾶς, κ[αὶ ἐ]ὰν τὸ τρίτον τῆς νῦν [- - - - -] (the rest is fragmentary).

sympathetic to the aspirations of the austere and conservative Sparta, which in addition had a special advocate
at this time in the philosopher Apollonius of Tyana,[1] whose
influence with the emperor is said to have been great.[2]
If, as Philostratus maintains, Sparta, under the influence of
Apollonius, turned her face once more against commercial
development, the strip of agricultural land to the south of
Cardamyle would seem a reasonable request, especially as
it included, in Thalamae, the alleged birthplace of the
Dioscuri.[3] Finally, remains of a Spartan inscription prove
that some arch or public building was set up there in honour
of Vespasian.[4] Thus, although there can be no absolute
proof, all the indications fit together to make it extremely
probable that it was Vespasian who included Thalamae,
and the region between it and Aegiae, in Spartan territory.
The lower course of the Pamisus must have formed the
boundary north of Thalamae, since Leuctra (between the
river and Cardamyle) continued to be Free Laconian.

(b) The West Frontier

From the coast at Cardamyle, the Spartan boundary
must have turned north-eastward to skirt the territory of
Free-Laconian Alagonia, turning then to the north to join
the river Choerius in the vicinity of the shrine of Artemis
Limnatis, the possession of which was traditionally con-
tested by Sparta and the Messenians.[5] Apart from fixing
the river Choerius (Sandava) as the boundary between
Messenia and the Free Laconians[6] (i.e. towards Alagonia
and Gerenia), the advisers of Augustus seem to have made
no clear ruling about the frontier here, for the Ager Dentheliatis in which the shrine lay continued to be in dispute,

---

[1] See further, pp. 158 f.

[2] Philostratus (Vit. Apoll. 220 f.) cites detailed advice given by the
sophist to the emperor on the subject of imperial government in general
and on the administration of the Greek-speaking provinces in particular,
and also quotes letters, conspicuously Laconic in style, exchanged between
the two (ibid. 225, 331).

[3] Paus. III, 26. 2 ; cf. III, 1. 4.

[4] I.G. V, i, 691. The inscription is preserved on a large fragment of
an architrave. The date of dedication was A.D. 77 (i.e. about the same
time as the survey of the boundaries was completed ; cf. below, p. 61).

[5] Cf. Paus. IV, 4. 2.   [6] Ibid. IV, 1. 1.

and the Messenians succeeded in being confirmed in possession of it by an award of the proconsul of Achaea, ratified
by the Senate, in A.D. 25.[1] From an imperial survey of
the boundaries between Messenia and Sparta which was
made towards the end of Vespasian's reign it seems probable
that this earlier decision was reversed by Vespasian, but
the evidence is not clear on the point.[2]

The nature of the document which preserves the survey
of boundaries made under Vespasian [3] must be made clear
before its significance can be fully understood. The inscription itself was found at Mavrommati, and was therefore set up at Messene. It represents the official record
of the boundary between Messenia and Sparta, as guaranteed
by a Roman surveyor at the beginning of A.D. 78. It
therefore represents the publication, for the benefit of
Messenians, of the boundaries as they existed in and after
A.D. 78. Only about half the original survey is preserved
(from the 23rd to the 48th ὅρος), and that in a very fragmentary condition. It is, however, possible to trace, with
a near approach to accuracy, the boundary in the southern
half, from the temple of Artemis Limnatis on the Sandava
river, along the western slopes of Taygetus, to the vicinity
of Mt. Malevo.

The detailed indications of the survey in this section
have been interpreted with great skill by Kolbe,[4] whose
discovery of three ὅροι still *in situ*, south of the Langada
Pass, greatly helps in the identification of the position of
others known only from the survey. But the actual position of the three boundary marks found by Kolbe does not
support his general conclusion that the boundary ran along

[1] *Cf.* Tac. *Ann.* IV, 43, where the earlier phases of the long dispute
are also mentioned. The evidence is fully discussed by Kolbe, *Ath. Mitt.*
XXIX (1904), pp. 375 ff.

[2] The boundary in the survey, as given from the Messenian point of
view (see further below), ends at the temple of Artemis, apparently excluding the temple itself. The temple was situated on the bank of the
river Choerius (Sandava) and apparently on the side remote from Messenia
(*cf.* below, p. 64). If this conclusion about the precise position of the
temple is right, it seems to imply that the temple itself was outside
Messenian territory under the arrangement attested by the survey.

[3] I.G. V, i, 1431.

[4] *Ath. Mitt.* XXIX (1904), pp. 364 f. To Kolbe also belongs the credit
of recognising the importance of, and first interpreting, this survey
represented by two fragments in the museum at Mavrommati.

the summit of Taygetus at an altitude of approximately 6,000 ft. They were found, according to his own account,[1] in the region south of the western end of the Langada Pass, in the vicinity of Pegadia [2] and the sources of the Sandava (Choerius) and therefore at an altitude of only about 2,000 ft.[3] And although Kolbe seems clearly right in identifying the συνροία which marked the position of one of the boundary marks mentioned in the survey [4] with the Langada Pass,[5] it is evident that a confluence of streams could not possibly occur at the summit of the pass over the highest ridge of Taygetus, whereas such a junction of streams does in fact occur at the western end of the pass.[6] It is clear, moreover, that the indications on the Roman survey are given in relation to a person proceeding directly along the frontier from one boundary stone to the next, for the most part by a well-defined path,[7] and that it was possible in every instance except one (where a swollen winter torrent made the normal procedure impossible for a short distance) [8] to measure the distances from one ὅρος to the next with a ten-foot measuring rod.[9] This could not have been done if the boundary stones had followed the actual summit of Taygetus. In that case the marks

---

[1] Cf. Sitz. Berl. Akad. 1905, pp. 60 f. and esp. p. 61.

[2] Ibid. The position of Pegadia is more precisely defined in Admiralty Handbook (route 75, mile 11) as north of Kampos, high on the slopes overhanging the gorge of Sandava, 3½ hours' distant from Kampos at alt. 2,904 ft. The name of the village implies proximity to the source of the river.

[3] Cf. preceding note. The altitude of the pass, where the ὅροι were found on the opposite side of the valley from Pegadia, is given by Kolbe (ibid.) as 2,000 m. (? 2,000 ft.).

[4] I.G. V, i, 1431, l. 20.

[5] Cf. Kolbe, Ath. Mitt. XXIX, 1904, pp. 364 ff.

[6] Cf. Kolbe, ibid. p. 367; Admiralty Handbook, route 74, mile 8½, records that many springs gush out of the rock at Lada, which is above the western end of the pass; cf. also Carte géologique internationale de l'Europe, which shows in this region a confluence of streams flowing to join the Nedon.

[7] E.g. ἐπὶ [δεξιὰ? κατα]βαίνουσιν (V, i, 1431, l. 3), ἐν καταβάσει (ll. 12, 36), [ἐπ' ἀριστερὰ ἀνα]βαίνουσιν (l. 31), ἐν τῇ διόδῳ (l. 26).

[8] Ibid. l. 16.

[9] The distances are given approximately in feet and, where preserved, are always in multiples of 50 except in one case (l. 33), where the number is 520. It may be observed that it was the normal practice of Roman surveyors to measure with a ten-foot measuring rod (Gromatici Veteres, Lachmann u. Rudorff, 1841, index s.v. decempeda).

would have had to be reached at any season of the year by arduous separate journeys from below. It is rather to be supposed, in view of these indications, that the ὅροι followed a normal route of communication along the western skirts of Taygetus.

This conclusion fits in with the approximate position of two ὅροι found about a century ago in the vicinity of Sitsova and Mt. Malevo near the northern end of Taygetus. Though their exact original location is uncertain, it would appear that one was first discovered on the western slopes of Mt. Golu to the east of Sitsova ; [1] the other was found on the slopes of Mt. Malevo about 4 miles further north.[2] The more northern of the two has been identified by Kolbe, from the form which the actual inscription takes,[3] with the third of the boundary marks mentioned in that part of the Roman survey which has been preserved.[4] The three ὅροι found by Kolbe, and the two found by Ross and Pernice, are thus seen to lie as nearly as possible on the same axis from north to south, and to the south of the three discovered by Kolbe the same line is continued further by the upper valley of the Sandava, which seems to be dry except in winter.[5] Along the side of this valley in the south, thence across country to the western end of the Langada Pass, and from there as far as Mt. Malevo, it was clearly possible, though in some places not easy, for the Roman surveyor

[1] *Cf.* Ross, *Reisen im Peloponnes* (1841), p. 3. Suspicious peasants, who feared that the evidence of the stone might lend support to a new arrangement of provincial boundaries then being made, are said to have transferred the stone to a more inaccessible place on the eastern side of the mountain.

[2] See the detailed sketch map, *ibid.* (*Ager Dentheliatis*).

[3] ὅρος Λακεδαίμονι πρὸς Μεσσήνην. The inscriptions on the ὅροι show a remarkable variety which was perhaps intended to make forgery more difficult.

[4] *Cf.* Kolbe, *Ath. Mitt.* XXIX, p. 365.

[5] This appears to be the deep valley running north to south described by Kolbe (*Sitz. Berl. Akad.* 1905, p. 61) as lying immediately to the west of the pass on which he found the three ὅροι. Its course in the gorge is not marked in the 1 : 1,000,000 contour map of Europe (Provisional edition, North J 34), but appears in the *Carte géologique internationale de l'Europe*. *Cf.* also *Admiralty Handbook* (1920), route 75, mile 11. The name χειμάρροος given to the Choerius in the Roman survey (l. 38) shows that the upper reaches at least were dry except in winter. Since Kolbe's visit was made in autumn, the stream in the valley would not be in evidence at the time.

to proceed direct from one boundary stone to the next, measuring as he went.[1] The indications given in the survey confirm the supposition that at the south end the way lay along the eastern side of the difficult gorge of the upper Sandava river,[2] ending almost certainly where the stream, attaining greater volume, bends sharply to the south-west.[3] Here the site of Artemis Limnatis, which marked the southern end of the frontier, is to be sought.

About 12 miles (as the crow flies) further north, the whole distance accounting for twenty-three boundary stones, lay the more northern of the stones discovered by Ross. Two further boundary marks to the north of this, accounting therefore for another mile or thereabouts, are mentioned at the beginning of the Roman survey as now preserved, the first of them being alluded to in the inscription itself as the twenty-third boundary mark from the beginning. It remains to discover, if possible, the line followed by the first twenty-two ὅροι in that section of the Roman survey which has not been preserved. Some allowance must be made for irregular spacing, the marks being probably set more closely where no natural features served to define the boundary,[4] but on the whole it seems safe to conclude that the missing section of the survey represented a stretch of about the same length—certainly not longer—compared with that covered by the part of the document which has survived. This consideration renders most unlikely Kolbe's suggestion that the missing part of the inscription was concerned with the frontier between

[1] From near the north end of the Sandava gorge there is now a track northwards to the Langada Pass which must join it near Lada ; cf. Kolbe (Sitz. Berl. Akad. 1905, p. 60). From Lada another path branches north to Tsernitsa, Sitsova, and the village of Anastasova on the southern slopes of Mt. Malevo (cf. Admiralty Handbook, route 74, mile 8½).

[2] I.G. V, i, 1431, ll. 32–38, mentions (immediately south of Kolbe's southern ὅρος) a κ[ορυφή ?], κοῖλον, ἀνάβασις, ἄκρον, κοῖλον, κορυφή, κρημνός, ἀπόκρημνος before the temple of Artemis Limnatis is reached (all these in the space of six ὅροι, or about 3 miles).

[3] I.e. at the point from which the river is marked on all the modern maps ; cf. above, p. 63, n. 5.

[4] Probably this was so in the case of the three ὅροι found by Kolbe, which cover a distance of less than 2 km., two of them being only 100 m. apart. Kolbe does not regard the two more widely spaced of these as being contiguous in the survey, but his reconstruction is perhaps not altogether convincing at this point in the inscription.

Messenia and Arcadia as well as with that between Messenia and Sparta,[1] and more especially in view of his supposition that a considerable deviation from the straight line occurred in that part of the frontier which still lay between Messenia and Sparta. On the other hand, the further extension of the same line about 12 miles north of Mt. Malevo would reach a point near the sources of the River Alpheus, a few miles to the east of ancient Asea, and this point appears to have marked the furthest northern limit of Spartan territory in the time of Pausanias.[2]

An apparent objection to this view arises from the inscription K on the twenty-fourth ὅρος from the beginning of the survey, which indicated an angle (καμπή) at this point.[3] Kolbe interprets this to mean that the frontier here diverged at a wide angle to the west away from the general northerly direction previously followed.[4] This supposed east-to-west stretch of unknown length, Kolbe postulates as necessary to include the region called Aegytis, which had belonged to Sparta in early times and belonged to it again, after various vicissitudes, under the Principate.[5] But in fact no sudden bend in the frontier was needed to include Aegytis, which, although it included the sources of the Carnion river,[6] must have lain mainly to the north-east of Mt. Malevo.[7] It is not difficult (as will presently be demonstrated) to find an alternative explanation of the καμπή ; and the supposition that the approximately straight line followed by the frontier to Mt. Malevo was continued still further northwards would fit in with the information which Pausanias gives about the general lie of the frontiers between Megalopolis, Messenia, Sparta and Tegea.[8]

[1] Cf. Ath. Mitt. XXIX, p. 375.   [2] See further below, pp. 68 ff.
[3] I.G. V, i, 1431, l. 5 : ἐπεγράφη κ.] τὸ δὲ γράμμα σημαίνει καμ[πή]. Very few restorations of the significant word are possible, and this one alone makes sense.
[4] Cf. Ath. Mitt. XXIX, pp. 372 ff.
[5] Cf. pp. 22, 67 f., and Strabo, X, 446.
[6] Paus. VIII, 34. 5.   [7] See below, p. 70, n. 2, and map.
[8] The basis which Pausanias provides for the reconstruction of these frontiers is as follows : (1) (Paus. VIII, 34, 1, 5) Point on the frontier between Megalopolis and Messene, along the main road between them. Distances are 22 stades from Megalopolis to the crossing of the Alpheus where the River Gatheatas joins it, 40 stades from here to ruins of Kromon, then 20 to Nymphae, another 20 stades to the Hermaion (boundary). Cf.

5

With regard to the interpretation of the καμπή, it is to be remembered that parts of the frontier between Messenia and Sparta had been in dispute for a very long period,[1] and had frequently been changed, returning more than once to the old line. Some of the boundary marks were on movable stones, but others were cut on the face of the living rock,[2] and so could not easily be removed. It is therefore quite possible that not all of the ὅροι recorded in the survey made under Vespasian were cut at the same time, and it may be suggested that the καμπή still recorded along this final line actually marked the angle of an earlier boundary. It might well refer to the period, of considerable duration, after Sparta had been deprived of Aegytis and Belbinatis by Antigonus Gonatas.[3] In support of this suggestion it may be observed that immediately to the north of Mt. Malevo, that is to say from a point corresponding to the K sign on the survey, a track crosses the ridge of Taygetus from west to east.[4] Since most of the range is impassable, this track would constitute a natural

Admiralty Handbook, route 72a, mile 16¼ (at Tsaousi, about 2½ miles N.W. of Meligala). (2) (Paus. VIII, 35. 1, 2) Point further east on the frontier between Megalopolis and Messenia. From Megalopolis the Alpheus is crossed at its junction with the tributaries Malos and Scyros (exact distance not given), the River Malos is kept on the right and crossed 30 stades later ; road ascends to Phaedria ; 15 stades from Phaedria is the boundary. *Cf. Admiralty Handbook*, routes 69b and 72b, mile 25¼. 45 stades (5⅝ miles) from the crossing of the Alpheus on this route gives a point about 3½ miles south of Leontari, 2 miles to the east of Mt. Hellenitsa and a little to the north of it. (3) (Paus. VIII, 35. 3) Point on the frontier between Megalopolis and Sparta. From Megalopolis to the crossing of the Alpheus, 30 stades ; from here to Phalaesiae (following the tributary Theius for some distance), 40 stades ; from Phalaesiae to the boundary at Belbina, 20 stades. *Cf. Admiralty Handbook*, route 69a, mile 16 (Chani of Chelmós, which corresponds with the description of Belbina in Paus. III, 21. 3 : τῆς δὲ χώρας τῆς Λακωνικῆς ἡ Βέλβινα μάλιστα ἄρδεσθαι πέφυκεν, ἥντινα διοδεύει μὲν τοῦ Εὐρώτα τὸ ὕδωρ, παρέχεται δὲ ἀφθόνους καὶ αὐτὴ πηγάς). (4) (Paus. VIII, 44. 7) The frontier between Megalopolis and Tegea is crossed 50 stades from Tegea along the main road. (5) (Paus. VIII, 54. 1) The frontier between Tegea and Sparta was marked by the River Alpheus. (On the precise significance of this statement, see further below, pp. 68 f.) All these boundaries are indicated on the accompanying map, *q.v.*

[1] See Kolbe's survey of these disputes (*Ath. Mitt.* XXIX, pp. 375 ff.).

[2] I.G. V, i, 1431, *passim.*   [3] *Cf.* above, p. 22.

[4] *Cf. Admiralty Handbook*, route 72b, mile 13½ ; *ibid.* route 69a, mile 4½ (branch path from Dyrrachi to Georgitsi, linking with a track to Kastania, and thence further east down a tributary to the valley of the Eurotas about 5 miles north of Sparta).

line of demarcation which may well have been followed by the ancient ὅροι at the period in question, especially in view of the tendency shown by the rest of the ὅροι in this region to follow the beaten track.[1] And additional support for the view that the K indicated a bend in the frontier towards the east rather than to the west may perhaps be seen in the later Roman meaning of the surveyor's mark in question : *Casa per K cappa nomen habens, ab orientali parte finis proximus venit.*[2] The rest of the definition is so peculiarly appropriate to the location of the K on the Messenian-Spartan frontier [3] that assimilation of the system of Greek surveyors' signs into the Roman system, in this branch of the science, seems the inescapable explanation.

Polybius says, referring to his own time, that Spartan territory lay between that of Messene and that of Tegea.[4] This implies that Aegytis had already then been restored to Sparta, and that the K on the frontier had consequently become out-of-date. The change was evidently a recent one when Polybius wrote, since an inscription records awards of neutral arbitrators in favour of Megalopolis in the period 164–148 B.C.[5] It is to be presumed that Sparta recovered this territory in the north at the general settlement in 146, Belbinatis and Aegytis both being restored together with Skiritis, with the result that the frontier towards Megalopolis was moved north as far as a line joining Belbina with one of the sources of the Alpheus.[6]

---

[1] *Cf.* above, p. 62.

[2] Innocentius *ap. Gromatici Veteres* I (1848), p. 322. The passage continues : *super se montem, et de monte descendit alveus, qui excurrit per finem de fundo supra scripto. Super se autem vallem, et in ipsa valle aqua viva, seqq.*

[3] See preceding note.   [4] Polyb. XVI, 17.

[5] *Cf.* Ditt. *Syll.*[3] 665, with note.—The decision of the arbitrators against Sparta in the instance here recorded confirmed an earlier decision of other Greek arbitrators, which in its turn confirmed a decision of Roman arbitrators in 164 B.C. The references in the inscription to the Achaean League make it clear that the date of the last award of all was still before 148 B.C. Livy, XXXV, 27 (referring to 192 B.C.) speaks of Tripolis (near Pellana) as the nearest piece of Spartan territory to Megalopolis. Although he uses the present tense, this cannot refer to his own time, but to the time of which he is speaking, since it implies that Belbinatis still belonged to Megalopolis.

[6] *Cf.* below, p. 69.

(c) The Northern Frontier

Pausanias has made it harder to ascertain the line of the frontier between Sparta and Tegea in his time by the remarkable statement that the River Alpheus marked the boundary.[1] The explanation probably lies in the difference of opinion which existed among Greek as well as among modern geographers as to which of the streams which go to form the Alpheus is to be regarded as its original constituent. In a limestone region where the rivers are constantly disappearing into underground channels and reappearing again, the actual course of any one stream is bound to remain a matter of dispute. Among the ancient writers, Polybius and Strabo both suppose the Alpheus to rise not far to the east of Asea, where it disappeared for the first time.[2] Pausanias, on the other hand, describes it as disappearing for the first time into the plain of Tegea,[3] and both from this observation and from his description of the earlier course of the river it seems clear that he is referring to the river now called Sarantopotamos.[4] Whether Pausanias was merely mistaken in supposing that the river in question disappeared into a chasm in the Tegean plain,[5] or whether (as has been commonly supposed by modern investigators of his account) the Sarantopotamos did actually flow in antiquity N.W. from Kryavrysi and disappear into the swamp of Taka,[6] S.W. of Tegea, it seems clear that the upper reaches of the stream from the vicinity of Vourvoura to Kryavrysi (in which stretch it flows approximately east to west) formed part of the boundary between Sparta and Tegea.[7] Ancient fortification walls and the remains of a hill-fort occur on the south side of the river about a mile from Kryavrysi ; this site has been

[1] Paus. VIII, 54. 1.
[2] Polyb. XVI, 17 ; Strabo, VIII, 3. 12 (343). The site of Asea is fixed with certainty (by the ancient references to the chasms into which the river disappears, and by the ancient remains) close to Phrankovrysis ; cf. Admiralty Handbook, route 72a, 15½ miles from Tripolitsa by road, 12¼ miles by rail, on the north of the railway (ibid. railway route xx). See further, Loring, J.H.S. XV (1895), p. 69, with map (1 inch = 1 mile).
[3] Paus, VIII, 54. 2.
[4] Cf. Neumann-Partsch, Geographie v. Griechenland (1885), p. 251.
[5] Cf. Loring, J.H.S. XV, p. 68.
[6] Reff. ibid.
[7] This view is taken by Loring, ibid.

with much plausibility identified as Caryae,[1] which is alluded to at various periods as a Spartan fortress on the frontier.[2]

About 4 miles to the north-west of this, and after the river has begun to flow towards the north, rock-cuttings and other remains of ancient fortifications, associated with black-glaze and other pottery, occur on a hill-site which has been identified with Oion in Skiritis.[3] Whether the actual identification is correct or not, the site obviously represents another point on the same frontier. Together with the fort just mentioned, this point would serve to control the most direct route from Tegea to Sparta, which must have followed the valley of the Sarantopotamos where it flows to the north.[4] By further prolonging in the same general direction north-westwards a line joining the two forts, we reach in about $2\frac{1}{2}$ miles the headwaters of the Alpheus where it rose [5] according to the general opinion of antiquity, and come very close to the point where the western frontier of Sparta must have ended.[6] It is hard to believe that Pausanias could have stated that the Alpheus formed the Spartan boundary towards Tegea if the river universally regarded as the Alpheus did not in fact do so in any part of its length, and it is therefore probable that the frontier in Pausanias' time followed the south bank of the river for about 2 miles and met the western boundary near Manari.[7] This conclusion would fit in with the distance from Tegea to the Megalopolitan frontier as given by Pausanias,[8] since it would imply what is probable in itself, that all three territories, Spartan, Tegean and Megalopolitan, met approximately at this point. The ancient site with fortification walls which Loring has identified as Eutaea [9] would on this interpretation of the line of the

---

[1] Loring, J.H.S. XV, p. 56. On the other hand it is possible that Caryae lay somewhat further east (cf. ibid. p. 55) and that the fortifications in question are really those of Leuctrum ὑπὲρ τῆς Μαλεάτιδος (cf. Xen. Hell. VI, 5. 24, and see further, Appendix I, p. 429, n. 3).

[2] Xen. ibid. (369 B.C.), Livy, XXXV, 27 (192 B.C.).

[3] Loring, ibid. pp. 61 f.

[4] Ibid. p. 62 ; cf. Admiralty Handbook, route 68, p. 469 (mile 50½).

[5] See map in J.H.S. XV, Pl. I.   [6] See above, pp. 64 f.

[7] Ten miles S.S.W. of Tripolitsa.

[8] Fifty stades distant from Tegea along the main road to Megalopolis (Paus. VIII, 44. 7).   [9] J.H.S. XV, pp. 50 f.

frontiers fall into its proper place on the Megalopolitan
frontier towards Spartan territory, and the hilly region
enclosed between the two angles of the frontier and lying
between the supposed site of Eutaea on the west and the
supposed site of Leuctrum in the east [1] will represent the
northern part of Aegytis. The precise extent of this region
towards the south is uncertain ; it appears to reach from
the upper waters of the Sarantopotamos in the north-east
to the source of the river Carnion in the south-west.[2]

(d) The East Frontier

Following the frontier along the Sarantopotamos to the
most southern of its sources on the slopes of Mt. Parnon,
we come very close to the pass over Mt. Parnon which,
according to Pausanias, was the meeting point of the
territories of Sparta, Tegea, and Argos.[3] Loring has given
convincing reasons for the identification of this pass as
the one which leads from Hagios Petros to Arachova, and
it actually lies about $2\frac{1}{2}$ miles N.E. of Arachova.[4] This,
then, represents the N.E. angle of Spartan territory. There
remains to be considered only the boundary between this
point and one in the extreme south between Gytheum
and Aegiae.[5] The N.E. angle already fixed lies some
5 miles or more to the west of the northern summits of the
main mountain range of Malevo, and the Free Laconian
town of Geronthrae lay on the west side of the same range
at its southern end. This makes it very unlikely that the
summit of the range marked the eastern frontier of Sparta,
and we have no closer guide to its actual course. The
mountain of Vrestena (Barbosthenes) which lies 6 or 7
miles to the south of Arachova [6] certainly lay inside Spartan
territory soon after the towns of the Perioikoi had first
been made independent.[7] Since the towns of the Perioikoi

---

[1] *I.e.* the site identified as Caryae by Loring ; *cf.* above, p. 69.
[2] *Cf.* Paus. VIII, 27. 4 : (Aegytis includes Scirtonium, Malea, Cromi,
Belbina, Leuctrum). On the probable position of Malea and Leuctrum
see above, p. 69, n. 1, and on Belbina, p. 65, n. 8.
[3] Paus. II, 38. 5–7 ; III, 1. 1.
[4] *Cf.* J.H.S. XV, p. 55, n. 111, and Pl. I, *ibid.*
[5] *Cf.* above, p. 57.
[6] *Cf.* J.H.S. XV, p. 65.
[7] *Cf.* Loring's account (*ibid.*) of the invasion of Philopoemen in 192
B.C. (Livy, XXXV, 27 ff.).

had been absorbed by Sparta at so early a date that no traditional frontiers can ever have existed between them and Sparta, it seems not unlikely that at the time of their liberation (195 B.C.) the Romans imposed a purely artificial frontier, running due north and south.[1] This line would actually end where on other grounds it is required to end, between Aegiae and Gytheum [2] (Las on the coast being Free Laconian). Croceae with its celebrated green marble quarries [3] would be excluded and so more easily available for exploitation by the Romans ; but on the other hand, the suggested frontier would include in Spartan territory slightly more than was claimed earlier as γῆ πολιτική as distinguished from γῆ τῶν περιοίκων.[4] A corresponding extension on the west of the area regarded as γῆ πολιτική is implied by the fixing of the boundary to the west of the ridge of Taygetus instead of to the east of it.

* * * * * * * *

It is now possible to attempt an interpretation of the general policy of the Roman government towards Sparta as illustrated by the arrangements made with regard to her territory in the later Republic and under Augustus and his successors. The main idea seems to have been to make the new Sparta resemble the old in every external respect, in so far as was compatible with arrangements made earlier as to the independence of Messenia and of the Perioikoi. It was neither possible nor desirable that these arrangements should be revoked, but the towns in Messenia which Augustus, and perhaps Vespasian, gave to Sparta could be regarded as remnants of her former power in Messenia, while the fringes of the γῆ πολιτική (referred to above), together no doubt with the rest of the country south of the Eurotas, might be looked upon as a survival of Perioecic territory. The inclusion of Skiritis in the north had been many times appealed for in vain by the

---

[1] It may be noted that a stretch of the German *Limes* just north of the Main illustrates exactly the same procedure.

[2] *Cf.* above, p. 57.   [3] For these see further below, pp. 73 f.

[4] *Cf.* Plut. *Agis*, 8, and on the interpretation of this passage, Appendix I, p. 429.

Spartans during the first half of the second century B.C., and was finally conceded by Rome, probably in 146 B.C.; [1] the concession is the more remarkable in that a whole series of Roman arbitrators had previously held the Arcadians to have the better claim, on the grounds that it was to them that the region had belonged ' at the time of the return of the Heraclidae to the Peloponnese '.[2] The consideration which eventually prevailed with the Roman government would therefore seem to have been that Skiritis had been an essential part of the Spartan state at least since the early sixth century, its possession being closely bound up with its military (and therefore automatically with its political) organisation.[3] In other words, it was a revival of the real traditional Sparta, not a hollow mockery, which the Roman government hoped to see in the *libera civitas* of the new period. Cynuria, which under the arrangements of the Principate lay outside Spartan territory, had never been a part of the Spartan state in the same sense as Skiritis, but a mere external possession, frequently in dispute between Spartans and Argives.

§ 2. *The Economic Resources of Sparta under the Principate*

With economic assets—apart from her good agricultural land—the new Sparta was not well provided; but this again may have been in accordance with the general purpose of restoring the traditional conservative state of antiquity. For example, Spartan territory under the Principate excluded all the marble quarries which produced the high-grade marbles prized by the Romans, and included only what was not suitable for export, namely the rather coarse blue-grey marble from the upper valley of the Oenus,[4] and a less plentiful yellowish marble from the same region,[5] white marble of rather poor quality from Vresthena [6] a little further south, and also from Gorani [7] (about 10 miles

---

[1] *Cf.* p. 67, n. 5.   [2] Ditt. *Syll.*[3] 665, l. 35.
[3] But on the λόχος Σκιρίτης, see further pp. 378 f.
[4] *Cf.* Lepsius, *Griechische Marmorstudien* (*Anhang zu. d. Abhand. König. Preuss. Akad. d. Wiss. Berl.*, 1890), pp. 34 f. : ' Kein edles Gestein '. The ancient cuttings are about 20 m. deep, but the quarries do not appear to have been used since ancient times.
[5] *Ibid.*   [6] *Cf.* P.W. XI, *s.v. Sparta* (1929), p. 1347.   [7] *Ibid.*

south of Sparta on the eastern slopes of Taygetus). All these local marbles, but especially the blue-grey from the quarries about 12 miles to the north of Sparta, continued to be used at Sparta for dedications of all kinds,[1] and for building purposes, from the archaic period onwards, and were still being used in later Imperial times.[2]

At no period do the Spartans appear to have made use (with a few insignificant exceptions in the case of *rosso antico*)[3] of the harder and finer marbles which lay in territory for long under their control, but outside their boundaries as those were fixed under the Principate. This applies to the fine white marble from Doliana south of Tegea, to the *rosso antico* and black marble of the Taenarum peninsula,[4] and to the green porphyry of Croceae.[5] This last stone was so much admired and prized by the Romans under the Principate[6] that the absence of any evidence whatever of its exploitation by the Spartans in this period in itself constitutes a strong argument for the view that the quarries lay outside the boundaries of the *libera civitas*. Other considerations which point to the same conclusion are that Sparta had now no port in the Laconian Gulf from which the porphyry could be exported, and that the presence near the quarries of a *dispensator domus Augusti* is attested by a Latin dedication to Castor and Pollux.[7] This makes it virtually certain that the quarries were an imperial monopoly.[8] As to the date when they first began to be exploited by the Romans, there is no evidence for this

[1] *Cf.* Tod and Wace, *Catalogue of the Sparta Museum* (1906), index, *s.v. Marble; ibid.* p. 102.

[2] *E.g.* for the seats from the Theatre (implying that the same marble was used for facing), B.S.A. XXVIII, pp. 35 f.

[3] *Cf.* Tod and Wace, *ibid.*

[4] A description of these is given by Bluemner, *Technologie*, III, pp. 42 f.

[5] *Ibid.* pp. 19 f.   [6] References, *ibid.*

[7] I.G. V, i, 1569 : *Diis Castori et Polluci sacrum Domus Augusti dispensator Dedit et dedicavit* . . . (Found near Croceae). The inscription is accompanied by a representation of the Dioscuri, for which see *Sparta Catalogue (Sculpture)*, p. 114. This is dated, apparently on grounds of style, to first century A.D., but seems to resemble in composition and style *ibid.* no. 121, which is assigned to first century B.C. A date early in the Principate seems to be indicated.

[8] Kolbe (I.G. *ibid.*) supposes that by the Dioscuri are meant here M. Aurelius and Verus, who may possibly have been worshipped as νέοι Διόσκουροι at Sparta (V, i, 447). But the suggestion is unlikely, since the relief (on local marble) conforms to a well-known Laconian type (*Sparta*

earlier than the first century A.D.,[1] and a statement of
Strabo which has commonly been assumed to indicate that
the working first began in the reign of Augustus does not
in fact bear that interpretation. What Strabo actually
says is that new quarries of large extent had recently been
opened ' on Taygetus ' to meet the demands of Roman
luxury ;[2] the description is perfectly appropriate to the
quarries of black marble and *rosso antico* in the southern
half of the Taenarum peninsula,[3] whereas Croceae is nowhere near Taygetus. It follows that the exploitation
and export of the marbles of the Taenarum peninsula was
wholly due to the Romans,[4] and began only with the
Principate ; that Sparta had never benefited from this
source in an earlier period, and did not acquire any fresh
revenues from it under the Principate. The Spartan port
of Cardamyle was too far north to have any part in the
export of these marbles.

Turning to metals, we find that iron ore occurs in what

Catalogue, ibid. pp. 113 f.). A dedication in gratitude to the Dioscuri
for a safe voyage (as in *ibid.* p. 113, fig. 14) seems more likely. But the
quarries at Croceae were under the special protection of the Dioscuri
(*cf.* Paus. III, 21. 4 : Διόσκουροι δὲ ἐπὶ τῇ λιθοτομίᾳ χαλκοῖ), probably
because the quarries were near the sea and because the marble was being
quarried for export. The connection of the imperial official in question
with the quarries is probable (1) in view of the place where the dedication
was found, (2) in view of the supervisory duties exercised by *servi Caesaris*
(all imperial *dispensatores* being apparently slaves ; *cf.* I.L.S., index
VI, *s.v. dispensator*) in other imperial quarries. *Cf.* I.L.S., 1600 : *Hy-
menaeus Caesaris ser. Thamyrianus a lapicidinis Carystiis.* . . . Other
parallels may be found in Hirschfeld, *Die Kaiserlichen Verwaltungsbeamten*
(1905), pp. 165–169. There is a parallel from the gold mines of Salonae
in Felicissimus, *aurariarum Delmatarum dispe(n)sator* (I.L.S., 1595).

[1] In addition to the evidence of the inscription considered above
(p. 73, nn. 7 and 8) the only indication of date is Paus. II, iii, 5 :
τοῦτο δὲ (*i.e.* baths at Corinth) Εὐρυκλῆς ἐποίησεν ἀνὴρ Σπαρτιάτης λίθοις
κοσμήσας καὶ ἄλλοις καὶ ὃν ἐν Κροκέαις χώρας τῆς Λακωνικῆς ὀρύσσουσιν.
Bluemner (*Technologie*, III, pp. 19 f.) observes in regard to this passage
that the date of the Eurykles in question is unknown ; from inscriptions
since discovered in Corinth it is now clear that its close connection with
the family of C. Julius Eurykles began about 40 A.D. (*cf.* below, pp. 183 f.).
But on general grounds a benefaction by Eurykles I is indicated, probably
in the late first century B.C. (*cf. ibid.* pp. 173 f.).

[2] Strabo, VIII, 5. 6 (367) : νεωστὶ δὲ καὶ ἐν τῷ Ταϋγέτῳ μέταλλον ἀνέῳξάν
τινες εὐμέγεθες, χορηγὸν ἔχοντες τὴν τῶν Ῥωμαίων πολυτελείαν.

[3] The name Taygetus (with its alternative Pentedaktylon) is given
in modern times to the whole range as far as Cape Matapan ; *cf.* General
Staff Map, Greece 1 : 1,000,000, Provisional Edition, North J34 (Athenai).

[4] In this case apparently by individual enterprise ; *cf.* above, n. 2.

was Spartan territory under the Principate near Kolines in Skiritis,[1] but there is no evidence of ancient working here. On the other hand, there is evidence of ancient working on a large scale in the Malea peninsula between the Free Laconian towns of Boeae and Asopus,[2] and also in the tip of the Taenarum peninsula.[3] It is clear that in the period when Sparta still possessed this region and exploited the Perioikoi, iron was extensively used by the Spartans themselves.[4] But evidence is lacking to suggest that, after they had lost control of the Perioikoi, the Spartans took up the manufacture of iron implements on their own account ; for the only ancient writer who provides evidence for iron-working in Laconia (as distinct from the mere use of iron) is Daimachus in his *Commentary on Siegecraft*,[5] written about a century before the Perioikoi became independent of Sparta.[6] Daimachus uses the vague description Λακω-νικὸν σιδήριον, which might apply equally to Sparta or the Perioikoi. In view of the known location of large ancient iron-workings in Free Laconian territory, it is extremely probable that from 195 B.C. onwards Sparta was forced to buy from her former subjects the ready-made implements which had no doubt been taken earlier without payment. On this hypothesis, too, the rapid decline of Spartan military power after Nabis becomes more easily understandable ; the difficulty of keeping up the supply of iron weapons must

[1] *Cf.* P.W.[2] VI, p. 1347.   [2] *Ibid.*
[3] *Cf.* Curtius, *Peloponnesos*, II, p. 206 (near Porto Quaglio).
[4] *Cf.* Xen. *Hell.* III, 3. 7 : ἀγαγόντα εἰς τὸν σίδηρον (near the Spartan Agora) ἐπιδεῖξαι αὐτὸν ἔφη πολλὰς μὲν μαχαίρας, πολλὰ δὲ ξίφη, πολλοὺς δὲ ὀβελίσκους, πολλοὺς δὲ πελέκεις καὶ ἀξίνας, πολλὰ δὲ δρέπανα. Iron spits about a foot long which have been preserved have been interpreted as currency (*cf. Artemis Orthia*, pp. 391 f.), but in view of this passage were no doubt actually used as spits, especially as the iron coinage seems to have taken the form of round coins (*cf.* Koehler, *Ath. Mitt.* VII, 1 f. on the iron coins of Tegea and Argos, also Hesych, *s.v.* πέλανορ. But Plut. *Lys.* 17 implies that iron ὄβελοι were used both by other Greek states and by Sparta). The wearing of iron rings at Sparta in Pliny's time (N.H. XXXIII, 9) was probably a custom of great antiquity.
[5] *Cf.* Steph. Byz. *s.v.* Λακεδαίμων (F.H.G. II, p. 442) : . . . καὶ ὅτι Σινωπικὸν καὶ Χαλυβδικὸν εἰς τὰ τεκτονικά, τὸ δὲ Λακωνικὸν εἰς ῥίνας καὶ σιδηροτρύπανα καὶ χαρακτῆρας καὶ εἰς τὰ λιθουργικά, τὸ δὲ Λύδιον καὶ αὐτὸ εἰς ῥίνας καὶ μαχαίρας καὶ ξυρία καὶ ξυστῆρας, ὥς φησι Δαίμαχος ἐν πολιορκη-τικοῖς ὑπομνήμασι λέ. From this it is clear that Laconian iron tools were exported, but that Laconian iron was not so good as that from the other sources mentioned for implements which required a sharp cutting edge.
[6] *Cf.* P.W. IV, 2, *s.v. Daimachus.*

have accelerated the collapse. Under the Principate it was no longer necessary to maintain an army,[1] so that the problem of the supply of iron implements became automatically less acute.

With regard to lead, the very extensive use of lead figurines at Sparta from archaic to early Hellenistic times,[2] taken in conjunction with the great rarity of lead figurines from other Greek sites,[3] obviously indicates that this metal was obtained locally. Lead workings, probably ancient, do in fact occur east of Cardamyle and near Arachova,[4] so that both these sources would be available to Sparta under the Principate. Neither region can have been under Spartan control from 222 to (at earliest) 146 B.C.,[5] and in the case of the mines near Cardamyle, not until the reign of Augustus. The long break may well explain the complete disappearance of the lead figurines from Spartan sites in the third century B.C.[6] and the failure to revive their manufacture when the mines once more became available. Under the Principate the lead seems to have been chiefly used for the manufacture of white lead ; objects made of lead continue to be very little in evidence on Spartan sites. Dioscorides mentions among the three best kinds of white lead, all from the east Mediterranean area, that made ἐν Λακεδαίμονι,[7] which implies that in his time (? second century A.D.) it was exported. Closer examination of the passage in Dioscorides also shows this development of the industry in Spartan territory to be subsequent to the grant of Cardamyle to Sparta by Augustus.[8] There appear in

---

[1] There were no shields to be found in Sparta in the time of Libanius (Liban. Orat. LXIV, 7).

[2] Cf. Artemis Orthia, p. 250. Over 100,000 of these come from the sanctuary of Artemis alone.

[3] Cf. ibid. p. 250. The examples mentioned from Bassae are likely to have come from Sparta ; those from Phlius and from the Argive Heraeum may be explained by the lead deposits near Corinth (cf. below, n. 7).

[4] Cf. O. Davies, Roman Mines in Europe, pp. 254 f.   [5] Cf. p. 21.

[6] Cf. Artemis Orthia, p. 252. On the evidence of stratification only, the latest examples are here dated c. 250 B.C. Historical considerations suggest that this date is somewhat too early.

[7] Diosc. V, 103. The other two kinds were from Rhodes and from Corinth.

[8] Pliny (N.H. XXXIV, 175) gives the same account of the manufacture of white lead as Dioscorides, but mentions only that produced in Rhodes. The source common to both appears to be King Juba II of Mauretania

fact to be the remains of more than one ancient lead-mine near Cardamyle,[1] and it seems likely that the white-lead industry was concentrated here, in the vicinity of the only Spartan port. In view of their inaccessibility from the rest of Spartan territory, the lead mines which were at one time worked at Arachova are more likely to have been exploited by the Argives at some time when this region belonged to them. But even in the region behind Cardamyle the Spartans are unlikely to have enjoyed the revenues from the lead-mines for very long, in view of the wholesale annexation of mining rights carried out all over the empire by Tiberius.[2]

Apart from the lead-working, there is no adequate evidence for any but rural industries in the whole of Spartan territory under the Principate. Some speculation has been aroused by the occurrence in Diocletian's edict of prices of *pellis Lacaena*, a leather intermediate in quality between two grades of Babylonian on the one hand, and Trallian and Phoenician leathers on the other. It seems clear from comparison of the Greek and Latin versions that the name was originally Latin, and to Greek merchants unfamiliar ; [3] this strongly suggests export to the west rather than to the rest of Greece or to the east. It is also clear that worked and finished leather, as distinct from hides (dressed or undressed) [4] is intended ; the kind of skin out of which the leather in question was produced does not come into consideration. It seems probable that each of the types of leather in question was always made out of its own

(*cf.* Pliny, N.H. XXXIII, 118, etc. ; Diosc. III, 96) who died early in the reign of Tiberius. The industry evidently developed about this time in Corinth and Sparta (Cardamyle).

[1] *Cf.* O. Davies, *op. cit.* p. 255, n. 6.

[2] *Cf.* Suet. *Tib.* 49 : *plurimis etiam civitatibus immunitates et ius metallorum . . . adempta.*

[3] The name is much corrupted in the surviving Latin versions of the Edict, the Aezani copy having *Pellis Lacceta* (C.I.L. III, 2, p. 814, l. 28) the Stratonicea copy *Pellis Laccitana* (? *Laccitena*, *ibid.* p. 809, l. 48). But the grammatically impossible forms in the Greek versions (δέρμα Λαχαίνου, *ibid.* p. 813, l. 31 ; δέρματος Λαχαίνου *ibid.* p. 816, l. 25) reveal clearly enough the original Latin form *Lac(c)aena;* the existing Latin versions may owe their curious form to confusion with Λακεδαιμόνια. The use of the single word δέρμα in the Greek versions to translate both *pellis* and *corium* indicates that the original list in general was made out in Latin.

[4] *Coria* of all kinds are listed in the next section of the Edict.

appropriate type of skin, and that the trade-name (*pellis Lacaena*, etc.) referred more particularly to the manner of tanning and dyeing. Another section of the Edict implies that this was certainly the case with ' Babylonian ' leather,[1] and the hypothesis would easily explain the trade-name *pellis Lacaena*, since the purple dye collected on the coasts of the south-eastern Peloponnese was well known to the Romans by the name Laconicum.[2] The purple fisheries were not in Spartan territory under the Principate, but in Free Laconian, and in any case were an Imperial monopoly before the time of Diocletian,[3] so that whether the leather industry was actually carried on in the same regions as those in which the dye was manufactured, or not, there seems to be no positive evidence for supposing that Sparta had any share in this part of the industry under the Principate. The Latin origin of the name of the leather in question indeed points to a non-Greek place of manufacture.[4] In modern times the well-wooded region round Kastanitsa (on the eastern slopes of Mt. Malevo, and therefore outside Spartan territory) provides both medicinal herbs and dyes, but, as would appear, rather on account of the lack of other natural resources than because the area is particularly well endowed in this respect.[5]

As far as the tanning was concerned, the leather industry might be carried on in antiquity almost anywhere in Greece, for many of the trees whose bark was used for this purpose by the Greeks are extremely widespread in all parts of the country.[6] But again there is no positive indication that

[1] *Cf.* § 9. 16 f. of the Edict (C.I.L. III, 2, p. 816, ll. 47 f.), *de soleis Babulonicis et purpureis et Foeniceis et alvis,* Βαβυλωνικῶν καὶ Φοινίκων καὶ λεύκων καὶ πορφύρων. Red or white ' Babylonian ' shoes are listed at the same price, *ibid.* l. 62. In § 10. 7 f. (*de zonis militaribus*) two grades of undyed ' Babylonian ' leather are mentioned for soldiers' equipment. The process was evidently applicable to the stouter types of leather.

[2] Pliny, N.H. XXXV, 44.

[3] *Cf.* I.L.S. 1575 : *proc. domini n. M. Aur. Severi Alexandri Pii Fel. Aug. provinciae Achaiae et Epiri et Thessaliae rat(ionis) purpurarum.*

[4] *Cf.* p. 77, n. 3.

[5] *Cf. Admiralty Handbook,* p. 439. The poverty of the hill districts in other natural resources may well explain the collection of medicinal plants in Laconia in antiquity (*cf.* Theophr. *Hist. Plant.* IV, 5. 2 ; IX, 15. 4, 8).

[6] *E.g.* oak, spruce-fir (πεύκη παραλία ἀγρία, *cf.* Theophr. *Hist. Plant.* III, 9. 1), sumach, alder, wild vine. See further, Daremberg-Saglio, *s.v. Coriarius.*

the industry was important in Spartan territory under the Principate. It is not improbable that some tanning was done in the vicinity of Cardamyle, Sparta's only port, for here suitable trees and shrubs might be found near the main source of supply (the forests of central Taygetus) of various animal skins, and shipping facilities were also available. This last point was also important in a period when Spartan military activity, and with it most of the home demand for leather, had disappeared. But it must be remembered that Spartan citizens, even under the Principate, were liable to heavy penalties for ' neglecting public affairs ', and in particular for engaging in commerce by sea,[1] so that those branches of the leather industry which have so far been considered are likely to have been almost exclusively in the hands of resident aliens. This hypothesis would well explain the large number of Roman villas of which there are still traces in the vicinity of Sparta,[2] the use of Roman *denarii* rather than Greek coinage [3] in a state otherwise so traditional in its outlook, and the presence in considerable numbers of alien settlers from other Greek states at Amyclae.[4]

But there was one lucrative activity in which even the most patriotic and traditionally minded Spartan might share, the provision of animals and animal skins, both for the leather industry and for the trade in wild beasts, which in the Roman Empire was of even greater importance. Hunting on Taygetus had been the traditional leisure occupation of the Spartans from the earliest moment that they took possession of this region,[5] and remained so in the time of

[1] Philostr. *Vit. Apoll.* 172. See further, p. 169. The details of the story are in accordance with the circumstances of the time (as, for example, the importance assigned to Gymnasiarchs and Patronomoi as well as to Ephors), and do not suggest anachronistic invention.

[2] *Cf. Sparta Catalogue*, p. 130, and below, p. 180, n. 1.

[3] *Cf.* above, p. 55. For the scarcity of Greek coins in Spartan territory in this period, *cf.* below, p. 192, n. 2.

[4] *Cf.* I.G. V, i, 515 (of unknown date ; thought from its lettering to belong to the Imperial period). The residents (οἱ κατοικοῦντες καὶ παρεπιδημοῦντες ἐν ᾿Αμύκλαις) include citizens of Messenia, Argos, Patrae, Corinth, Sicyon, Megalopolis. A fairly large number is implied by the appointment of a special Spartan ἐπιμελητής to look after them.

[5] *Cf. Od.* VI, 102 f. The recurrence of the same theme in Virg. *Georg.* III, 44 ; *Aen.* I, 498 f. may be due to mere literary imitation, but the references to Spartan hunting dogs (*Georg.* III, 345, 405) clearly imply their actual use in Virgil's time.

Claudian, who makes particular reference to the supply of wild beasts from here for the triumph of Stilicho in A.D. 404.[1] They would certainly be among those sent to Rome by sea,[2] for the Spartan port of Cardamyle was conveniently accessible from the main hunting grounds on the middle stretch of Taygetus, which Pausanias says was actually known by the name of θῆραι.[3] In view of the large number of wild beast shows given by the emperor Augustus,[4] it seems not improbable that Cardamyle was given to Sparta mainly on this account, although the traffic in animal skins must also have been considerable. Pausanias mentions particularly wild goats, boars, deer and bears from Taygetus ; in modern times wolves, lynxes and jackals have also been found there.[5] All these were valued for their skins in Roman times,[6] as well as for menageries and for the arena.

Since the whole of the central Taygetus range, and not merely its eastern side, was included in Spartan territory under the Principate, it is clear that the luxurious and (in the case of wild beast shows) somewhat barbarous tastes of the Romans must have brought increased and constantly growing prosperity to at least a section of the population of Sparta. It can scarcely be doubted that this section was the old landed aristocracy[7] and its protégés, for even on the assumption (which is indeed probable) that the hunting forests of Taygetus were the property of the state, only the members of this class can have had the independent means, the leisure, and the training in boyhood required for successfully engaging in so arduous and dangerous a pursuit. By the end of the Julio-Claudian period the Spartan aristocracy were probably already wealthy from this source, and the still greater increase in the traffic in wild beasts which began in the Flavian period would continue the process still further.

On the other hand, it is clear that for the rest of the population practically no resources were open other than agriculture, and this is likely to have been confined almost

---

[1] Claud. de cons. Stilich. III, 257 f., 300.   [2] Ibid. 325 f.
[3] Paus. III, 20. 5.   [4] Suet. Aug. 43, cf. Pliny, N.H. VIII, 64.
[5] Cf. Curtius, Peloponnesos, II (1852), p. 308, n. 5.
[6] Cf. C.I.L. III, 2, p. 816.
[7] For the restoration of this class to power in the second century B.C. see p. 50.

entirely to the fertile and productive valley of the Eurotas.
From the surrounding hills only a very meagre living could
be derived, and it would not appear that any numerous class
below the peasant-proprietor level had existed at the time
of the revival of the traditional constitution in the second
century B.C.[1] Those who did exist might easily find em-
ployment with the rich proprietors or with resident Greek
or Roman merchants engaged in the wild beast trade ;
a few would be absorbed by the small development of
industry round Cardamyle.[2] The peasant-farmer class is
likely to have been prosperous, for the circumstances which
had affected Sparta adversely in the second century B.C.[3]
were now entirely changed. The natural fertility of the
country [4] was no longer offset by the necessity under which
its potential cultivators found themselves of constantly
neglecting it to protect their borders from hostile attack.
The disappearance of the citizen army meant that there
were plenty of free farmers to cultivate the land, and that
there was no longer a large population of non-producers
to feed. The presence in the country of Roman merchants
and of other foreign residents provided a new home market
for agricultural produce. The longer the archaic Sparta
survived, the greater the interest which foreign visitors
took in its institutions and its festivals ; [5] this provided an
additional market for home produce. On the other hand,
the disappearance of the Helots meant a shortage of labour,
and would tend to substitute orchard for tillage. It is not
therefore particularly surprising to hear of a completely
new development in the history of Laconian agriculture, the
export of olive oil from the country.[6]

Nor is it likely that the Spartan state as a whole suffered
under the Principate from the lack of public revenues which
had overtaken it in the period of Achaean domination.[7]
Not only had a great deal of territory north of Sparta itself

---

[1] *Ibid.* The last expulsion of freed labourers by Philopoemen (*cf.*
p. 40) would sufficiently account for the absence of a numerous ' working
class '.

[2] *Cf.* pp. 76, 79.   [3] *Cf.* pp. 41 f.
[4] *Ibid.*   [5] *Cf.* p. 264.

[6] Sidon. Apoll. *Carm.* V, 44. In the fifth century A.D. Sparta itself
seems to have been deserted (*cf.* P.W.[2] VI, p. 1453) but the poet is no
doubt reflecting in this particular instance the conditions of an earlier age.

[7] *Cf.* Paus. VII, 13. 7.

6

been restored, but since the reign of Augustus Sparta had
enjoyed the revenues from the isolated possessions of
Thuria and Cythera,[1] which in the latter case at least must
have been considerable.[2]

All these considerations make it unlikely that Sparta
under the Principate was afflicted, at least during the
first two centuries while Roman commerce flourished,
with the decline of the free population which is said to have
befallen Greece in general.[3] The country would be quite
capable of supporting at least the four thousand (or rather
more) adult male citizens of the peasant-farmer class who
were established in possession by Cleomenes III, the number
regarded as representing the full number in the Apella in
earlier times.[4] Even if only about half the available good
agricultural land (exclusive of Cythera) was in their hands,
they would still just reach the level of the more prosperous
peasant-farmers of modern Greece.[5] Allowing for a small
artisan class in addition, we may suppose as a rough
estimate that the total citizen population during the period
of prosperity under the Principate amounted to about
20,000,[6] exclusive of Cythera. In earlier times the citizen
population had tended gradually to fall,[7] but greater
political security and the absence of wars would check the
tendency ; on the other hand, no considerable increase in
numbers was likely to occur in a country almost wholly
devoid of industries, occupied mainly by peasant-farmers,
and fixed in its ancient social habits.

About the middle of the third century the series of
Spartan inscriptions which will form the subject of the

[1] Cf. p. 56.
[2] For the agricultural products and purple fisheries of Cythera cf.
P.W. XII, i, p. 210. In 424 B.C. a tribute of 4 talents was imposed by
Athens, the inhabitants being left in possession (Thuc. IV, 57). Under
the Principate, though probably not from the beginning, the purple
fisheries were probably reserved as an Imperial monopoly (cf. p. 78, n. 3,
but some doubt arises from the fact that Cythera, as belonging to Sparta)
was not properly speaking a part of Achaea. Strabo's statement (VIII,
363) that C. Julius Eurykles held Cythera ἐν μέρει κτήσεως ἰδίας is easily
reconciled with Dio, LIV, 7. 2 (cf. p. 56, n. 4) by supposing that Eurykles
leased the greater part of it from the Spartan state.
[3] Cf. Plut. De defectu oraculorum, 8.
[4] Cf. p. 18, n. 6.   [5] Cf. Appendix I, p. 430.
[6] Adopting the rough-and-ready estimate of antiquity, that the males
of military age represented a quarter of the total population.
[7] See further, pp. 350 f.

following chapters comes to an end. This indication of decline is only to be expected, in view of the general confusion and collapse of commerce in the Roman empire at that period, and in view of the new era of insecurity which opened for Greece with the first invasions of the Goths.[1] But it was the invasion of Alaric in 396, not the gradual working of natural causes, which caused the final abandonment of the ancient city.[2]

[1] *Cf.* Jornandes, *De reb. Get.* 27.
[2] See further, Gibbon, *Decline and Fall*, Vol. V., Chap. XXX.

CHAPTER III

THE EPHEBIC ORGANISATION

§ 1. *The Nature of the Evidence*

Until the excavation of the temple of Artemis Orthia [1] provided us with a large number of inscriptions relating to the athletic and musical contests of the Spartan boys, our information about their training was very scanty. The pseudo-Xenophon [2] gives a rather vague general account of the whole system, stressing the advantages of accustoming boys to physical hardships and gymnastic exercises ; Aristotle [3] confines himself to general criticism, pointing out the tendency of the Spartan education to develop the fierce and untamed instincts (τὸ θηριῶδες) at the expense of the more civilised side of human nature. The account given by Plutarch [4] provided almost our only information about the details. From Plutarch we knew that the Spartan boys were first taken from the charge of their parents at the age of seven, and they were organised in ' herds ' (ἀγέλαι) in which the big boys had authority over the little boys. A lexicographer has furnished the further information that the leader of the ἀγέλη was called βουαγός,[5] ' leader of the bull-calves ', and abundant evidence for this has now been provided by the inscriptions. There

---

[1] Excavated by the British School at Athens 1906–1910. The results have been collected and published in J.H.S. Supplement, Vol. V (*The Sanctuary of Artemis Orthia*), ed. R. M. Dawkins ; 1929.

[2] *Resp. Lac.* II, 12–IV, *fin.* Throughout the present work references from this treatise will be cited in accordance with the chapter-numbers of existing editions. In a forthcoming work I shall seek to show that a misplaced chapter must have been originally the first, and that Xenophon was not the author. See p. 490, n. 2.

[3] *Pol.* VIII, 4. 1 ff.   [4] *Lycurg.* 16–21.

[5] Hesych. *s.v.* βούα. ἀγέλη παίδων (Λάκωνες). βουαγόρ. ἀγελάρχης, ὁ τῆς ἀγέλης ἄρχων παῖς. The same word ἀγελάρχης properly belongs to the animal which was the leader of a herd of oxen (*cf.* Suidas, *s.v.*). The precise meaning of the name βοαγός (βουαγόρ being the Spartan dialect form) is examined below, pp. 95 f.

was a similar or apparently similar organisation of the boys in ' herds ' among the Cretans in the fourth century B.C., but the question of origins and the possible direct connection between the two systems [1] cannot profitably be discussed except on the basis of a more detailed knowledge of the Spartan system than is provided by the literary writers.

Here the inscriptions of the Roman period come to our assistance. These fall into two main classes, those commemorating successes in the contests organised for the young Spartans (παιδικὸς ἀγών), on account of which the victors dedicated sickles to the goddess Orthia, and secondly, records of careers and lists of magistrates,[2] in which adult Spartans mention titles and distinctions which they originally acquired during their early training, before reaching the age of manhood or soon after. With the exception of one or two inscriptions of earlier date, the great mass of this epigraphical material upon which our generalisations must be based belongs to the Imperial period, and almost exclusively to the Flavian period and later : and it may be asked how far we are justified in drawing conclusions from such late evidence about the ἀγωγή referred to by writers of the fourth century B.C., who ascribed the origin of the system to Lycurgus. To this question the following answers may be made : (1) one inscription probably dates back to the fourth century B.C., and implies precisely the same organisation as we find in the later inscriptions ; (2) ancient writers say that it was the ' Lycurgan ' ἀγωγή which Philopoemen abolished and which the Romans restored ;[3] (3) supposedly, 'Lycurgan' customs were flourishing in the first and second centuries A.D., and Lycurgus himself was several times regarded as the *Eponymos* of the year.[4]

---

[1] See further, pp. 218 f.

[2] I.G. V, 1 (1912), contains the inscriptions from the temple of Artemis Orthia afterwards published by Woodward (in *Artemis Orthia*, J.H.S. Suppl. Vol. V (1929), Chap. X). Further inscriptions from the Theatre and elsewhere are published by Woodward in B.S.A. Vols. XXVI, XXVII, XXIX (excavations of 1924–1927). The epigraphical material available before the excavation of the temple of Orthia is collected in C.I.G. Vol. I, Part IV (1878) and in I.G. V, i.

[3] *Cf.* p. 46, nn. 1, 3.   [4] See further below, pp. 160, 467.

§ 2. The Age-classes

The publication of the inscriptions from the Orthia temple has resulted in a re-studying of the literary evidence which was first discussed by Müller,[1] but so far no final conclusion can be said to have been reached. The great problem which still remains to be solved concerns the age at which the systematic training of the boys began, and the number of years it lasted. Some recent answers to these questions may be summarised. Kahrstedt's answer [2] to the first is that we do not know when the training began. The inscriptions mention age-classes—μικιχιζόμενοι, πρατοπάμπαιδες, ἀτροπάμπαιδες, and a higher grade called μελλειρονεία, all in order of seniority, but no inscription mentions specifically in years the age of a boy under training. Kahrstedt accordingly thinks it possible that the four classes just enumerated, which are the only ones mentioned in the inscriptions, refer to the oldest groups of the boys only, and that the smaller boys may have left no trace in the inscriptions.[3]

It is more generally held that μικιχιζόμενοι, πρατοπάμπαιδες, ἀτροπάμπαιδες and μελλείρενες are all boys under thirteen years of age. In support of this view a Scholiast on Herodotus is cited, who says, ' Among the Lacedaemonians a boy is called in the first year ῥωβίδας, in the second προμικιζόμενος, in the third μικιζόμενος, in the fourth πρόπαις, in the fifth παῖς, in the sixth μελλείρην '.[4] Two of these

---

[1] Müller, Dorians (1830), Vol. II, Chap. V. Rostovtzeff (Bleitesserae, 1905, p. 66) refers to the work of Shebelew ('Αχαϊκά, Petersburg, 1904, in Russian) as the first scientific consideration of the Spartan age-classes. I have not been able to utilise this work, but in view of the fact that no inscriptions which mention the age-classes of the boys were found at Sparta before the excavation of the temple of Orthia began in 1906, the conclusions of Shebelew must need re-consideration in the light of more recent evidence.

[2] Kahrstedt, Sparta u. seine Symmachie (1922), pp. 342 f. Kahrstedt is only indirectly concerned with the training of the boys, and does not therefore discuss it in detail.

[3] Kahrstedt, op. cit. p. 343, n. 1.

[4] Schol. ad Herod. IX, 85 (to explain the meaning of the term Εἴρην): Παρὰ Λακεδαιμονίοις ἐν τῷ πρώτῳ ἐνιαύτῳ ὁ παῖς ῥωβίδας καλεῖται, τῷ δευτέρῳ προμικιζόμενος (Codd. προκομιζόμενος), τῷ δὲ τρίτῳ μικιζόμενος, τῷ τετάρτῳ πρόπαις, τῷ πέμπτῳ παῖς, τῷ ἕκτῳ μελλείρην· ἐφηβεύει δὲ παρ' αὐτοῖς παῖς ἀπὸ ἐτῶν ΙΔ' μέχρι καὶ Κ'. On the Scholiast's statement about the duration of the ephebic training (fourteenth to twentieth year), see, below, p. 91, and additional note, p. 247.

names (μικιχιζόμενος for μικιζόμενος, and μελλείρην) recur in the inscriptions ; hence it appears that the names in the inscriptions must be concerned with the third to the sixth year of training mentioned by the Scholiast, and that the terms πρατοπάμπαις and ἀτροπάμπαις in the inscriptions must correspond respectively to πρόπαις and παῖς in the list of year-classes given by the Scholiast. By 'the first year' the Scholiast is usually understood to mean the year in which the boys' training first began, which, according to Plutarch, was when he was seven years old.[1]

On this assumption we arrive at the conclusion that the inscriptions relating to the Boys' Contests at Sparta are concerned solely with boys from the beginning of their tenth to the end of their thirteenth year.[2]

Let us now consider the main difficulties in the way of this interpretation. What are its implications ? In the first place we are struck by the great interest taken by the state in the training of the little boys under thirteen as compared with the Epheboi, who according to the same Scholiast on Herodotus, were boys between the ages of fourteen and twenty.[3] Several classes of athletic and musical contests are arranged for the younger boys, the victors dedicate sickles to Artemis Orthia, the leaders (Boagoi) of a 'herd' (ἀγέλη) of little boys record the fact that they held this position much later in life, when they are already holding the chief offices of the state. Similarly, boys called κάσεν in the Agelae record the fact later in life. The training of the Epheboi, on the other hand, has apparently left no trace whatever in the inscriptions. These conclusions cannot fail to seem peculiar. We know from our literary sources that mock battles were organised for

[1] Plut. Lycurg. 16.
[2] Cf. Tillyard in B.S.A. XII (1906), pp. 386 ff. ; Woodward in B.S.A. (1909), pp. 44 ff., and in Artemis Orthia (1929), p. 286 ; Nilsson in Klio, XII (1912), pp. 308 ff. ; Kolbe, I.G. V, 1 (1912), pp. 179. Swoboda, (Busolt-Swoboda, Griech. Staatskunde, II (1926), pp. 694 ff.) gives a very complete summary of all the available evidence. All these authorities hold approximately the same view about the Spartan παῖδες, viz. that the inscriptions of the παιδικὸς ἀγών are concerned solely with boys below their thirteenth birthday. Nilsson and Swoboda have developed a further theory about the Eirenes, on which see further, pp. 89 f.
[3] Cf. above, p. 86, n. 4. The only inscription which calls a Spartan boy ἔφηβος is I.G. V, i, no. 1186. The boy died at the age of fifteen. There are lists of ἔφηβοι from other towns in Laconia and Messenia.

the Epheboi,[1] and that the whole training of the Spartan boys became much more strict when they reached the verge of manhood,[2] their conduct and achievements being carefully watched in order to discover whether or not they were fitted to enjoy the full privileges of citizenship afterwards.[3] It would therefore be very strange if they were never mentioned in any of the inscriptions relating to the athletic training of the Spartan boys, while their younger brothers under the age of thirteen received so much prominence. And still harder is it to account, on this theory, for dedications of sickles in connection with the παιδικὸς ἀγών by boys who call themselves συνέφηβοι—'Epheboi with' some other boy, for the Scholiast cited above distinctly says that Spartan boys were Epheboi from the age of fourteen to the age of twenty.[4] As Woodward says, the only interpretation of the word συνέφηβος which is possible on his own view (namely, 'Ephebos with' a Boagos) implies that the name had 'a certain elasticity in its application, for we can scarcely suppose that the victor at the age of ten waited till he was an ἔφηβος before recording his success and dedicating his sickle to the goddess'.[5] This supposition of elasticity in the use of the term cannot, however, be considered a satisfactory explanation of what must remain, so long as the main theory is accepted, a very curious fact indeed ; namely, that the activities of the real Epheboi are never mentioned in these inscriptions, while their name is given to younger boys who had apparently no right to use it.

Moreover, the theory that the παιδικὸς ἀγών concerns only boys under thirteen breaks down in the face of Plutarch's evidence about the age of Melleirenes. Plutarch

[1] Paus. III, xiv. 8–10 ; xx, 8.

[2] Xen. Resp. Lac. III, 2 : ὅταν γε μὴν ἐκ παίδων εἰς τὸ μειρακιοῦσθαι ἐκβαίνωσι . . . τηνικαῦτα πλείστους μὲν πόνους αὐτοῖς ἐπέβαλε (ὁ Λυκοῦργος), πλείστην δὲ ἀσχολίαν ἐμηχανήσατο. This group is called by the writer παιδίσκοι (ibid. § 5) as opposed to ἡβῶντες (iv, § 1) who are already ἄνδρες.

[3] Ibid. § 3 : ἐπιθεὶς δὲ καὶ ὥ τις ταῦτα φύγοι, μηδενὸς ἔτι τῶν καλῶν τυγχάνειν, ἐποίησε μὴ μόνον τοὺς ἐκ δημοσίου ἀλλὰ καὶ τοὺς κηδομένους ἑκάστων ἐπιμελεῖσθαι ὡς μὴ ἀποδειλιάσαντες ἀδόκιμοι παντάπασιν ἐν τῇ πόλει γένοιντο.

[4] ἀπὸ ἐτῶν ΙΔ' μέχρι καὶ Κ'.

[5] Artemis Orthia, p. 291. There is, in addition, reason to think that the 'sickle' was in reality a military weapon (see pp. 254 f.) and would therefore be a very strange prize for boys of ten.

makes the following statements : [1] (1) the Melleirenes (whom the Scholiast mentions as the oldest of his six age-groups) were the oldest of the boys (τῶν παίδων οἱ πρεσβύτατοι) (2) the Eirenes were in their second (?) year out of boyhood (οἱ ἔτος ἤδη δεύτερον ἐκ παίδων γεγονότες) ; (3) ' The Eiren at the age of twenty years commanded his subordinates in the battle of the boys '. The last statement, assigning a definite age to the Eiren, receives confirmation from Photius who explains the cognate word πρωτείραι as οἱ περὶ εἴκοσι παρὰ Λάκωσι.[2] We should naturally conclude that a Melleiren was a boy of nineteen, in his twentieth year.

According to Nilsson, his own view, which makes the ῥωβίδαι boys in their eighth year and μελλείρενες boys in their thirteenth year, reconciles the statements of Plutarch with those of the Scholiast. He argues that Plutarch implies an interval of a year between the Melleiren and the fully fledged Eiren ; for Plutarch says the Eiren is ἔτος δεύτερον ἐκ παίδων γεγονώς, not ἔτος πρῶτον ἐκ παίδων γεγονώς. This argument is not cogent, for δεύτερον ἔτος ἐκ παίδων could equally well mean, according to the normal Greek usage, ' the next [3] year after boyhood '. But for the sake of discussion we may suppose with Nilsson that it means ' the second year out of boyhood '. According to Nilsson's theory ' the first year out of boyhood ' would be a holiday year following the thirteenth birthday : the training would begin again at the fourteenth birthday and continue until the twentieth birthday, and during all these six years the young man would be an Eiren. For Nilsson wishes to identify the period of Ephebic training, defined by the Scholiast on Herodotus as lasting from the age of fourteen to the age of twenty, with the training of the Eirenes.

The improbability of this holiday-year theory has already pointed out by Swoboda : [4] there is the further objection that Nilsson's scheme makes the training of the

---

[1] Plut. Lycurg. 17 : Εἴρενας δὲ καλοῦσι τοὺς ἔτος ἤδη δεύτερον ἐκ παίδων γεγονότας, μελλείρενας δὲ τῶν παίδων τοὺς πρεσβυτάτους. οὗτος οὖν ὁ εἴρην ἔικοσι ἔτη γεγονὼς ἄρχει τε τῶν ὑποτεταγμένων ἐν ταῖς μάχαις καὶ κατ' οἶκον ὑπηρέταις χρῆται πρὸς τὸ δεῖπνον.
[2] Photius, s.v. κατὰ πρωτείρας ; cf. Hesych. κατὰ πρωτείρας· ἡλικίας ὄνομα οἱ πρώτειρες παρὰ Λάκωσι.
[3] Cf. Herod I, 82 : δευτέρῃ ἡμέρῃ—' on the next day '.
[4] Op. cit. p. 696, n. 3.

Eirenes end the year before the age at which, according
to Plutarch, Eirenes held their authority over the younger
boys. For Plutarch's Eiren is εἴκοσι ἔτη γεγονώς ; on the
analogy of Nilsson's seven-year old ῥωβίδαι, who according
to him are to be identified with Plutarch's ἑπταετεῖς γενομένους,[1] Plutarch's Eiren must be twenty years old, that is,
in his twenty-first year. But Nilsson's Eiren would cease
to be such on attaining his twentieth birthday ;[2] this follows
inevitably from the statement of the Scholiast already referred to,[3] which implies six year-classes of Epheboi, not
seven. The conclusion is unavoidable that Nilsson has
misinterpreted Plutarch's εἴκοσι ἔτη γεγονώς as meaning ' in
his twentieth year ',[4] whereas it should really be ' in his
twenty-first ' ; and that he is mistaken in regarding the
Eirenes as themselves Epheboi. Plutarch evidently means
that the Eirenes had already passed the stage of Epheboi.

It must therefore be concluded that Nilsson fails in his
attempt to reconcile the statements of the Scholiast on
Herodotus and those of Plutarch. Swoboda frankly realises
that his own interpretation of the Scholiast cannot be reconciled with Plutarch's statements, and he therefore rejects
the evidence of Plutarch. So must all others who hold
the theory that the age-classes mentioned in the inscriptions
are those of little boys under thirteen.

But the rejection of Plutarch's evidence is a serious
matter for those whose own theories are ultimately based
upon a statement of Plutarch himself. They have assumed that when the Scholiast on Herodotus speaks of
' the first year ' he must mean the eighth year of the boys'
age, simply because Plutarch says that the boy's state
training began at that age.[5] But the Scholiast may not

---

[1] Cf. below, n. 5.
[2] Nilsson says (Klio, XII, p. 310) : ' Folglich entspricht die Altersstufe
der Iranes (i.e. Εἴρενες) der physischen Ephebie, der Pubertät, und erlischt
daher auch passend mit dem 20 Jahr, wie der Glosse (i.e. the Scholiast on
Herodotus) zu entnehmen ist '.
[3] Cf. above, p. 86, n. 4.
[4] Cf. Nilsson (ibid.) : ' der Wortlaut dieser Stelle lässt sich wenigstens
ebenso gut zu, dass der Jüngling erst im 20 Jahr, nachdem er schon einige
Jahre Iran gewesen war, eine Befehlstellung erhalten könnte '.
[5] Plut. Lycurg. 16 : πάντας εὐθὺς ἑπταετεῖς γενομένους . . . εἰς ἀγέλας
κατελόχιζε ; cf. Woodward in B.S.A. XV, p. 45 (' the first two years of
his state training, namely, in his eighth and ninth years ') and Kolbe in
I.G. V, i, p. 79 (octavum annum agens).

mean this at all, and in view of the great difficulties in the way of accepting the theory built up on this assumption, it is surely better to look for another interpretation which will account for the epigraphical evidence without rejecting Plutarch's plain statement about the age of the Eirenes.

There is a very simple and satisfactory solution of the difficulty, namely, to suppose that the Scholiast is speaking of the Ephebic training only, and that his concluding remark (ἐφηβεύει δὲ παρ' αὐτοῖς παῖς ἀπὸ ἐτῶν ΙΔ' μέχρι καὶ Κ') [1] is put in to explain what has gone before ; for if he had not gone on to explain that Ephebic training at Sparta lasted from the age of fourteen to the age of twenty his readers might well have been surprised, and a little incredulous, that it could last for six whole years. In other Greek states three years was the normal length of training for Epheboi.

If we adopt this interpretation of the Scholiast, the μικκιχιζόμενοι (vel sim.) of the inscriptions (μικιζόμενοι in the Scholiast) [2] are to be regarded as boys of sixteen (i.e. in their seventeenth year) : πρατοπάμπαιδες, ἀτροπάμπαιδες and μελλείρενες must be regarded as the names (in ascending order) of the year-classes next above the μικκιχιζόμενοι.[3] The Synepheboi then fall into their proper place among the boys of these ages ; in other words, among the Epheboi. The Melleirenes will be in their twentieth year ; Plutarch must be supposed to be using ' boy ' (παῖς) as synonym for ' Ephebos ' when he says that these ' about-to-be-Eirenes ' are ' the oldest of the Boys ' (παῖδες). The Eirenes will no longer be Epheboi : as Plutarch expresses it, in their twenty-first year (εἴκοσι ἔτη γεγονότες) they will be ' passing the next year after boyhood '.[4] This arrangement will be in effect the one suggested by Kahrstedt.[5]

[1] Cf. above, p. 86, n. 4.
[2] There are many varieties of spelling (μικιχιδδόμενοι, μικκιχιδδόμενοι, etc.) but always in the reduplicated form in the inscriptions. The shortened form μικιζόμενος occurs only in the Scholiast on Herod. IX, 85.
[3] Cf. A.O. 2 (= I.G. V, i, 256). A κάσεν dedicates three sickles in commemoration of victory in the μῶα contest as μικκιχιδδόμενος, πρατ[οπάμ]παις and [ἀτροπάμπαις]. A βοαγός might be βοαγὸς μικκιχιδδομένων (A.O. 36, 45, etc.) or βοαγὸς πρατοπαμπαιδων (A.O. 33, ? 88). It is therefore practically certain that πρατοπάμπαιδες and ἀτροπάμπαιδες were the two year-classes above the year-class μικκιχιδδόμενοι.
[4] Cf. above, p. 89.   [5] Cf. above, p. 86.

Before this reconstruction of the outlines of the system is discussed in greater detail, it is necessary to meet some objections which might naturally be raised at this stage.

Nearly all the names of the year-classes mentioned in the inscriptions and in the Scholiast's list seem inappropriate to Epheboi over fourteen. The name ῥωβίδας for the boy of fourteen (which does not occur in the inscriptions, but only in the Scholiast) is in fact the only name which would be appropriate, since it might well indicate that they had reached the beginning of maturity.[1] Is it possible that boys of seventeen and eighteen were called πάμπαιδες (' small boys ') [2] and boys of sixteen μικκιχιζόμενοι (' very little boys ') ? [3] Even the name παῖδες seems inappropriate ; yet this is used of all the year-classes up to, and probably including, that of the Melleirenes,[4] while τὸ παιδιχόν is frequently employed as a generic name for all the contests in which the age-groups in question took part.[5] This has not unnaturally been interpreted to mean that only young boys, as opposed to Epheboi, took part in them.[6]

But the use of the word παῖς by our literary authorities does not support this view : it goes rather to show that it might be used as the Latin *puer* was used, to denote much

[1] From ῥώννυμι ? *Cf.* also Lat. *robur.*

[2] πάμπαιδες (without prefix) occur as an age-group in lists of athletic victors from Boeotia (I.G. VII [= C.I.G. I], 1764, 2871) and Euboea (*cf.* Kavvadias, 'Εφ. 'Αρχ. 1897, 195), as distinguished from παῖδες. Hesych. *s.v.* ἄμπαιδες (*sic*) would suggest that the word could also be used without a prefix at Sparta. πρατο-πάμπαιδες are doubtless πρῶτο-πάμπαιδες, *i.e.* the first, or youngest, group of πάμπαιδες. They were younger than ἀτροπάμπαιδες (*cf.* I.G. V, i, 279 = A.O. 27 : 'Ονασικλείδας Φιλοστράτου νεικάσας κασσηράτοριν πρατοπαμπαίδων, ἀτροπαμπαίδων, εἰρένων δὲ κελοῖαν) : Kretschmer's suggestion that the ἀτροπάμπαιδες were the ' well-grown ' (ἀτρός = ἁδρός) πάμπαιδες therefore seems probable. ἁδρός is frequently used of older boys (*cf.* Plut. *Lycurg.* 17 ; Plato, *Rep.* V, 466e).

[3] μικκιχιζόμενοι is apparently from μικκός (= μικρός) : ' tiny ' in relation to the ' small ' πάμπαιδες, who are older. See preceding note.

[4] I.G. V, i, 296 = A.O. no. 41 : Νεικάγορος Σωσιδάμου Εὐδάμῳ κάσεν νεικάσας κελοῖαν καὶ μῶαν καὶ καθηρατόρειν καὶ μῶαν καὶ ἀπὸ μικχιζο-μένων μεχρὶ μελλειρονείας τοῦ(ς) Γααόχους καὶ 'Ασάνεα τὴν τῶν παίδων πάλην, 'Αρτέμιτι 'Ορθεία. *I.e.* ' the wrestling matches of the boys in honour of Poseidon and Athena ' (lit. the wrestling match of the Earth-Shaker and that called 'Ασάνεια, *i.e.* 'Αθάναια). The date is either ± 100 or towards the middle of the second century A.D.

[5] τὸ παιδιχόν is mentioned in inscriptions three times in connection with πρατοπάμπαιδες (I.G. V, i, 270, 273, 340), once in connection with ἀτροπάμπαιδες (I.G. V, i, 278).

[6] *Cf.* B.S.A. XV, pp. 44 ff.

older boys or young men. Plato certainly uses it of young men up to the age of twenty,[1] and we have noticed already that Plutarch calls a young man in his twenty-first year ' in the next year out of the παῖδες '. The indiscriminate use of either the word ἔφηβοι or the word παῖδες to describe the young Spartans who were whipped in the annual ceremony at the altar of Orthia serves as a further illustration of the same usage.[2] Plutarch, who is one of the writers who refers to the victims as παῖδες, elsewhere calls them ἔφηβοι, though otherwise describing the ceremony in almost the same words. But an even more cogent argument, as putting the age of the lads referred to beyond possible doubt, is the application of the name παῖδες to the Epheboi in Athenian inscriptions. These speak of the young men of eighteen to twenty inclusive as παῖδες τῆς πρώτης, δευτέρας, τρίτης ἡλικίας.[3] A likely explanation of the usage, which admittedly differs both from that usually adopted by literary writers [4] and (apparently) from that of common speech,[5] is that it arose from the close association

[1] *Rep.* VII, 537*b*. *Cf.* also Dio Chrys. XXI, 13 (of a boy of sixteen or seventeen).

[2] *Cf.* Plut. *Lycurg.* 18 : καὶ τοῦτο μὲν οὐδὲ ἀπὸ τῶν ἐφήβων ἄπιστόν ἐστι, ὧν πολλοὺς ἐπὶ τοῦ βωμοῦ τῆς Ὀρθίας ἑωράκαμεν ἀποθνήσκοντας ταῖς πληγαῖς. *Cf* Philostr. *Vit. Apoll.* 260, Paus. III, 16. 10, Suidas, *s.v. Λυκοῦργος*, all of whom use the word ἔφηβοι. For the use of παῖδες in the same connection, *cf.* Plut. *Inst. Lac.* 239*c.* : οἱ παῖδες παρ' αὐτοῖς ξαινόμενοι μάστιξι δι' ὅλης τῆς ἡμέρας ἐπὶ τοῦ βωμοῦ τῆς Ὀρθίας Ἀρτέμιδος μέχρι θανάτου πολλάκις διακαρτεροῦσιν. The curious story in Xen. *Resp. Lac.* II, 9, relating to the stealing of cheeses from the altar at the whipping ordeal is also referred to the παῖδες.

[3] I.G. II, 444–450, 452 (second century B.C.). Girard (Dar.-Sagl. *s.v. Epheboi*, p. 633, n. 228) doubts the identification of these three classes of παῖδες with the Epheboi. But the following considerations seem to be conclusive : (1) The παῖδες are enrolled in the Athenian tribes (I.G. ibid. pass. *Cf. Ath. Pol.* 42. 1 : ἐγγράφονται δ'εἰς τοὺς δημότας ὀκτωκαίδεκα ἔτη γεγονότες). (2) Among the contests in which they take part is the ὁπλομαχία with heavy shield and sword (I.G. II, 446, l. 74, etc.). Instruction in this began at the age of eighteen in the fourth century B.C. (*Ath. Pol.* 42. 3). The distinction made in the later inscriptions relating to the *Theseia* between παῖδες and ἔφηβοι may be explained either as a social one, or on the supposition that ephebic training in the narrower sense now began a year later (*i.e.* at nineteen) and that one group of contests was limited to the second and third year of παῖδες (19 and 20 groups).

[4] *Cf. e.g. Resp. Lac.* III, IV (classification into παῖδες, μειράκια, ἡβῶντες) ; Xen. *Hell.* V, iv, 32 (a Spartan gives the classification as παῖς, παιδίσκος, ἡβῶν).

[5] In the Spartan inscriptions relating to gymnastic contests the classification is into παῖδες, ἀγένειοι, ἄνδρες (I.G. V, i, 19, 663).

of the Epheboi with the army organisation. It seems to have been the general practice in the Greek states in the period of their independence to draw upon the class of νεώτατοι (i.e. the three or four age-classes below that of ἥβη) [1] in circumstances of special emergency, or to assist in home defence during the absence of the main citizen army.[2] Although these lads were grown-up in relation to the younger boys, in relation to the older men liable for regular military service they would seem mere children ; hence as a characteristic military usage the generic name of παῖδες, and at Sparta, the special colloquial nicknames of ' little uns ' (μικκιχιδδόμενοι) and the others for which it is even harder to find an English parallel. The name προμικιζόμενος (more correctly προμικκιχιδδόμενος) mentioned by the Scholiast is clearly derived from μικκιχιδδόμενος, and so probably means the age-class who had still a year before they could be called upon for military service with the νεώτατοι. Incidentally this explanation of the names will also serve to explain why the inscriptions from Sparta which relate to the Ephebic organisation fail to mention any age-class below that of μικκιχιδδόμενοι. For the class which could be directly useful from the military point of view was naturally the one to which any Greek state directed its attention with a view to its training ; there is no good reason for supposing that Sparta was exceptional in this respect, but rather for suspecting that the extension of the system of public education backwards to include much younger boys [3] was a comparatively late development due to the impact of philosophical theories about education. That the prize given for successes in the παιδικὸς ἀγών was an ancient military weapon [4] not only testifies to the great antiquity of this part of Spartan

---

[1] The age of ἥβη was fixed at the completion of the twentieth year, as implied by the Scholiast on Herodotus (cf. p. 86, n. 4). It is not possible to accept Kahrstedt's view (Sparta u. seine Symmachie, p. 294, n. 2) that the time of ἥβη was variously reckoned according to individual development, since a precise definition according to age is implied by the Spartan law which dispensed from military service outside Laconia all who were above forty years ἀφ'ἥβης (Xen. Hell. V, iv, 13 ; cf. Busolt-Swoboda, op. cit. p. 705).

[2] Cf. Thuc. I, 105 ; II, 13 (Athens) ; V, 64 (Sparta).

[3] Boys entered the Agelae at the age of seven (Plut. Lycurg. 16).

[4] On the Drepanon see further, pp. 254 ff.

education, but also reinforces the opinion that the so-called παῖδες were in reality of age for military service in an emergency.

§ 3. *The Social Structure of the Agelai*

In the preceding account of the Ephebic organisation no account has so far been given of the Boagoi, those who held authority over the Agelai (' herds ') of Epheboi. Discussion of this subject was postponed in order that the relation of the Boagoi to ' Kasens ' and ' Synepheboi ' might be considered in detail.

Hesychius defines the meaning of Boagos as ' the boy who was leader of the Agela '.[1] Before the inscriptions relating to the contests in the Orthia sanctuary were found, other epigraphical evidence from Sparta seemed to throw doubt on Hesychius' statement that the Boagoi were ' boys ', for the word Boagos only occurred in lists of senior magistrates (ephors, members of the Gerusia, etc.), and seemed to indicate public office held at the same time, or at least after the person in question had become a full citizen.[2] But since the excavation of the temple of Orthia the pendulum has swung in the opposite direction, and the Boagoi are believed to belong themselves to the age-groups between ῥωβίδας and μελλείρην,[3] since they make dedications to Orthia on account of contests won by members of the Agelai.

But there are objections to this view. Not only is it

---

[1] *Cf.* p. 84, n. 5.

[2] This view is discussed by Boeckh (who finally rejects it) in C.I.G. Vol. I (1878), Part IV, *Introd.* p. 612. Gilbert (*Staatsalter.* I², 69) and Szanto (Pauly-Wissowa, R.E. III, 572) consider that the Boagoi must have been young men older than the age-classes of which they were ἀγελάρχαι.

[3] Kahrstedt (*op. cit.* pp. 343, 344) supposes the Boagos for each βούα (= ἀγέλη) to have been appointed from the members of the year-class of which the ἀγέλη was composed. *Cf.* Busolt-Swoboda (*Griech. Staatskunde*, p. 696, n. 1), ' die zahlreichen von einem βουαγός . . . besonders von einem βουαγὸς μικιχιζομένων, gesetzten Siegesinschriften beweisen, wie Nilsson . . . richtig bemerkt hat, dass die Buai Knaben von derselben Altersklasse vereinigten und der Buagor zu der Altersklasse seiner Bua gehörte '. The views expressed in B.S.A. Vols. XII (353 ff.) ; XIV (79 ff.) ; XV (44 ff.) and by Kolbe in I.G. V, i, p. 79, are quoted in support of this statement, and a still more recent expression of it will be found in *Artemis Orthia*, p. 290 (Woodward).

hard to believe that a distinction conferred in boyhood [1]
could last through life (as the lists of magistrates which
preserve the title of Boagos imply that it did),[2] but the
statement of Hesychius that the Boagos was a ' boy '
conflicts with what we are told by the author of the
Respublica Lacedaemoniorum and by Plutarch. Both these
writers imply that the Boagoi were drawn from the class
of Eirenes,[3] that is, they had reached the age of twenty
years. And after all, we should perhaps not press too closely
Hesychius' statement that the Boagos was a ' boy ', for
he (or his source) is above all anxious to make clear that by
ἀγελάρχης he means not the leader of a herd of oxen (which
would be the normal meaning of the word) but the leader
of the so-called ' herd ' of boys. It is further probable that
παῖς is here used in the technical sense instead of ἔφηβος.[4]
The author probably knows that the Boagoi were leaders
of Agelae in the Ephebic organisation, but there is no reason
to think that he has any special information about their age.

There is in fact no evidence, apart from Hesychius'
statement, that the Boagos belonged to the same age-class
as the Agelae of which he was in charge. For in the inscriptions from the Orthia sanctuary in which Boagoi are
mentioned, they are called a great many times βοαγὸς
μικιχιζομένων,[5] and twice βοαγὸς πρατοπαμπαίδων.[6] But
never, be it observed, is a Boagos called (*e.g.*) βοαγὸς μικιχιζόμενος (for the one inscription which is supposed to record
this is restored at the crucial point) [7] and never is he de-

---

[1] According to the view maintained above (pp. 91 f.), the ' boys '
in question were between their fourteenth and twentieth birthdays ;
the common view that they were between seven and thirteen would
make it still harder to believe that a distinction conferred at so early an
age could last through life.

[2] It will be shown later (pp. 102 ff.) that the names Kasen and
Synephebos, when they occur in the lists of magistrates, indicate not so
much a personal distinction as a difference of social and political status.

[3] [Xen.] *Resp. Lac.* II, 11 : ἔθηκε τῆς ἴλης ἑκάστης τὸν τορώτατον τῶν
εἰρένων ἄρχειν ; cf. Plut *Lycurg* 17 : καὶ κατ᾿ἀγέλας αὐτοὶ προΐσταντο
τῶν λεγομένων εἰρένων ἀεὶ τὸν σωφρονέστατον καὶ μαχιμώτατον. For Plutarch's
definition of the age of the Eirenes, cf. above, p. 89.

[4] *Cf.* pp. 92 f.

[5] I.G. V, i, 283, 288, 289, 292, 294, 300, 302, 304, 305, 306, 310, 312,
314, 324, 325.

[6] *Ibid.* 273, 340.

[7] A.O. no. 49 . . . βουαγὸς . . . μικιχιζόμε[νος (similarly restored in
I.G. V, i, no. 276\.

scribed by any adjective which would imply that he himself
belonged to one of the age-classes enumerated by the
Scholiast or mentioned in the inscriptions relating to the
activities of the boys. On the other hand, those boys who
are called ' Kasen ' in the dedications to the goddess made
on account of their victories in the boys' contests are always
described as κάσεν μικιχιζόμενος, κάσεν πρατοπάμπαις,[1] etc.,
but never as κάσεν μικιχιζομένων or under any similar
formula. It is clear from this form that they belonged
themselves to the age-class in question. Similarly, in the
case of the Synepheboi, the formula employed in inscriptions
indicates that they too belonged themselves to the age-class
mentioned in connection with them.[2] The consistent use
of the different formula (βοαγὸς μικιχιζομένων, etc.) in the
case of the Boagoi must surely indicate a difference in age.

There is also an exceptional case to be considered in this
connection, that of a Boagos named Philochareinos, who
appears to have been attached to the same year-group
μικιχιδδόμενοι in two different years,[3] in the Patronomate
of Sejanus and in that of Biadas, a thing plainly impossible
if the Boagos in question himself belonged to the year-group
μικιχιδδόμενοι. Kolbe denies the identity of the Boagos
mentioned in the two inscriptions,[4] and it is true that he
is called in one case ' Philochareinos son of Lysippos ',
and in the other ' C. Julius Philochareinos '. But the
existence of two identical lists of members of the Gerusia
for these same two years,[5] in spite of the fact that membership of the Gerusia was annual in the period of the Principate,[6]
strengthens the case for identifying Philochareinos as the
same Boagos in both years. For it seems evident that the
years of Sejanus and Biadas were consecutive ones, and
that they were marked by some internal or external crisis
which prevented the holding of elections in the second year
of the two. Boagoi, then, appear to have been regarded
as on a level with magistrates to this extent at least, that

[1] Cf. I.G. V, i, 256, 270, 278, 298.
[2] Ibid. 286 (A.O. no. 43): συνέφηβορ . . . μιχιχιδδόμενορ ; I.G. V, i,
287 (the only other inscription which mentions a Synephebos in connection
with an age-class) provides no evidence on the question, since it merely
mentions that a Synephebos was victor in the κελοῖα μικιχιζομένων.
[3] I.G. V, i, 292, 294.   [4] Cf. ibid. 294.
[5] I.G. V, i, 111 ; B.S.A. XXVI, pp. 169, 193.   [6] Cf. pp. 138 f.
7

in a year when no elections were held, no Boagoi were appointed either. But this implies, further, that Boagoi in general were older than the μικιχιδδόμενοι to whom they were often attached, and in particular, that the Boagos Philochareinos was not himself a μικιχιδδόμενος in either of the years when he acted as the Boagos of that group. The same argument would make the Boagoi older than the πρατοπάμπαιδες,[1] and if more evidence about the contests of ἀτροπάμπαιδες and Melleirenes had been preserved, we should doubtless have the direct evidence that Boagoi were older than these classes also. It is, however, implied by Plutarch that authority over the Epheboi was exercised only by young men of not less than twenty years old,[2] and putting together all these indications, we may say that there is a strong probability that the Boagoi had already reached the age of the Eirenes (twenty years), and that the pseudo-Xenophon is referring to the Boagoi, without directly naming them, when he says that Lycurgus put ' the keenest of the Eirenes ' in command of each ἴλη of παῖδες.[3] This implies that the Boagoi were an officer-class among the age-group of Eirenes, and that they were chosen to command the various sub-divisions (i.e. year-classes) of the Agelae.

The objection which will naturally be made against the view that the Boagoi did not themselves belong to the year-classes of the Epheboi is that they frequently dedicated sickles and commemorated their victory in the παιδικὸς ἀγών. Moreover, the different kinds of contest open to the παῖδες make quite a long list,[4] and there is no reason to distinguish the contests won by Boagoi from those won by a Kasen or any other dedicator. The list of contests won by Boagoi seems in fact to be precisely the same as the list of contests won by Kasens, and not essentially different from the list of contests won by Synepheboi, though in the case of Synepheboi the evidence is too scanty to permit of any certain conclusion.

The answer to this objection, and the alternative view which will now be put forward about the Boagoi, depends upon an examination of the material collected in the Ap-

---

[1] Cf. p. 96.   [2] Cf. p. 89, n. 1.
[3] Cf. p. 96, n. 3.   [4] Cf. pp. 121 f.

pendix, where as complete a list as it has been possible to compile of all the Boagoi, Kasens and Synepheboi who are known to us up to the present [1] will be found, together with what is known about the dates of their athletic victories (if such are recorded), and particulars of the offices they held in later life.

One of the conclusions which seems to follow from the study of this evidence is that the dedication of a sickle in commemoration of a victory in the παιδικὸς ἀγών was, in general, only permitted to a Kasen in the period before Hadrian. From this time onwards (and as we may suspect, from the date of one of Hadrian's two visits to Sparta in A.D. 125 and 128) a Boagos, although he had not actually competed,[2] had apparently the exclusive right to claim the victory on behalf of any victor in his year-class (μικιχιδ-δόμενοι vel. sim.), and to dedicate the sickle. For out of twelve recorded victories by Kasens, only one belongs to the period after Hadrian's visit,[3] and in this case the date may be as late as the reign of Caracalla, by which time the rule had perhaps again been relaxed. It would seem that Synepheboi did not come under the same rules as Kasens, for, while there are only three surviving dedications all told by Synepheboi in the παιδικὸς ἀγών, two belong to the period after Hadrian's visit.[4]

Thus far, then, we may arrive at the following conclusions upon the relation between Kasens, Synepheboi and Boagoi. The Kasens were in some way inferior to both the other classes, since over a long period they were not allowed to claim their own victories. But this inferiority of the Kasens was not, in respect to the Synepheboi, one of age ; for it has been shown that the Synepheboi were equally capable with the Kasens of being μικιχιδδόμενοι. The Boagoi, on the other hand, were apparently senior in years to both the other classes.

Before proceeding further with the epigraphical evidence, it will be well to notice the meaning indicated for the name

---

[1] The evidence is taken from I.G. V, i (1912), *Artemis Orthia* (1929) and B.S.A. Vols. XXVI, XXVII, XXIX (1925, 1926, 1928).

[2] This follows from his age. *Cf.* above, pp. 95 f. But I.G. V, i, 258 (cited below, p. 106) implies that the Boagos in any case shared the right to dedicate on account of his protégé's victory.

[3] See Appendix IV, § 3 B, p. 456, no. 2.   [4] *Ibid.* p. 459, § 6, Aa.

Kasen on etymological grounds. Hesychius appears to be referring to the Spartan Kasens in defining κάσιοι (a plural which in fact is never found in the inscriptions,[1] nor in literary Greek either) as οἱ ἐκ τῆς αὐτῆς ἀγέλης ἀδελφοί τε καὶ ἀνεψιοί.[2] The lexicographer (or more probably his source) obviously connects the Spartan term with the classical Greek κάσις, a brother, but at the same time regards it as not precisely identical with κάσις in its classical literary meaning, for he also defines κάσης (sic) as ἡλικιώτης ' one of the same age ', that is, a contemporary in the Agelai, with which alone the definition is directly concerned.

The opinion of an ancient authority that the Spartan κάσεν is to be connected with the classical Greek κάσις, but is not precisely identical in meaning with it, is much to be preferred to a modern theory that κάσεν is really καθ'ἕν, ' at one with ' ;[3] this idea is indeed disproved by the fact that there could be one Kasen attached to three Boagoi,[4] and three Kasens attached to one Boagos.[5] Woodward, who rejects the καθ'ἕν theory, concludes on the basis of Hesychius that a boy presumably called himself Kasen to another person ' because he was his brother or his cousin '.[6] But as will be shown presently, the inscriptions afford proof of the distinct social inferiority, throughout life, of the Kasen class in relation to those persons to whom they were Kasens.[7] This rules out the literal interpretation of Kasen as ' brother or cousin '.

The connection between the words κάσις (or κάσεν, evidently its Spartan form) and κασίγνητος may help us here. Evidently ' born brothers ' are somehow different from mere ' brothers '. This provides a useful clue to the true meaning of the word κάσεν at Sparta. Is it not possible that when κάσις (or κάσεν) is used in its technical sense it implies a fictitious blood relationship, not a real one ? If this hypothesis be adopted, many of the most

---

[1] No plural of κάσεν occurs in any of these inscriptions.
[2] Hesych. s.v. κάσιοι.
[3] Cf. Kretschmer, Glotta III, p. 272 ; Hoffmann, S.G.D.I., IV, p. 684.
[4] Cf. I.G. V, i, 298.   [5] Cf. Appendix IV, § 4, p. 458.
[6] Cf. Artemis Orthia, pp. 290 f. Woodward also assumes that it was always to a Boagos that a boy was Kasen. For objections to this view see further below, pp. 105 f.
[7] See further below, pp. 102 f.

puzzling features of the Kasen relationship become clear ; for instance, the fact that grown men are proved by the Spartan inscriptions often to have claimed the relationship of Kasen to some holder of high office in the state, and in particular, to persons who in the great majority of cases may be shown to have held the office of Patronomos, the magistrate who gave his name to the year. So commonly does this occur that it was once believed that a Kasen stood in the Kasen-relationship not to another boy or youth at approximately the same stage of educational training as himself, but directly to the Patronomos.[1] Apart from the question whether this theory is true or false,[2] how is the practice of retaining the name of κάσεν from boyhood into ripe manhood to be explained ? There would be no particular credit in having been born, by a mere accident, the brother of a person destined to be distinguished later, and it is therefore hard to believe that so fortuitous a circumstance would have been mentioned frequently in lists of magistrates ; on the other hand, there would be some point in stressing the fact that a distinguished person had once selected one for his *adoptive* brother, for this would presumably depend not upon accident but upon merit.

Let us then consider further the suggestion that a Kasen was not a real brother, but an adoptive brother, and if the latter, in what sense we should use the word ' adoptive ' in this connection. Some such distinction may well be what the source of Hesychius intended to convey by his cryptic statement that κάσιοι (*sic*) were ἀδελφοί τε καὶ ἀνεψιοί. If cousins could come as near to being Kasens as could brothers, then clearly a Kasen was not a blood-brother. The modern Italian use of *cugino* for an adoptive brother [3] suggests the true interpretation, although it still remains to be ŝeen in what sense Kasens may have been ' adoptive '.

---

[1] This view, first put forward by Boeckh (C.I.G. I) is still accepted by Kolbe in I.G. V, i, with the consequence that Kolbe's list of Patronomoi includes the names of any persons who are recorded as having had either a Kasen or a Synephebos. Woodward (A.O. p. 290) rejects this view in favour of the supposition that a Kasen was always Kasen to a Boagos ; for the case against this alternative see below, pp. 105 f.

[2] The theory of Boeckh and Kolbe must in fact be rejected in view of the considerations advanced below, pp. 105 f.

[3] *Cf.* Petrocchi, *Nuovo Diz. Ital.* 1913, *s.v. cugino*.

The new suggestion agrees with the evidence of the Spartan inscriptions in so far as these indicate a distinct difference of social class between those who were Kasens and those to whom Kasens were attached. It will be shown later, from a more detailed examination of the names of those who had Kasens, that they belonged to the most distinguished Spartiate families,[1] whereas there is reason, as will presently be shown, for thinking that none of the Kasens can be regarded in this light. Further, there is a conspicuous difference between the names of Kasens who record victories in the contests of the boys and those who appear in the lists of magistrates. The names of Kasens of the second category all conform, with the single exception of Sosikrates son of Epaphrodeitos, for which there may be some special explanation, to a single pattern,[2] the Kasen's name being the same as the name of his father.[3] Not a single Kasen who records a victory in the contests of the boys has a name of this form. These facts strongly suggest that before a Kasen could hold office in the state he had to be in some way legally adopted and change his name ; a certain number of the names of Synepheboi [4] seem to show that in some cases the Synepheboi also had to conform to this rule ; this point will be further discussed below in connection with the difference between Kasens and Synepheboi.

It is perhaps desirable to examine more closely the case of Sosikrates son of Epaphrodeitos, who is the only known exception to the rule that Kasens who become magistrates have names of the ' A son of A ' type. Sosikrates is also marked out from other Kasens among the magistrates in that he held, some time late in the reign of Trajan or under Hadrian,[5] the office of Diabetes, which appears to have been held by no other Kasen. The reason for this may have been the considerable expense involved in the office, which was that of president of one of the four

---

[1] See below, pp. 111 f.

[2] See Appendix IV, § 3, A (p. 454).

[3] For this reason the reading in line 4 of the inscription published in B.S.A. XXVI, p. 202(e) cannot be accepted.

[4] Appendix IV, § 6, B (p. 459).

[5] I.G. V, i, 65. For the date of the Patronomos Lysippos son of Philochareinos, cf. Appendix IV, § 8, p. 465.

gymnastic Phylae.[1] But Sosikrates son of Epaphrodeitos seems to have been a man of exceptional wealth, since he would appear to have been closely related—probably as his father—to C. Iulius Epaphrodeitos, a very wealthy man who in A.D. 163 made a distribution of money to each member of the Gerusia and provided a banquet for the whole city for ten days in succession.[2] Sosikrates may well, therefore, have been allowed to enter upon a public career without changing his name, in consideration of the way in which he (like his son after him) used his wealth for the benefit of his city. It is evidently a very special case which does not affect the general rule.

The peculiarity which has been observed in the names of all other Kasens than Sosikrates who hold office serves to elucidate the relation between the Kasen and his ' adoptive brother ' as we provisionally called the person to whom he was Kasen during the period of his preliminary training among the boys. If Kasen means ' adoptive brother ', it does not mean adoptive in the legal sense. There were evidently two distinct processes. First came the formal selection of a boy as his Kasen by another person[3] at the stage of the boy's gymnastic training in the Agelai : this act made the boy a Kasen. Later came the act of legal adoption which enabled the Kasen to hold office in the state. A certain class of the citizens had evidently to pass through both these stages before they could hold office : to be selected as Kasen at the initial stage of the boys' training was an indispensable preliminary qualification.

The names of the Kasens in the lists of magistrates, considered in relation to the names of the respective persons to whom each was Kasen, show that there is no question of legal adoption (that is, of adoption by one person of another into his own family, perhaps as the heir to his

[1] See below, p. 154.
[2] I.G. V, i, 1346. For the text and the date of this inscription see Part II, p. 343, n. 1. Its exact place of origin is not recorded, ' the south of the Peloponnese ' alone being mentioned. But it certainly belongs to Sparta : (1) because the decree in question is issued by the Gerusia, whereas those from other Laconian towns in this period were always issued by the Ephors and Demos ; (2) the office of ἀγρέτης implied by ἀγρετεύσαντα (l. 3) is also implied by the title of Hippagretes at Sparta ([Xen.] *Resp. Lac.* IV, 3).
[3] See further below, pp. 110 f.

property) between the Kasen and the person to whom he
stood in that relationship.   For example, Chaleinos, son of
Chaleinos (Kasen-list, no. 8), Kasen of Enymantiadas, is
presumably the adoptive son of Chaleinos and has taken
his adoptive father's name instead of his original one, but
there is no reason to suppose that he is also the adoptive
brother of Enymantiadas, in other words, no reason to
suppose that it was the father of that person, to whom
another was Kasen, who adopted that Kasen afterwards in
order to enable him to embark upon a public career.   It
is true that our evidence is too scanty to permit this
negative conclusion to be drawn in more than a few particular instances.   In support of the contention we may
cite the family trees of Seidektas, who held the office of
Patronomos early in the reign of Hadrian,[1] and of Brasidas,
who was Patronomos soon after A.D. 150.[2]   The family
trees of both these men have been reconstructed by Kolbe [3]
so fully that it is possible to say without hesitation that
the adoptive fathers of their respective Kasens (Philippus
son of Philippus, and Dekmos (sic) son of Dekmos) were
not in any way related to themselves : certainly it was not
the fathers of Seidektas and Brasidas who afterwards
adopted their sons' Kasens.

Who, then, did adopt the Kasens to enable them to
enter upon public office ?   The names of their adoptive
fathers seem to show just what we should expect, namely
that the Kasens had to be adopted by a man who belonged
to the same privileged circle as those who had Kasens.
Thus the Kasen who later became a magistrate under the
name of Agathokles son of Agathokles bears in his public
life the name of a man to whom someone else (Sosidamus
son of Sosidamus) was Kasen.   Other Kasens in the lists
of magistrates bear names which connect them with
persons who were Boagoi ; thus the Kasens Neikokrates
son of Neikokrates, and Neikandros son of Neikandros,
have (adopted) names which connect them with the family
of the Boagos Neikandros son of Neikokrates ; similarly,

[1] I.G. V, i, 32 A.
[2] I.G. V, i, 71 ; cf. Appendix IV, § 8 (p. 467), under A.D. 157.
[3] Cf. I.G. V, i, 537 (Seidektas) and 591 (Brasidas).   Both belong to
distinguished priestly families (cf. I.G. V, i, 497, 537), hence the completeness with which their family trees are known.

the Kasen Diokles son of Diokles, has an (adopted) name which connects him with the family of the Boagos Damokrates son of Diokles.

The assumption commonly made, that every Kasen was Kasen to a Boagos,[1] would enable us to draw without further argument the conclusion that the ' privileged circle ' into which Kasens aspiring to a magistracy had to be adopted consisted of those families whose members were eligible to be Boagoi. This indeed was probably the case, but it is not a conclusion which can be reached without further examination of the lists of those who had Kasens and those who were Boagoi, for the evidence seems to show that it was never to a Boagos as such that a boy or man stood in the relationship of Kasen, even though it was possible for a man who had been Boagos also to have a Kasen or Kasens. The evidence is as follows. Thirty-six names of Boagoi who actually mention that title occur in I.G. V, i. In only one case (or possibly two cases, both furnished by one inscription which will be discussed presently) can the holder of the title Boagos be identified with a person to whom other persons were Kasens ; for although a few names coincide in both lists, it can be shown from the evidence of date in all other cases than the above-mentioned exception, that the Boagoi are not the same persons as their namesakes in the list of ' patrons of Kasens '.[2] The inscriptions found since the publication of I.G. V, i, furnish no instances of Boagoi actually called by that title whose names recur in the list of patrons of Kasens.

The one certain exception among the inscriptions published in I.G. V, i, is that of Teisamenos, the possible exception is that of Iamos. Both certainly had Kasens, for they shared the Kasen Charixenos son of Damokratidas, with a third person (Kritodamos), and Teisamenos appears to have had two other Kasens in addition (Kleon son of Kleon, and Sosibios son of Sosibios),[3] Teisamenos certainly,

---

[1] Cf. above, p. 101, n. 1.

[2] Those who had Kasens will henceforward be referred to as ' patrons of Kasens ' for the sake of convenience. It should be clearly understood, however, that the word is not used in the exact sense of the Latin *patronus* (which would be a relationship between adults) but to describe a similar relationship between boys in the Agelai.

[3] For these details see Appendix IV, § 5 (p. 458).

and Iamos probably, was a Boagos. The evidence for this
is a metrical inscription [1] in which two Boagoi are mentioned, apparently brothers, of whom the first is Teisamenos,
and the name of the other is lost but was of the form ∪∪—
in the dative. The missing name may well be 'Ιάμῳ, especially in view of the fact that Teisamenos and Iamos are both
names in the family of that celebrated seer, Teisamenos of
Elis (a descendant of the original Iamos) who for his services
was granted the full privileges of Spartan citizenship, together
with his brother, in reward for his promise to act as sooth-
sayer for Sparta before the battle of Plataea. [2] In the
seventh line of the inscription in question the name Τεισαμενῶι is followed by a space for one letter, and then comes
an incomplete letter which Kolbe interprets as an initial Σ,
but which might be part of the second letter Α of the name
'Ιάμῳ. [3] Thus epigraphical, metrical and historical considerations combine to favour the restoration of the name
Iamos as that of the other Boagos referred to in this inscription, and Kolbe's suggestion that the name Iamos
should be restored at the beginning of the first line of the
inscription as the name of the Synephebos who set up the
dedication, must therefore be rejected.

There is therefore reason to think that Iamos as well
as Teisamenos was a Boagos as well as the patron of a
Kasen. Yet the inscription just discussed, which is the
only evidence that either of them was a Boagos, is a dedication set up not by a Kasen, but by a Synephebos. There
is nothing remarkable in the fact of the same person having
both Kasens and Synepheboi attached to him: the
Patronomos Seidektas mentioned above had at least one

---

[1] I.G. V, i, 258 :

["Ιαμος 'Ορθείη]ι δρεπάν[ην| τὰ κελ]οῖα κρατήσα[ς] |
[χώρ]ωι ἐν ἡγαθέωι| [θῆκ]εν ὅμηρα λαβών |
Συνστέφομαι δάφνηι| σολοειδεῖ τοῖσι βοαγοῖς |
Τεισαμενῶι Σ[∪ ∪ –] παισὶν 'Αριστο[λόχ]ου·
[Πρῶτο]ς δ' 'εκ πάν[τ]ων συν[εφήβων ε]ἴλον [ἄ]εθλον
[– ∪ ∪ – ∪ ∪]οις ϙ . . ∪ ∪ – ∪ ∪ –

[2] Cf. Herod. IX, 33 f. Memory of the original Iamidae was kept alive
in Pausanias' time by the preservation of their tomb at Sparta (Paus.
III, 12. 8), and the daughter of a Spartan Teisamenos about A.D. 200
claims to be descended ἀπ' 'Ιαμιδῶν (I.G. V, i, 599).

[3] The first line of the dedication may easily be restored without the
aid of the name Iamos, as ['Αρτέμιδ' 'Ορθείη]ι κ.τ.λ.

Synephebos [1] as well as his Kasen Philippos son of Philippos. But the fact that only two Boagoi (including Iamos) can be shown also to have had Kasens, and that these two, in the inscription in which they are called Boagoi, appear as ' patrons ' not of Kasens but of Synepheboi, justifies the suspicion that the ' patrons ' of Kasens were not Boagoi, whereas patrons of Synepheboi were. For the number of names preserved, both of ' patrons ' of Kasens and of Boagoi, is fairly large, and since the names of so many individuals in both classes recur in several inscriptions, we should naturally expect to find several cases in which ' patrons ' of Kasens were called Boagoi, if a Kasen were always Kasen to a Boagos. On the other hand, since it has been shown already in the case of Teisamenos and Iamos that the patron of a Synephebos could be a Boagos, it is evident that the *argumentum ex silentio* must not be pushed too far : all the ' patrons ' of Synepheboi in the list could be Boagoi even though the fact that they were Boagoi does not happen to have been explicitly recorded in the inscriptions which have been preserved ; and similarly, some ' patrons ' of Kasens may have been Boagoi although the fact does not happen to be recorded.

Further conclusions upon this subject can only be reached when we have considered what can be known about the Synepheboi, for it is evident that the problem of the Kasens and the problem of the Synepheboi are intimately bound up together.

In the case of the Synepheboi there is good reason to think that Boagoi, and only Boagoi, could be their ' patrons ' in the Agelai. The evidence is as follows.

In one list of magistrates, the names of the five Nomophylakes are followed by the words βοαγὸς καὶ συνέφηβοι.[2] This strongly suggests that the first name was that of a Boagos, the rest the names of the Synepheboi attached to him.[3] Two other inscriptions relate to Synepheboi

[1] I.G. V, i, 59, 66. In no. 59 the names of both Synepheboi are lost, and the second entry may be due to careless repetition of the same name (*cf.* Appendix IV, § 6, n. 4).

[2] B.S.A. XXVI, p. 167.

[3] For more than one Synephebos attached to the same person compare the case of Seidektas (above) and the Synepheboi of Damokrates son of Diokles (I.G. V, i, 493).

who distinguished themselves in the καρτερίας ἀγών.[1] One is set up in honour of Marcus Aurelius Kleonymos, Synephebos of Sextus Pompeius Gorgippos son of Onasikrates, and the expense of the inscription is defrayed by 'the mother of the Boagos',[2] who must be the mother of Sext. Pomp. Gorgippos, since her father's name, Eudamos, is also the name of another son of the same Onasikrates,[3] and it was a common practice for a boy to be given the name of his maternal grandfather. A similar inscription is set up in honour of Marcus Aurelius Euarestos son of Zoilos, Synephebos to two persons,[4] and in this case the cost is defrayed by 'the Boagoi'.[5] If when a Synephebos has only one Boagos, 'the mother of the Boagos' defrays the cost of the inscription, whereas when a Synephebos has two Boagoi 'the Boagoi' pay the expenses, we naturally conclude that the Synephebos in each case was personally attached to the Boagos or Boagoi in question. Finally, we may cite the portrait-herm set up in honour of one Damokrates son of Diokles, by his Synepheboi (συνέφηβοι Δαμοκράτους) at the time when these were still in the Agelai.[6] Damokrates is not actually called Boagos in this inscription, but he calls himself so in a dedication set up in commemoration of a victory in the contests of the boys, and therefore about the same time.[7]

A general comparison between the status of the Synepheboi and that of the Kasens, both in the Agelai and in later life, may help us to decide whether it is likely that Synepheboi (in the Agelai) were boys whose 'patrons' were Boagoi, Kasens (in the Agelai) boys whose 'patrons' were not Boagoi.

As regards the age at which Kasens and Synepheboi acquired these relationships, no distinction can be drawn.

---

[1] See below, pp. 134 f.
[2] I.G. V, i, 653b : ποδδεξαμένης τὸ ἀνάλωμα τῆς ἀξιολογωτάτης καὶ πάντα ἀρίστης Αὐρ. Ἁγίου (sic) τῆς Εὐδάμου τῆς τοῦ βουαγοῦ μητρός.
[3] Ibid. no. 559.
[4] Cf. I.G. V, i, 258 (discussed above, pp. 106 f.), where the same person is Synephebos to three others.
[5] Ibid. 653a : ποδδεζαμένων τὸ ἀνάλωμα τῶν βοαγῶν.
[6] Ibid. 493 : παῖδες ἀνίκατοι, σθεναροὶ, κρατεροὶ συνέφηβοι.
[7] Ibid. 293 : Ἀγαθῇ τύχῃ. Δαμοκράτης Διοκλέους βουαγὸς ἐπὶ πατρονόμου Τιβ. Κλαυδίου Σηιανοῦ νεικήσας τὸ παιδικὸν μῶαν Ἀρτέμιδι Ὀρθείᾳ ἀνέθηκε (c. A.D. 150).

We have seen already [1] that Synepheboi did not necessarily become Synepheboi at a later stage in the boys' training than Kasens became Kasens, for there are instances of Synepheboi as well as of Kasens at the stage of μικκιχιδ-δόμενοι. Again, the Kasen, like the Synephebos, might be one of a number attached to the same ' patron ' in the Agelai : there are no grounds for suggesting that each ' patron ' had several Synepheboi but only one Kasen, nor for thinking that each patron must have both Synepheboi and Kasens. It seems in fact to have been extremely rare for the same person to have both.[2] Here in fact a difference between Synepheboi and Kasens emerges : whereas it was not at all uncommon for a person to be a Kasen, to be a Synephebos was much more rare. We know at present the names of only seventeen Synepheboi as against those of about fifty Kasens [3] in the same period, and if we take into consideration the inscriptions which preserve the mention of a Kasen or a Synephebos without preserving the actual name, the proportion becomes over sixty Kasens as compared with twenty Synepheboi. This suggests that it was a greater distinction to be a Synephebos than to be a Kasen, but whether the act of selection as Synephebos conferred that greater distinction, or whether the class from which the Synepheboi were drawn possessed it from birth through some social difference, is not easy to determine. On the one hand, seven out of the thirteen Synepheboi who are known to have been magistrates have names of the ' A son of A ' type, which we have observed to be typical of the Kasens who became magistrates. This suggests that a high proportion of the Synepheboi were drawn from the same unprivileged class as the Kasens, and like them, had to be legally adopted before they could enter upon office in the state. On the other hand, a much higher proportion of the Synepheboi than of the Kasens are exempt from this condition ; indeed, the single exception to the

---

[1] Above, p. 99.
[2] Teisamenos (above, p. 105), and possibly Iamos (*ibid.*), seem to be exceptional in having both Kasens and Synepheboi. Though several names coincide in those of ' Patrons ' of Kasens (Appendix IV, § 3) and ' Patrons ' of Synepheboi (Appendix IV, § 6) they can be shown to belong to different persons in every case with the possible exception of Longinus.
[3] See Appendix IV, § 3, A, B. (pp. 452 f.).

' A son of A ' type in the list of Kasens who held high office appears to have been a very special case which in no way forbids us to regard the rule of adoption as practically universal.[1] One Synephebos at least, the son of a Spartan aristocrat and a high-born Roman lady, seems to have ranked as of noble birth.[2] A hypothesis which appears to account for all the known facts is that the Kasens belonged to a class which did not automatically possess the right of entry into the Agelai at all, and owed their own inclusion wholly to the fact of having been selected as Kasens, whereas the Synepheboi were selected from among those already in the Agelai, Kasens and non-Kasens alike.

This explanation would be in accordance with the suggestion made earlier, that Synepheboi were boys whose ' patrons ' were Boagoi, Kasens boys whose ' patrons ' were not Boagoi, for it would obviously be a greater distinction, and a mark of higher ability, bravery or prowess, to be selected by the leader of an Agela rather than by a younger lad of the rank and file. The fact that there are instances of both Kasens and Synepheboi attached to the same person [3] is of course no objection to this theory, for a boy might well ' adopt ' a Kasen or Kasens before he became Boagos, and adopt a Synephebos or Synepheboi afterwards. It is true that this arrangement might lead to a certain amount of confusion later : the case of Neon son of Neon, who in one list of magistrates is called ' Synephebos of Damares ' and in another ' Kasen of Damares ' [4] is an indication that it did. If a Synephebos lacked some qualification (whatever it was) and could only enter upon a public career through the way of legal adoption by another citizen, the distinction between Kasen and Synephebos would cease to have any significance in his later career and a mistake might very easily be made, when the lists of magistrates were being made up, in a case where the distinction mattered so little.[5]

[1] See above, p. 102.
[2] Cf. I.G. V, 1, 259. The boy was priest of Apollo of Amyclae. Cf. also Appendix IV, § 6 (p. 459), no. 8.
[3] See above, p. 106 (Teisamenos).   [4] I.G. V, i, pp. 38 and 68.
[5] The mistake would not be likely to arise with a name not of the ' A son of A ' form, for in that case the magistrate was almost certainly not an ex-Kasen : for one exception to this rule see, however, the case of Sosikrates son of Epaphrodeitos (above, p. 102).

It is now time to consider whether the inscriptions throw any light on the reason why Kasens, and many Synepheboi, coming up from the training groups of the boys could only hold office under certain conditions, and why the class or classes from which they were drawn apparently could not hold office at all. For the ex-Boagoi, and the ' patrons ' of Kasens in the Agelai, evidently possessed from the beginning of their career the right to proceed to public office if elected : as the Romans would say, they had *ius honorum*, and were thereby marked off from the rest. Do the inscriptions reveal any inferiority of birth (for that is the reason which naturally suggests itself) which would explain the position of Kasens, Synepheboi and the class from which they were drawn ? For it must be remembered that the Kasens and Synepheboi in the Agelai have themselves already achieved a certain distinction in acquiring the right to these titles ; they must be drawn from a much larger class of which only a few could ever hope to rise to office in the state.

It is fortunately possible to deduce the evidence which we require from an examination of the names which are preserved of individuals of these various categories (Boagoi, ' patrons ' of Kasens, Synepheboi, Kasens and others).[1] The lists of names extend over a period of about 250 years, from the second half of the first century B.C.

From these lists we observe first of all a constant repetition of names in the lists of Boagoi and ' patrons ' of Kasens. It is clear from the repetitions that the same names recurred in the same family for several generations, and evident, moreover, that in spite of the large number of names only a comparatively small number of families is represented. Close family relationship can be traced between many of the Boagoi, as also between Boagoi on the one hand and ' patrons ' of Kasens on the other, for there seems no reason to suppose a social distinction between these two classes, nor does the privilege of being Boagos seem to have been restricted to a still more limited number of families.

Here, then, we seem to have evidence that only the

---

[1] This material has been collected in Appendix IV (pp. 442 f.), together with a list of those dedicators on account of victories in the boys' contests who were neither Boagoi, nor Synepheboi, nor Kasens.

members of a small privileged group of families could
' adopt ' Kasens or Synepheboi in the Agelai. It will be
convenient to refer to them henceforward as the Privileged
Families since that name appears to be justified by the
indications of their social superiority as compared with the
members of the other two groups (Kasens and Synepheboi).

These indications are, first that the use of the Roman
name is noticeably more common among the members of
the Privileged Families than in either of the other two
classes.[1] It is true that Spartans of this period did not
always record their possession of Roman citizenship when
they had it—perhaps for fear of revealing freedman origin
—but it can scarcely be accident that while twenty-nine
names in the list of members of Privileged Families testify
to Roman citizenship, there are only two Kasens in the
whole list (one apparently of freedman origin [2]), and only
four Synepheboi, with the Roman names which mark their
Roman citizenship. The proportion of those who reveal
Roman names is about one in three among the Privileged
Families, about one in thirteen among the Kasens and
Synepheboi taken together. And among the Kasens taken
separately only two are prepared to reveal their Roman
citizenship in a total of about fifty.[3] The members of the
Privileged Families may be said to flaunt their Roman
citizenship, the Kasens and Synepheboi (if they possessed
it) to conceal it.

Moreover, in the list of members of Privileged Families
there are several whose ancestors must have received Roman
citizenship (and in their case certainly by official grant,
not as freedmen) very early, as the added names of Sextus
Pompeius and C. Iulius indicate, whereas two of the four
Synepheboi with Roman names are called ' Marcus Aurelius ',
one ' Marcus Ulpius ', and the fourth, ' Tiberius Claudius '.
It is obvious that members of distinguished (and therefore
probably wealthy and high-born) families would be the first

[1] On the general subject of Roman citizenship among Spartans, cf.
H. Box, J.R.S. Vol. XXI, pp. 200 f. ; XXII, pp. 165 f.

[2] See further below, pp. 113 f.

[3] It is difficult in some cases to decide whether the repetition of the
same name indicates the same person or not, since it is not always possible
to ascertain the date of the inscription or the age of the persons concerned.
Hence the precise number of Boagoi, etc., in these lists cannot be stated.

to receive the honour of Roman citizenship officially granted, and likely that Roman citizenship would continue to be given to them in this way more frequently than to the rest.

The argument from the distribution of Roman citizenship is strengthened by the discovery that all the hereditary Spartan priesthoods appear to have belonged to the members of the Privileged Families whose names occur in our lists. The reasons for this conclusion are fully discussed in another section of this work,[1] and it is not necessary to do more than refer to it here. The same applies to the evidence that the members of the Privileged Families were many of them descended from the families of the Spartan kings, as for example the bearers of the names Gorgippos and Gorgion, whose forbears can be shown to have been among the royal ancestors of Nabis.[2]

With regard to the social and political status of the Kasen-class, if Kasens in general had to be adopted and to change their names before they could become magistrates, they evidently belonged in origin to a different social class from the rest of those eligible to hold office. This conclusion is further supported by the fact that no Kasen whose name appears in the list of magistrates ever holds the office of Patronomos, although such Kasens are apparently eligible for every other office.[3] The office of Patronomos apparently remained the preserve of a limited number of aristocratic families, none of whose members were ever Kasens. Any inferiority of social origin is not unnaturally concealed by the non-committal new names of the office-holding Kasens, but the hint of an explanation appears in one case among the names of Kasens who record victories in the παιδικὸς ἀγών. Damion son of ' Anthestios Philokrates ',[4] was actually the son of M. Antistius Philokrates,[5] whose *praenomen* almost certainly shows him to have acquired his Roman citizenship through M. Antistius

---

[1] See Appendix V, pp. 471 f.

[2] *Cf.* Homolle, *Bull. Hell.* XX (1896), pp. 505 f.

[3] For the offices held by Kasens, see Appendix IV, § 3. Sosikrates son of Epaphrodeitos, who is in other respects exceptional (*cf.* above, pp. 102 f.), is the only Kasen recorded as having held the office of Diabetes.

[4] *Cf.* Appendix IV, § 3, B, no. 4.

[5] *Cf.* B.S.A. XXVI, pp. 170 (E2), 195 f.

8

Labeo,[1] the celebrated jurist of the reign of Augustus. But since Antistius Labeo was consistently in open opposition to Augustus [2] (and on that account never rose above the praetorship), he is most unlikely ever to have held the office of proconsul of Achaea, which would be the normal explanation of the appearance of his *nomen* and *praenomen* among Spartan citizens, namely among those upon whom he was empowered to confer Roman citizenship in his public capacity. It is also to be observed that no Spartan Antistii are known outside the family of M. Antistius Philokrates (in the second half of the first century A.D.) and his son Damion, and if the name had come in through an official grant of citizenship we should expect to find other families holding it, as in the case of the Spartan Sex. Pompeii, C. Julii and P. Memmii.[3] But there is an obvious alternative explanation, namely that the ancestor of M. Antistius Philokrates in the reign of Augustus was a freedman. But if a Roman freedman, then certainly this ancestor was not a Spartan citizen. Either he himself or a son must have been the first of his family to settle in Sparta, Philokrates (in the third generation ?) acquiring full citizenship and the right to hold office only through the medium of the Kasen system.

Since the whole system of the Kasen relationship is obviously an archaic survival into Roman times, it may be suggested that it was through this avenue that Xenophon was advised to enter his sons for the Spartan Agoge,[4] presumably with a view to acquiring Spartan citizenship. The whole arrangement is clearly of the greatest significance in relation to the social and political organisation of Sparta in the archaic period.

It is, however, to be observed that, in the case of the ' unadopted ' Kasens, many of their names connect them

---

[1] M. Antistius Labeo (P.I.R.[2] p. 144, no. 760) is the only one of the twenty-seven Antistii cited in P.I.R. *ibid.* who has the *praenomen* Marcus. His father may have had the *praenomen* Marcus, but with the *nomen* Pacuvius, the *nomen* of the jurist being accounted for by adoption into the *gens Antistia* (*cf.* reff. cited in P.I.R. *ibid.*). Antistii of Greek origin among those cited in P I.R. (*ibid.* nos. 767–769, *cf.* 751) appear to derive their Roman name from C. Antistius Vetus (*ibid.* no. 770).

[2] *Cf.* Syme, *The Roman Revolution*, p. 482.

[3] *Cf.* I.G. V, i, Index II.   [4] Plut. *Ages*, 20.

with the Privileged Families ;[1] here the status of the
mother may well provide the explanation of inferiority.
It should be borne in mind that citizens of other Laconian
towns independent of Sparta had not the right of intermarriage (ἐπιγαμία) with Spartans, at least in the Roman
period,[2] so that children of Spartiate fathers, but of mothers
who were ' foreign ' in the sense of coming from one of the
Laconian towns, might form a large class in Sparta, and
might possibly account for most of the class from which
Kasens and Synepheboi were drawn.

It remains to check the conclusions which have been
reached so far with the help of the list of boys who won
victories in the boys' contests, but were neither Boagoi
nor Kasens nor Synepheboi.[3] So far as their names are
concerned, these may all be members of Privileged Families :
but our ignorance of the origin of their mothers' parents
prevents us from being certain that this was the case. We
observe, however, that one of them (Onasikleidas son of
Philostratos) becomes a Boagos later,[4] while three of them
eventually become Patronomoi, from which office it seems
clear that Kasens were excluded.[5] Whether Synepheboi
were also excluded the scantiness of our evidence prevents
us from determining.[6]

In view of what has already been said, it will occasion
no surprise that the very numerous inscriptions provide no
case of a Kasen or Synephebos becoming a Boagos.[7] This
appears to justify the conclusion that although it was in a
sense a distinction to be chosen as a Kasen or a Synephebos,
the Kasens in general, and some of the Synepheboi [8] were

---

[1] Cf. Appendix IV, § 3, B, nos. 1, 3, 4, 9, 10. Aristokritos, the father
of no. 10, apparently belonged to the Herakleidai (cf. Poralla, s.v.) but the
name does not occur among those of the Privileged Families of the
Principate.

[2] Cf. I.G. V, i, 961 : Cotyrta makes a special grant of this privilege,
among others, to a Spartan (? late second century B.C.).

[3] Cf. Appendix IV, § 7.

[4] I.G. V, i, 36 ; cf. 279.   [5] Cf. above, p. 113.

[6] Cf. B.S.A. XXVII, pp. 239 f.   The Neon son of Neon, who was
συνπατρόνομος of Lampis in the second century A.D. (see Appendix IV,
§ 8, under 164-5 A.D.) seems to have been the son of a man of the same
name who was either Kasen or Synephebos to Damares.

[7] Cf. Appendix IV, §§ 1-6.

[8] I.e. those with names of the ' A son of A ' type (cf. Appendix IV,
§ 6, B).

nevertheless marked out not as superior to the ordinary members of the Agela, but as inferior to them. It was evidently a privilege for those who became Kasens to be admitted at all, and in view of this it is extremely unlikely that any from the class from which they came were admitted except as Kasens.

To sum up the evidence, we may suppose that the Agelai contained altogether three social classes, (1) members drawn from the Privileged Families, who might select Kasens and Synepheboi, (2) the rank and file, who could neither select nor needed to be selected, (3) a third class consisting entirely of Kasens, drawn from a much larger class whom we may call the Unprivileged, as they were apparently ineligible for office except through admission to the Agelai. Boagoi appear to have been free to select their Synepheboi from among the members of any of these classes.

We are now able to determine more precisely the position of the Boagoi. They were the members of the most distinguished families who, having gone through the Ephebic training with credit themselves, could be chosen when they had reached the age of twenty years to hold authority over the age-classes of the Epheboi.

The evidence from the period of the Principate has now probably been pushed as far as it will go in the direction of accounting for Boagoi, Synepheboi and Kasens. It has revealed the existence of the Privileged Families and tells us a good deal about some of them,[1] it has enabled us to see how the boys' training was used to select promising material from the ranks of the Unprivileged, and has thrown light on the methods of legal adoption which enabled these selected candidates later to hold office in the state. Several points still remain obscure : in particular, the precise ground of distinction between this class of the Privileged and the Unprivileged, and the question whether the Unprivileged were citizens of Sparta at all. But one thing is clear ; the institutions which have been discussed in this chapter cannot have been the result of modifications introduced in the boys' training by the Roman government. It was clearly in the interests of the Romans that the old Spartan

---

[1] See further, Chap. V.

ἀγωγή should be revived and encouraged, just as it was in the interests of Rome to promote *Collegia Iuvenum* throughout the empire. But in a *civitas libera,* as Sparta was under the Principate, the Roman government could not have introduced for the first time an organisation so oligarchical in character (if the Unprivileged were included in the citizen body) or so liberal, if they were not citizens but could become so by the means described above. Neither is it in the least likely that the Spartans invented on their own account a system so archaic in character at so late a period in the history of their city. The emphasis laid upon this distinction of birth by the Privileged Families cannot have been an invention of the Roman period, or it would never have been recognised by the Unprivileged, if these last were included in the Spartan citizen body. And if they were not included, and the arrangements about Synepheboi and Kasens was a device for keeping up the number of the citizen body, this was a need which had been felt long before the Roman period, and much more acutely, because the safety of the inhabitants and the preservation of their property depended upon it, which was no longer the case under the protection of Rome. There is therefore every reason to think that the inscriptions relating to Boagoi, Synepheboi, and Kasens in the Roman period may be regarded as evidence for the earlier organisation of Sparta.[1]

The immense importance of the whole system of Ephebic training in determining the character of the Spartan state cannot be over-estimated. This applies both in the sphere of social life and to the constitution. It is obvious that the elaborate system of graded privilege on which the ἀγωγή was built up tended to the preservation of a conservative and authoritarian régime, and after examining the organis- ation in detail, we may fully agree with the writers of the Roman period who stress the significance of the abolition of the Ephebic training in 188 B.C.,[2] and may also realise the full implications of its revival after no more than two or three age-groups of the citizens had been seriously affected by the abolition.

---

[1] The relation of the whole system to the early Cretan organisation is discussed in Part II, pp. 218 f.

[2] *Cf.* above, pp. 46 f.

§ 4. *The Agoge in its Educational Aspect*

It remains to examine the inner nature of the training included in the Agoge, as this is illustrated in the inscriptions of the Roman period ; and also to consider, for the sake of more complete understanding of the historical development of Sparta, how far in this respect there was real continuity from an earlier period.

From at least as early as the fourth century B.C., foreign observers formed the opinion that the Spartan educational system had the defect of developing mere animal ferocity at the expense of the gentler and more civilised instincts, although these last might be thought of even greater importance in making men amenable to discipline.[1] This may, however, have been an erroneous impression, due to the prominence given at the Gymnopaedia, when strangers were present, to a pitched battle fought without weapons between two opposing camps of Epheboi.[2] Pausanias [3] ascribes the institution of these μάχαι to Lycurgus, and the accompanying ritual, involving the nocturnal sacrifice of a puppy to the god of war on the eve of the battle, as well as the extreme barbarity of the contest itself, supports the view that they were of very ancient origin. This ' battle ' was held in an open space called *Platanistas*, surrounded by a dyke and approached only by two bridges at opposite ends. The object of each side was to push the opposing side into the water, and the fighting itself, though done without weapons, was of the most violent and barbarous character ; the lads fought and kicked and bit those on the opposing side and ' tore each others' eyes out ' ; no wonder that spectators from other states came to the conclusion that Spartan education paid too much attention to the development of τὸ θηριῶδες. The same impression might easily result from witnessing the annual whipping competition at the altar of Orthia,[4] another occasion when foreign audiences were admitted. And that there was real

---

[1] *Cf.* Arist. *Pol.* VIII, iv, 1 f.

[2] *Cf.* Plato, *Laws* I, 633 B, C : καρτερήσεις . . . ἔν τε ταῖς πρὸς ἀλλήλους ταῖς χερσὶ μάχαις κ.τ.λ. ; Paus. III, xiv, 8 ff. ; Hesych. *s.v.* λιμνομάχαι· παῖδες οἱ πυκτεύοντες τόπῳ Λίμναις καλουμένῳ ; Plato (*ibid.*) gives the information that the μάχαι were held at the Gymnopaedia. For the presence of foreign visitors at this festival, *cf.* Philostr. *Vit. Apoll.* 258.

[3] Paus. III, xiv, 8.   [4] See further below, pp. 260 f.

danger to life and limb in these encounters is indicated by the dispensation from passing through the *Agoge* which was granted to the heirs-apparent of the two royal houses and to no other Spartan citizen.[1] Nor can it be denied that the theory underlying the whole Spartan system of education was that boys were just so many wild or half-wild animals, to be treated as such until they were tamed,[2] and not to be allowed to lose their wild characteristics altogether. This idea explains their organisation in ἀγέλαι or ἶλαι and the name Boagos ('leader of the bull-calves') for the leader of each Agela. It also explains why they were made to go without clothes or shoes, baths or soap, to pluck the river reeds with their bare hands to make their beds, to range the woods for their food or learn to steal it.[3]

But the mere fact that Plato, convinced as he is that instruction in the arts and particularly in music is indispensable to the proper training of the young, still patently admires the Spartan system of education, and obviously thinks of the products of that system in his description of his auxiliaries in the ideal city as ' fierce and gentle dogs ' —this in itself throws doubt on the popular belief that the Spartans completely overlooked the value of the arts in education. When the evidence of the inscriptions of the Roman period is further examined, this suspicion will be seen to be justified.

By far the most commonly mentioned of the various contests in honour of Orthia are μῶα, κελοῖα,[4] and καθθηρατόριον.[5] The meaning of μῶα can hardly be in doubt. The word itself is evidently the old Dorian form of Μοῦσα :[6] Hesychius gives the more specific meaning ' a kind of song '.[7] It is clear therefore that Μῶα was a musical competition.

---

[1] Plut. *Ages.* 1. Agesilaus himself actually passed through the Agoge, because he was not at that time the nearest heir to the throne.

[2] Simonides' epithet δαμασίμβροτος for Sparta (*cf.* Plut. *ibid.*) is literally appropriate.

[3] *Cf. Resp. Lac.* II, 3, 4, 6 ; Plut. *Lycurg.* 16, 17.

[4] Variant spellings, κελέα, κελήα, κελεία, καιλοῖα, κελῦα.

[5] Variant spellings, κατθηρατόριον, κασσηρατόριον.

[6] For the disappearance of the *sigma*, *cf.* I.G. V, i, 213. 2, νικάhας (*c.* V, B.C.), *ibid.* 329 (*c.* II, A.D.), νεικάας. Hesych. preserves the aspirate in μῶα (*cf.* n. 7).

[7] Hesych. *s.v.* Μῶά. ὠδὴ ποιά.

The name κελοῖα (*vel. sim.*) does not give so clear a clue, but a dedication to Orthia on account of a victory in this contest ends with the following couplet : [1]

Εὔστομον [2] εὐτροχάλου γλώσσης τοδ' ἄεθλον ἀείρας,
Παρθένε, σοὶ δρέπανον Τιμοκράτης ἔθετο.

Since the dedicated sickle is referred to as ' the prize of a nimble tongue ', we may conclude that the κελοῖα was some kind of recitation or invocation.[3] Since one (fragmentary) dedication of a sickle seems to record the prize as being won for accompanying the human voice (γᾶρυν ὀπ[άδων]),[4] it may be assumed that this musical accompaniment was what was meant by μῶα as distinct from κελοῖα.

The name καθθηρατόριον (or its variants) clearly has something to do with hunting, but the discussion of its precise nature must be postponed for the present.[5]

In addition to these three contests, which are all mentioned very frequently in the inscriptions, we have also to account for the ' contest of endurance ' καρτερίας (*sc. ἀγών*), which is only mentioned in one inscription,[6] also for ὁ εὐβάλκης (*sc. ἀγών* ?) and for ὁ κυναγέτας (*sc. ἀγών* ?).[7] The καρτερίας ἀγών has been interpreted both in modern times and by Philostratus[8] as another name for the famous Flogging Ordeal ; ὁ εὐβάλκης has been regarded as yet another name for this, while ὁ κυναγέτας has been supposed to be an alternative name for the καθθηρατόριον.[9] The meaning of the last two words is certainly closely allied, but it is doubtful whether this interpretation will suit all the texts. More detailed discussion of the nature of these various contests must be postponed until we can arrive at some closer knowledge of the organisation of them.

[1] A.O. 4 ; *cf.* B.S.A. XIII (1907), p. 199.
[2] Perhaps a mistake for εὔστομος. The nominative would seem to be required by the sense.
[3] *Cf.* κλύω, κέλομαι.
[4] A.O. 3. The victor is also referred to as ὑμνοτόκος, *i.e.* not ' singing ' but ' giving rise to song '.
[5] See further below, pp. 123 f.
[6] A.O. 37 : . . . αι 'Α[λκά]στῳ ϙάσεν ἐπὶ ϝατρονόμου Δεξιμάχου νικάσ[α]s τον τᾶς καρτερίας ἀ[γ]ῶνα 'Ορθείᾳ. On the καρτερίας ἀγών, see further below, pp. 134 f.
[7] On these contests see further below, pp. 126 f.
[8] *Vit. Apoll.* 259.
[9] This is the view expressed by Woodward (A.O. pp. 288 f.).

Both in the four mutilated inscriptions which mention ὁ κυναγέτας or ὁ εὐβάλκης and in the other dedications relating to the contests of the Epheboi, we find that the name of the contest is frequently qualified by the addition of the words τὸ παιδιχόν placed in apposition to it.[1] It is usually supposed that the words τὸ παιδιχόν are an unnecessary addition, that they merely explain that the victory in question was one of the Boys' Contests. But it may be that the addition is significant, and that the words τὸ παιδιχόν distinguish the competitions open to all age-classes of Epheboi from those which were limited to a particular section. The records of victories appear to put this hypothesis beyond reasonable doubt. By comparing the inscriptions which mention the contests in question in connection with the names of age-classes we arrive at the following results. Those inscriptions in which the name of a contest is further qualified as τὸ παιδιχόν may be considered first. τὸ παιδιχὸν κασσηρατόριον is won by a βοαγὸς μικκιχιζομένων several times,[2] once by a κάσεν πρατοπάμπαις,[3] once by a κάσεν ἀτροπάμπαις.[4] τὸ παιδιχὸν μῶα is won by a συνέφηβος μιχιχιδδόμενορ[5] and at least once by a βοαγὸς πρατοπαμπαίδων.[6] Two inscriptions mention victories in τὸ παιδιχὸν μῶαι by the same competitor in two different years.[7] τὸ παιδιχὸν κελοῖα is won in two cases by a κάσεν μικιχιζόμενος,[8] and one inscription records the success of the same boy in this competition in two different years.[9] Thus it seems reasonable to conclude that all the three year-classes μικιχιζόμενοι, πρατοπάμπαιδες and ἀτροπάμπαιδες were eligible for

---

[1] E.g. I.G. V, i, 272 : Φιλόστρατος Πασικλέος νικάσας τὸ παιδιχὸν μῶαν Ὀρθείᾳ ; cf. ibid. 280 (νικάσας τὸ παιδιχὸν κελοίᾳ) ; ibid. 278 (τὸ παιδιχὸν καθθηρατορίῳ) ; A.O. 16 (τὸ παιδιχὸν κελέαι (sic) [καὶ ?] εὐβάλκει) ; I.G. V, i, 268 (τὸ παιδιχὸν κετεύων (sic) ἐν τῶι εὐβάλκει καὶ κυναγέται).
[2] I.G. V, i, 283, 288, 294 (= A.O. nos. 36, 45, 52).
[3] I.G. V, i, 298 (= A.O. no. 35).   [4] I.G. V, i, 278 (= A.O. no. 27).
[5] I.G. V, i, 286 and add. p. 303 (= A.O. no. 43).
[6] I.G. V, i, 273 ; cf. 340 (= A.O. nos. 33, 88). In the second of these inscriptions the restoration is uncertain ([βοαγ]ὸ̣ς̣ [πρατοπαμ]π̣αίδ̣[ων]).
[7] I.G. V, i, 262 (= A.O. 13) : Σίων Δαμίππου νικάσας τὸ παιδιχὸν μώιαι ἐπὶ Τιμάρχου καὶ Πολυδ[άμαν]τρος Ὀρθε[ίαι] ; I.G. V, i, 269 (= A.O. no. 19) : Ξενοκλῆς Ξενοκλέος ἐπὶ·Εὐετέος νικάας τὸ παιδιχὸν μώιαι Ὀρθείαι καὶ ἐπὶ Ἱππάρχου ὡσαύτως.
[8] I.G. V, i, 281, 334 (= A.O. nos. 34, 84).
[9] Cf. below, p. 127 (A.O. 16).

all the three contests qualified by the addition of τὸ παιδιχόν. As to the Melleirenes we have no definite evidence, since they are never mentioned in connection with any particular contest, although it is certain from one inscription that they were eligible for some at least of the contests for παῖδες.[1] It may be by accident that no mention of them has been preserved in connection with τὸ παιδιχὸν (μῶα, κελοῖα or κασσηρατόριον); or on the other hand it is possible that they were excluded from these particular contests.

Turning to the evidence for contests, entries for which were restricted to boys of particular age-classes, we may notice first, an inscription which records that Onasikleidas 'won the contest κασσηρατόριον of the πρατοπάμπαιδες and of the ἀτροπάμπαιδες, and the contest κελοῖα of the εἴρενες'.[2] Similarly, a boy records his victory in 'the contest κελοῖα of the μικιχιζόμενοι'.[3] Woodward has expressed the opinion that these apparent examples of contests restricted to particular age-classes 'seem capable of explanation as due to a loosely descriptive use of the genitives'; [4] that is to say, Onasikleidas would have been more accurate had he said that he won the κασσηρατόριον when πρατοπάμπαις and when ἀτροπάμπαις, and the κελοῖα when εἴρην. But against this explanation it may be urged that the Eirenes were no longer classed as παῖδες,[5] so that in any case εἰρένων κελοῖα cannot refer to the same κελοῖα as that which was included in τὸ παιδιχόν. Since, therefore, we must admit a separate κελοῖα-contest for Eirenes, why should we refuse, giving the natural explanation to the other genitives, to admit the possibility of separate contests for the other age-classes, that is, to suppose that there was a κελοῖα, a μῶα and a κασσηρατόριον limited to μικιχιζόμενοι, a κελοῖα, a μῶα and a κασσηρατόριον limited to πρατοπάμπαιδες, and similarly for ἀτροπάμπαιδες and μελλείρενες? The evidence is not, however, sufficiently complete to establish

---

[1] Cf. above, p. 92, n. 4.

[2] I.G. V, i, 279 (= A.O. 31): Ὀνασικλείδας Φιλοστράτου νεικάσας κασσηρατόριν πρατοπαμπαίδων, ἀτροπαμπαίδων, εἰρένων δε κελοῖαν.

[3] I.G. V, i, 287 (= A.O. 44): Μ.Οὔλπιος Ἀριστοκράτης Καλλικράτους συνέφηβος Ἰουλίου Εὐρυκλέους νεικήσας κελο[ῖ]αν μικιχιζομένων ἐπὶ Κλαυδίου Ἀττικοῦ Ἀρτέμιτι Ὀρθείᾳ χαριστήριον. The fragmentary inscription A.O. no. 63 seems to provide another example of the κελοῖα μικιχιζομένων.

[4] A.O. p. 287.   [5] Cf. above, pp. 88 f., 92, n. 4.

this interpretation in detail, since the inscription about Onasikleidas, referred to above, is the only one which mentions a victory by a πρατοπάμπαις or ἀτροπάμπαις in any one of these contests unqualified by the addition of τὸ παιδιχόν, and in this inscription only the one contest κασσηρατόριον is involved. There is no reason to postulate separate contests of this kind for Boagoi only ; inscriptions in which the same βοαγὸς μικιχιδδομένων claims victories in three separate contests (unqualified by the addition of τὸ παιδιχόν) in the same year [1] refer in fact to victories won by boys in the group of μικιχιδδόμενοι for which the Boagos in question was responsible.[2] It may be that the number of contests arranged for μικιχιζόμενοι only was larger than the number of contests arranged for any one of the other year-classes only. This hypothesis would help to explain the very high proportion of all victories won by μικιχιζό-μενοι, although the proportion of victories won by this class in the open contests (τὸ παιδιχόν) is also high,[3] and perhaps may to some extent be explained by the nature of the contests themselves.

It would be natural for the younger lads to excel in competition in singing and recitation, as the contests μῶα and κελοῖα are thought to have been, but it is hard to understand the proficiency of the youngest age-class in the καθ-θηρατόριον, if this was a rough hunting game, as the name

[1] A.O. nos. 67, 68, 69 (victories in μῶα, κασσηρατόριον and κελοῖα).
[2] See above, p. 99.
[3] Out of the ten inscriptions recording victories in τὸ παιδιχιόν which also mention the age-class of the victor (A.O. nos. 27, 33, 34, 35, 36, 43, 45, 52, 84, 88) six record victories by μικιχιζόμενοι. Woodward (B.S.A. XV, p. 48) who thinks that all contests were open to all the six year-classes (from ῥωβίδαι upwards) without distinction of age, supposes that the two youngest classes were too young and inexperienced to have stood a chance against the older boys, and that the high proportion of victories recorded by μικκιχιζόμενοι may be explained by supposing that as it was more creditable to win at this age than in one of the older groups, nearly all the μικκιχιζόμενοι took care to commemorate their victories, whereas the older boys did not. This explanation is not very convincing as applied to boys of seven to twelve (as Woodward supposes them to be) : it becomes less convincing when applied to Epheboi above the age of fourteen, for whereas boys of nine might easily sing, play or dance better than boys of ten to twelve, it is hard to see what could be better done by boys of sixteen (as μικκιχιζόμενοι were on the theory now being maintained) than by young men of seventeen to nineteen. Thus the theory that they were prodigies could not account for a high proportion of victories by the lowest year-class.

124 ANCIENT SPARTA

suggests. It seems not unlikely that it was the name of a dance. Some support to this idea is given by the names and descriptions of other Greek dances in the list given by Pollux, who, after mentioning one called 'The Lion' adds that there were also certain Spartan dances of a terrifying character;[1] he also mentions another dance called μορφασμός, not necessarily Spartan, which was 'an imitation of all kinds of animals'.[2] And unless we admit that the Spartan καθθηρατόριον was a dance, there is apparently no room in the general scheme of Spartan ephebic training in the Roman period for what was regarded at an earlier period as one of its essential features, and was still extensively practised in Roman times if we may judge from Athenaeus' account of Spartan dances[3] and from Pausanias' reference to the dances of the Epheboi at the festival of the Gymnopaedia.[4]

The place of the dance in the education of the young is considered at length in Plato's Laws, and it is there suggested that it may have an important influence in producing ἀνδρεία in the grown citizen—that virtue which above all others the Spartan state desired to inculcate.[5] So closely, in fact, do the general views there expressed about the purpose of education coincide with the theory which underlies the Spartan training that it is worth while to examine this section of the Laws more closely. The characters of the dialogue are agreed that the bravery of the citizen (ἀνδρεία) is demonstrated in two ways, by endurance (καρτερήσεις) against pain and discomfort[6] on the one hand, by καρτερήσεις against pleasure (ἡδονή) on the other.[7] We are reminded by this of the καρτερίας ἀγών,[8] and since the second manifestation of ἀνδρεία is also explained by Plato as the true meaning of σωφροσύνη,[9] it seems not improbable that a reference to Spartan education underlies

[1] Pollux IV, 14. 103 : ὁ δὲ λεών, ὀρχήσεως φοβερᾶς εἶδος : ἦν δέ τινα καὶ Λακωνικὰ ὀρχήματα δειμαλέα.
[2] Ibid. : ὁ δὲ μορφασμὸς παντοδαπῶν ζώων μίμησις ἦν.
[3] Athen. XIV, p. 631.   [4] Paus. III, 11. 9.
[5] Cf. Thuc. II, 39. 2 : καὶ ἐν ταῖς παιδείαις οἱ μὲν (sc. the Spartans) ἐπιπόνῳ ἀσκήσει εὐθὺς νέοι ὄντες τὴν ἀνδρείαν μετέρχονται. The stress still laid on ἀνδρεία in the Roman period is illustrated by many inscriptions (cf. I.G. V, i, 472, 527, 565, 566, 652, 653, 660).
[6] Laws, 633 B.   [7] Ibid. 635 B, C.
[8] Cf. above, p. 120, n. 6.   [9] Laws, 647 D.

the whole passage in the *Laws*. For σωφροσύνη too was regarded as an essential part of the virtue of the Spartan citizen, not only in classical times but also in Roman Sparta.[1]

In Plato's dialogue, the Spartan Megillus is at first inclined to think that the laws of Lycurgus were designed chiefly to ensure the development of the first kind of καρτερία, endurance of pains : he suggests that the laws against drunkenness and festive gatherings indicate Lycurgus' wish to bring up his citizens in ignorance of pleasures altogether.[2] But the Athenian goes on to point out [3] that the pleasures of childhood are by no means unimportant in forming character ; the attitude to ἡδοναί in childhood is expressed in childish ways, namely in dancing and singing. It is at this stage that σωφροσύνη must be inculcated in the future citizen, through a proper training in music and the dance, calculated to produce a realisation of rhythm and harmony. There are right and wrong types of music and dance, and only the right types should be practised, as was done in Egypt. The test of the right types must be that they shall be those which give most pleasure to persons of the best education and character.[4]

The Cretan replies that the only places in which this principle is really carried out in practice, and where only certain types of music and dancing are permitted, are Crete and Sparta.[5]

It follows that the dance (ὄρχησις) as well as music was regarded as of the highest value in developing σωφροσύνη in the youth of Sparta in Plato's time, and when we turn to another fourth century account of Spartan dances, that of Aristoxenus of Tarentum,[6] we find that his description of the Pyrrhic dance as performed there in his own time

---

[1] For Spartan σωφροσύνη in the fifth century B.C. see Thuc. I, 79 ff. Archidamus, ἀνὴρ καὶ ξυνετὸς δοκῶν εἶναι καὶ σώφρων, recommends the Spartans to consider the project of war σωφρόνως (I, 80. 2), says that their σωφροσύνη ἔμφρων is best proved by their having maintained the freedom and high repute of their city (84. 3), that the reason why they are so amenable to discipline is that αἰδὼς σωφροσύνης πλεῖστον μετέχει (84. 6), that the young are educated ξὺν χαλεπότητι σωφρονέστερον than to disobey the laws (*ibid.*). For the stress laid on σωφροσύνη in Sparta in Roman times, *cf.* I.G. V, i, index, *s.v.* σωφροσύνη, σώφρων.

[2] *Laws*, 636 E *seq.*   [3] *Ibid.* II, 653 A–654 D.

[4] *Ibid.* 658 E–659 A.   [5] *Ibid.* 660 B.

[6] *ap.* Athen. XIV, 630 *e* ff. ; *cf.* IV, 139 *e* (dances at the Hyacinthia).

agrees very well with the supposition that it was called
καθθηρατόριον, or the ' hunting-dance '.[1] For Aristoxenus
describes it as like a Dionysiac dance, the dancers carrying
thyrsuses to throw instead of spears, also fennel rods and
torches ; [2] and it cannot be doubted that the real Dionysiac
dance, which was performed with the same equipment,
was the representation of a hunt.[3] Moreover, there were
several forms of Pyrrhic dance in early times,[4] as was
natural when it was danced by boys, Epheboi, and grown
men alike ; [5] and the torches [6] used in the version described
by Athenaeus provide so much more likely a derivation
for the name πυρρίχη than the fanciful ones adduced by
ancient writers that it is tempting to regard the Pyrrhic
dance as performed in Aristoxenus' time as itself of early
origin, and not merely (as Aristoxenus himself supposed
it to be) a later modification of the early war-dance. There
may always have been the distinction between the warrior-
dance of the grown men, danced with shields and spears,
and the hunting dance of the Epheboi, which was no doubt
very similar except for the absence of weapons, for
Aristoxenus describes his ' present-day Pyrrhic dance ' as
' a preparatory training for war ' (προγύμνασμα οὖσα τοῦ
πολέμου). He further says that this dance was performed to
the finest music and strictest (?) rhythms : [7] it would therefore have the general educational value demanded by Plato
as well as the special value of providing a training for war,[8]
which was no doubt more fully recognised in early Sparta.

The passage in Plato's *Laws*, discussed above, also helps
to throw light on ὁ εὐβάλκης and ὁ κυναγέτας,[9] which have

---

[1] On the possible origin of the καθθηρατόριον see p. 256.
[2] Athen. XIV, 631a : ἡ δὲ καθ' ἡμᾶς πυρρίχη διονυσιακή τις εἶναι δοκεῖ
ἐπιεικέστερα οὖσα τῆς ἀρχαίας. ἔχουσι γὰρ οἱ ὀρχούμενοι θύρσους ἀντὶ
δοράτων, προΐενται δ'ἐπ' ἀλλήλους, καὶ νάρθηκας καὶ λαμπάδας φέρουσιν.
[3] See Roscher, *s.v. Mainaden*, p. 2251. Dionysus himself is ἄναξ
ἀγρεύς and κυναγέτας, the Maenads κύνες δρομάδες.
[4] Cf. Dar.-Sagl. *s.v. saltatio*, pp. 1030 f.
[5] *Ibid.* p. 1032. Athen. *loc. cit.*, says that all children in Sparta over
the age of five years learnt the Pyrrhic dance.
[6] Perhaps originally to assist in driving the animals from their lairs ?
[7] Athen. XIV, 631b : τακτέον δ 'ἐπὶ τῆς πυρρίχης τὰ κάλλιστα μέλη καὶ
τοὺς ὀρθίους ῥυθμούς.
[8] Athen. XIV, 628 f., quotes a poem of Socrates expressing this belief :
οἱ δὲ χόροις κάλλιστα θεοὺς τιμῶσιν ἄριστοι ἐν πολέμῳ.
[9] See above, p. 120.

been thought to be the names of separate contests, in spite of the difficulty of explaining their masculine form. It now seems more likely that these are the names of standard pieces for recitation to music.[1] ' The Valiant One ' and ' The Hunter ' would be subjects appropriate to performance by the virtuous citizens of the future (according to Spartan standards) in Plato's time, and the hypothesis that set pieces survived under these titles into Roman times provides a reasonable explanation of the four Spartan inscriptions in which they are mentioned as a part of the performances in τὸ παιδιχόν. The text of these four inscriptions, which all appear to belong to the first century B.C., is as follows : [2]

1. (A.O. no. 11) Δάμιππος 'Αβολήτου ἐπὶ Σιδάμου νικάσας τ[ὸ] παιδιχὸν ἑọ - - - - μώαι [καὶ κυνα]γέτα[ι].

2. (A.O. no. 16) Λαχάρης Λαχάρεος νικάας τὸ π[αιδι]χὸν κελέạ[ι καὶ ?] εὐβάλκ[ει ἐπὶ πατ]ρονόμ[ω - - - - - -]δα καὶ Σọ - - - καὶ Κλεοξ[ένω - -] καὶ δέρει - - - - νίκαθρον Β[ορθέαι].

3. (A.O. no. 18) Πρατιάδας 'Αρίστωνος νικάας τὸ παιδιχὸν κετεύων (sic) ἐν τῶι εὐβάλκει καὶ κυνạγέτ[αι].

4. (A.O. no. 84) - - - - ς Δαματρίου - - - - κάσεν μικι[χιζό-μενο]ς ὑπὸ πα[τρονόμω ? - - -]ạνδρω νι[κάσας] κελείαι τὸ [παιδιχὸν ? τ]ὸ τῷ εὐβάλ[κει καὶ τῷ] κ[υ]νạγέ[ται].

In these four inscriptions, εὐβάλκης and κυναγέτας are associated with the musical contest (μῶα) and with the ' invocation ' (κελοîα, κελεία) but in no example are they associated with the καθθηρατόριον.[3] The third inscription in the list makes it clear that the contest κελοία [4] was won ' in the εὐβάλκης and the κυναγέτας ', thus explaining νι[κάσας] κελείαι τὸ [παιδιχὸν τ]ὸ τῷ εὐβάλκει in the next example. It is thus evident that ὁ εὐβάλκης was a variety

[1] As examples of this usage may be cited the titles of the Linos-song (Iliad XVIII, 570) and the Paian (see Leaf's note, ·Iliad l.c.).
[2] The text is cited from Artemis Orthia, pp. 303 f., and the dating is that suggested by Woodward, ibid.
[3] Woodward would deduce from this and from the apparent resemblance in the meaning of the words that the καθθηρατόριον was identical with the κυναγέτας, the name καθθηρατόριον being introduced in the first century A.D. ; cf. A.O. pp. 288 f.
[4] Assuming κετεύων in the text to be an engraver's mistake for κελεύων, Woodward is compelled to reject this emendation (cf. A.O. p. 290) on account of his interpretation of the meaning of εὐβάλκης, etc., as violent physical contests.

of the contest κελεία, and it therefore seems necessary to restore in the second inscription in the list νικάας τὸ π[αιδι]χὸν κελέα[ι ἐν τῶι] εὐβάλκ[ει, and similarly in the first νικάσας - - - - - - - μώαι [ἐν κυνα]γέται.[1] This last example seems to show that the same poem set to music might be used either as a test of ability to play the music on some instrument (μῶα) or to chant the poem itself (κελοῖα).

In the second of these inscriptions (A.O. no. 16) the words καὶ δέρει,[2] which have not yet been satisfactorily interpreted, can best be explained in the same way as ὁ εὐβάλκης and ὁ κυναγέτας, as the title of a piece of music or a recitation. On the analogy of the datives τῷ εὐβάλκει and τῷ κυναγέται which are used in recording victories in the other two contests, δέρει would also appear to be a dative, and may come either from δέρος, meaning a skin, fleece or hide, or from δερεύς, ' The Flayer '.[3] This gives little guide to the real nature of the song, which might be concerned with the legend of the slaying of Marsyas, or with the story of Jason and the golden fleece, or possibly with the Homeric type of leather shield and breastplate combined [4] which apparently continued to be used by the Spartans longer than by other Greeks ; [5] and again, if the title was ' The Shield ', the meaning might be either literal, as in Tyrtaeus' exhortations to battle, or metaphorical, being concerned with some form of divine protection,[6] as in Alcman's *Partheneion*.[7]

But since the meaning of the companion contests, εὐβάλκης and κυναγέτας, is clear enough, namely ' The Valiant Man ' [8] and ' The Hunter ', and since all three musical pieces were suitable for competitions of Spartan

---

[1] The letters εο ascribed to l. 3 of A.O. 11 seem more likely to be ἐγ, immediately preceding [κυνα]γέται and intended to be read after μώαι.

[2] Woodward's transcription in A.O. 16 suggests a doubt about the last letter of δέρει which does not appear in Kolbe's version (I.G. V, i, 267). But the socket for a sickle would preclude a word with any letter other than ι for its fifth. The possibility of a longer word cannot be excluded, but the suggested connection with Artemis Dereatis (I.G. V, i, 267, n. ; cf. Paus. III, 20. 7) is unlikely, since the names of the other contests connect them not with a goddess, but with male divinities or heroes.

[3] This form is not actually preserved elsewhere, but cf. δορεύς.

[4] Cf. Leaf, *Iliad* Vol. I, Appendix 8, § VIII.

[5] See further, pp. 379 f.

[6] Cf. the similar use of σάκος.   [7] Cf. pp. 266 f.

[8] It may be noticed that Eubalkes (and Eualkes) occurs as a Spartan proper name ; cf. A.O. p. 289.

Epheboi, probability on the whole favours the interpretation of τὸ δέρος as a warlike song called ' The Shield '. One recalls the recommendation which Plato makes in the Republic, that all songs should be suppressed in the training of the young men who are to be the defenders of their city save those which display the reactions of the brave and self-controlled man in battle or in other violent pursuits, and the reactions of the noble and self-controlled man in his peaceful relations with gods or men.[1] The general resemblance of the ideal state of the Republic, at least in its practical outlines, to Sparta makes it extremely likely that Plato wrote this section about the censorship of poetry and music with Spartan rules on the subject in his mind. But since it is Plato's constant criticism of Sparta that the system of education there was too rigorous, and concentrated too exclusively on the production of a race of soldiers,[2] it seems reasonable to conclude that at Sparta the second type of permissible poetry, concerning itself with εἰρηνικαὶ πράξεις, was completely overshadowed by that which concerned πᾶσα βίαιος ἐργασία, and that the musical contests of the Epheboi were confined mainly to elegies such as those of Tyrtaeus,[3] supplemented in the field of less stately rhythms by poems on such subjects as the Calydonian boar-hunt, which would be a suitable theme for a poem called ὁ κυναγέτας. So far as Tyrtaeus at least is concerned, there is good reason for thinking that his poems continued to play an important part in Spartan education for many centuries even after Plato's time,[4] and it may well be that the poem called ὁ εὐβάλκης at least was one of these. That the other two musical contests at present under discussion may also date back to an early period is strongly suggested by the fact that the Spartans themselves called all their traditional dances, tunes and songs ' Cretan '.[5] Songs by new poets

---

[1] *Rep.* III, 399 *a*, *b* ; *cf.* also the whole of the preceding argument from 395c onwards.   [2] *Cf. e.g.*, *Laws*, I, 630 D.

[3] From Plato, *Laws*, I, 629 B, we learn that the youth of Sparta in the fourth century were fed on the poems of Tyrtaeus *ad nauseam*.

[4] *Cf.* Jaeger, *Paideia*, Vol. I (translated by Highet, 1939), p. 93, also his essay in *Sitz. Berl. Akad.* 1932, *Tyrtaios über die Wahre Arete.*

[5] *Cf.* Strabo, X, 4. 18, 481 (citing authorities whose names he does not mention) : τήν τε ὄρχησιν τὴν παρὰ τοῖς Λακεδαιμονίοις ἐπιχωριάζουσαν καὶ τοὺς ῥυθμοὺς καὶ παιᾶνας τοὺς κατὰ νόμον ἀδομένους καὶ ἄλλα πολλὰ τῶν νομίμων Κρητικὰ καλεῖσθαι παρ' αὐτοῖς ὡς ἂν ἐκεῖθεν ὁρμώμενα.

9

and composers are therefore very unlikely to have been admitted at a late period for performance at the traditional festivals.

The type of musical contest which has just been under consideration would no doubt be classed by Plato under the heading of ' tests of endurance (καρτερήσεις) in relation to pleasures ' in the training of the Spartan Epheboi. We now have to consider καρτερήσεις in relation to pain, the other kind of endurance discussed in Plato's Laws.¹ This side of the Ephebic training receives more notice from the literary writers, but has left less definite evidence in the Spartan inscriptions. Of the Lycurgan institutions directed to the production of bravery in this sense the Spartan in Plato's Laws distinguishes the common meals (where apparently food was scanty), the gymnastic exercises, hunting, and fourthly, hand-to-hand battles and ' a sort of stealing in which many blows are given on every occasion '.² The mock-battles of the Epheboi in Roman times have already been described,³ and are no doubt a survival of those alluded to in the Laws. The blows received in ' a sort of stealing ' (ἐν ἁρπαγαῖς τισι) have been supposed to refer to the whipping ordeal at the altar of Orthia, for the pseudo-Xenophon says that the boys who were being whipped were trying to steal as many cheeses as possible from the altar of Orthia.⁴ It is true that none of the writers of the Roman period who describe the whipping ordeal ⁵ mention the cheeses, but it can scarcely be doubted that the ' victor of the altar ' (βωμονίκης) mentioned in several inscriptions of this period was the victor in the whipping ordeal, and if the ordeal resulted in a victory for one Ephebos only, it seems reasonable to suppose that the one who succeeded in carrying off the greatest number of cheeses from

¹ Cf. above, p. 124.
² Laws, I, 633 B : ἔτι τοίνυν καὶ τὸ τέταρτον ἔγωγε πειρῴμην ἂν λέγειν τὸ περὶ τὰς καρτερήσεις τῶν ἀλγηδόνων πολὺ παρ' ἡμῖν γιγνόμενον ἔν τε ταῖς πρὸς ἀλλήλους ταῖς χερσὶ μάχαις καὶ ἐν ἁρπαγαῖς τισι διὰ πολλῶν πληγῶν ἑκάστοτε γιγνόμενον.   ³ Cf. above, p. 118.
⁴ (Xen.) Resp. Lac. II, 9 : ὡς πλείστους δὴ ἁρπάσαι τυροὺς παρ' Ὀρθίας καλὸν θείς, μαστιγοῦν τούτους ἄλλοις ἐπέταξε, τοῦτο δὴ δηλῶσαι καὶ ἐν τούτῳ βουλόμενος ὅτι ἔστιν ὀλίγον χρόνον ἀλγήσαντα πολὺν χρόνον εὐδοκιμοῦντα εὐφραίνεσθαι. The verbal similarities between this passage and the passage from the Laws cited in note 2 above strongly suggest that they refer to the same thing.
⁵ For a discussion of this, see further, pp. 260 f.

the altar, enduring a fresh rain of blows each time as he ran the gauntlet through a line of floggers, was the victor, in Roman as in earlier times.

The six inscriptions of the period of the Principate which mention a βωμονίκης [1] give no help in deciding at what stage in the training of the Ephebos this ordeal was imposed, but since the victor carried the title βωμονίκης throughout his career,[2] as indeed the pseudo-Xenophon also implies in his description of the cheese stealing,[3] we may presume that each Ephebos went through the ordeal only once in the course of his training. It would have been far less of a distinction if each boy had at least six chances of becoming βωμονίκης. It is scarcely likely that so rigorous a test of endurance was imposed upon young boys under the age of Epheboi, and although the ancient writers who refer to the whipping speak indiscriminately of παῖδες and of ἔφηβοι, we have seen that Epheboi in the 14–20 age-classes are normally called παῖδες. The conclusion of Rose [4] that ' all young Spartans were scourged ' therefore needs some modification. We cannot, on the other hand, infer from the four decrees of the city of Sparta granting a statue to βωμονίκαι, that the scourging ordeal was a passing-out test for the oldest class of Epheboi, for these honours were not necessarily given *because* the person in question was βωμονίκης but may have been given because, being incidentally βωμονίκης, he was conspicuous for ἀνδρεία,[5] which (as we have already seen from the passage in Plato's *Laws*) [6] had a very comprehensive and significant sense at Sparta, and will be further discussed below, or for ἀρετή which again is a term of special meaning at Sparta.[7]

In connection with these tests of endurance of pain we may here consider the difficult question of the Sphaireis,

----

[1] I.G. V, i, 554, 652, 653, 653b, 654, A.O. 144. These inscriptions all seem to belong to the latter part of the second century A.D., though there is no guide except the lettering for the dating of I.G. V, i, 654.

[2] *Ibid.* no. 554 ; a statue base set up in honour of Ti. Claud. Sophron, βωμονίκης, σύνδικος καὶ δαμοσιομάστης and ἐξηγητὴς τῶν Λυκουργείων ἐθῶν (for these offices, see p. 160).

[3] *Cf.* p. 130, n. 4.   [4] *Cf.* below, p. 261.

[5] I.G. V, i, 652 (ἀνδρείας χάριν) ; 653b (ἀνδρείας χάριν, cf. no. 653, a similar decree referring to the same βωμονίκης, where (ἀρετῆς) χάριν is restored) ; 654 (ἀρετᾶς χάριν) ; A.O. 144 has no corresponding phrase, but the βωμονίκης is called εὐψυχότατος.

[6] *Cf.* above, p. 124.   [7] *Cf.* p. 146.

132 ANCIENT SPARTA

who are mentioned in several inscriptions of the Roman period, and are defined somewhat inadequately by Pausanias as ' those ceasing to be Epheboi and beginning to be counted among the men '.[1] It is not clear whether he means that the Sphaireis had already ceased to be Epheboi (like the Cretan ἐγδραμόντες [2]), that is, were above the age of twenty, or were still Epheboi in the 19–20 age-group (Melleirenes,) about to be classed with the men. The evidence about the age of the Boagoi [3] points to the former conclusion, for a Boagos could be πρεσβὺς σφαιρέων,[4] and on the analogy of the πρεσβύς of the boards of Ephors, Nomophylakes, etc., who was himself an Ephor or a Nomophylax, the πρεσβύς of the Sphaireis must have been himself a Sphaireus.

Since most of the inscriptions which refer to the Sphaireis seem to be concerned with some team-game,[5] which may conceivably have been a ball game,[6] it has naturally been concluded that Sphaireis means simply ' the ball-players ', from the word σφαῖρα in its commonest usage. But a more likely interpretation, in view of the general purpose of the physical education of the young Spartans, which was to train soldiers, is the derivation from σφαῖρα, a boxing glove. In the Laws, Plato describes the various military exercises most useful in training the citizens for war, and makes his Athenian advocate boxing contests with the σφαῖραι, instead of with the ordinary straps which were worn for less serious boxing[7]. The σφαῖραι were evidently more like modern

[1] Paus. III, 14. 6 : ἐς τοῦτον τὸν Δρόμον ἰόντι . . . ἔστι δὲ ἄγαλμα Ἡρακλέους, ᾧ θύουσιν οἱ σφαιρεῖς· οἱ δέ εἰσιν οἱ ἐκ τῶν ἐφήβων ἐς ἄνδρας ἐρχόμενοι συντελεῖν. [2] Cf. Kahrstedt, Sparta, p. 353.
[3] Cf. above, pp. 95 f. [4] I.G. V, i, 686.
[5] Cf. I.G. V, i, 674–688. A typical example is no. 676 : Ἐπὶ Ἀγαθοκλέους τοῦ [Κ]λεοφάντου, βιδύου δὲ Ξένωνος τοῦ Ξενοστράτου, διαβέτεος δ[ὲ] Φιλέρωτος τοῦ Θεοξένο[υ], σφαιρεῖς Λιμναέων οἱ νικάσαντες τὰς ὠβάς, ὧν πρέ[σ](βυς) Ἐπάγαθος Σ[ωκράτους . . . (a list of twelve names follows). No. 674, with fourteen names of σφαιρεῖς, is complete. On the Limnaeis, etc., cf. pp. 163 f.
[6] The tops of the stelae on which these Sphaireis-inscriptions are engraved have pediments, in the gable of which a circular object is represented which may be a ball. On the other hand this is a very obvious decoration for a triangular space. For an illustration see B.S.A. XIII (1907), p. 214. A possible ball game, if this interpretation is followed, is described by Pollux, IX, 104.
[7] Plato, Laws, VIII, 830 B : ἀντὶ ἱμάντων σφαίρας ἂν περιεδούμεθα, ὅπως αἱ πληγαί τε καὶ τῶν πληγῶν εὐλάβειαι διεμελετῶντο ἐς τὸ δυνατὸν ἱκανῶς. In 830 E this kind of boxing is again referred to as the σφαιρομαχία, and described as the nearest possible imitation of real warfare.

boxing gloves, making the hand look like a ball, and so protecting it that the wearer could deal much heavier blows than he could when wearing only straps round his knuckles.[1] Now we are told by the author of the *Lacedaemoniorum Respublica* that the oldest classes of Spartan youths, in the last stage of their training, were divided into two groups, three hundred specially selected by the Hippagretae, and the rest, and the members of each of these two groups engaged in boxing matches with members of the other whenever they met.[2] Presumably therefore they went about continually wearing σφαῖραι, their ball-like boxing gloves. Whether the team matches in which, as the inscriptions tell us,[3] the Sphaireis took part were boxing matches or a ball game is not important, but the evidence on the whole favours the first interpretation.[4]

Unfortunately the author of the *Respublica* is confused about the age of these ἡβῶντες, as he calls them ; for he goes on to speak of the next age-group, under the name of ' those who have passed the age of ἥβη ', as eligible for the

---

[1] It was apparently not until the late nineteenth century that boxers again made ' the discovery that the glove fight is a more trying and dangerous form of contest than the old knuckle fight ' (see Bernard Shaw, *Note on Modern Prize-Fighting*, appended to *Cashel Byron's Profession*).

[2] (Xen.) *Resp. Lac.* IV, 6 : καὶ γὰρ πυκτεύουσι διὰ τὴν ἔριν ὅπου ἂν συμβάλωσι· διαλύειν μέντοι τοὺς μαχομένους πᾶς ὁ παραγενόμενος κύριος.

[3] *Cf.* above, p. 132, n. 5.

[4] τὰ σφαιρομαχία is mentioned by Eustath. *ad Od. θ.* 372 as a traditional ἀγών at Sparta, and another Scholiast, *ad loc.* mentions a traveller called ' Pius ' as having watched it there. This implies that τὰ σφαιρομαχία went on at Sparta in the time of the Sphaireis inscriptions. But the meaning of ἡ σφαιρομαχία (of which τὰ σφαιρομαχία is presumably a variant ; referring to the public contests) seems always to be ' boxing-match ', not ' ball-game ' : it definitely refers to boxing in Plato (*cf.* above, p. 132, n. 7), and in Pollux, III, 150, citing Aristomenes Comicus (fifth century B.C., *cf.* Meineke's *Frag. Com. Graec.* II, p. 734). Polybius (XVI, 21) says of a high Greek official in Egypt, *c.* 200 B.C. that he spent most of the day σφαιρομαχῶν καὶ πρὸς τὰ μειράκια διαμιλλώμενος ἐν τοῖς ὅπλοις, which implies that the σφαιρομαχία was one of the recognised military exercises and was engaged in by pairs of combatants, not by teams only. The σφαιράρχης mentioned in an inscription on a grave-stele of Egyptian Thebes (C.I.G. III, 4794) seems likely therefore to have been a military trainer and boxing expert. There is no reason whatever (apart from the derivation from σφαῖρα, which is ambiguous) for supposing the Spartan Sphaireis to have been merely ball players except the ball-like object, probably a mere decoration and in any case more like a disc, in the apices of the stelae referring to them.

highest offices,[1] and in Sparta in his time at least office-holding was permitted only to men who had reached the age of thirty. In fact, the three hundred selected by the Hippagretae must be identical with the three hundred ἱππεῖς καλούμενοι mentioned by Herodotus and Thucydides,[2] and since these fought as hoplites, it is certain that they must have passed the age of ἥβη,[3] which was twenty years. The passage cited above from Pausanias [4] suggests that he, too, suffers from the same confusion, and in view of the association of the ' boxers ' in the Respublica with the three hundred Hippeis, it seems necessary to conclude that the Sphaireis were no longer Epheboi, but were taken from the 20–22 age-group,[5] and that the Phylae in which they were organised had nothing to do with the Agelae, but were part of a quasi-military organisation. This is also implied by the different cults with which the two classes are associated, the Sphaireis with the Dioskouroi and with Herakles,[6] the Epheboi exclusively with Artemis and Apollo.

We now come back to the question of ὁ καρτερίας ἀγών. From the passage in Plato's Laws cited earlier it now appears that this cannot be a competition similar to any of those already described ; neither should it be identified with the whipping ordeal, for the ideal of καρτερία is that which the whole training of the young Spartan is directed to produce, and this includes endurance not only of pains, but of pleasures. It seems, therefore, more likely that the καρτερίας ἀγών is a comprehensive test which takes into account the whole training of the Ephebos, that in fact it is a sort of graduation, the passing out into manhood. Two inscriptions refer to it, one directly,[7] the other indirectly.[8] The second is engraved on a columnar statue-base similar to those which bear inscriptions referring to

---

[1] Resp. Lac. IV, 7 : τοῖς γε μὴν τὴν ἡβητικὴν ἡλικίαν πεπερακόσιν ἐξ, ὧν ἤδη αἱ μέγισται ἀρχαὶ καθίστανται, κ.τ.λ.

[2] Herod. VIII, 124 ; Thuc. V, 72. [3] See further, pp. 388 f.

[4] Cf. p. 132, n. 1. [5] See further, pp. 388 f.

[6] Cf. above, p. 132, n. 1, and for the Dioskouroi, the symbols on the stele illustrated in B.S.A. XIII, p. 214.

[7] I.G. V, i, 290 : [ὁ δεῖνα . . . Ἀλκά]στῳ [κ]ᾷσεν ἐπὶ πατρονόμου Δεξιμάχου νικάσας τὸν τᾶς καρτερίας ἀγῶνα Ὀρθείᾳ (c. A.D. 150).

[8] Ibid. 653a : ἁ πόλιρ Μᾶρκον Αὐρῆλιν Εὐάρεστον Ζωΐλω, συνέφηβον Μ. Αὐρηλίω Ἀριστοκράτηρ τῶ Δαμαινέτω καὶ Τιβερίω Κλαυδίω Εἰρανίωνορ τῶ Ὑγείνω, ἐπιφανῶρ καρτερήαντα, ποδδεξαμένων τὸ ἀνάλωμα τῶν βουαγῶν (second half of second century A.D.).

βωμονῖκαι, and the form of the inscription itself is also strikingly similar.[1] The similarity between these two groups of inscriptions has already been noticed by others, and has led to the conclusion that the βωμονῖκαι were victors in the καρτερίας ἀγών, which has therefore been identified with the Whipping Ordeal at the altar of Orthia. But there remains yet another small group of four inscriptions, all of the second century A.D. and therefore of approximately the same date as the other two groups. In this third group the formula is again similar,[2] and in three of the four cases the inscriptions are engraved on statue-bases similar to those of the other two groups. Of the four inscriptions two [3] record that the person in question was honoured by the city for courage and for nobility of life (ἀνδρείας καὶ βίου σεμνότητος ἕνεκα), one [4] that he was honoured ' for courage and for the αἰδώς (a combination of reverence for himself and reverence for others) which he displayed towards all ' ; the fourth [5] mentions only that the honour was given ' for courage '.

Altogether then we have ten [6] similar inscriptions to take into account, some of which mention that the recipient of the honour was a βωμονίκης, one that he was distinguished for καρτερία, nearly all the rest (including those which mention a βωμονίκης) that he received the honour for ἀνδρεία. We may reasonably infer from this that the fact that the recipient of the honour was a βωμονίκης was incidental (as has been suggested earlier),[7] that ἀρετή in one or perhaps two cases, and καρτερία in another, are synonymous with ἀνδρεία in all the rest, and that ἀνδρεία is the real reason for the grant of a statue by the city.[8] We have noticed that in two cases the honour is granted for ἀνδρεία combined with σεμνότης βίου : this brings the support of Plato to the theory that the καρτερίας ἀγών is a final

---

[1] Cf. e.g., I.G. V, i, 653b : ἡ πόλις Μαρ. Αὐρ. Κλεώνυμον τὸν καὶ Ὕμνον Ὕμνου βωμονείκην, συνέφηβον τοῦ ἀξιολογωτάτου Σεξ. Πομ. Γοργίππου τοῦ Ὀνασικράτους, ἀνδρείας χάριν προσδεξαμένης τὸ ἀνάλωμα τῆς ἀξιολογω- τάτης καὶ πάντα ἀρίστης Αὐρ. Ἁγίου τῆς Εὐδάμου τῆς τοῦ βουαγοῦ μητρός.
[2] Cf. above, p. 134, nn. 7 and 8.   [3] I.G. V, i, 472, 660.   [4] Ibid. 565.
[5] Ibid. 564.   [6] Cf. above, p. 131, n. 5, p. 134, n. 8, above, nn. 3, 4, 5.
[7] Cf. above, p. 131.
[8] It is difficult to believe the view that the statues were set up in honour of boys who distinguished themselves exclusively in the Whipping Ordeal, as is maintained, for example, in Artemis Orthia, p. 358.

comprehensive examination for the purpose of selecting the most ' courageous ' (ἀνδρειότατος, εὐψυχότατος) in the Platonic sense of the one who excels the rest not only in endurance of pains but in endurance of pleasures. For it is precisely those who rise superior to the temptations of pleasures who are called in Plato's *Laws* σέμνοι : [1] in accordance with Plato's other definition [2] this is a synonym for σώφρονες. βίου σεμνότητος ἕνεκα in the inscriptions must therefore mean ' for σωφροσύνη ', in other words, that the person in question has excelled in the tests for σωφροσύνη, namely, in the various musical competitions of the Epheboi which have already been described.[3] The word ἀνδρεία must be used in the inscriptions of the Roman period sometimes with its more comprehensive Platonic meaning, sometimes with the more restricted sense of endurance of the physical tests of endurance to which the Epheboi were continually subjected.

The general conclusion seems to be that the καρτερίας ἀγών at the age of twenty, closing a young man's Ephebic training, corresponded to the ἀριστοπολιτείας ἀγών [4] at the age of sixty, when a Spartan citizen retired from military service and was excused from the obligations of the younger citizen. The καρτερίας ἀγών marked the beginning of his military career, the ἀριστοπολιτείας ἀγών its end. In the earlier scrutiny as in the later, qualities other than mere physical courage played an important part, and on closer examination the Spartan inscriptions of the Roman period are seen to corroborate the impression conveyed by Plato, that the education of young men at Sparta was far less calculated to brutalise than the opponents of Spartan militarism at all periods have suggested. On the other hand, it must be remembered (in view of the evidence about the selection of Kasens) that the whole system of the Agelae was aristocratic ; it did not provide education for all who were in some sense citizens of Sparta, still less for all inhabitants of Laconia.

[1] *Laws*, 633 C, D : Εὖ γε ὦ Λακεδαιμόνιε ξένε, λέγεις. Τὴν ἀνδρείαν δέ, φέρε, τί θῶμεν ; πότερον ἁπλῶς οὕτως εἶναι πρὸς φόβους καὶ λύπας διαμάχην μόνον, ἢ καὶ πρὸς πόθους τε καὶ ἡδονὰς καί τινας δεινὰς θωπείας κολακικάς, αἳ καὶ τῶν σεμνῶν οἰομένων εἶναι τοὺς θυμοὺς μαλάττουσαι κηρίνους ποιοῦσιν ; ΜΕ. Οἶμαι μὲν οὕτω, πρὸς ταῦτα ξύμπαντα.
[2] *Cf.* above, pp. 124 f.   [3] *Cf.* above, pp. 125 f.
[4] See further, p. 159, also B.S.A. XXVII, pp. 242 (no. 33) f.

CHAPTER IV

THE GERUSIA AND THE MAGISTRACIES IN HELLENISTIC AND ROMAN SPARTA

§ 1. *General Evidence of Continuity*

The inscriptions of the Principate show that in its broad outlines the constitution of Sparta remained the same as it had been at an earlier period. The fiction of popular sovereignty was maintained ;[1] but as in earlier times, the Gerusia and the Ephors seem to have shared between them the real direction of affairs. The question whether the disappearance of the kings made any real difference to the constitution, in a period when war-leaders were no longer required, is one which it will only be possible to answer after the detailed evidence has been considered.[2] Some new or hitherto unknown boards of magistrates appear for the first time in this period, notably the Patronomoi, whose institution is ascribed to Cleomenes III,[3] and who are frequently mentioned in the inscriptions of the Principate. Other collegiate magistracies of which the names appear for the first time in the inscriptions of the Roman period may in fact have a long history. This is suggested in some cases by the very archaic flavour of the names of the magistracies themselves, as for example the Bidyoi,[4] Diabetai,[5]

---

[1] *Cf.* above, p. 48, n. 3.

[2] A full answer to this question depends upon the interpretation of the constitutional position of C. Julius Eurykles.

[3] *Cf.* above, p. 19.

[4] In the inscriptions the most common form is βίδυοι, though βίδεοι also occurs. Both these are therefore to be preferred to the form βιδιαῖοι (only in Paus. III, xi, 2 ; xii, 4). The initial letter is certainly a survival of the digamma, as in Βωρθία (*cf.* ἴδυοι Hesych., Phot., etc.), and the name must be derived from ἰδεῖν, thus forming an exact parallel to ἔφοροι (from ὁρᾶν). The Bidyoi in Pausanias' time were the ' overseers ' of the Epheboi (Paus. *loc. cit.*).

[5] *I.e.* διάϜεται (*cf.* preceding note). The name clearly refers to the annual tenure, as contrasted with an office held for life, or during the holding of some festival. On their functions, see below, p. 154.

and Damosiomastai.[1] The name ἐμπέλωροι,[2] which is said to have been the Spartan equivalent for Agoranomoi, suggests that the Agoranomoi of the later inscriptions were also of much earlier origin than their typically Hellenistic title would suggest. As for the Nomophylakes, who may be seen from the inscriptions to have played an important part in the administration of later Sparta, the existence of nine Nomophylakes in late fourth-century Cyrene, in a constitution in other respects closely modelled on that of early Sparta,[3] makes it probable that Sparta already had Nomophylakes in an earlier period. The minor magistracies of Sparta may quite easily have escaped notice in the ill-informed literary sources and in the scanty inscriptions which relate to that early time.

§ 2. *The Later Gerusia and its Relation to the Magistracies*

But in spite of a number of general similarities, there had been some considerable changes in the constitution since the time of Aristotle. The most conspicuous change was in the constitution of the Gerusia, which was now no longer a body of elders, elected for life from the highest class of citizens.[4] Membership had now become annual, though a longer term of office might be acquired through re-election. To take one example of a list of Gerontes, the senior member at the head of the list is recorded as holding office as Geron for the fifth time, one of his colleagues is holding office for the fourth time, eight for the third time, six for the second time.[5] A fifth tenure of the

---

[1] I.G. V, i, 47, 554 (in both cases σύνδικος καὶ δαμοσιομάστης, the second title being perhaps merely a more archaic name for the first). The meaning is probably ' public investigators ', from μαστεύω ; *cf.* the Rhodian and Delphian μαστροί (Ditt. *Syll.*³ 338, 339, 340, 672), the magistrates of the same name attested for Pellene by Aristotle's *Constitution of Pellene* (*cf.* Harpocrat. *s.v.* μαστῆρες· ἔοικεν ἀρχή τις εἶναι ἀποδεδειγμένη ἐπὶ τὸ ζητεῖν τὰ κοινὰ τοῦ δήμου) and the μαστῆρες of fourth-century Amorgos (Ditt. *Syll.*³ 963).

[2] Hesych., *s.v.*, *i.e.* ' guardian of merchandise ' (ἐμπολή-οὖρος, combined in Doric form).

[3] *Cf.* p. 16. The number (9) of the Cyrenean Nomophylakes suggests an early origin, being presumably connected with the three Dorian tribes.

[4] On the early Gerusia, see further, pp. 211 f.

[5] I.G. V, i, 97 (late first century A.D.).

office does not seem to have been unusual ;[1] in one case a sixth tenure is recorded.[2] It is clear from many inscriptions that these years of office were not, in the normal course, held consecutively, but with intervals between them in which other offices could be held.[3] But it does not appear that the interval between terms of office in the Gerusia was legally required, for a case of immediate re-election of the πρεσβὺς γερόντων has been recorded.[4] This would seem to imply that the annual Gerontes of later times were not liable to be called to account for their conduct in office, any more than the life-holders of the same office in Aristotle's time.[5]

Was there still, as in earlier times, a minimum age-qualification of sixty years [6] in the annually reconstituted Gerusia ? This question admits of no clear answer in the present state of our knowledge, though it may be possible to answer it when the list of Eponymoi of the first and second centuries after Christ has been finally reconstructed, and this task is by no means beyond the range of possibility.[7] To suppose that the minimum age-qualification was still in force would imply, it is true, that a large number of public offices were frequently filled in this period by men over sixty, for the inscriptions frequently mention men who held the offices of Ephor and Nomophylax, as well as others of

---

[1] Cf. I.G. V, i, 97, 306 ; B.S.A. XXVI, p. 163, A9 ; p. 164, A3 ; p. 166, B8 ; p. 170, E1.

[2] B.S.A. XXVI, p. 164, A5.

[3] E.g. I.G. V, i, 32A (early in Hadrian's reign). Agathokles, son of Stephanos, holds the offices of Nomophylax and Ephor between his first and his second years of office in the Gerusia.

[4] Ibid. 254 (first century B.C.) : γεροντεύσας τρὶς καὶ πρεσβὺς γενόμενος δὶς κατὰ τὸ ἑξῆς. The tenure of office for a second year by all the members of the Gerusia in the years of Sejanus and Biadas (cf. above, p. 97) seems too exceptional to be used as definite evidence that any member of the Gerusia could be re-elected to a second term of office without an interval.

[5] Cf. Arist. Pol. II, 9. 26.

[6] Plut. Lycurg. 26, cf. [Xen.] Resp. Lac. X, 1. Kahrstedt (Sparta, p. 246, n. 3) has argued on the evidence of Ar. Lysistr. 980 (πᾶ τᾶν 'Ασανᾶν ἐστιν ἁ γερωΐα ;) that the official Spartan name of the council was not γερουσία but γερωχία, derived from γέρας ἔχειν and having no reference to the age of the members. But in fact γερωΐα (γερωhία in earlier inscriptions, as may be inferred from I.G. V, i, 213) is merely the normal Spartan dialect form for γερουσία, and so preserves the allusion to the advanced age of the members of the council.

[7] See Appendix IV, § 8 (list of Patronomoi).

lesser importance, between their first and later tenures of office in the Gerusia. But so far as it is possible to tell from the provisionally reconstructed list of Eponymoi (Patronomoi), in few if any of these cases would the holder of an office (other than that of Geron) be over the age of seventy, and the offices in question are so little likely to have been onerous in character at this late period that little harm to the state could result from the practice of holding office late in life.[1] There is, on the other hand, a certain amount of prosopographical evidence which suggests a reduction before the second century A.D. in the minimum age-limit, perhaps to the age of fifty, which was already the lower limit for Gerontes at Cyrene in the late fourth century B.C.[2] At Sparta, the Kasens of Teisamenos appear at first sight to have been in the Gerusia only about twenty-five years after victories in the Agelae.[3] This would suggest a minimum age for Gerontes of only about forty years. But five or six years' difference in age between different Kasens of the same ' patron ' is possible, and the dates of Patronomoi cannot be fixed with complete precision. A minimum age of fifty years therefore seems not improbable.

There is indeed an inscription of uncertain date, but from all internal indications belonging to the fourth or third century B.C., which might be thought to prove that very soon after Aristotle's time, if not before, the minimum age-qualification for Gerontes had already been removed altogether. It is supposed to record a case of a man being a member of the Gerusia at the same time as his own paternal grandfather,[4] but the text need not bear that interpretation. It runs as follows : Νικοσθενίδας ταῖ Παhιφαῖ γεροντεύων ἀνέσηκε αὐτός τε καὶ ho τῶ πατρὸς πατὴρ Νικοσθενίδας, προβειπάhας τᾶ(ς) σιῶ ποτ' 'Ανδρίαν συνεφορεύοντα

---

[1] It is clear from the inscriptions recording careers that there was no fixed rule about the order in which offices should be held, or as to whether they should be held after or before a man first entered the Gerusia ; consequently no conclusions as to the age at which the offices of Ephor and Nomophylax were held in early times can be drawn from the fact that under the Principate these offices were often held after a man had entered the Gerusia.

[2] Cf. Hermes, LXIV (1929), p. 434, § iii.

[3] Cf. Appendix IV, § 1, No. 84.

[4] Cf. Kolbe (I.G. V, i, 1317) : Una senatoris munere functi sunt Nicosthenidas avus et nepos.

ἀνιστάμεν Νικοσθενίδαν ἐν τῶι ἱερῶι, ͱον(?) [1] καὶ σὺν καλῶι χρῆσται. We may notice first the singular γεροντεύων; if grandfather and grandson had been members of the Gerusia at the same time γεροντένοντες would have been more appropriate. A satisfactory explanation which avoids this unlikely assumption is that the elder Nikosthenidas, when Ephor, believed himself to have been instructed by Pasiphae to set up a statue of a fellow-Ephor in her shrine. Whether from lack of funds (and according to Aristotle it was a common thing for Ephors to be financially embarrassed) [2] or for other reasons, he failed to comply with the requirement of the goddess in his own lifetime, and the obligation was finally fulfilled by his grandson late in life [3] (having reached the age to be a member of the Gerusia). Both grandfather and grandson could properly be said to have put up the statue if the money set aside for the purpose by the grandfather was eventually used. There is therefore no definite evidence of a removal of the age-qualification at any period.

But as regards the number of its members, the Spartan Gerusia of the Principate seems to have undergone modification since the fourth century B.C. The evidence is somewhat confusing. An inscription of the reign of Augustus or of Tiberius mentions ' the twenty-eight Gerontes ', if the last word, of which only the top part of the first three letters remains, is rightly restored.[4] This suggests that the original number [5] was kept after the suppression of the kingship and still persisted under the Principate. Yet several complete lists of Gerontes are extant, of which one at least is earlier than the inscription just mentioned, and belongs to the first century B.C. ; [6] while others belong to

---

[1] *I.e.* the statue of Andrias, not (as suggested by Kolbe, *loc. cit.*) of the elder Nikosthenidas.

[2] Arist. *Pol.* II, 9. 19.

[3] The lapse of a long interval between the injunction of the goddess and its fulfilment is indicated by the word ποτε (l. 5), perhaps also by the name *Andrias* (' the statue ') which may have been invented later when the actual name of the Ephor in question had been forgotten.

[4] I.G. V, i, 16.

[5] Thirty, including the two kings, *cf.* Plut. *Lycurg.* 6.

[6] I.G. V, i, 93, 94. Both are assigned to the first century B.C. by Kolbe, but the only evidence for the date of no. 94 is the mention of Lachares, son of Herklanos, who may be a later descendant of C. Julius Eurykles rather than his father, *cf.* p. 461, n. 3.

the second century A.D. : [1] in all these lists the number of names is only twenty-three.[2] In consequence it has been suggested that the five Ephors were *ex officio* members of the Gerusia [3] and so made up the number to twenty-eight : an earlier suggestion that the number twenty-three was augmented by a college of six Patronomoi and their six σύναρχοι [4] has been refuted by Wilamowitz' restoration of the inscription above referred to, which speaks of a council of twenty-eight.

Yet there are objections to Kolbe's view. For in the first place, if we suppose that the number twenty-eight was reached by the inclusion of a college of five magistrates, there is no particular reason why the Ephors should be preferred to the Nomophylakes, who were also a board of five,[5] and who, unlike the Ephors, are not referred to as if they were quite distinct from the Gerusia.[6] But further, it is clearly implied by several inscriptions giving accounts of careers that neither of these magistracies carried with them membership of the Gerusia. An inscription cited earlier [7] records that a man was Nomophylax and then Ephor in the years which followed his first membership of the Gerusia, and only ' Geron for the second time ' after he had been Ephor.

A theoretical way out of these difficulties would be to suppose that the name Gerontes (or Gerusia) was kept strictly for the twenty-three, while the augmented council with its five *ex-officio* members was called ἁ βουλά, or ἁ βουλὰ τῶν κή. But this apparently was not the case : the name Gerontes seems to be used as a synonym for βουλά in two inscriptions [8] apart from the one already mentioned,[9] of which the restoration is not quite certain.

---

[1] I.G. V, i, 97 (reign of Trajan) ; B.S.A. XXVI, p. 169, C9 and 10 is *c*. A.D. 150 (*cf*. Woodward's comments, *ibid*. p. 193). The date of A3–5 (*ibid*. p. 164) depends on the date of the Patronomate of L. Volussenus Aristokrates, which must fall some time in the reign of Trajan (*cf*. p. 465).

[2] Including the πρεσβὺς γερόντων, but excluding the secretary.

[3] *Cf*. Kolbe, I.G. V, i, p. 37.

[4] Tod, *Catalogue of Sparta Museum*, p. 12.

[5] The Bideoi, in spite of Pausanias' statement (III, xi, 2) that they were five in number, were in fact a board of six (*cf*. I.G. V, i, 136–138).

[6] *Cf*. the letters quoted by Josephus, *Antiq*. XIII, 166 : Λακεδαιμονίων ἐφόροις καὶ γερουσίᾳ καὶ δήμῳ.

[7] Above, p. 139, n. 3.   [8] I.G. V, i, 11 and 18.   [9] Above, p. 141, n. 4.

There seems, then, to be no satisfactory complete explanation of the discrepancy between the twenty-three Gerontes and the Gerusia (or *Boula*) of twenty-eight. This suggests that we have to deal with another real change of organisation since the time of Aristotle, involving the selection of the Gerusia partly from independently elected and partly of *ex-officio* members, the last-named being members of a college of magistrates which so far has not been identified. As to the date of this change in number, we have so far no direct indication of its having occurred earlier than the inscription of the first century B.C. already mentioned,[1] although the possibility must be borne in mind that it was connected with the change from life to annual membership, which for various reasons is probably to be ascribed to Cleomenes III.[2] It seems worth while to consider other possible explanations of the discrepancy between twenty-three and twenty-eight in the hope that further light may incidentally be thrown on the problem of the reorganisation of the Gerusia in general.

To explain this discrepancy of five, we must evidently look for a board of five which is not either the Ephors or the Nomophylakes (for reasons already given) or any of the boards of six magistrates (Bideoi, Agoranomoi, etc.)[3] in which all the members seem to be on exactly the same footing. Perhaps the explanation is after all to be found in the Patronomoi, for although there existed in any one year a board of six Patronomoi, assisted by six σύναρχοι,[4] one of the Patronomoi in each year held quite an exceptional position as Eponymos, in this respect succeeding to the position which in an earlier period had been held by the president of the board of Ephors, and it was to him in particular that the six σύναρχοι (also called συνάρχοντες τῆς πατρονομίας)[5] were attached. There is one case of

---

[1] *Cf.* above, p. 141, n. 6.   [2] *Cf.* below, p. 145.

[3] On the Bideoi, see above, p. 142, n. 5. On the other boards of six, see below, pp. 162, 164.

[4] *Cf.* I.G. V, i, 48 (second half of first century B.C.). After each of the first six names the title *Patronomos* is added ; the rest are collectively described as σύναρχοι. This college was completed by a secretary, three assistant secretaries, and a ὑπηρέτας. For more than one Patronomos in office in the same year, see also B.S.A. XXVII, p. 239 (no. 31, of the second century A.D.), where a man is called συνπατρονόμος of Lampis.

[5] I.G. V, i, 505.

two sets of six συνάρχοντες attached to a single Patronomos, apparently in the same year ; [1] this may mean either that the board of six σύναρχοι was reconstituted (at least in the period in question) twice yearly, or that the position of the Patronomos in this particular instance was exceptional. But in either case the status of the σύναρχοι is revealed as much inferior in dignity and importance to that of the Eponymos Patronomos, and the earlier list of six Patronomoi and six σύναρχοι (already referred to) [2] indicates that the σύναρχοι were also subordinate to the five colleagues of the Eponymos Patronomos. It is obviously to these latter, and not to the σύναρχοι (συνάρχοντες) that the title συμπατρονόμος is appropriate. The συνάρχοντες are evidently comparable to the Paredroi (assessors) of senior magistrates at Athens, whereas the συμπατρονόμοι were themselves magistrates. A side-light on their judicial functions, which explains their need for assessors, is provided by an inscription concerning the administration of the Leonidean Games. Persons upon whom fines are imposed in connection with them, and who wish to dispute the fine, are to have their case decided by οἱ πεπατρονομηκότες τῆς τρίτης ἡμέρας.[3] This implies that the Patronomoi, assisted by their assessors either singly or collectively, shared out among themselves the duty of presiding in the courts on the various days on which sessions were held. Since there were apparently two Patronomoi in session on any day of the courts, it is implied that the Eponymos shared in some matters exactly the same functions as the five συμπατρονόμοι. Thus, from one point of view, the Patronomoi might be regarded as a board of five, from another point of view as a board of six magistrates, but there is no justification for regarding them as a board of twelve.

The reasons for suggesting that five Patronomoi each year (the συμπατρονόμοι of the Eponymos) made up the

[1] I.G. V, i, 541, 544. Both seem to refer to the ' fourth Patronomate of Lycurgus', when the god's human substitute was P. Memmius Pratolaus (late second century, A.D.).

[2] Above, p. 143, n. 4.

[3] I.G. V, i, 18 B (early Hadrian). The ' third day ' seems likely to reflect the influence of Roman judicial procedure (the *comperendinatio*) and so means not the third day of the Leonidean Games, with which the Patronomoi had no direct connection, but the next day but one of the law-courts.

full number of the Gerusia to twenty-eight may be summarised as follows. (1) Cleomenes III is said to have set
up Patronomoi in place of the Gerusia.[1] Though not literally true, this statement seems to preserve in garbled form
a tradition that Cleomenes set up a board of Patronomoi
to take over the deliberative functions of the Gerusia, so
that the Council as a whole sank to the position of a mere
ratifying body.[2] (2) The radical changes which have already
been noted in the composition of the later Gerusia support
the view that Cleomenes III did in fact alter its constitution
very considerably. This is a reason for accepting Pausanias'
statement that Patronomoi succeeded (in some sense) to
the functions of the Gerontes. (3) The office of Patronomos
still remained, under the Principate, the preserve of a
specially privileged class, whereas Kasens were eligible for
office as Gerontes.[3] In this respect the Patronomoi inherited a privilege which had formerly belonged to the
Gerontes,[4] whereas the ranks of the Gerontes were thrown
open to all citizens who were eligible for office in the state
at all. (4) Whereas in the time of Aristotle jurisdiction
was shared between the Gerusia and Ephors (except for the
very small part played by the kings), in Roman times the
Patronomoi appear as the normal presiding magistrates in
criminal trials,[5] but the court was apparently still the
Gerusia.[6] This arrangement implies a very close association
persisting between Patronomoi and Gerusia in Roman times,
and contributes another of the indications that it was the
college of Patronomoi (exclusive of the Eponymos) who
went to make up the full Gerusia of twenty-eight. (5) The
name Patronomoi itself suggests that their function was to
supervise the Gerusia, not so much on account of a possible
parallel between Sparta and the Romans, who called their
senate *patres*, as on account of the obvious analogy with

---

[1] P. 19, n. 3.
[2] *Cf.* I.G. V, i, 11 : καθὰ καὶ οἱ γέρον]τες ἐπέκριναν (full formula attested
by *ibid.* 18 A).
[3] *Cf.* p. 113.
[4] *Cf.* Arist. *Pol.* II, 9. 22 ; *cf.* V, 6. 11 (the Gerontes καλοκἀγαθοί and
their election δυναστευτική).
[5] I.G. V, i, 18 B (*cf.* above, p. 144, n. 3) is concerned with the infringe-
ment of a law of the Spartan Demos regulating the conduct of business at
the Leonidean festival.
[6] *Cf.* p. 55.

10

the Paidonomos, whose function was to supervise the boys, and the Gynaikonomoi, whose function was to supervise the girls and women. The existence of the Paidonomos at Sparta early in the fourth century B.C. is attested by the *Respublica Lacedaemoniorum;* [1] the Gynaikonomoi are first revealed to us by the inscriptions of the Principate, but their appointment is said to have been κατὰ τὰ ἀρχαῖα ἔθη καὶ τοὺς νόμους,[2] and the existence of gymnastic training and contests for girls at a much earlier period [3] would seem to have necessitated the institution of an official comparable to the Paidonomos in the case of the girls. The Gynaiko-nomoi are a very close parallel to the Patronomoi in that they were six in number, a president with five σύναρχοι.[4] On the analogy of the other two offices, therefore, *Patronomoi* must be interpreted as those who controlled the πάτερες. But this cannot mean that they controlled all adult male Spartans, in other words, that their functions were confined to the sphere of manners and morals, for not all adult male Spartans can have been fathers, and the name would in that case imply that the authority of the Patronomoi stopped short just where it was most needed, namely to chastise those Spartan citizens who wilfully avoided parenthood.[5] On the other hand, since membership of the early Gerusia was ' the reward of virtue ',[6] and since in Spartan eyes to become a father was an indispensable part of civic virtue, all the Gerontes must certainly have been fathers. Thus the name Patronomoi would be entirely appropriate if it meant ' controllers of the Gerusia '.

It may be finally concluded, therefore, that it was the Patronomoi (exclusive of the Eponymos) who made up the number of the later Gerusia to twenty-eight, and it is perhaps worth noticing that in that case the full council together with its secretary (γραμματεὺς βουλῆς) and the Eponymos-Patronomos would correspond in number to the Gerusia of the regal period augmented by the two kings.

With regard to the exceptional position and the functions

---

[1] (Xen.) *Resp. Lac.* II, 2.
[2] *Cf.* B.S.A. XXVI, p. 165, B 1, β (reign of Trajan).
[3] *Cf.* (Xen.) *Resp. Lac.* I, 4.   [4] *Cf.* I.G. V, i, 170.
[5] *Cf.* Plut. *Apopth. Lac.* X, 14.
[6] *Cf.* Dem. *Lept.* 107 ; Arist. *Pol.* II, 9. 22 ; Aesch. *Timarch.* 181 ; [Xen.] *Resp. Lac.* X, 3.

of the Eponymos-Patronomos, we can only hazard guesses about their origin, since there is no direct evidence for an Eponymos-Patronomos at all before the reign of Augustus.[1] In the Spartan tile-stamps of the second century B.C. the personal name of the Eponymos is always given without his title,[2] thus leaving it uncertain whether at that period the president of the board of Ephors had already ceased to be the Eponymos or not. It is clear from the inscriptions that the Patronomos was Eponymos throughout the period of the Principate. But on grounds of general probability it is likely that a Patronomos took the place of the Eponymos Ephor much earlier than the evidence for this appears in the inscriptions, in fact, from the reign of Cleomenes III. For it is recorded that Cleomenes was determined to reduce the power of the Ephors,[3] and this information hangs together with the statement of Pausanias that he instituted the Patronomoi, if both statements are interpreted in the light of the substitution of a Patronomos for the Chief Ephor as Eponymos.

After considering the functions of the Eponymos-Patronomos in greater detail, it may be well to summarise the reasons for thinking that Cleomenes III was in fact responsible for both the main changes in the Gerusia, the change in number and the introduction of annual re-election. The change in number can be accounted for by the inclusion of Patronomoi, and the institution of Patronomoi has been shown to imply that reduction in the powers both of Gerusia and of Ephors which was one of Cleomenes' principal aims. But the abolition of life-membership in the Gerusia would also greatly reduce the power of that body, and on that account is a reform likely to have been introduced by Cleomenes. Further, it seems clear that the Patronomoi

---

[1] Cf. I.G. V, i, 261, 265, 266, 267. Three of these inscriptions appear from coincidence of names to be contemporary with the lists of *Tainarioi*, for which see below, pp. 152 f. No. 265, which records a victory in the boys' contests by Lachares, son of Herklanos, is supposed by Kolbe (*ibid.*) to refer to Lachares the father of C. Julius Eurykles ; in that case he might be identical with the Lachares who was Strategos of the Lacedaemonian League in 77-6 B.C. (V, i, 1146). But it is extremely improbable that a Spartan who died before the battle of Actium had a father with the Latinising name of Herklanos, and a later descendant of C. Julius Eurykles is more likely to be the subject of V, i, 265 (*cf.* also, p. 461, n. 3).

[2] I.G. V, i, 886 *seq.* For the date, *cf.* p. 47, n. 4.   [3] *Cf.* p. 19.

were always annually elected, otherwise the chief Patronomos could not have acquired the position of Eponymos magistrate. But if Cleomenes had allowed the twenty-three Gerontes to hold their office for life, while the Patronomoi who made up their number to twenty-eight were only appointed for a year, the influence of the Patronomoi over the Gerusia could only have been negligible, instead of paramount, as Cleomenes obviously intended. This implies that tenure of office by Gerontes was also reduced to one year by Cleomenes.[1]

An interesting side-light on the new system is provided by the story of the exile of twenty-four prominent Spartans in 150 B.C.[2] The number of these men, who are described as πρωτεύοντες τὰ πάντα ἐν Σπάρτῃ, surely connects them with the Gerusia of twenty-three (exclusive of Patronomoi) together with the usual Secretary (γραμματεὺς βουλῆς).[3] Their names were sent to Sparta by the Achaean Strategos in response to a request by the Gerusia (whether including or excluding the Patronomoi is not clear) that he should nominate ὁπόσους ἡγοῖτο ἀδικεῖν in the dispute which was then in progress with the Achaean League. To demand the ejection of the whole of the existing Council, that is, of the Gerusia in the narrower sense, as being responsible for the direction of Spartan foreign policy, would be a typical piece of Achaean tyranny. Pausanias relates that a mock trial was then held, the twenty-four going into voluntary exile (in anticipation of speedy restoration by the Romans) before sentence of death was passed upon them.[4] The δικαστήριον to which Pausanias refers could well be the Court of the Patronomoi, the evidence for whose judicial competence in later times has already been mentioned.[5] From I.G. V, i, 48,[6] it is natural to conclude that it consisted of all six Patronomoi (including the Eponymos) together with the six assessors (σύναρχοι).

This interpretation of the affair of the twenty-four Spartans is admittedly conjectural, the only reason for

---

[1] Polybius (VI, 45) mentions the life-tenure of the Gerontes, but the context makes it clear that he is merely discussing the views of Ephorus and other ancient authorities.

[2] Cf. p. 50. [3] Cf. I.G. V, i, Index, iv, 3.
[4] Paus. VII, 12. 8. [5] Cf. above, pp. 144 f.
[6] Cited above, p. 143, n. 4.

suggesting it being that it is in keeping both with the general political circumstances of the time and with the scattered evidence about the Gerusia and the Patronomoi which has already been assembled. But it does further provide a completely satisfactory explanation of the συναρχία referred to in many later Spartan inscriptions, of which I.G. V, i, 448, comes nearest to revealing the truth.[1] It records the setting up of a statue of Caracalla διὰ συναρχίας τῆς περὶ Μάρ|κον Τάδιον Φιλοξενίδην. A list of the Gerontes follows, with the same M. Tadius Philoxenidas as their πρεσβύς (γέροντες ἐπὶ Ἰούλ. Δαμ . . . ὧν πρεσβὺς Μᾶρκος Τάδιος Φιλοξενίδης). Why should the name συναρχία be used, apparently as a synonym for the Gerusia,[2] if not because, as the evidence already considered has led us to conclude, the Gerusia was now composed of *two* colleges, the Gerontes in the narrower sense (the twenty-three), and the five Patronomoi (exclusive of the Eponymos) ? The Gerontes in the narrower sense may be supposed to have exercised the same functions as the older Gerusia except for its criminal jurisdiction—an important reservation, involving the loss of all its real power. The Patronomoi succeeded to the powers of criminal jurisdiction formerly exercised by the Gerusia, and probably (if Cleomenes III had his way about the Ephors) to the powers of criminal jurisdiction formerly exercised by the Ephors as well. Both colleges appear to have combined to consider matters of foreign policy generally ; there is direct evidence for this in the case of a grant of Proxenia[3] and in the matter of the statue of Caracalla to which reference has already been made.

The evidence about the way in which the Patronomoi were selected under the Principate, so far as it goes, bears

---

[1] Cf. also I.G. V, i, index, iv, 2, s.v. συναρχία.

[2] Since the same man in this case is both πρεσβὺς γερουσίας and the chief official of the συναρχία, it appears impossible to regard the πρεσβὺς συναρχίας (cf. V, i, 37, 480, 504, 1505 ; B.S.A. XXVI, p. 166 B8) as presiding in a separate unidentified college (cf. Woodward, B.S.A. ibid. p. 186).

[3] Cf. I.G. V, i, 4 : πόθοδον ποιησαμένου Δαμίωνος τοῦ Θεοκρίτου Ἀμβρακιώτα περὶ προξενίας καὶ ἐπελθόντος ἐπί τε τὰς συναρχίας καὶ τὸν δῆμον, κ.τ.λ. The date is uncertain, but the supposition that it belonged to a period in which there were no Ephors or Gerusia (cf. Kolbe, ibid.) is invalidated by the evidence of V, i, 448, discussed above.

out the view that this body possessed greater prestige and influence than the twenty-three Gerontes. Men adopted from the lower ranks of the citizen body (as the Kasens were) [1] appear never to hold the office of Patronomos, though they may hold any other office in the state, including membership of the Gerusia.[2] This implies a further degrading of the Gerusia by Cleomenes III, by the admission of all classes into the council previously reserved for the Privileged Families.[3]

The Spartan inscriptions of the period of the Principate do not necessarily, or even probably, provide a reliable guide to the full activities of the Gerusia and Patronomoi, or even of the magistrates in general. The apparent preoccupation with festivals and games is probably misleading. No doubt there was a smaller amount of important business to be transacted, under the beneficent protection of the Roman Empire, than in a less happy but more exciting age. But since it was not the custom in the earlier Sparta to commemorate any of the activities of government on stone, the absence of any documents other than lists of Gerontes and magistrates, inscriptions recording athletic victories and the setting up of statues, does not mean that the government in this period concerned itself wholly with trivialities. The administration of a fairly extensive territory and the maintenance of an extremely elaborate ephebic system would entail a good deal of routine work, judicial and otherwise, which in the inscriptions has left no trace. The lists of magistrates, which suggest at first sight merely a mania on the part of individuals for seeing their names perpetuated on walls, may in fact have a strictly practical purpose, as making possible the dating of all sorts of legal contracts, which would be bound to come into existence in a period when citizens were no longer forbidden to possess money or engage in trade.

These general considerations forbid us to assume that the Eponymos Patronomos, who occupied in the period under review a position of dignity and prestige comparable to that of the Archon Eponymos at Athens, was wholly con-

---

[1] *Cf.* pp. 102 f.
[2] For evidence on this point see Appendix IV, § 3, *A.*
[3] *Cf.* above, p. 145, n. 4.

THE GERUSIA AND THE MAGISTRACIES 151

cerned with the supervision of games and festivals, as the inscriptions would at first sight imply. The office was sometimes combined with that of chief Gymnasiarch,[1] the official chiefly responsible at Sparta in Roman times, as in other Greek cities, for the general supervision of athletic festivals and for providing (often out of his own pocket) the heavy expenses which they entailed. Hence the references in inscriptions to the προνοία and φιλοτιμία of an Eponymos Patronomos who twice combined his duties with those of chief Gymnasiarch.[2] Since there is no indication in the Spartan inscriptions of the existence of Gymnasiarchs before the late first century after Christ, since the title itself has nothing specifically Spartan about it, and since in other Greek cities the Eponymos often combined his office with that of Gymnasiarch,[3] it seems likely that the chief Patronomos already fulfilled these expensive duties much earlier in the Roman period and that it was only when the celebration of the ancient festivals became (as it would appear) one of the main industries of Sparta [4] that a Gymnasiarch was appointed to share in the growing burden of expense, for which the resources of any one magistrate would be inadequate. A similar development led to the appointment of assistants to the chief Gymnasiarch in other Greek cities.[5] The gradual imposition upon the eponymous magistrate of what was to become an intolerable burden was no doubt natural in view of the position of prestige which he occupied, and in view of his appointment only from the highest social class.[6] But the existence of evidence for it does not mean that the financing of festivals was his chief or original

[1] Cf. I.G. V, i, 535, 539. The Gymnasiarch in question is not to be confused with the minor gymnasiarchs attached to the gymnasia (cf. B.S.A. XXVII, p. 228 : γυμνασίαρχος ἐν τοῖς ιβ') who were perhaps only occasionally appointed, as were assistants to the chief Gymnasiarch in other Greek cities. See further on the Gymnasiarchy in general Dar. Sagl. s.v.
[2] Cf. I.G. V, i, 535. In this case the personal expense to the Patronomos (ἥν αὐτόθεν ὑπέστη) is directly mentioned.
[3] Cf. Dar. Sagl. s.v. Gymnasiarchia, p. 1678, n. 40.
[4] Cf p. 81 ; below, p. 264.
[5] Cf. Dar. Sagl. ibid p. 1679. The heavy expenses of Gymnasiarchs at Sparta are implied by the compliments paid to them in inscriptions on their statues (γυμνασιαρχῶν λαμπρῶς, φιλοτείμως καὶ μεγαλοπρέπως, μεγαλοψύχως, vel. sim. cf. I.G. V, i, 464, 480, 481, 486, 487, 492, 494, 506, 555, 557, 560, 561). [6] Cf. above, p. 150.

function. The more obscure indications to the contrary have already been considered. On the other hand, the importance of the financial aspect of his activities in Roman times may well explain the possibility of holding the office twice [1] (a practice otherwise undesirable because tending to confusion in the dating of legal documents), and the absence of a minimum age-qualification. This is implied by the instance of a son who took his father's place as Patronomos,[2] and also by the custom of holding numerous other offices later than the Patronomate.

Turning to the activities of the Gerusia, we find it apparently (but no doubt only in appearance) concerned entirely with the setting up of statues of distinguished citizens or emperors, and with the supervision of the various Spartan cults.

The Gerusia and the magistrates were represented in all associations for worship, even in θίασοι of which the members were in a humble social position. An association for the worship of Helen and the Dioscuri in the first century B.C. has among its members, and evidently as representatives of the state, one Bideos, one member of the Gerusia, one Ephor, one Nomophylax and one Gynaikonomos, although the main body of the members is made up of lyre-players, wreath-makers, bakers, etc.[3] The state is similarly represented in an association for the worship of the goddess Damoia (apparently at Thalamae) in the reign of Hadrian ; [4] but the representation varies from year to year, there being in one year two Bideoi, two Gerontes, one Ephor, one Nomophylax,[5] in another the five Ephors, in another one each of the Bideoi, Gerontes, Ephors and Nomophylakes,[6] in another year one Bideos only. The Gerusia and the magistrates must have been hard put to it to maintain supervision of all the various cults and the θίασοι connected with them, and it is no wonder if they were sometimes less well represented than the regulations required.

The lists of Ταινάριοι, apparently an association for the worship of Poseidon at Taenarum in the late first century

---

[1] I.G. V, i, 480 : ἐπὶ Γ. 'Ιουλίου Λακῶνος τὸ β'.
[2] Ibid. 280.   [3] I.G. V, i, 209 ; cf. 206.
[4] Ibid. 1314.   [5] Ibid. 1314, §a.   [6] Ibid. 1315.

B.C.[1] are particularly interesting in this connection. Each
list gives the members for a particular year, dated by the
name of the Eponymos, but no titles of magistrates are
mentioned, nor is any indication given of the occupation
of the members, except in the case of the various heralds,
cooks, etc., who were connected with the organisation of
the cult, and whose names appear after the rest. These
persons seem to have continued in office, sharing the various
duties in turn, for several years, since several of their names
are duplicated in the three lists which we possess ; but
among the rest there are no names which occur more than
once in the three lists, from which it may be inferred that
the list of members changed every year. Such an organisation makes it extremely unlikely that we have here to do
with an ordinary θίασος of a private nature. A curious
feature is that although all three lists are complete, two of
them contain the names of forty-two men apart from the
minor officials of the *collegium*, but the third has only
thirty-eight. This suggests that a collegiate board of four
magistrates is absent from the list of thirty-eight, and that
the full complement was made up by twenty-three Gerontes,
five Ephors, five Nomophylakes, five Bideoi (since these
various magistrates are all normally represented in other
Collegia) and a board of four which still requires to be
identified. The Patronomoi cannot be fitted into the
number, and supposing that the general explanation here
given of the *Tainarioi* is right, the omission of the Patronomoi

---

[1] I.G. V, i, 210–212. Kolbe (*ibid.*) assumes from the absence of Roman
praenomina and *nomina* that the date is not later than the first century
B.C., but gives too little weight to the occurrence of Γάιος as the equivalent
of a Greek personal name (Ποσίδιππος Γάιου) in 212, l. 12, and to the
obviously Latin title κοιακτήρ (*i.e. coactor*) in 211, l. 53. The generation
after Julius Caesar seems to be implied by Ποσίδιππος Γάιου, also by
Ἀγησίνικος Λαχάρεος in 210, l. 16 (*cf.* the family tree of Eurykles on
p. 204), but a date not later than Augustus' complete separation of the
Eleutherolaconian League from Sparta (about A.D. 10 ; *cf* Appendix III,
pp. 435 f.) is implied by the fact that at the time of these inscriptions
Sparta still had some control of a cult at Taenarum. Wilhelm's suggestion
that the cult was transferred to Sparta when Taenarum was lost is unconvincing. It seems not unlikely that the most recent of a series of
inscriptions relating to the cult at Taenarum were kept when Sparta
lost control of the town, as a proof of control up to that time, and in the
hope of its eventual recovery. The name of Agesinikos son of Lachares,
evidently a younger brother of C. Julius Eurykles I, is compatible with
this interpretation.

is not to be wondered at, since they were magistrates of comparatively late origin, whereas the *Tainarioi*, being undoubtedly connected with the festival called *Tainaria*, must be regarded as ancient. The Spartan *Tainaria* is referred to by Hermippus in the fifth century B.C.[1]

An obvious explanation suggests itself in the officials in charge (Diabetae)[2] of the four local associations, called Phylae in the inscriptions, of the Ephebic organisation— the *Limnaeis, Konooureis, Pitanatai* and *Neopolitai*. On the assumption that the names preserved in the Sphaereis inscriptions[3] represent all the divisions which existed,[4] and that they belonged to an organisation exclusively gymnastic (as opposed to political) in character, the hypothesis that the Diabetae of these ' Phylae ' were the four additional officials represented in the list of *Tainarioi* provides a very satisfactory explanation. The only connection which Sparta can have had with Taenarum in the first century B.C., when it was politically independent, was the religious one, and we know from an earlier inscription that athletic contests were everywhere a feature of the cult of Poseidon.[5]

This explanation would not satisfy those who believe that there actually existed more than four of these so-called Phylae, and that they were not purely gymnastic in character, but political divisions of the whole citizen body. On this subject more will be said later.[6] But whatever the explanation of the missing four names, the complete lists of forty-two suggest an explanation of the μικρὰ ἐκκλησία, referred to only by Xenophon,[7] but implied also by the existence in later times of a μεγάλη ἄπελλα at Gytheum ; for it may be observed that in his account of the conspiracy of Cinadon Xenophon gives the number of ' Spartiatae ' in the Agora, apart from the main crowd

---

[1] *Steph. Byz. s.v.: Ταίναρος. λέγεται καὶ ταιναρίζειν, ὡς ʽΕρμιππος Θεοῖς. καὶ σε τί χρὴ παραταιναρίζειν* ; *cf.* Hesych. *s.v.: Ταινάρια· παρὰ Λακεδαιμονίοις ἑορτὴ Ποσειδῶνος· καὶ ἐν αὐτῇ Ταιναρισταί.* The *Ταιναρισταί* need not necessarily be identical with the *Ταινάριοι* ; they may represent the performers in the games.

[2] *Cf.* I.G. V, i, 32A, B, 34, 676–683.
[3] V, i, 676 *seq.* On the Sphaereis, see pp. 131 f.
[4] On this point see further, pp. 163 f. [5] *Cf.* I.G. V, i, 213.
[6] See § 4 below, p. 163. [7] Xen. *Hell.* III, iii, 8.

of about four thousand, as 'about forty' including a king, the Ephors and the Gerontes.[1]

§ 3. *Lycurgan Features in the Later Constitution*

If Cleomenes III was right in maintaining that in the early Lycurgan constitution the position assigned to the Ephors was one of secondary importance,[2] the Spartan constitution under the Principate was in this respect at least 'Lycurgan'. In the conduct of foreign affairs the Ephors had sunk to the position of mere secretaries, who received and passed on the letters of foreign powers to their own government,[3] and despatched copies of decrees of their own Gerusia to other states.[4] In Pausanias' time the statues of Zeus Xenios and Athenia Xenia, protectors of strangers, stood hard by the office of the Ephors in the Spartan Agora,[5] and this implies that foreign ambassadors addressed themselves in the first instance to the Ephors in Pausanias' time. The survival of an ancient practice seems excluded in this case, since in the fifth century B.C. the Spartans still called enemies who were at war with them ξένοι.[6] Their cults of Zeus Xenios and Athena Xenia can therefore scarcely have been very ancient. The same applies to the formal supervision which the Ephors in this late period exercised over the issue of coinage, as attested by the copper coins inscribed *ΕΦΟΡΩΝ*. The existence of otherwise similar coins inscribed *ΓΕΡΟΝΤΩΝ* or *ΝΟΜΟ-ΦΥΛΑΚΕΣ* indicates that such powers as the Ephors possessed in this field were purely formal.[7] In the judicial

---

[1] *Ibid.* § 5.   [2] *Cf.* pp. 19 f.

[3] I.G. V, i, 8, 9 (two letters addressed Λακεδαιμονίων ἐφόροις καὶ τᾶι πόλει, probably first century B.C.) ; *ibid.* 30 : Λακεδαιμονίων ἐφόροις [καὶ τᾶι πόλει] (121 B.C.) ; *ibid.* 961 ; *cf.* Joseph. *Antiq.* XIII, 5-8 (*c.* 145 B.C. ?) : Λακεδαιμονίων ἐφόροις καὶ γερουσίᾳ καὶ δήμῳ. The unimportant part played in the negotiations by the Ephors is revealed by their absence from the prescript of the letter of an emperor (I.G. V, i, 17 : [Λακεδαιμονί]ων βουλῆι καὶ τῶι [δήμωι χαίρειν]).

[4] I.G. V, i, 1566. Λακεδαιμονίων ἔφοροι καὶ ἁ πόλ[ις Δελφῶν τοῖς ἄρχουσι καὶ τᾶι πόλ]ει χαίρειν (c. 29 B.C.).

[5] Paus. III, xi, 11.   [6] Herod. IX, 11, 53.

[7] *Cf.* B.M. Cat. Pelop. p. 126, nos. 58–61, pl. xxv, 3, 4 : (*ΕΦΟΡΩΝ*) ; *ibid.* p. 125, nos. 51–53, pl. xxiv, 16 (*ΝΟΜΟΦΥΛΑΚΕΣ*), *ibid.* p. 126, nos. 56, 57, cf. B.M. Cat., *ibid.*, Introd., p. L (*ΓΕΡΟΝΤΩΝ*). According to Head (H.N.², p. 436) and Kolbe (I.G. V, i, p. xvi, l. 148) these coins

sphere the power of the Ephors seems to have been reduced to nothing by the creation of the Patronomoi. The cessation of foreign wars deprived them of their ancient powers of levying troops and determining where the army should fight. It can only be supposed that Pausanias is guilty of an anachronism in saying of the Ephors in his own time that they conducted the most important business of the state as well as in the statement that one of them was the Eponymos.[1] It is, however, possible that they still presided in the public assembly, for the inscriptions occasionally mention ratification by the δᾶμος (the name Apella is no longer found) of decisions of the Gerusia,[2] and the continuance of popular elections is implied by the part played by the Damos in electing the holder of the title ἀριστοπολιτευτής (or ἀριστοπολείτης).[3]

The Ephors themselves were still elected, as in early times ' from the people '.[4] This may be deduced from the fact that men of the rank of Kasen were eligible for the office.[5] But the ' Privileged Families ' were not excluded from the Ephorate, as is shown by the instance of a Boagos who became Ephor.[6] In this respect the old traditions were followed, for although in early times men of any social class were eligible, some of the Ephors were in fact men of the highest stratum of society.[7] In the seniority of its holders, too, the later Ephorate probably resembled the

belong to the period after Claudius, but they seem more likely to belong to the later Republic, since the group inscribed by the Ephors cannot otherwise be distinguished from those inscribed by the Gerontes or Nomophylakes, and some coins of both these last groups have a small head stamped as countermark which is thought, on good grounds, to represent Augustus (Artemis Orthia, p. 395, no. 36).

[1] Paus. III, xi, 2 : τά τε ἄλλα διοικοῦσιν τὰ σπουδῆς μάλιστα ἄξια καὶ παρέχονται τὸν ἐπώνυμον.

[2] Cf. I.G. V, i, 18 B. 10 ; ἐκύρωσεν ὁ δῆμος. The reference to the disposal of fines (ibid. 1. 6 ; χωρήσει εἰς ἃ ἂν ὁ δῆμος ἐθελήσῃ καὶ οἱ ἄρχοντες κρείνωσι) suggests that the real decision lay with the ἄρχοντες (i.e. συναρχία, Gerusia ?) as in early times (cf. Plut. Lycurg. 6, on the reversal of ' crooked decisions ' made by the Damos).

[3] Cf. below, p. 159. [4] Cf. Arist. Pol. II, 9. 19.
[5] See Appendix IV, § 3 A. [6] I.G. V, i, 32 B.
[7] E.g. Cheilon, whose name connects him with the royal houses, and who is said to have been a member of the Gerusia (Alcidamas ap. Arist. Rhet. II, 23. 11) as well as Ephor, and the Ephor Agesilaos, who was the uncle of Agis IV (Plut. Agis. 12, 16) and one of the richest men in Sparta (ibid. 6).

office in early times, although there is no direct evidence for a minimum age-qualification for the early Spartan Ephors, the only indication of it being the lower age-limit of fifty years for Ephors in the late fourth-century Constitution of Cyrene.[1] In the case of the later Spartan Ephors, a high age-qualification is suggested by the fact that they appear to hold this office last of all, after most of the other magistracies and membership of the Gerusia.[2] It is doubtful whether there is a single exception to the practice of holding the Ephorate after at least one term of office in the Gerusia, for the one inscription which might suggest the contrary does not in fact do so.[3] As a rule an Ephor has already been Nomophylax as well as Geron.[4] Thus we may infer that the later Ephorate made up in dignity for what it lacked in real importance.

The Ephors do, however, appear to have possessed in this period a general supervisory authority over the lives of the citizens and an obligation to see that the traditional laws are kept. They had possessed these powers at an earlier period,[5] and this was apparently how their ancient name of ἔφοροι, ' overseers ', was interpreted by Cleomenes III and in later times. Thus for a long period (μεχρὶ πολλοῦ) the work of Dicaearchus of Messene (a pupil of Aristotle) on the Spartan constitution is said to have been read annually in the council-house of the Ephors to the assembled Epheboi.[6] The curious statement of the lexicographer Timaeus that there were five senior and five junior Ephors at Sparta [7] points in the same direction, for it implies that the functions of the Ephors were of the same kind as those of the five

---

[1] Cf. Hermes, LXIV (1929), pp. 432 f. (l. 33). It may be noted that the minimum age for Gerontes at Cyrene at this time was ten years lower than for Gerontes at Sparta. This perhaps implies an original age-qualification of sixty years both at Cyrene and at Sparta.

[2] Cf. I.G. V, i, 31, 32, 34, 39, 40, 65, 71.

[3] V, i, 40 (career of Agathokles son of Aristokles) does not mention membership of the Gerusia before the Ephorate, but implies that the Gerusia had been entered earlier by the mention of the position of πρεσβὺς γερουσίας later in the career.

[4] Cf. Woodward, B.S.A. XXVI, p. 191.

[5] Cf. (Xen.) Resp. Lac. VIII, 3 ; it was their function καταπλῆξαι τοὺς πολίτας τοῦ ὑπακούειν, ζημιοῦν ὃν ἂν βούλωνται, ἐκπράττειν παραχρῆμα.

[6] Cf. F.H.G. II, p. 241. 21.

[7] Timaeus Soph., Lex. Platon. (ed. Ruhnken) s.v. ἔφοροι πέντε μείζους καὶ πέντε ἐλάττους.

Bideoi,[1] who, as we learn from Pausanias, and as the inscriptions also suggest, were generally responsible for supervising the athletic activities of the Epheboi.[2]

In the middle of the first century A.D. some light is thrown on the general supervisory authority of the Ephors by the account which Philostratus gives of the visit of the sophist Apollonius of Tyana to Sparta. Philostratus attributes to the influence of Apollonius during his visit in Nero's reign a great revival of enthusiasm at Sparta for all the ancient customs, although he also implies that so far from having been allowed to fall into disuse, some of them were being enforced almost too strictly at the time of Apollonius' visit.[3] The reform most needed seems to have been in the matter of dress ; Apollonius is said to have been officially approached at Olympia by envoys from the Spartan government begging him to visit Sparta ; and the effeminate toilet and attire of these ambassadors produced such a bad impression upon him that he wrote immediately to the Ephors upon the subject. This letter resulted in the issuing by the Ephors of an edict abolishing such practices for the future and restoring the ancient austere traditions in dress and physical training.[4]

While it would be rash to assume the absolute historical accuracy of Philostratus' account, it is certainly an interesting coincidence that the vast majority of the inscriptions of the Roman period which relate to the organisation of the physical and gymnastic training of the boys begin with the reign of the Emperor Nero.[5] Only a few stray inscriptions of this class can be dated earlier, and those apparently all belong to the first century B.C.[6] And this coincides with the information from literary sources, for although we know from these that the ἀγωγή was restored quite early in the second century B.C. after a temporary suppression, and was still alive in Livy's time,[7] there is

---

[1] Cf. above, p. 137, n. 4.

[2] Paus. III, xi, 2 ; cf. I.G. V, i, 676, 677, 679, 680, etc.

[3] On this point see further below, p. 161.

[4] Philostr. Vit. Apoll. 167 : ὡς ἐκείνους κήρυγμα ποιήσασθαι δημοσίᾳ τήν τε πίτταν τῶν βαλανείων ἐξαιροῦντας καὶ τὰς παρατιλτρίας ἐξελαύνοντας ἐς τὸ ἀρχαῖόν τε καθισταμένους πάντα, ὅθεν παλαῖστραί τε ἀνήβησαν καὶ σπουδαὶ καὶ τὰ φιδίτια ἐπανῆλθε καὶ ἐγένετο ἡ Λακεδαίμων ἑαυτῇ ὁμοία.

[5] Cf. the Tables of Boagoi and Kasens, Appendix IV, §§ 1, 3.

[6] Appendix IV, § 3, B, n. 4.   [7] Cf. above, pp. 50 f.

no later evidence from literary sources of the existence of the characteristic training of the boys until we reach the time of Plutarch.

The Spartans appear to have sought and followed the advice of the Sophist Apollonius with the same respectful awe which was characteristic of their earlier attitude to professional philosophers.[1] The Ephors invited him to their council-house and asked him what he thought of their laws. ' Excellent teachers ', was the reply, ' but it needs assiduous pupils to bring their teachers credit '.[2] Philostratus says that Apollonius made further practical suggestions which were actually put into effect,[3] and mentions a list of complimentary titles with which he was rewarded, including those of ' Father of the Youth ' and βίου νομοθέτης. Both of these titles are in themselves quite credible Spartan titles for the period.[4]

But on the whole it seems probable that the element of truth in this story is that there was in fact a conspicuous revival of the more archaic and peculiarly Spartan institutions about the end of the first century, and rather too late for Apollonius to have played any direct part in it. Thus, for example, the ἀριστοπολειτείας ἀγών, which appears to be a revival in slightly different form of the ancient method of electing new members of the Gerusia [5] seems to have been revived early in the reign of Trajan, the first holder of the title ἀριστοπολείτης being Ti. Flavius Charixenus, ἀθλοθέτης of the Uranian and of the Leonidean Games about A.D. 97. A formal election to the title by Gerusia and Demos was held,[6] apparently each year, in view of the exceptional title αἰώνιος ἀριστοπολείτης.[7] But in view of the annual election of all Gerontes, the title could no longer have any direct connection with the holding of the office of Geron.

---

[1] E.g. Hippias of Elis (Plato, Hipp. Maj. 283B ff.), Dicaearchus of Messene (cf. above, p. 157), Sphaerus the Borysthenite (Plut. Cleom. 2), and many others.

[2] Philostr. Vit. Apoll. 171.　　　　[3] Ibid. 258.

[4] Cf. I.G. V, i, 589 : μητέρα εὐσεβείας καὶ δήμου καὶ βουλῆς (c. A.D. 160) ; 598 : πατρὸς] νόμων καὶ πόλεως (C. III ?), and the much commoner υἱὸς πόλεως and υἱὸς βουλῆς (ibid. Index IV, 4).

[5] Cf. Plut. Lycurg. 26, Arist. Pol. II, 9. 27. The basis of selection was proof of political virtue by the holding of all offices, cf. Dar.-Sagl. s.v. Lacedaemoniorum Respublica, pp. 896 f.

[6] I.G. V, i, 467 ; cf. 541, 542.　　　　[7] Ibid. 468, 504, etc.

New, or apparently new, offices designed to secure that the laws should actually be kept are found for the first time from the reign of Domitian onwards. Thus the office of Nomodeiktes is first found (in the inscriptions so far known to us) late in the reign of Domitian ; [1] a σύνδικος ἐπὶ τὰ ἔθη (to be distinguished from other σύνδικοι who are probably financial officials [2]) in inscriptions of the reign of Hadrian and later in the second century ; [3] ' Instructors in the Lycurgan customs ' (διδάσκαλοι οἱ ἀμφὶ τὰ Λυκούργεια ἔθη) in the reign of Marcus Aurelius and Verus,[4] and an ' Expositor of the Lycurgan customs ' (ἐξηγητής τῶν Λυκουργείων ἐθῶν) late in the second century.[5] In the present state of our evidence it is impossible to say whether the three last-mentioned offices, or any two of them, existed at the same time or not, nor precisely when any of them came into existence. The names of the two last would suggest that both were of a fairly permanent character, and the absence of the mention of a year in which Ti. Claud. Sophron held the office of ἐξηγητής in an inscription which mentions the year when he was Damosiomastes [6] suggests that it was a life-office. It seems possible that in the ἐξηγητὴς τῶν Λυκουργείων ἐθῶν we have a revival of the ancient office of Paidonomos, and that his function was to exercise a general supervision of education and discipline among the boys and Epheboi.[7] The title of Paidonomos is not found among the Spartan inscriptions at any period. The διδάσκαλοι ἀμφὶ τὰ Λυκούργεια ἔθη could be assistants to the ἐξηγητής.

With regard to the σύνδικοι ἐπὶ τὰ ἔθη, their title suggests that they had judicial functions, and although further information is lacking, it seems reasonable to suppose on general grounds that their function was to interpret the meaning of the Lycurgan laws in their application to

---

[1] In the Patronomate of Kleodamos (B.S.A. XXVI, p. 183), assigned to 93/4 in the reconstructed list (below, p. 464). The Nomodeiktas Sosidamus held office under at least five Patronomoi, covering about twenty years (cf. Appendix IV, § 3, A, n. 6, p. 455). A life office seems to be implied.

[2] Cf. I.G. V, i, 47, 554 : σύνδικος καὶ δαμοσιομάστης. On the Damosiomastai, cf. p. 138, n. 1.   [3] I.G. V, i, 65 ; B.S.A. XXVII, p. 234 (F4).
[4] I.G. V, i, 500.   [5] Ibid. 554.   [6] Ibid. 554.
[7] Cf. Resp. Lac. II, 2, and for the functions of Paidonomoi in ancient aristocracies in general, Arist. Pol. VII, 17. 5–7.

individual behaviour in the society of the second century A.D. For however much the Spartans at this period might pride themselves upon their retention of ancient customs, it is obvious that in many respects fundamental changes had occurred, as for example in the possession of money, the development of trade and normal intercourse with foreigners. A purely literal interpretation of the law might easily result in public impeachment for wearing too long a moustache, or for not wearing a beard,[1] or being in possession of money.

A case of this sort is said actually to have occurred during the visit of Apollonius in the reign of Nero. A certain young man of distinguished family, descended from the navarch Callicratidas, had a hereditary passion for the sea and consequently followed the life of a merchant, spending his time in voyages to Carthage and to Sicily instead of remaining in Sparta and dedicating himself to a career of public office, as the laws of Lycurgus required. Consequently he found himself awaiting trial before the Ephors —a public trial (δημόσιος ἀγών) on the charge of ' offending against the moral code ' (ἀδικῶν περὶ τὰ ἤθη).[2] Apollonius is said to have convinced him privately of the error of his ways, and then to have gone to the Ephors and begged him off. The details of this story may be apocryphal, but it obviously represents a state of affairs which might easily arise, and it is interesting and perhaps significant that the function of trying such cases is here attributed to the Ephors, whereas somewhat later they would presumably come before the σύνδικοι ἐπὶ τὰ ἔθη. A possible explanation of the appearance of all these new offices is that a more rigid enforcement of the ancient customs, dating from the later Flavian period, was found to give the Ephors too much power over the private lives of citizens, so that it was considered desirable to distribute the powers in question over three or four colleges of magistrates, some of whom at least were less advanced in years than the Ephors appear to have been.

A last survival of the ancient Syssitia (or Phiditia) is found in this late period in the common meals of the various

[1] Cf. p. 366.   [2] Philostr. Vit. Apoll. 172.

colleges of magistrates. The epigraphic evidence relates
to the Ephors, Nomophylakes and Agoranomoi [1] though
the title πρέσβυς φειδειτίου is preserved only in the case of
the Agoranomoi and for an unknown board of magistrates. [2]
The number of ἔνσιτοι seems to have varied between one and
two. Sometimes σπονδοφόροι are mentioned in addition,
the Ephors in one case having as many as four, with one
ἔνσιτος. The Phidition of the six Agoranomoi, which
included also eight σύναρχοι, was in one case brought up by
the addition of ἔνσιτοι to a total of seventeen ; but it is
evident that there was no fixed rule about the number
of additional members. The five Nomophylakes appear
as a rule to have added two not in office to their number,
the Ephors about five. The surviving epigraphical evidence
covers as nearly as possible the period A.D. 100–200. It
is impossible not to suspect that Plutarch's statement that
the Lycurgan Syssitia (which he says were also called
Phiditia) contained ' about fifteen members more or less ' [3]
is founded merely on the practice of the Spartan colleges
of magistrates, even though it appears to be drawn from
an earlier literary source and not from his own direct
observation. [4] The same criticism probably applies to his
description of the secret ballot (achieved by squeezing or
refraining from squeezing pellets of bread) which was held
before the admission of new members.

The ancient Delphic oracle which was said to have
instructed Lycurgus to carry out certain reforms, φυλὰς
φυλάξαντα καὶ ὠβὰς ὠβάξαντα [5] left an echo in the Phylae of
later Sparta and in the Oba of Amyclae ; [6] but whether and in
what sense these divisions were survivals of the ancient
tribal organisation is a matter for detailed enquiry.

[1] I.G. V, i, 53, 64, 65, 71, 89, 128, 129, 155 and 1507.
[2] *Ibid.* 128 (a college identified as that of the Agoranomoi by the eight
σύναρχοι, cf. 129), 155.
[3] Plut. *Lycurg.* 12. 2 ; cf. Schol. Plato, *Laws*, 633A : οἱ συσσιτοῦντες
δέκα ἦσαν.
[4] See further, p. 245, n. 1 ; Plut. *Cleom.* 8 implies that the Ephors had
their own Syssition already in the reign of Cleomenes III,
[5] Plut. *Lycurg.* 6. See further, Appendix VI (pp. 477 f.).
[6] I.G. V, i, 26 (second or first century B.C.) is a decree of the *Oba* of
Amyclae relating to its own officials (three Ephors and a secretary).

§ 4. The Nature of the Phylae

The Sphaireis-inscriptions [1] preserve the names of four Phylae, the *Limnaeis, Konooureis, Neopolitai, Pitanatai,* and Pausanias in his account of the whipping of the Epheboi, (III, 16. 9) also mentions four, the *Limnatai, Kynosoureis,* 'those of Mesoa and of Pitane'. Earlier in this chapter it has been assumed that the number was in fact four, on the assumption that the 'Mesoans', being the only ones in Pausanias' enumeration which do not correspond to the evidence of the Sphaireis-inscriptions, are identical with the *Neopolitai.* The alternative name could easily be explained on the supposition that the ancient village of Mesoa [2] grew in size in later times and acquired the more imposing name of Neapolis. Apart from this passage in Pausanias, which may well be taken from an earlier author, there is no good evidence for the survival of the name Mesoa into the period of the Principate,[3] but even if it were reliably attested, the simultaneous existence of an alternative name is clearly possible. Moreover, the Sphaereis of the Phyle *Neopolitai* are at pains in one inscription to describe themselves as οἱ ἀρχαῖοι ; [4] this also indicates that *Neopolitai,* which naturally suggested a recent origin, was not their original name. In any case it is evident from the names *Limnatai* (or *Limnaeis*), *Pitanatai* and ἐκ Μεσόας that the divisions in question were all connected with definite localities.[5] *Neopolitai* must therefore mean ἐκ Νεασπόλεως. A further reason for supposing that the total number of these Phylae was four is that the *Pitanatai* appear to have been one of four divisions of Eirenes at the time of the invasion of Xerxes.[6]

Other historians, influenced by the possibility of a direct

[1] *Cf.* above, pp. 131 f., 132, n. 5.
[2] To which the poet Alcman is said to have belonged (Suid. *s.v.*).
[3] Little weight can be attached to I.G. V, i, 515, Δαμάτριον 'Αριστάνδρου ΜΙΓΟ . . . the last word restored Μεσο[άταν]. The inscription is now lost.
[4] I.G. V, i, 677 : σφαιρεῖ]s οἱ ἀρχαῖοι [Νεοπολειτῶν] οἱ νικάσαντες κ.τ.λ. The length of the lacuna imposes the restoration [Νεοπολειτῶν] in preference to Πιτανατῶν, Λιμναέων or Κονοουρέων.
[5] For Pitane, *cf.* Herod. III, 55 : 'Αρχίη . . . αὐτὸς ἐν Πιτάνῃ συνεγενόμην· δήμου γὰρ τούτου ἦν.
[6] The name of Amompharetus, the captain of the λόχος Πιτανάτης at Plataea (Herod. IX, 53), was inscribed with three others on the separate grave of the Eirenes (*ibid.* 85).

connection between the number of the early Phylae (of
which they suppose these later ones to be survivals) and the
five Ephors and other boards of five magistrates at Sparta,
have concluded that οἱ ἐκ Μεσόας were a fifth Phyle, and
that five was the total number.[1] A similar argument has
led others who have considered the problem to suppose
that there were in all six Phylae, for there are several boards
of six magistrates at Sparta (e.g. the Patronomoi, Gynaiko-
nomoi and Agoranomoi), at least in later times. Those
who maintain this view accept the five names already mentioned, including οἱ ἐκ Μεσόας, and add one more.

As to the identification of this supposed sixth Phyle
there is no general agreement. Kahrstedt and Swoboda
believe it to have been based on a place-name Dyme,[2] on
the strength of Hesychius' statement that there was a
Spartan Phyle of this name.[3] But as Ehrenberg has
pointed out,[4] this information from Hesychius probably
rests on a confusion with the early Dorian tribe Dymanes,
and merits no serious attention. The Hylleis, Pamphyloi
and Dymanes which occur in many Dorian states were
certainly quite unlike the later Spartan Phylae connected
with Laconian villages. There is no other evidence for
the existence of a Spartan village of Dyme.

A more generally accepted view is that Amyclae was
the basis of a sixth Phyle.[5] This theory rests on the evidence
that an Oba τῶν Ἀμυκλαιέων existed in the Hellenistic
period [6] and that inscriptions of the first and second century
mention a φυλὴ Λιμναέων on the one hand,[7] and an ὠβὰ
Λιμναέων on the other.[8] On the assumption that φυλή
and ὠβά were synonymous terms, it is also possible to
explain the phrase which occurs in several of the Sphaireis-
inscriptions, σφαιρεῖς Λιμναέων (vel. sim.) οἱ νικάσαντες τὰς
ὠβάς. The Obae in question, according to this interpretation, were the Konooureis, Neapolitai and Pitanatai else-

---

[1] Cf. C.A.H. III, p. 560.
[2] Kahrstedt, Sparta u. seine Symmachie (1922), p. 19 ; Swoboda (Busolt-
Swoboda), Griech. Staatsk. 1926, p. 645, n. 3.
[3] Hesych, s.v. Δύμη.   [4] Cf. Hermes, LIX (1924), pp. 27 f.
[5] Cf. Niccolini, Riv. di Storia Antica (1905), p. 95 ; Neumann, Hist.
Zeitschr. (1906), p. 42 ; Pareti, Rend. Accad. Linc. (1910), pp. 173 f. ;
also in Storia di Sparta arcaica, Vol. I (1920), pp. 173 f. ; Kolbe in I.G. V,
i (1913), p. 144 ; Ehrenberg, Hermes, LIX (1924), pp. 27 f.
[6] I.G. V, i, 26.   [7] Ibid. 564.   [8] Ibid. 688.

where referred to as φυλαί.[1] Amyclae, then, would appear to have been another of these.

The difficulty for this theory is that the ancient oracle-Rhetra (φυλὰς φυλάξαντα καὶ ὠβὰς ὠβάξαντα) clearly implies that the Obae were either subdivisions of the Phylae, or were separate from them altogether. If the Phylae and Obae of the late period were genuine survivals of the early ones, the supposed assimilation could not have occurred ; if, on the other hand, they were artificial creations of a later period, the famous oracle-Rhetra (known to Plutarch, and so presumably to the Spartans themselves in his time) would have forbidden the interpretation that Phylae and Obae were the same. In either case it seems necessary to find an interpretation of the Phylae and Obae mentioned in the inscriptions which does not patently contradict the ancient oracle. So far as the phrase σφαιρεῖς Λιμναέων (vel. sim.) οἱ νικάσαντες τὰς ὠβάς is concerned, the explanation is easy ; the Phyle could be the whole Ephebic association, comprising young men of all age-classes and covering the whole field of their activities ; the Oba could be a sub-division of the Phyle comprising only the Sphaireis, and perhaps existing only for the purpose of their athletic competitions, in other words, an athletic team.

The Oba τῶν Ἀμυκλαιέων with its three Ephors need not necessarily be an association of the same kind. In fact the inscriptions imply that it was of a different kind, for the chief officials of the Amyclaean Oba were of their own choosing, and the whole organisation seems to have been modelled on that of the independent Laconian towns, with three annual Ephors like Geronthrae and Taenarum [2] and (as we learn from another inscription) [3] an ἐπιμελητής, again like Taenarum.[4] The officials of the Phylae Limnaeis, etc., on the other hand, were the Bideoi and a Diabetes,[5] who were magistrates of the Spartan state, and a single πρεσβὺς Λιμναέων. When the φυλὴ Λιμναέων wished to honour one of its members, the city of Sparta (ἡ πόλις) set up the statue ; [6] when the ὠβὰ τῶν Ἀμυκλαιέων did the

---

[1] Ehrenberg (Hermes LIX, p. 28) would explain the double name by supposing Oba to be the archaic one, Phyle to have been introduced later in imitation of the Athenian usage.

[2] I.G. V, i, 1114, 1240.   [3] Ibid. 515 ; cf. above, p. 163, n. 3.
[4] Ibid. 1241.   [5] Ibid. 676, etc.   [6] Ibid. 564.

same, the Amyclaeans themselves solemnly passed a δόγμα, as did Gytheum [1] and other independent states.[2] It is clear that Amyclae enjoyed some kind of municipal organisation which was conceded by Sparta on the score of the exceptional antiquity and alleged early importance of the town.[3] But how was this organisation to be described ? πόλις was an obvious misnomer, since it was not independent ; φυλή too evidently suggested dependence ; ὠβά was undoubtedly an ancient name, and uncertainty about its original meaning would be an advantage rather than the reverse.

Officials called ἐπιμεληταί have been supposed to suggest identity of character between the Oba of Amyclae and the Phylae of the Sphaireis inscriptions, for there is some reason to think that each of the Phylae in question, like Amyclae, had an ἐπιμελητής.[4] But Ehrenberg is mistaken in supposing that there were altogether six Spartan ἐπιμεληταί [5] (as there would be if his theory about the six Phylae were right) ; the fact seems to be that there was only one ἐπιμελητής of the city of Sparta (ἐπιμελητὴς τῆς πόλεως),[6] assisted sometimes by five σύναρχοι.[7] It has already been demonstrated in the case of the Patronomoi that the σύναρχοι of Spartan magistrates were not themselves magistrates, but assessors.[8] This explains the fluctuation in the number of σύναρχοι attached to the Agoranomos,[9] and demonstrates the impossibility of basing any conclusion about the number of the Phylae upon the number of a magistrate together with his σύναρχοι. The single ἐπιμελητής of the city found his counterpart in the single ἐπιμελητής at Taenarum to whom reference has already been made, and in the single ἐπιμελητής of Coronaea [10] (otherwise called Corone) on the Messenian Gulf. The fact is that the word ἐπιμελητής has a very vague

---

[1] I.G. V, i, 1208.

[2] As for example, Sparta itself (ibid. 5. l. 14, τὰ δεδογμένα).

[3] Cf. Ephorus ap. Strabo, VIII, 364.

[4] Cf. I.G. V, i, 682 (a Sphaireis-inscription of the Limnaeis) : . . . ἐπιμελη]τοῦ δὲ τῆς φ[υλῆς καὶ γυμνασιάρ]χου Αὐρ. Ἀπο[λλ - - -] κ.τ.λ.

[5] Cf. Hermes, LIX, p. 27.   [6] Cf. I.G. V, i, 32A (reign of Hadrian).

[7] Ibid. 133, 135. No. 134, giving three σύναρχοι, is presumably incomplete.   [8] Cf. above, pp. 143 f.

[9] Five σύναρχοι in I.G. V, i, 124, six ibid. 127, eight ibid. 128.

[10] Ibid. 34, 35, 44 (all second century A.D.). This was a Spartan official, but the appointment obviously does not mean that there was a Phyle of Coronaea.

and general connotation, and no real link need be supposed
to exist between its meanings in various contexts.
The co-existence in the later Sparta of colleges of
magistrates which normally numbered five with others
which normally numbered six, and the absence of any
definite rule about the number in some collegiate magistracies,[1] makes it clear that elections were not in that period
conducted on the basis of representation of tribes. They
may still, so far as we know, have been conducted in the
' childish ' fashion derided by Aristotle, who appears to be
referring to selection from and by the whole citizen body
without restriction.[2] At all events, since in the Roman
period close relatives are often found holding the same
magistracy together in the same year,[3] as also Boagoi
together with their Synepheboi,[4] and ' Patrons ' together
with their Kasens,[5] it seems likely that only the president
of the board (πρεσβύς) was elected at all, and that it was
left to him to co-opt his colleagues. In any case the equal
representation of Phylae is clearly excluded as an explanation. But there is in fact no indication that the Phylae
which have been the subject of this discussion had any
functions except in connection with the Ephebic organisation, to which the passage in Pausanias also relates them.
In the inscriptions they are mentioned only in connection
with the Sphaereis and with athletic activities generally.
Thus Avidius Agathangelos, Λακεδαιμόνιος Πιτανάτης, is
recorded as winning the wrestling match of the ἀγένειοι
at the Euryklean games,[6] and another inscription, set up
by his Boagos, commemorates his ἀνδρεία.[7] 'Ανδρεία was
the special quality of the Sphaireis, as we see from the
inscription honouring a Sphaireus of the Phyle Konooureis;[8]

---

[1] *E.g.* the Bideoi, who were sometimes five (Paus. III, xi, 2 ; B.S.A.
XXVI, p. 166, B5), sometimes six (I.G. V, i, 136–138, 556 ; B.S.A. *ibid.* B3,
XXVII, p. 221).

[2] *Cf.* Arist. *Pol.* II, 9. 23, 27, with Plut. *Lycurg.* 26.

[3] *Cf.* I.G. V, i, 97 (a list of the Gerusia, *c.* A.D. 120) which contains
an elder and a younger Aristokles Καλλικράτους and (as secretary) Jul.
Pollio Ρούφου, known to be a member of the same family ; *ibid.* 129
shows brothers acting together as Agoranomoi. Prosopographical investigation would reveal many similar instances.

[4] *Cf.* B.S.A. XXVI, p. 167, C3(β), a list of Nomophylakes ending with
the words Βοαγὸς καὶ Συνέφηβοι.

[5] *Cf.* I.G. V, i, 109 ; 137 with 99 ; Appendix IV, § 3B, note 3.

[6] I.G. V, i, 663.   [7] *Ibid.* 472.   [8] *Ibid.* 566.

this enables us to identify as another testimony to athletic merit the inscription relating to a πρέσβυς τῆς Λιμναέων φυλῆς,[1] an official who is also mentioned in the Sphaereis inscriptions.[2] Finally, the Phyle *Konooureis* set up a statue of Ti. Claud. Harmoneikos, who was a Gymnasiarch.[3] There are no other known inscriptions relating to Phylae, or for that matter, to Obae.

It seems safe to conclude, therefore, that the Phylae of the Roman period at Sparta were four in number, and that they were wholly athletic organisations, unconnected with the citizen body except in so far as the state directly controlled the activities of the Epheboi.

[1] I.G. V, i, 564.　　　　[2] *Ibid.* 676.　　　　[3] *Ibid.* 480.

CHAPTER V

THE FAMILY AND DESCENDANTS OF C. JULIUS EURYKLES

THERE is already a considerable bibliography on the subject of C. Julius Eurykles and his immediate descendants,[1] but the last word has not yet been said on the subject, for there can as yet be no certainty about the position which Eurykles and his son Lakon occupied at Sparta in the Julio-Claudian period, and little interest has hitherto been taken in the part played in Spartan life by later members of the same family. This family is interesting historically for two reasons, first on account of the exceptional constitutional position usually supposed to have been occupied by Eurykles in the reign of Augustus, and by his son Lakon in the reign of Claudius, and secondly because Eurykles and his descendants belonged, as will be shown later, to that stratum of Spartan society which in an earlier chapter has been described as the ' Privileged Families '.[2] The family of Eurykles provides a good illustration of the way in which this class monopolised the highest offices for generation after generation, and how its power and prestige was secured by intermarriage and by the judicious expenditure of its wealth.

The question of the constitutional position of the first Eurykles and the first Lakon so far known to us is of particular interest in relation to the underlying assumption of the present work, which is that Spartan institutions of the early period were preserved almost unchanged into the

---

[1] *Cf.* Weil, *Ath. Mitt.* VI (1881), pp. 10 ff. ; Kjellberg, *Klio*, XVII (1921), pp. 45 ff. ; Ditt. *Syll.*³ 786–790, with notes ; Kolbe in I.G. V, i, pp. xv, xvi, 307 ; Pauly-Wissowa RE, *s.v. Iulius* (309 and 495) and *Eurykles;* A.J.A. (1926), pp. 389 ff. ; Kornemann, *Neue Dokumente zum lakonischen Kaiserkulte* (1929).

[2] *Cf.* Chapter III, esp. pp. 111 ff.

Principate. If it be true that C. Julius Eurykles was permitted by Augustus to reign at Sparta as a sort of tyrant, and that his son Lakon occupied a similar position under Claudius, this would mean a considerable dislocation of the earlier constitution of Sparta under the Julio-Claudian emperors, a dislocation which could hardly fail to leave its mark in later times. Such petty tyrants might easily have introduced for the first time all sorts of archaising features which were not genuinely archaic at all. The whole theory of the tyranny of Eurykles and Lakon therefore calls for careful examination.

This, the generally accepted view, rests mainly on the evidence of coins inscribed ἐπὶ Εὐρυκλέους,[1] and ἐπὶ Λάκωνος,[2] and upon references by Strabo to C. Julius Eurykles which appear to confirm the view that he held a sort of tyranny at Sparta in the reign of Augustus. Strabo calls Eurykles ὁ καθ' ἡμᾶς τῶν Λακεδαιμονίων ἡγεμών, and says that he held the island of Cythera as his private possession.[3] It might seem a natural conclusion that Eurykles was tyrant of Sparta, and in this way exercised his control over the island. But Strabo tells us further that Eurykles ' was thought to have made improper use of the friendship of Caesar (i.e. Augustus) [4] to make himself supreme over them (i.e. the Spartans), but his rule (ἀρχή) speedily came to an end '.[5] He has been saying immediately before that the Spartans had for long been tranquil and contented under Roman protection and implies that this tranquillity was only momentarily interrupted by the affair of Eurykles, whatever it was. The translation of the following sentence

[1] Cf. Weil, op. cit. p. 13 ; B.M. Cat. Peloponnesus, 1887, pp. 127, 128. The coins from the Orthia site (cf. Artemis Orthia, p. 395) include no examples of coins of Eurykles differing from those published in B.M. Cat., loc. cit.

[2] Weil, loc. cit., B.M. Cat., loc. cit. On a recently discovered hoard of coins of Lakon see further below, p. 184, n. 4. No coins of Lakon have been found on the Orthia site.

[3] Strabo, VIII, 5. 1 (363) : Κύθηρα . . . νῆσος εὐλίμενος, πόλιν ἔχουσα ὁμώνυμον, ἣν ἔσχεν Εὐρυκλῆς ἐν μέρει κτήσεως ἰδίας, ὁ καθ' ἡμᾶς τῶν Λακεδαιμονίων ἡγεμών.

[4] Cf. Plut. Ant. 67.

[5] Strabo, VIII, 5. 5 (366) : νεωστὶ δ' Εὐρυκλῆς αὐτοὺς ἐτάραξε δόξας ἀποχρήσασθαι τῇ Καίσαρος φιλίᾳ πέρα τοῦ μετρίου πρὸς τὴν ἐπιστασίαν αὐτῶν, ἐπαύσατο δ' ἡ ἀρχὴ ταχέως, ἐκείνου μὲν παραχωρήσαντος εἰς τὸ χρεών, τοῦ δ' υἱοῦ τὴν φιλίαν ἀπεστραμμένου τὴν τοιαύτην πᾶσαν.

in Strabo's passage is obscure, and has formerly been interpreted to mean that Augustus permitted Eurykles to rule with a certain measure of independence, of which his (Augustus') son Tiberius subsequently deprived him.[1] But from an inscription recently discovered at Gytheum it now appears that this interpretation must be rejected, and that Strabo must mean that Eurykles 'gave in to necessity' (ἐκείνου μὲν παραχωρήσαντος εἰς τὸ χρεών), that is to say, realised that he must not try the patience of Augustus too far, while his own son Lakon was 'altogether averse to that kind of friendship', namely, friendship with an emperor.[2] The Gytheum inscription is dated in the reign of Tiberius, but before the death of Germanicus in A.D. 19 [3] and is concerned with festivals in honour of Augustus, Tiberius, Livia, Germanicus, Drusus, Flamininus,[4] and lastly Eurykles and Lakon, in other words, of Καισάρεια and Εὐρύκλεια, such as were established also at Sparta.[5] The significant point is that Eurykles is spoken of in the Gytheum inscription as already dead, the festival being arranged 'in his memory' (εἰς μνήμην Γαίου 'Ιουλίου Εὐρυκλέους), whereas in the case of Lakon the festival is 'in his honour' (εἰς τείμην Γαίου 'Ιουλίου Λάκωνος).[6] Kornemann points out that this inscription must be later in date than a letter of Tiberius to the people of Gytheum permitting them to organise the worship of Augustus, and in a more limited sense, the worship of himself. The date of this letter seems to be some time in the year A.D. 15,[7] and it is very probable that the festivals of the Καισάρεια and 'Εὐρύκλεια were organised as soon as permission was received, either later in this year or in A.D. 16.[8] Now if Dittenberger was right in supposing that Tiberius had deprived Eurykles of his exceptional position in Sparta,[9]

[1] So Kornemann, op. cit. p. 14, following Dittenberger (Syll. II³, 787, n. 2). Taylor and West take the same view in A.J.A. XXX (1926), p. 390.
[2] Cf. above, p. 170, n. 5: ἐκείνου μὲν παραχωρήσαντος could also be taken literally, meaning that Eurykles went into exile from Sparta. This possibility is strengthened by Joseph. B.J. I, 26. 4, and also by inscriptions concerning Eurykles' son and grandson from Corinth, on which see further below, pp. 183 f.
[3] Kornemann, op. cit. p. 20.   [4] Cf. above, p. 29, n. 5.
[5] For these festivals at Sparta see I.G. V, i, nos. 71b, 86, 168, 550, 603, 655, 664, 665, 666, and below, p. 181, n. 1.
[6] Kornemann, op. cit. p. 15.   [7] Ibid. p. 16.
[8] Ibid. p. 20.   [9] Cf. above, n. 1.

he must have done this between his accession in September
A.D. 14 and the death of Eurykles, that is in the first two
years of his reign. The disgrace of Eurykles would in that
case be so recent in A.D. 16 that Gytheum could not
possibly have ventured to institute a festival in his memory,
and in honour of his son Lakon, especially a festival so
closely connected with the imperial cult itself. The evidence
of the Gytheum inscription therefore forbids us to accept
Dittenberger's hypothesis. Eurykles must have ' given in
to necessity ' already in the reign of Augustus. The evidence
for Lakon's fall from favour under Tiberius, and for the
position which he later occupied under Claudius, will be
further considered after the other evidence for the career
of Eurykles has been examined.

It is usually held that Eurykles acquired his supremacy
at Sparta early in the reign of Augustus, as a reward for
the services which he had offered to that emperor when he
was still Octavian, at the battle of Actium.[1] Weil believes
that one of the coins of Eurykles, with the inscription
KAIC(AP) on the obverse and ἐπὶ Εὐρυκλέους on the
reverse, bears the portrait of Octavian before he became
emperor.[2] Both the general assumption, and the particular
argument derived from this coin, create difficulties when
considered in relation to the literary sources. For example,
Strabo's statement that Eurykles held Cythera as his
private possession,[3] which not unnaturally has been taken
to mean that Eurykles was tyrant of Sparta, is difficult
to reconcile both with the early coin and with Strabo's
statement that Eurykles' supremacy very soon came to
an end, because we know from Dio that Cythera was only
given to Sparta in 21 B.C.,[4] having previously been an
independent member of the Lacedaemonian League.[5] The
chronological discrepancy between the early coin and the

---

[1] Cf. A.J.A. XXX (1926), p. 389.
[2] Cf. Ath. Mitt. VI (1881), p. 13. Kjellberg (Klio, XVII, 1921, p. 49)
rejects this view, pointing out that the simple inscription Καῖσαρ without
the addition of Σεβαστός, is retained in many instances after Octavian's
assumption of the title Augustus in 27 B.C. On the other hand, the coin
in question bears a strong resemblance to the coins of Augustus issued
in the Eastern provinces between 27 and 20 B.C. (B.M. Cat. Imp. Coins, I,
Pl. XVI, nos. 5–8).
[3] Cf. above, p. 170, n. 3.
[4] Dio, LIV, 7.   [5] Cf. Appendix III.

evidence of Josephus about Eurykles is, as will be shown presently, very much wider than this.

These initial difficulties seem to justify a doubt whether either Eurykles' possession of Cythera, or the appearance of his name on the coins, really prove him to have been local prince of Sparta. But since the evidence of the coins is generally regarded as incontrovertible proof that this was so, discussion of it must be detailed and is better postponed until the literary evidence has also been examined in more detail. The difficulty about Cythera admits of a simple solution, since it is not necessary to suppose that Eurykles was tyrant of Sparta even though he possessed enormous estates in Cythera, and was even the sole landowner in the island apart from the state. Strabo's statement only attributes private ownership of land there to Eurykles (ἔσχεν - - ἐν μέρει κτήσεως ἰδίας).[1] Augustus is likely to have stipulated when he gave Cythera back to Sparta in 21 B.C. that his protégé Eurykles should be allowed to retain any estates which he already possessed in the island ; the greater part of what remained was probably held by him on lease from the Spartan state.[2] In any case it is certain that the great wealth of the immediate descendants of Eurykles himself was independent of Eurykles' possessions as ' tyrant ', since they continued to hold it after Eurykles had been driven into exile.[3]

The evidence of Josephus introduces a serious chronological difficulty into the usual interpretation of Eurykles' position at Sparta, which as we have seen supposes him to have acquired supremacy there early in the reign of Augustus. From Josephus it appears that about 7 B.C.[4] Eurykles was instrumental in bringing about a conspiracy of the two sons of Herod of Judaea against their father, and that this happened *before* Eurykles attempted to make himself supreme at Sparta. Josephus' account of Eurykles has

[1] *Cf.* above, p. 170, n. 3. As a possible explanation of Eurykles' possessions in Cythera, apart from hereditary estates which might be owned by any aristocratic Spartan family in a town of the Perioikoi, it may be noted that hereditary γῆς ἔγκτησις was regularly given to πρόξενοι and εὐεργέται of towns in the Lacedaemonian League including Cythera, in the period after 195 B.C. ; *cf.* I.G. V, i, index, p. 343, *s.v.* ἔγκτησις. *Ibid.* no. 961 gives an instance of a Spartan receiving it.

[2] *Cf.* above, p. 82, n. 2.

[3] *Cf.* below, p. 182.　　　　[4] *Cf.* C.A.H. Vol. X, p. 335.

been frequently cited, but has apparently not been studied in its proper context, with the result that Eurykles' visit to Judaea has usually been assumed to fall during his ' tyranny ', after he had supposedly been for many years local prince of Sparta.[1] It is therefore desirable that Josephus' account should be examined in detail.

According to Josephus' story, shortly before Eurykles' visit there was discord at the court of Herod between himself and his sons, and also between the two sons of his second wife, Alexander and Aristobulus, and Antipater, who was the son of a former wife divorced by Herod. Alexander was married to the daughter of king Archelaus of Cappadocia, who was therefore interested in maintaining the peace between Alexander and Herod. Archelaus himself actually visited Judaea for the purpose of diverting to someone else Herod's suspicions of Alexander's designs ; and having at length succeeded in this, was sent back to Cappadocia with rich gifts both from Herod himself and from members of Herod's family.[2]

Not long after this [3] there arrived at the court of Herod the Spartan Eurykles, who is described by Josephus as ' not without distinction in his own country '[4] and ' a much cleverer intriguer than Archelaus '.[5] His motive, according to Josephus, was ' to enrich himself in order to make himself king '[6]—that is, naturally, king of Sparta, not king of Judaea, for his subsequent movements plainly showed that to stay in Judaea was not his aim. Bringing with him gifts, to ingratiate himself with Herod and other members of his family, he very soon collected from them much larger sums than he had brought, for he contrived to receive money from Antipater as a reward for giving information against his half-brother Alexander,[7] and also fifty talents from Herod as a reward for revealing a sup-

---

[1] This interpretation is adopted in A.J.A. XXX (1926), p. 389 (L. R. Taylor and A. B. West), also by Kjellberg in *Klio*, XVII (1921), pp. 44–58.
[2] Josephus, *Bell. Jud.* I, 25.   [3] *Ibid.* 26.
[4] *Id. Ant. Jud.* XVI, 10. 1 : Εὐρυκλῆς ἀπὸ Λακεδαίμονος οὐκ ἄσημος τῶν ἐκεῖ. This description corresponds to what is known about Eurykles' descent and his private wealth (*cf.* above, pp. 172 f.).
[5] πολὺ τῶν Ἀρχελάου στρατηγημάτων δυνατώτερος.
[6] *Bell. Jud.* I, 26. 1 : πόθῳ χρημάτων εἰς τὴν βασιλείαν προσφθαρείς. . . . οὐδὲν ἡγεῖτο τὴν καθαρὰν δόσιν, εἰ μὴ δι' αἵματος ἐμπορεύσαιτο τὴν βασιλείαν.   [7] *Ant. Jud.* XVI, 10. 1.

posed plot against their father on the part of Alexander and Aristobulus.[1] Not content with these ill-gotten gains, and fearing the discovery of his nefarious schemes, Eurykles then proceeded to the court of Archelaus of Cappadocia, from whom he collected further large sums on the ground that he had finally reconciled Archelaus' son-in-law Alexander to Herod.[2] Finally he returned to Greece, ' to use the proceeds of his crimes for equally discreditable ends ', and was at length banished from Sparta,[3] after being twice arraigned before Augustus on the charge of ' filling Achaea with revolution and destroying the allegiance of the cities '.[4]

Given Josephus' own hypothesis that Eurykles at the time of his visit to Judaea was aiming at making himself king at Sparta—an assumption which will have to be further considered in the light of the other available evidence—Josephus' story does not appear in the least improbable. We naturally ask why Eurykles fixed upon Herod of Judaea as his victim, but the answer is obvious. In the first place, the great wealth of Herod at this time must have been proverbial in all the countries bordering on the Aegean.[5] The new temple at Jerusalem had just been rebuilt on a magnificent scale. Moreover, Herod had been generous in his gifts to the chief cities of Achaea, including Sparta itself.[6] This was a part of Herod's general profession and practice of Philhellenism,[7] which again may well have been an encouragement to the Spartan adventurer. The coinage issued by Herod, with its Greek types and inscriptions, must have made his Philhellenism widely known. And finally, the Jews of Judaea in this period believed that

---

[1] *Ant.* XVI, 10. 1., also *Bell. Jud.* I, 26. 4.

[2] *Ant.* and *Bell. Jud.*, *ibid.*   [3] *Ibid.*

[4] δὶς γοῦν ἐπὶ Καίσαρος κατηγορηθεὶς ἐπὶ τῷ στάσεως ἐμπλῆσαι τὴν Ἀχαίαν καὶ περιδύειν τὰς πόλεις (*Bell. Jud.* I, 26. 4). There is no authority other than the Roman government which could be deprived of the cities, hence the στάσις in question must be revolt from Rome rather than civil strife in the separate cities concerned. Strabo's allusion (*cf.* above, p. 170, n. 5: νεωστὶ δ'Εὐρυκλῆς αὐτοὺς ἐτάραξεν) is in accordance with this interpretation.

[5] *Cf.* C.A.H. Vol. X, pp. 330 f.

[6] Joseph. *Bell. Jud.* I, 21. 11. Josephus' list of Herod's benefactions to Greek cities is confirmed by inscriptions in the case of Athens (I.G. III, 550, 551) and Berytus (*C.R. Acad. Inscr.* 1927, p. 243) so there is no reason to doubt it in the case of Sparta.

[7] C.A.H. Vol. X, p. 329.

special ties of kinship, of great antiquity, united them to Sparta. For although modern scholars are inclined to reject as a forgery the document in I *Maccabees* which purports to record a treaty of friendship concluded on this basis between the Jews and Sparta about 145 B.C.,[1] Josephus records this same document in perfect good faith ;[2] evidently then Jewish readers of I *Maccabees* regarded the treaty as genuine and the kinship with Sparta as an established fact. Josephus accordingly thinks it perfectly natural that a close friendship should spring up between Herod and his distinguished Spartan visitor, on account of the state from which he came.[3]

It remains to show that this story of Josephus, which assumes that Eurykles at the time of his visit to Sparta was still merely a distinguished citizen of Sparta, and implies that he was never permitted by Augustus to make himself tyrant there, is not only credible in itself, but is also in accordance with the other evidence at our disposal. The first question to be considered is whether it conflicts with Strabo's account, which is two generations earlier than that of Josephus, and contemporary with Eurykles himself. This at first sight appears to be the case ; we have already seen that Strabo's references to Eurykles himself as ἡγεμών, and to his ἀρχή and ἐπιστασία,[4] have been interpreted as evidence that Eurykles held a recognised position at Sparta, as local prince or despot under the authority of Augustus.[5] But it should be observed that Strabo describes Eurykles as *aiming at*, but not necessarily acquiring, ἐπιστασία over the Spartans (δόξας ἀποχρήσασθαι τῇ Καίσαρος φιλίᾳ πέρα τοῦ μετρίου πρὸς τὴν ἐπιστασίαν αὐτῶν), a statement which may well correspond to Josephus' description of Eurykles at the time of his visit to Judaea as πόθῳ χρημάτων εἰς τὴν βασιλείαν προσφθαρείς. The statement of Josephus might literally be interpreted to

---

[1] I *Macc.* 12. 6–18. A summary of recent views on this and similar documents in the books of *Maccabees* will be found in C.A.H. Vol. VIII, pp. 710 ff.   [2] Joseph. *Ant. Jud.* XIII, 5. 8.

[3] *Id. Bell. Jud.* I, 26. 1 : καὶ γὰρ ὁ βασιλεὺς διὰ τὴν πατρίδα, καὶ πάντες οἱ περὶ αὐτὸν ἡδέως προετίμων τὸν Σπαρτιάτην. The emphasis with which Josephus here refers to Eurykles as ' the Spartan ' strongly suggests that τὴν πατρίδα refers to Sparta in particular rather than Greece in general

[4] *Cf.* above, p. 170, n. 5.

[5] See the authorities cited above, p. 169, n. 1.

mean that Eurykles had hopes of reviving the kingship
at Sparta, with himself (as a descendant of one of the royal
families) as the first king. With regard to the position
which he actually did succeed in attaining, it would be rash
to base any conclusions on the meaning of a word so vague
as ἀρχή, which may signify anything from an annual office
to the despotic rule of a tyrant : [1] if Strabo means that
Eurykles actually made himself *for a short time* [2] supreme
at Sparta, this is not inconsistent with Josephus' account.

As to the meaning of ἡγεμών in this context, an example
of its application to a client prince has yet to be discovered,
and Strabo himself refers to these as βασιλεῖς, δυνασταί,
and in one case as τύραννος.[3] What is more, the history
of the word ἡγεμών, and the general manner of its use in
Strabo's time, are against the view that Strabo intended
by it in Eurykles' case an autocratic ruler. It commonly
meant in Strabo's time, and for several centuries before and
after him, any army commander ; usually the commander-
in-chief,[4] but not necessarily so.[5] It would not be going
too far to say that ἡγεμών was the exact equivalent in the
Hellenistic period of στρατηγός.[6] Since Eurykles was
probably the commander of the only contingent at Actium
from the province of Achaea which fought on the side of
Octavian, and was in any case conspicuous in the fighting
as some sort of commander,[7] Strabo might well refer to him

[1] Herod. V, 59. 6, uses it of the rule of Peisistratus, Thuc. VI, 54. 5,
55. 1, 2 of the rule of Hippias.   [2] He says ἐπαύσατο δ' ἡ ἀρχὴ ταχέως.
[3] Strabo XIV, 658, referring to the dynast Nicias of Cos.
[4] For Strabo's time, *cf.* Dion. Hal. V, 60 (of a Roman general in the
early wars with the Latins, contrasting his behaviour with οἱ καθ' ἡμᾶς
ἡγεμόνες) ; *ibid.* V, 61 (of the generals of the Latins at war with Rome).
[5] *Cf.* Plut. *Pyrrhus*, 29 (of the captains in the army of Pyrrhus invading
Laconia), also the Spartan metrical inscription (I.G. V, i, 724 : τόνδε
ποτὲ Σπάρτα Βότριχον, ξένε, πολλὸν ἄριστον | ἀνδρῶν αἰχμητᾶν ἔτρεφεν
ἀγεμόνα),
[6] Hence the common use of ἡγεμών as the title of Roman provincial
governors, as an alternative to στρατηγός. In a dedication at Delos
commemorated in B.C.H. VI, p. 36, no. 68 (ὑπέρθυρον ἦν ἀνέθηκαν Ἀχαιοὶ
καὶ ὁ ἡγεμὼν Θεόξενος), the word is evidently used of the Strategos of the
Achaean League, since a prominent official in the League is clearly indicated, and the title ἡγεμών is not otherwise known as an official title in
its organisation.
[7] There is reason to doubt the position of a mere captain of a pirate
vessel ascribed to Eurykles in the anecdote related by Plutarch. *Ant.* 67,
since in his list of the allies of Octavian (*ibid.* 61) Plutarch omits to notice
that Sparta took the opposite side from all the rest of Achaea and joined

as ' the Spartan general '—(or he may mean merely ' the Spartan army captain ')—' of our own time ' (ὁ καθ' ἡμᾶς Λακεδαιμονίων ἡγεμών) for this reason alone. But there is admittedly a certain ambiguity in the use of the word ἡγεμών to describe a prominent Spartan, since this title was apparently used, at least from the early fourth century, of the Spartan kings in their capacity as commanders-in-chief of the army ;[1] ἡγεμών in this sense appears to take the place of the earlier ἀρχαγέτης,[2] and that it was commonly so used is indicated by Appian's curious statement that Spartan kings (βασιλεῖς) were in command at the battle of Pharsalus,[3] it being a well-known fact that the kingship at Sparta came to an end a century and a half before that time. Appian was presumably confused by the word ἡγεμόνες in one of his sources.

That Eurykles himself liked to be referred to as ἡγεμών and welcomed the ambiguity inherent in the title is not impossible ; it has been pointed out that this is consistent with Josephus' account of his career, and it is not inconsistent with that of Strabo, which undoubtedly implies that he was aiming to acquire some sort of supremacy at Sparta. What might at first sight appear to be discrepant with Strabo's account is Josephus' statement that the actual charge brought against Eurykles was one of treason against the Roman Empire, of attempting to detach the cities of Achaea from their allegiance to Rome.[4] But there is no real discrepancy here. For it must be remembered that Sparta was a *civitas libera*, and that with the internal affairs of such states the emperors made it their policy to abstain from interference.[5] If, therefore, certain elements

Octavian (*cf.* Paus. IV, 31. 1, 2). Eurykles had a personal grudge against Antony which would explain his temporary adoption of a new role in the hope of being personally responsible for Antony's death ; but he enjoyed the favour of Augustus after Actium to so marked an extent (*cf.* above, pp. 170 f., below, p. 179) that he must surely have commanded the Spartan contingent in that campaign.

[1] [Xen.] *Resp. Lac.* XI, 9 ; *cf.* XIII, 6 ; Arist. *Pol.* III, 14. 3.
[2] *Cf.* the oracle quoted in Plut. *Lycurg.* 6.
[3] App. *B. C.* II, 70.　　　　[4] *Cf.* above, p. 175, n. 4.
[5] *Cf.* Pliny, *Ep.* VIII, 24. There can be no doubt that this policy dates from the reign of Augustus, since the Roman administrative machinery was then far less developed than it was a century later, and to devolve responsibilities upon *civitates liberae* was therefore even more desirable than in the later period.

in Sparta wished to enlist the support of Augustus in bringing about the overthrow of a man whom they suspected of trying to acquire too much power in the Spartan state (as Strabo implies), they would have to show that the interests of Rome were threatened, not merely those of Sparta. Otherwise they would certainly have been told to settle their own internal quarrels.

An anecdote related by Plutarch reveals that the spokesman of the actual accusers, on one of the two occasions when Eurykles was arraigned before Augustus,[1] was a representative of another family of the Spartan aristocracy,[2] and no doubt it was this class, jealous of Eurykles' great wealth and personal influence, who were chiefly anxious to overthrow him. The anecdote shows that Augustus, although he showed great patience and forbearance with the accusers, nevertheless made it clear that he considered their allegations to be trifling and unfounded.[3] The only conceivable support for them which can be found in the surviving non-literary evidence lies in the extent of Eurykles' benefactions in various cities of Achaea. The case of Gytheum, where Eurykles' generosity led to the establishment of the *Eurykleia*, has already been noticed.[4] The same inscription calls him εὐεργέτης of the whole League of Free Laconians as well as of Gytheum.[5] An inscription from Asopus in Laconia, where Eurykles was rewarded with the title εὐεργέτης for his generous bequest for the purpose of supplying the gymnasium with oil,[6] provides

[1] Cf. above, p. 175, n. 4.
[2] A descendant of Brasidas (cf. Plut. Reg. et Imperat. Apopthegm. Augustus, 14). The high position of this family at Sparta under the Principate is revealed by the inscriptions (cf. I.G. V, i, , p. 131).
[3] Plut. ibid. The accuser is reported as saying εἰ ταῦτά σοι, Καῖσαρ, οὐ φαίνεται μεγάλα, κέλευσον αὐτὸν ἀποδοῦναί μοι Θουκυδίδου τὴν ἑβδόμην. Augustus was at first angry at this impertinence and ordered the offending descendant of Brasidas to be removed from his presence in custody, but on learning of his distinguished descent, recalled him and allowed him to go free with a mild rebuke. The point of the allusion to Thucydides is not clear, but it possibly referred to the disastrous consequences for Athens which followed from disregarding at first as of no importance the arrival in Sicily of the Spartan Gylippus with his four ships (cf. Thuc. VII, 3 f.; VI, 104). It is at all events clear from the anecdote that Augustus regarded the allegations against Eurykles as without foundation.
[4] Cf. above, p. 171.
[5] εὐεργέτου τοῦ ἔθνους καὶ τῆς πόλεως ἡμῶν ἐν πολλοῖς γενομένου.
[6] I.G. V, i, 970. This bequest started a hereditary connection with Asopus, cf. ibid. 971, referring to a descendant, C. Julius Eurykles Herklanos

180 ANCIENT SPARTA

a further illustration of this. Nor did he forget the Roman business men in Laconia, who record their gratitude in a recently discovered bilingual inscription from Gytheum,[1] evidently from the base of a lost statue of Eurykles. Further afield, Corinth had Eurykles to thank for magnificent baths, decorated with Laconian marble ;[2] Athens set up statues of him and of his son Deximachus.[3]

All this lavish generosity might suggest to the suspicious that Eurykles, to use the expression of Josephus, was ' using his ill-gotten gains for equally discreditable ends '. But Augustus had not the same reasons for dislike and suspicion as had the prominent Jews with whom Eurykles came into contact in Judaea, or the prominent Spartans who resented the greater prominence and prosperity of Eurykles. Similar widespread benefactions were perhaps used to prefer a charge of treason against Herodes Atticus,[4] but there can be little doubt that Augustus, like Marcus Aurelius, and less jaundiced than Eurykles' enemies, remembering also his services at Actium and perhaps those of his father Lachares before him,[5] dismissed the accusations as ungrounded when Eurykles was first arraigned before him.

On the other hand, the attack made upon Eurykles by the members of other prominent families in Sparta was evidently successful in bringing about his exile from his native city. Josephus says simply φυγαδεύεται,[6] leaving it uncertain whether the sentence of banishment was imposed by Augustus or by the Spartans. The fact that Sparta was a *civitas libera*, and the continued honour in which Eurykles was permitted by Augustus to be held at Gytheum [7] and probably at Asopus also,[8] constitute strong

---

[1] Kornemann, *op. cit.* p. 6 : C. *Iulium Lacharis f. Euruclem cives Romani in Laconica qui habitant negotiantur benefici ergo.* Γάϊον Ἰούλιον Λαχάρους υἱὸν Εὐρυκλέα Ῥωμαῖοι οἱ ἐν ταῖς πόλεσιν τῆς Λακωνικῆς πραγματευόμενοι τὸν αὐτῶν εὐεργέτην.

[2] Paus. II, 3. 5 : τὸ δὲ ὀνομαστότατον αὐτῶν (*sc.* of the baths in Corinth) πλησίον τοῦ Ποσειδῶνος. τοῦτο δὲ Εὐρυκλῆς ἐποίησεν, ἀνὴρ Σπαρτιάτης, λίθοις κοσμήσας καὶ ἄλλοις καὶ ὃν ἐν Κροκεαῖς χώρας τῆς Λακωνικῆς ὀρύσσουσιν.

[3] Ditt. *Syll.*[3] 787, 788.   [4] *Cf.* P.I.R.[2] II, p. 178.

[5] Lachares had been put to death by Antony for ' piracy ' (Plut. *Ant.* 67) ; which may well mean that he had been interfering on Octavian's behalf with the transport of troops and supplies from Italy for use by Antony.   [6] Josephus, *B.J.* I, 26. 4.

[7] *Cf.* above, p. 171.   [8] *Cf.* above, p. 179, n. 6.

reasons for supposing that the sentence of exile was pronounced by the Spartans themselves, not by the emperor.[1] However, since Eurykles was a Roman citizen, he presumably had the right of appeal to the emperor,[2] and it is therefore to be presumed that Augustus confirmed the sentence for reasons of policy, though probably with regret, in view of his personal confidence in Eurykles. The confirmation of the Spartan sentence of exile would account for the second occasion on which Eurykles, according to Josephus, was arraigned before Augustus.

It was no doubt the emperor's influence which prevented the sentence of banishment from being extended to Eurykles' son Lakon, whose own downfall was postponed until late in the reign of Tiberius.[3] Moreover, Lakon and his son continued until that time in full enjoyment of the family property at Sparta,[4] so that Eurykles cannot have had his property confiscated when he was sent into exile.

It would not be difficult for Eurykles' enemies at Sparta, once they gained the upper hand, to find plausible reasons for imposing sentence of exile upon him in accordance with their own laws. An alleged attempt to make himself tyrant would be enough, even if it had not succeeded, for a tyranny was obviously incompatible with the existing constitution.[5] Mere lavish display of wealth might in itself be enough, in view of its supposed tendency to corrupt the citizens, to justify sentence of exile.[6] But fear of Augustus' displeasure, in view of his known personal friendship with Eurykles, must have made Eurykles' enemies anxious to

---

[1] The *Eurykleia* at Sparta (*cf.* I.G. V, i, 71, 86, etc.), if founded in honour of the first Eurykles, constitute a difficulty whether his exile is attributed to the emperor or to the Spartans themselves. Since none of the dateable inscriptions referring to these games can be put earlier than the middle of the second century A.D., it is not improbable that the Spartan Eurykleia were founded in honour of C. Iulius Eurykles Herklanos, on whom see further below, pp. 188 ff.

[2] Although the evidence about the status of Roman citizens in *civitates liberae* is in general inconclusive (*cf.* Mommsen, *Droit Public Romain*, VI, ii, pp. 334 ff.), for Sparta at least their right of appeal to the emperor is attested by I.G. V, i, 21, for which see above, p. 55.

[3] Tac. *Ann.* VI, 18. See further below, pp. 182 ff.

[4] See further below, p. 182.

[5] *I.e.* with the Republican constitution maintained under the protection of Rome, *cf.* Chap. I, p. 51.

[6] *Cf.* (Xen.) *Resp. Lac.* VII, 6 ; Plut. *Lys.* 19 (444A).

shift the responsibility for his ejection from themselves to the emperor, if they could do so. Only when this expedient failed did they take the more risky alternative.

Eurykles' son Lakon seems to have saved himself from a similar fate by studiously avoiding any suspicion of being at all friendly with the emperor.[1] It may incidentally be pointed out that Strabo in commenting upon this must be writing of the reign of Augustus, for Tiberius is most unlikely to have tolerated overtures of personal friendliness from any of his subjects, however distinguished in their own province. In any case Strabo could not foresee developments which might occur after about A.D. 19.

It would appear that the enemies of the family at Sparta made a more successful attack upon Eurykles' son Lakon and grandson Argolicus in the reign of Tiberius. Relating the events of the year A.D. 33, Tacitus says that Tiberius at that time sent into exile Pompeia Macrina the wife of Argolicus, Argolicus himself and his father Lakon having been 'afflicted' by the emperor previously.[2] Tacitus does not say what form their punishment took, but since Lakon and a son Spartiaticus are later found still alive and still wealthy,[3] it is to be supposed that Tiberius 'afflicted' them only with one of the milder forms of exile. Nor does Tacitus mention the date of their punishment, but the exile of Pompeia Macrina was presumably connected with it and took place not long afterwards, so that it is reasonable to connect the accusations brought against these two 'primores Achaeorum', as Tacitus calls them, with the widespread trials and persecutions which followed the discovery of the conspiracy of Sejanus.[4] Tiberius had a particular reason for being nervous about the allegiance of the cities of Achaea at this time, for immediately after the death of Sejanus an impostor claiming to be Germanicus' son Drusus had appeared in southern Greece, and had been received with great excitement and acclama-

[1] Cf. above, p. 170, n. 5.
[2] Tac. Ann. VI, 18 : etiam in Pompeiam Macrinam exilium statuitur, cuius maritum Argolicum socerum Laconem e primoribus Achaeorum Caesar adflixerat.
[3] See below, pp. 186 f., on the τρυφή of Spartiaticus before his exile, and for the wealth of both men when in exile in Corinth, the inscriptions cited below, p. 183, n. 6, init. [4] Tac. Ann. VI, 3–9, 14, 18 ff.

tion wherever he went.[1] It was no doubt unfortunate for Lakon and Argolicus that several of the towns of the Free Laconians, where the family of Eurykles was very popular,[2] were also great admirers of Germanicus ;[3] it might also be thought suspicious that Lakon was a friend and benefactor of a distinguished citizen of Pisa, the son of a man who had set up a statue of Germanicus at Olympia.[4] Since Tiberius, not unnaturally, was at this particular time at his most suspicious, it was a favourable moment which any enemies of Lakon in Sparta could easily turn to account to bring about his downfall.[5] Whether the emperor believed the accusations for long, or how long Lakon was in exile from Sparta, is not known ; both Lakon and his son Spartiaticus appear to have settled not long afterwards in the Roman colony of Corinth, where they both had distinguished municipal careers which cannot have been until after their reinstatement by the emperor, and must have begun either during the reign of Gaius or even before the death of Tiberius.[6]

---

[1] Tac. *Ann.* V, 10 (Ed. Fisher, Oxford Text).　　[2] *Cf.* above, p. 179.

[3] *Cf.* I.G. V, i, 1411 (Asine), 1394 (Corone). The honours paid to Germanicus at Gytheum (*cf.* above, p. 171) need imply no more than flattery of the imperial family in general.

[4] Ditt. *Syll.*[3], 792.

[5] Tacitus implies that Tiberius was prone to believe false accusations at this time (*cf. Ann.* VI, 9 : *sive ficto habita fides*).

[6] *Cf.* the two Latin inscriptions from Corinth, A.J.A. XXX (1926), pp. 389 ff. (1) *Ti. Claudi. Caesar. Aug. Germanici. Procurator. C. Iulio. C. f. Fab. Laconi. Augur. Agonothet. Isthm. et Caesareon. II vir. Quinq. Cur. Fla. Aug. Cydichus. Simonis. Thisbeus. b.m.* (2) *C. Iulio. Laconis. f. Euryclis. n. Fab. Spartiati[co]. Procuratori. Caesaris. et. Augustae. Agrippinae. Trib. Mil. equo. p[ub]. [ex]ornato. a. Divo. Claudio. Flam. Divi. Iuli. Pontif. II vir. Quinq. iter. Agonotheti. Isthmion. et Caesa(reon). [S]ebasteon. Archieri. Domus. Aug. [in]. perpetuum. Primo. Achaeon [. . .] ob. virtutem. eius. et. animosam. [fusi]ssimamque. erga. domum. divinam. et. erga. coloniam. nostr. munificentiam. Tribules. tribu. Calpurnia. patrono.* The second inscription almost certainly belongs to the period 54–59, when Agrippina was still alive. Claudius is less likely than Nero to have been referred to as ' Caesar ' ; the probability is that Spartiaticus held under Nero the same procuratorship as his father had held (*cf.* the first inscription) under Claudius, and that both were in charge of imperial estates in Achaea.

The approximate dates of their municipal offices may be deduced from the fact that II viri (Quinquennales) in Roman colonies had to take the municipal census at the same time as the census was taken in Rome ; *cf.* I.L.S. 6085 (*Lex Iulia Municipalis*), ll. 142 ff. Caesar's law applies specifically only to Italy, but was presumably extended also to colonies in the provinces, otherwise great confusion would arise. The taking of

In the reign of Claudius, Lakon is found holding an equestrian procuratorship, presumably in charge of imperial estates in the province of Achaea,[1] and his son Spartiaticus, later to hold a similar post under Nero,[2] was given the *equus publicus* by the emperor.[3] Before the discovery of the Latin inscriptions from Corinth which record these appointments, Lakon was universally thought to have been reinstated by Claudius and installed as local prince of Sparta, in the position which his father Eurykles is thought to have held before him. The coins of Claudius' reign with the inscription ἐπὶ Λάκωνος were thought to be sufficient proof of this.[4] It has been suggested that the

the census in Corinth during the reign of Claudius must therefore have fallen in 43, 48 (censorship of Claudius himself) and 53, and in the reign of Nero in 58 and 63. Since after being II vir Quinq. Lakon held two more municipal offices still under Claudius, he must have been II vir Quinq. either in 43 or in 48. Since after being II vir Quinq. iter. Spartiaticus held one more municipal office (Agonothetes), followed probably by the election as *archiereus* in the Achaean League, before 59 (in view of the date of inscr. 2 above), he cannot have been II vir Quinq. iter. later than 53. Since it may be regarded as certain that Lakon and Spartiaticus were not elected II viri Quinquennales for the same year ; and since in view of his own age (see further below, pp. 185 f.) as well as of his age relatively to his son, Lakon is likely to have held the highest civil office at Corinth earlier than Spartiaticus, it is fairly certain that Lakon was II vir Quinq. in 43, and Spartiaticus II vir Quinq. for the first time in 48.

But already before becoming II vir Quinq. Lakon had held at least two other municipal offices, those of Flamen Aug. and Curio (note that in the two inscriptions under discussion, the municipal posts are mentioned respectively in inverse order and in the order in which they were held) ; and it is probable that he had also held the minor municipal offices of quaestor and aedile which are not mentioned at all in either inscription. The *cursus honorum* of Lakon and Spartiaticus at Corinth illustrate the close correspondence between the constitutions of the two Caesarian colonies of Corinth and Urso ; both have election by tribes instead of curiae, augurs, flamines, a patronus, II viri Quinquennales, etc. Since it was the rule at Urso that no one might be elected to any of these offices who was disqualified from becoming decurion (*cf*. I.L.S. 6087, *Lex Coloniae Genetivae Iuliae*, § CI ; *cf*. § CV) ; and since Caesar laid it down for all Roman colonies that no candidate should be accepted for the office of decurion ' who had been condemned by a criminal court at Rome, whereby his residence in Italy had been rendered unlawful ' (I.L.S. 6085, ' *Lex Iulia Municipalis* ', l. 118), it is clear that the verdict passed on Lakon and Spartiaticus about A.D. 32 had been reversed by Caligula, if not by Tiberius himself at the end of his reign.

[1] *Cf*. preceding note.

[2] *Cf*. inscription 2 cited above, p. 183, n. 6.   [3] *Ibid*.

[4] *Cf*. I.G. V, i, introd. p. xvi, *sub a*. A.D. 37. I am indebted to the kindness of Mrs. Shear for the following note upon an unpublished hoard of these coins in her possession : ' The hoard consists of two large groups

discovery that Lakon was a procurator of Claudius constitutes no difficulty for the generally accepted theory ; but in all the parallels, cited in support of this view, the petty princeling enjoys senatorial, not merely equestrian rank.[1] There could be very little dignity attached to the holding of a mere procuratorship of imperial estates, and moreover, the administrative work involved would seriously interfere with the management of a client kingdom, even a kingdom of the size of Sparta, which was not so very small after all.

If it be suggested that Lakon held his procuratorship only at the beginning of the reign of Claudius, as the first indication that he had been restored to the imperial favour, and was permitted to give it up later when he became prince of Sparta, a difficulty arises about his age. This point does not appear to have been considered in discussions about his ' Principate '. Yet it can be shown that Lakon was already some years over sixty when Claudius came to the throne, and even that eccentric emperor can scarcely have thought him likely to make a success of being local prince of Sparta at so advanced an age, especially seeing that he had a son who was obviously a more suitable candidate.

With regard to the age of Lakon, it must be remembered that his father Eurykles was already old enough to hold some sort of command at Actium, and since the traditional constitution was then in force, it seems reasonable to assume that he was at least thirty years old at the time.[2] His close personal friendship with Augustus is a further argument in favour of this view, since it would be easier to explain if the two men were of the same age. Lakon is not, therefore, likely to have been born much after

of coins, 217 of one type and 205 of another. The first group has on the obverse a variety of portraits of the Emperor Claudius with some form of the accompanying legend *ΤΙ. ΚΛΑΥΔΙΟΣ/ΣΕΒΑΣΤΟΣ*. On the reverse is represented a nude male figure, the Apollo Karneios, with the legend *ΛΑ ΕΠΙ ΛΑΚΩΝΟΣ*. In the second set of coins the obverse type is a Zeus head, supplemented more often than not by the letters *ΛΑ* in various arrangements about the heads. The reverses show the jugate heads of the Dioscuri with *ΛΑ ΕΠΙ ΛΑΚΩΝΟΣ* or simply *ΕΠΙ ΛΑΚΩΝΟΣ* in diverse positions.   [1] *Cf.* A.J.A. XXX, p. 398.
    [2] This being the age at which full citizenship was attained (*cf.* Plut. *Lycurg.* 25).

20 B.C. in view of the age of his father. But the age of his own son Spartiaticus shows that it is impossible that Lakon can have been born later than 20 B.C.

With regard to Spartiaticus, the Latin inscription concerning him from Corinth makes it possible to correct an erroneous deduction which has formerly been made from a passage of Musonius relating to his exile. Musonius is quoted as saying that the Spartan Spartiaticus was a conspicuous example of the benefits which might come from being exiled, since previous to his exile he had been for many years (ἀπο πολλοῦ) constantly suffering in his lungs on account of his idle and luxurious life, but his exile by putting an end to his luxurious life completely cured him.[1] The exile of Spartiaticus was naturally assumed from this passage to fall towards the end of his life, the *terminus ante quem* being A.D. 65, since Musonius was writing to encourage himself immediately after his own exile, which occurred in that year.[2] But the Latin inscription from Corinth shows that Spartiaticus was far from having had an idle and luxurious life from about the end of the reign of Tiberius ;[3] his long record of municipal posts in Corinth strongly suggests that his exile from Sparta, with its resulting reformation in his character, had already taken place at the time when he began to hold them. In fact no other alternative is possible, for if it be suggested that Spartiaticus, *after* his active career at Corinth and in the imperial service, suddenly took to a life of idleness at Sparta some time after A.D. 55 (the earliest possible date for the Corinth inscription) there was scarcely time for him to be ἀπὸ πολλοῦ τρυφῶν καὶ νοσηλευόμενος and also to be exiled before 65. On the other hand, the hypothesis that his τρυφή and ill-health belonged to the period *before* the Corinthian career makes a reasonable story ; like his father Lakon, who was particularly careful not to appear to be friendly with the

---

[1] *Ap.* Stobaeus, *Floril.* XL, 9 (Teubner) : καὶ ἴσμεν τινας χρονίων νοσημάτων ἐν τῷ φεύγειν ἀπολυθέντας, ὥσπερ ἀμέλει Σπαρτιατικὸς οὗτος ὁ Λακεδαιμόνιος, ὃς ἀπὸ πολλοῦ ἔχων τὸ πλευρὸν κακῶς κἀκ τούτου πολλάκις νοσῶν διὰ τὴν τρυφήν, ἐπειδὴ ἐπαύσατο τρυφῶν ἐπαύσατο καὶ νοσηλευόμενος. Musonius is evidently referring to Spartiaticus, son of Lakon, since he clearly implies that he was a well-known figure in Achaea, as the first provincial high-priest for life of the imperial family in Achaea (*cf.* above, p. 183, n. 6) would certainly be.

[2] Ditt. *Syll.*[3] 790, n. 1.   [3] *Cf.* above, p. 183, n. 6.

emperor, Spartiaticus would be anxious not to call down upon himself the fate of Eurykles by making himself conspicuous in public life at Sparta, and so would naturally avoid holding office there. The length of his municipal career at Corinth makes it probable that he was exiled from Sparta at the same time as his father, about A.D. 31 ; he would naturally not be mentioned in this connection by Tacitus, whose primary interest in mentioning the two Achaean nobles at all was the connection of the otherwise unknown Argolicus with Pompeia Macrina. A brother-in-law would be too distant a relative to deserve a mention. But if, as now seems likely, Spartiaticus was ἐκ πολλοῦ τρυφῶν καὶ νοσηλευόμενος in A.D. 31 or 32, he cannot have been much less than thirty years old at that time. It is therefore highly improbable that his father was born later than 20 B.C., and to draw the conclusion which chiefly interests us at the moment, Lakon must therefore have been already over sixty at the beginning of the reign of Claudius.

Even if Claudius the administrator may be imagined obtuse enough to attempt to impose an elderly estate agent upon the Spartans as their *Princeps*, Claudius the antiquarian is surely most unlikely to have so far flouted the traditions of a famous state which was a living monument of antiquity. It is true that he set up client kings once more in a few regions which had ceased to be client kingdoms before his reign, and if there were a strong case for believing that Sparta had actually been governed as a client kingdom under Augustus, Claudius might perhaps be supposed to have allowed his respect and admiration for Augustus to override his respect and admiration for ancient political institutions. But it has been shown that, apart from the possible evidence of the coins, no such strong case exists for Eurykles' supposed ' Principate ', and that the literary evidence even conflicts with it.

With regard to Lakon, the epigraphic evidence from Corinth makes his supposed ' Principate ' appear improbable to say the least, for it strongly suggests that Lakon and his son not only held offices in Corinth but actually resided there. Yet their Roman sentence of exile must already have been revoked not later than the beginning of the reign of Claudius, to permit of their both holding Roman public offices. A likely explanation of their failure to return to Sparta is that the sentence of exile imposed by Tiberius had been followed up by sentence of exile passed by the *libera civitas* itself,[1] involving, *inter alia*, the confiscation of such of the family estates as lay within Spartan territory.[2] The existence at Sparta in later times of a public official with the title of πράκτωρ τῶν ἀπὸ Εὐρυκλέους [3] fits in with this explanation, but would constitute a difficulty if we are to suppose that Eurykles' son became prince of Sparta under Claudius, since it appears to imply that the ancestral estates there had been sequestrated, and continued to be so after Lakon's lifetime.

In short, the final conclusion to which both the literary and the epigraphical evidence leads us is that neither Eurykles nor Lakon was installed as local prince of Sparta under the emperors. This conclusion appears to be directly contradicted by the evidence of the coins, with the legend ἐπὶ Εὐρυκλέους in the reign of Augustus, and ἐπὶ Λακῶνος in the reign of Claudius.[4] But it is unnecessary to assume that a contradiction is involved. For in the first place, the Lakon of the coins need not be the son of Eurykles ; and in the second place, the legends ἐπὶ Εὐρυκλέους and ἐπὶ Λακῶνος need not imply that either of these persons was local prince of Sparta.[5]

With regard to the identity of the Lakon of the coins, it is certain that another Lakon than the son of Eurykles son of Lachares was alive at Sparta in the reign of Claudius, and was of a suitable age to be the one referred to on the coins. This follows from the age of C. Julius Eurykles Herklanos L. Vibullius Pius, whose father was called Lakon, and who was still alive when Antinous died in A.D. 130,

---

[1] *Cf.* above, pp. 180 f.

[2] Estates lying outside Spartan territory, as for example, at Gytheum and Asopus (*cf.* above, p. 179) would, of course, not be affected, so that no difficulty arises about the *munificentia* of Lakon and Spartiaticus while domiciled at Corinth (*cf.* above, p. 183, n. 6).

[3] B.S.A. XXVI, p. 166, B9 (towards the end of Hadrian's reign, *cf.* *ibid.* pp. 188 f. for the dates of the Eponymoi concerned in this inscription). Woodward suggests that the revenues from the estates of Eurykles were devoted partly to the celebration of the Eurykleia, but *cf.* above, p. 181, n. 1.

[4] References above, p. 170, nn. 1 and 2.   [5] See further below, pp. 192 f.

but died soon afterwards.[1] Even if Herklanos was ninety years old at the time of his death, he must have been born not earlier than about A.D. 40, when Lakon son of Eurykles I was already sixty at least.[2] But there is good reason for thinking that the date of Herklanos' birth actually lay between the limits A.D. 60–70,[3] which would make it wholly impossible for him to be the son of the Lakon who was son of Eurykles I.

In addition to the chronological difficulty, there is the further difficulty concerning the confiscation by the Spartan state of the property in Spartan territory of the family of

[1] On the evidence of the inscription from Mantinea, Ditt. *Syll.*[3] 841.

[2] *Cf.* above, pp. 185 f.

[3] This conclusion rests upon Herklanos' connection with Pompeius Falco (P.I.R.[1] III, p. 134, n. 68) who bears all Herklanos' names (Vibullius Pius Julius Eurycles Herculanus), just as Herklanos himself bears the name of Vibullius Pius (*cf.* I.G. V, i, 380). Falco's son also bears the names of Herklanos (P.I.R. *ibid.* p. 70, n. 492), and the most likely explanation of the custom seems to be some sort of legal adoption, no doubt involving an inheritance of property. For this close tie to arise, Herklanos and the elder Falco must have come into close personal contact, and it is not difficult to discover, from what is known from inscriptions about their respective careers, how and when this contact took place. For the elder Falco, *cf.* P.I.R. *loc. cit.*: he was appointed military tribune of Legio X Fretensis in A.D. 97, then was quaestor, trib. pl., praetor peregrinus, legatus of Legio V Macedonica in the Dacian War of 101–103, legatus of Lycia and Pamphylia, legatus of Judaea and of Legio X Fretensis 107–109, consul suffectus *c.* 109, XV vir sacris faciundis, curator viae Traianae, legatus of Moesia Inferior from about 116, legatus of Britain *c.* 120–122, proconsul of Asia *c.* 128, and was still alive *c.* 140. The Roman career of Herklanos is given in I.G. V, i, 1172 (from Gytheum, in Greek) as quaestor pr. pr. of Achaea, trib. pl., praetor, legatus of Baetica, legatus of Legio III (not further specified). This point in his career must already have been reached before 115, the date of I.G. V, i, 380 (from Cythera), which gives him the additional name of L. Vibullius Pius, which he had evidently not yet acquired when *ibid.* no. 1172 was inscribed. He must therefore have come into contact with Pompeius Falco some time before 115. In view of Falco's *cursus*, this can scarcely have happened either when Herklanos was quaestor of Achaea or when he was legatus of Baetica ; the likely times are either when Herklanos was tribune and praetor in Rome, or when he was legatus of ' Legio III ', or at both these times, *i.e.* (in view of Falco's career) either in Rome between 98 and 100, or in Judaea 107–109, or both. Since Legio III Gallica was permanently stationed in Syria (*cf.* Ritterling's article in P.W. *s.v.*, *Legio*) at the time of Falco's governorship of Judaea and command of Legio X Fretensis, Herklanos not improbably met Falco as legatus of III Gallica (the other two Third Legions existing at this time are ruled out of account, III Cyrenaica because it was not at this period commanded by a legatus, and III Augusta because its commander held an independent position with propraetorian authority, and a Greek holder of the post would be unlikely to allow it to remain

Eurykles I.[1] These reasons make it impossible to suppose that Herklanos was the son of Eurykles' son Lakon I, and he must be supposed to be the son of some other Lakon. Two inscriptions from Laconia, in which Herklanos is called Γ. Ἰουλίου Λάκωνος υἱός, ἔκγονος Εὐρυκλέους,[2] present no objection to this view, since from them no definite conclusion can be drawn about the relationship of Herklanos to Eurykles I. The word ἔκγονος is ambiguous, meaning in various contexts ' descendant ', ' great-grandson ' or ' grandson '.[3] In the first case, the inscription may mean ' descendant of the well-known Eurykles ' (i.e. of the Eurykles noted for his benefactions in the reign of Augustus), but would imply that Herklanos was not the son of Lakon I. But if ἔκγονος means ' grandson ' in this context, then the name Eurykles becomes quite colourless, and may refer to some quite unknown member of the family. There were after all at least two other holders of the name at Sparta of whom we know something,[4] in addition to the Eurykles who was too friendly with Augustus.

Kolbe has distinguished from Lakon I, and has identified with the father of Herklanos, another Lakon (' Lakon II ') who was Patronomos himself and whose son, also called Lakon (' Lakon III '), and on this theory a brother of

unnoticed in an inscription about himself). The senatorial posts of the two men in Rome may also easily have coincided. With regard to their respective ages, it is likely that Herklanos, being a Greek, began his Roman career at rather a later age than Falco, and this supposition fits in with the fact that it was Herklanos who gave his name (and presumably the promise of a legacy) to Falco. Falco probably held his praetorship c. 100 at the lowest possible age (30) ; he is unlikely to have been more than c. 50 at the time of his appointment as governor of Britain c. 120, or more than 60 when he became proconsul of Asia c. 128. The later limit for Herklanos' birth is therefore somewhat before 70 ; the earlier limit is fixed by the nature of the two active but not senior military commands which followed his praetorship, beginning probably c. 102. He is not likely to have been much over 40 when appointed to the first of these ; the earlier limit of his birth therefore appears to have been c. A.D. 60. Evidence cited in connection with the entry of his Kasen into the Gerusia (p. 445, n. 38) makes the earlier limit more likely than a later date.

[1] Cf. above, p. 188.   [2] I.G. V, i, 971 (Asopus), 1172 (Gytheum).
[3] Cf. Liddell and Scott (ed. Stuart Jones), s.v. ἔκγονος. ' Descendant ' or ' great-grandson ' seem to be the only uses illustrated in the Spartan inscriptions.
[4] Namely, the C. Julius Eurykles Herklanos under discussion, and a younger C. Julius Eurykles who dedicated in the Paidikos Agon as Boagos (i.e. aged 20) c. A.D. 134 (I.G. V, i, 287).

Herklanos, on one occasion held the office of Patronomos as substitute for his father. That these Lakons were members of the same family as Herklanos is indicated by their Roman name of C. Julius,[1] but the date of the office of Lakon III as substitute-Patronomos cannot be so late as Kolbe suggests (reign of Trajan),[2] and in fact can hardly be later than the end of Vespasian's reign.[3] This date would be compatible with the view that Lakon II is to be identified with the man whose name appears on the coins of Claudius' reign, but makes it likely that his son Lakon III was the father of Eurykles Herklanos rather than (as suggested by Kolbe) his elder brother.

It may seem strange that an otherwise obscure Lakon, of whom there is very little to be said except that he was not improbably the grandfather of Eurykles Herklanos, and that he held the office of Patronomos, should have his

[1] Cf. I.G. V, i, 480.

[2] Ibid. 280, 281, 480. Woodward's suggestion of a date in the reign of Claudius rests presumably on the supposition that the elder Lakon of this pair is identical with the Lakon of the coins of Claudius' reign. Kolbe's rejection of this date as too early by half a century rests on the argument that Ti. Claudius Harmoneikos, who was gymnasiarch and of mature age in the second patronomate of Lakon (i.e. on Kolbe's view, the second patronomate of Lakon II, not of Lakon III), was a member of the Gerusia c. A.D. 100 and was still alive in Hadrian's reign (cf. I.G. V, i, 275 n. and the stemma, ibid. p. 131). This argument is fallacious for this reason: it now appears that there were two holders of the name of Ti. Claudius Harmoneikos, one a son of Pratoneikos (B.S.A. XXVI, p. 168, C6), the other, honoured as gymnasiarch in I.G. V, i, 485, a son of Pleistoxenos. The son of Pratoneikos was in the Gerusia some time in Trajan's reign (B.S.A. ibid. p. 192) and may or may not be identical with the Geron Ti. Claud. Harmoneikos of I.G. V, i, 97; but there is nothing to prevent us from identifying the son of Pleistoxenos with the substitute Patronomos of I.G. V, i, 275, and also with the gymnasiarch of 'the second patronomate of Lakon' (ibid. 480). I.G. V, i, 275 must be dated about A.D. 70 (cf. Appendix IV, § 8, under this year). But with regard to the more precise determination of the date of I.G. V, i, 280, when Lakon III was substitute-Patronomos for Lakon II, a point which seems hitherto to have escaped notice is that the Kasen Thrasybulus Callicratis f. who in that year dedicated in the Paidikos Agon was the contemporary within two or three years of two others, who were members of the Gerusia in the Patronomate of C. Julius Philokleidas c. A.D. 120 (I.G. V, i, 97; cf. Appendix IV, § 8, Chronological Note B). All three as Epheboi were Kasens of Enymantiadas; that they were contemporaries follows from the nature of the Kasen-relationship, discussed in Chap. III, esp. pp. 103 ff. In view of this, and of the indications for the age of Gerontes, the date of the patronomate of Lakon (III), acting for his father, was probably about A.D. 75. [3] See preceding note, ad fin.

name inscribed on considerable issues of coins covering
apparently the greater part of the reign of Claudius.[1]   What
makes these coins and their inscription ἐπὶ Λάκωνος appear
even more significant than would be the case in a state which
normally coined money is that Sparta in the first century
and a half of the Principate very rarely issued coins,[2] following in this respect the traditional Spartan policy of the pre-
Macedonian period.   In view of Claudius' policy of restoring
client princes elsewhere,[3] it would seem a natural inference
from these coins that the Lakon whose name they bear
was set up by that emperor as client prince of Sparta.
Similarly, *mutatis mutandis*, for Eurykles as far as his coins
are concerned ; yet it has been shown that there are very
serious if not unsurmountable difficulties in the way of
supposing that Eurykles was set up as client prince of
Sparta.

But is the inscription ἐπὶ Λάκωνος (or ἐπὶ Εὐρυκλέους)
in any case an indication of autocratic rule ? [4]   The coins
of known Greek tyrants and dynasts do not bear out this
supposition ; such rulers never appear to use the inscription
ἐπὶ with their name in the genitive, but use either their
name in the nominative without prefix, or more frequently,
their name in the genitive with or without the prefix βασιλέως.
This applies to Dion of Syracuse,[5] Hieron II [6] and his son
Gelon,[7] Euagoras I [8] of Cyprus, Maussolus of Caria and
his successors.[9]

---

[1] *Cf.* above, p. 184, n. 4.

[2] The only known Spartan issues of the period of the Principate before
Hadrian are copper coins with inscriptions of Eurykles or Lakon (A.O.
p. 395 ; *B.M. Cat. Pelop.* (Laconia), nos. 62–72).   From Hadrian onwards
almost every reign is represented until the middle of the third century,
the change being evidently due to Imperial rather than to Spartan policy,
since it occurs also in the history of other Greek coinages from Hadrian
onwards.   Though few Roman coins of any part of this period, and none
between Hadrian and Trebonianus Gallus, have survived on the Orthia
site (A.O. p. 396) it is evident that they were in fact in circulation in
Sparta during that time (*cf.* above, p. 55).   [3] *Cf.* C.A.H. X, pp. 752 f.

[4] As is assumed in *B.M. Cat. Pelop.* Introd. p. 1 : ' It is observable
that these names (*i.e.* of Eurykles and Lakon) alone, among those of
Spartan magistrates, are preceded by the preposition ἐπί, a fact indicating
that their rule in Laconia was of a different and more absolute nature
than that of other magistrates '.

[5] *Cf.* Head, H.N².   (1911), p. 430.   The attribution to the Syracusan
Dion is not certain.

[6] *B.M. Cat. Coins (Sicily)*, pp. 208 f.   [7] *Ibid.* pp. 210 f.

[8] *Ibid.* (*Cyprus*), pp. 56 f.   [9] *Ibid.* (*Caria and Islands*), p. 181.

It may be objected that all these were independent rulers, while Eurykles must in any case have recognised his dependence on Augustus. But there is no parallel for the ἐπὶ Εὐρυκλέος inscription on the coins of any of the semi-independent dynasts of the last century B.C. or of the reign of Augustus. The coins of Aristion, tyrant of Athens set up by the general of Mithridates VI in 88 B.C.,[1] have the name and title of king Mithridates and the simple nominative ' Aristion ' on the reverse.[2] Similarly, Nikias of Cos, apparently an older contemporary of Eurykles,[3] inscribed his name in the nominative on the obverse of his coins, if indeed the coin ascribed to him is genuine.[4] The ' high priest and dynast ' of Olba in Cilicia, during the second triumvirate and in the reign of Augustus, inscribes his name and official titles on his coins in the genitive,[5] but the preposition ἐπί does not occur.

In fact the use of ἐπί in coin inscriptions seems to indicate a position the reverse of autocratic. In all periods we find it used of the ordinary magistrates in the Greek towns,[6] and from the reign of Augustus onwards Greek coins are frequently inscribed in this way in order to date them by the Roman governor of the province.[7]

Turning to Sparta, we find ἐπὶ τοῦ δεῖνος employed in the way common throughout Greece, as a means of dating inscriptions on stone by the eponymous magistrate of the year, who at Sparta at this period was the Patronomos. But the coins bearing the names of Eurykles and Lakon are evidently not to be so explained, in view of the strong reasons for thinking that the coins in question, at least so far as those of Lakon are concerned, cover a fairly long

---

[1] C.A.H. IX, p. 244.   [2] Eckhel, Vol. II, p. 219.
[3] Cf. above, p. 177, n. 3.   [4] Cf. Eckhel, II, p. 601.
[5] ἀρχιερέως καὶ δυνάστου (Eckhel, III, pp. 62–64) ; cf. Strabo, XIV 5. 10 (672).
[6] E.g. at Nicomedeia in Bithynia, Mytilene, Apollonia in Ionia, Clazomenae, Smyrna, Priene, Magnesia on the Maeander (cf. Eckhel, II, pp. 431, 506, 509, 511, 516, 519, 528, 529, 554–558). The magistracies represented are ἄρχων, στρατηγός, γραμματεύς, and at Clazomenae ἡγεμών. (The last-named seems to be unique as the name of a magistracy.) All these coins belong to the period of the Principate.
[7] E.g. the coinage of the towns of Ionia (Eckhel, II, 519, 555–558), Bithynia (ibid. 400 ff.), Crete (ibid. 300–303). The inscription is sometimes ἐπὶ ἀνθυπάτου - -, sometimes the name of the governor alone is mentioned (as ἐπὶ Κορνηλίου Λύπου) without his title.

series of years.[1] There is, however, an alternative possibility, that the life-priesthood of Augustus was the office referred to in these two cases. Nor is this a mere hypothesis ; in setting up a statue of the emperor Trajan in A.D. 115 the city of Sparta [2] has it commemorated in the inscription that the statue was dedicated ἐπὶ ἀρχιερέος διὰ βίου τῶν Σεβαστῶν . . . Γ. Ἰουλίου Εὐρυκλέους Ἡρκλανοῦ,[3] in the life-high-priesthood of the emperors of C. Jul. Eurykles Herklanos, whom we have reason to identify as the grandson of the Lakon whose name is inscribed upon the coins of Claudius. Moreover, it is known that Eurykles Herklanos was the son and grandson of high priests for life of the emperors,[4] so that the Lakon of the coins, if he was the grandfather of Herklanos, was certainly also high priest for life of the emperors. If it was appropriate to mention the name of the high priest of the emperors in setting up a statue of an emperor, it was equally appropriate to do so in issuing a series of coins stamped with the emperor's head ; in fact, it seems not too much to say that, but for preconceived notions about the 'tyranny' of Eurykles I, this explanation would long ago have occurred to historians, for parallels are not lacking from other Greek cities for the dating of the local issues of coins by the high priest for life of the emperors.[5]

[1] Cf. above, p. 184, n. 4.

[2] The inscription (I.G. V, i, 380) appears to have been found in Cythera, but this island belonged to Sparta at the time (cf. p. 56, n. 4) and the πόλις referred to must certainly be Sparta.

[3] I.G. V, i, 380 ; cf. ibid. 971, 1172.

[4] Ibid 971 : ἀρχιερέα διὰ βίου τῶν Σεβαστῶν ἀπὸ προγόνων.

[5] Cf. Eckhel, III, p. 149 (Cotiaeum, Phrygia), ἐπὶ Γ. Ἰού. Ποντικοῦ Ἀρχιερε. (coin of Macrinus) and ἐπὶ Γ. Ἰού. Ποντικοῦ Ἀρχιερέως (coin of Philip senior) ; it is clear that C. Julius Ponticus must have had a life-high-priesthood ; whether a life office is referred to or not remains uncertain in the examples from Apamea (Phrygia), Eckhel, III, pp. 133, 141, ἐπὶ Μ. Αὐρ.Ἀλεξάνδρου Β. (or Βελ ? = βελτίστου) ἀρχι. Ἀπαμέων, on coins of the two Philips, father and son ; also ibid. III, p. 147 (from Cidyessus, Phrygia, coin of Domitian), ἐπὶ Φλαουίου Πιναρίου Ἀρχιερέως ; and ibid. II, p. 437 (Cius, Bithynia, coin of Domitian and Domitia), ἐπὶ ἀρχιερέως Κλαυδ. Βίαντος Κιάνων. Dating by the life-priesthood (not high-priesthood) of the emperor appears for certain on coins of Pergamum in the reign of Commodus (cf. Eckhel, II, p. 471 : ἐπὶ Αὐρ. Κελ. ἱερέως διὰ βίου τῶν Σεβ. Περγαμηνῶν ; coins of Augustus from Pergamum inscribed Μ. Φούριος ἱερεύς may possibly belong to this class, cf. Eckhel, ibid.) ; also on coins of Perperene (ibid. p. 475, reign of M. Aurelius : ἐπὶ . . . ἱερέως διὰ βίου τῶ. Σεβ. Γλύκωνος).

The only missing link which might lead us to hesitate in accepting this theory is that we do not know for certain that Eurykles I was high priest of Augustus at Sparta, since there are reasons for rejecting the supposition that Eurykles Herklanos, who calls himself ἀρχιερεὺς διὰ βίου τῶν Σεβαστῶν ἀπὸ προγόνων [1] was the grandson of Eurykles I, or was even directly descended from him.[2] There are, however, other indications which make it extremely probable that Eurykles I held this position. The letter of Tiberius to the free-Laconian town of Gytheum, already referred to,[3] shows that both Eurykles I and Lakon I were very closely connected with the imperial cult there, and were sufficiently distinguished in that connection to be commemorated in the games established in honour of the imperial family. It is not known that the imperial cult already existed at Sparta in the reign of Augustus, but since there was already a Καισαρεῖον at Gytheum before Augustus' death,[4] it is unlikely that the much more important metropolis of Sparta would allow itself to be eclipsed in this respect.[5] Eurykles was a very likely candidate for the high priesthood, in view of his distinguished descent,[6] his great wealth, and his close friendship with Augustus. Finally, the choice of his grandson Spartiaticus (son of Lakon I) as the first high priest of the emperors for the province of Achaea [7] suggests that there was already existing in the family the tradition of holding the same office in a more limited sphere.

It has been pointed out that the coins inscribed ἐπὶ Εὐρυκλέους apparently belong to an early period of Augustus' reign,[8] but this circumstance presents no difficulty to the view that Eurykles' name appears on them because he was high priest for life of Augustus, for the cult was established at Pergamum and at Nicomedia as early as 29 B.C.,[9] and

---

[1] Cf. above, p. 194, n. 4.   [2] Cf. above, pp. 188 f.

[3] Cf. above, pp. 171 f.

[4] Cf. Kornemann, op. cit. (above, p. 169, n. 1), pp. 2 f.

[5] Cf. the rivalry displayed by the cities of Asia in applying for the right to have the temple for the imperial cult, Tac. Ann. IV, 55.

[6] Cf. p. 197, n. 5.   [7] Ditt. Syll.³ 790.   [8] Cf. above, p. 172, n. 2.

[9] Dio, 51. 20 ; Dio's statement that the cult at Pergamum was intended from the first as a cult for the whole province Asia is confirmed by an inscription (cf. Gardthausen, Augustus u. seine Zeit., Vol. II (1891), pp. 253 ff.).

Augustus may well have thought it desirable to lay the foundations of the worship of himself as soon as possible in those Hellenistic cities in which national feeling was likely to be strongest. Sparta was just as likely to be one of these as were the capitals of the Pergamene kingdom and of Bithynia.

It seems justifiable, therefore, to draw the general conclusion that the names of Eurykles (I) and Lakon (II) occur upon the Spartan coins not because they were tyrants of Sparta, but because they were high priests for life of the imperial cult. Whether Lakon I and Spartiaticus enjoyed the same distinction until their exile under Tiberius is not at present clear ; this depends upon the descent of Lakon II, whose father, and possibly grandfather also, were certainly high priests for life of the emperors, as we know from I.G. V, i, 971.[1]

Even though there are good reasons for thinking that Lakon II was not directly descended either from Lakon I or from Eurykles I,[2] indirect descent from Eurykles I seems to be proved by Eurykles Herklanos' description of himself as ἔκγονος Εὐρυκλέους,[3] for it has been shown to be virtually certain that Lakon II was the grandfather of Herklanos. Two potential forbears of Lakon II among the immediate descendants of Eurykles I are not open to the objections which rule out Lakon I and Spartiaticus. These are C. Julius Krateinos, of whom all that is known is that he was a son of Lakon I, and may or may not have shared his father's exile,[4] and C. Julius Deximachos, to whom the Athenians set up a statue, together with one of his father Eurykles I.[5] There are very good reasons, though not reasons which are immediately apparent, for believing that C. Julius Deximachos actually was the grandfather of Lakon II, and this assumption has been incorporated in the proposed family tree of the family of Eurykles set forth at the end of this chapter.

With regard to C. Julius Deximachos, the question which first requires to be answered is whether the Athenian inscription mentioned above refers to the same Deximachos

[1] Cf. above, p. 194.   [2] Cf. above, pp. 188 f.
[3] Cf. above, p. 190.
[4] Cf. I.G. V, ii, 541.   [5] Ditt. Syll.³ 788 ; cf. 787.

as appears in a list of a college of Agrippiastae from Sparta, dated 18–12 B.C.[1] It is obvious that if two different persons are the subject of these inscriptions, as Kolbe supposes,[2] they were both Spartans and they lived at the same time. An ostensible difficulty in regarding them as one and the same person is that the C. Julius Deximachos in the Athenian inscription is called ' son of Eurykles ', whereas C. Julius Deximachos who was senior member of the college of Agrippiastae appears to be called, according to the restoration in I.G. V, i, 374 (a bilingual inscription), ' son of Pratolaos '. But a serious difficulty in the way of this restoration is that it does not agree with the normal practice, either Latin or Greek, in the recording of names,[3] whereas under the assumption that Pratolaos here is the name not of the father but of the grandfather of Deximachos, it is possible to suppose that the normal procedure was followed.[4]

Another interesting fact which requires to be taken into account in this connection is that both Deximachos and Pratolaos are names otherwise unknown among the C. Julii of Sparta, but occurring several times among the P. Memmii. This may be seen from Kolbe's proposed tree,[5] covering the second half of the first, and the first three-quarters of the second century A.D.

[1] I.G. V, i, 374.
[2] Cf. I.G. V, i, 307 (proposed tree of Eurykles' family).
[3] In the Roman half of I.G. V, i, 374, the name appears as C. Julius [4 letter-spaces, Dexi]machus Pratola [- -], in the Greek half as Γά]ιος Ἰούλιος [5 letter-spaces, Δε]ξίμαχος Πρα[- -. If we suppose with Wilhelm that what is missing is the tribe-name only, it is possible to restore the appropriate tribe Fab. in the missing space of the Roman half (allowing a space for the stop as in the rest of the Roman part of the inscription), Φαβία in the corresponding gap in the Greek. But to put the tribe-name before the father's name is extremely rare if not unparalleled, and this is a strong objection to Wilhelm's theory.
[4] I.e. in the Roman half C. Julius [C. f. Dexi]machus Pratola[i n.], in the Greek half Γά]ιος, Ἰούλιος [Γα. υἱὸς (or Γ. υἱὸς) Δε]ξίμαχος Πρα[τολάου ἔκγονος (or υἱωνός)]. It may be noticed that the recording of a Roman tribe-name in Spartan inscriptions is extremely rare, occurring only in no. 533 in I.G. V, i.
[5] Cf. I.G. V, i, p. 117. There are several objections to this tree in detail ; e.g. P. M. Deximachus II, who is 42nd from the Dioscuri, is placed only a generation, or at most two generations later than C. Julius Eurykles Herklanos, who is 36th from the Dioscuri (I.G. V, i, 971), and the gap in age suggested between P. M. Pratolaos IV and P. M. Spartiaticus II, if they were brothers, seems unduly long. But these points do not affect the argument at present under discussion.

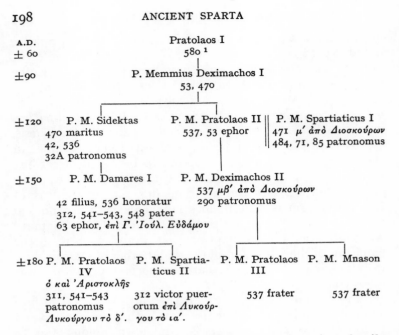

A.D.   Pratolaos I
± 60   580 [1]

±90   P. Memmius Deximachos I
                              53, 470

±120   P. M. Sidektas   P. M. Pratolaos II ‖ P. M. Spartiaticus I
          470 maritus   537, 53 ephor   ‖ 471 μ′ ἀπὸ Διοσκούρων
          42, 536   ‖ 484, 71, 85 patronomus
          32A patronomus

±150   P. M. Damares I   P. M. Deximachos II
                                   537 μβ′ ἀπὸ Διοσκούρων
          42 filius, 536 honoratur 290 patronomus
          312, 541–543, 548 pater
          63 ephor, ἐπὶ Γ. Ἰούλ. Εὐδάμου

±180 P. M. Pratolaos P. M. Spartia-   P. M. Pratolaos   P. M. Mnason
      IV   ticus II   III
      ὁ καὶ Ἀριστοκλῆς
      311, 541–543   312 victor puer-   537 frater   537 frater
      patronomus   orum ἐπὶ Λυκούρ-
      Λυκούργου τὸ δ′. γου τὸ ια′.

In addition, the same cycle of names appears in a family of the later first century B.C., reconstructed by Kolbe as follows :—[2]

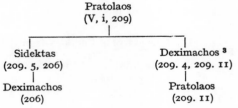

                    Pratolaos
                    (V, i, 209)

      Sidektas   Deximachos [3]
      (209. 5, 206)   (209. 4, 209. 11)
      Deximachos   Pratolaos
      (206)   (209. 11)

At this period the name of P. Memmius does not occur in Spartan inscriptions, and there is an overwhelming probability in favour of its having been introduced through P. Memmius Regulus, proconsul of Achaea about A.D. 35.[4] The persons named in the tree given above are therefore almost certainly members of the same family as their later

---

[1] These numbers refer to the inscriptions in I.G. V, i.

[2] Cf. I.G. V, i, 307.

[3] This Deximachos is identified by Kolbe (I.G. V, i, p. 307) with C. Julius Deximachos of ibid. no. 374, but no Roman name appears in either of the two inscriptions on which the tree cited above in the text is based.

[4] Cf. P.I.R¹. II, p. 364.

namesakes in the tree of the P. Memmii,[1] and this being so, the Deximachos, son of Pratolaos, mentioned in I.G. V, i, 209, cannot be identified with any C. Julius Deximachos, as Kolbe proposes, without further explanation. But a ready explanation suggests itself in the adoption of a P. Memmius Deximachos (if we may so describe by anticipation a member of a family which only later acquired the *nomen* Memmius) by a C. Julius. All the known facts would seem to be accounted for by supposing that the Deximachos, son of Sidektas in the tree cited above,[2] was adopted by C. Julius Eurykles I, and was the ancestor of the later bearers of the names C. Julius Lakon and C. Julius Eurykles who were distinguished at Sparta from the reign of Claudius onwards. Adoptions of this kind may be seen from the inscriptions to have been extremely common in Sparta throughout the period of the Principate.

Such an adopted son would naturally appear in a Latin inscription, if his full descent were given, as *C. Julius C. f. Deximachus Pratolai n.*, which fits in with the probable restoration of I.G. V, i, 374.[3] But like very many other Spartans,[4] he may also have assumed a new name upon adoption ; and if, in accordance with the practice usual among Roman citizens, he took his adoptive father's name in full, and combined with it a cognomen of Roman adjectival form, derived from the gentile name of the family in which he was born,[5] we should have a complete explanation of the names of the later C. Julius Eurykles *Herklanos*,[6] and also of a mysterious Lachares Ἡρακλανοῦ whose date lies between that of Deximachos and that of the later Eurykles.[7] For the P. Memmii, to which family Deximachos

---

[1] It may further be noted that the Sidektas in Kolbe's tree cited above had also a daughter Eurybanassa (I.G. V, i, 209), who likewise has a later namesake among the P. Memmii (*ibid.* 507, 573, 574) but in no other family so far as is known.

[2] *I.e.* the nephew of the Deximachos identified as C. Julius Deximachos by Kolbe.   [3] *Cf.* above, p. 197, nn. 3 and 4.

[4] *Cf.* I.G. V. i, 32B (Damokles Δαμοκλέους ὁ καὶ Φιλοκράτης), and similar uses of ὁ καί with the alternative name, *ibid.* nos. 305, 314 ; B.S.A. XXVI, p. 163, A9.

[5] A later Spartan example of this practice is M. Valerius Ulpianus Aphthonetos (I.G. V, i, 323), evidently a descendant of earlier bearers of the name M. Ulpius Aphthonetos (*ibid.* 61, 104) who had been adopted into a family of the *gens Valeria*.   [6] *Sic. cf.* P.I.R. II, p. 189, no. 199.

[7] *Cf.* Appendix IV, § 7, n. 3.

belonged by birth, claimed to be descended from Herakles ; [1] thus *Heraklanos* was the nearest possible approximation to a Roman adoptive cognomen such as *Octavianus* which a Greek, till then without Roman citizenship, could assume on being adopted, if he wished at the same time to stress both his new-found possession of Roman citizenship and his aristocratic Greek descent. For Roman citizenship, being rare among Spartans at this period, was doubtless a much-prized possession ; on the other hand, no one could possibly suspect of being a freedman a Greek with the name of C. Julius Eurykles Heraklanos ὁ καὶ Δεξίμαχος.

An adopted son of C. Julius Eurykles I might easily continue to prosper in Sparta, and his descendants after him, in spite of the exile by Tiberius and by the Spartans themselves of the real son of Eurykles I and of his descendants, especially if the blood-relations of the adopted son were as influential in Sparta as the P. Memmii obviously continued to be.[2]

The occurrence of the names of Spartiaticus and Lakon both in the family of Eurykles I and in that of the P. Memmii [3] strongly suggests that the two families were related quite independently of the Deximachos who may be supposed to have been adopted by Eurykles I ; and in view of the severance which occurred through the exile of Lakon I and his sons in the reign of Tiberius, the relationship must date back before that time. It seems reasonable to suppose that the Deximachos adopted by Eurykles I was already a blood relation, and in any case it appears that we must consider Eurykles I and his descendants, and this family of P. Memmii, as merely two branches of the same family. The fortunes of their members are those of a single powerful clan, and the inscriptions of the Principate

---

[1] *Cf.* I.G. V, i, 471 : *Π. Μέμμιον Σπαρτιατικὸν ἔκγονον ῾Ηρακλέους καὶ ῾Ραδαμάνθυος, μ᾽ ἀπὸ Διοσκούρων.* Descent from the Dioscuri as well as Herakles is also claimed by Eurykles III, Herklanos II (*ibid.* 1172).

[2] See following note.

[3] The inscriptions record more than one P. Memmius Spartiaticus (*cf.* I.G. V, i, index) and a P. Memmius Lakon (B.S.A. XXVI, p. 201, γ). It is true that the name Spartiaticus also occurs in a Spartan family of Ti. Claudii (*cf.* stemma in I.G. V, i, p. 131), but the occurrence of the name Pratolaos, characteristic of the P. Memmii, in three successive generations of this family of Ti. Claudii in the second century, indicates a family connection also between these Ti. Claudii and the P. Memmii.

permit us to trace in the most striking fashion the extent of that clan's influence at Sparta during the first two centuries of the Principate, while there are some indications that the same family was influential also in the latter part of the Roman Republic.[1] Their influence under the Principate no doubt rested to a great extent upon imperial favour, which is manifested by the continued tenure by the same clan of the priesthood of Augustus. For about two centuries this priesthood was a life office, and for most of that time it was held by members of the same clan ; when it passed from Eurykles I and his direct descendants through their downfall, it passed to the grandfather and father of Eurykles Herklanos and to Herklanos himself, who died about A.D. 130. Then there was a break in the tradition, for the next holder of the life priesthood of the emperors was one C. Pomponius Alkastos,[2] who obviously had no immediate connection by birth with our C. Julii or P. Memmii.[3]

The life priesthood of Pomponius Alkastos creates two difficulties for the historian, for not only does it appear that there was a much younger male relative [4] of Eurykles Herklanos alive at the time when Alkastos held this office after Herklanos' death, but it would also appear from I.G. V, i, 59, that Alkastos was already holding the priesthood in question in the patronomate of Hadrian, which must fall earlier than the death of Herklanos in c. A.D. 130. It does not seem possible to interpret otherwise what remains of the heading of this inscription, giving the patronomate of Hadrian as the date, nor in view of the repetition of

---

[1] A Sidektas, a Pratolaos and a Damares (all names characteristic of the later P. Memmii) appear among the Patronomoi of this period (cf. I.G. V, i, index, p. 342).

[2] Cf. B.S.A. XXVII, p. 242. Woodward dates his posts as Patronomos, chief Nomophylax and Ephor in the decade A.D. 130–140, cf. I.G. V, i, 116 n. But according to I.G. V, i, 59 he was Nomophylax already in the patronomate of Hadrian.

[3] His son C. Pomponius Aristeas (cf. Appendix IV, §1, no. 12) does, however, make the claim made by both the C. Julii and the P. Memmii to be descended both from Herakles and from the Dioscuri (I.G. V, i, 495. For this claim made by members of the other two families in the same period, cf. ibid. 463, 471, 537, 971, 1172, 1399). A distant family relationship between Eurykles Herklanos and C. Pomponius Alkastos is therefore likely to have existed.

[4] Cf. below, p. 202, n. 3.

exactly the same titles after Alkastos' name in other inscriptions, can the title here be otherwise restored than as ἀρχιε[ρεὺς τῶν Σεβ.]. But it may be noted that I.G. V, i, 59, in contrast with the later inscriptions relating to Alkastos, does not say that his priesthood was a life office, and herein may be the clue to the puzzle. From other examples it is clear that the life high · priesthood of the emperors at Sparta is to be distinguished from the mere high priesthood, and it may be that for some reason Alkastos was promoted on the death of Eurykles Herklanos from the position of mere high priest of the emperors to that of high priest for life.[1] Is it not possible that the reason for passing over the young namesake of Eurykles Herklanos was that he was still too young to hold so dignified an office ? The younger Eurykles was Boagos about four years after the death of Herklanos,[2] and so was about sixteen at the time of the latter's death. From another inscription it seems probable that he was Herklanos' great-nephew, adopted as his heir.[3]

It is not improbable that Alkastos was chosen to succeed to the high priesthood because he was the eldest possessor at the time of the hereditary right to call himself 'Ηρακλείδης καὶ Διοσκουρίδης.[4]

This break in the tradition, by which the imperial priesthood passed to another family, seems to have been followed soon afterwards by a more fundamental change, the transformation of the life priesthood of the emperors into an annual one. In the next generation after C. Pomponius Alkastos a Ti. Claudius Spartiatikos, possibly

[1] In I.G. V, i, 65, which belongs to the year of Damokles (see B.S.A. XXVI, p. 201, 2β, for the restoration of the name of the Eponymos of this year) Alkastos is called ἀρχιερεὺς διὰ βίου τῶν Σεβαστῶν. The probable date of Damokles (see list of Patronomoi, Appendix IV, § 8, A.D. 131/2, with notes) fits in with the supposition that this is after Herklanos' death.

[2] In the year of Atticus (I.G. V, i, 287). Eurykles must have been a Boagos at the time to have a Synephebos (cf. above, pp. 110 f.).

[3] This interpretation is favoured by the inscription on Herklanos' tomb at Sparta (I.G. V, i, 489 : ἐπι]μελουμένης [τῆς ἀναθέσεως . . .] τῆς ἀνεψ[ίας]. This duty could scarcely have been left to a niece or female cousin if adult male relatives had been living, but a niece whose young son was the heir would be likely to fulfil it.

[4] Cf. above, p. 201, n. 3, and I.G. V, i, 36, [ὁ δεῖνα] τοῦ τῶν ['Ηρακλεί]δων γένους πρεσβύτατος (c. A.D. 150).

connected with the family of the P. Memmii,[1] was ἀρχιερεὺς δὶς τῶν Σεβαστῶν,[2] and there seems to be no later recorded instance of a high priest of the emperors at Sparta holding the office either διὰ βίου or κατὰ γένος. Members of a family of Sex. Pompeii are later found holding the office, apparently as an annual one.[3] The institution of an annual instead of a life priesthood must have occurred about the middle of the second century, and since about this time there was a year of political upheaval (νεωτερισμοί) in Sparta, serious enough to prevent the normal annual elections, though Ephors were elected,[4] it seems permissible to suspect a connection between these upheavals and the change in the nature of the priesthood of the emperors, which permanently closed to all the prominent aristocratic families their hopes of enjoying added prestige and influence through this office. Political disturbances might easily happen when the descendants of Eurykles Herklanos, of whom there evidently were some, found themselves deprived of their traditional life priesthood of the emperors on the death of Herklanos, but may not have happened until after C. Pomponius Alkastos had held the life office for some time, that is to say, when the younger Eurykles and his Synepheboi and Kasens were old enough to make their presence felt in political affairs. There is some reason to think that the emperor himself intervened.[5]

From this time onwards the family of Eurykles ceases to be conspicuous at Sparta ; at all events, it leaves no more trace in inscriptions. But for the very reason that the family of Eurykles was not exceptional, but typical of several families of the Spartan aristocracy, its disappearance leaves no effect on social and political life, which may be seen from the inscriptions to have gone on as before for at least another century.[6] There were other ' descendants

[1] Cf. above, p. 200, n. 3.   [2] I.G. V, i, 525.
[3] Cf. ibid. 557, 559 (Sext. Pompeius Onasikrates and his son Eudamos). The son held a large number of other priesthoods, and in each case mentions that he held them κατὰ γένος. This implies that the imperial priesthood was no longer hereditary, since in this case it is not said to be held κατὰ γένος, and if it was no longer hereditary, it is most unlikely that father and son held it for life.
[4] Cf. B.S.A. XXVII, p. 234, F4, and on the date of this inscription, Appendix IV, § 8, note D (p. 469).   [5] Cf. Appendix IV, ibid.
[6] See the lists of ' Patrons ', Boagoi, Kasens, Synepheboi and Patronomoi (Appendix IV).

of Herakles and the Dioscuri ' [1] to insist upon the observance
of the traditional ceremonies and institutions, knowing
well that the ' Lycurgan ' régime more than anything else
was calculated to preserve the social and economic supremacy
of a small class.

THE FAMILY OF EURYKLES

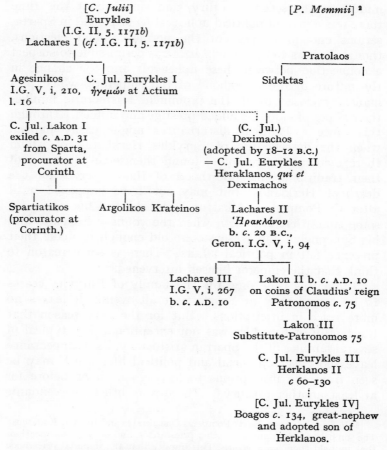

[C. Julii]
Eurykles
(I.G. II, 5. 1171b)
Lachares I (cf. I.G. II, 5. 1171b)

[P. Memmii] [2]

Agesinikos — C. Jul. Eurykles I
I.G. V, i, 210, ἡγεμών at Actium
l. 16

Pratolaos
Sidektas

C. Jul. Lakon I
exiled c. A.D. 31
from Sparta,
procurator at
Corinth

(C. Jul.)
Deximachos
(adopted by 18–12 B.C.)
= C. Jul. Eurykles II
Heraklanos, qui et
Deximachos

Spartiatikos
(procurator at
Corinth.)
Argolikos Krateinos

Lachares II
'Ηρακλάνου
b. c. 20 B.C.,
Geron. I.G. V, i, 94

Lachares III   Lakon II b. c. A.D. 10
I.G. V, i, 267   on coins of Claudius' reign
b. c. A.D. 10   Patronomos c. 75

Lakon III
Substitute-Patronomos 75

C. Jul. Eurykles III
Herklanos II
c 60–130

[C. Jul. Eurykles IV]
Boagos c. 134, great-nephew
and adopted son of
Herklanos.

[1] See further, Appendix V (The Hereditary Priesthoods).
[2] On the meaning of the bracket see pp. 198 f.

THE EARLIER SPARTA

CHAPTER VI

THE EARLY SOCIAL ORGANISATION IN SPARTA AND CRETE

AMONG the more obvious conclusions to be drawn from the detailed study of Sparta in Roman times, it appears that the Ephebic organisation was a survival intact, or almost intact, from a much earlier period, that it was used for the purpose of perpetuating the rigid social classes which were the basis of all political life, and in particular, in order to select at an early age a class from which could be drawn the future holders of magistracies. The assembling of this later evidence has also told us something more about the relations of Sparta with the Perioikoi, and about the probable extent of Spartan territory before the Perioikoi became subject or any advance was made into Messenia.[1] Some further light has also been thrown on the nature of Spartan cults, especially that of Orthia, which the inscriptions of the Roman period prove to have been closely connected with the Ephebic organisation. It is now time to consider how these conclusions work out in detail when brought into connection with what is known about Sparta in the far more obscure archaic period.

The obscurity which envelops all Spartan institutions at any period before the end of the fifth century B.C. is ultimately due, as Thucydides has remarked, to deliberate Spartan policy. A state permanently organised for war naturally observes at all times what for normal states are merely the special precautions which must be adopted in time of war. Such scraps of information as were allowed by the Spartan government to filter through to the outside world were specially calculated either positively to mislead,

---

[1] See Appendices I and III.

or at least to give away no secrets. So far as we can tell
after fairly exhaustive excavation of the likely sites in
Sparta itself, no inscriptions were in that earlier period
put up recording lists of magistrates, decrees of the Gerusia,
laws passed by the Apella or any of the matters of general
public interest which are commonly recorded by normal
Greek states at all periods of their history. A few inscriptions concerning victories at cult festivals, and dedications to various gods, are all that remain, and probably all
that ever existed, of epigraphical evidence for this earlier
epoch. The evidence which remains is almost exclusively
literary, if we leave out of account for the time being that
argumentum ex silentio of which so much has been made,
the absence of archaeological remains after the beginning
of the sixth century B.C.

A bare list of the pre-Hellenistic literary authorities
for the history and institutions of Sparta will serve to indicate at once the inequalities and chronological gaps in
this class of evidence. From the early poets Terpander
of Lesbos, Thaletas the Cretan, Polymnestus of Colophon,
Tyrtaeus of doubtful origin, Alcman of Sardis, Sacadas
of Argos (all of whom wrote before about 625 B.C.) [1] we
pass straight to the historians of the later fifth century
and after—Herodotus, Hellanicus, Thucydides, Xenophon
and Ephorus, and to the philosophers of the Athenian
school—Socrates, Plato and Aristotle, and their lesser
satellites. This seems to exhaust the list of pre-Hellenistic
authorities who were known to the Greeks themselves, and
it may be observed that, with the possible exception of
Tyrtaeus, not one of them was a Spartan.

The philo-Laconian philosophers found much to interest
them in the early poets, especially in Tyrtaeus, who provided them with material for the study of Spartan institutions from the moral and educational points of view, these
being the aspects of Sparta which chiefly interested them.
But the strictures of Aristotle upon Spartan institutions
in his own day make it clear that the panegyrics upon

[1] On these poets and their dates see further Farnell, *Greek Lyric Poetry*
(1891). Sacadas is associated with musical victories in the Pythian
Games early in the sixth century (Paus. VI, 14. 10) but his activity at
Sparta seems to fall before that of Alcman. Terpander, the earliest of
the series, appears to belong to the first half of the seventh century.

Sparta by his philosophical contemporaries were called forth by an idealised Sparta which had never at any time existed as they imagined it.[1] A bare knowledge of the outlines of the Spartan constitution provided these admirers of Sparta with all they required for philosophical discussion ; there was no need for them to probe further into the precise way in which the various institutions actually worked in practice.[2] Aristotle, who is no admirer of Sparta, is also in a different category from the scientific point of view ; not because he investigates the facts about Sparta (for this he does not appear to do) but because he pursues in considerable detail a different method, the method of comparing the known institutions of Sparta with those of other states. The value and results of this method of study merit detailed consideration ; whether Aristotle has himself been successful in it or not, it remains the only possible line of approach other than the argument from those later survivals which have formed the subject of inquiry in the first part of this work.

For the inadequacy of the information possessed by the great fifth-century historians is immediately apparent ; Thucydides confesses himself baffled ; Herodotus has carried away from Sparta a few stories about the early kings, some confused traditions about Lycurgus,[3] a detailed account of the pomp and ceremony and general dislocation of public life involved in a royal funeral (which he is unlikely to have seen),[4] and other unimportant details about the respect paid to the kings. From Thucydides' sole piece of detailed information about the Spartan state, his account of the army organisation at the battle of Mantinea,

[1] See further, the illuminating study of Ollier, *Le Mirage Spartiate* (1933).

[2] The treatise on Sparta by the pseudo-Xenophon falls into this category. See further, Appendix VII (pp. 490 f.).

[3] See below, pp. 329 f.

[4] In view of Herodotus' visit to the battlefield of Papremis soon after 460 (*cf.* Mahaffy, *History of Greek Literature*, p. 118), it seems unlikely that he was himself present at Pleistarchus' funeral in 458. The information about the Spartan kings may be taken at second hand from Charon of Lampsacus (*cf.* below, p. 335, n. 1), especially in view of the fact that the parallel of remission of debts to cities in the Persian empire by Persian kings on their accession (Herod. VI, 59) would no longer apply when Herodotus was writing, but would apply at the time of the accession of Xerxes.

modern writers have deduced theories about the rapid extinction of the Spartan stock which can be shown to be quite unsound ; [1] from the evidence of Herodotus also, as a result of studying it in too great isolation, modern scholars have drawn conclusions as to the constitutional development of Sparta which will not square with the evidence of other kinds and from other sources.[2] Xenophon was in a different position from his two predecessors in that he served as a mercenary captain in the Spartan army, and was for many years settled on an estate in Elean territory granted to him by Sparta. This should have given him a better opportunity for knowing the facts about Sparta than historians who merely visited Sparta as complete outsiders, and that only in a period when Athenians and pro-Athenians were inevitably suspect. Yet he, too, like his predecessors among the historians, expressed opinions about Sparta which Polybius regarded as preposterous,[3] and although the *Constitution of Sparta* ascribed to him contains much that is of the greatest interest, any estimate of its value as evidence must depend upon the exact date of its composition as well as upon its authenticity.[4]

Enough remains of the work of the early poets to show that this could not provide the later Greek historians and students of constitutions with any appreciable amount of detailed evidence about Sparta, though Ephorus and no doubt others sedulously collected such scraps of definite evidence as could be found in their poetry.[5]

In general it seems clear that philosophers and historians of the fourth century B.C. who were particularly interested in Sparta had even less direct material to work upon than is accessible to modern scholars, because they had not the evidence of survivals which lasted on into a less secretive age.

---

[1] See below, pp. 348 f.   [2] See below, pp. 319 f., 330 f.

[3] *Cf.* below, p. 217.

[4] It is assumed in the present work that the treatise is not by Xenophon. See further, Appendix VII.

[5] *Cf.* Ephorus, frag. 53 (Müller), quoting Tyrtaeus on the first Messenian War ; *ibid.* frag. 64, quoting Alcman on the Spartan *Andreia*. Herodotus (III, 52) alludes to ' all the poets ' as evidence for the earliest history of Sparta.

§ 1. *Ancient Comparisons*

What conclusions, then, may be reached through the comparative method employed by Aristotle, his contemporaries and his immediate successors? Their comparison is directed mainly to Crete, so that we possess in the surviving inscriptions from the Cretan towns the means of testing the validity of the alleged resemblance to Sparta. Many of the similarities pointed to by Aristotle [1] are too superficial to be significant, as for example, the Ephorate, which Aristotle compares on the one hand to the board of ten Cretan Kosmoi, on the other hand to the Carthaginian Council of the Hundred and Four.[2] Apart from the difference in number, Aristotle himself mentions a significant difference in the mode of election, the Ephors being elected from all the citizens without distinction, the Kosmoi only from certain aristocratic families.[3]

But what is more important is the difference in allocation of functions between the Kosmoi as compared with the Spartan Ephors, for this clearly shows the board of Kosmoi to have developed in the same way as the Athenian Archons, through distributing over a larger number the functions originally united in the sole person of the king. Aristotle himself notices particularly the military functions of the Kosmoi ; [4] but although all may have exercised some direct military authority in the field (differing incidentally in this respect from the Spartan Ephors),[5] one Kosmos, in particular, had the title of στραταγέτης, and so corresponded to the Athenian Polemarch, while another was called κόσμος ξένιος, being particularly concerned with jurisdiction involving aliens ; yet another appears to have had

---

[1] It is not improbable that Ephorus is the real source of the various inconsistencies and inaccuracies in Aristotle's account. Compare especially *Pol.* II, 10. 1–10 with Ephorus, fr. 64 (Müller), *Pol.* II, 9. 17 with Ephorus, fr. 18.

[2] *Pol.* II, 10. 6 ; II, 11. 3.   [3] *Ibid.* II, 10. 10.

[4] *Cf. Pol.* II, 10. 6 : βασιλεία δὲ πρότερον μὲν ἦν, εἶτα κατέλυσαν οἱ Κρῆτες, καὶ τὴν ἡγεμονίαν οἱ κόσμοι τὴν κατὰ πόλεμον ἔχουσιν.

[5] *Cf. ibid.* III, 14. 3, 14 : the Spartan kingship at that period is still στρατηγία τις αὐτοκρατόρων καὶ αΐδιος. The two Ephors who went with the king on campaign, at least from the early fifth century (*cf.* Hdt. IX, 76 ; Xen. *Hell.* II, iv, 36 ; *Resp. Lac.* 13. 5), were there not to command in the field but to take part in any negotiations which might be necessary with the enemy (*cf.* Xen. *Hell.* II, iv, 35–38). On the limits of the powers of the Ephors in relation to military matters see further below, pp. 403 f.

14

charge of ἀστικαὶ δίκαι, involving citizens only, and more than one were called γνώμονες,[1] meaning perhaps 'interpreters of the law'. The allocation of different classes of suits to the various Kosmoi differs in detail from the Athenian system, but the underlying principle is the same in both cases.

Among the Spartan Ephors, on the other hand, there seems to have been no differentiation of functions at any period, with the exception that one of them gave his name to the year (until the Patronomos took over this privilege) and so perhaps presided at their meetings and in the Ecclesia. The Ephors can be seen to have acted always as a board, or, as in the case when two were sent with a king on campaign, as delegates of that board.[2] It was as a board that they had the right of calling all magistrates and the kings themselves to account for their actions.[3] Apart from this they did indeed preside individually (subject no doubt to ratification by the whole college of Ephors) over certain judicial suits, but it is to be noted that all the suits in question belonged to the single category of δίκαι συμβολαῖαι,[4] the basis of distribution among the various Ephors thus being not generic, as was the case in Athens and Crete, but purely quantitative.

Another conspicuous difference between the Spartan Ephors on the one hand, and the Cretan Kosmoi and Athenian Archons on the other, is that the Ephors could not be called to account themselves, but (as already mentioned) had the power of calling to account all other holders of office (including the kings). They were in fact above the laws.[5]   On the other hand, the Cretan Kosmoi

---

[1] For the titles of the various Kosmoi see the epigraphical references cited by Kohler and Ziebarth, Das Stadtrecht von Gortyn (1912), p. 44.

[2] The right of concluding peace belonged exclusively to the whole board of Ephors (cf. Xen. Hell. II, ii, 12, 13 ; 17, 18), hence both Agis and Lysander refused to treat directly for peace with Athens.   Yet the two Ephors, at the same time with Pausanias in Attica were competent to conclude peace (ibid. II, iv, 38) which implies that they were official delegates of the whole board.   [3] Cf. Arist. Pol. II, 9. 26.

[4] Cf. ibid. III, i. 10 : οἷον ἐν Λακεδαίμονι τὰς τῶν συμβολαίων δικάζει τῶν ἐφόρων ἄλλος ἄλλας, οἱ δὲ γέροντες τὰς φονικάς, ἑτέρα δ'ἴσως ἀρχή τις ἑτέρας.

[5] Cf. ibid. II, 9. 23 : ἔτι δὲ καὶ κρίσεών εἰσι μεγάλων κύριοι, ὄντες οἱ τυχόντες, διόπερ οὐκ αὐτογνώμονας βέλτιον κρίνειν, ἀλλὰ κατὰ τὰ γράμματα καὶ τοὺς νόμους.

and the Athenian Archons could individually be called to account and deposed even in the middle of their term of office.[1] The Cretan and Athenian arrangement may be regarded as normal among Greek states in which the original functions of the king were distributed among a college of chief magistrates, but the Spartan arrangement is distinctly abnormal. Moreover, the fact that at Sparta the kings continued to be the supreme generals in the field,[2] whereas this was the first royal prerogative to be undermined in the vast majority of Greek states, throws further doubt on the assumption commonly made that the Ephors were brought into existence for the express purpose of reducing the powers of the kings. But whatever may have been their origin, it is certain that the office in its developed form was totally different in all essential points from the Cretan Kosmoi. The only resemblances which survive examination are the absence of property qualification for the office in both cases (noted by Aristotle),[3] and the fact that in the pre-Roman period letters and embassies from other states were addressed to the Boule and the Kosmoi of Crete, and to the Ephors and Gerusia, or Ephors and Polis, of Sparta.[4] Neither of these resemblances is important enough to outweigh the differences.

In their respective aristocratic councils there is another instructive resemblance between the Cretan towns and Athens, and here, too, the supposed resemblance between Crete and Sparta breaks down. In the Cretan towns the Boule (to which Ephorus seems to have given the name of Gerusia, in a deliberate attempt to strengthen his own theory of resemblance with Sparta[5]) was composed exclusively of those who had held the office of Kosmos.[6]

---

[1] For the Kosmoi, cf. Arist. Pol. II, 10. 13 ; for the Archons, Dem. LVIII, 27, 28.

[2] Cf. above, p. 209, n. 5.   [3] Cf. Arist. Pol. II, 10. 10.

[4] For Crete, cf. Ditt. Syll³ 528, 622 ; for Sparta, I.G. V, i, 8–10.

[5] The name Gerusia does not occur in the Cretan inscriptions, where it is referred to as ἁ βουλά. Aristotle seems to be aware of this ; cf. Pol. II, 10. 6 : οἱ δὲ γέροντες (sc. of Sparta) τοῖς γέρουσιν, οὓς καλοῦσιν οἱ Κρῆτες βουλήν, ἴσοι. But Ephorus ap. Strabo, X, 484, uses about the Cretan institution the expression τοῖς γέρουσι καλουμένοις. This may well be an instance of his deliberate use of the same names to describe Cretan and Spartan institutions in order to increase the apparent resemblance, a device of which he is accused by Polybius (VI, 46).

[6] Arist. Pol. II, 10. 10 ; Ephorus ap. Strabo, X, 484.

Similarly, the Athenian Areopagus was composed exclusively of those who had held the office of Archon, in this case by automatic enrolment of retiring holders of the office. Although he does not directly say so, Aristotle seems to imply by the criticisms which he brings against the Spartan Gerusia but not against the Cretan Boule, that the Cretan Boule was also automatically recruited from retiring Kosmoi, whereas the Spartan Gerontes were democratically elected. In any case the eligibility of all citizens without distinction of class for the Ephorate debarred many ex-Ephors from entering the Gerusia. Turning to the points of resemblance between the Spartan Gerusia and its Cretan counterpart, we find that in both cases membership was for life, that it was limited to the aristocracy, and that there was some kind of test of moral character and of past service to the state. This last point is, in fact, far more vaguely stated in regard to Crete than in regard to Sparta,[1] and rouses the suspicion that Ephorus, who is our only authority for it in the case of Crete,[2] may have been pushing his list of resemblances to the furthest limit in order to prove his main case that the two constitutions were closely connected. It is highly probable that early aristocratic councils in all Greek states required a certain standard of personal probity and loyalty to the constitution in their new members. The Athenian Areopagus is again a case in point, and provides an equally good parallel to the typical Cretan Boule in the other two respects cited as evidence for resemblance between Spartan and Cretan constitutions. In the Areopagus also membership was for life, and until the reforms of Solon must have been limited to the Eupatridae, who alone at that time were eligible for the archonship.

The only useful conclusion to be drawn from the somewhat superficial resemblance between the Spartan Gerusia and the typical Boule of the Cretan towns is that, in both these regions, the early aristocratic council, which had been typical of the majority of Greek states in the period when aristocratic government was general, persisted unaltered into a late period, because, for reasons which differed some-

---

[1] For Sparta, cf. Arist. Pol. II, 9. 25.

[2] For Crete, cf. Ephorus ap. Strabo, X, 4. 22 (484) : καθίστανται δ'εἰς τοῦτο τὸ συνέδριον οἱ τῆς τῶν κόσμων ἀρχῆς ἠξιωμένοι καὶ τἆλλα δόκιμοι κρινόμενοι.

what in the two cases, it was not called upon to face the competition of new and more democratic institutions.[1] There is certainly no valid evidence here, any more than in the case of the Ephors and Kosmoi, to justify the ancient belief that either the Spartan constitution was derived from Crete, or *vice versa*. From what has already been said, it may be seen that in certain respects the constitutions of the Cretan towns and of Sparta reached the conditions regarded in the fourth century B.C. as similar by developing along different lines.

Aristotle and his contemporaries saw in the Spartan Helot system another instance of resemblance to Crete. The evidence is somewhat confused and confusing, and it is perhaps not possible to give a final estimate of its significance until a detailed study of the Spartan treatment of Messenia, which must be postponed for the present,[2] has been made. The question concerns the alleged resemblance of the Helots to the class of agricultural labourers in Crete who are called by Aristotle ' Perioikoi ' [3] and in another passage δοῦλοι.[4] Various later writers give a more detailed account of Cretan serfdom in its various forms [5] which makes it probable that the class to which Aristotle is actually referring is the ἀφαμιῶται or κληρωταί, the latter term being certainly the normal Greek version of the former, which must be regarded as the technical Cretan one.[6]

---

[1] In the case of Crete, because the harbours were poor, and the island consequently lay off the beaten track of commerce after it ceased, with the coming of the Dorian Greeks, to be controlled by a people who were themselves active in developing maritime enterprise. Aristotle attributes Cretan conservatism mainly to the remoteness of the island (*Pol.* II, 10. 12, 15). In the case of Sparta, direct contact with all external influences was deliberately avoided for political reasons.

[2] See further, pp. 289 f.

[3] *Pol.* II, 10. 5, *cf.* II, 9. 3 ; *cf.* also Busolt, *Griech. Gesch.*[2] I, p. 341 n.

[4] *Pol.* II, 5. 19.

[5] *Cf.* Onesicritus (a historian employed by Alexander the Great) *ap.* Strabo, XV, 34 (701), comparing Spartan Helots to Cretan ἀφαμιῶται ; Sosicrates (Rhodius ?) *ap.* Athen. VI, 264, a : Σωσικράτης δ'ἐν δευτέρῳ Κρητικῶν· τὴν μὲν κοινήν, φησί, δουλείαν οἱ Κρῆτες καλοῦσι μνοίαν, τὴν δὲ ἰδίαν ἀφαμιώτας, τοὺς δὲ ὑπηκόους περιοίκους· τὰ παραπλήσια ἱστορεῖ καὶ Δωσιάδας ἐν τετάρτῳ Κρητικῶν. The ἰδία δουλεία referred to by these three writers may in fact be seen from the Gortyn Code to bear no resemblance whatever to the Spartan Helot system. See further below, pp. 214 f.

[6] That it was not normally current in Greek appears from three glosses of Hesychius (ed. Schmidt, 1858) : ἐφημίαι· ἄγροι, καὶ *βελτίονα φήμης*,

But whether the land-lots to which they were attached were their own or belonged to someone else is a matter of some doubt. For the curious thing is that Aristotle, in spite of his statement that the ' Perioikoi ' (as he mis-leadingly calls them) were slaves (δοῦλοι) most clearly implies that they enjoyed a separate system of laws of their own, distinct from those of the state within whose borders they worked.[1] The natural conclusion to be drawn from this seeming contradiction is that the class of the Cretan agricultural labourers in question were *not* slaves, but in a position ' intermediate between slavery and freedom ' (μεταξὺ ἐλευθέρων καὶ δούλων), as a Greek grammarian of the late third century B.C. expressed it.[2] The Gortyn Code reinforces this conclusion by its references to the large fines imposed upon any ' slave ' (δοῦλος, Ϝοικεύς) found guilty of abduction of a free man or woman,[3] or of adultery,[4] and by the right of a slave-woman (Ϝοικέα) married to a slave to restitution of her property in case of divorce.[5] The same conclusion also results from a passage cited from

where the reading should probably be καὶ βέλτιον ἀφημίαι ; *cf*. Schmidt *ad loc*., and the other two glosses, ἀφημιάστους· ἀγροικίας (with Schmidt's likely emendation, ἀφημίας· τὰς ἀγροικίας), and ἀφημοῦντας· ἀγροίκους, the last form being probably due to a mistaken derivation from ἀφ' ἡμῶν. A Doric form, ἀφαμία, may be inferred both from the Cretan word ἀφαμιῶται under discussion, and from words connected with πέπαμαι (πᾶμα, ἐχεπάμων, παμῶχος, etc.), the change from π to φ being common in many Greek dialects, while the prefix α- may have been added either for the sake of euphony or as the result of a mistaken connection with ἀπό. The meaning of ἀφαμία is thus clearly identical with κλῆρος in the sense of a possession in the form of land.

[1] *Cf. Pol*. II, 10. 3 : διὸ καὶ νῦν οἱ περίοικοι (*sc*. of Lyktos) τὸν αὐτὸν τρόπον χρῶνται αὐτοῖς (*sc*. τοῖς τοῦ Μίνω νόμοις), ὡς κατασκευάσαντος Μίνω πρώτου τὴν τάξιν τῶν νόμων. Aristotle implies that the Dorian colonists of Lyktos brought their own code of laws with them, but found a similar code already in existence among the ' Perioikoi ', whom they made their subjects, but who continued to be governed by the laws of Minos in their original form when the later (Dorian) colonists no longer used even the similar ones

[2] Callistratus, ὁ Ἀριστοφάνειος, *ap*. Pollux, III, 83. (That Callistratus is the source of the passage in Pollux appears clearly from the citation in Athen. VI, 263 e.) For a suggested ultimate source of this passage in Callistratus, comparing Cretan *Klarotai* and *Mnoitai* with Spartan Helots, etc., see further below, p. 215, n. 3.

[3] Col. ii, ll. 5 f. (Kohler u. Ziebarth, *op. cit.* p. 4). The fine is 200 staters.

[4] *Ibid*. ll. 27 f. The fine is 200 staters, twice the amount payable for the same offence by a man of free birth.

[5] *Ibid*. col. iii, l. 41.

Dosiadas, who seems to have been a writer of repute on Cretan institutions. This speaks of a class of Cretan ' slaves ' liable for the general contribution made to the upkeep of the public *Syssitia* of the citizens ; each ' slave ' paid one Aeginetan stater,[1] the equivalent of five or six days' wages for a free labourer. It is not improbable that an equal amount was levied from the so-called ' slaves ' for other purposes.[2] Such a contribution is incompatible with the status of slaves (δοῦλοι) in the normal Greek sense, even if we suppose that the Cretan class referred to had not the free right of disposal of the property in question.

Moreover, the Cretan *Klarotai* are compared by Greek writers to two other classes of agricultural serfs, the Thessalian Penestai and the Mariandynoi of Heraclea Pontica,[3] neither of whom were slaves in the normal Greek sense. In both these cases the origin of the serfdom was regarded as contractual, individual owners recognising their permanent obligation to protect and not to expel the labourers settled on their land, the serfs, on the other hand, being bound to work the land and to render up a proportion of the annual yield to their overlord, but being capable of owning property of their own.[4]

[1] *Cf.* Dosiadas *ap.* Athen. IV, 143a. Dosiadas is cited as a reliable authority on Crete by Diod. V, 80. 4. On his date see further below, p. 234.

[2] *Cf.* Arist. *Pol.* II, 10. 8 : ἀπὸ πάντων γὰρ τῶν γινομένων καρπῶν τε καὶ βοσκημάτων, καὶ τῶν ἐκ δημοσίων καὶ φόρων οὓς φέρουσιν οἱ περίοικοι τέτακται μέρος τὸ μὲν πρὸς τοὺς θεοὺς καὶ τὰς κοινὰς λειτουργίας, τὸ δὲ τοῖς συσσιτίοις.

[3] *Cf.* the passage of Callistratus, ὁ ᾿Αριστοφάνειος, referred to above, p. 214, n. 2, and for the parallel between Cretan *Klarotai* and Thessalian Penestai, Aristotle's Συρακοσίων Πολιτεία (F.H.G. II, p. 170, no. 219). All three are compared in Plato's *Laws*, VI, 776 D, E, and the prominence thus given to the otherwise obscure Mariandynoi strongly suggests a native writer of Heraclea Pontica as the original source of the comparison, especially in view of the detailed information given about the Mariandynoi by other Greek writers (*cf.* following note, also F.H.G., index *s.v.*, especially *ibid.* III, 13. 9, citing Nymphis of Heraclea, who wrote a history of his native city in the first half of the third century B.C.). The most likely source of the passage in Plato's *Laws*, and also of the passage in the Stoic Posidonius cited in the following note, is the sophist Bryson of Heraclea Pontica, said by Theopompus (*ap.* Athen. XI, 508 d) to have been much drawn upon and even plagiarised by Plato, and several times quoted by Aristotle (references in F.H.G. II, p. 27, n.).

[4] For the Penestai *cf.* Archemachus of Euboea *ap.* Athen. VI, 264 a : παρέδωκαν ἑαυτοὺς τοῖς Θετταλοῖς δουλεύειν καθ᾿ ὁμολογίας, ἐφ᾿ ᾧτε οὔτ᾿ ἐξάξουσιν αὐτοὺς ἐκ τῆς χώρας οὔτε ἀποκτενοῦσιν, αὐτοὶ δὲ τὴν χώραν αὐτοῖς

It is by no means easy to understand how a feudal
system of this kind, which might appropriately be described
as ' intermediate between slavery and freedom ' could
possibly be compared to the Spartan Helot system as the
majority of the later writers agree in describing it. But
even the fourth-century evidence about the Helots is con-
tradictory ; on the one hand we are told that the Spartans
declared war on them every year,[1] which implies that they
had no recognised rights in law, on the other hand, their
position is described in terms very much like those applied
to the Thessalian Penestai and the Mariandynoi, implying
that they were only ' bound to the soil ' in the sense that
their masters had no right to displace them from it.[2]

A possible explanation of the contradiction is that
Aristotle and his contemporaries were thinking not of the
old-style Helots, but of a class who should more properly
have been designated ' Neodamodeis ', namely ex-Helots or
descendants of ex-Helots, who had been established on
lands of their own with the perpetual obligation to military
service and presumably without the right to move from their
κλῆροι.[3] The natural tendency in all periods when such
a system has been adopted is for a new type of serfdom
to develop, and consequently the old name Helots was not
inappropriate even though the class in question were in
theory free men. With regard to the date at which this
system first became common in Sparta, isolated examples
have already been cited dating from the late fifth century,[4]
so that it was demonstrably already in existence in the

ἐργαζόμενοι τὰς συντάξεις ἀποδώσουσιν. . . . καὶ πολλοὶ τῶν κυρίων ἑαυτῶν
εἰσιν εὐπορώτεροι. Demosthenes' allusion to the mounted Penestai of
Menon of Pharsalus (Dem. XXIII, 199) supports the foregoing description.
So far as it goes, Posidonius' description (ap. Athen. VI, 263 d) of the
Mariandynoi is similar : 'Ηρακλεώταις ὑπετάγησαν, διὰ τέλους ὑποσχόμενοι
θητεύσειν παρέχουσιν αὐτοῖς τὰ δέοντα, προσδιαστειλάμενοι μηδενὸς αὐτῶν
ἔσεσθαι πρᾶσιν ἔξω τῆς 'Ηρακλεωτῶν χώρας, ἀλλ' ἐν αὐτῇ μένειν τῇ ἰδίᾳ
χώρᾳ. This last passage implies a hereditary arrangement prohibiting
the transfer of serfs from one estate to another.
[1] Arist. ap. Plut. Lycurg. 28.
[2] Cf. Ephorus, fr. 18 (F.H.G. I, p. 238) : τοὺς δ' Ελείους . . . κατὰ
κράτος ἁλῶναι πολέμῳ, καὶ κριθῆναι δούλους ἐπὶ τακτοῖς τισιν, ὥστε τὸν
ἔχοντα μήτ' ἐλευθεροῦν ἐξεῖναι, μήτε πωλεῖν ἔξω τῶν ὅρων τούτους. Similarly,
Myron of Priene (F.H.G. IV, p. 461, fr. 1) : καὶ παραδόντες αὐτοῖς τὴν
χώραν ἔταξαν μοῖραν, ἣν αὐτοῖς ἀνοίσουσιν ἀεί.
[3] Cf. Chap. I, p. 39.   [4] Cf. ibid.

time of Plato and Aristotle and their immediate predecessors among the sophists.[1] But this explanation is un-
satisfying because the Neodamodeis, as has been demonstrated earlier,[2] were settled not on private land but on
state land ; they were τρόπον τινα δημόσιοι δοῦλοι, in
Strabo's phrase,[3] and in this respect quite unlike the Cretan
ἀφαμιῶται (κληρωταί) attached to the lands of individual
masters. That the ἀφαμιῶται were private, not public
serfs (who were called μνωῖται), is directly stated in our
authorities.[4]

If there is indeed a real parallel between serfdom in
Sparta and serfdom in Crete, the ancient literary authorities
have certainly not succeeded in making it clear,[5] with the
result that, so far, the alleged resemblances between Sparta
and Crete seem to fall to the ground ; and we may be
tempted to reach the same general conclusion, though by
arguing along different lines and in greater detail, as that
reached by Polybius, who asks how ' Ephorus, Xenophon,
Callisthenes and Plato, the most learned of the ancients '
can ever have persuaded themselves that the constitution
of Sparta was similar to those of the Cretan towns.[6]

Polybius also finds a striking difference in economic
organisation, but since his argument depends on the assumption that in Sparta each citizen possessed an equal
amount of land, it cannot be taken too seriously.[7] None
the less, we do not find and cannot expect to find great
similarity in the economic laws of states which were so
differently situated from the economic point of view as

[1] Cf. above, p. 215, n. 3.   [2] Part I, pp. 38 f.
[3] Strabo, VIII, 5. 4 (p. 365).
[4] Cf. above, p. 213, n. 5. The name μνωῖται is genuine Cretan, being
cited from the Κρητικαὶ Γλῶσσαι of the Cretan Hermonax (ap. Athen.
VI, 267 c), and recurring in Pollux, III, 83. Hermonax explained it as
εὐγενεῖς οἰκέται, which may be reconciled with the statement of Sosikrates
that the μνωῖται were ' public slaves ' on the assumption that the word
is derived from δαμνάω (cf. δμῶες from δαμάζω) and meant slaves taken
in war as opposed to hereditary serfs. It is true that the ἀφαμιῶται were
also said to have been reduced to slavery through war (cf. Callistratus
('Αριστοφάνειος) ap. Athen. 263 e : ἀφαμιώτας δὲ τοὺς κατ' ἀγρόν, ἐγχωρίους
μὲν ὄντας, δουλωθέντας δὲ κατὰ πόλεμον), but this was presumably thought
to have occurred at the time of the Dorian conquest of Crete, since the
ἀφαμιῶται are described as natives, not foreigners.
[5] See further below, pp. 301 f.   [6] Polyb. VI, 45.
[7] Polyb. ibid. On the problem of land-ownership in Sparta, see further
above, pp. 13 f. (with Appendix I) ; below, pp. 245 f.

Sparta on the one hand and the Cretan towns on the other. Whereas Sparta could expand over the whole of the fertile valley of the Eurotas and beyond it into the rich lands of Messenia, the little towns of Crete, each hemmed into its narrow little valley and none being provided with good harbours, found no easy solution either in immediate territorial expansion or in colonial enterprise ; they were forced instead to frame their marriage laws with a view to discouraging further growth of the population.[1] This is in direct contrast with Sparta, where more men were always needed to hold down an ample and (for a long period) ever-expanding territory. Since the Spartan marriage laws, of which one of the main objects was to encourage the growth of the population,[2] were universally attributed to ' Lycurgus ', it is strange that the Greek writers who stressed the direct connection between the Cretan and the Lycurgan systems did not observe an obvious contradiction here. The law of marriage being so fundamental a part of all early systems of Greek law, and indeed of the whole social and political structure, it is inconceivable on this ground alone that ' Lycurgus ' took his code of laws from Crete, or any Cretan legislator from ' Lycurgus '.

§ 2. *Resemblances in Social and Feudal Structure*

In the face of all these contrasts, a strong resemblance is all the more striking and significant. And in spite of those conspicuous differences, which must have existed from an early period, probably from the eighth century B.C. when the hereditary monarchies were breaking down, and the Cretan Kosmoi came into existence, there is still a remarkable resemblance between the life-long military or quasi-military training of the Spartans and of the Cretans, between the organisation of the Agelae in each case, and between the Spartan Syssitia and the Cretan Andreia. As the two sets of institutions existed in the time of Ephorus and Aristotle they actually manifested a good many differences ; but further examination, especially in the light of what has now emerged from the study of the later Spartan

[1] *Cf* Arist. *Pol.* II, 10. 9.
[2] *Ibid.* II, 9. 18 ; *cf.* (Xen.) *Resp. Lac.* I, 7, 8.

inscriptions, will show that the Cretan Agelae and Andreia at an earlier period than the fourth century B.C. were much more like the corresponding Spartan organisations than they later became.

To consider first the Cretan Agelae, according to Ephorus' account, οἱ ἐπιφανέστατοι τῶν παίδων καὶ δυνατώτατοι (a phrase which clearly means ' influential boys of noble family ') were left to form their own bands of followers of their own age, and the father of the boy who thus collected a group of others round him made himself responsible in general for the organisation of the sport and physical exercises of the whole band and for the discipline of its members.[1] The band was formed of ' the bigger boys ' according to Ephorus' account, and when the organisation was fully developed the lower age-limit for membership was seventeen,[2] but the upper limit is unknown.[3] An inscription from Dreros, of the third century B.C. records the terms of the oath of loyalty taken by the members of the Agelae to the state, apparently on first attaining the status of adult citizens.[4] At this period, therefore, the state exercised strict control over the organisation, as is implied by Ephorus' statement that the members of the Agelae

[1] Ephorus ap. Strabo, X, 483 : οἱ δὲ μείζους εἰς τὰς ἀγέλας ἄγονται. τὰς δὲ ἀγέλας συνάγουσιν οἱ ἐπιφανέστατοι τῶν παίδων καὶ δυνατώτατοι, ἕκαστος ὅσους πλείστους οἷός τέ ἐστιν ἀθροίζων· ἑκάστης δὲ τῆς ἀγέλης ἄρχων ἐστὶν ὡς τὸ πολὺ ὁ πατὴρ τοῦ συναγαγόντος, κύριος ὢν ἐξάγειν ἐπὶ θήραν καὶ δρόμους, τὸν δ' ἀπειθοῦντα κολάζειν. τρέφονται δὲ δημοσίᾳ. An account follows of the organised mock battles of the Agelae with one another, resembling those of the Spartan Agelae ; cf. Part I, Chap. III, p. 118. The same information in similar phraseology occurs in an alleged excerpt from Heraclides (F.H.G. II, pp. 211 f.).

[2] Cf. Hesych. s.v. ἀπάγελος· ὁ μηδέπω συναγελαζόμενος παῖς· ὁ μέχρι ἐτῶν ἑπτακαίδεκα. Κρῆτες.

[3] Dar.-Sagl. s.v. Agelai, suggests that membership of the Agelai lasted ten years, but this is not proved by Hesych, s.v. δεκάδρομοι, which refers rather to Cretan citizens who had served ten years in the army.

[4] Cf. Guarducci Inscr. Creticae I (1935), pp. 83 f. ; Michel, Recueuil, no. 23 ; Ditt. Syll.³ 527. Dittenberger (ibid., n. 6) maintains that the Agelaoi are taking the oath on first entering the Agelae, but from l. 85, implying that they are of age to marry, it seems more likely that they are passing out of them (cf. Eph. ap. Strabo, X, 482). The further description of them as ἄζωστοι and πανάζωστοι implies too young an age for service as hoplites (cf. Hesych. s.v. ἄζωστος· ἄνοπλος, ἄστολος), while ἐγδυόμενοι (l. 100) is appropriate to service (as γυμνῆτες) in defence of the boundaries (l. 150 ; cf. Ath. Pol. 42. 4). The parallel ceremony at Lato applied to ἐγδραμόντες (S.G.D.I. 5075, l. 20 f.), probably implying escape from legal tutelage.

were maintained at state expense.[1]   The Athenian Epheboi
at the same period were also maintained by the state,[2]
and their oath of loyalty to the state also offers a close
parallel to the Cretan custom [3] : we may therefore conclude
that the Cretan Agelae were transformed at some point
in their history—perhaps as late as the fourth century B.C.
—into an Ephebic organisation resembling that which was
beginning to be common throughout the Greek world at
that time.   But the individual choice exercised in the
forming of each Agela, and the authority of the father of
the boy who formed it over his son's Agela, would seem
to be a survival from a much earlier period, designed to
secure the influence of individual nobles by providing
them from an early age with a loyal band of carefully selected
followers.   For such an arrangement, in which the initiative
belongs not to the state but to individual nobles (for in actual
fact it was the father and not his young son who organised
the Agela) bears the evident stamp of antiquity ; and since
as a rule there would be several sons and consequently
several Agelae attached to the one family, the arrangement
would go far to ensure the continued influence of that particular family in the next generation, especially in view of
the warlike feuds between noble families which were a
feature of Cretan life.[4]

Now it is clear from the analysis of the Spartan inscriptions of the Principate that there is a close parallel
between the organisation of the Cretan Agelae in their
earlier, or ' feudal ' period, and the selection of a group of
Kasens by a member of one of the Spartan ' Privileged
Families '.[5]   They were his so-called ' brothers ', even
though they can be shown to have belonged to a lower
social class, and went through the training of the *Agoge*

[1] Ephorus, *loc. cit.* (*cf.* above, p. 219, n. 1).
[2] Arist. *Ath. Pol.* 42. 3.   [3] *Cf.* Dar.-*Sagl. s.v. Epheboi*, p. 624.
[4] *Cf.* Arist. *Pol.* II, 10. 14.
[5] *Cf.* Part I (Chap. III), p. 103.   There is no evidence for the view
sometimes held that the Cretan Agelae (differing thereby from the Spartan
ones) were composed exclusively of boys drawn from the noble families
(*cf. P.W. s.v., Kreta*, p. 1818 : ' Die Hetairie war eine aus der Junglingsgenossenschaft hervorgegangene Schichtung der Bevölkerung, an der
nur diejenigen teilnahmen die zur ἀγέλη gehörten, also nur die vom Herrenstande '.   Ephorus says merely that it was boys of noble family who
collected the members of the Agela.

with him. In later life they still remained attached to him, preserving the record of their Kasen relationship as part of their personal name. The record of all this lies in inscriptions which belong to a period when the Kasen relationship has for long been made to serve the interests of the state as a whole ; it has become a means of raising new recruits for the office-holding class ; or as Plato expressed it in the Republic [1] (quite evidently thinking of Spartan institutions), a means of promoting members of the ' bronze ' class among the population into the ' silver ' class, or in the terms of his scheme for the ideal state, of promoting members of the ' artisan ' class into the class of ' auxiliaries ' who were to be the warrior section and defenders of the state from its foes. But as in the case of the corresponding Cretan institution, the Spartan one clearly had a feudal origin, and went back to a period when state control was negligible except when the whole people were at war. That such a period existed in the case of early Sparta is even more evident than in the case of other Greek states, in view of the long continuation of an organisation κατὰ κωμάς and the retarded development of a localised city of Sparta.

Literary evidence concerning the Kasen class at Sparta enables us to carry our detailed knowledge of it further back than do the inscriptions, and to corroborate the belief that, like the corresponding Cretan organisation, it had a feudal origin. This appears from Phylarchus' description of a class whom he calls Mothakes, but who are without doubt to be identified with the Kasens. ' The Mothakes ', he says, ' are persons brought up with the Spartans (σύντροφοι τῶν Λακεδαιμονίων).[2] For each citizen boy, in order to increase his own influence, causes one, two, or more boys to be sharers of his upbringing. These Mothakes are of free birth, though not Spartiates [3] (ἐλεύθεροι μέν, οὐ μὴν Λακεδαιμόνιοι), and

---

[1] Rep. III, 415 B, C.

[2] Phylarchus ap. Athen. VI. 102, p. 271 e. The same information appears in Aelian (V.H. XII. 43), who further adds that the navarch Callicratidas and Gylippus were also Mothakes. Cf also Schol. Arist. Plutus 279 : οἱ δὲ Λάκωνες τοὺς παρατρεφομένους τοῖς ἐλευθέροις παῖδας μόθωνας καλοῦσιν.

[3] Hesych. s.v. μόθακες goes further and defines them as οἱ ἅμα τρεφόμενοι τοῖς υἱοῖς δοῦλοι παῖδες. This directly contradicts Phylarchus' statement

they share the whole of his education. They say that Lysander the conqueror of Athens was actually one of them and became a citizen on account of his bravery.' The allegation that the class in question were ' not citizens ' or ' not Lacedaemonians ' is (in the light of what we now know about the complicated grades of citizenship which existed at Sparta [1]) a pardonable confusion which need not delay us further here. Its inaccuracy is sufficiently illustrated by the supposition that the ·navarch Lysander was ' not a citizen '. What is more significant for the present purpose is the striking resemblance to the method by which the Cretan Agelae were formed. This appears even more clearly from a passage of Aelian,[2] who says (attributing the origin of the institution to Lycurgus) that the Mothakes were boys ' whom fathers sent out with their sons to share their exercises in the gymnasia ', and who went through the *Agoge* with them. But while there seems to be exact resemblance between the Spartan Mothakes and the following of the noble young Cretans on the one hand, there is surely complete identity between the Mothakes and the Kasens on the other. The inscriptions prove in the case of the Kasens the inferior social status which the literary sources attribute to the Mothakes ; while the ex-Kasens could under certain conditions hold magistracies, ex-σύντροφοι (*i.e.* Mothakes) could in certain circumstances become generals and navarchs. The ex-Kasens continued in after life to be known as ' Kasen of so-and-so ' ; the ex-σύντροφοι could give their former leader in the Agela valuable military assistance on occasion, as Cleomenes III demonstrated as late as 228 B.C.[3] How in the face of these resemblances is it possible to distinguish between Kasens and Mothakes ? The alternative name admits after all

that they were ἐλεύθεροι ; *cf.* also Schol. Arist. *Plut.* 279 (cited in preceding note) and Ael. *V.H. loc. cit.* The modern suggestion that they were the sons of Helots (*cf.* Liddell and Scott, *ed.* Stuart Jones, *s.v.*) is an unsatisfactory compromise for which there is no evidence whatever. The explanation of the confusion is doubtless to be found in the existence of several grades of citizenship at Sparta.

[1] As revealed by the inscriptions relating to the παιδικὸς ἀγών. *Cf.* above, Chap. III, and see further below, pp. 353 f.

[2] Ael. *V.H.* XII, 43.

[3] *Cf.* Plut. *Cleom.* 8 : Θηρυκίων δὲ καὶ Φοῖβις, δύο τῶν συντρόφων τοῦ Κλεομένους, οὓς μόθακας καλοῦσιν, ἐπηκολούθουν στρατιώτας ὀλίγους ἔχοντες.

of a very simple explanation. It has been shown that
Kasens were, as their name implies, ' adoptive brothers ',[1]
and this name refers to their relation to the boy who had
selected them to be brought up with himself, being in fact
the technical term corresponding to σύντροφοι ;[2] the name
Mothakes, on the other hand, may be supposed to refer,
if accurately used, exclusively to the adult status of this
class. It seems obvious that its true derivation is from
μόθος (battle),[3] and that the Mothakes were originally the
military following of the noble Spartan who (like his Cretan
counterpart) had built up for himself a following from a
youthful age. That the name Mothakes has left no trace
in the inscriptions need not surprise us in view of the late
date of the inscriptions, which reflect a period in which there
are few traces of the original feudal relationship of the
Kasen class to their noble patrons except in the Agelae.

But the parallel between this evidently ancient social
organisation in Sparta and in Crete is not limited to the
Kasen class and its Cretan counterpart ; it applies also to
the Spartan relationship of Boagos and Synepheboi.[4] It
has been shown from the Spartan inscriptions that a Boagos
was the leader of an Agela, but himself beyond the age of
membership of the Agelae, a member of the Privileged
Families, who selected as his Synephebos a younger companion, still of the age to be in an Agela, who might be
either of his own rank entirely, or who at least had some
connection with the nobility.[5] The distinction of being a
Synephebos, like that of being a Kasen, lasted through
life and gave a passport of entry to certain offices which
otherwise might have been denied to the person concerned.[6]

An evident literary allusion to this institution occurs
in the *Respublica Lacedaemoniorum* attributed to Xenophon.
The author explains the somewhat different attitude of

---

[1] *Cf.* Part I, Chap. III, pp. 101 f.

[2] σύντροφοι appears as an alternative name for Mothakes in Phylarchus
(*cf.* above, p. 221, n. 2) and Plutarch (*cf.* above, p. 222, n. 3), and by
implication in Schol. Arist. *Pl.* 279 (*cf.* above, p. 221, n. 2).

[3] *Cf.* κώμαξ from κῶμος, βώμαξ from βῶμος. Hesych. and the Schol.
on Arist. *Pl.* 279 explain Mothon, which was either a normal variant or
a deliberate perversion of Mothax, to mean ' braggart ' or ' slavish person '.
But surely this meaning is secondary.

[4] *Cf.* Chap. III, pp. 107 f.   [5] *Cf.* pp. 110 f.   [6] *Cf. ibid.*

Sparta as compared with other Greek states towards any close friendship of a young man with a boy younger than himself by saying that Lycurgus thought it made all the difference whether the ' lover ' (ἐραστής) were concerned only with the nobility of character of his younger friend or merely with his physical attractiveness ; in the latter case there was no justification, but in the former and supposing the ἐραστής himself to be a young man of noble character, there could be no finer education for the younger boy.[1]

Turning to Crete, we find Ephorus, in exactly the same period as the literary sources which explain the true meaning of ἐραστής at Sparta,[2] explaining the meaning of the terms ἐραστής and κλεινός in Crete.[3] The passage from Ephorus has not been sufficiently fully preserved for us to know whether Ephorus himself drew the obvious parallel between Sparta and the Cretan towns here ; if so, he had hit upon a real similarity in this case even though, in general, he pushed the comparison between Sparta and Crete much too far. Actually the Cretan ritual which, according to Ephorus, went with the ἐραστής-κλεινός relationship does not appear to have had a parallel in Sparta, and its very peculiarity is a guarantee that Ephorus has not invented it. In fact Ephorus himself is said to have described it as unique.[4] It appears then that in its technical application, the term ἐραστής in Crete denoted a young man of noble family [5]

---

[1] *Resp. Lac.* II, 13 : ὁ δὲ Λυκοῦργος ἐναντία καὶ τούτοις πᾶσι γνούς, εἰ μέν τις αὐτὸς ὢν οἷον δεῖ ἀγασθεὶς ψυχὴν παιδὸς πειρῶτο ἄμεμπτον φίλον ἀποτελέσασθαι καὶ συνεῖναι, ἐπῄνει καὶ καλλίστην παιδείαν ἐνόμισεν. A similar allusion to the Spartan custom in the fourth century B.C. occurs in Xen. *Conv.* VIII, 35. It was natural that other Greeks who did not agree with this point of view should take a cynical view of the Spartan practice (*cf.* Hesych. *s.v.* λακωνίζειν, Λακωνικὸν τρόπον).

[2] *Cf.* preceding note.

[3] *Cf.* Ephorus *ap.* Strabo, X, 4. 21 (483). The name ἐραστής in this connection is not one of Ephorus' inventions designed to increase the apparent similarity to Sparta (*cf.* above, p. 211, n. 5) ; he explains that the technical Cretan term was actually φιλήτωρ. It seems not improbable that it was alternatively φιλητής, since this would explain the double meaning of ἐραστής and κλέπτης which so much puzzled the ancient philologists (*cf.* Suidas, *Etym. Magn. s.v.* φιλητής), the function of the Cretan φιλητής being ἁρπάζειν (see further below).

[4] Ephorus *ap.* Strabo, X, 4. 21 (483) : ἴδιον δ'αὐτοῖς τὸ περὶ τοὺς ἔρωτας νόμιμον· οὐ γὰρ πειθοῖ κατεργάζονται τοὺς ἐρωμένους ἀλλ' ἁρπαγῇ, κ.τ.λ.

[5] *Cf. ibid.*: ὡς ἐξομολογούμενος ὅτι ἀνάξιος ὁ παῖς εἴη τοιούτου ἐραστοῦ τυγχάνειν. The noble birth of the ἐραστής is not stated in so many words but it is quite definitely implied by the whole account.

(as were the Spartan Boagoi), already old enough to be a member of one of the Andreia [1] or men's clubs (as were the Boagoi) who carried out a ritual ' kidnapping ' (ἁρπαγή) of some boy (παῖς, in Cretan κλεινός) in the face of opposition from the boy's comrades. The younger boy for his part must be worthy of admiration on account of his manly virtues,[2] and Ephorus implies that he also was of high social class, though not necessarily so distinguished as the ἐραστής. Here we may note the resemblance so far to the Synepheboi. The ἐραστής gave notice of the intended kidnapping to the friends of the κλεινός some days beforehand, so that they could band themselves together to resist if they thought the ἐραστής unworthy ; otherwise they made only a token resistance, and the boy was carried off by his kidnapper, first to his own *Andreion* and then into the country for eight weeks (the maximum time allowed by law) together with all his friends, and the whole company spent their time in celebrations and in hunting together, the ἐραστής providing the means through the costly presents —impossible for a poor man—which he gave to his κλεινός. One of these presents was always a soldier's cloak which continued to be worn by the ex-κλεινός at all public festivals for the future, until he grew out of it, when another distinctive dress for ex-κλεινοί was worn instead. This detail, and the name παρασταθείς which was the proper designation of the boy who had been carried off in this fashion, being clearly equivalent in meaning to παραστάτης (a comrade in arms) give the clue to the meaning of the whole institution ; its purpose was similar to that of the Agelae, namely to provide the young noble with a close following in war, but in this case the choice made by the ἐραστής looked to a less remote future and to a more aristocratic following than when he had himself been of an age to form an Agela. This aspect of the institution is further illustrated by an anecdote in Aelian which purports to apply to a particular example of the Cretan ἐραστής-παρασταθείς relationship, and from which it appears that it was as an intrepid soldier that the

---

[1] Ephorus, *loc. cit.*: πέρας δὲ τῆς ἐπιδιώξεώς ἐστιν ἕως ἂν ἀχθῇ ὁ παῖς εἰς τὸ τοῦ ἁρπάσαντος ἀνδρεῖον.

[2] *Cf.* Plato, *Laws*, I, 633 B : ἐράσμιον δὲ νομίζουσι οὐ τὸν κάλλει διαφέροντα, ἀλλὰ τὸν ἀνδρείᾳ καὶ κοσμιότητι. *Cf.* the Spartan requirement, above, p. 224, n. 1.

15

ἐραστής was above all anxious to shine in the eyes of his younger protégé.[1]

Both Ephorus and Aelian stress the nobility of character and behaviour displayed by both the parties to this relationship, and one would conclude from Ephorus' account that there was no justification for the cynical view taken by other Greek states of the Cretan attitude in this matter.[2] Thus from the point of view of public morals also the theory of this peculiar institution was the same in Crete as in Sparta, and in particular it was thought to conduce to valour in the military sphere. But here again our information applies to the period when both in Crete and in Sparta the state had assumed wider control than can have existed in any earlier period, and it seems probable that originally the institution was less lofty and from the material point of view more practical in its aims than it had become in the time of Ephorus and Xenophon, the obvious aim at that more remote period being to secure the power and influence of the wealthy nobles. For, as in the case of the Spartan Synepheboi, it is to be observed that the Cretan παρασταθέντες (whose name as we have seen denotes the followers of their patrons in war) enjoyed also special privileges in the state in adult life, a distinctive dress and the most distinguished seats at public festivals. To be selected as a παρασταθείς or Synephebos would, therefore, become an object of ambition ; hence no doubt the evident pride with which the Spartan Synepheboi record their status in inscriptions later in life,[3] hence also the Cretan view, mentioned by Ephorus, that for handsome boys of noble birth it was a disgrace not to be so chosen.[4] To judge from Ephorus' account one would conclude that in Crete every φιλήτωρ (ἐραστής) who adopted a κλεινός as his future follower in war was himself the παρασταθείς of some other noble. Such

---

[1] Cf. Ael. De Nat. An. IV, 1. The description of both ἐραστής and boy tallies here with that given by Ephorus, the boy being described as μειράκιον ὥρᾳ διαπρεπὲς καὶ τὴν ψυχὴν ἀνδρεῖον καὶ πρὸς τὰ κάλλιστα τῶν μαθημάτων πεφυκὸς εὖ καὶ καλῶς, καλούμενον δὲ δι' ἡλικίαν ἐς ὅπλα μηδέπω.

[2] As in the case of Sparta (cf. above, p. 224, n. 1), the Cretan practice called forth unfavourable comments outside Crete (cf. Plato, Laws, I, 636 C, D).

[3] Cf. p. 167, n. 4 (one example of many).

[4] Ephorus, ibid. : τοῖς δὲ καλοῖς τὴν ἰδέαν καὶ προγόνων ἐπιφανῶν αἰσχρὸν ἐραστῶν μὴ τυχεῖν.

a system, however, would be bound to lead to great confusion and is therefore improbable in itself, and the otherwise close resemblances between the Cretan arrangement and the Synephebos-Boagos relationship makes it more improbable. Like the Boagoi, the Cretan ἐρασταί must have belonged to a specially privileged class in the state, and the nobility of birth of the class of παρασταθέντες is probably exaggerated by Ephorus.

It seems not improbable that the specially-privileged class in Crete who as boys selected their Agela, and as young men their παρασταθέντες, should be identified with the Hippeis, who in the time of Ephorus continued to be obliged to furnish the cavalry. The existence of a class of Hippeis both in Crete and in Sparta was noted by Ephorus as one of the parallels between the two,[1] there being, however, the attendant difference (or so he himself believed) that in Sparta the Hippeis were no longer obliged actually to furnish horses.[2] Consequently it seems reasonable to identify with the class of Hippeis at Sparta mentioned by Ephorus the ' Privileged Families ' for whom our evidence is the later Spartan inscriptions, the class which furnished the Boagoi and the ' patrons of Kasens ' in relation to the Ephebic organisation, and who in political life were alone eligible for certain offices, including (in the period before its reorganisation by Cleomenes III) admission to the Gerusia. In terms of military organisation, the whole scheme clearly goes back, both in Sparta and in Crete, to a period before the adoption of the hoplite system, and since it is common to both these regions, to a period much more remote than that.

Below the class of Hippeis both in Crete and Sparta we

---

[1] Ephorus ap. Strabo, X, 4. 18 (481) : τῶν δ'ἀρχείων τὰ μὲν καὶ τὰς διοικήσεις ἔχειν τὰς αὐτὰς καὶ τὰς ἐπωνυμίας, ὥσπερ καὶ τὴν τῶν γερόντων ἀρχὴν καὶ τὴν τῶν ἱππέων, πλὴν ὅτι τοὺς ἐν Κρήτῃ ἱππέας καὶ ἵππους κεκτῆσθαι συμβέβηκεν· ἐξ οὗ τεκμαιροῦνται πρεσβυτέραν εἶναι τῶν ἐν Κρήτῃ ἱππέων τὴν ἀρχὴν· σώζειν γὰρ τὴν ἐτυμότητα τῆς προσηγορίας · τοὺς δὲ μὴ ἱπποτροφεῖν.

[2] Ibid. On the 300 Spartans of the age of ἥβη chosen each year by the three Hippagretae (Resp. Lac. IV, 3), see Appendix VII, p. 496. These appear to have been the class of which Ephorus was thinking, since they no longer served as cavalry. But Ephorus as usual is confused ; we know from Xenophon that there was in addition at Sparta a class of richer citizens who in his time were still obliged to furnish horses (Appendix VII, ibid.). The true parallel between Sparta and Crete in regard to the Hippeis (i.e. the social class) lies here.

are now in a position to distinguish at least two social grades, the highest of these being the class from which in Crete the παρασταθέντες were drawn, and from which in Sparta the Synepheboi were drawn. Reasons have already been suggested for supposing this grade of society also to have originated in a ' feudal ' period before state control of the population was at all highly developed. As to the third class, they furnished in Crete the rank and file of the Agelae, in Sparta the Kasens (with their alternative name of Mothakes). But below these again there seems to be yet a fourth class, which though not socially inferior to the third yet missed certain of their privileges, namely those who in Crete were not chosen to be members of an Agela, and those who in Sparta did not become Kasens. It has been shown on the evidence of the Spartan inscriptions that the Spartan Agelae at least included members who were neither Kasens nor Synepheboi,[1] an arrangement which may well be due to later modification by the state of an organisation which originally had been exactly like the early Cretan one, that is to say in which the nobles alone decided who should be in the Agelae. Some of these, on the evidence of their names, belonged to the noble families ; none of them are likely to represent the class from whom Kasens were drawn. This last stratum of the Spartan population should rather be identified with the Ὑπομείονες or ' Inferiors ', who are known to have been politically discontented and to have ranged themselves on the side of the Helots, Perioikoi and the oppressed section of the population generally.[2] The corresponding class in Crete must obviously be distinguished from the Klarotai since it is inconceivable that the Agelae of the feudal period were drawn from this class of semi-serfs.[3] They are perhaps to be identified with the *Aphetairoi* (non-members of Hetaeriae) who are mentioned in the Cretan inscriptions ;[4] in any case failure to reach a certain property qualification appears to have involved exclusion from the Hetaeriae.[5]

---

[1] *Cf.* Part I, Chap. III, p. 115.

[2] *Cf.* Xen. *Hell.* III, iii, 6, referring to the time of the conspiracy of Cinadon, 397 B.C. Xenophon gives no further information about the Hypomeiones here, and they are not mentioned elsewhere.

[3] *Cf.* above, pp. 213 f.

[4] See further below.   [5] *Cf.* below, p. 232.

A tabulation of the corresponding social classes in Sparta and in Crete, based on the preceding account but given with some reservations as regards the application of the Cretan technical names, may help to make clearer the general arrangement in both.

SPARTA	CRETE
Class	
1. *Hippeis* (*i.e.* ' Privileged Families ').	*Hippeis.*
2. *Synepheboi.*	*Parastathentes.*
3. *Mothakes* (Kasens) and other ex-members of Agelae.	*Agelaoi.*[1]
4. *Hypomeiones.*	*Aphetairoi* (*Apageloi*)[2]
5. *Neodamodeis.*[3]	*Klarotai.*

There is reason to think that in Gortyn at the time of publication of the later law code there was no longer any effective distinction between classes 4 and 5 ; in other words, that all above the class of *Klarotai* were now compulsorily passed through the Agelae. For in the classification of fines for assault [4] only three social classes are recognised : (1) Free-born persons ; (2) those whose parents are ἀφέταιροι ; (3) slaves (δοῦλοι). From the amounts of the prescribed fines it is apparent that Class 2 were in a position intermediate between slavery and freedom, and so are to be identified with the *Klarotai*; [5] from their name it is also apparent that this class were not eligible for the Hetaeriae, in which (since the classification in this section of the code is clearly exhaustive) *all* above their class must have been included. Since at this period admission to the Hetaeriae depended on passing through an Agela, [6] it may be supposed that the reduction of the number of social classes reflected in the Gortyn Code was consequent upon the transformation of

---

[1] Supposing this name to mean, in earlier times at least, those who had passed through the Agelae and were now adult citizens, as well as boys actually in the Agelae. This meaning is supported by the oath taken by the ἀγελάοι of Dreros (third century B.C.), *cf.* Ditt. *Syll.*[3] 527, and above, p. 219, n. 4.

[2] Hesych. *s.v.* ἀπάγελος gives ὁ μηδέπω ἀγελαζόμενος παῖς, i.e. ' a boy too young to be in an Agela '. But *cf.* preceding note.

[3] This class at Sparta may not have come into existence until the time of the Peloponnesian War, *cf.* above, pp. 39 f.

[4] Gortyn Code, col. ii, 2–10 (M.A.L. III, 1893, p. 107, with Comparetti's translation and notes, *ibid.* pp. 125, 160).

[5] *Cf.* above, pp. 213 f.

[6] This seems the natural conclusion from Ditt. *Syll.*[3] 527, l. 95 f. (cited below, p. 231, n. 3).

the Agelae into an Ephebic organisation under the direct control of the state. There were no longer any persons above the grade of *Klarotai* who were not in the Agelae. That the early Cretan classification of society was, in general, more elaborate seems clear from the way in which the Agelae were then recruited by members of the nobility. The table of social classes given above, as far as Crete is concerned, is intended as a reconstruction of what the general scheme was like before the state assumed control of the Agelae.

The obvious questions which arise out of the establishment of these hierarchies in early Crete and Sparta are : (1) What point in the scale was fixed in each case for the enjoyment of citizen rights ? (2) How were these classes related to the groups which partook of common meals (Syssitia, Phiditia or Andreia in Sparta, Andreia in Crete) ? The two questions are in fact closely connected, membership of a Syssition in the case of Sparta, and of an Andreion in the Cretan states, being the *sine qua non* of citizenship.[1] But since it is not at all likely, in view of the different way in which state institutions developed in Sparta as compared with Crete,[2] that any significant conclusion could be drawn from a comparative study of Sparta and the Cretan towns in the matter of eligibility for citizenship, this investigation is best confined for the purpose of the present study to Sparta only, and will be considered in another place.[3] On the other hand, enough evidence has already been adduced to show that the organisation of society in Sparta and Crete, from the non-constitutional point of view, was in early times similar to some extent at least, and so it may be profitable to examine the extent of possible further resemblance between the Spartan Syssitia and the Cretan Andreia. Evidence about the Spartan Syssitia is in fact self-contradictory and impossible to interpret as it stands, and it seems not impossible that comparison with the Cretan arrangement may clear up obscurities in the Spartan one. What can be discovered about the Cretan Andreia

---

[1] For Sparta, *cf.* Arist. *Pol.* II, 9. 31, 32 ; II, 10. 7 ; for Crete, Dosiadas *ap.* Athen. IV, 143a : διῄρηνται δ'οἱ πολῖται πάντες καθ' ἑταιρίας · καλοῦσι δὲ ταύτας ἀνδρεῖα.

[2] *Cf.* above, pp. 209 f.   [3] See below, pp. 245 f.

independently of the alleged similarities to the Spartan Syssitia which we find in Ephorus and works dependent on him ?

§ 3. The Relation of Andreion and Hetaireia

According to Dosiadas, in a passage already cited,[1] all the citizens in the Cretan towns were members of associations (ἑταιρεῖαι) which the Cretans themselves called ἀνδρεῖα. The name ἀνδρεῖα is attested by inscriptions of the third century B.C.,[2] but so is the name ἑταιρεῖαι in the same period in the case of Dreros,[3] and for a somewhat earlier period in the Gortyn Code, as has been already mentioned. It therefore seems not improbable that Dosiadas has employed by accident, as it were, a word which was in fact the correct technical term in some Cretan states, although he himself clearly uses it with its more common and non-technical meaning of any kind of association whatsoever. On the other hand, it has been suggested that the two names were not interchangeable, that ἑταιρεία was properly speaking the name of the association, ἀνδρεῖα properly speaking the common meals shared by the members of such an association.[4] This interpretation fits in with the evidence of the Gortyn Code and with that of inscriptions from other Cretan towns in the third century B.C., but as will be seen presently, does not agree with all the available evidence. A final decision on the subject is best postponed for the present.[5]

With regard to ἀνδρεῖα, the statement of Dosiadas that all the citizens were eligible for them is corroborated for the second half of the third century B.C. by inscriptions

---

[1] P. 230, n. 1.   [2] Cf. below, p. 232, n. 1.

[3] Cf. Ditt. Syll.[3] 527 (oath of the Agelaoi of Dreros), ll. 95 f.   If the Kosmoi do not in any year administer the prescribed oath to the Agelaoi 500 staters fine is to be paid by each of them, and the amount of the fine (the negative in l. 124 being certainly due to a mistaken repetition of ὅσα κα μὴ πράξωντι in l. 120), ταῖς ἑταιρείαις δασσάσθωσαν ταῖς ἐμ πόλει καὶ αἱ πεί τινεν οὐρεύωντι Δρήριοι. On the meaning of αἱ πεί τινεν οὐρεύωντι (frontier garrisons) see Dittenberger's notes 19, 40.

[4] Cf. Ditt. Syll.[3] 527, n. 38.   This opinion appears to be followed by De Sanctis, Atthis, pp. 42 f.   Ephorus also limited the name ἀνδρεῖα to the meals (cf. Ephorus ap. Strabo, X, 480-1).

[5] See further below, pp. 238 f.

relating to Priansos, Hierapytna and Lyktos. Priansos and Hierapytna on the one hand, and Hierapytna and Lyktos on the other, concluded at this period agreements for joint citizenship (ἰσοτελεία) which involved, amongst other things, the admission of all the citizens of the one town to the ἀνδρεῖα of the other at all public festivals.[1] It is also evident from the context that the main purpose of the meeting together of the citizens on those occasions was to share in a common meal.

The common meals at Lyktos are described in detail by Dosiadas : ' The Lyktians arrange their common meals (τὰ κοινὰ συσσίτια) as follows. Each contributes to his association (εἰς τὴν ἑταιρίαν) one-tenth of the produce of his crops, and the government of the state apportions the revenues of the state [2] to the halls of meetings of each group.[3] Each slave (τῶν δὲ δούλων ἕκαστος) [4] also contributes an Aeginetan stater per head. The citizens are all distributed into associations (ἑταιρίαι) which they call ἀνδρεῖα. And the supervision of the common meal itself (τοῦ συσσιτίου) is in the hands of a woman, who is given in addition three or four commoners [5] to help in the preparation and serving ;

[1] Cf. Cauer, Delectus,[2] 119 (Priansos and Hierapytna) ll. 35 f. The Kosmoi of either city have the right to attend the meetings of the Kosmoi of the other and the right to a seat in their Ecclesia : ἐν δὲ τοῖς ἡροικοῖς καὶ ἐν ταῖς ἄλλαις ἑορταῖς οἱ παρατυγχάνοντες ἑρπόντων παρ' ἀλλάλος ἐς ἀνδρήιον καθὼς καὶ οἱ ἄλλοι πολῖται (i.e. not as ξένοι, who could be invited in any case, but as πολῖται on equal terms with the citizens of the state in which the festival was being held). For the agreement between Hierapytna and Lyktos, cf. ibid. 117, ll. 1 f. : ἑρπόντων δὲ οἱ Ἱεραπύτνιοι τοῖς Λυττίοις ἐς τὰ [. 12 .] Λύττιοι τοῖς Ἱεραπυτνίοις ἐς τὰν εὐάμερον τα[. 7 .] ὁ δὲ κόσμος τῶν Ἱεραπυτνίων ἑρπέτω Λυττοῖ ἐς τὸ ἀρχεῖον, κατὰ ταὐτὰ δὲ καὶ ὁ τῶ[ν Λυττίων κόσμος ἑρπέτω ἐν Ἱεραπύτνοις ἐς] τὸ ἀρχεῖον. In view of the close resemblance to the Priansos-Hierapytna agreement just cited, it seems certain that the first of the two lacunae in this passage should be filled by the words [ἀνδρήϊα καθὼς], the second no doubt contained the name of a public festival.

[2] I.e. presumably, the tenths which have been subscribed. But some phrase may have been omitted at this point in the excerpt, referring to other contributions to the revenues of the state by Lyktian property owners. Cf. Arist. Pol. II, 10. 8.

[3] This interpretation of εἰς τοὺς ἑκάστων (sc. τῶν ἀνδρείων or τῶν συσσιτίων) οἴκους is necessitated by the reference to the οἶκοι δύο for each Syssitia mentioned later in the same passage.

[4] I.e. each Klarotas. Cf. above, p. 213.

[5] τῶν δημοτικῶν. The expression stresses a difference of social status compared with the members. According to Pyrgion ap. Athen. IV, 143e, those chosen to serve were the youngest members.

and each of these is provided with two servants to carry
the ξύλα (rough wooden trays ? [1]), whom they call καλοφόροι.
Everywhere throughout Crete there are in the buildings
set apart for common meals [2] two rooms (οἶκοι) of which
they call one the Andreion (i.e. " the men's hall ") and the
other the " sleeping-room " in which they entertain strangers
for the night.   And in the room for meals there are, first,
two tables called guest tables,[3] at which strangers who are
present sit, then the tables for the rest.   The same share
is apportioned to everyone who is present, except that
to the boys (τοῖς δὲ νεωτέροις) [4] only half a share of meat
is given, and they do not touch anything else.   Further,
there is a drinking vessel of water and wine mixed set for
each table ; all the persons at the common table drink of
this in common, and after they have finished their meal
another is set before them.   And for the boys (παῖσι) a
common mixing bowl is prepared.   The older men if they
wish to do so are permitted to drink more.   The woman
who presides in the Syssitia [5] takes from the table in the
sight of everyone the best of the fare, and places it before
those who have won renown in war or on account of their
wisdom.   And after the meal they are accustomed first of
all to deliberate about public affairs, and after this they
recall great deeds done in war and rehearse the praises of
their brave men, thus exhorting the young to deeds of
valour.'

[1] Cf. the servant called ὁ ἐπὶ τῶν ξυλῶν, Hermipp. ᾿Αρτοπ. fr. 5 (Meineke).
At all events the servants in the Cretan Andreia are unlikely to have
carried clubs or other kind of wooden weapons.
[2] ἡ συσσιτία seems to mean the building, as distinct from τὰ συσσίτια,
the meals which were held there.
[3] Pyrgion ap. Athen. IV, 143e, speaks of only one guest table in each
Syssitia.
[4] According to Pyrgion, loc. cit., the half-share was given to the 'little
sons sitting under their father's chairs '.   Cf. also Ephorus ap. Strabo,
X, 4. 20 (483) : τοὺς μὲν οὖν ἔτι νεωτέρους εἰς τὰ συσσίτια ἄγουσι τὰ ἀνδρεῖα,
χαμαὶ δὲ καθήμενοι διαιτῶνται μετ' ἀλλήλων κ.τ.λ.
[5] ἡ προεστηκυῖα τῆς συσσιτίας ; i.e. not over the association, but in the
dining-hall, as above, note 2.   The title of θοιναρμοστρία held by members
of distinguished families at Sparta in the Roman period, and apparently
connected with various cults (cf. I.G. V, i, index, vi, 2) may well represent
the survival of an early Spartan parallel to the Cretan usage.   θοῖναι is
used in the special sense of banquets of a Phratria (suggesting a close
parallel to the meals of these Cretan Hetaeriae) in the constitution of the
Phratria of the Labyadae at Delphi (Inscr. Iurid. Gr. II, ii (1904), p. 190 D).

Now it is quite clear that this passage is the source of Aristotle's remarkable and quite incredible statement in the *Politics* that the Cretan system of Syssitia provided meals at the public expense for all, women and children as well as men. The summary account of the organisation with which Aristotle prefaces this astonishing piece of information coincides exactly in sense and to a certain extent in verbal expression with the passages just cited from Dosiadas.[1] Moreover, the passage in Dosiadas, carelessly read no doubt by Aristotle's source (? Ephorus) rather than by Aristotle himself, might easily lead to the conclusion drawn by Aristotle (again no doubt following Ephorus), since a woman did preside over the serving, and children did attend at the common meals. We therefore get a *terminus ante quem* in the earlier fourth century B.C. for the Κρητικά of Dosiadas, and it further seems probable that he, and not Ephorus, is to be recognised as the fountainhead of all the detailed information which has come down to us, not only about the Cretan Syssitia, but about other Cretan social institutions. This is an important conclusion from the point of view of the present inquiry, since it means that this information about Cretan social institutions is far more likely to be reliable than it would have been if it had been collected in the first place by a writer who was setting out with the express purpose of pointing out the close parallels between Sparta and Crete. So far as can be seen from the other fragments of his work which have been preserved, Dosiadas had no interest whatever in Sparta.

We therefore seem entitled to conclude that the description in Dosiadas is a reliable account of the organisation of the Cretan common meals in the early fourth century B.C., and so far as it goes, the evidence from the inscriptions of the third century B.C., already mentioned, is in accordance

---

[1] *Cf.* Arist. *Pol.* II, 10. 7 f. : ἐν μὲν γὰρ Λακεδαίμονι κατὰ κεφαλὴν ἕκαστος εἰσφέρει τὸ τεταγμένον . . . ἐν δὲ Κρήτῃ κοινοτέρως· ἀπὸ πάντων γὰρ τῶν γιγνομένων καρπῶν τε καὶ βοσκημάτων, καὶ ἐκ τῶν δημοσίων καὶ φόρων οὓς φέρουσιν οἱ περίοικοι, τέτακται μέρος τὸ μὲν πρὸς τοὺς θεοὺς καὶ τὰς κοινὰς λειτουργίας, τὸ δὲ τοῖς συσσιτίοις, ὥστ' ἐκ κοινοῦ τρέφεσθαι πάντας, καὶ γυναῖκας καὶ παῖδας καὶ ἄνδρας. The passage in Dosiadas could not on the other hand possibly have been deduced from the one in the *Politics* or from its counterpart in Ephorus.

with it. With regard to the size of gathering which is
implied, it was not too large to be entertained together in
one room (οἶκος) and to be waited upon by three or four
young men each with the assistance of two servants to
fetch and carry. The two guest tables had also to be provided for, not to speak of the little boys who accompanied
their fathers. These were not too numerous to be looked
after by a single *Paidonomos* appointed for the purpose ; [1]
however well-behaved they were he can scarcely have
kept more than fifty in order. It seems unlikely that more
than two hundred persons can have been provided for all
told, including the children, or that there were ever more
than twelve tables (one for each assistant) including the
two guest tables. The number at each table cannot have
been very large, since only one drinking cup (ποτήριον)
was provided for each, and was only refilled once. Half
a pint of watery wine altogether for each man would be a
modest allowance, but it would be a very large drinking
cup which would hold more than three pints.[2] This implies
a maximum of twelve adults at each table. The conclusion is reinforced by the fact that the little boys who
were present had a mixing bowl (κρατήρ) prepared for them,
whereas each table had only a drinking cup (ποτήριον).

On the other hand, the total number entertained cannot
have been very small, for the keynote was evidently sim-
plicity and austerity, and therefore nine or twelve men
to wait at table implies a total of about 80–100 diners,
exclusive of the children.

With regard to eligibility for attendance, it is certain
from the name *Andreion* given both to the gathering itself
and to the room in which it was held that membership was
restricted to adult men. Moreover, the picture of women
taking part in ' deliberations on public policy ' after the
meal, in a Greek state, is patently ridiculous. But the

[1] *Cf.* Pyrgion *ap.* Athen. IV, 143 e.
[2] The drinking vessels used in the Spartan Syssitia were not of earthen-
ware (which was used only at special feasts and celebrations) but wood
(πισάκναι, Hesych.), made in the shape of a leather bottle, hence called
also κώθωνες. *Cf.* Polemon Iliensis *ap.* Athen. XI, 483 c. The normal
capacity of such a κώθων of archaic form seems to have been four κοτύλαι
(about 2 pints). *Cf.* Alexis Comicus (fourth century B.C.) *ap.* Athen.
loc. cit. εἶτα τετρακότυλον ἐπεσόβει κώθωνά μοι παλαιὸν οἴκων κτῆμα.

statement of Dosiadas that ' all the citizens ' were eligible for membership does not necessarily imply that all the adult free males were included, since it is quite possible that citizenship depended on a property qualification which excluded a large part of the population. The way in which the expenses of the common meals was defrayed in fact supports this interpretation, and moreover indicates that membership of the group which shared in the common meals was at Lyktos, and at the period when Dosiadas was writing, confined to landholders, who alone could pay the annual tenth of their produce in kind.[1] The δημοτικοί who did the serving [2] were not necessarily or even probably members of the Andreion. Aristotle seems to be wrong in maintaining that there was any difference between the Cretan and the Spartan systems in the matter of contributions to the Syssitia.[3] In both cases property controlled by individuals was the basis of the contributions.

A last point of interest which emerges from Dosiadas' account is that the levy of one-tenth implies that the common meals at that period were not limited to public festivals, but were a daily occurrence. For the remaining nine-tenths of the farm produce would be no more than enough in the average case to provide for the year for a wife, unmarried daughters, infant sons and those in the Agelae, domestics and farm servants.[4] One-tenth of the whole produce would be far too high a levy if it were intended to provide the food of the master of the estate only at public festivals.

It is now time to bring the account of Dosiadas into relation with what has already been established on the basis of other evidence about the early social organisation of Crete. We have seen that the fundamental purpose of the Agelae and also of the system of selecting older supporters by the nobles was to protect the interest of their

---

[1] This appears even more clearly from the version in Arist. *Pol.* II, 10. 8 (*cf.* above, p. 234, n. 1) than from Dosiadas *loc. cit.* which last seems to have suffered some abridgement at this point, and so omits the reference to a tenth of the βοσκήματα, mentioning only καρποί.

[2] *Cf.* above, p. 232, n. 5.　　　　　　　　[3] *Cf.* Arist. *Pol.* II, 10. 7, 8.

[4] Note that the contributions of the *Klarotai* were reckoned separately (*cf.* above, p. 234 and note 4 *ibid.*) so that their upkeep does not come into question.

own family group ; and it has been shown that the whole
system implies the existence in early times of a well-defined
association, partly hereditary and partly selected irre-
spective of birth, in which groups of brothers of noble
family, each with his own following of inferiors, were united
by their father into a single association, the father in his
turn also having been connected from youth upwards with
his brothers and their respective followers in the same way.
In spite of the existence of some social differences, the whole
group, as has been demonstrated,[1] was in a sense aristocratic
in character, in that it still excluded the rank and file of
the population ; and it is possible to make a rough estimate
of its average size. If we suppose that each boy of noble
family collected an Agela round him of ten or twelve
others, and on reaching manhood acquired in addition
three or four *Parastathentes*,[2] this would imply a special
following for each member of the *Andreion* of about fifteen
or somewhat fewer. If now we imagine a family group
among the nobles consisting of three middle-aged brothers,
ten grown-up sons among them, and an aged father, the
whole association will comprise about 200 members. The
size would naturally vary considerably according to the
number in the aristocratic family which was its nucleus,
according to its local prestige, and according to whether
its own numbers tended to grow or to dwindle, but in any
case would be comparable to the size of the Andreia as
described by Dosiadas, especially having regard to the
improbability of all members being present at the common
meals on each occasion.

A group such as has been described would very appropriately be described as a ἑταιρεία, since it would be
literally an association of ἑταῖροι in the specialised sense
of comrades in war. This suggestion is at variance, however,
with others made by modern authorities ; it has been maintained, for example, that the Cretan Hetaeriae were purely
aristocratic,[3] and that they were purely hereditary from

---

[1] *Cf.* above, pp. 227 f.

[2] This number is suggested on account of the close resemblance of
the Cretan *Parastathentes* to the Spartan *Synepheboi*. *Cf.* Part I, Chap.
III, pp. 108 f.

[3] *Cf.* Kohler u. Ziebarth, *Das Stadtrecht von Gortyn* (1912), p. 46 : ' Hetärie
ist eine aus der Junglingsgenossenschaft hervorgegangene Schichtung
der Bevölkerung, an der natürlich nur diejenigen teilnahmen, welche

very early times, even if not in origin.[1] But neither of
these views rests upon any secure foundation ;[2] and it seems
fair to say that the new facts which have been observed
about the Spartan Kasen-system, reacting as they necessarily
must upon our interpretation of the early social organisation
of Crete, make these earlier interpretations of the character
of the Cretan Hetaeriae inherently improbable. For even
though there may continue to be doubt about points of
detail, one thing at all events must now be clear, that both
in Sparta and in Crete the aristocratic families sought to
maintain their power and prestige by continually drawing
upon fresh blood from outside their ranks.

It is true that the alternative view, rejected here, appears
to rest on the assumption that the Hetaeria was a much
smaller organisation than is now being suggested, coinciding
rather with what has been for convenience described as
the ' aristocratic nucleus ' of the association which it is
now proposed to identify as the Hetaeria. This consideration raises once more the question of whether *Hetaeria*
and *Andreion* are synonymous terms, and of what in any
case is the original and true meaning of *Andreion*. Although
later writers appear to use the plural ἀνδρεῖα of the meals,
this does not seem to have been the usage in the time of
Alcman, whose phrase φοίναις δε καὶ ἐν θιάσοισιν Ἀνδρείων,[3]
certainly seems to imply that the Andreia were the associations which held the feasts and banquets ; having already
given two names for the banquets, the poet is most unlikely
to have added yet a third, namely Andreia. But this passage
is admittedly not conclusive.

zu der ἀγέλη gehörten, also nur die von Herrenstande'. There is no evidence
whatever that the Agelae were limited to the aristocracy, and although
it may be concluded from the oath of the Agelaoi of Dreros (Ditt. *Syll.*[3]
527) that all members of the Agelae passed into Hetaeriae, there is no
evidence that the Hetaeriae were exclusively composed of these even at
this late period.

　　[1] *Cf.* De Sanctis, *Atthis* (1912), p. 43 : 'A poco a poco ciò diviene regola.
Nella eterià, fatta ereditaria, non si ammettono se non i figli de suoi membri
. . . La eteria sie è cambiato in fratria'. With the possible parallel between Hetaeria in Crete and Phratria in other Greek states this is not
the place to deal. But De Sanctis' view does not appear to rest upon any
definite evidence. The interest taken by the Cretan Hetaeria in adoptions
(De Sanctis, *ibid.*) certainly provides no proof that it was purely hereditary
in character.

　　[2] See two preceding notes.　　　　[3] Alcman *ap.* Strabo, X (482).

There is, however, a further piece of evidence which does not appear to have been taken into account in this connection. This is the well-known ' Testament of Epikteta', the classic Greek example of a document establishing a testamentary trust.[1] The date appears to be about 200 B.C. ; the place of origin is not mentioned in the inscription itself but has been identified with great probability by Boeckh as Thera, mainly from the personal names which it contains. It comes in any case from a Dorian state in which there were Ephors, and further examination of it will show that it not only contains other points of resemblance to Sparta, but implies a system of law closely similar to the Cretan. In these features alone it establishes further links between Sparta and Crete, but its immediate interest in connection with the Cretan and Spartan Andreia is that it concerns the organisation of a body of trustees which is called τὸ κοινὸν τοῦ ἀνδρείου τῶν συγγενῶν, ' the council of the Andreion of kinsmen ', or sometimes simply ὁ ἀνδρεῖος (sc. σύλλογος). This κοινόν appears to be nothing more nor less than a council of the adult male members of a single agnatic group.[2]

The testatrix Epikteta makes her kinsmen responsible for the upkeep of a *Heroon* built in memory of her husband, her two sons, and herself,[3] and provides for an annual festival to be held in the building, at which all the relatives of all ages and both sexes are to be present. The members of the κοινόν itself, which receives the building as a bequest and assumes responsibility for it, are all men, as the name κοινὸν τοῦ ἀνδρείου itself implies. From the list which is given of the twenty-five members of this body, it is clear that they are also literally συγγενεῖς.[4] Those who are to attend the annual festival are also relatives—the wives of

---

[1] *Cf. Inscr. Jur. Gr.*, no. xxiv ; C.I.G. II, 2448.

[2] *I.e.* the group of kindred descended from a common ancestor in the male line.

[3] All these are referred to as ἥρωες (Col. iv, 15–20). Compare the Spartan use of the word ἥρως of any dead person (I.G. V, i, index, *s.v.*).

[4] *Cf.* C.I.G. 2448, col. iii, 14 f. At the head of the list comes Epikteta's son-in-law, then the name of her adopted brother : among the rest are two pairs of brothers, four brothers of another family, and probably three pairs of fathers and sons, to judge from pairs of names like Prokleidas son of Evagoras and Evagoras son of Prokleidas. Only in four cases does the relationship of the names to others in the list fail to appear.

the twenty-five, their daughters below marriageable age (unless these are ἐπίκλαροι, in which case they are to come with their husbands),[1] their sons both below and above the age of maturity (τὰ δὲ ἄρσενα καὶ ἐν ἁλικίᾳ γενομένα). The children of these are likewise to attend, and certain other married women relatives [2] with their husbands.

The second half of the inscription represents a decree passed by the body of twenty-five, which constitutes itself a legal κοινόν with regularly appointed officials [3] and with a treasury and archives, for the purpose of carrying out the terms of Epikteta's will. Since it is the implied intention of the testatrix, and the expressed intention of the κοινόν, that these arrangements should remain in force for all time,[4] we should expect to find somewhere in the document, which is complete as it stands, provision for future recruitment of the κοινόν. Since, however, it is merely assumed that it will be hereditary,[5] we must conclude that the distinction between the members of the κοινόν τοῦ ἀνδρείου τῶν συγγενῶν and the συγγενεῖς as a whole was already clearly recognised —in other words, that this κοινόν existed, at least potentially, before the will of Epikteta was made. Before that time it was perhaps not a legal ' person ' capable of undertaking the joint responsibility for a bequest, but that its corporate existence was already recognised before the will, at least by the relatives, is implied by the words of the will itself, in which Epikteta speaks of herself as having summoned τὸ κοινὸν τοῦ ἀνδρείου τῶν συγγενῶν to hear the terms of the bequest in the first instance,[6] before it was accepted and before the constitution of the κοινόν was drawn up.

---

[1] Implying that an ἐπίκληρος could be married at an age below that usually permitted for marriage.

[2] Apparently sisters of members of the κοινόν. See below, p. 241, n. 2.

[3] An ἀρτυτήρ (treasurer) ἐπίσσοφος (general organiser and secretary), ἐγδανεισταί to arrange for the investment of the funds (col. vi, 24 ff.). The Ephors mentioned in the heading of the decree of the κοινόν (col. iv, 1) may be officials of the κοινόν itself rather than magistrates of the state. Their president Himertos appears among the list of members of the κοινόν.

[4] Col. viii, init.: ἃ δέ κα δόξει τοῖς πλείοσι τοῦ κοινοῦ, ταῦτα κύρια ἔστω πλὰν ὑπὲρ διαλύσεως. Ὑπὲρ δὲ τούτου, μὴ ἐχέτω ἐξουσίαν μηθεὶς μήτε εἶπαι μήτε γράψαι, ὡς δεείσῃ διαλῦσαι τὸ κοινόν, εἴ τὰς θυσίας τὰς προγεγραμμένας εἰ τῶν τοῦ κοινοῦ τι κακῶσαι ἢ διελέσθαι ἢ τοῦ ἀρχαίου τι καταχρήσασθαι. Cf. also col. ii, l. 10 f.

[5] Col. iv, l. 28-30.   [6] Col. i, 22, 26.

The inscription permits us to draw certain conclusions about the distinction between the members of τὸ κοινόν τοῦ ἀνδρείου and the rest of the συγγενεῖς. For in the first place, male children even above the age of maturity (τὰ δὲ ἄρσενα καὶ ἐν ἁλικίᾳ γενομένα)[1] may be excluded from the κοινόν, so that the qualification for membership was not simply a matter of sex or of reaching the age of maturity. Again, since groups of brothers appear among the members of the κοινόν, but do not appear in the list of συγγενεῖς (though this included the wives and children and sisters[2] of members of the κοινόν), it may be inferred that the qualification for membership was not the position of eldest male heir. Again, since fathers and their sons are included in the κοινόν at the same time, the qualification cannot have been that of eldest male representative of the family. A positive conclusion may be drawn from the inclusion within the κοινόν of the husband of the testatrix' daughter, Epiteleia, who is an ἐπίκληρος, whereas the husbands of the ἐπίκληροι of persons still alive and belonging to the κοινόν are included only among the rest of the συγγενεῖς. Evidently inheritance of property belonging to a member of the family—or, to be more precise, the right to the enjoyment of it, where the husband of an ἐπίκληρος was concerned[3]—was a necessary qualification for membership

---

[1] See above, pp. 239 f.

[2] The inclusion of sisters of members of the κοινόν is illustrated by the section of the family tree set out below. (Names in brackets represent persons already deceased, those in italics represent members of the κοινόν).

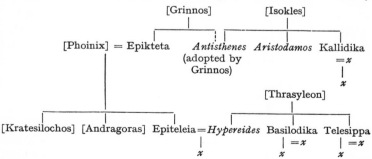

[3] In Cretan law the husband of the ἐπίκληρος had the usufruct of half her property (Gortyn Code, II, 45 f. ; VII, 29–35) but was not the owner of it (*ibid.* VI, 7–25, 31–34). Similar provisions were made in Athenian law (*cf.* Dem. XLIII, 54).

of the κοινόν. Inheritance of the appropriate share of the family property by the children during the father's lifetime was, however, not forbidden by Cretan law,[1] and the hypothesis that this was also the case in the Dorian state from which the inscription comes provides a satisfactory explanation of the appearance of fathers and sons together as members of the κοινόν. Finally, the absence of brothers of members of the κοινόν from the list of συγγενεῖς can be satisfactorily explained on the hypothesis that here, as in Crete, there was no system of primogeniture : if any sons inherited a part of their father's property before his death, all the sons of the same father must receive their portions at the same time. No case could then arise in which one brother would be qualified to be a member of the κοινόν while others were only qualified for inclusion among the συγγενεῖς.

To sum up : the *Andreion* of the kinsmen is composed of all the male relatives above the age of ἥβη—presumably twenty years—who have inherited property, either during or after their father's life-time, presumably from some person included among the whole group of συγγενεῖς. The detailed evidence of the inscription confirms the opinion already expressed, that the kinsmen in question are the members of a single agnatic group. This conclusion may seem at first sight unjustified, since on a first examination there is more evidence for the inclusion among them of Epikteta's relatives than of the relatives of her husband,[2] and the testament itself clearly shows that a married woman (unless she was an ἐπίκληρος) ceased on marriage to belong to her father's family and entered that of her husband.[3] But from the fact that Epikteta had an adopted brother, and apparently no natural brothers, it may be supposed that

---

[1] The Gortyn Code permits the father to give their portions to the children during his lifetime, but does not require him to do so (col. iv, 23–31).

[2] *Cf.* above, p. 241, n. 2. None of the names of the members of the κοινόν can with certainty be connected with Epikteta's husband Phoinix, though it seems not improbable that the Evagoras-group (see above, p. 239, n. 4) was connected with a man who bore the name of ' the Phoenician '. Both names suggest a connection with Cyprus.

[3] *Cf.* C.I.G. 2448, col. iii, 27 f. : πορευέσθωσαν δὲ καὶ αἱ τούτοις συνοικοῦσαι γυναῖκες καὶ τὰ τέκνα αὐτῶν, τὰ μὲν θήλεια ἕως κα ᾖ ὑπὸ τὸν πατέρα, κ.τ.λ.

she had acquired the property of which she disposes in her will as an ἐπίκληρος of her father's property,[1] and as an ἐπίκληρος, had been married to a member of her father's family, probably a brother of her father or his brother's son.[2] It is clear that Epikteta's daughter, as the only one left of the children of Phoinix,[3] was ἐπίκληρος not only of her mother's property, but also of that of her father, so that her husband must have been not only a near relative of her father, but also of her maternal grandfather, thus providing another close link between the male and female sides of the family, and corroborating the view that the συγγενεῖς of this inscription represent an agnatic group.

It is to be observed that the full significance of this document can only be explained by reference to the Gortyn Code and its regulations concerning the inheritance and disposition of the family property in Crete. Certain points in the Code have already been used to illustrate the meaning of Epikteta's will : [4] the Code also enables us to understand the extent and limits of Epikteta's power of disposing of the property which she had inherited, and in particular, why her daughter's consent was required.[5]

Here, then, is a document from a Dorian state, with a system of private law revealing at every point its close similarity to the Cretan, in which a body called ' the *Andreion* of the kinsmen ' owns and controls property in the joint interest of a single agnatic group.[6] But this is precisely

---

[1] *Cf.* Gortyn Code, col. viii, 40–43 (M.A.L. III, 1893, p. 116) : πατ-οωιῶκον δ'ῆμεν ἆι κα πατὴρ μὴ ἦι ἦ ἀδελπιὸς ἐς τῶ αὐτῶ πατρός. If there are adopted brothers (as in Epikteta's case) the Gortyn Code provides that the ἐπίκληρος shall have equal shares of the property with them (*ibid.* col. x, 52 f.).

[2] *Cf.* Gortyn Code, col. vii, 15 f. The Athenian law was similar (*cf.* Dem. XLIII, 54). The Spartan arrangement was no doubt also similar (*cf.* Herod. VI, 58 : δικάζειν δὲ . . . πατρούχου δὲ παρθένου πέρι, ἐς τὸν 'ικνέεται ἔχειν) but its precise provisions are unknown. For a late survival of the practice, *cf.* Appendix V, p. 471. (Claudia Damostheneia I.)

[3] *Cf.* above, p. 241, n. 2.

[4] *Cf.* above, nn. 1, 2 ; p. 241, n. 3 ; p. 242, n. 1.

[5] Epikteta was a widowed ἐπίκληρος : as such her position is defined by the Gortyn Code, col. viii, 25–36 ; ix, 1–24 (commentary in M.A.L. III, 1893, p. 216). The widowed Cretan ἐπίκληρος may dispose of the property (col. ix, 1–24), but on the analogy of the widowed husband of an ἐπίκληρος who leaves children at the time of her death, only with the consent of the children when they are of mature age (col. vi, 31 f.).

[6] *Cf.* above, pp. 24 f.

the form of family organisation, the existence of which we have seen reasons, on quite other grounds, to assume in Crete. A further point of resemblance is that Epikteta's kinsmen may be seen from the evidence of some of their names to belong to the highest Dorian aristocracy.[1] It does not follow from the existence of this inscription that the whole of society in the Dorian state in question was organised in clearly defined agnatic groups. The evidence of the Cretan Andreia points rather to the conclusion that this applied only to the aristocracy, for it seems hard to resist the general inference that the Spartan and Cretan Andreia, like the one mentioned in Epikteta's will, were kinship groups. The existence of two totally different kinds of Andreia, one concerned only with private property and the other only with the public rights of citizens, seems most unlikely, especially in view of the close connection, both in Sparta and in Crete, between the enjoyment of citizen rights and the holding of a land-lot.

To account for all the evidence so far considered, the following definitions may be proposed. The *Andreion* (in the Cretan states, Sparta, and the unknown Dorian state in which Epikteta made her will) was a closely related group [2] of adult male kindred in the male line, all owners of property, and belonging to the aristocratic stratum of society. The συγγενεῖς were the larger family groups, including also female relatives, to which the members of the Andreion belonged.[3] The *Hetaireia* was a more artificial organisation, composed of an Andreion together with all the male dependents which the various members of the *Andreion* had severally acquired, either before reaching the age of manhood, or soon after becoming members of the Andreion.[4] The *Syssitia* were the common meals of the Hetaireia, to which members of the Andreion were also permitted to bring their young sons below the age of entry

[1] As pointed out by Boeckh (commentary on C.I.G. II, 2448).

[2] The evidence of Epikteta's will suggests that the members of the Andreion were all descended from a single male ancestor in the generation previous to the earliest generation represented in the Andreion itself.

[3] Note that neither the *Andreion* nor the larger group of συγγενεῖς corresponds to the typical Greek *Genos*, but is a closer and smaller group (*cf.* the οἶκος in fourth-century Athens, discussed by Beauchet, *Droit Privé Athénien*, I (1897), pp. 19 f.). [4] *Cf.* pp. 241 f.

into the Andreion. Two passages from later authors which imply a very much smaller membership for the Syssitia, and recruitment by co-optation,[1] are probably to be explained by confusion between these ancient Syssitia and the various colleges of magistrates, augmented by additional members, who took their meals together, not only in Sparta but in other states as well, in later times.[2]

§ 4. *Conclusions*

Traces of the archaic Hetaireiai survived, as proved by the evidence from other states beside Sparta, into Hellenistic and Roman times. But it is clear that their common meals were not the same as the Syssitia which existed in the time of Herodotus.[3] For the archaic Syssitia of the ' feudal ' age (if we may venture to call it so on account of many resemblances to medieval feudalism) must have excluded the great majority of the free population, including as members only the aristocracy and their picked followers. But in the fifth century and later the Syssitia included all who were liable for service as hoplites, the qualification being possession of a citizen land-lot.[4] A significant change had taken place in the interval, namely the transition from a feudal organisation of society, calculated to maintain the influence of a small number of noble families, to a state organisation, in which society was united under a single central authority. This may well have been the fundamental meaning of the reformation ascribed to Lycurgus. The main administrative change involved would be the assignation of land-lots (on public land acquired by conquest) to a large class of hitherto landless Spartans, thus putting them on a level with the members

---

[1] *Cf.* Plut. *Lycurg.* 12 (on the meaning of κεκαδδίσθαι at Sparta), Schol. Plato, *Laws*, 633 A (commentary on an observation about Syssitia by the Spartan Megillus). Both passages describe the same secret ballot with the aid of pieces of bread, and both are evidently derived from the same source, which, to judge from the description of the Spartan ' black broth ' which follows in Plut. *ibid.*, was Aristotle's pupil Dicaearchus of Messene (*cf.* Athen. IV, 141b). The Scholiast and Plutarch differ slightly as to the number of σύσσιτοι, the Scholiast giving it as ten, and Plut. as ἀνὰ πεντεκαίδεκα καὶ βραχεῖ τούτων ἐλάττους ἢ πλείους.

[2] *Cf.* Part I, pp. 161 f.

[3] *Cf.* Herod. I, 65 : τὰ ἐς πόλεμον ἔχοντα, ἐνωμοτίας καὶ τριηκάδας καὶ συσσίτια . . . ἔστησε Λυκοῦργος. [4] *Cf.* Arist. *Pol.* II, 9. 32.

of the archaic *Andreia*. New Hetaireiai could then grow up around the new *Andreia*, and new Syssitia of which the new full citizens and their picked dependents were the members. Thus would arise a new united state, fully and efficiently organised for war. For this characteristically Dorian social structure was obviously not one which favoured the rapid growth of a strong united state. In Crete, as is well known, feuds between the noble families were still of frequent occurrence in Aristotle's time and later ; [1] in Sparta, according to the extremely probable statement of Thucydides, lawlessness and internal strife went on ' longer than in any other known state ', [2] until the reformation ascribed to Lycurgus.

The probable date, the details, and the further political implications of this significant change will be considered at length in later chapters.[3] It is enough for the present to note that the imposition of a later upon an earlier social organisation would account for the conflicting evidence which exists about the later distribution of property in Sparta. Frequent allusions occur to the great wealth of individual Spartans [4] at a period when the ' Lycurgan ' constitution was in full force, although under the Lycurgan laws the citizens were all ' Equals ' (ὅμοιοι), as being the possessors of land-lots all of equal size. On the hypothesis now being put forward, an aristocratic minority would still continue to enjoy their individual fortunes from their private estates.

In Sparta of the ' feudal ' period all political power was evidently in the hands of the Hippeis, the class of large landowners whose name survived in the τριακόσιοι ἱππῆς καλούμενοι of much later times.[5] The predominance of a similar class in other Peloponnesian states in the period covered by the Homeric poems is suggested by the descrip-

[1] *Cf. Pol.* II, 10. 13 f.
[2] Thuc. I, 18. 2 : ἐπὶ πλεῖστον ὧν ἴσμεν χρόνον στασιάσασα. Herod. I, 65 : τὸ δὲ ἔτι πρότερον τούτων, καὶ κακονομώτατοι ἦσαν σχεδὸν πάντων Ἑλλήνων. [3] See further, pp. 346 f., 418 f.
[4] References in Dar-Sagl. *s.v. Lacedaemoniorum Respublica* (Fustel de Coulanges), p. 890.
[5] *Cf.* Thuc. V, 72. 4. The Three Hundred are to be distinguished from the actual cavalry of the fifth and fourth centuries, on whom see further below, p. 376.

tion ἱππόβοτος applied to Argos [1] and Elis,[2] and by the epithets ἱπποβότης applied to Atreus [3] of Mycenae, and ἱππότα applied to Nestor [4] of Pylos and Phyleus [5] of Ephyra and Dulichium. The existence in later times of the class called Hippobotae who monopolised political power in Chalcis provides a reason for regarding as more than merely conventional the Homeric epithets in question. As is well known, the Homeric poems contain no direct reference to Dorians in the Peloponnese,[6] and presumably reflect conditions of society in the Mycenean age. No doubt, therefore, the aristocracy among the Dorian invaders continued in this respect the traditions of an earlier age ; [7] the rest of their peculiar social organisation, on the other hand, would appear to have been brought in by themselves, since in historical times it is found in several Dorian states of high antiquity, but, so far as we know, not in other parts of the Greek world.

[1] *Il.* II, 287, etc.   [2] *Od.* XXI, 347 ; *cf.* IV, 635 f.
[3] Eur. *Or.* 1000 ; *Iph. Aul.* 1059. The epithet is obviously traditional here, not invented by Euripides.   [4] Il. II, 601, etc.
[5] Il. II, 628.   [6] See, however, pp. 275 f.

[7] The continued significance of the horse in early Dorian Sparta is reflected in the great popularity of votive offerings representing horses from the earliest deposits onwards ; *cf.* A.O. Index, *s.v. Horses*, and on the preponderance of the horse among all animal votives from the Orthia site, *ibid.* p. 157.

Additional Note on the Spartan age-classes: see also pp. 86 et seq.

In my discussion of the Spartan age-classes I interpreted the well-known scholium on Herodotus to mean that the six age-classes named in it comprised the *ephebia*, instead of preceding it, as is commonly held by those who assign the names of the classes to the ages from seven to thirteen. In *Amer. Journ. Philol.* LXII (1941), p. 499 f. (inaccessible to me owing to war conditions when this book went to press), A. Diller has publ:shed the same gloss from a new source, an MS. of Strabo (*Parisinus* 1397), which contains the significant variant ἐφηβεύει μὲν γάρ where the version formerly known (see above, p. 86, n. 4) has ἐφηβεύει δέ. The new version confirms my interpretation of ἐφηβεύει δέ as an example of the deictic use of the particle. Both versions may now clearly be seen to imply that the names describe the year-classes of the *ephebia* itself. Those who still reject my interpretation of the age-classes must now deny entirely the authenticity of both glosses.

CHAPTER VII

THE CULT AND FESTIVAL OF ORTHIA

THERE is no institution in which the Sparta of Roman times more clearly displays its continuity with the ancient Sparta than in the cult of Orthia. It is the object of the following chapter to demonstrate this point of view more clearly in general, and in particular to reveal continuity at a more remote period (so far as this cult is concerned) between early Dorian Sparta and the Mycenean age which preceded it. Continuity with the Mycenean age in cults and in social organisation generally was more likely to develop under a feudal organisation of society like that which has been demonstrated in the preceding chapter than would have been the case in a unified state. The study of the transition from the 'feudal' to the 'Lycurgan' Sparta will be continued in later chapters, to which we may refer the reader who has no wish to delve further into the problem of remote origins, or who is no longer in doubt about the thesis of continuity. The present chapter is in the nature of a digression from the main track of the work.

As we have sought to demonstrate at length in an earlier section,[1] the study of the inscriptions relating to the παιδικὸς ἀγών leads to the general conclusion that the contests were mainly musical in character, comprising competitions in dancing (καθθηρατόριον, the hunting-dance), in playing on some instrument (μῶα) and in reciting to music (κελεία, the invocation). The names of the set-pieces (ὁ εὐβάλκης, ὁ κυναγέτας, possibly ὁ δερεύς, 'the Flayer') all suggest a close connection with the hunting-dance and may well be part of a ritual in honour of the goddess which was of great antiquity, and which, at the time to which the inscriptions refer, had in all probability lost the more barbarous character which it must have had originally. It seems in fact not unlikely that these inscriptions give an

[1] *Cf.* Part I, pp. 119 f.

indication of the identity of the Spartan Orthia which has not so far received the attention it deserves.

It has already been suggested by Nilsson [1] that the Peloponnesian Artemis was a direct survival from the Cretan goddess, whose close connection with wild life in all its manifestations, and as a natural corollary, with hunting, is proved beyond all doubt by the remains at Cnossos.[2] This suggestion has been denied in so far as it applies to the Spartan Orthia, on the grounds that nothing pre-Dorian was found on the site of the temple of Orthia herself,[3] and that the identification of Orthia with Artemis is itself of late origin in Sparta, no recorded examples of the usage being earlier than the Flavian period.[4] For these reasons Rose supposes Orthia to have been a purely local Spartan goddess, whose cult was adopted by a certain number of other Greek states [5] on account of the political prestige of Sparta. The series of ivory plaques and figurines of Oriental style, found in the temple of Orthia, which represent a πότνια θηρῶν, winged and grasping in each hand an animal by the neck or by the tail, are explained by him as the work of local artists strongly influenced by the Oriental art of the time ; he does not believe that they indicate a real Oriental influence upon the cult, still less the adoption at Sparta of a non-Greek goddess.

These objections to the theory of the Mycenean origin of Orthia have not so far been challenged, and Nilsson's suggestion about the Peloponnesian Artemis in general is not accompanied by any attempt at direct proof so far as Orthia is concerned. But the literary evidence gives room for some doubt as to the supposed lateness of the identification of Orthia with Artemis, since the goddess Orthosia is directly identified with Artemis by Pindar [6] and by

[1] *Minoan-Mycenean Religion* (1927), pp. 432 f.
[2] References in Sir Arthur Evans, *Palace of Minos* (index volume, 1936), *s.v.* ' Goddess '.
[3] *Cf.* H. J. Rose, *The Cult of Artemis Orthia* (A.O. Chap. XII, p. 399).
[4] *Ibid.* p. 401.
[5] *Ibid.* p. 400 : ' Inscriptions and references prove that more or less the cult of Orthia, Orthosia or Orthasia existed in Athens, Megara, Epidaurus, one or two places in Arcadia, Elis, Byzantium, and perhaps Thera '.
[6] In *Olymp.* III, 46 f. Pindar identifies Orthosia with the Istrian (? Tauric) Artemis.

Herodotus,[1] and the name Orthosia (Doric form Orthasia [2])
is a not unusual variant, or perhaps a rationalisation,[3] of
the name Orthia. Moreover, it is very hard to believe,
with Rose, that Spartan artists in the seventh century
B.C. represented their local goddess in exactly the same way
as Oriental Greek artists represented Artemis the πότνια
θηρῶν,[4] but yet had no conception of the identity of the
two. Nor is it permissible to argue (in support of Rose's
contention) that this ' Oriental ' way of representing the
goddess ceases with the disappearance of the ivories, about
the end of the seventh century B.C., proving it alien to
Spartan conceptions of their goddess. Evidence to the
contrary is found in the cheap lead figurines which accompany the ivories as votive offerings, supplant them about
the end of the seventh century, and afterwards persist for
several centuries, being especially plentiful in the sixth,
to which period nearly 69,000 from the shrine of Orthia
have been assigned. Representations of the winged goddess
holding animals are, it is true, rare in this series, being
confined to a few larger examples in the later seventh
century B.C.[5] But it is evident that the vast number of
figures of a winged goddess with the same characteristic
tall headdress as in the ivories, but without animals, and
holding rings or garlands in each hand instead (e.g. Pl. 3,
Fig. 11), also represent the πότνια θηρῶν : the animals
have been omitted (the rings perhaps being a survival from
the curve of their necks or tails),[6] on account of the technical difficulty involved in reproducing the early type completely on a very small scale [7] in these flat and obviously
cheap lead figurines. A further modification of the earliest
type is seen in the figures of a goddess between two horse

[1] Herod. IV, 87 (cult of Artemis Orthosia at Byzantium).
[2] As on the Laconian II plate found below the sand level on the Orthia
site (A.O. p. 16).
[3] I.e. ' She who makes straight ', according to the Scholiast on Pindar
Olymp. III, 52. The identity of Orthosia with Orthia is accepted by
Rose (cf. p. 249, n. 5.)
[4] For examples cf. A.O. Pl. XCI, 1, 2 ; XCII, 2 ; XCVIII ; in Pl.
CVII the goddess has a horse with her in addition, in Pl. XCII, 2, a snake.
[5] Cf. A.O. pp. 260, 261e, 263f, 273b.
[6] Cf. e.g., ibid. p. 260, Fig. 120.
[7] The average height of the figurines is about 2 inches.

heads [1] which occurs from the seventh century onwards. In publishing the lead votives, Wace points out that a crude aniconic type, in which the figure of the goddess is reduced to a geometrical representation of her dress, the two rings being still attached at the sides, is characteristic of the examples of the earlier seventh century and persists to the end of the sixth.[2] The objects like gridirons and the spiked rings (Pl. 2), which persist even longer,[3] are without doubt a further degeneration of the same type. Side by side with these types, beginning in the later seventh century, are found large numbers of representations of various animals,[4] the deer, the animal specially associated with Artemis, being particularly common from the sixth century onwards.[5] There seems then to be overwhelming evidence that the goddess worshipped at this shrine, even after the cessation of any direct Oriental influence which may have come from Asia Minor in the seventh century, was a πότνια θηρῶν, and that she was popularly identified at Sparta with Artemis from an early period.

As a result of his study of the lead votives, Wace is inclined to conclude that although the actual sanctuary of Orthia does not go back beyond the Iron Age, the goddess herself had descended from the Bronze Age, her connection with the Minoan-Mycenean civilisation being attested by the recurrence on the Orthia site of several jewellery types or cult objects, such as pillars and double axes, which are characteristic of the Mycenean Age.[6] This idea is capable of further illustration. For example, although it has been denied that the lead figurines representing winged goddesses or female figures wear Mycenean dress, and has been maintained that the costume is Dorian,[7]

[1] Cf. A.O., Pl. X, XXII, 4, 5 (terra-cotta); CLXXII, 1 (ivory, early seventh century); p. 266, Fig. 123 (lead, all periods before 500 B.C.). This type is particularly interesting on account of its connection with cults in South Italy. Cf. also Pl. 2, no. 7.   [2] Cf. A.O. p. 259.
[3] E.g. A.O. Pl. CXCIX, 23–26, CC. 22. For examples of the later seventh and sixth centuries, cf. ibid. Pl. CLXXXV, CXCIV. In the sixth century the spiked wreaths greatly outnumber all other types put together (ibid. p. 281).
[4] Ox-heads, horses, goats, cocks, lions, fish, bulls and deer (cf. Pl. 2, nos. 18–29, A.O. pp. 262, 269, 276, 279, 282).   [5] Ibid. pp. 281 f.
[6] Ibid. p. 282. For the double axes, see below, p. 257, n. 6.
[7] A.O. p. 280.

on closer examination the so-called ' Dorian ' costume
represented in the lead figurines (though not in all the Spartan
representations of Orthia) is seen to be an underdress with
an all-over diagonal pattern, usually worn underneath a
very full bell-shaped skirt with many flounces.[1] This
skirt must certainly have given rise to the ' gridiron ' votives
already mentioned, and must therefore have been regarded
as characteristic. Since the reduction of these figurines
to their simplest geometric terms in some of the contemporary and later votives implies that they were intended
as representations of the cult-image of the goddess, we must
therefore suppose that the image was dressed in detachable
clothes, to suit the aspect of the goddess which it was
desired to stress at any particular time. The φᾶρος offered
to Orthia in Alcman's *Partheneion* [2] may well have been a
divided flounced skirt of the kind just described. The
lead figurines show a certain variation in the pattern of
the skirt which is consonant with the theory of the annual
offering of a robe. It is also possible that the diagonal
pattern of the underdress really represents a wicker framework
for the bell-shaped skirt. Some such device would certainly
be necessary in clothing a primitive ξόανον in a flounced
skirt, and the story that the statue of Orthia at Sparta was
found held upright in a thicket of willows (hence the cult-
name Lygodesma) [3] provides support for this suggestion.

[1] An example of the under dress is seen in Pl. 3, nos. 4, 19. It also
occurs on some of the ivory plaques, *e.g.* A.O., Pl. XCVI, 2, XCVIII, 2,
where it may clearly be seen to be worn under other draperies. The
overskirt is shown in many of the figurines divided down the front (*cf.*
Pl. 3 of the present work, nos. 1, 5, 7).

[2] The meaning of φᾶρος in the passage of Alcman is fully discussed
by Kukula (*Philol.* LXVI, 1907, pp. 222 f.) who concludes that it was
a robe, not a ploughshare. *Cf.* also *Hermes*, LXXIII, 1938, pp. 448 f.
It is perhaps worth noting that the Spartan women wove a new robe
each year for Apollo of Amyclae (Paus. III, 16. 2).

[3] *Cf.* Roscher, *Lex. Mythol.*, *s.v. Lygodesma*. The name of Artemis
Phakelitis at Tyndaris in Sicily, which, like Sparta in the case of Orthia,
claimed to have the original ξόανον of the Tauric Artemis, is similarly explained. Since there is no direct connection between Sparta and Tyndaris,
a colony founded by Dionysius I of Syracuse as a home for the exiled
Messenians after the Peloponnesian War, and since the cult-names are
different even though they have the same explanation attached to them, it
seems probable that the explanation was suggested by the appearance of
the ξόανον itself in each case. The attempt to find a special ritual significance in the connection of Orthia with λύγοι (*cf.* Wide, *Lakonische Kulte*,
114, and *cf.* below, p. 261) seems therefore to be misguided.

It may perhaps seem a difficulty in the way of this explanation of the variety of costume among the lead figurines that those of the same period show the goddess sometimes with and sometimes without wings (Pl. **3** nos. 9, 11). But the curious fact that the wings are shown springing from the waist in front of the figure,[1] instead of from her shoulders, seems to suggest that painted wooden wings, perhaps made in one piece with a false front, could be affixed to the image when it was desired to represent the goddess as πότνια θηρῶν. The legend of Daedalus and Icarus may well preserve a genuine tradition of the method of early sculptors in wood in making winged statues, namely, that they made and affixed the wings separately. In the case of the statue of Orthia, the junction of the wings would be concealed by the tight belt which is always a part of the costume of Orthia, as of that of the Cretan goddess and her votaries.

As to the rest of the costume, some of the ivories and a few of the lead figurines which seem to represent Orthia show her wearing a tightly fitting bodice, but in the majority of the lead figurines she is shown without any bodice at all, thus crudely representing the extremely low décolletage of the true Minoan tradition (Pl. **3,** nos. 2, 4). To complete the resemblance in costume, the tall headdress also corresponds to that of the Minoan goddess.[2]

But in addition to the connection implied by the resemblance of costume, the direct descent of Orthia from the Cretan goddess is also indicated by other considerations. It would appear that the usual Greek πότνια θηρῶν has no male divinity attached to her cult;[3] but Orthia, like the Cretan goddess, has a Master of Animals associated with her, represented like herself in several of the Spartan ivories as a winged figure grasping birds or animals in each hand.[4] It is true that the later Spartan cult, like other

[1] Cf. A.O. Pls. CLXXXII, 1, 5, 9; CLXXXVIII, 2–10, 12, 15 (on lead figurines); also on the ivories, ibid. Pl. XCII, XCIII.

[2] Cf. Pl. **6.** The dress of the Cretan goddess is discussed in *Palace of Minos*, I, pp. 500 f. (other references in Index Volume, s.v. Goddess), in its origin being assigned (op. cit. Vol. I, p. 197) to Syrian influence in the M.M.I. period. For the headdress of the Cretan goddess, cf. op. cit. Vol. I, pp. 500 f.   [3] Cf. Nilsson, op. cit. p. 442.

[4] Cf. A.O. Pl. XCIX, 1, 2, also the unwinged male figure clasping two winged monsters, ibid. Pl. CV. It seems possible that the 'winged Dionysus' worshipped at Amyclae (cf. Paus III, 19. 6) was a survival of this deity.

Greek cults of Artemis, stressed the virginity of the goddess.[1]
If the earlier Cretan religion had done the same, as Sir
Arthur Evans believes,[2] a mystical faith had been able to
regard the goddess as at the same time the Great Mother.
This possibility was denied to the more logically minded
Greek ; but to turn the male consort into Apollo, the brother
of the goddess, was an easy way out of the difficulty, and
in this guise the consort survived.[3]

Both in Crete and in Sparta the goddess specialises in
the use of the bow, surviving with this attribute in Crete
as Diktynna or Britomartis into the period when lead figurines representing the goddess armed with the bow are
offered to Orthia in Sparta.[4] Whether this goddess represents Orthia herself or one of the συγκαθειδρευμένοι θεοί
worshipped in her shrine [5] is uncertain. In spite of the
flounced skirt (shown in some examples), they can scarcely
represent the cult image of Orthia, since the difference of
attitude between them and the figurines already discussed
is too great. It is rather to be supposed that the many
aspects under which the Cretan goddess was worshipped
led to a multiplication of deities in a later period, of whom
the goddess with the bow in Orthia's shrine is one. At all
events, the goddess with the bow seems to be conceived of
rather as a goddess of war than as a goddess of hunting,
to judge from the close resemblance of the figurines in
question to representations of Athena.[6] But here again we
find a continuation of the tradition of the Cretan goddess,
who likewise appears at Cnossos armed with weapons of
war, a long sword and a sickle,[7] and at the same time is
encircled with snakes which suggest an origin for the snakes
of Athena. The sickle of the Cretan goddess (Pl. 4 *a*) is
particularly interesting in view of the choice of this weapon
at Sparta as the prize for all the competitions in the παιδικὸς
ἀγών. Actual examples of these Spartan iron sickles

---

[1] *Cf.* A.O. p. 367, no. 169. 1 (archaic inscription), p. 298, no. 4 (of
Roman date).   [2] *Cf. P. of M.* Vol. II, p. 48.
[3] See further below, pp. 270 f.   [4] *Cf.* A.O. Pl. CXCVI, 2, 3.
[5] I.G. V, i, 602 (early third century A.D.).
[6] The goddess wears a crested helmet and aegis fringed with snakes
(*cf.* A.O. CXCVI, 2, 3).
[7] On the Cretan armed goddess, see *P. of. M.* III, pp. 467 f. ; IV, pp.
849, 937, Fig. 907.

which have survived (Pl. 1) show that they were smaller in size (about 14 inches) than the Cretan weapon would appear to have been to judge from the representations of it in Cretan art (Pl. 4 *a*, *b*). But comparison of these last with the Spartan sickles will show the close correspondence in form, and should in itself be a convincing refutation of the idea that the object carried by the Cretan goddess, and by the young warrior on the Hagia Triada Cup (*cf.* Pl. 4 *b*), is a sprinkler for holy water, made of ' a wisp of hair attached to a rod '.[1] A weapon of very similar form is illustrated on a silver *rhyton* from Mycenae,[2] and this may be the direct ancestor of the Spartan one. That the Spartans actually did make use of a sickle-shaped weapon of war in the fifth century B.C. is attested by Xenophon's references to their ξυήλη,[3] which by the lexicographers is said not only to have been like a sickle (δρέπανον), but sometimes even to have been called a sickle.[4] It also seems significant that one of Xenophon's passages in question relates to a Spartan exile among the Ten Thousand, who had fled from Sparta while still a boy because he had killed another boy by accident with a ξυήλη.[5] This strongly suggests that the sickle-like weapon was used in the military training of the boys in the *Agoge* at that time, and if so, that it was already given as a prize for the competitions associated with the cult of Orthia. In any case it is far more probable that the δρέπανον, or more accurately ξυήλη, was awarded as a prize to the Spartan *Epheboi*, even in later times, as being an ancient military weapon than on account of some

---

[1] *Cf. P. of M.* IV, **, p. 936, and *ibid.* p. 792, n. 1, where it is compared to the *aspergillum* of the Roman *pontifices*. The identification of it as ' a long *falx*-like halberd ' (Hall, *Aegean Archaeology*, p. 63) is on the face of it much more likely, since in both the Cretan representations it is associated with a long sword, and the figure described by Sir Arthur Evans as a ' young prince ' stands face to face with another warrior armed with a spear.

[2] *Cf. P. of M.* III, p. 94 ; J.H.S. XIII, p. 199. The right-angled objects lying on the ground in this siege-scene are here identified as throw-sticks, but since all the warriors depicted are naked and are using their bows and arrows, any other weapons they possess must necessarily lie on the ground until they are required in hand-to-hand fighting.

[3] Xen. *Anab.* IV, 7. 16 (μαχαίριον ὅσον ξυήλην Λακωνικήν, a weapon useful for fighting at close quarters and cutting off heads) ; *ibid.* 8. 25.

[4] *Cf.* Hesych. *s.v.* ξυάλη· ξιφίδιον, ὅ τινες δρέπανον λέγουσι ; Pollux, I, 10. 137 (ξυήλη Λακωνική) ; Suidas, *s.v.* ξυάλη.

[5] Xen. *Anab.* IV, 8. 25.

connection, otherwise unattested, with agriculture.[1] Thus the connection of Orthia with a particular type of weapon of war has its close parallel, and not improbably its ultimate origin, in the cult of the Cretan goddess.

The same may be said about the connection of both cults with hunting, attested on the one hand by the bull-fights over which the goddess presided at Cnossos,[2] on the other by the καθθηρατόριον in honour of Orthia, which, however, in later Greek times, appears to have been transformed into a violent and terrifying kind of dance.[3] Finally, the close connection of both goddesses with navigation is significant and must not be overlooked.

Among the many indications that the Cretan goddess was regarded as Mistress of the Sea,[4] Sir Arthur Evans cites the decoration on a gold signet-ring from Candia (cf. Pl. 5 b), which represents a scene precisely paralleled on an ivory plaque dedicated to the Spartan Orthia (Pl. 5 c). In both of these a male figure is seen at the stern of a ship filled with rowers, greeting or being greeted by a female figure who wears the typical costume of the goddess for that period. The Candia ring is supposed to show the goddess about to depart on a sea voyage, but this interpretation makes it difficult to explain the sacred tree and what appears to be an image of the goddess in the field above the ship itself. These features, absent from the Spartan version, rather suggest the safe arrival of a ship which has sailed under the protection of the goddess as represented by her sacred tree and her own image. On the Spartan plaque too, the sailors furling the sails and the man fishing off the prow suggest safe arrival in port rather than the imminence of departure. Moreover, the Spartan plaque is itself an inscribed dedication to the goddess, and as such is more likely to represent the dedicator's safe return from a voyage than the departure of the goddess overseas. It is to be supposed that the ships carved on limestone blocks found in the same shrine [5] also represent thank-offerings to Orthia for a safe voyage.

---

[1] As tentatively suggested by H. J. Rose (cf. A.O. p. 406).
[2] Cf. P. of M. I, p. 447 ; II, p. 649 ; III, p. 207 ; IV, pp. 20, 39.
[3] On the καθθηρατόριον, see pp. 123 f.
[4] Cf. P. of M. II,* pp. 249 f.   [5] A.O. p. 195, no. 69, 69a ; Pl. 74.

The list of close parallels between the cult of the Cretan goddess and that of Orthia is thus seen to be long and may perhaps be said to be convincing, but for two possible objections. These are the alleged absence of Mycenean remains from the Orthia site,[1] and the close connection of the Spartan goddess with horses, apparently the only animal unconnected with the worship of the Cretan goddess. Not only are limestone carvings of horses one of the commonest of the inscribed dedications to Orthia, but the number of horses among the various classes of small offerings is said by the excavators to be greater than that of all the other animal votives put together.[2] It has recently been observed that the comparison of the maidens to horses in Alcman's *Partheneion*, a work written for a festival of Orthia, is probably connected with the prominence of horses in the cult.[3] What the precise significance of the horse was in the worship of Orthia is not known, but it must have been on account of its use in hunting, in athletic festivals, and in war, and more generally, on account of the interest taken by the aristocratic class of *Hippeis* in the cult ; and since the horse was not used at all for riding in Minoan Crete,[4] there is an obvious explanation of its absence from all the monuments connected with the Minoan goddess.

With regard to the *argumentum ex silentio*, it must first be noted that the absence of pre-Dorian remains from the Orthia site is not complete. The pre-600 deposit, below the sand, yielded ten Mycenean engraved gems, one of them with the design of a double axe,[5] which is of frequent occurrence among the later objects from the site.[6] The number of Mycenean objects is certainly small, and they may have been brought there in post-Mycenean times. On the other hand, it would be rash to assume this, since the temple was built on the bank of a river subject to floods, which in fact have washed away part of the Roman building, and which led to the abandonment of an earlier temple and the general raising of the level of the precinct about

---

[1] *Cf*. above, p. 249, n. 3.   [2] *Cf*. A.O. p. 157.
[3] *Cf*. J. A. Davison, *Hermes*, LXXIII, 1938, pp. 455 f.
[4] *P. of M*. IV, ii, p. 830.   [5] A.O. pp. 378, 382, Fig. 146.
[6] *Cf*. *ibid*. pp. 159, no. 12, 199, 238, no. 9, 254, 264, 270, 383, no. 3, 384 ; Pls. LXXXV, CLXIII, CCII, 2, 4 (in all materials).

17

600 B.C.[1] Since the earliest altar of all lies in the part of the site most vulnerable to floods,[2] it is *a priori* probable that the first shrine was completely washed away by the river. But even if the first shrine on this site was post-Mycenean, it does not follow that the cult did not originate in the Mycenean Age. It may have been introduced into Sparta from elsewhere, just as the cult of Orestes was introduced from Arcadia in the sixth century B.C.[3] The long and unbroken history of the shrine of Orthia shows that if the same thing had happened here, it must have happened at or before the first Dorian occupation. The supposition that the cult was taken over direct from the former inhabitants of Laconia in the Mycenean Age is strengthened by the presence of other cults in Sparta which must be pre-Dorian in origin—those of Cassandra at Amyclae [4] and of Diktynna in Sparta itself.[5] The name Orthia is, however, said by some ancient authorities to be derived from a mountain in Arcadia,[6] a derivation supported by the analogies of Zeus Lykaios whose name was derived from Mt. Lykaion in Arcadia,[7] and of Diktynna the goddess of Mt. Dikte in Crete. It certainly seems much more likely that the name Orthia came from that of a mountain with precipitous sides than from the straightness of the ancient image,[8] since there can have been very few archaic ξόανα, if any, which did not share this characteristic. And since it is well known that in the pre-Dorian period the Arcadian-speaking Greeks had a much wider distribution, both in

---

[1] *Op. cit.* pp. 5 f.

[2] *Ibid.*; *cf.* Pls. I and II B. The danger of floods may have been the real reason for keeping the image of the goddess at Mesoa, instead of in the temple, except at the time of the festival (Paus. VII, 20. 8).

[3] *Cf.* Herod, I, 67, 68.   [4] Paus. III, 19. 6.

[5] *Id.* III, 12. 8 ; *cf.* III, 14. 2. See further Appendix V, pp. 472 f.

[6] *Cf. Schol.* in Pind. *Olymp.* III, 52 (Abel) : 'Ορθωσία ἡ ῎Αρτεμις παρὰ τὸ 'Ορθώσιον, ὅπερ ἐστὶν ὄρος 'Αρκαδικόν· ἔστι δὲ καὶ ῎Ορθιον ὄρος 'Αρκαδίας, ἀφ' οὗ καὶ ἡ θεὸς 'Ορθὶς (sic) καὶ 'Ορθωσία καλεῖται. Another Scholiast has 'Ορθωσίᾳ· τῇ ἐν 'Ορθωσίῳ ὄρει 'Αρκαδίας τιμωμένῃ 'Αρτέμιδι. Hesych. *s.v.* 'Ορθία, gives the same explanation of the name, but derives it more vaguely from a χωρίον 'Αρκαδίας. The mountain is not otherwise known, either as ῎Ορθιον or as 'Ορθώσιον ὄρος, but see further below, p. 259, n. 4.

[7] *Cf.* Paus. VIII, 38. 6.

[8] *Cf.* Paus. III, 16, 11, for this idea, which is accepted by Rose in A.O. pp. 403 f., and by Farnell (*Cults of the Greek States*, II, p. 453, n. *b*). The adjective ὄρθιος is used of Mt. Taygetus by Strabo (VIII, 363 *init.*).

the Peloponnese and outside it, than they had in classical times,[1] it seems not improbable that the cult of Orthia in Sparta originated among the Greek-speaking inhabitants of that region in the Mycenean Age.[2] The Spartan belief that her image had been brought to them by Orestes is thus seen to be not without foundation.[3] It seems certain, however, that the goddess herself was by no means confined to the central and western Peloponnese in Greek times but was widely recognised in the regions where the civilisation of Crete penetrated, and that in the Bronze Age she was 'the lady of the straight-sided mountain '[4] only in the Arcadian-Greek-speaking part of the Peloponnese. Without further evidence than we possess, the history of the Messenian cult of Orthia is now impossible to trace, but since it was closely associated with the Spartan one,[5] which clearly proclaims itself a cult of the aristocracy, its origin must at all events go back to the time before the enslavement of Messenia by Sparta in the eighth century B.C.

It may seem strange that a goddess normally at home on a mountain, as the Cretan goddess was,[6] and also her Arcadian descendant, should have her temple at Sparta located in marshy ground by a river.[7] This fact may not be unconnected with the rites peculiar to the shrine, for it suggests that Orthia was believed to have the power to bring or to avert pestilence,[8] which belonged to Apollo and Artemis in popular belief.

[1] Cf. Myres, Who Were the Greeks ? pp. 152 f.
[2] The Arcadian cult of Zeus Lykaios, which seems to have existed in Sparta in Alcman's time (cf. Wide, Lakonische Kulte, p. 11) may well have had a similar history, since it also was apparently Cretan in origin (cf. Paus. VIII, 38. 2). [3] Cf. Paus. III, 16, 7.
[4] The mountain probably had another name, just as ' the sacred peak ' (ἱερὰ κορυφή) or ' Olympos ' were used as alternatives for Mt. Lykaion (cf. Paus. VIII, 38. 2). It seems likely to be identical with Mt. Lykone near Hysiae on the summit of which was a temple of Artemis Orthia (Paus. II, 24. 5). [5] Cf. below, n. 7, and p. 269.
[6] Cf. P. of M. I, pp. 156 f.
[7] The site was called τὸ Λιμναῖον (Paus. III, 16. 7). The village called Λίμναι on the borders of Sparta and Messenia also had a temple of Artemis (Paus. IV, 31. 3). Strabo (VIII, 362) says that the Spartan temple took its name from the Messenian one.
[8] Cf. Farnell, Cults of the Greek States, II (1896), p. 467; IV (1907), p. 408, n. 211.

It has been recently observed that Alcman, by bringing the heliacal rising of the constellation of the Pleiades into connection with the festival of Orthia for which his *Partheneion* was written, provides evidence for dating that festival between May 17 and 19.[1] This is precisely the time of the month when the festival of the Thargelia was held in honour of Apollo and Artemis at Athens. Both at Athens and in various Ionian states the Thargelia was accompanied by the expulsion or castigation of *Pharmakoi*, the scapegoats upon whom the gods were supposed to visit their wrath, in order that the coming harvest might be spared.[2] In some states the *Pharmakoi* were merely expelled from the city boundaries, in some they were stoned, in others beaten with rods.[3]

To these last instances of the treatment of *Pharmakoi* the annual scourging of the Spartan Epheboi is an obvious analogy, and it is possible that we have here the true explanation of the remarkable rite which has attracted the attention of both ancient and modern writers upon Sparta. It is true that in all the states for which the rite of the *Pharmakoi* is recorded either criminals or poor persons hired for the purpose were chosen as the victims, but this may be regarded as a degeneration of the original custom, the essence of which must have been the belief that valued members of the community must be hurt in order to avert the wrath of the deity.[4] The annual scourging of the adolescent boys might well be thought in very early times to have this effect, and the conspicuous conservatism of Sparta would certainly preserve the early form of the rite long after it had been modified by all other states. The ancient reason given for the scourging by the Spartans themselves was that it was a propitiatory rite, instituted to avert the insanity, civil strife and plagues with which the goddess had previously afflicted the state. This certainly is the meaning of the story which Pausanias

[1] Cf. *Hermes*, 73, 1938, pp. 449 f.

[2] On *Pharmakoi*, see P.W. *s.v. Thargelia*.

[3] *Cf.* Hipponax, Frg. 37B, 9B, 14, 2D (*cf.* P.W. *s.v. Thargelia*, p. 1293).

[4] A similar belief is implied in the story of the ring of Polycrates, which he cast into the sea because it was his most valued possession (Herod. III, 40 f.).

heard in the second century A.D.,[1] but that it was believed many centuries earlier that Orthia needed to be propitiated is shown by the introductory section to Alcman's *Partheneion*, of which the theme is ἔστι τις σιῶν τίσις, reinforced by examples of many heroes who incurred the wrath of the gods.[2]

Modern writers have suggested that the whipping was in reality a pre-nuptial rite to secure fertility,[3] but in that case it seems unlikely that *all* the Epheboi, rather than those of marriageable age, would have had to undergo the ordeal. There is also the objection that whipping to secure fertility seems in general to be confined to women.[4] On the other hand, a passage cited from the περὶ παροιμιῶν of Clearchus of Soli (*ap.* Athen. XIII, 555*c*) might conceivably illustrate the whipping of men for this purpose : ἐν Λακεδαίμονι (φησὶ) τοὺς ἀγάμους αἱ γυναῖκες ἐν ἑορτῇ τινι περὶ τὸν βωμὸν ἕλκουσαι ῥαπίζουσι. But it seems more likely that this is simply a confused account of the Orthia ceremony itself, especially as the victims are implied to be all young men, the accompanying explanation (ἵνα τὴν ἐκ τοῦ πράγματος ὕβριν φεύγοντες φιλοστοργῶσί τε καὶ ἐν ὥρᾳ προίωσι τοῖς γάμοις) being suggested partly by the known discouragement of celibacy at Sparta and partly by the custom in other states of submitting women to ritual whipping to secure fertility.

This passage from Clearchus, who was a pupil of Aristotle, incidentally tends to upset the theory of Rose, based upon the relative lateness of references which with certainty apply to the scourging of the Epheboi, that the scourging was itself of late origin.[5] It is evident that many

[1] Paus. III, 16. 9. The further belief that it was a survival of human sacrifice is generally rejected by modern critics.
[2] *Cf. Hermes*, LXXIII, 1938, pp. 441 f.
[3] *Cf.* J.R.S. XIX (1929), pp. 81 f. The λύγοι in which the cult statue was entwined have been thought to indicate that the beating was done with willow-rods, on account of the power of promoting fertility which they were believed to have (*cf.* Thomsen in *Archiv für Religionswiss.* IX, 1906, pp. 397 f.). But *cf.* above, p. 252, n. 3.
[4] J.R.S. *ibid.* pp. 78 f. Among many instances there cited of ritual flagellation, both Roman and Greek, the only example of whipping applied to men, apart from the flogging of the Spartan Epheboi, is Hesych. *s v.* Μόροττον. ἐκ φλοιοῦ πλέγμα τι, ᾧ ἔτυπτον ἀλλήλους τοῖς Δημητρίοις. We have no further indication of the purpose of this whipping. There is clearly no reason to think that the beating of the *Pharmakoi* (*cf.* above, p. 260, n. 2) was intended to promote fertility.   [5] *Cf.* A.O. p. 405.

peculiar religious rites of high antiquity must have passed
unnoticed by travellers from other states in a period when
such things were common everywhere ; it was only at a
time when they were beginning to die out that they began
to seem remarkable and worthy of comment.

Rose cites as possible fourth-century B.C. references to
the whipping of the Epheboi a passage in Plato's *Laws* [1]
which he considers too vague to be significant, and one
in the *Respublica Lacedaemoniorum* ascribed to Xenophon,
which must on Rose's view represent a different ceremony
though reasons have already been given for thinking otherwise. [2] The writer says [3] that it was regarded as honour-
able to steal as many cheeses as possible ' from Orthia ' [4]
while running the gauntlet of the whips of those who
were posted to stop the stealing. He goes on to say
that this custom taught the boys that speed, not lazi-
ness, was what really paid, since it meant that they received fewer blows, also that lasting glory might come
out of endurance of pain for a while. This description implies
that at some festival the boys were required to make their
way to a pile of cheeses belonging to Orthia and to steal as
many as possible in the face of opposition from young
men armed with whips. These are probably to be identified
with the μαστιγοφόροι of the Paidonomos, drawn from the
class of young men over the age of ἥβη, who are mentioned
by the author of the *Respublica* earlier in the same chapter. [5]
The quickest, the bravest and the most resourceful would
naturally carry off the most cheeses, and the winner acquired lasting glory from his success.

But it may be shown that this description is not inconsistent with the accounts of the whipping ordeal which
are found in later writers. A popular explanation of the
origin of the custom, which appears in Plutarch, [6] strongly

---

[1] Cited above, p. 130, n. 2.   [2] *Ibid.*

[3] *Resp. Lac.* II, 9: καὶ ὡς πλείστους δὴ ἁρπάσαι τύρους παρ' 'Ορθίας,
καλὸν θείς, μαστιγοῦν τούτους ἄλλοις ἐπέταξε, τοῦτο δὴ δηλῶσαι καὶ ἐν τούτῳ
βουλόμενος ὅτι ἔστιν ὀλίγον χρόνον ἀλγήσαντα πολὺν χρόνον εὐδοκιμοῦντα
εὐφραίνεσθαι. δηλοῦται δὲ ἐν τούτῳ ὅτι καὶ ὅπου τάχους δεῖ ὁ βλακεύων
ἐλάχιστα μὲν ὠφελεῖται, πλεῖστα δὲ πράγματα λαμβάνει.

[4] This is a common meaning of παρά τινος with verbs of receiving,
obtaining, etc. (Liddell and Scott, *s.v.*). It is unlikely that the meaning
here is ' from the temple of Orthia '.   [5] *Resp. Lac.* II, 2.

[6] Plut. *Arist.* 17.

implies that it was the same as that described in the *Respublica*. ' The blows inflicted on the Epheboi at Sparta around the altar ' are by Plutarch explained as a ' dramatic representation ' (μιμήματα) of an incident which was supposed to have occurred in the Persian Wars. When Pausanias was sacrificing just before the battle of Plataea, a horde of Lydians swooped down and carried off or scattered the utensils and various properties being used in the sacrifice (τὰ περὶ τὴν θυσίαν) ; and Pausanias and his officers, not having arms with which to defend themselves, drove them off with rods and whips. In this way the popular explanation interpreted not only the whipping of the Epheboi, but also the ' procession of Lydians ' [1] which followed it. The story clearly indicates that the Epheboi, far from being drawn up in lines or presented in succession to be whipped, had to make some sort of attack upon the altar, which was defended by the μαστιγοφόροι. Since the Epheboi imitated the alleged attack of the Lydians, they must have carried off some of Orthia's property from the altar, and here the account tallies with the stealing of cheeses mentioned in the *Respublica*. But further, Plutarch's account also tallies with that of Pausanias, who ascribes the origin of the whipping to a set battle round the altar between four supposed early Spartan tribes [2] in which many were killed, after which Lycurgus, on the injunction of an oracle, instituted the whipping of the Epheboi to propitiate the goddess. Thus Pausanias also implies that the whipping ordeal was an imitation of a sort of battle. He also says that the priestess of Orthia stood by holding the wooden image of the goddess, which grew inordinately heavy if the scourgers failed to exert all their strength. This would explain (on the hypothesis that the author of the *Respublica Lacedaemoniorum* is referring to the same ceremony) why in the *Respublica* the cheeses are said to be stolen ' from Orthia '. Finally, the reference to ' lasting glory ' [3] as the reward of the victor in the cheese-stealing contest accords

---

[1] See further below, p. 266.

[2] The four groups to which he refers under the names of Limnatae, Konoooureis, Mesoatae and Pitanatae (Paus. III, 16. 9) are now known from the late inscriptions to have been divisions of the Epheboi in Roman times, not early tribes. *Cf.* pp. 163 f.

[3] πολὺν χρόνον εὐδοκιμοῦντα εὐφραίνεσθαι (*cf.* p. 262, n. 3, above).

well with the title of βωμονίκης which in the time of Pausanias
was given at the time of the victory and held for life.[1]

There is therefore very good reason for rejecting the
idea that the whipping ordeal was a late innovation introduced to satisfy the ' sadistic taste ' of the third century
A.D.[2] On the explanation given above it was neither late
nor exceptionally cruel, though undoubtedly rather barbarous. The reference to it in the *Respublica Lacedaemoniorum* omits, it is true, any mention of spectators, whereas
under the Principate large audiences drawn from all over
Greece came to watch the whipping,[3] but this in itself
indicates no general decline in public taste, since on the one
hand the audiences from other Greek cities at the Spartan
Hyacinthia and Gymnopaedia in the same period were
just as large,[4] and on the other, we cannot assume from the
silence of earlier writers that there were no foreign audiences
at Orthia's festival in the fourth century. They may well
not have been so large, because in the fourth century the
preservation of very ancient religious ceremonies was
doubtless more widespread and therefore less remarkable.
But as a final argument against the notion that under the
Principate the Epheboi were simply drawn up in lines to
be flogged for the whole of the day (and Plutarch says that
the ceremony lasted the whole day),[5] it would ill accord
with all that we know of the peace-loving, philosophy-
loving Greeks of that period, who would appear to
have found their chief pleasure in attending lectures on
abstract philosophical topics, if they crowded from all
parts of Greece to look on all day at so barbarous a
spectacle.

How does the alternative explanation of the whipping
fit in with the suggestion that it is to be brought into
connection with the widespread practice of scourging
Pharmakoi ? Obviously the characteristic Spartan system
of physical training of the boys must have had a strong
influence upon the original rite, and no doubt accounts

---

[1] I.G. V, i, 554, 652, 653, 653b, 654. The victor in 653b must have
been successful very near to the time of Pausanias' peregrinations. *Cf.*
above, p. 131, and Plut. *Inst. Lac.* 41 : καὶ ὁ περιγενόμενος ἐν τοῖς μάλιστα
ἐπίδοξός ἐστι.   [2] A.O. p. 405.   [3] Philostr. *Vit. Apoll.* 258.
[4] Philostr. *ibid.*   [5] Plut. *Inst. Lac.* 40.

for the competitive and sporting element [1] which was probably the most interesting part from the point of view of the spectators. It seems, however, to be significant that the connection between the whipping and the stealing of property from a deity recurs in a popular explanation of the rite of chastising the *Pharmakoi*. ' Pharmakos ' was supposed to be the name of a man who was stoned by the companions of Achilles for stealing the sacred bowls (φιάλαι) of Apollo, and this incident was supposed to be commemorated at the Athenian Thargelia,[2] although in fact the stoning (as opposed to whipping) was part of the Ionian rather than the Athenian rite.[3] This story recalls both the supposed ' Lydians ' who stole or scattered τὰ περὶ τὴν θυσίαν when Pausanias was sacrificing before Plataea, and the stolen cheeses mentioned in the *Respublica Lacedaemoniorum*. To provide a logical justification for this chastisement, it was evidently thought necessary that the *Pharmakoi* selected as scapegoats should make a show of stealing the property of the deity, and sacred bowls were an obvious choice for the purpose. But if the broad, flat shallow bowls called φιάλαι [4] were once used, then by a natural transition cheeses might be substituted, as being approximately the same size and shape,[5] and (in Sparta at least) far less difficult to replace after the kind of mêlée described above than the original φιάλαι would have been.

Thus we conclude that in Roman Imperial times, and at least as far back as the beginning of the fourth century B.C., the real nature of the whipping ceremony was not the long drawn-out sadistic spectacle imagined by some modern writers, but a rough and brutal but exciting display of activity and endurance.

Turning to a fresh aspect of the festival of Orthia, we may find another parallel between it and the Athenian Thargelia in the musical and gymnastic competitions. These in the case of the Athenian festival took place on the

[1] This is proved independently of the account in the *Resp. Lac.* by Pausanias' reference (III, 16. 9) to the four sections of the Epheboi, the *Limnatai, Konooureis, Mesoatai* and *Pitanatai*.
[2] Harpocr. *s.v.* φαρμακός.   [3] *Cf.* Daremberg-Saglio, *s.v. Thargelia*.
[4] Illustrations and references in Smith, *Dict. Antiq. s.v. Patera*.
[5] The γαυλοί in which cheeses were made (*cf.* P.W. *s.v.* Käse, p. 1492) could also be used as drinking vessels (*cf* Theocr. 5. 104).

second day, after the ceremony of driving out the *Pharmakoi* on the first. Now, according to Plutarch, the whipping of the Spartan Epheboi was immediately followed by a ' procession of Lydians '.[1] Since the whipping lasted all day, this procession must have taken place at night, and it may be identical, or a part of it may be identical, with the procession of maidens in honour of Orthia for whom Alcman wrote his *Partheneion*. It is well to remember the principle which Plutarch recalls in his *Instituta Laconica*, κόραις καὶ κόροις κοινὰ τὰ ἱερά.[2] This demands that some connection between the whipping contest and the song of the maidens to Orthia be found. Alcman's maidens, who wear festal costume and the μίτρα Λυδία, are bringing a robe [3] to the goddess, and their song is written to be sung just before the dawn.[4] It is to be supposed, in view of the origin assigned by Plutarch to the ' procession of Lydians ', that there were male ' Lydians ' as well as the maidens in Lydian costume, and that a procession of men or boys in Lydian costume occupied the earlier part of the night. There is a striking resemblance here (already commented upon by Kukula),[5] to the torchlight procession at the Ephesian Plynteria ; and it may well be, as Davison has suggested,[6] that the Spartan festival in honour of Orthia combined elements which in other states were divided among more than one festival in the month Thargelion.

With regard to the ' Lydian ' costume, which presumably remained traditional from Alcman's time until that of Plutarch, it may be questioned whether it was really Lydian at all. At all events, Alcman's description of it would apply equally well to the costume of the Minoan goddess (Pl. **6, 5** *a*). These are the poet's words :

οὔτε γάρ τι πορφύρας
τόσσος κόρος, ὥστ' ἀμύναι,
οὔτε ποικίλος δράκων
παγχρύσιος, οὐδὲ μίτρα
Λυδία νεανίδων . . .
. . . ων ἄγαλμα
οὐδὲ ταὶ Ναννῶς κόμαι (κ.τ.λ.).

[1] *Cf.* above, p. 263. [2] Plut. *Inst. Lac.* 35 (239*b*).
[3] *Cf.* above, p. 252, n. 2. [4] *Cf. Hermes*, LXXIII, 1938, p. 449.
[5] In *Philol.* LXVI, 1907, pp. 224–228. [6] Hermes, *loc. cit.* p. 450.

The coloured faience statuette of the Minoan goddess shows her wearing the typical flounced skirt and tight laced bodice worn also by the goddess Orthia, but the striking resemblances to the attire of Alcman's maidens are the tall, almost conical cap (μίτρα), the snakes wreathed round the waist and upper part of the figure, and the flowing hair. Other statuettes of this Cretan goddess show her with a single snake only,[1] and in view of the other resemblances of costume it seems highly probable that the Spartan votaries of Orthia wore their golden imitation snake (ποικίλος δράκων παγχρύσιος) as a survival of the Minoan ritual.[2] The tall headdress is represented in many of the lead figurines of the goddess Orthia,[3] and in Alcman's time might well be called ' Lydian ', since it persisted in western Asia Minor for centuries,[4] and of all the peoples of Asia Minor it was the Lydians who in Alcman's time came most into contact with the Greeks. It is true that the darker portions of the dress of the Minoan goddess as it appears in the faience statuette are brown rather than purple,[5] but this seems likely to be due to technical difficulties in the firing, for it is known that the purple dyeing of fabrics was practised in Minoan Crete, and the colouring of the patterns in other examples of Cretan faience varies from purplish-brown to pure lilac.[6]

Once Alcman had embodied in a famous poem the idea that the headdress was Lydian, it would be natural for spectators at the festival to assume that the whole curious costume of the maidens (supposing that it continued to survive until Plutarch's time) was Lydian too. Certainly nothing more un-Greek could be imagined at any period after Alcman wrote. The tradition that the night procession

[1] *Cf.* Pl. 4a, and *P. of M.* IV, p. 194, Figs. 149, 150.

[2] Votive snakes in various materials are a fairly common offering at Orthia's shrine (*cf.* A.O., index, *s.v. Snakes, ibid.* Pl. XCIII, 2). In the night ritual performed by Alcman's maidens they would be especially in place, as emphasising the chthonic aspect of the goddess.

[3] *Cf.* Pl. 3, nos. 15, 17, 19.

[4] *Cf.* Evans, *P. of M.* IV, p. 197. In the early seventh century B.C. it is found represented on the ' Pontic ' vases (*cf.* Pfuhl, *Malerei u. Zeichnung*, III, p. 36, no. 156).

[5] For a coloured reproduction, *cf. P. of M.* I (frontispiece).

[6] *Cf. P. of M.* I, p. 490, and for the method of firing, *ibid.* p. 489, n. 3. Evidence for the Minoan use of murex is cited, *ibid.* IV, p. 111, n. 5.

represented ' Lydians ' thus explains itself, and it would be a waste of time to see in it any special significance for the origin or nature of the cult.

Alcman's *Partheneion* provides some further indications of the nature of the nocturnal procession and of the celebrations which followed it. A certain test of endurance seems to have been imposed upon the maidens, comparable to that imposed upon the boys in the whipping ordeal. Though Alcman's poem was no doubt meant to be sung by divisions of the choir, in strophe and antistrophe, it by no means implies a static gathering. The ten maidens, under their choir-leader Agesichora, bearing their offering for the goddess, are met by Agido (not one of the ten, but probably priestess of Orthia) [1] who comes to tell them that the sun is rising. There is evidently no time to lose ; the need for haste no doubt explains the comparison of the chorus-leader and of Agido to race-horses.[2] The rising of the Pleiads immediately after is a moment of peculiar supernatural danger, threatening to wreck the efficacy of the whole ritual ;[3] but it is safely overcome, not so much by the counterglow from the glittering apparel of the maidens [4] and the brightness of their hair, as by the intervention of the goddess of the Dawn [5] and through the wise direction of the chorus-leader.[6] After admiring the θωστήρια (presumably a sacred feast prepared either for Orthia

---

[1] Since she comes out to receive the offering from the maidens, and since it is evidently particularly important that by direct praise or blame of her (*cf.* l. 43 f., Diehl) the chorus shall not attract the attention of malign influences to her at the moment of handing over the offering. Her name also connects her with the royal house of the Agiadae, and there is reason to think that the royal families monopolised the chief priesthoods at Sparta. *Cf.* Appendix V. [2] Ll. 45 f.

[3] Ll. 60 f. This seems to be the point of the statement that the Pleiads, ' rising like Sirius ' (though they were normally small and dim) ' contend with us ' (μάχονται).

[4] Ll. 64 f. : οὔτε γάρ τι πορφύρας | τόσσος κόρος, ὥστε ἀμύναι, κ.τ.λ.

[5] There is no need to identify Aotis, as is commonly done, with Orthia herself, and no positive reason for doing so. The point surely is that the light of dawn extinguishes the baleful Pleiads.

[6] Ll. 77, 90 f. : Agesichora's chief service, apart from assuring the proper rendering of the ritual song, seems to have been her ban on praising Agido (*cf.* above, n. 1). In view of the character of the poem, it seems unlikely that this was a joke, or dictated by jealousy as some commentators have maintained. Fear of the jealousy of the gods seems much more likely.

herself or for her worshippers) [1] and joining in prayers to the gods with Agido, Agesichora is able to tell her chorus that their own prayers have been answered and that the dawn has released them from their toils (πόνων γὰρ | ἄμιν ἰάτωρ ἔγεντο).[2] The chorus replies that through Agesichora ' they have attained to lovely peace '.[3]

The relief here expressed would be inappropriate after the short and uneventful walk from the little town of Sparta to the temple of Orthia on its outskirts ; it implies rather that the journey has been a long and arduous one. It seems therefore not improbable that it was on the occasion of this annual festival that the Spartan maidens visited the temple of Artemis at Limnae on the borders of Messenia,[4] about 12 miles distant from Sparta by the mountain path,[5] a shrine which was said to have given its name to the temple of Orthia at Sparta.[6] That the same goddess was worshipped at both temples is clear from a dedication made to Orthia at the Messenian shrine,[7] and the pilgrimage of Spartan maidens to the Messenian shrine was evidently regarded as an important occasion by the state, since one of the two kings accompanied it.[8] The gathering on the Messenian border may well, therefore, have occupied the evening before the procession back to Sparta, for which Alcman wrote his poem. The long journey would well explain why Alcman's maidens felt tired.

The mention of θωστήρια in Alcman's poem indicates that the second day of the festival was to be a joyous celebration, after the rites of purification were safely over. At the Athenian Thargelia gymnastic and musical competitions were held on this day ; at the festival of Orthia there appears to be no indication of gymnastic competitions in the usual sense—foot-races, javelin throwing and the like. The purely physical exercises involved appear, to

---

[1] Cf. Hesych. : θωστήρια . . . εὐωχητήρια καὶ ὄνομα (ἑορτῆς ?). The Scholiast on the Partheneion has θωστήρια ἑορτή.　　　　[2] Ll. 87 f.
[3] Ll. 90 f. Bowra (Greek Lyric Poetry (1936), p. 34) thinks this may refer to the end of a Messenian War in Alcman's time, but this seems most unlikely. It is surely peace in the metaphorical sense which is meant.
[4] Cf. Paus. IV, 4. 2.
[5] For the identification of the site, see above, p. 64, and map (Pl. 10).
[6] Cf. above, p. 259, n. 7.　　　[7] I.G. V, i, 1376.　　　[8] Paus. IV, 4. 2.

judge from the list of prizes, to have been confined to the
καθθηρατόριον, the violent dance which presumably first
originated as a hunt.[1] More orthodox gymnastic competitions seem to have been reserved for the festival of Apollo,
the Hyacinthia, which must have been held at almost
exactly the same time in the spring as that of Orthia, namely,
about the middle of May.[2]

The celebrations at the Hyacinthia were in all other
respects extremely similar to those attested for Orthia's
festival,[3] and it seems not impossible that the Hyacinthia
was a more characteristically Greek expression of the same
general religious ideas, and had developed in purely Greek
time, whereas the Orthia festival preserved the reminiscences of a far more ancient origin, its roots going back
to Mycenean times. This apparent doubling of what was
essentially the same festival would serve to explain the
disappearance of Orthia's male consort, who naturally
turned into the brother-god Apollo when she was identified
with the Greek Artemis, but who in earlier times seems to
have been more like the Greek Poseidon.[4]

The many parallels with the Athenian Thargelia certainly cannot be said to prove beyond doubt that the various
rites and celebrations associated with the worship of Orthia
at Sparta fitted together in detail in the way that has been
suggested. They do, however, appear to provide a further
clue to the real nature of the Spartan Orthia-cult as it existed
in the historical period. But the clue must be taken in
conjunction with the evidence for Orthia's descent from
the Minoan-Mycenean goddess, for this evidence shows
beyond doubt that the Spartan goddess was by no means
exclusively a fertility-goddess and a protectress from

[1] Cf. Part I (Chap. III), pp. 123 f.
[2] Cf. Roscher, Lexikon, s.v. Hyakinthos, p. 2762. On the time when
the festival of Orthia was held, cf. above, p. 260.
[3] The first day of the festival was one of mourning, the second of joyous
celebration, with feasting and various performances by the youth of both
sexes—hymns in honour of Apollo to the music of lyre and flute, archaic
dances, a procession in the theatre on horseback, and two-horse chariot
races for the maidens. Cf. the Spartan Polycrates ap. Athen. IV, 139d.
[4] Cf. the series of lead figurines, A.O. Pl. CXCVI. The horse and
chariot races which were evidently a special feature of the Hyacinthia
(cf. preceding note) point in the same direction, as being more appropriate
to Poseidon than to Apollo.

plagues ; she was also a goddess of war and of hunting, and well fitted to become the patroness of all the warlike and manly pursuits to which the population of Dorian Sparta, or at least the aristocratic section of it,[1] devoted itself so completely.   And because in the Cretan-Mycenean religion the goddess completely overshadowed the god, for this reason, as we may venture to suppose, the Spartans continued to entrust to Orthia, rather than to Apollo, the training and protection of their boys and young men as well as of their maidens.

[1] The predominance of the horse among the animal votives offered at the shrine of Orthia (*cf.* above, p. 247, n. 7) suggests that the worship of the goddess was largely confined to the Spartan aristocracy.

CHAPTER VIII

THE SUBJECT POPULATION
(Perioikoi and Helots)

THE two preceding chapters lead to three general conclusions which must affect our interpretation of the earliest relations between Sparta and those peoples in the Peloponnese who became directly subject to her, namely, the Perioikoi of Laconia, and the Messenians. These general conclusions are, first, that what historians have been accustomed to regard as purely Spartan institutions were in the social sphere widely shared by other Dorian Greeks. This conclusion follows from the comparison of Spartan social institutions and those of Dorian Crete. The second general conclusion, based upon the wide diffusion of the Orthia-cult and its contacts with pre-Dorian Crete and with Arcadia, is that the common social structure which Sparta shared with other Dorian Greek states goes back to a very early period indeed, in fact to a period not long after the Dorians had settled in the Peloponnese. It is hard to see how in any other way a pre-Dorian cult could become, at Sparta, the very focal point round which their most fundamental social institutions centred. The third general conclusion is that the common Dorian tradition, which in the social sphere Sparta shared, was not in fact purely Dorian, but a mixed culture in which earlier elements were incorporated.

What is the bearing of these general conclusions upon a problem still obscure, the manner in which the Perioikoi of Laconia became subject to Sparta? And do they tend to confirm or otherwise the ancient belief that there were Spartan Helots in Laconia before the Spartan conquest of Messenia? [1] These are two of the main questions with

[1] This theory, based on a supposed derivation from the Laconian place-name Helos is first found in Hellanicus (F.H.G. I, p. 54, fr. 67), was probably accepted by Thucydides (cf. I, 101. 3), and reappears in Ephorus (F.H.G. I, p. 238, fr. 18) and Pausanias (III, 20. 6).

which this chapter will be concerned, and in seeking an answer to them, we shall find the constitutional relation of the Perioikoi and of the Helots to Sparta in later historical times gradually becoming more clear. Only then will it also be possible, to see more clearly the bearing of the later epigraphic evidence from the Free Laconian towns upon their relation to Sparta in the time of their dependence.

We possess at present no archaeological evidence either in the Peloponnese or elsewhere, which might throw light on the early movements of the Dorians. The various theories which are held upon the matter at the present time are therefore of necessity based upon general considerations, especially upon the distribution of the various Greek dialects, and relate to two main questions. Was the Dorian conquest in Laconia slow or rapid ? Did the previous inhabitants remain, or were they driven out ? The views of Busolt, Glotz, and Eduard Meyer may be cited as typical answers to these questions.

Glotz, following the account of Spartan expansion in Laconia given by Pausanias,[1] supposed the Dorian conquest to have been very slow ;[2] remaining for long entrenched in the middle valley of the Eurotas with Sparta and Amyclae as their main centres, they did not begin their real expansion until about the end of the ninth century, then rapidly subjected first the northern Eurotas valley, then the towns already existing on the slopes of Parnon on the East, including Geronthrae, finally the lower valley of the Eurotas, including Helos. ' Partout ils asservirent les vaincus.' The process was completed, according to Pausanias, in the reign of the ninth king in the Agiad line.

Busolt rejects the account in Pausanias on the ground that it contradicts an earlier tradition, accepted by the Spartans themselves, who believed (or so Busolt interprets Herodotus, VI, 52)[3] that Aristodemus, the father of the twin kings Eurysthenes and Procles, occupied the whole of Laconia outright.[4] On Busolt's view, the Dorian

---

[1] Paus. III, 2. 2–7. [2] Glotz, *Hist. Grecque*, I (1925), p. 343.
[3] Herod. VI, 52 : Λακεδαιμόνιοι γὰρ ὁμολογέοντες οὐδενὶ ποιητῇ λέγουσι αὐτὸν Ἀριστόδημον . . . βασιλεύοντα ἀγαγεῖν σφεᾶς ἐς ταύτην τὴν χώρην τὴν νῦν ἐκτέαται, ἀλλ' οὐ τοὺς Ἀριστοδήμου παῖδας.
[4] *Cf.* Busolt, *Gr. Gesch.* I², pp. 206 f. ; Busolt-Swoboda, II (1926), pp. 633 f.

18

invaders, uniting in the central Eurotas valley, where they made their standing camp in the vicinity of Sparta, overran the whole country almost immediately after their first appearance, the valley of the Eurotas first, then the hilly surrounding country. The richer land round the river was taken by the invaders as πολιτικὴ χώρα, and divided into approximately equal lots for the victorious Dorians ; this was the origin of the Spartan κλῆροι. The previous inhabitants of this land, of south-Achaean stock, were reduced to the condition of serfs bound to the soil, the original Helots. In the surrounding hill country the inhabitants (on Busolt's view, of the same south-Achaean stock as the rest)[1] were allowed to continue in occupation without becoming serfs, but did become subject to the Dorians under the name of Perioikoi. The persistence of the name πόλεις is to be explained, on Busolt's view, by the retention of a shadow of liberty. It implies that towns had already developed in this region before the Dorian invasion, a hypothesis which Busolt considers to be borne out by the survival of Cyclopean walls at Geronthrae.[2]

In contrast with Busolt and Glotz, many historians believe the Perioikoi to have been Dorians.[3] A supporter of this theory is Eduard Meyer,[4] who suggests the possibility that the Dorians may not have overwhelmed the earlier inhabitants outright, but may have served at first as mercenaries, gradually increasing in numbers until they were able to overwhelm the overlords for whom they fought. This interpretation he believes to be supported by the Dorian occupation, not of the lands nearest to them, but of the south and east of the Peloponnese and of Crete. In any case he believes, mainly as it would appear in view of the history of the Germanic and other similar conquests,[5] that the Dorian conquest in the Peloponnese was slow, probably lasting above a hundred years. Long-continued resistance at some points, notably Argos and Corinth,

[1] This thesis is supported on philological grounds (Achaean survivals in the Laconian dialect) by Meister, Solmsen and others (ref. in Busolt-Swoboda, I, pp. 113, n. 3, 136, n. 1. But see further below, pp. 277 f.

[2] Cf. B.S.A. XI (1905), pp. 91 f.

[3] Cited by Busolt-Swoboda, II, p. 637, n. 3.

[4] Ed. Meyer, Gesch. d. Altertums², III (1937), pp. 2 f. (followed in the main by Roussel, Sparte (1939), p. 42). [5] Cf. ibid. III, i, pp. 572 f.

seems to be indicated by the tradition that the Dorians occupied strong points near by.[1] In the course of long wars the earlier inhabitants were gradually restricted to the mountains of Arcadia and to the west coast north of Messenia ; in Argos, Laconia and Messenia the population became wholly Dorian in race and in speech. In the case of Messenia, Meyer believes an early Dorian invasion to be indicated by the story in Iliad, XI, 690 f., of a raid upon Pylos by Herakles :

ἐλθὼν γὰρ ἐκάκωσε βίη Ἡρακληείη
τῶν προτέρων ἐτέων, κατὰ δ᾿ ἔκταθεν ὅσσοι ἄριστοι,
δώδεκα γὰρ Νηλῆος ἀμύμονος υἱέες ἦμεν·
τῶν οἶος λιπόμην, οἱ δ᾿ ἄλλοι πάντες ὄλοντο.

Meyer's interpretation of the passage receives support from the description, in the *Catalogue,* of the coming of Tlepolemus (υἱὸς βίης Ἡρακληείης), to Rhodes, where he established his followers in three tribes, founded three cities, and brought nine ships to the attack on Troy.[2] A reference to the Dorians and their characteristic three tribes is surely intended here.

But a further piece of Homeric evidence for the penetration of Dorians into Messenia at any early date gives additional support to Meyer's theory. This is the appearance of a place-name Δώριον in the *Catalogue,*[3] in company with other names which locate it somewhere in northern Messenia. This is the significant fact ; the uncertainty about its precise location among the Greeks of the Roman period is of little importance.[4] ' The Dorian fort ' (Δώριον τεῖχος) seems the most likely interpretation of the name, in view of the traditions, already mentioned, that Dorian strongholds were established near Corinth and Argos. It seems to be widely agreed that the *Catalogue* is even earlier in date than the *Iliad* as a whole ;[5] the occurrence of the

[1] For Dorian occupation of the hill Solygeios near Corinth, *cf.* Thuc. IV, 42 : for their occupation of the Temenion near the sea south of Argos, Strabo, VIII, 368 ; Paus. II, 38. 1. The cult of Temenos here was peculiar to Dorians (Paus. *loc. cit.*).

[2] *Il.* II, 654–670. The Dorian predilection for threes and multiples of three is further discussed below, pp. 341 f., 392 f.

[3] *Il.* II, 594.   [4] *Cf.* Strabo, VIII, 350 ; Paus. IV, 33. 7.

[5] Bowra (*Tradition and Design in the Iliad* (1930), p. 135) thinks Homer ' hit on the expedient of incorporating an old poem giving the list of troops who gathered at Aulis '.

name *Dorion* in the passage in question is therefore good reason both for thinking that the tradition of Dorian forts near Corinth and Argos was a genuine one, and for assigning to a date much earlier than the first Messenian War the appearance of the Dorians in Messenia.

There is also an argument to be drawn from the use of the Dorian dialect and Dorian proper names in Rhegium, which was founded at the time of the outbreak of the first Messenian War, being a joint colony of Chalcidians from Euboea and Italian Cumae, and Messenians who, immediately before the invasion of their country, fled to escape death at the hands of the Spartans.[1] Now the dialect of the Chalcidian Greeks (Euboeans) was Ionian,[2] and that of the pre-Dorian population of Messenia was (almost certainly) Arcadian ; [3] the survival of Dorian Greek in the joint Chalcidian-Messenian colony [4] must therefore be due to the fact that the Messenians, who formed the aristocracy in the colony,[5] were themselves Dorians, not preDorians. But this implies that at least a section of the Messenians (probably the aristocracy, since it was these refugees who provided the hereditary kings in Rhegium) were already Dorians before the Spartans invaded Messenia in the eighth century. This also is the most natural explanation of the universal adoption by the Messenians, in the period after their liberation in the fourth century, not only of the Dorian dialect but of the pure Dorian cult of Apollo Karneios [6] and of the Dorian calendar.[7] If the

---

[1] *Cf.* Heracl. Pont. fr. 25 (F.H.G. II, p. 219) ; Strabo, VI, 257 ; Paus. IV, 23. 6. The chronology of Pausianas' account is confused, but the main fact of the Messenian origin of Anaxilas and his ancestors (explicitly mentioned by all three authorities) is supported by the re-naming of Zancle as Messene (Herod. VII, 164 ; Thuc. VI, 4, corroborated by the evidence of coins) at a time (*c.* 493) when fresh Messenian colonists were not available.

[2] *Cf.* J. L. Myres, *Who Were the Greeks ?* (1930), p. 158.

[3] *Ibid.* p. 149, Fig. 7.

[4] *Cf.* Ditt. *Syll.*³ 715 (second century B.C.). The reappearance of the Dorian form *Messana* on the coins of Zancle-Messene (previously recolonised by Ionians from Samos) *c.* 480–476 is attributed by Hill (*Hist. Greek Coins*, 1906, pp. 29 f.) to re-annexation by Anaxilas of Rhegium.

[5] *Cf.* Strabo, *loc. cit.* : διόπερ οἱ τῶν Ῥηγίνων ἡγεμόνες μέχρι Ἀναξίλα τοῦ Μεσσηνίων γένους ἀεὶ καθίσταντο.

[6] *Cf.* I.G. V, i, 1390 (Andania, 92 B.C.), also at Thalamae (Paus. III, 26. 5) and at Cardamyle (*ibid.* § 7 : καθὰ Δωριεῦσιν ἐπιχώριον).

[7] *Ibid.* 1447 (Messene, third century, B.C.). The month Agrianios mentioned here is also common to Sparta, Rhodes and Cos, *cf.* Dar.-Sagl.

Messenians, or at least those who now acquired political
power among the Messenians, had felt themselves to be
non-Dorian they would have eagerly seized this opportunity
to throw off a forcibly-imposed Dorian culture. There is
no difficulty in finding obvious parallels to this development in modern times. Even if, in Busolt's phrase, the
Messenians had become ' Dorianised ' in language [1] during
the period of their subjection, and were no longer able to
recover the old language, surely they would have adopted
the Boeotian or Achaean calendar rather than the Spartan
in the fourth century B.C., and would have refrained from
perpetuating the office of ephor,[2] and from retaining the
names of Dorian legendary heroes for their tribes.[3]

Thus it appears certain that whether the Dorian conquest
in the Peloponnese was slow or rapid, a Dorian aristocracy
at least [4] had already established itself in Messenia before
the Spartan invasion of that region, and was already in
process of establishing itself at the original time of composition of the Homeric Catalogue.[5] But what is true of
Messenia is *a fortiori* true of Laconia outside the Eurotas
valley, the coastal area and the islands on the east and south,
and the slopes of the Parnon range on which Geronthrae
was situated. In view of the wide distribution of the Dorian
invaders, over many of the islands as well as in the Peloponnese, and already in Crete, and in Rhodes and neighbouring
islands, at the time of composition of the earliest Homeric

s.v. Calendarium, pp. 829, 832. A month $\Phi υ\lambda\lambda\iota(\kappa\acute{o}s)\cdot$ at Messene (I.G.
ibid.) must be connected with the month Phyllikos (I.G. IX, index) and the
cult of Apollo Phyllios (Strabo, VIII, 435), both in that part of Thessaly
from which the Dorians were reputed to have wandered (Herod. I, 56 ;
cf. Myres, *op. cit.* pp. 163 f.). The months Mnaster (I.G. *ibid.*, Messene),
Laphrios (*ibid.* 1145, from Gytheum, which also has Hyakinthios) ; Lykeios,
(*ibid.* 932, from Epidaurus Limera, which also has Karneios) may perhaps
be added to the names of Spartan months known either from literary
sources or from inscriptions (Agrianios, Artemitios, Gerastios, Hekatom-
beios, Hyakinthios, Karneios, Phloiasios : *cf.* Dar.-Sagl. *ibid.* I.G. V, i,
index VI, 4). Lykeios also occurs as the name of a month in Pthiotis
(Dar.-Sagl. *ibid.* p. 828).   [1] Busolt-Swoboda, II, p. 639.
    [2] *Cf.* Polyb. IV, 4 (ephors at Messene, 222 B.C.).
    [3] *Cf.* I.G. V, i, 1433.   The tribe-names Hyllis and Kleolaia (or Kleodaia ?
cf. Herod. VII, 204 ; VIII, 131), if not the rest, must clearly be pure Dorian
in origin.   [4] On this point see further below, pp. 288 f.
    [5] An attempt to give more precise indications of chronology in regard
to the Dorian invasion of the Peloponnese will be found in the following
chapter (pp. 335 f.).

poems, it is (to say the least) extremely improbable that the south and east coastal districts of the Peloponnese were not overrun by the Dorians at the same time as the rest.

This must have been generally believed at least as early as the sixth century B.C., since Hecataeus of Miletus mentioned a sacred snake kept at Taenarum, which was said to have been ' brought by Herakles to Eurystheus '.[1] Herodotus also believed the Laconian Perioikoi, as well as the Messenians, to be of Dorian origin, for he contrasts them with the autochthonous Cynurians, who ἐκδεδωρίευνται ὑπό τε 'Αργείων ἀρχόμενοι καὶ τοῦ χρόνου, and gives a clear location to all the other non-Dorian races of the Peloponnese outside Laconian territory.[2]

But the evidence of similar social institutions, considered in an earlier chapter, provides clear evidence that the Dorians of the Eurotas valley were *not* isolated, for many generations after their settlement in Peloponnese, from the Dorians of Crete and other islands by a fringe of non-Dorian Perioikoi. The close similarity of complex social institutions proves that a more or less homogeneous Dorian culture, or more correctly, a mixed Dorian and pre-Dorian culture, existed over the whole of the area in question.[3] Busolt's picture of a Dorian ' Standlager ' in the central Eurotas valley,[4] from which the Dorians established a purely political conquest over the territory of the Perioikoi, is completely opposed both to general probability and to the new evidence considered in the present work. The Dorian invaders of the Peloponnese were certainly not few, but exceedingly numerous, quite able to overrun the whole of Laconia and Messenia as well as Argolis, and to remain as the ruling aristocracy in all of them. It is possible that historians who take the contrary view have been unduly influenced by the belief held in antiquity, and by the

[1] Hecataeus *ap.* Paus. III, 25. 5.   [2] Herod. VIII, 73.
[3] That is, over the area indicated by the language-map (*cf.* Myres, *Who were the Greeks ?*, p. 84, Fig. 3).
[4] Busolt-Swoboda, *ibid.* p. 633. Ed. Meyer appears to have a similar though not identical conception, believing the Dorians in the Peloponnese to have been at first united in a single army (*op. cit.* p. 253). It is hardly necessary to point out that in that case they cannot have been employed as mercenaries, as Meyer also suggests.

Spartans themselves at least as early as the time of Tyrtaeus, that the little state of Doris in central Greece was the metropolis of all the Dorians.[1] But as Myres has shown conclusively from the distribution of the dialects, the inhabitants of Doris can have been no more than an off-shoot from the main Dorian migration southwards.[2]

With regard to the length of time occupied by the conquest, it is very doubtful whether in the absence of archaeological evidence we can find any other to guide us, and the archaeological evidence would in any case need to be considerable in amount and wide in distribution, comparable to that existing for the Villanovans in Italy, to be of any use. It has been suggested on the basis of ancient genealogies that the Dorian invasion of the Peloponnese occurred about 1140 B.C.[3] It has also been suggested that the earliest Geometric pottery goes back to about 1000 B.C.[4] The lapse of so long a period between the invasion and the appearance of the new pottery might reasonably be regarded as evidence of a long period of disturbance before civilisation revived. But it must be admitted that neither basis of the argument is certain. The genealogies in question admit of more than one inter-pretation and may in this case indicate a later date for the conquest ;[5] the Geometric pottery in the Peloponnese is dated at its lower end from finds in central Laconia, which are themselves dated from the late historical tradition which represents the conquest of Laconia by Sparta as having begun only about 800 B.C.[6] This particular ancient account not only conflicts with an earlier Spartan one, but is, as we have seen, on general grounds improbable. It is too easily explained by the desire of later annalists to expand a mere list of royal names into a plausible (or apparently plausible) account. It can have no more validity than the similar attempts of Greek and Roman annalists to write a history of the exploits of the kings of Rome.

But although there is at present no definite conclusion to be drawn from the genealogies or from the pottery, the

---

[1] Cf. Tyrtaeus, fr. 2 (Diehl). Erineon in Doris is meant (cf. Thuc. I, 107. 2).   [2] Myres, op. cit. p. 149 f.
[3] Ibid. p. 304.   [4] Cf. p. 336, n. 5.   [5] See further below, pp. 336 f.
[6] Cf. Myres, op. cit. p. 477, citing Strabo and Pausanias.

evidence of assimilation by the Spartans of pre-Dorian cults at an early period [1] points to a gradual rather than to a sudden conquest. Taken in conjunction with the early evidence for Dorians in Messenia and for Dorian forts in other parts of the Peloponnese besides Laconia, it suggests that the Dorians came in everywhere (perhaps not by land from the north, but by sea), at first in comparatively small, but later in ever-growing numbers. Meyer's theory that they may at first have been employed as mercenaries seems not improbable in the light of the amalgamation of cultures, and would explain an apparently long gap before the emergence of the new pottery, because the invaders would for long be employed mainly in fighting against each other. The same hypothesis would also explain the isolation of the various groups of Peloponnesian Dorians and their hostility to one another, as seen particularly in the case of Spartans and Argives, and Spartans and Messenians.

Busolt, as we have seen, believes a tradition held by the Spartans in the fifth century B.C. to outweigh all these other considerations. But apart from a vagueness of wording which leaves the real meaning uncertain,[2] the account of this tradition in Herodotus is based wholly on the Spartan interpretation of their own king-lists, which may have some significance for mere chronology, in particular for the approximate date of the invasion, but can have no value otherwise, as being mere unadorned lists of names. This subject will be treated at length in a later chapter.[3] There is indeed a sense in which there can be a real folk-memory going back to a very remote past, a tradition namely which is attached to particular localities by the survival of place-names or peculiar cults, as for example the cult peculiar to Dorians at the Temenion near Argos, which has been mentioned earlier.[4] But such evidence reveals its full significance only to the researcher who can collect and compare it ; the peoples whose own

---

[1] The cult of Orthia, cannot, by its very nature and importance at Sparta, be regarded as an instance of a cult adopted comparatively late in order to appease the conquered. The same applies to the cult of the Dioscuri, the ' brothers of Helen '.

[2] *Cf.* above, p 273, n. 3. ' Aristodemus led them to the land which they now possess.'   [3] Pp. 333 f.   [4] *Cf.* p. 275, n. 1.

past inheritance it was were certainly not possessed of the full story. Thus, for example, we find Thucydides, in his attempt to reconstruct the early history of the Greek race, forced back upon a few scattered archaeological remains and the evidence of the Homeric poems,[1] which is still available to us at the present day. Later Greek historians (such as Strabo and his predecessors) who made any attempt at critical investigation were obviously, as may be seen from their works, in the same position. Similarly Herodotus, desiring to give some account of the history of the eastern coastal region of the Peloponnese and the outlying islands in the period previous to the war between Sparta and Argos for the possession of the Thyreatis, says ' once all the land as far as Malea belonged to the Argives, both the mainland, and the island of Cythera and the rest of the islands '.[2] This passage, interpreted by some historians as evidence that Cythera was still subject to Argos until about 600 B.C.[3] must in actual fact be derived from the line of Homer which Thucydides (I, 9) also quotes concerning Agamemnon— πολλῇσιν νήσοισι καὶ Ἀργεϊ παντὶ ἀνάσσειν.[4] It provides no evidence whatever for the political condition of this region in the period after the Dorian conquest.

When Herodotus speaks of the Laconians subject to Sparta in his own time there is no reason to doubt his information. They lived in ' many cities ' (πόλιες πολλαί),[5] a statement only to be expected in view of the long list of Free Laconian towns which existed in later times,[6] which at the same time it renders most unlikely Busolt's suggestion that the name πόλεις survived among the Spartan Perioikoi merely because there had been πόλεις in this region in the period before the Dorian invasion at the beginning of the Iron Age. The Cyclopaean walls of Geronthrae may possibly be evidence for a Mycenean town here, for Geronthrae is fifteen to twenty miles inland both from the east and the south, perched high on the hillside and in every way corresponding to Thucydides' description of

[1] Cf. Thuc. I, 9.   [2] Herod. I, 82.
[3] Cf. Kolbe, I.G. V, i, p. 176. The anecdote about Cheilon (Herod. VII, 235) which is quoted in support of this view has no bearing upon the date when the Spartans first occupied the island.   [4] Iliad II, 108.
[5] Herod. VII, 234 (quoting Demaratus' conversation with Xerxes).
[6] See Part I. Appendix III.

those ' older cities ' which were built to keep their inhabitants safe from pirates in the days of the Sea-Raiders. But what of Gytheum, Las, and in fact almost all the towns which later became Free Laconian ? Those were built on the sea-shore itself (ἐπ' αὐτοῖς τοῖς αἰγιαλοῖς), and so must be classed on Thucydides' view with those towns ὅσαι νεώτατα ᾠκίσθησαν, owing their origin to a more settled and prosperous period when piracy had come to an end.[1] It is true that Helos, Las, and Oetylus, all sea-coast towns, are mentioned by the Homeric *Catalogue* [2] in the list of Lacedaemonian cities, but as we have seen from references to Dorians in the *Catalogue*,[3] this does not mean that they existed before the coming of the Dorians. Nor would they have been allowed to be built afterwards if this region had been politically subjugated by the Dorians of Sparta, as Busolt assumes, immediately after the first coming of the Dorians. In other words their existence implies a fairly long period of independence for the mixed Dorian-Achaean population of the coastal region before the political conquest by Sparta.

There are the same reasons for thinking that Dorian Greeks had long been in control of this region before the Spartan conquest as there are for thinking that the civilisation of Messenia was predominantly Dorian before the Messenian Wars, namely the persistence of Dorian cults, the Dorian Calendar,[4] and typically Dorian political institutions, in what had been the towns of the Perioikoi, for long after they had been freed from the Spartan yoke. The universal use of the Dorian dialect, to which the inscriptions of these Laconian towns testify, might be due (if we had not other reasons for believing the Perioikoi to be themselves predominantly Dorian) to Spartan tyranny ; the same cannot be said of the other survivals, which could be maintained or abandoned at will. And although the Perioikoi are not known to have gone to the length of open revolt as the Messenians did on occasion, we have Xenophon's authority for their intense hatred of the Spartans [5] during the period of their dependence.

---

[1] *Cf.* Thuc. I, 7. 1, 8. 3, and see further, Myres, *op. cit.* p. 457.
[2] *Iliad* II, 380 f.   [3] *Cf.* p. 275.
[4] Evidence for this is cited above, p. 276, n. 7.
[5] Xen. *Hell.* III, iii, 6.

With regard to the later survival of Dorian cults the evidence is scanty, but Apollo Karneios was still worshipped in Roman times on a hill outside Las, and a statue of Herakles stood outside the walls of the ancient city [1] which was in ruins in Pausanias' time. Apollo Karneios was also worshipped at Oetylus, where an ancient *Xoanon* of the god still stood in the Agora in Pausanias' time. [2]

The chief magistrates in all the towns of the Perioikoi after their liberation from Sparta appear to have been ephors, for whom there is epigraphic evidence at Boeae, [3] Cotyrta, [4] Epidaurus Limera, [5] Geronthrae [6] in the group of towns east of the Eurotas, at Gytheum, [7] Pyrrhicus, [8] Taenarum, [9] Hippola, [10] Oetylus, [11] Cardamyle [12] and Gerenia [13] in the central promontory. Most of the inscriptions concerned date from the second and first centuries B.C. ; in the case of Taenarum the evidence relates only to the first half of the third century A.D., but it is certain that the magistracy is an ancient survival here, not a new invention in view of its existence much earlier in other Laconian towns. Nor was the ephorate copied from Sparta, for in the few inscriptions from Laconian towns where the number of ephors is recorded, it is always three, [14] not five. This in itself suggests an ancient Dorian survival, and a connection with the three Dorian tribes. But the strongest reason for believing the ephorate to be a widespread Dorian institution [15] rather than a Spartan one is that Messene, which was an entirely new city created after the liberation of Messenia from Sparta, proceeded to institute ephors. [16] Their number is unknown, but at all events they can scarcely have been imitated from the arch-enemy, Sparta. The states outside the Peloponnese which are known to have had ephors

[1] Paus. III, 24. 6, 8.   [2] *Ibid.* 25. 10.   [3] I.G. V, i, 952.
[4] *Ibid.* 961, 964, 965, 966.   [5] *Ibid.* 931, 932.
[6] *Ibid.* 1114 (3 ephors, uncertain date).
[7] *Ibid.* 1144, 1145, 1146, 1524.   [8] *Ibid.* 1281, cf. 1524.
[9] *Ibid.* 1240, 1241 (3 ephors in A.D. 213 and 238).
[10] *Ibid.* 1336.   [11] *Ibid.* 1294.
[12] *Ibid.* 1331 (? 3 ephors).   [13] *Ibid.* 1336.
[14] *Ibid.* 1114 (Geronthrae), 1240 (Taenarum), possibly 1331 (Cardamyle).
[15] As Müller believes (*Dorians*, II, p. 115). See further on this question, pp. 402 f.   [16] *Cf.* Paus. IV, 4 (referring to 222 B.C.).

are all Dorian, namely Thera,[1] Cyrene [2] and the Tarentine colony Heraclea ;[3] and among these Thera at least can scarcely be supposed to have owed its ephors to Spartan influence, for although it was said in antiquity to be a Spartan ' colony ', there was no more reality in this than in the similar assertions made about Melos, Lyktos, and Selge [4] in Asia Minor. Any town of Dorian origin came to be claimed as a colony of Sparta for the same political reasons which led Athens to claim that all Ionian states were colonised from Attica.

Since Gytheum existed as a walled town in the period of Spartan domination,[5] it may be assumed that the cities of the Perioikoi in general had the privilege of a certain amount of self-government, which would make possible the survival of ephors even under the supervision of a Spartan ἁρμοστής.[6] The survival of public assemblies is less likely, and in any case such assemblies are likely to have been of very rare occurrence in early times, before the Spartan conquest of the Laconian towns in question. It seems more prudent to ascribe to direct Spartan influence the survival of the name μεγάλαι ἀπέλλαι for the public assembly at Gytheum [7] after it had become independent, and to suppose that Gytheum had in the past received preferential treatment among the towns of the Perioikoi because it was indispensable as a naval base.[8] This might have the effect of making Gytheum less reluctant than the rest to copy Spartan institutions.

---

[1] Ephors (number unknown) are mentioned in the Testament of Epikteta (C.I.G. 2448, col. i, l. 1). *Cf.* above, p. 239.

[2] Their earliest mention at Cyrene (number unspecified) is in Heracl. Pont. (F.H.G. II, p. 212, fr. 4), implying that they had only minor judicial powers. We may suspect a radical change in the office either at the time of the reorganisation by Demonax of Mantinea, or in the middle of the fifth century when the monarchy was overthrown. The increase in the number of tribes and the general democratisation referred to by Arist. *Pol.* VI, 4. 17 f. may account for the ephors mentioned in the late fourth-century constitution (*Hermes*, 1929, p. 437) being five in number.

[3] *Inscr. Jur. Gr.*, no. XII, col. i, l. 1.   [4] *Cf.* Strabo, XII, 570.
[5] *Cf.* Xen. *Hell.* VI, v, 32.   [6] See below, p. 288, n. 6.

[7] I.G. V, i, 1144 (c. 70 B.C.), l. 20 : δι' ἃ ἔδοξε τῶι δάμωι ἐν ταῖς μεγάλαις ἀπελλαῖς. The same name at Sparta is implied by Xen. *Hell.* III, iii, 8 (οὐδὲ τὴν μικρὰν καλουμένην ἐκκλησίαν συλλέξαντες) and by the Spartan term ἀπελλάζειν (Plut. *Lycurg.* 6). On the ' μικρὰ ἐκκλησία ' at Sparta, *cf.* p. 154.   [8] *Cf.* Xen. *Hell.* VI, v, 32.

The evidence for archaic Dorian institutions in the towns of the Perioikoi must not be allowed to eclipse the evidence of the existence of a pre-Dorian element. Philologists have found considerable influence of a pre-Dorian dialect in the dialect of the Spartans [1] which implies the existence of the same element in the territory of the Perioikoi also. The cult of Artemis Limnatis, which has been shown to be pre-Dorian,[2] is found at Boeae,[3] and that of Artemis Issoria (possibly the same goddess) at Teuthrone.[4] Las worshipped Artemis Diktynna.[5] The name of Pyrrhicus was locally derived from the Curetes of Crete.[6] The ubiquitous cult of the Dioscuri, common to Sparta also, is another argument in favour of the supposition that a pre-Dorian stratum existed in the population.

This pre-Dorian population would certainly be reduced to political subjection by the invading Dorians. The various grades of serfdom which existed among the Cretan Dorians in later times, and the evidence for feudal institutions in earlier times, proves that subjugation of non-Dorians, not expulsion, was the policy pursued by the Dorian invaders in Crete. We have seen that there is abundant evidence for the same course of development among the Spartans, that this is in fact the origin of their peculiar social institutions in later times. There can scarcely be any doubt that in the other Laconian towns too the same process took place; we shall presently have occasion to notice the same thing in pre-Spartan Messenia also.[7] The ancient authors are therefore likely to be right in assuming the existence of Helots among the Spartans before the conquest of Messenia, even if they are wrong about the origin of the name εἵλωτες.[8] The majority were doubtless a lower stratum of the pre-Dorian population of the Eurotas valley, subjugated soon after the Dorian invasion; others were probably taken from the other Laconian peoples (who had previously reduced the same element to serfdom) when they in turn became subject to Sparta. For the reduction of the previously free Laconian towns to the status of Perioikoi

---

[1] Cf. p. 274, n. 1.   [2] Cf. pp. 251 f., 269.   [3] I.G. V, i, 952.
[4] Paus. III, 25. 4 ; cf. 14. 2.   [5] Paus. III, 24. 9.
[6] Ibid. 25. 2.   [7] See below, pp. 288 f.
[8] Cf. p. 272, n. 1. The true derivation is clearly from ἑλεῖν.

involved the annexation of some of their land, either as Spartan royal estates, or as πολιτικὴ χώρα. Since the kings were owners only of a small quantity of γῆ ἐξαίρετος, *i.e.* ' land exempted from distribution ',[1] in each of a number of towns of the Perioikoi,[2] it may be assumed that a much larger amount was assigned on the occasion of each fresh conquest to the Spartan state as πολιτικὴ χώρα,[3] corresponding to the Roman *ager publicus*. But as in Italy, so in Laconia, this land was not necessarily distributed to citizens, but for the most part remained in the possession of its former owners, who may possibly have paid a tax on it in the form of a proportion of the produce, if Kahrstedt is right in so interpreting the καλάμη referred to by Hesychius.[4] The contemptuous name ('stalks') implies that it was very poor quality corn, grown on land which the Spartans did not think it worth while to annex outright. But at Geronthrae, Acriae, Helos and Gytheum, the towns of the Perioikoi nearest to Sparta and bordering on the Eurotas, πολιτικὴ χώρα must have been actually annexed by the Spartans for distribution to their own citizens,[5] and the serfs who formerly worked this land for overlords in Geronthrae, Acriae, Helos, and Gytheum would pass with the land into the hands of Spartan owners as Helots. Many of them doubtless worked the land round Helos and so naturally gave rise to the misunderstanding about the origin of their name.

At the other end of the Eurotas valley it seems clear that πολιτικὴ χώρα sufficient to provide land for 4,500 Spartan citizens was annexed after the Spartan conquest in the region between Caryae and Sellasia (Skiritis), since

---

[1] *Cf.* the inscription relating to Brea (Tod, *Gk. Hist. Inscr.* 44, l. 10) : τὰ δὲ τεμένη τὰ ἐχσῃρημένα ἐᾶν καθάπερ ἐστί, καὶ ἄλλα μὴ τεμενίζειν.

[2] *Resp. Lac.* 15. 3 (on the privileges assigned by Lycurgus to the Spartan kings) καὶ γῆν δὲ ἐν πολλαῖς τῶν περιοίκων πόλεων ἀπέδειξεν ἐξαίρετον τοσαύτην ὥστε μήτε δεῖσθαι τῶν μετρίων μήτε πλούτῳ ὑπερφέρειν. This implies that only a very small share of land went to the kings from any one town.

[3] This phrase is applied to Spartan public land by Polyb. VI, 45.

[4] *Cf.* Kahrstedt, *Sparta u. Seine Symmachie*, p. 25, etc. But the gloss in Hesychius (καλάμη τὸ τέλος † ὃ ἔδει ? † φέρειν τοὺς παροίκους (*sic*) is incomplete and the meaning far from certain.

[5] For Geronthrae and the settlement of Spartans there, *cf.* Paus. III, 2. 6, 22. 6, who says that the original population (whom he wrongly describes as 'Achaeans') were driven out at the time of the Spartan conquest.

this area was actually set aside for distribution to Spartan citizens by Agis IV.[1] But this does not necessarily mean that the land in question, which was of very inferior quality, had actually been distributed in an earlier period ; it rather implies that, since it was of poor quality, the least possible opposition to its use by the state for distribution would arise in the third century B.C., and further, that it had not actually been so distributed in the past. It is more likely that it was one of the regions from which ' καλάμη ' was collected. For if, as seems probable, the land round the mouth of the river was actually annexed for Spartan κλῆροι after conquest, this would provide room for about another 4,500 lots, with the further implication, if the land in the north was annexed too, that already before the conquest of Messenia the number of Spartan citizens provided for in this way had at least equalled, if not passed, the largest number (9,000 or 10,000) [2] which is said to have existed at any time. These considerations with regard to the size of the Spartan citizen population have an obvious bearing upon the date of the Spartan conquest of the Perioikoi, but the subject cannot profitably be further discussed except in connection with the evidence for political changes at Sparta, and is best postponed for the present.[3] At all events it can safely be assumed that the conquest was a process which took some considerable time, since it involved a succession of attacks upon separate towns, many of which must have had at least as large a population as Sparta, and that the conquest of all Laconia was complete before the conquest of Messenia began. This last conclusion follows not only from considerations of general probability, but from the fact that towns with the status of Perioikoi were established in Messenia itself.[4]

The extent of the resentment which the Laconian Perioikoi felt against Sparta [5] does not necessarily mean that they were harshly treated. If they had actually been oppressed, they would surely have revolted long before the Thebans destroyed Spartan supremacy in the Peloponnese, for their united population was many times as large

---

[1] See Part I, Appendix I.   [2] See further, pp. 350 f.
[3] See further, below, pp. 424 f.   [4] Cf. pp. 298 f.   [5] Cf. above, p. 282.

as that of Sparta, and they possessed raw materials (in particular, iron), and the resources for working them, without which the Spartans could not make war.[1] The total number of the Perioikoi with the property qualification of hoplites (excluding the Perioikoi of Messenia) was assessed at over three times the number of Spartans so qualified, 30,000 Perioikoi to 9,000 Spartans under the original ' Lycurgan ' arrangement,[2] and 15,000 Perioikoi to 4,500 Spartans according to the land distribution scheme of Agis IV.[3] Yet the largest number of hoplites ever known to have been called out from the towns of the Perioikoi, 5,000 for the campaign of Plataea,[4] was only equal to the number of the Spartan hoplites, and represented a levy of only one-sixth of their own total. The allied states in the Peloponnesian League in the fifth century were required on occasion to provide a two-thirds levy of the total number available.[5]

But although the Perioikoi were in many respects privileged, and were free to carry on their own economic life, it was natural that states with the traditions of free Dorians should resent the marks of their subordination to Sparta, the tribute imposed on a part of their land, the presence in some cases at least of a Spartan governor (ἁρμοστής) [6] with a Spartan garrison, and the lack of any voice in deciding the foreign policy which they were called upon to support.

To determine how towns of the Perioikoi came to be established round the coasts of Messenia, the nature of the conquest of Messenia itself must first be investigated. It has already been shown that a Dorian aristocracy must have been established in Messenia as early as in Laconia itself, and this fundamental fact must affect our interpretation of the settlement imposed upon the country by the Spartans. For as in Laconia, so in Messenia, the

---

[1] Cf. pp. 74 f.   [2] Plut. Lycurg. 8 ; cf. Arist. Pol. II, 9. 16, 17.
[3] Plut. Agis. 8.   [4] Herod. IX, 11 (described as λογάδες).
[5] Thuc. II, 10, 47 ; III, 15.

[6] A ἁρμοστής is attested by an inscription at Cythera (I.G. V, i, 937 ? fourth century B.C.) and probably at Oetylus (ibid. 1295, of uncertain date), in the last case with a garrison of mercenaries. The Κυθηροδίκης ἀρχή mentioned by Thuc. IV, 53 (with a garrison of Spartan hoplites) doubtless had the actual title of ἁρμοστάς.

survival of many pre-Dorian cults [1] and some traces of a pre-Dorian dialect [2] bear witness to a mixture of population, and lend support to the Greek tradition that in Messenia the pre-Dorian population as a whole was not driven out, but remained in the country when the land was divided among the Dorian conquerors.[3] On the other hand it would appear that at least a part of the pre-Dorian aristocracy escaped overseas, for the Neleidae of Pylos gave their name to descendants in Athens and in Ionia, perpetuating other Messenian names in Miletus at least.[4] It is natural to suppose that it was the common people and the agricultural labourers [5] who, lacking the resources of the aristocracy, remained behind. This would lead to the development of the same kind of feudal society in Messenia in the centuries immediately following the Dorian invasion as developed in Crete and in Sparta itself, and indeed we have direct evidence for this in a passage of Tyrtaeus which Pausanias (the only ancient author who quotes it) interprets quite differently. Pausanias (IV, 14.5) quotes two fragments, which he supposes to refer to the Messenians reduced to serfdom by the Spartans after the first Messenian war. The first is usually accepted as evidence that the Helots handed over to the Spartans half the produce of all the land they worked :

ὥσπερ ὄνοι μεγάλοις ἄχθεσι τειρόμενοι,
δεσποσύνοισι φέροντες ἀναγκαίης ὑπὸ λυγρῆς
ἥμισυ πᾶν ὅσσων καρπὸν ἄρουρα φέρει.[6]

The second is interpreted by Pausanias as an allusion to the compulsory mourning imposed by the Spartans upon the Messenians when a Spartan king died :

[1] Thalamae claimed the birthplace of the Dioscuri (Paus. III, 26. 2), Leuctra worshipped Alexandra (Cassandra) the daughter of Priam (ibid. 26. 5), the cult of Zeus of Ithome was reputed to be pre-Dorian in origin (Paus. IV, 3. 9).
[2] Cf. Paus. III, 26. 9 : . . . στέφανος, ὃν οἱ Μεσσήνιοι κίφος καλοῦσι τῇ ἐπιχωρίῳ φωνῇ.
[3] Cf. Paus. IV, 3. 6 : Μεσσηνίων δὲ τῶν ἀρχαίων οὐκ ἐγένετο ὑπὸ τῶν Δωριέων ὁ δῆμος ἀνάστατος, ἀλλὰ βασιλεύεσθαί τε συγχωροῦσιν ὑπὸ Κρησφόντου καὶ ἀναδάσασθαι πρὸς τοὺς Δωριέας τὴν γῆν.
[4] Cf. Paus. II, 18. 9 (Neleidae in Athens), Tod, Greek Hist. Inscr. 35 (in Miletus, c. 450 B.C.).
[5] Cf. the passage of Pausanias cited above, n. 3. The emphasis should probably be placed on the words ὁ δῆμος here.   [6] Tyrt. fr. 5, Diehl.

19

δεσπότας οἰμώζοντες ὁμῶς ἀλοχοί τε καὶ αὐτοί,
εὖτέ τιν᾽ οὐλομένη μοῖρα κίχοι θανάτου.[1]

To elucidate the second passage Pausanias quotes (though without naming his authority) Herodotus' description of Spartan royal funerals.[2] According to Herodotus, when a king died, a man and a woman from each free Spartan household were obliged, on pain of a heavy penalty, to put on mourning, a stipulated number of Perioikoi from all parts of Laconia were obliged to attend the funeral, and Helots as well as the free population were present on the occasion in large numbers. Pausanias (or perhaps the source whom he is following) quite obviously modifies this information to fit his own interpretation of the passage in Tyrtaeus, informing us [3] that at the deaths of kings *and other persons in authority* (καὶ τῶν ἐν τέλει, who are nowhere mentioned by Herodotus) both men and women were required to attend *from Messenia* (Herodotus says from Laconia) in black garments, and a penalty for disobedience was imposed upon these (whereas Herodotus says it was upon Spartans who omitted to go into mourning that the punishment was inflicted). It is clear, therefore, that no authority whatever can be attached to Pausanias' elucidation of the second of the passages in question.

When both passages are considered in the light of the rest of the poem in which Tyrtaeus seeks to call out all the energies of the Spartans for the second Messenian War, it seems very doubtful whether Pausanias has come anywhere near to the truth in his interpretation of them. Pausanias is evidently thinking of the Messenians as having already been reduced by the Spartans in the First Messenian War to the position of serfdom which was that of the Helots in the period after the Second War. ' Like asses weighed down by great burdens ' is indeed appropriate to describe the later Helots. But it seems most unlikely that the poet of Sparta would so speak of them, implying that after the First Messenian War the Spartans themselves had oppressed the Messenians in this fashion, and that having become their masters, they had obliged their Messenian serfs to put on a mock pretence of grief whenever one of their Spartan

---

[1] Tyrt. fr. 5, Diehl.   [2] Herod. VI, 58.   [3] *Cf.* Paus. IV, 14. 4.

overlords died. Moreover, it is abundantly clear from the rest of Tyrtaeus' poem that the Messenians in general had not been treated in this fashion after the First Messenian War, for the second war is to be a struggle between opposing hoplite armies :

καὶ πόδα παρ' ποδὶ θεὶς καὶ επ' ἀσπίδος ἀσπίδ' ἐρείσας,
ἐν δὲ λόφον τε λόφωι καὶ κυνέην κυνέηι.[1]

Each Spartan in the front line is exhorted to stand firm and be courageous :

οὗτος ἀνὴρ ἀγαθὸς γίγνεται ἐν πολέμωι,
αἶψα δὲ δυσμενέων ἀνδρῶν ἔτρεψε φάλαγγας
τρηχείας . . . .[2]

If the Messenians by the time of Tyrtaeus have become ' asses weighed down by great burdens ', toiling to produce the fruits of the soil demanded by their Spartan masters, who are these warriors with crested helmet and shield, fighting in their ' rugged phalanx ' in Spartan fashion ? But the answer is clear ; Tyrtaeus in this poem is seeking not only to exhort the Spartans to battle, but to justify the cause for which they are fighting. It is the Messenians, that is, the Dorian aristocracy in Messenia, who are being accused of oppressing their serfs, while the serfs in their turn are derided for their stupid loyalty to their masters in the face of oppression. An objection may be raised to this interpretation on the ground that Tyrtaeus implies that Messenia had already been completely subjugated by the Spartans in the First Messenian War two generations earlier, and complete conquest, it may be argued, would involve the acquisition by the Spartans of any agricultural serfs or other labourers who had earlier tilled the land for the Messenian landowners. This we have seen to be the interpretation of Pausanias, who bases his opinion on the lines of Tyrtaeus :

ἡμετέρωι βασιλῆι, θεοῖσι φίλωι Θεοπόμπωι,
ὃν διὰ Μεσσήνην εἵλομεν εὐρύχορον,[3]

and upon the evidence of the same poet for the long duration of the war :

ἀμφ' αὐτὴν δ' ἐμάχοντ' ἐννεακαίδεκ' ἔτη
νωλεμέως ἀεί, ταλασίφρονα θυμὸν ἔχοντες

---

[1] Tyrtaeus, fr 8, l. 31 (Diehl).   [2] Ibid. fr. 9, ll. 20 f.
[3] Tyrt. fr. 4, ll. 1, 2 (Diehl), cited by Paus. IV, 6. 5.

αἰχμηταὶ πατέρων ἡμετέρων πατέρες·
εἰκοστῶι δ'οἳ μὲν κατὰ πίονα ἔργα λιπόντες
φεῦγον Ἰθωμαίων ἐκ μεγάλων ὀρέων.[1]

Strabo, citing the last five lines as evidence, arrives at the same conclusions, that as a result of the First Messenian War Sparta got possession of Messenia and divided up the land among her own citizens,[2] and that the second war was made necessary by a Messenian revolt.[3] Pausanias also supposes that a revolt was the cause of the second war.[4]

In assessing the value of this evidence from Tyrtaeus, the contemporary soldier-poet of the Second Messenian War, and his ancient interpreters, we have to bear in mind, first, that neither Strabo nor Pausanias thought that there could be any better evidence than that of Tyrtaeus ; Pausanias in fact rejects various statements about the Messenian Wars made by a later literary writer because they conflict with what is said by Tyrtaeus.[5] Secondly, it is clear that no other passage in the whole of Tyrtaeus' *Eunomia* as it was known to Strabo and Pausanias provided better evidence for the nature of the settlement of Messenia made after the First Messenian War than those lines which they have quoted.

The question to be decided is therefore this : do the lines quoted by Strabo and Pausanias in fact bear the interpretation which those authors have placed upon them ? And apart from the difficulty of explaining how a people reduced to the position of unarmed agricultural serfs could organise a fresh war in which (on the evidence of Tyrtaeus) they fought as hoplites, there is a difficulty about the name Μεσσήνη. Strabo and Pausanias naturally assume that

---

[1] Ll. 4–8, *ibid.*, cited by Paus. IV, 15. 2 (ll. 4–6), IV, 13. 6 (ll. 7, 8). and by Strabo, VI, 3. 3 (279), *cf.* VIII, 4. 10 (362).

[2] Strabo, VI, (280) : τὴν μὲν οὖν Μεσσηνίαν κατενείμαντο, κ.τ.λ. *Cf.* VIII, (362) : τὴν μὲν πρώτην κατάκτησιν αὐτῶν (*sc.* τῶν Μεσσηνίων) φησι Τυρταῖος ἐν τοῖς ποιήμασι κατὰ τοὺς τῶν πατέρων πατέρας γένεσθαι.

[3] Strabo, VIII, 362.   [4] Paus. IV, 15. 1, *cf.* 6. 2.

[5] *Ibid.* 6. 4 (referring to the prose work by Myron of Priene). Rhianos, the third-century Cretan poet who sang the exploits of the legendary Messenian hero Aristomenes in the second Messenian War, did not touch upon the first war at all (*ibid.* 6. 2). The fictitious character of both these later accounts (on which Pausanias has drawn for his detailed history of the Messenian Wars) was pointed out by Grote (*Hist. of Greece*, II, pp. 579 f.), and has been more recently reaffirmed by Schwartz (*Philologus*, XCII, i, 1937, pp. 19 f.).

Tyrtaeus uses it as it could be used in their own times, to mean the whole of Messenia from the borders of Triphylia southwards.[1] But this usage cannot be traced back to a period earlier than the late fifth century B.C., and then only in Aristophanes.[2] The earlier prose writers use Μεσσήνιοι, Μεσσηνία, or γῆ Μεσσηνίς [3] in speaking of the whole country, while Μεσσήνη appears to be a poetic form imitated from Homer, applicable to a small part of the historical Messenia only. In Odyssey, XXI, 15, which may well be the passage of which both Tyrtaeus and Pindar [4] are thinking when they use this form of the name, Μεσσήνη seems to refer to a region near Pherae at the head of the Messenian Gulf,[5] though the ancient writers are anxious to connect it with the Homeric ' Messe ' which Homer enumerates among the cities of Lacedaemon.[6] In view of the other imitations of Homer which are a conspicuous feature of the *Eunomia*,[7] it seems scarcely likely that Tyrtaeus used the name Μεσσήνη in quite a different sense from that which it bears in Homer ; and yet another indication that it had in early times a much more restricted application than that which was given to it in the Roman period is that early in the fifth century the tyrant Anaxilas of Rhegium, who claimed Messenian descent,[8] named his

---

[1] *Cf.* Vespasian's survey (I.G. V, i, 1431) *pass.* ὄρος Λακεδαίμονι πρὸς Μεσσήνην ; similarly in Strabo himself (VIII, 4. 7, 361, etc.).

[2] *Lysistr.* 1141.

[3] Herod. always uses Μεσσήνιοι ; for the other forms *cf.* Thuc. IV, 3. 2 ; 41. 2.

[4] *Cf. Pyth.* IV, 221 f. : ἐγγὺς μὲν Φέρης κράναν Ὑπερῇδα λιπὼν | ἐκ δὲ Μεσσάνας Ἀμυθάν. As in *Od.* XXI, 15 (see following note), Messene is here located near Pherae.

[5] *Od.* XXI, 15 f.: τὼ δ'ἐν Μεσσήνῃ ξυμβλήτην ἀλλήλοϊν | οἴκῳ ἐν Ὀρσιλόχοιο δαΐφρονος. The home of Orsilochus was Pherae (*Od.* III, 488).

[6] *Il.* II, 582. On the meaning of this passage, see further below, p. 294. According to Strabo (VIII, 364) some authorities believed ' Messe ' to be short for ' Messene ' !

[7] *E.g.* fr. 3, l. 1 (Diehl) : ἀργυρότοξος ἄναξ ἐκάεργος Ἀπόλλων ; fr. 4, l. 7 : κατὰ πίονα ἔργα λιπόντες (*cf. Il.* XII, 283) ; fr. 7, l. 7 etc. : ἐνὶ προμάχοισι πεσόντα (*cf. Od.* XVIII, 379, etc.) ; fr. 7, l. 3 : ἄλκιμον ἐν φρεσὶ θυμόν ; (*cf. Il.* XIII, 487, XXII, 475) ; fr. 8, l. 5 : θανάτου δὲ μελαίνας | κῆρας (*cf. Il.* II, 302, III, 360, VIII, 70) ; fr. 8, l. 25 ; τινασσέτω ὄβριμον ἔγχος (*cf. Il.* III, 357, XX, 163). The use of λαός in fr. 8, l. 13, is also Homeric, the description of the great shield in fr. 8, ll. 22 f. is out of keeping with Spartan military equipment in Tyrtaeus' time (see further below, p. 361) and must also be put down to imitation of Homer.

[8] *Cf.* above, p. 276, n. 1.

Sicilian colony ' Messana '. His own ancestors claimed to
have fled from Messenia on the eve of the first Spartan invasion and therefore from the border territory ; nor is there
any reason (apart from patently faked later tradition) to suppose that any political unity existed in Messenia as a whole
between the time of the Dorian invasion and that of the
Spartan conquest.[1] There seems, therefore, little likeli-
hood that an early name for the whole country, of which
their own place of origin was but a small part, would be
preserved by the exiles at Rhegium. Nor again is there
any parallel for a Greek colony, founded by a city-state,
which took its name from a whole large region comparable
to the size of what was known after the complete Spartan
conquest as Messenia.[2]

A more likely explanation of the origin of the name $M\epsilon\sigma\sigma\acute{\eta}\nu\eta$
would seem to be that the Homeric ' Messe ' (i.e. ' the middle
region ', $\mu\acute{\epsilon}\sigma\sigma\eta$ $\gamma\hat{\eta}$?) [3] meant originally the border territory
between the late Mycenean kingdoms of Pylos and Lacedae-
mon, persisting there even after the collapse of these kingdoms
through the advent of the Dorians, until its original meaning
was forgotten, and it was believed to be the name of a
lost town, with $M\epsilon\sigma\sigma\acute{\eta}\nu\eta$ as its territory. Then when
political unity was restored on the Laconian side through
the advance of Spartan conquests, the name $M\epsilon\sigma\sigma\acute{\eta}\nu\eta$
came to be extended gradually westward until by the time

[1] O. Müller (Dorians, I, p. 70) is probably right in suggesting that the
story of Cresphontes' unification of all Messenia (propagated by Euripides)
was first invented by the Athenians as political propaganda.   It would
certainly help anti-Spartan activities in this part of the Peloponnese during
the Peloponnesian War.

[2] The town of Arcadia in Crete claimed a pre-Dorian origin, and is in
fact likely (on philological grounds) to have been a settlement dating from
the period of the great migrations.   The origin of the name in this case
must therefore be racial rather than regional.

[3] It is generally agreed that the author of the Catalogue had no detailed
personal knowledge of the Peloponnese.   If ' Messe ' in the passage in
question (Il. II, 582, the only one in Homer which mentions the name)
was intended to mean a town (which is not necessarily the case) this does
not necessarily mean that such a town existed.   No trace of an ancient
town of Messe existed in Strabo's time (cf. VIII, 5, 3, 364) ; the Messe
known to Pausanias (III, 25. 9) seems to have been a new town built
on the coast near the ruins of the ancient Hippola, and to have owed its
name entirely to the search for Homeric origins which was popular in Greece
at that period.   In this case it was only necessary to keep pigeons to give
verisimilitude (cf. Il. II, 582 : $\pi o\lambda v\tau\rho\acute{\eta}\rho\omega\nu\acute{a}$ $\tau\epsilon$ $M\acute{\epsilon}\sigma\sigma\eta\nu$).

of Tyrtaeus it meant a part of western Messenia (as the whole country was later called) up to and including Mt. Ithome. The extension of the name westwards to the head of the Messenian Gulf may be traced in Homer. Thus in *Il.* II, 581–585 ' Lacedaemon ' includes ' Messe ' and towns as far up the west coast of the Maina peninsula as Oetylus ; in *Il.* IX, 149–153, representing a somewhat later stage, ' the last cities of sandy Pylos ' include Pherae at the head of the Gulf in the north, and Cardamyle in the south. Since Cardamyle is over 20 miles distant from Oetylus, and since the towns of Leuctra, Pephnos, and Thalamae in between preserved pre-Dorian cults, and so are likely to have been already in existence when the Iliad was being written,[1] an advance of the Laconian frontier northward is clearly indicated by the later passage. A further stage is reached in *Od.* XXI, 13, where ' Lacedaemon ' has come to include Pherae,[2] to the region round which the name Messene is now attached. Finally, in Tyrtaeus the name Messene is extended as far as the region round Mt. Ithome ; there is no indication from his poem that it extended any further westward or northward.

Thus the Homeric evidence throws some light on the gradual nature of the Spartan conquest of the Perioikoi, and links on to the evidence of Tyrtaeus for the situation reached two generations before his own time in such a way as to suggest that the First Messenian War was merely a continuation of the gradual conquest which had been going on for several generations before that. Judging from the strong opposition from hoplite forces which still confronted the Spartans in the Second Messenian War, it is to be supposed that two generations after Theopompus all northern, western and southern Messenia still remained to be conquered, and that the Μεσσήνη which was already in Spartan possession meant only the fertile alluvial valley of the Pamisus (Pirnátsa) south of the sandstone ridge (itself immediately to the south of the river-confluence) which separates it from the upper plain of Stenyclarus.[3] The extremely fertile lower plain, which is also well defined on either side by sandstone hills, bore in ancient times the

---

[1] *Cf.* above, p. 289, n. 1.   [2] *Cf.* above, p. 293, n. 5.   [3] See map at end.

appropriate name of *Μακαρία* ;[1] this, then, is the region
referred to by Tyrtaeus as

$$Μεσσήνην \; ἀγαθὸν \; μὲν \; ἀροῦν, \; ἀγαθὸν \; δὲ \; φυτεύειν,$$[2]

a description which is by no means applicable to the whole
of what was known later as Messenia.[3] To the east and
northeast of the valley of the Pamisus is a rising table-land
of sandstone and marl, ending in the series of mountain-
ridges which form the heart-shaped system of Mt. Kyparissia.
The most westerly and highest of these ranges falls steeply
at first to the broad terrace called Kámpos, then in narrow
terraces to the coastal plain. The peninsula which lies to
the west of the Messenian Gulf is also mountainous in the
north, the limestone mass of Mt. Lykódemo (alt. 3,140 ft.)
falls steeply to the sea in the east, though more gently in
the west. The remainder of the peninsula is occupied by
broken hilly country and narrow coastal plains. The
alluvial plain of Stenyclarus to the north of the plain of
Macaria is (as the name itself implies) very much more
limited in extent, and being perfectly flat and surrounded
by steep hills, it tends to become marshy in the rainy season.
Thus, in spite of its favoured climate and plentiful water
supply, Messenia as a whole is better adapted to pasturage
than to agriculture, and this is in fact the impression conveyed by a fragment of Euripides.[4]

It seems very doubtful whether much more of Messenia
than the plains of Macaria and Stenyclarus were ever
divided up as Spartan *κλῆροι*, for the two plains together
(c. 49,920 and 19,200 acres) would easily provide holdings
for 3,000 Spartans on the basis of 22 acres to the *κλῆρος*
which is indicated by the scheme proposed by Agis IV,[5]
and 3,000 is the number of extra *κλῆροι* which is said (according to the most probable account) to have been added
by King Polydorus,[6] the colleague of Theopompus the victor

---

[1] Strabo, VIII, 361. [2] Fr. 4, l. 3 (Diehl).

[3] *Cf. Admiralty Handbook* (1920), Vol. I, pp. 33 f., from which the
accompanying description of the country is taken.

[4] Eur. fr. 452 (*ap.* Strabo, VIII, 366) :

κατάρρυτόν τε μυρίοισι νάμασι
καὶ βουσὶ καὶ ποίμναισιν εὐβοτωτάτην,
οὔτ' ἐν πνοαῖσι χείματος δυσχείμερον,
οὔτ' αὖ τεθρίπποις ἡλίου θερμὴν ἄγαν.

[5] *Cf.* Appendix I, pp. 429 f. [6] *Cf.* Plut. *Lycurg.* 8.

of the First Messenian War. But too much stress must not be laid on the number 3,000, not only because there are variants in the story of how the supposed grand total of 9,000 κλῆροι was made up,[1] but because Spartan χιλιαστύες appear in fact to have stood in early times for the cube of nine instead of the cube of ten.[2] On this basis the plain of Macaria alone would provide κλῆροι for exactly three χιλιαστύες (2,187) of Spartans at the rate of between 22 and 23 acres per head, and the supposition that at the end of the First Messenian War Spartan conquests stopped short at the barrier between this and the upper plain is in accordance with the strong Messenian tradition that the fighting in the Second War centred round the plain of Stenyclarus,[3] and that it was at this time that the ancient city of Andania (eventually restored by the Thebans and re-populated with recalled Messenian exiles) was destroyed.[4]

What is the value of this later Messenian tradition? The view which we take about this must depend to a great extent on the interpretation of evidence, other than Messenian tradition, of what happened to Messenia as a whole as a result of the final Spartan conquest. The literary tradition is late, vague and confused in chronology; Pausanias (an account derived from Callisthenes?)[5] assumes that only the population of the coastal district escaped from the country, to settle eventually for the most part in Sicilian Messana,[6] which was not itself founded until nearly two hundred years later. The rest of the Messenians, with the exception of a few who settled in Arcadia,[7] became Helots

---

[1] *Ibid.* The alternative accounts were (1) that Lycurgus made all 9,000 κλῆροι (improbable in view of the fact that the majority of conquests were made *after* the reforms), (2) that Lycurgus and Polydorus each made 4,500 (which fails to account for conquests made in the second Messenian War), (3) that Lycurgus made 6,000 and Polydorus 3,000. The truth may well be that Polydorus was responsible for three χιλιαστύες, the other lots being assigned at various times. On the real meaning of these figures in relation to the population see further, pp. 424 f.

[2] See further, pp. 341 f.   [3] *Cf.* Paus. IV, 15. 7 f.

[4] Paus. IV, 26. 6: τὴν γὰρ 'Ανδανίαν οἱ Μεσσήνιοι καὶ Οἰχαλίαν οὐκ ἔφασαν ἀνοικεῖν, ὅτι αἱ συμφοραί σφισιν ἐγεγόνεσαν ἐνταῦθα οἰκοῦσιν. It was, however, soon afterwards restored (*cf.* I.G. V, i, p. 266).

[5] *Cf.* n. 7 below.   [6] Paus. IV, 23. *Cf.* above, p. 276.

[7] Callisthenes *ap.* Polyb. IV, 33; Paus. IV, 22. 1, 2; 23, 1, 3. Some confirmation of the tradition of Messenian settlements in Arcadia is provided by Arist. fr. 90 (F.H.G. II, p. 134) in which the meaning is expounded of the words Μεσσηνίους ἐκβαλεῖν ἐκ τῆς χώρας καὶ μὴ ἐξεῖναι χρηστοὺς

of the Spartans. The Messenians who were collected and brought back by the Thebans at the time of the founding of Messene were (according to Pausanias) nearly all the descendants of the Helots who had been freed by the Athenians at Pylos, settled by them at Naupactus, turned out by the Spartans at the end of the Peloponnesian war, and who had then migrated to Cyrenaica or (in small numbers) had joined their kinsmen at Messana in Sicily. It is hard to see how any real tradition could survive even for a hundred years, much less for about two hundred and fifty years, among a people who had all been treated as the Spartans are said to have treated the Helots, depriving them of every vestige of education and personal liberty. But in his account of the Helot Revolt of 464 B.C. Thucydides mentions that the insurgents were joined by two towns 'of the Perioikoi', Thuria and Antheia (?).[1] These two towns at the head of the Messenian Gulf were Messenian, not Spartan, as also were towns of ancient origin farther south which continued in existence. Cardamyle, described by Herodotus as ἡ Λακωνική,[2] could scarcely have been so described unless it had the same status as the Laconian Perioikoi; Alagonia, Gerenia, Leuctra and Thalamae could hardly have appeared in later times in the list of towns of the Free Laconians[3] if their status also had not been that of Perioikoi in the time of Spartan domination. Sparta, in fact, appears to have treated eastern Messenia differently from the more remote hill-country in the west, which could not be kept so closely under surveillance. The Messenian population was ejected from the ancient site of Methone and refugees from Nauplia were settled there;[4] Nestor's Pylos and the surrounding country became a

ποιεῖν, occurring in a Spartan treaty with Tegea. Aristotle interprets μὴ χρηστοὺς ποιεῖν as 'not to kill', but the real meaning is probably 'not to enfranchise', cf. Polyb. ibid.: αὐτοὺς Ἀρκάδες ὑποδεξάμενοι . . . ὁμεστίους ἐποιήσαντο καὶ πολίτας.

[1] Thuc., I, 101. The MSS. have Θουριᾶταί τε καὶ † αἰθνεεῖς, αἰθιεῖς, ἐθεεῖς † Stephanus Byz. supposed the passage to refer to a town Aἰθαία, citing Philochorus as well as Thucydides. The survival of the Homeric Antheia (Il. IX, 151) is attested by I.G. V, i, 1426 (from Messene, c. 300 B.C.) l. 1 (ΑΝΟΓΙΔ as preserved). The name Ἀνθειεῖς could easily give rise to the MSS. variants in Thuc. loc. cit., and Antheia was certainly near Thuria, since some later authorities supposed (as Thuc. evidently did not) that the Homeric Antheia was later called Thuria (cf. Strabo VIII, 360).

[2] Cf. Herod. VIII, 73.   [3] Cf. p. 56.   [4] Paus. IV, 35. 2.

desert ; [1] at Asine the existing population was allowed to remain because it claimed to be Dryopian, not Messenian.[2] A great part of the western hill-land must have been as deserted as the coast, visited only by young Spartans in training for the Crypteia,[3] and garrisoned only sporadically and when special need arose.

But in eastern Messenia where it bordered on Laconia Spartan administration seems to have been exactly the same as in subject Laconia, the towns being allowed to continue a semi-independent existence. Thuria was perhaps brought under more direct Spartan control later, as a result of the part it played in the Helot Revolt, since in Roman times it was again directly administered by Sparta [4] instead of being included in Messenia or in the League of Free Laconians. But in any case it seems clear that several πόλεις of Messenian origin continued to exist on the eastern shore of the Messenian Gulf, and here (as also in Sicilian Messana) it would be natural for anti-Spartan Messenian traditions to survive. Refusal to accept the obviously fictitious details about the Messenian Wars with which the Messenians after recovering their independence consoled their national pride, and in particular, refusal to accept the story of the exploits of their national hero Aristomenes, does not necessitate the complete rejection of the whole tradition. Thus we have no reason to doubt that the plain of Stenyclarus was the centre of the fighting in the Second Messenian War and that Arcadians, Argives and Eleans were called in as allies. It is also probable in itself that once the Spartans were in control of the plain of Stenyclarus all resistance collapsed, since the plain commands the routes from Messenia into Elis and Arcadia, and its loss would automatically cut the rest of Messenia off from Elean, Arcadian and Argive assistance.

The general conclusions to be drawn about the Spartan conquest of Messenia are therefore these. A predominantly

---

[1] Cf. Thuc. IV, 3. 2 : τὸ χωρίον (sc. Pylos) . . . φύσει καρτερὸν ὂν καὶ ἔρημον αὐτό τε καὶ ἐπὶ πολὺ τῆς χώρας ; ibid. 3 : πολλὰς ἔφασαν εἶναι ἄκρας ἐρήμους τῆς Πελοποννήσου ; ibid. 29. 4 (Sphacteria) : διὰ τὴν ἀεὶ ἐρημίαν.
[2] Paus. IV, 34. 9. Their kinship with Dryopian Hermione was re-iterated about 200 B.C. in an invitation sent to that city to join in the celebration of a local cult (I.G. IV, 679). [3] Cf. pp. 374 f. [4] Cf. p. 56.

Dorian civilisation, of an early feudal type, but centring round independent πόλεις, was in existence in Messenia when first the Spartans invaded the country. Although the aristocracy was Dorian, the population as a whole preserved many of the traditions of Nestor's kingdom ; in other respects no distinction of race or culture can be found between Messenians and non-Spartan Laconians. The conquest of the Messenian coastal region on the east of the Messenian Gulf, and the transformation of the autonomous πόλεις into towns of the Perioikoi, preceded the First Messenian War. The First Messenian War meant the annexation of the plain of Macaria, together with the serfs who had formerly been cultivating it for Messenian overlords. These serfs formed the majority of the later Spartan Helots. The Second War, two generations later, meant the destruction of Andania and occupation of the plain of Stenyclarus by the Spartans, and the deliberate depopulation by the Spartans of most of the rest of the country, with the exception of Methone and Asine, where non-Messenian settlements were allowed to remain, with the status of Perioikoi.[1] The half-empty uplands and coastal plains were probably useful recruiting grounds for Messenians employed by the Spartans on army service.[2] That agricultural labourers from the κλῆροι were drawn upon for this purpose seems scarcely likely, both on general grounds, and because the treatment meted out to these, at least in the century following the Helot Revolt, was said to be deliberately calculated to make them as unfit for all military pursuits as possible,[3] whereas some ex-Helots were made use of to serve as permanent garrisons, with the status of Neodamodeis.[4] The Helots who were promised their freedom as a reward for running supplies into Sphacteria,[5] and the two thousand distinguished for their νεότης and φρόνημα who actually received it soon afterwards [6] can hardly have been agricultural serfs bound

---

[1] This is implied in the case of Methone by Thucydides' description of it (II, 25) as Μεθώνη τῆς Λακωνικῆς, and by its existence at that time as a walled town. Asine is mentioned as a walled town in Thuc. IV, 13, and as on a footing with Helos, ibid. 54. [2] See further, pp. 382 f.
[3] Cf. Myron of Priene (of uncertain date, condemned by Paus. IV, 6. 4, for his inaccuracy), fr. 1 (F.H.G. IV, p. 461), Aristotle ap. Plut. Lycurg. 80.
[4] See further, pp. 216 f. [5] Thuc. IV, 26. 6. [6] Ibid. 82.

to the soil,[1] but they may well have sprung from the still untamed population of western Messenia, and may easily account for the class of Helots upon whom the Spartans declared war every year.

There is nothing in the name εἵλωτες itself, which corresponds closely in meaning to the Roman *dediticii*, to suggest the legal status of serfdom, and it seems likely that there were in fact two or more grades among the un-free population of Messenia under Spartan domination, of whom the ἀδέσποτοι (mentioned by Myron of Priene among various grades of emancipated Helots) [2] were perhaps the more or less uncontrolled class, not bound to κλῆροι, who have been under consideration. The same author also mentions ἀφέται, who were doubtless freed Helots permitted to live where they chose ; ἐρυκτῆρες, whose name suggests that they were employed on garrison duty but were not yet freed (otherwise they would come into the category of νεοδαμώδεις),[3] and δεσποσιοναῦται, who were employed (presumably in the early fourth century) in the fleet. According to the same authority, the δεσποσιοναῦται were emancipated already, but their name does not suggest it.

There is no need to doubt the existence of these classes half-way between serfdom and freedom among the population subject to Sparta on the score of the unfavourable account of Spartan treatment of the Helots which has prevailed in the general tradition, for it is extremely likely, as Müller pointed out,[4] that this unfavourable account is due to deliberate Athenian political propaganda. On the contrary, the names given by Myron, in this passage, for the various intermediate grades of ex-serfs are peculiar to Sparta, and so create a strong presumption in favour of the existence of the classes in question, since they are unlikely to have arisen from inaccurate comparison with Crete or elsewhere. The existence of these classes half-way between serfdom and freedom does seem after all to justify the opinion of Aristotle's contemporaries, reflected in later writers also, that there was in a sense a parallel between the Spartan Helots and the Cretan Perioikoi ; [5]

---

[1] For these *cf.* Ephorus, fr. 18 (F.H.G. I, p. 238), cited above, p. 216, n. 2.
[2] Myron of Priene *ap.* Athen. VI, pp. 271 f.   [3] *Cf.* pp. 39 f.
[4] *Cf.* above, p. 294, n. 1.   [5] *Cf.* pp. 213 f.

the probable explanation of the view would seem to be that the name Helots is used here in a wider sense (like *dediticii*) to include the half-emancipated Messenian population as well as the rest. No real distinction could be drawn between them and the Perioikoi of the semi-independent towns.

On the other hand, the parallel assumed by Aristotle and others between Spartan Helots and Cretan ἀφαμιῶται also seems to be valid, in view of the evidence from Tyrtaeus that there was a class of bondsmen in Messenia already paying to overlords half the produce of the land they worked before the Spartan conquest. Passages already cited about the Spartan Helots, mixing strict truth with exaggeration, allow us to infer that the Spartans continued the system [1] and although there is no direct evidence that the stipulated payment continued to be one-half the produce, it may be assumed that the Spartans are unlikely to have improved the lot of their serfs, and could scarcely oppress them in this respect more severely, even in good agricultural land like the plain of Macaria, if they wished to keep them fit for work at all. Moreover, there seems to be confirmation of the view that the Spartan Helots paid one-half of the produce in the information which Plutarch gives about the size of the Spartan κλῆροι,[2] taken in conjunction with Herodotus' figure of seven Helots to each Spartan which he mentions for the battle of Plataea.[3] The κλῆροι were large enough to produce 70 medimnoi of barley for the Spartan owner and 12 for his wife ; this implies provision for a Spartan family of seven, and the requisite amount would be produced on 11 or 12 acres of good Messenian or Laconian land, whereas the amount available for each κλῆρος was at least twice this area. ' Seven Helots to each Spartan ' would therefore seem to be a computation based on the number of Helots on each κλῆρος, occupying half of the whole estate, and accounting for about 22 acres altogether. As an assessment of the actual number of Helots employed at Plataea the figure given by Herodotus is therefore almost certainly worthless ; nor can it be employed as the basis for estimating the total non-Spartan population of Messenia for the reason already given, that not all the Helots were employed on Spartan κλῆροι.

[1] *Cf.* p. 216, n. 2.   [2] Plut. *Lycurg.* 8.   [3] Herod. ix, 10. 29.

With regard to the dating of the Spartan conquest of Laconia and of the two Messenian Wars, it is best to postpone detailed consideration until more has been said about the general basis of Spartan chronology, which will be dealt with in the following chapter. But it may be mentioned here that the chronology of the two Messenian wars rests on a firm non-Spartan foundation, for the first Messenian war was immediately preceded by the foundation of Rhegium, and immediately followed by the foundation of Tarentum, and the lapse of two generations between the end of the first and the beginning of the second war was a period short enough to be contained within living memory in the time of Tyrtaeus. But the nineteen years' duration of the first war [1] is as likely (or even more likely) to have been derived from the known dates of the foundation of the two western colonies as the other way round. For the official dates of the final solemn founding of Greek colonies (as opposed to the date of foundation of the unofficial enterprises which usually preceded the official founding) have been suspected without reason. There were all sorts of legal reasons (in particular, the means of proving ownership of land then first allotted to the colonists) why a record of this date should be preserved in the colony.[2] The date actually preserved for the foundation of Tarentum is 708 B.C.,[3] which accords well both with the general colonising activity in Sicily and South Italy at that time, and with the evidence from Homer and later literary authorities for the history of Spartan conquests in Laconia and the eastern coastal strip of the Messenian Gulf before the first Messenian war. The earlier conquests can well have occurred towards the middle of the eighth century B.C.

It appears then, from the evidence considered in the foregoing account, that the process of Spartan conquests beyond Taygetus was gradual, allowing for recuperation by Sparta after each new war, and for consolidation of the position gained. Western Messenia remained, however, incompletely subjugated—no very serious threat to Sparta

[1] Tyrt. fr. 4 (Diehl).
[2] For a fuller discussion of this question see my article in B.S.R. XIV (1938), pp. 128 f.
[3] *Cf.* Clinton, *Fast. Hell.* I, p. 174. The foundation date of Rhegium has not been preserved.

in view of its small, scattered, and non-urban population, and even an asset as providing a perpetual military training-ground. It further appears that the conquest of Messenia involved no completely new problem of government at any stage, since its population was similar in race and in social organisation to already-subjugated Laconia. These considerations destroy the grounds for a hypothesis commonly made, that the conquest of Messenia involved Sparta in the necessity for complete political and social reorganisation. But a fuller evaluation of the theory of the late origin of the ' Lycurgan ' organisation is necessary, and will form the subject of the following chapter.

CHAPTER IX

THE DATE OF THE LYCURGAN REFORMS

§ 1. MODERN THEORIES

The British excavations at Sparta have been thought to prove that it was only about the end of the seventh century B.C. that Sparta ceased to be a normal Greek state and became a perpetually armed camp with all her energies concentrated upon the training of her citizens for war. From that time onwards, it has been suggested, Spartan art was strangled, and Sparta said farewell to the civilisation depicted by Alcman and Tyrtaeus in the seventh century. ' The city where life had been as beautiful as anywhere in Greece, became a barracks.' [1]

This theory, which involves the dating of the reform known as the *Eunomia*, that is, the beginning of all the typically ' Lycurgan ' institutions, as late as about 600 B.C., seems now to have met with general acceptance. It is certainly a plausible hypothesis that the final conquest of Messenia, by first giving Sparta economic self-sufficiency and a vast population of agricultural serfs to keep in subjection, not only facilitated but also made necessary the transformation of the whole citizen population into an army of highly trained professional soldiers. But when the ancient authors are unanimously agreed in attributing the reforms ascribed to Lycurgus to at least two centuries earlier than this, very convincing proof to the contrary must be required before the tradition can be rejected.

And if the arguments put forward in support of this theory are examined, none of them appear to be very convincing. These arguments are : (1) the strangling of Spartan art after the seventh century B.C. ; (2) the appearance of five Ephors and five *Agathoergoi*, implying

[1] C.A.H. III, p. 564. The theory outlined above is the one advanced by Wade-Gery, *op. cit.* (1925), 558 f.

the existence of five tribes in place of three early Dorian tribes ; (3) the chronology implied by Herodotus' account of the reforms of Lycurgus.[1]

It is hard to understand how the evidence about Spartan art in the sixth century B.C. can ever have led to the conclusion that it had already received its death-blow at the beginning of the century. As even supporters of this view admit, a new temple of Orthia [2] and the temple of Athena Chalkioikos were built in the sixth century, and the Spartan could still make beautiful pottery in the half-century 600–550 B.C. It has more recently been pointed out that it was not until the beginning of the sixth century that Sparta began to export the pottery which is attributed to her on a large scale to all parts of the Mediterranean.[3] It was during the succeeding half century that this pottery reached its highest development, easily rivalling the Corinthian wares with which it is closely connected ; and when it came to an end, with the third quarter of the sixth century,[4] its end was probably not unconnected with the failure of inspiration from Corinth.[5] Corinthian pottery of artistic merit ends about the middle of the sixth century,[6] and if the same argument which the supporters of the view under discussion apply to Sparta were applied to Corinth, we should have to conclude that Corinth transformed herself into a military barracks rather earlier than Sparta. The absurdity of this conclusion calls for no comment.

That there was a cessation of foreign imports about the end of the seventh century or the beginning of the sixth seems certain. The carved ivory objects found in large numbers in the earlier Orthia-temple,[7] and the gold

---

[1] Herod. I, 65.

[2] The probable date of the rebuilding of the temple of Orthia is about 585 B.C. *Cf.* Lane in B.S.A. XXXIV (1933–1934), p. 135.

[3] Lane, *op. cit.* p. 178.

[4] *Ibid.* pp. 150, 153. The chronology adopted earlier for Laconian pottery by Droop postulated a much longer duration, well into the fifth century, but this view no longer seems to be tenable for the reasons given by Lane, *loc. cit.*   [5] *Ibid.* p. 150.

[6] *Cf.* Payne, *Necrocorinthia*, p. 331. ' It cannot be denied that, with the later sixth and fifth centuries, the Corinthian tradition comes to rather an inglorious end.' There is little evidence for the continuation of the animal frieze style in Corinthian vase-painting after the middle of the sixth century.   [7] See *Artemis Orthia*, p. 204, Pl. XCI f.

ornaments described by Alcman,[1] and other luxuries associated with foreign trade, are no more to be found in later Sparta. But Plutarch gives the correct and obvious explanation of this : there was no money.[2] The well-known ban on gold and silver coinage must have been imposed soon after its first introduction into the Peloponnese, or at least when its demoralising effects began to be felt at Sparta. There is no need to suggest the hypothesis of a complete constitutional and social reorganisation. If the ' Lycurgan ' constitution was there earlier, the ban on coinage was necessary to its preservation and would quickly have the desired effect. ἁ φιλοχρηματία Σπάρταν ὀλεῖ turned out in the fourth century to have been a true prophecy.[3] But the alliance between Thrasybulus of Miletus and Periander of Corinth (c. 615 B.C.) would prove a further discouragement to the trade of Ionia with the southern Peloponnese, especially if it was accompanied, as is not unlikely, by the construction of the Diolkos across the Isthmus.

In short, the archaeological evidence does not favour the view that the end of the seventh century, or even the middle of the sixth, brought any marked change in the policy of Sparta towards foreign influences in art or commerce. The change which gradually occurred in that period is rather to be ascribed to influences affecting the Greek world as a whole, in particular to the Persian conquests, and the consequent cutting of communications between Lydia and Greek Asia Minor and Greece proper. The resulting interruption of the flow of Asiatic imports into Greece lasted long enough for economic conditions and requirements to change utterly in the interval, and even when commerce with Asia Minor was re-established after the Persian wars, the policy of Athens towards the Delian League diverted it away from the Peloponnese, leaving Laconia dependent, in overseas trade, upon Egypt and

---

[1] Cf. p. 266.

[2] Cf. Plut. Lycurg. 9 : οὐδ' εἰσέπλει φόρτος ἐμπορικὸς εἰς τοὺς λιμένας, οὐδὲ ἐπέβαινε τῆς Λακωνικῆς οὐ σοφιστὴς λόγων, οὐ μάντις ἀγυρτικός, οὐχ ἑταιρῶν τροφεύς, οὐ χρυσῶν τις, οὐκ ἀργυρῶν καλλωπισμάτων δημιουργός, ἅτε δὴ νομίσματος οὐκ ὄντος. ἀλλ' οὕτως ἀπερημωθεῖσα κατὰ μικρὸν ἡ τροφὴ τῶν ζωπυρούντων καὶ τρεφόντων αὐτὴ δι' αὑτῆς ἐμαραίνετο.

[3] Cf. Plut. Agis, 5 ; Lycurg. 30, and above, p. 5.

Libya.[1] But in the meantime, the Greek export trade in pottery and other *objets d'art* seems also to have been completely captured, so far as the Persian market at least was concerned, by Athens;[2] so that such commercial art as had previously existed in Laconia, as in Corinth and elsewhere, would automatically come to an end for want of purchasers.

With regard to the absence of foreign poets in Sparta in later periods, which is in striking contrast to the number of them who worked there before about 625 B.C.,[3] the suggestion that they were banned as the result of a sudden change of policy is not the only possible explanation. A very obvious and likely one is the failure of Sparta to follow the lead of other Greek states in introducing an electrum or silver currency, since at no time can these foreigners have produced their work for nothing,[4] and once the more negotiable currency was introduced they would certainly prefer this form of payment to any other. The tyrants, who attracted so many poets and artists to their courts in the sixth and fifth centuries, were no doubt already proving generous patrons in the seventh century, and consequently both poets and artists were more likely to be drawn to Corinth and Sicyon than to Sparta in this period.

This explanation of the disappearance from Sparta of the foreign poets appears the more probable in view of the fact that foreign philosophers did not cease to teach and to reside there, although teaching on moral and political philosophy could have been at least as subversive as any foreign poetry. The Ionian monists, the fourth century sophists, the third century Stoics, all visited Sparta and were allowed to teach there.[5] But all these, even the

[1] *Cf.* Thuc. IV, 53..

[2] For convincing evidence of the Athenian monopoly (from late C. VI onwards) at commercial sites near Antioch on the Orontes *cf. Antiquaries Journal*, XVII (1937), pp. 6 f.

[3] Terpander of Lesbos, Thaletas the Cretan, Polymnestos of Colophon, Tyrtaeus, Alcman of Sardis, Sacadas of Argos. Sacadas is associated with musical victories at the Pythian games in the early sixth century (Paus. VI, 14. 10), but his activity at Sparta seems to fall before that of Alcman (*cf.* Plut. *De Mus.* 12).

[4] As witness the story of the wealth acquired by Arion in Italy and Sicily (Herod. I, 24).

[5] *E.g.* Thales and Pherecydes (Plut. *Agis*, 10), Anaximander (F.H.G. III, p. 581, fr. 27), Hippias (Plato, *Hippias Maj.* 283b f.) and probably many others in the third century B.C. (*cf.* p. 1, n. 3).

reputedly mercenary sophists,[1] had good reasons for coming apart from consideration of pecuniary reward, namely to learn something at first hand of the peculiar Spartan institutions which were so greatly admired by almost all Greek moral and political philosophers, and perhaps also to pick up a few more of the profound and pithy sayings (γνῶμαι, ἀποφθέγματα) for which the Spartans as individuals were so famous. According to Plato, not even the early gnomic poets disdained this abundant source of wisdom,[2] and the less profound of the later sophists must have found them a welcome addition to their lecturers' stock-in-trade. Since the earlier philosophers who visited Sparta all belonged to the landed aristocracy, and since the later sophists were able to command very high fees for their lectures elsewhere,[3] the absence of pay at Sparta did not matter to them. But since from the time when lyric and elegiac poetry became divorced from philosophy, foreign poets are unlikely to have had the same motives as the philosophers for visiting Sparta, the economic factor produced its natural effect at an early stage, and after money had been introduced everywhere else they came to Sparta no more. The only Spartan poet we hear of is one Dionysodotus, whose paeans to Apollo were sung at the Gymnopaedia together with those of Thaletas and Alcman.[4] The date of Dionysodotus is unknown, but must certainly have been later than the sixth century B.C.[5] From this instance it is clear that the writing of poetry was not despised at Sparta or regarded with disapproval, but a people naturally so serious and so severely practical could not be

[1] Cf. Plato, Hippias Maj. 282C f.
[2] Cf. Plato, Protagoras, 342, E—343A.
[3] Cf. Plato, Hippias Maj. 282D, E. Hippias himself is said to have earned 2½ talents in Sicily in a very short time, taking more than 20 minas at the little town of Inycus alone, and in competition with the more famous Protagoras who was there at the same time. But at Sparta, enthusiastic though the Spartans were about his lectures, he received no pay at all (ibid. 284 C).　　　　[4] Sosibius Laco, fr. 5 (F.H.G. II, p. 626).
[5] Both from the order in which the three poets are mentioned, and from the name Dionysodotus itself, it seems unlikely that he belonged to a time earlier than the fifth century B.C. at the earliest. It seems improbable that the worship of Dionysus was introduced into Sparta until long after it had become common in the rest of Greece, especially as it occupied a very minor position among the Spartan cults in later times (cf. I.G. V, i, 559).

expected to keep alive any enthusiasm for poetry and the arts after the foreign exponents of them had ceased to visit them. Though the exploits of Sparta in the Messenian wars were commemorated for posterity, those of Thermopylae and Plataea went unsung. No action on the part of the state needs to be postulated to explain this decline.

The continuance of the visits of foreign philosophers to Sparta suggests that there has been some misunderstanding about the significance of ξενηλασίαι (the word is normally used in the plural) at Sparta. This misunderstanding has occurred in ancient as well as in modern times. It is not the case that foreigners were permanently and automatically excluded from Sparta,[1] even in the period when the law permitting ξενηλασία was certainly in force. This we know from references to the welcome which was given to them at certain festivals;[2] references to their exclusion, on the other hand, seem to refer to special action taken in special circumstances, as for example when Athenians and citizens of towns in the Athenian Confederacy were expelled in the months before the outbreak of the Peloponnesian War.[3] It seems probable that this measure was only taken after Sparta and her allies had decided that Athens had ' broken the truce ', and that the Peloponnesian League must fight,[4] especially as the purpose of the expulsion was said in Athens to have been to prevent the enemy from learning of military secrets and preparations.[5] Another instance of wholesale

---

[1] Plutarch (Lycurg. 27) appears to assume this on quite inadequate grounds, since the rule which he cites applies only to the expulsion of τοὺς ἀθροιζομένους ἐπ' οὐδενὶ χρησίμῳ, as also does the allusion in Aristoph. Av. 1016: ὁμοθυμαδὸν| σποδεῖν ἅπαντας τοὺς ἀλαζόνας δοκεῖ. For other references to ξενηλασία not cited here, see Daremberg-Saglio, s.v. Xenelasia.

[2] Cf. esp. Cratinus ap. Athen. IV., 138e: ἆρ' ἀληθῶς τοῖς ξένοισιν ἔστιν, ὡς λέγουσ', ἐκεῖ| πᾶσι τοῖς ἐλθοῦσιν ἐν τῇ κοπίδι θοινᾶσθαι καλῶς;. The κοπίς banquets were a part of several different festivals (cf. Athen. IV, 138e–140a). Hospitality to foreigners at Spartan festivals in general is stressed by Xenophon (Memor. I, 2. 61), by the Schol. on Aristoph. Pax, 622, and at a much later date by Marcus Aurelius (Medit. XI, 24). Sparta was normally full of foreigners at the festival of the Gymnopaedia (cf. Plut. Ages. 29), and foreigners came from all parts of Greece to see the Whipping Ordeal at the festival of Orthia (cf. p. 264, n. 3).

[3] Thuc. I, 144.   [4] Cf. I, 87.

[5] The same explanation is evidently alluded to in Pericles' Funeral Speech, cf. Thuc. II, 39: καὶ οὐκ ἔστιν ὅτε ξενηλασίαις ἀπείργομέν τινα ἢ μαθήματος ἢ θεάματος, ὃ μὴ κρυφθὲν ἄν τις τῶν πολεμίων ἰδὼν ὠφεληθείη, πιστεύοντες οὐ ταῖς παρασκευαῖς τὸ πλέον καὶ ἀπάταις ἢ τῷ ἀφ' ἡμῶν αὐτῶν ἐς τὰ ἔργα εὐψύχῳ.

expulsion of foreigners, mentioned by Theopompus, was justified by an acute shortage of food in Laconia.[1] But except in such special circumstances, the expulsions seem to have been confined to individual foreigners who, by making a display of wealth [2] or by plotting against the state, seemed likely to endanger its life or its existing institutions. Against such individuals the ephors were empowered to take action at any time.[3]

As to the famous system of physical training which at Sparta took the sons of citizens when they were seven years old and kept control of them throughout their active life, the records of Spartan victories at Olympia do not favour the view that it was only introduced quite suddenly about 600 B.C. The time when Spartan victories in all contests of the Olympic games were most frequent precedes this date : the greatest activity of the Spartans at Olympia is in fact the whole of the seventh century B.C. ; about 580 B.C. it practically ceases for three-quarters of a century.

Except for victories in 556 and 552 no more Spartan successes are recorded until a series of four-horse-chariot victors begins about 510 and lasts until towards the end of the fifth century.[4] This is the reverse of what we should expect if the theory of the late origin of the ' Lycurgan ' constitution were right. In that case the οἰκίαι τεθριπ- ποφόροι, the rich and noble families who could afford to keep up four-horse chariots, could scarcely have made their mark at Olympia after 600 B.C. ; the numerous victories of the Spartans in all contests would begin with the introduction of intensive physical training at the time of the supposed reform. The more probable deduction from the facts is that the intensive gymnastic training had

[1] Dar.-Sagl. *s.v. Xenelasia*, p. 1007, n. 1, quoting F.H.G. I, p. 311, no. 197.

[2] This is represented ([Xen.] *Resp. Lac.* 14) as a standing justification for ξενηλασίαι in the period before the victory over Athens. *Cf.* also Herod. III, 148, on the expulsion of Maeandrius the Samian in the time of Cleomenes (implying that other foreigners were allowed to remain in Sparta on that occasion). [3] *Cf.* Herod. *ibid.*

[4] For details of Spartan victories at Olympia, see Förster, *Die Olympische Sieger* (1891). The first Spartan victor appears in 720 B.C., the majority before that time having been Messenians. From 416 B.C. there is a break in the series of Spartan chariot victors until 384, and so again after 368 until near the end of the fourth century. After the end of the fourth century B.C. there are practically no more Spartan victors.

been in force throughout the seventh century B.C.[1] and probably much earlier, but that from the time when Sparta began to acquire her Confederacy in the Peloponnese, military activity and a more purely military type of training took the place of the one which had produced the athletic victors.

It is not quite clear whether the supporters of this theory about the late introduction of the Lycurgan constitution and laws suppose the system of common meals to have existed previous to the army reforms and the introduction of intensive physical training or not.   Certain it is that no part of the sixth and fifth century organisation was more closely associated with Lycurgus by Spartan tradition than the Syssitia ; certain also that no part of that organisation was more conducive to barrack life and the perpetual concentration of the citizens on thought of war.   Yet Alcman, who is supposed on the view under discussion to reflect the freer life of a pre-Lycurgan aristocratic society, speaks of the common meals of the *Andreia* as already in existence [2] ; and in addition to this piece of evidence it has now been shown that the *Andreia* represent one of the closest points of resemblance with Crete, and are clearly a survival from the very earliest times, inasmuch as in both cases they are an integral part of a structure of society which, whatever branch of it we examine, preserves archaic features.

Another argument adduced in support of the view that the typical ' Lycurgan ' institutions developed late, after the Messenian Wars, is concerned with a supposed change in the number of the citizen tribes.   In the time of Tyrtaeus there were three of these, the Hylleis, Pamphyloi and Dymanes,[3] which also appear in other Dorian states.   For the early sixth century, according to the theory under

---

[1] The lists of victors include winners in 632 and 628 of the boys' boxing contests and Pentathlon, in each case in the first contest of the kind.

[2] *Cf.* C.A.H. III, 558.   Alcman is attributed to the period just before the ' Messenian Revolt ' ; the Lycurgan reforms are supposed to have been the outcome of the new economic and political position produced by that revolt (*ibid.* p. 560).   It may, however, be contended, to overcome this difficulty, that what the reforms of about 600 B.C. did was to extend to all social classes an institution which had previously been confined to the aristocracy, and in fact a radical reconstruction of the basis of citizenship is postulated by those who maintain this theory.

[3] *Cf.* Tyrtaeus, fr. I, 8 (Diehl.).

consideration, a five-tribe organisation is implied by the existence of boards of five magistrates. ' Our first evidence, perhaps, of the new Five Tribes ', says Wade-Gery, ' is the board of five arbitrators who adjudged Salamis to Athens (c. 570 B.C.) : we meet the five annual *Agathoergoi* about 560 B.C.'[1] He assumes that the five ephors are a further case in point.

But in the first place, more detailed inquiry into the numbers in the various boards of Spartan magistrates has shown that there is no connection whatever between the number in the college and the number of the tribes,[2] any more than there was at Athens between the nine archons and the four, or later ten, tribes ; or in the Cretan states between the three Dorian tribes and the ten Kosmoi. In the second place, there is no satisfactory evidence for the date of the first appearance of any of these boards of five. The assumption of so late a date for the institution of the ephors directly contradicts Spartan tradition, which ascribed them to king Theopompus in the eighth century.[3] The date of the adjudication of Salamis to Athens by five Spartan arbitrators[4] is uncertain, but is more likely, in view of the character of the Athenian inscription relating to the founding of the cleruchy there, to have occurred near the end of the sixth century than about 570 B.C.[5] And in the third place, Pindar's account of the founding of the colony of Etna by Hiero of Syracuse (after 478 B.C.) implies that three Dorian tribes still persisted at Sparta at that time. For after mentioning the tribe Hylleis in connection with the other settlers (πόλιν . . . ῾Υλλίδος στάθμας . . . ἐν νόμοις ἔκτισσ '), he passes on to the Lacedaemonians who were sent,

---

[1] C.A.H. III, p. 562. For *Agathoergoi* (oldest of Hippeis), cf. Herod. I. 67.

[2] For the period of the Principate, cf. p. 166. That this organisation was a survival from early times follows from the argument developed in Part I as a whole.   [3] Cf. p. 405, n. 4.   [4] Plut. *Solon*, 10.

[5] The early date for the inscription is accepted by Judeich (*Ath. Mitt.* XXIV, 1899, p. 333, n. 1) and Hicks-Hill (*Greek Hist. Inscr.* 4). Cf. however, De Sanctis, *Atthis* (1911), p 359, who believes the cleruchy to have been founded by Cleisthenes, and Tod, *Gr. Hist. Inscr.* (1933), no 11, who assigns the inscription on grounds of epigraphy to ' the latter part of the sixth century '. The only time when Spartan arbitration is likely to have been asked for by Athens during this period is in the period of pro-Spartan government between the overthrow of Hippias and the reforms of Cleisthenes.

evidently in considerable numbers, to join the colony, and says :

ἐθέλοντι δὲ Παμφύλου
καὶ μὰν Ἡρακλειδᾶν ἔκγονοι
ὄχθαις ὑπὸ Ταϋγέτου ναίοντες ἀεὶ μένειν τεθμοῖσιν ἐν Αἰγιμίου
Δωρίοις· ἔσχον δ' Ἀμύκλας ὄλβιοι.[1]

It is impossible to doubt that Pindar knew the facts about the foundation of Etna. Is it likely that the Lacedaemonian colonists were in reality giving up their own institutions in settling there, and consenting to go back to an arrangement which their own state had abandoned more than a century before ? But it happens that there is an even later indication of the persistence of the three-tribe arrangement at Sparta in the three hundred *Hippeis*,[2] whose selection was in the hands of three *Hippagretae ;*[3] and in fact the whole military organisation of the Spartan citizens (as opposed to that of the light-armed) in Pindar's time may be shown still to have been based on a three-tribe, not on a five-tribe arrangement.[4]

This is not, however, an opinion generally held at the present time. Many historians believe, mainly on the evidence of a λόχος Πιτανάτης named from a village of Pitane, that five new local regiments at some time took the place of the three Dorian tribal regiments. Of this change which he ascribes with the rest to about 600 B.C. Wade-Gery says : ' The significance of this reform was first and foremost *military:* the Spartan army henceforward (until a further reorganisation in the fifth century) consisted of five regiments recruited by locality, instead of three regiments recruited by descent '.[5] He believes the first certain evidence for the five regiments to be at the battle of Plataea in 479.[6] The evidence for these supposed

---

[1] Pind. *Pyth.* I, 120 f. Aristophanes refers to the rich Spartans of his own day as τῶν Ἡρακλειδῶν . . . τῶν Παμφύλου (*Plut.* 382 f., with Schol. *ad loc.*) but this may mean no more than ' Dorian Spartans '.

[2] *Cf.* Thuc. V, 72. 4 : οἱ τριακόσιοι ἱππῆς καλούμενοι.

[3] [Xen.] *Resp. Lac.* IV, 3.   [4] See further, pp. 394 f.

[5] C.A.H. III, p. 560. Wade-Gery maintains substantially the same view in *Class. Quart.* XXXVIII (1944), pp. 119 f., though with the substitution of Oba for Phyle as the unit of locality. Difficulties in this interpretation of the Oba are considered above, pp. 164 f.

[6] *Ibid.* p. 562. (Presumably on account of the λόχος Πιτανάτης mentioned in Herod. IX, 53).

five *Lochoi* is as follows. (1) A scholiast on Aristophanes complains that the poet is careless in implying that there were only four Spartan *Lochoi*, because ' the number of *Lochoi* at Sparta is not four but five, called *Edolos*, *Sinis*, *Arimas*, *Ploas*, *Mesoages:* Thucydides, however, says there were seven without the Sciritae '.[1] Approximately the same names as the five given by the scholiast on Aristophanes appear in a scholiast on Thucydides.[2] (2) Aristotle is variously quoted by the lexicographers as having said (a) that there were five Spartan *Lochoi*,[3] (b) that there were seven *Lochoi*,[4] (c) that there were six *Morai*.[5] (3) Photius, who says that Aristotle speaks of seven *Lochoi*, says that Thucydides says there were five.[6]

Out of all this confusion it seems to emerge that the two scholiasts stand alone, unsupported by Thucydides or by Aristotle. Aristotle said there were six of the large regiments called *Morai:* Harpocration appears to be citing the passage in question *verbatim* and gives this number.[7] The same number is given by the fourth century writer on the Spartan constitution,[8] and six is also the number of the normal regiments given by Thucydides, who implies that the *Lochos* (as he calls it) raised by Brasidas, as well as that composed of Sciritae, was an addition to the regular citizen army.[9] The name *Lochos* may have caused some of the confusion, since it was more properly applied to a sub-division of the regiment to which Aristotle gave its correct name of *Mora*,[10] but since both in Thucydides' time and in

---

[1] Schol. Arist. *Lysistr.* 453 : ὅτι καὶ παρ' ἡμῖν εἰσὶ (sc. τέσσαρες λόχοι μαχίμων γυναικῶν) : παρὰ ταῖς γυναιξὶν ὑπάρχουσι δ λόχοι· τοῦτο δέ φησιν, ὅτι καὶ παρὰ Λακεδαιμονίοις τέσσαρες ὑπάρχουσι λόχοι οἷς κέχρηται ὁ βασιλεύς. τέσσαρες λόχοι· ἀργότερον τὰ Λακώνων ἔοικεν ἐξείργασθαι ὁ ποιητής. λόχοι γὰρ οὐκ εἰσὶ τέσσαρες ἐν Λακεδαίμονι, ἀλλὰ ε, Ἔδωλος, Σίνις, Ἀρίμας, Πλόας, Μεσσοάγης. ὁ ἐ Θουκυδίδης ζ φησὶ χωρὶς τῶν Σκιριτῶν.

[2] Schol. Thuc. IV, 8, λόχοι Λακεδαιμονίων πέντε, Αἰδώλιος, Σίνις, Σαρίνας, Πλόας, Μεσοάτης ; cf. Hesych. s.v. Ἔδωλος. λόχος Λακεδαιμονίων οὕτως ἐκαλεῖτο.

[3] Hesych. s.v. λόχοι : Λακεδαιμονίων φησὶν Ἀριστοφάνης τέτταρας· πέντε γάρ εἰσιν, ὥς φησιν Ἀριστοτέλης.

[4] Phot. s.v. λόχοι : Λακεδαιμονίων δ, ὡς Ἀριστοφάνης· Θουκυδίδης δὲ ε, Ἀριστοτέλης ζ.

[5] Harpocrat. s.v. μόρων· Ἀριστοτέλης φησὶ ὡς εἰσὶ μόραι ἓξ ὠνομασμέναι, καὶ διῃρῆνται εἰς τὰς μόρας Λακεδαιμόνιοι πάντες. [6] Cf. above, n. 4.

[7] Cf. above, n. 5. The name μόρα is confirmed by (Xen.) *Resp. Lac.* XI. 4 (Λυκοῦργος) μόρας μὲν διεῖλεν ἓξ καὶ ἱππέων καὶ ὁπλιτῶν.

[8] See above, n. 7. [9] Thuc. V, 67. 1. [10] See p. 357, n. 4.

Aristotle's time the *Lochos* was a quarter of the *Mora*, it is clear that the information given by the scholiasts on Thucydides and Aristophanes cannot refer at all to the period covered by Thucydides, the writer of the *Respublica Lacedaemoniorum* and Aristotle. The scholiasts themselves certainly belong to some time after Aristotle,[1] and the present tense is used by one, and implied by the other, in enumerating the five names of *Lochoi:* the probability is therefore that they are speaking of their own period rather than preserving a tradition which goes back to the period before Thucydides. This probability is increased by the reflection that the Spartan *Lochoi* were not themselves the main regiments, but subdivisions of them : for the subdivision by quarters, which goes through the whole Spartan army organisation in Thucydides' time and continues in the fourth century,[2] can scarcely have superseded an earlier subdivision by fifths, especially if the basis of the earlier division was five local tribes, as the theory under consideration maintains. Are we to suppose that one of these tribes had been wiped out of existence by Thucydides' time ? But we have seen that our earliest evidence for their existence comes from the period of the Principate.[3] Surely, then, if the basis of the lesser army divisions was local tribes, we should conclude from our evidence that there were four of these in Thucydides' and Aristophanes' time and still four in the fourth century, and that the fifth was added later, perhaps at some stage in the fortification of the city, and therefore not earlier than the beginning of the third century B.C. But even this hypothesis breaks down in view of the discrepancy of names : only one ($M\epsilon\sigma o\acute{a}\tau\eta s$) in the list of five given by the two scholia coincides with those of the apparently local divisions which occur in Roman times,[4] and even in this case $M\epsilon\sigma o\acute{a}\gamma\eta s$ rather than $M\epsilon\sigma o\acute{a}\tau\eta s$ may well be the true form, $M\epsilon\sigma o\acute{a}\tau\eta s$ having been influenced by the existence of the place-name. Here, incidentally, it may be pointed out how misleading is the description of

---

[1] The scholion on Thucydides appears in a late and poor manuscript, and seems likely to be derived from the scholiast on Aristophanes' *Lysistrata*, since it merely repeats the same five names in the same order.

[2] See below, p. 357.   [3] *Cf.* Part I, pp. 163 f.

[4] *Cf.* Part I, pp. 163 f., where reasons are given for thinking that there were four of them, not five.

the localities Mesoa, etc., as 'the quarters of Sparta town ',[1] at least with reference to the period before the inclusion of them within the town walls which for the first time gave them a definite boundary. More than one modern historian appears to make this assumption,[2] although the truth was pointed out by Müller when he first examined the question of the supposed five local tribes in 1839.[3] Müller connects the κῶμαι into which Thucydides says that Sparta was divided [4] with these local divisions (the *Phylai*), but points out that the local *Phylai* remained separate until the συνοικισμός, which Thucydides plainly says had *not* taken place in his own time. In Thucydides' time the Spartans still lived κατὰ κώμας, in separate villages, 'after the ancient fashion of Greece '. Müller very plausibly suggested that it was the building of the walls of Sparta in the Macedonian period which transformed the local *Phylai* for the first time into the divisions of a unified town.

It has been shown that the theory under discussion breaks down in the attempt to connect the *Lochoi* with local administrative divisions. There remains, as a logical possibility at least, the alternative of connecting the largest military units, properly called *Morai*,[5] with the local *Phylai*. But apart from the difficulty involved in the number of the *Morai*, which early in the fourth century B.C. is said to have been six from the time of Lycurgus,[6] there is a further serious difficulty. In the only period of which we know anything at all of its organisation, apart from the time when it was presumably based on the non-local Dorian tribes, the recruitment of the *Morai* was independent of local administrative divisions. During the war with Corinth in 394 B.C. the men of Amyclae were released from *all* the *Morai* to attend an ancient festival.[7] Whether Amyclae was actually on a par with the other local divisions, as Wade-Gery and Ehrenberg believe, makes no difference

---

[1] C.A.H. III, p. 560.

[2] *Cf.* Ehrenberg, cited above, Part I, Chap. IV, p. 164, n. 5.

[3] K. O. Müller, *Dorians*, II, pp. 47 f.

[4] Thuc. I, 10. 2 : ὅμως δὲ οὔτε ξυνοικισθείσης πόλεως οὔτε ἱεροῖς καὶ κατασκευαῖς πολυτελέσι χρησαμένης, κατὰ κώμας δὲ τῷ παλαιῷ τῆς Ἑλλάδος τρόπῳ οἰκισθείσης, φαίνοιτ' ἂν ὑποδεεστέρα.

[5] Diod. XV, 32 : τὴν δὲ μόραν ἀναπληροῦσιν ἄνδρες πεντακόσιοι, *cf.* below, p. 357, n. 4.   [6] [Xen.] *Resp. Lac.* XI, 4.   [7] Xen. *Hell.* IV, 5. 11.

to the force of this argument : in any case the presence of
men from a single locality in all the *Morai* must imply
that there was no direct connection between the *Morai*
and the local *Phylai*.

With regard to the λόχος Πιτανάτης, Thucydides, who
denies that any such λόχος existed[1] is presumably thinking
of the Spartan army, the hoplite regiments of fully adult
citizens. But Herodotus mentions that Amompharetos,
the captain of the Pitanate *Lochos*, was an Eiren, and that
the Eirenes who fell in the battle were buried in a separate
tomb from all the rest of the Spartan citizen troops.[2] He
also records the names of three other Eirenes besides
Amompharetos who fell in the battle,[3] having no doubt
found them all recorded in the inscription on the tomb.
According to Herodotus' Spartan informants, three of the
four were the most distinguished of all the Greeks at Plataea
for bravery, and the fourth (who was killed before the battle
began) for beauty.[4] This implies that all four were
captains,[5] and therefore that the Eirenes were brigaded
separately in four *Lochoi* which took their names from
villages ; it also fits in with the evidence for local divisions
of Sphaireis in the Roman period, among which Pitanatae
are included.[6] In view of Herodotus' information about
the tomb of the Eirenes at Plataea, it seems clear that
there were never five of these groups. The appearance in
the later inscriptions of the name Νεοπολῖται among the
number may easily be accounted for by supposing that the
ancient village of Mesoa[7] grew later into a larger community
to which the name of Neapolis was given.

[1] Thuc. I, 20. 4.
[2] Herod. IX, 85. It is also worth noting that the Pitanate *Lochos*
revived in the time of Caracalla was also composed of νεανίαι (Herodian,
IV, 8. 3). [3] Herod. *ibid.*, *cf.* IX, 71, 72.
[4] *Ibid.* 71, 72. In Herodotus' own opinion, private jealousies had
something to do with this account, and the bravest Spartan was actually
Aristodamos, not an Eiren. We may infer that his informants were
members of the Privileged Families, and that Aristodamos was not.
[5] Judging from the example of Athenian casualty lists, the name of
the commander, if he fell in the fighting, would be inscribed at the head
of each list (*cf.* I.G. I², 929, 943, 950, 953). I.G. V, i. 1 ('Εχεμμᾶ λόχος),
implies that a Spartan captain's name would be conspicuous on the tomb
even if he were not killed.
[6] *Cf.* pp. 163 f.
[7] Of which Alcman is said to have been a resident (Suidas, *s.v.* 'Αλκμάν).

In fact there is no satisfactory evidence either that there were five local divisions of Sparta in the pre-Hellenistic period, or that there were ever five main army divisions, or that in Sparta local administrative divisions at any time formed the basis either of the military units or of political representation. Our knowledge of the constitution and military organisation of the Athenian democracy makes it dangerously easy to assume such a connection in other Greek states of which we have less knowledge : this knowledge should at all events not be allowed to influence our view of the development of the constitution of Sparta, which was universally acknowledged in antiquity to be utterly different from that of Athens.

The last argument employed by the supporters of the view that the reforms attributed to Lycurgus occurred about 600 B.C. is drawn from the account of Herodotus. It is said that Herodotus relates the history of the Arcadian wars of the early sixth century as if they were the immediate consequence of the reform of the Spartan constitution by Lycurgus.[1] At first sight the chapters in question do indeed appear to support this interpretation, but a more detailed examination of them in the light of other ancient traditions about the early history of Sparta, will reveal quite clearly that this was not Herodotus' meaning. The further discussion of this is best postponed for the present, but will be returned to later.[2] It will appear in due course that although Herodotus may have been confused himself about the chronology, he intended to follow the usual Spartan tradition that Lycurgus belonged to the ninth century B.C. It is therefore impossible to base a new chronology of the Spartan constitution, differing from that of all other ancient writers, upon the assumption that Herodotus in these chapters brings forward information unknown to all other surviving literary sources.

§ 2. THE ANCIENT TRADITIONS

(i) *The Olympic Discus*

It can be shown that ancient opinion was overwhelmingly in favour of dating the reforms of Lycurgus at least as early

---

[1] *Cf.* C.A.H. III, p. 562. [2] See further below, pp. 329 f.

as the first half of the ninth century B.C.[1] But the existence in antiquity of a rival view, which assigned Lycurgus to the time of the first Olympiad, may be thought to deprive this otherwise consistent tradition that the reforms were of great antiquity of any basis of fact whatever. Modern historians indeed have utilised the ancient belief in the partial responsibility of Lycurgus for the establishment of the ' Olympic truce ' to support their own theories, based mainly upon archaeological arguments, as to the late origin of Lycurgan institutions in Sparta.[2] It seems therefore desirable to examine the pedigree of the divergent tradition about Lycurgus first ; the historical value of the one more widely held in antiquity, if it has any, will then be more clearly seen.

As his immediate authority for the view that Lycurgus was concerned together with the Elean Iphitus in the foundation of the Olympic festival and the institution of the ' Olympic truce ', Plutarch cites in his *Life of Lycurgus* the work of Hermippus.[3] This was presumably Hermippus of Smyrna, a philosopher of the third century B.C. who wrote, among other works, lives of the famous ancient lawgivers. Hermippus, however, did not invent the story, but merely recorded the opinions of others, among whom was Aristotle, as appears from the more detailed account of the evidence for the date of Lycurgus which Plutarch gives earlier in the same work. Since the precise meaning of Aristotle is not clear (as will be shown presently) the passage of Plutarch is best quoted in full. He says : [4]

οἱ μὲν γὰρ Ἰφίτῳ συνακμάσαι (sc. τὸν Λυκοῦργον) λέγουσι, ὧν ἐστι καὶ Ἀριστοτέλης ὁ φιλόσοφος, τεκμήριον προσφέρων τὸν Ὀλυμπίασι δίσκον, ἐν ᾧ τοὔνομα τοῦ Λυκούργου διασώζεται καταγεγραμμένον. οἱ δὲ ταῖς διαδοχαῖς τῶν ἐν Σπάρτῃ βεβασιλευκότων ἀναλεγόμενοι τὸν χρόνον, ὥσπερ Ἐρατοσθένης καὶ Ἀπολλόδωρος, οὐκ ὀλίγοις ἔτεσι πρεσβύτερον ἀποφαίνουσι τῆς πρώτης Ὀλυμπιάδος.

[1] See below, pp. 327 f.
[2] Lenschau (*e.g.*) *Die Entstehung des Spartanischen Staates, Klio*, XXX, 1937, pp. 271 f., even maintains that the connection with the Olympic truce associates Lycurgus with the war between Sparta, allied with Elis, and Pisa *c*. 590–580 B.C. This theory is not supported by any detailed examination of the sources, and is in fact in disagreement with them.
[3] *Cf.* Plut. *Lycurg.* 23 : φασί τινες, ὡς Ἕρμιππος μνημονεύει.
[4] Plut. *Lycurg.* 1.

This passage clearly reveals the divergent views held about the date of Lycurgus in the third century B.C. and later. It also appears from it that Plutarch thought that Aristotle thought that the occurrence of the name of Lycurgus on the inscribed Olympic discus proved that Lycurgus assisted in the organisation of the first Olympiad, 776 B.C. Whether this was in fact what Aristotle thought is a question for further discussion.

Two other writers of the second century A.D., Phlegon of Tralles and Pausanias, give much fuller accounts of the history of the Olympic festival, which furnish some indication of the way in which this tradition about Lycurgus was built up. The fullest account is that of Phlegon. Tracing the history of the festival at Olympia, Phlegon says that the original one founded by Heracles and various mythical personages fell into disuse for a long and indefinite period.[1] Unfortunately the text is uncertain in the passage in which Phlegon indicated the date when this period ended, but both on account of other information which he gives in the same passage, and on purely textual grounds, it is to be supposed that he fixed the end of the period of neglect in question 28 Olympiads (108 years) before the refounding of the festival in 776 B.C.[2] At the end of this time, general *stasis* having broken out in the Peloponnese, the Olympic festival was restored, with a view to restoring ὁμονοία, by Lycurgus of Sparta, Iphitus of Elis, and Cleisthenes of Pisa, after consultation of the Delphic oracle, which instructed them to proclaim a truce for all states which took part in the festival. The Olympic discus which

---

[1] *F. Gr. Hist.* (Jacoby), 2 Teil B (1929), pp. 1160 f.

[2] *Cf.* Phlegon, *ibid.* 1. 15 : μετὰ Πεῖσον καὶ Πέλοπα, ἔτι δὲ Ἡρακλέα, τοὺς πρώτους τὴν παγήγυριν καὶ τὸν ἀγῶνα τὸν Ὀλυμπίασιν ἐνστησαμένους, ἐκλειπόντων τῶν Πελοποννησίων τὴν θρησκείαν χρόνωι τινι, εἰς †ὃν ἀπὸ Ἰφίτου† Ὀλυμπιάδες ὀκτὼ πρὸς ταῖς εἴκοσι καταριθμοῦνται εἰς Κόροιβον τὸν Ἠλεῖον, καὶ ἀμελησάντων τοῦ ἀγῶνος, στάσις ἐνέστη κατὰ τὴν Πελοπόννησον. Λυκοῦργος δὲ . . . καὶ Ἴφιτος, κ.τ.λ. Wilamowitz seeks to emend the text by removing ἀπὸ Ἰφίτου in l. 17, but this would still not make sense. What is required by the sense is rather χρόνωι τινι, εἰς Ἴφιτον, ἀφ' οὗ, κ.τ.λ. Iphitus and Lycurgus would then be dated to 108 years before Coroebus won the foot-race, *i.e.* before 776 B.C. This is in accordance with Phlegon's genealogy of Lycurgus, which makes him son of Prytanis and fifth from Procles. The tables of Spartan kings from which this information is taken show that Prytanis must have been supposed to live about four generations before 776 B.C. See further below, pp. 334 ff.

laid down the conditions under which the festival was to
be held was then inscribed by the Elean *Hellanodikai*.
But the Peloponnesian states did not obey the injunctions
of the oracle, and a plague and failure of the crops led to a
second and then a third appeal to the oracle by οἱ περὶ
Λυκοῦργον, resulting finally in the Eleans receiving the
admitted right to organise the festival.[1] The Eleans then
proposed to assist the Spartans in the siege of Helos, but
were discouraged by the oracle, who told them to concen-
trate on κοινόδικος φιλίη in the quadriennial festival. The
first five Olympiads were held without the victors being
crowned, in the sixth (*sc.* after 776 ?)[2] ' King Iphitus ' was
sent again to Delphi to consult the oracle about the desirability of crowning the victors, and in ' the seventh Olympiad '
(*sc.* after 776), Daikles of Messenia, victor in the στάδιον,
was first to be crowned. *I.e.* Phlegon thought that Lycurgus
and Iphitus were concerned with the foundation of the
Olympic festival in 776, and this agrees with Plutarch's
interpretation of Aristotle.

Pausanias begins his account of the earliest history of
the Olympic festival, on the authority of 'Ηλείων οἱ τὰ
ἀρχαιότατα μνημονεύοντες (V, 7.6), with a long list of mythical
founders beginning with ' Heracles the Idaean Dactyl '
from Crete. Oxylus, the founder of the kingdom of Elis,
is said to have led to the discontinuation of the festival
until the time of Iphitus by accidentally killing his brother
with a discus (*cf.* V, 4.1, 5). Then follows a shorter version
of the account given by Phlegon of Iphitus' refounding.
Pausanias mentions only one consultation of the oracle,
and that by Iphitus only, which resulted in the authorisation to the Eleans to hold the festival. Lycurgus is not
said in Pausanias' account to have taken any part in the
refounding, but is merely mentioned as a contemporary

[1] Phlegon, *ibid.* 8 : τούτων χρησθέντων οἱ Πελοποννήσιοι ἐπέτρεψαν
τοῖς 'Ηλείοις ἀγῶνα τιθέναι τῶν 'Ολυμπίων καὶ ἐκεχειρίαν ἀγγέλλειν ταῖς
πόλεσιν. *Cf.* the abbreviated account from the same source in Schol.
Plato, *Rep. V*, 465 : οἱ δὲ (*i.e.* Iphitus, Lycurgus and Cleisthenes) τοῖς
'Ηλείοις ἐπιτρέπουσι διαθεῖναι τὸν ἀγῶνα. This seems to be the main
point of the whole story. See further below, pp. 326 ff.
[2] But *cf.* above, p. 321, n. 2. Phlegon is trying to reconcile two inconsistent accounts, and ' King Iphitus ' (whose kingship is denied by
Paus. V, 4. 5) may be a ' double ' invented to account for the discrepancy
of 108 years.

of Iphitus. From the account in V, 8.5–7 (*cf.* VIII, 26.4) it is clear that Pausanias referred the refounding of the festival to 776 B.C., when Coroebus won the foot-race.

All these three accounts therefore agree in assigning Iphitus' refounding of the festival to 776 B.C. It has already been mentioned that this belief goes back at least to the authorities cited by Hermippus in the third century B.C.[1]

But in spite of the apparent concurrence of Aristotle, it is doubtful whether this dating for Lycurgus and Iphitus rests on any reputable early authority. This may be seen from consideration of the source of Pausanias' account, which may well be the source of all three, allowing for further embroidery by Phlegon. All the indications point to Ephorus. The story of the first foundations of the Olympic festival by 'Heracles the Idaean Dactyl' occurred in Ephorus,[2] as also the story which Pausanias tells of how Oxylus and the Dorians conquered Elis from Arcadia, driving out the Epeians as the result of a single combat between the Aetolian slinger Pyraechmes and Degmenes the Epeian archer.[3] Ephorus also mentioned the foundation of the Olympic games by Iphitus.[4]

With regard to the source of Aristotle's account, citing the authority of the Olympic discus, the evidence is less clear. But probability again points to Ephorus, who is known to have appealed to similar authority in support of the connection of Oxylus with Aetolia, in this case a metrical inscription from the base of the statue of Oxylus in the agora at Elis.[5] In the *Politics* Aristotle uses Ephorus as his main authority for all information about Sparta, and in particular he accepts the same date for Lycurgus as Ephorus.[6]

The interesting thing is that this date, according to Ephorus, was the early one, 'sixth from Procles and five

[1] *Cf.* above, p. 320.
[2] *Ap.* Diod. Sic. V, 64. The story itself is much older than Ephorus (*cf.* Pindar, *Olymp.* II, 5 ; XI, 51).
[3] Ephorus *ap.* Strabo, VIII, 3. 33 (357), *cf.* Paus. V, 4. 1, 2.
[4] *Ap.* Strabo, VIII, 3. 33 (358).
[5] Ephorus *ap.* Strabo, X, 3. 2 (463–464).
[6] *Cf. Pol.* II, 10. 2 (Lycurgus the guardian of Charillus). For the generation of Charillus (sixth from Procles) see the table of Spartan kings (below, p. 334). For Ephorus' view that Lycurgus was 'sixth from Procles' *cf.* Strabo, X, 481.

generations after the Dorian colonisation of Crete ',[1] or in the seventh generation after the Dorian conquest of Laconia. Since the Dorian conquest of Laconia ('Return of the Heracleidae') was already assigned by Thucydides to eighty years after the fall of Troy,[2] this gives a date for Lycurgus early in the ninth century B.C. Moreover, Pausanias, who assigns Lycurgus together with Iphitus to 776 B.C. in his account of the Olympic festival, elsewhere in his work accepts Ephorus' date and puts Lycurgus in the reign of Agesilaus ; [3] it must therefore be supposed that the late date for Lycurgus and Iphitus which appears in Pausanias' account of the Olympic festival is derived not from Ephorus, but from his Elean informants.[4] It must also be supposed that Plutarch misunderstood Aristotle in supposing him to assign Iphitus and Lycurgus to the first Olympiad, 776 B.C.

This misunderstanding might quite easily arise in view of the difficulty of making a distinction in the form of wording between the foundation by Iphitus and the much more famous foundation of 776 B.C. A form of words which might equally well describe the foundation of 776 B.C. was in fact used by Ephorus both of that of Iphitus and of the foundation by 'Heracles the Idaean Dactyl '.[5] In point of fact the foundation by Iphitus seems no more likely to be historical than that by the Dactyl, in spite of the supposed evidence of the Olympic Discus ; and there is no wonder that later writers following Ephorus tended to confuse it with the foundation of 776 B.C. which formed the basis of Greek chronology. A similar difficulty arose in making a distinction between the dates of Olympic victories in the pre-776 period after Iphitus, and after 776. This indeed is probably the true explanation of Pausanias' confusion about the date of Iphitus and Lycurgus, for as the passage in Phlegon shows, the common source drawn upon by both spoke of ' the sixth Olympiad ' and ' the seventh

---

[1] Strabo, loc. cit.
[2] Thuc. I, 12. See further below, pp. 334 f.
[3] Paus. III, 2. 4. For the date assigned to Agesilaus see below, p. 334.
[4] Paus. V, 7. 6 ; cf. above, p. 323.
[5] Cf. Eph. ap. Diod. V, 64 : Ἡρακλέα . . . θεῖναι τὸν ἀγῶνα τὸν τῶν Ὀλυμπίων ; Eph. ap. Strabo, VIII, 3. 33, 358 : Ἴφιτόν τε θεῖναι τὸν Ὀλυμπικὸν ἀγῶνα.

Olympiad ' obviously meaning by this twenty and twenty-four years respectively after the date of Iphitus' refounding. But Pausanias, like some of his predecessors and like the modern editors of Phlegon,[1] has not unnaturally concluded that these dates are 756 and 752 B.C., with the corollary that Iphitus and Lycurgus belong to 776. It is quite possible that Ephorus himself was guilty of the same chronological confusion as Pausanias, for the idea that there were two Lycurguses 108 years apart occurs already in Timaeus.[2]

Although literary evidence for the inscribed discus which mentioned Iphitus carries us back no further than the fourth century B.C., the discus itself actually existed, and was seen and described by Pausanias. From him we learn that the lettering ran round it in a circle,[3] so that it probably had an archaic appearance. But it must certainly be regarded as a forgery, whether it was supposed to refer to 776 B.C. or to a century earlier. An inscription in Greek lettering dating from the early ninth century B.C. may be regarded as a virtual impossibility, and even had it existed it is certain that it could not have been deciphered by the Greeks of the fourth century B.C. And although an inscription on bronze of 776 B.C. may conceivably have existed, the Eleans at all events cannot have maintained that the discus cited by Aristotle and seen by Pausanias was inscribed at the time of the Olympic festival of 776 B.C., because at that time it would have been quite inappropriate to the occasion, discus-throwing not having been introduced until the Pentathlon was instituted in the eighteenth Olympiad (i.e. 708 B.C.).[4] This was during the period in which the Eleans were in charge of the festival and of the records of the victories won in the various contests on each occasion. It follows that their own interpretation of the Iphitus-discus, at the time when it was

---

[1] Cf. Jacoby, loc. cit. pp. 1161, 1162.

[2] Timaeus ap. Plut. Lycurg. 1. Cf. also Cic. Brut. 10 and De Rep II, 10. 18 (the last-named passage also preserving the interval of 108 years between the two).

[3] Paus. V, 20. 1 : ὁ δὲ τοῦ Ἰφίτου δίσκος τὴν ἐκεχειρίαν ἣν ἐπὶ τοῖς Ὀλυμπίοις ἐπαγγέλλουσιν οἱ Ἠλεῖοι, ταύτην οὐκ ἐς εὐθὺ ἔχει γεγραμμένην, ἀλλ' ἐς κύκλου σχῆμα περίεισιν ἐπὶ τῷ δίσκῳ τὰ γράμματα.

[4] Paus. V, 8. 5–7.

first inscribed, was that it referred to the ninth-century date. The difficulty about the late introduction of discus-throwing was overcome by the supposition that many contests which had existed in a very early period were afterwards forgotten, and only gradually reintroduced after 776 B.C.[1]

The explanation is patently unconvincing, and suggests that at some time the Eleans had a good reason for forging a document to prove that they controlled the Olympic festival from a period earlier than 776 B.C. Such a reason is known to have existed when Elis fell under Spartan domination c. 400 B.C.,[2] for there was some hesitation and discussion before Elis was allowed to retain her control over the sanctuary at Olympia, it being pointed out that ' this control did not belong to Elis in antiquity '.[3] Now in Ephorus' account of the history of the festival, great stress appears to have been laid on the fact that it was the Spartans themselves who came to the help of Elis and helped her to recover complete control of the sanctuary on three occasions, after 748 B.C. (the eighth Olympiad) when they assisted in the overthrow of Pheidon of Argos,[4] immediately after the thirty-fourth Olympiad (644 B.C.), when they assisted Elis against Pantaleon of Pisa,[5] and in 572 B.C. when they helped Elis to crush Pisa completely, the Pisans having then shared in the control of Olympia for a little over a century.[6] Moreover, in the same account it was pointed out by Ephorus that until the twenty-sixth Olympiad (676 B.C.), when the Pisans first claimed a share in the administration, the festival had been in the sole control of the Eleans from the time of the Dorian conquest of Elis.[7]

---

[1] Paus. V, 8. 5–7.

[2] The Elean War is variously dated within the limits 402–397 B.C. (ref. in *Class. Quart.* XXXIX, p. 22, n. 4).

[3] *Cf.* Xen. *Hell.* III, ii, 31 : τοῦ μέντοι προεστάναι τοῦ Διὸς τοῦ Ὀλυμπίου ἱεροῦ,. καίπερ οὐκ ἀρχαίου Ἠλείοις ὄντος, οὐκ ἀπήλασαν αὐτούς. The Spartans would presumably have preferred at that time to accept the ' demonstrations of ancient mythology ' on which the claim of the Pisans was based (*cf.* Diod. XV, 78, referring to the Pisan Ἀνολυμπίας of 364 B.C.).

[4] Ephorus *ap.* Strabo, VIII, 3. 33, 358.

[5] Ephorus, *ibid.* 355 ; *cf.* 362 ; Paus. VI, 22. 2.

[6] Strabo, VIII, 355. The help given by Sparta on the last two occasions is here confused ; *cf.* Paus. VI, 22. 4.

[7] Ephorus *ap.* Strabo, *ibid.* Strabo himself rejects the evidence of legend for the period before 776, and adds ἐγγυτέρω δὲ πίστεως, ὅτι μέχρι

Hence it may be assumed that the evidence of the discus was intended to prove that this earlier claim on the part of Elis, going back far beyond the first Olympiad, had been recognised also by the Spartans, and even enforced by them, no less a person than their own lawgiver Lycurgus himself having given his sanction to it.

Since Sparta, as we have seen, allowed the Eleans to retain their control c. 400 B.C., but still denied their claim that they were the original possessors of the sanctuary, it may be supposed that the discus had not been accepted as a historical document before this time, as it certainly would have been accepted by the Spartans, had it then existed, throughout the period when they supported the claim of Elis to Olympia. The Spartan denial c. 400 B.C. of the justice of the Elean claim also implies that the discus did not then seem to the Spartans convincing, although it probably produced a sufficient element of doubt, and of prejudice in favour of Elis, to make it impolitic for Sparta to deprive the Eleans of their control.

All the evidence therefore points to the conclusion that the Eleans forged the discus c. 400 B.C. to serve a particular purpose, and that the inscription on it, together with a legendary account of the period from Oxylus to Iphitus, was incorporated by Ephorus in his history of the sanctuary.[1]

It is only after the time of Ephorus that doubt appears as to whether Iphitus and Lycurgus (and no doubt other legendary or half-legendary figures besides) belonged to the early ninth century or to the time of the first Olympiad.[2]

τῆς ἕκτης καὶ εἰκοστῆς Ὀλυμπιάδος ἀπὸ τῆς πρώτης, ἐν ᾗ Κόροιβος ἐνίκα στάδιον Ἠλεῖος, τὴν προστασίαν εἶχον τοῦ τε ἱεροῦ καὶ τοῦ ἀγῶνος Ἠλεῖοι. It has sometimes been assumed that the interruption of Elean control at the twenty-sixth Olympiad refers to Pheidon's celebration of the festival, but Strabo himself goes on to explain (ibid.) that what happened after the twenty-sixth Olympiad was that Pisa acquired a share in the control until deprived of it by the Spartans (cf. also Clinton, F.H. I, 660 B.C., where further evidence and the true explanation is given). Pheidon's celebration must be dated 748 B.C., as by Paus. VI, 22. 2, since this date agrees with the information that he was 'tenth from Temenos' and a contemporary of the founder of Syracuse (cf. Clinton, ibid. p. 248).

[1] It may also have been incorporated by Hippias of Elis about the same time in his Ὀλυμπιονικῶν Ἀναγραφή, as Wade-Gery believes (Class. Quart. XXXVIII, p. 5, n. 3). Hippias is said by Plutarch, however, to have 'based his work on nothing worthy of credence' (Numa, 1).

[2] A discrepancy of about 100 years in the date of Pheidon of Argos appears already in the time of Herodotus, who puts him in the later seventh

The conception of a first Olympiad 108 years before the first Olympiad was too difficult an idea to be readily accepted. But it is interesting to find that in spite of the natural tendency to prefer the later date for the real first Olympiad, the supposed connection with Iphitus did not succeed in displacing Lycurgus the lawgiver from his securely anchored position in chronology in the ninth century B.C. Timaeus (as has been mentioned already) [1] even went to the length of supposing *two* Lycurguses, the famous lawgiver being the earlier, and in this he was followed by Cicero. Other reputable chronographers of the Hellenistic period and later refused to bring down either Iphitus or Lycurgus below the first half of the ninth century B.C., over a hundred years before the first Olympiad.[2] It is only the very late and second-rate authorities who believe in the later date.[3] This goes to show that in the general tradition, including that of the Eleans who apparently forged the discus, the date of Lycurgus fixed the date of Iphitus, and certainly did not itself depend upon the date of the discus.

But what evidence fixed the date, real or supposed, of Lycurgus ? Was there any justification for this persistent earlier tradition that Lycurgus propounded his laws about a hundred years before the first Olympiad (of 776 B.C.) ? About this we may notice a difference of opinion as early as the fifth century B.C. Hellanicus attributed everything in the Spartan constitution to Eurysthenes and Procles, the supposed first founders of Sparta, without even mentioning Lycurgus.[4] This is no doubt the origin of the

century (*cf.* VI, 127) instead of in the generation of Archias the founder of Syracuse (*cf.* above, p. 326, n. 7 *ad fin.*). This might at first sight seem to suggest that the story of Iphitus' founding of the Olympic games had already been invented at the time of Herodotus, and that the historian reckoned from 776 B.C. when he should have reckoned from 884 B.C. But the true explanation seems to be confusion between the two ἀναλυμπιάδες of Pheidon in alliance with Pisa (the eighth Olympiad, 748 B.C.) and of the Pisans under Pantaleon (the thirty-fourth, 644 B.C., *cf.* Paus. VI, 22. 2).   [1] *Cf.* above, p. 325, n. 2.

[2] The earlier date for Lycurgus and Iphitus is accepted by Eratosthenes, Apollodorus, and the other chronographers whose work depends upon these. Timaeus also ascribed Lycurgus the lawgiver to the earlier date, although he knew the alternative story, *cf.* preceding note.

[3] These are, in addition to Pausanias, Phlegon and Plutarch (above, pp. 322 f.) Velleius, I, 6. 3 ; Athenaeus, XIV, 635 f (the last-named claiming universal support for this view in his own time).

[4] *Cf.* Ephorus *ap.* Strabo, VIII, 366.

statement in the *Respublica Lacedaemoniorum* that the law-giver Lycurgus lived 'at the time of the Heracleidae '.[1] On the other hand, the Spartans themselves in the fifth century believed in a later date, as we know from Herodotus, who is the earliest extant author who mentions Lycurgus. 'As the Spartans themselves say ' (says Herodotus) Lycurgus brought these reforms from Crete when he was acting as guardian for his nephew Leobotas, who was king of Sparta.[2] In the list of Agiad kings which Herodotus gives elsewhere,[3] Leobotas appears at the fourth generation after Aristodemus, the founder of the Spartan kingdom at the 'Return of the Heracleidae', and at the twelfth generation before the invasion of Xerxes. Since Herodotus reckoned three generations to a century,[4] he supposed himself when writing this passage (if he thought about it) that Lycurgus lived about 880 B.C., or about a century before the first Olympiad. This reckoning (based it is to be observed on the Spartan list of Agiad kings) gives a date singularly close to what was apparently the Elean date for Iphitus, Lycurgus' reputed contemporary, *viz.* 108 years before the first Olympiad of 776 B.C. The Eurypontid tradition in Herodotus' time about Lycurgus would seem to place him two generations later,[5] which may possibly account for Thucydides' statement that at the end of the Peloponnesian war the constitution of Sparta had lasted unchanged for rather more than four hundred years.[6] But if these two Spartan sources differ in detail, they both agree in placing the reforms of Lycurgus in the ninth century B.C.

The Spartan king-lists themselves call for further investigation, but in the meantime, it is necessary to dispose of a modern interpretation of Herodotus' account (which has already been referred to)[7] of Lycurgus' reforms which seeks to show that the information contained in it actually proves the received Spartan dating for them to be about two centuries too early.[8] For Herodotus says that one of

---

[1] (Xen.) *Resp. Lac.* X, 8.   [2] Herod. I, 65.
[3] *Id*. VII, 204. (See list on p. 334.)   [4] *Id*. II, 142.
[5] In the reign of Charillus. See further below, pp. 331 f.
[6] Thuc. I, 18 (referring like Herodotus to the beginning of Eunomia after a long period of disorder).   [7] *Cf*. above, p. 319.
[8] *Cf*. C.A.H. III, p. 562.

the immediate consequences of those reforms was an
aggressive foreign policy, including an attack on Arcadia,
which the theory in question would identify with an unsuccessful war against Tegea in the reign of Leon and
Hegesicles, early in the sixth century B.C.

Herodotus introduces a brief account of early Sparta
à propos of Croesus' inquiry about the contemporary condition of the Greek states. Croesus learnt, says Herodotus,
that at this time the Spartans had just won a war with the
Tegeans, against whom the two previous kings, Leon and
Hegesicles, had conducted unsuccessful campaigns. The
rest of Herodotus' narrative appears to be a digression
comparable to that which he has just given in connection
with a similar Lydian inquiry about Athens. Sparta was
at this time a state which enjoyed an excellent form of
government (Eunomia) though it had in former times been
the worst-governed state in Greece. This change, says
Herodotus, came about through the reforms of Lycurgus ;
and as a result of these reforms Sparta immediately (αὐτίκα)
' shot up and throve ', developed a more aggressive foreign
policy, attacked Arcadia, and was ignominiously defeated
by the Tegeans, who bound their Spartan prisoners in the
very chains which they had brought with them in the
expectation of measuring out the conquered territory.
Herodotus seems in concluding his account to speak of
only two wars, the earlier unsuccessful one, and the recent
successful one in the reign of Anaxandridas and Ariston,
just before Croesus' inquiry, and his account has been so
interpreted by some modern scholars, with the consequence
that the Lycurgan reforms are brought down to about
600 B.C.

This theory rests on the acceptance of the most unlikely
of several possible interpretations of Herodotus' chronology
in this passage. These alternatives are, first, that by his
phrase ' the former war ' [1] against Tegea Herodotus meant
all the long series of unsuccessful wars waged by Sparta
against Tegea from the time of the Lycurgan reforms to
the reign of Anaxandridas and Ariston. This interpretation
is favoured by Herodotus' references in the same passage

---

[1] Cf. Herod. I, 67 init.: κατὰ μὲν δὴ τὸν πρότερον πόλεμον συνεχέως αἰεὶ
κακῶς ἀέθλεον πρὸς τοὺς Τεγεήτας, κατὰ δὲ τὸν κατὰ Κροῖσον χρόνον, κ.τ.λ.

to a state of chronic hostilities between the two cities.[1]
A second possibility is that Herodotus inadvertently confused in his account two unsuccessful wars separated by a
long period, exactly as he has done in the case of the wars
between Athens and Aegina.[2] His habit of digressions
naturally made it easy for chronological confusion of this
sort to arise, and they do not necessarily imply that confusion existed in the mind of the author as well as in his
narrative. The third possibility, which appears to be the
basis of the theory now under consideration, is that there
was only *one* unsuccessful war which Herodotus mistakenly
transformed into two ; [3] this was the war against Tegea in
the reign of Leon and Hegesicles.

This last alternative must be regarded as the most unlikely of the three for the reason that Herodotus was certainly
not the originator of the idea of two widely separated wars.
The story of the ill-fated invasion with fetters comes from
a Tegean, not from a Spartan source, being the account
which was told to travellers at the temple of Athena Alea
who were shown the dedicated fetters there. This appears
clearly not only from Herodotus but also from Pausanias,
who was shown the same fetters many centuries later.[4]
But in the Tegean account the war was firmly associated
with the Spartan king Charillus, for whom there is no room
in the Eurypontid king-list after Theopompus the victor in
the first Messenian War, and who cannot therefore be
brought down lower than the first half of the eighth century
B.C. The Tegeans said that Charillus had been taken
prisoner with the rest of the Spartans, but had been released
on making a solemn (but as it turned out, treacherous)
engagement with the Tegeans that the Spartans should

---

[1] *Cf.* the preceding note (συνεχέως αἰεὶ) ; also I, 67. 2 : ἐπειδὴ αἰεὶ
τῷ πολέμῳ ἐσσοῦντο ὑπὸ Τεγεητέων ; I, 68. 1 : ἐούσης γὰρ τοῦτον τὸν χρόνον
ἐπιμειξίης πρὸς τοὺς Τεγεήτας (*i.e.* peaceful intercourse was exceptional) ;
I, 68. 6 : καὶ ἀπὸ τούτου τοῦ χρόνου, ὅκως πειρῷατο ἀλλήλων (' whenever
they attacked one another ') πολλῷ κατυπέρτεροι τῷ πολέμῳ ἐγίνοντο
οἱ Λακεδαιμόνιοι.
[2] *Cf.* Herod. V, 81, 89, where attacks by Aegina upon Athens in 506
are confused with attacks in 487.
[3] *Cf.* C.A.H. III, p. 562 : ' Herodotus stultifies his narrative by implying
that the Reform took place several centuries before those immediate
consequences which gave him occasion to mention the matter at all.'
[4] Herod. I, 66 *ad fin.; cf.* Paus. VIII, 47. 2, III, 7. 3.

never again attack Tegea.[1]   The details of the story sound circumstantial, and the main fact of these early hostilities between Sparta and Arcadia is confirmed by the close and friendly relations which certainly existed between Arcadia and Messenia during the wars of Sparta and Messenia.[2]   In fact Charillus, son of Polydectes, may fairly be said on the strength of this Tegean account to be a historical figure, even if his precise date remains uncertain.[3]

A further reason for accepting Herodotus' account of the two widely separated unsuccessful wars as it stands is that Pausanias, who gives the Tegean story of the ' fetter ' war in much greater detail than Herodotus, also accepted direct from Herodotus the historian's distinction between the early ' fetter ' war and the later unsuccessful Spartan attempt in the reign of Leon and Hegesicles.[4]   It may confidently be asserted, therefore, that the chronology of the Arcadian wars offers no support whatever to the theory that the Lycurgan reforms at Sparta were as late as 600 B.C. or anywhere near that date.

But although it would appear, as has been shown, that Spartan opinion in the middle of the fifth century agreed that these reforms were to be dated in the region of four centuries earlier than their own time, the rival claims of the two royal houses, both of which wanted to attach Lycurgus to their own family, and uncertainty about the sequence of kings in the Eurypontid house, made a certain discrepancy in the dating of Lycurgus inevitable even at that period. The account of Herodotus, which makes Lycurgus guardian of Leobotas, follows in this the Agiad tradition, but Ephorus and those who followed him preferred the Eurypontid version which made Lycurgus guardian of Charillus,[5] and it is certain from the appearance even in

---

[1] Paus. VIII, 48. 5.

[2] *Cf.* Tyrtaeus (?) *ap.* Strabo, VIII, 4. 10 (362) ; Polyb. IV, 33.   The joint citizenship and ἐπιγαμία accorded by Arcadian towns to dispossessed Messenians (Polyb. *loc. cit.*) was forbidden in the final treaty between Sparta and Tegea (*cf.* Plut. *Quaest. Graec.* 5, where, however, an erroneous explanation of the phrase χρηστοὺς ποιεῖν is cited from Aristotle).

[3] See further below, p. 334.

[4] *Cf.* Paus. III, 2. 3 (allusion to Herodotus) ; III, 7. 3 (Tegean war of Charillus) ; III, 3. 5 ff. (story of the bones of Orestes and the war under Leon and Hegesicles).   Pausanias' narrative is full of verbal reminiscences of Herodotus' account.

[5] *Cf.* Arist. *Pol.* II, 10. 2, Plut. *Lycurg.* 3, and οἱ πλεῖστοι *ap.* Plut. *ibid.* 1.

Herodotus of the name ' Eunomus ' (*sic*) in the Eurypontid king-list, where Charillus' father Polydectes ought to be, that the Eurypontid house claimed for their family even at that time the honour of producing Lycurgus and through him the *Eunomia*.

The bearing of these rival claims to Lycurgus upon the chronological problem can best be seen from an examination of the Spartan king-lists themselves.

(ii) *The Spartan king-lists of the period before the Persian Wars and the extent of their value as a basis for Chronology*

The origin of the double kingship at Sparta is attributed by all ancient authors at all periods to the birth of twin sons, Eurysthenes and Procles, to Aristodemus, who was himself sixth in descent from Heracles according to the Greek method of reckoning. This part of the genealogy may therefore be left out of account in considering the growth of the tradition, and for the present purpose the lists become of interest only where the divergences begin, with the names which follow Eurysthenes in the Agiad house and Procles in that of the Eurypontidae. It is surely a significant fact which calls for further examination that the divergences are confined to the names of the Eurypontid kings, the names in the Agiad succession being unvarying and in the same order in all authors. For the sake of comparison, two lists of the Eurypontid kings are set side by side in the table below with the agreed list of the Agiads ; the two Eurypontid lists are taken respectively from Herodotus (list A) and Pausanias (list B), who give them in the most complete form, but certain variations which occur in other writers will also have to be considered.

In considering the historical validity of these lists, the first question which arises is whether any value whatever can be attached to the names or even to the number of generations which purport to go back to a period several hundreds of years before the introduction of writing. The Greek chronographers did not feel this to be a difficulty, and it is worth noticing that even those Alexandrian scholars who might reasonably claim to be making a scientific approach to the subject of early chronology by the collation of myths as well as of historical writings, the mathematician Eratosthenes and his later followers, took the Spartan king-lists as the basis of their definite scheme of dating.[1] But this conviction of the chronological reliability of the Spartan king-lists does not begin with Eratosthenes ; it is even more clearly the basis of the chronology

		Eurypontidae.		
Generation	*Agiadae.*[2]	(A)[3]		(B)[4]
I	Eurysthenes	Procles		Procles
II	Agis	Euryphon		Soos
III	Echestratus	Prytanis		Eurypon
IV	Leobotas	Polydectes		Prytanis
V	Doryssus	Eunomus		Eunomus
VI	Agesilaus	Charillus		Polydectes
VII	Archelaus	Nicander		Charillus
VIII	Teleclus	Theopompus		Nicander
IX	Alcamenes	Anaxandridas		Theopompus
X	Polydorus	Archidamus		Archidamus
XI	Eurycrates		[Anaxilaus]	Zeuxidamus
XII	Anaxander		[Leotychidas]	Anaxidamus
XIII	Eurycratidas		[Hippocratidas]	Archidamus
XIV	Leon	Agasicles[5]	[Agesilaus]	Agasicles
XV	Anaxandridas	Ariston[6]	[Menares]	Ariston
XVI	Cleomenes, Leonidas	Demaratus[7]	Leotychidas	Demaratus

of those predecessors of Eratosthenes who gave lower dates than he did for the Fall of Troy and the Return of the Heraclidae. For the ' Return ', the date given by Phanias of Eresus (a disciple of Aristotle) was 56 years lower than that of Eratosthenes, and that of Callimachus (librarian at Alexandria before Eratosthenes) was one year higher than that of Phanias. The three dates translated into terms of modern chronology are thus (Eratosthenes) 1103 B.C.,

[1] *Cf.* Clinton, F.H. I, pp. 124 ff., for the dependence upon Eratosthenes' chronology of Apollodorus, Diodorus and Eusebius. The use of the Spartan king-lists as the basis of chronology between the Trojan War and the first Olympiad is attested by Diodorus (I, 5 ; *cf.* Euseb. *Chron.* 166).

[2] Herod. VII, 204 (descent of Leonidas, who was Cleomenes' half-brother). *Cf.* also Paus. III, 2, III, 3, and for the names as far as Alcamenes, Diod. cited by Euseb. *Chron.* 166 f.

[3] Herod. VIII, 131. The names in square brackets are those of collaterals of the direct line, the actual tree given by Herodotus being that of Leotychidas, so that not all the names necessarily represent kings.

[4] Paus. III, 7. The omission of Anaxandridas between Theopompus and Archidamus could be explained as above, note 3, since Pausanias' list contains only the names of kings.

[5] Herod. I, 65 Hegesicles.   [6] Herod. I, 67.   [7] Herod. V, 75.

'in the 624th year before Xerxes' invasion of Greece ' ;
(Callimachus) 1048 B.C. ; (Phanias) 1047 B.C.[1] The two last
dates are quite obviously arrived at by reckoning back in
accordance with the Spartan king-lists seventeen generations, at three generations to a century,[2] from the invasion
of Xerxes to the beginning of the reign of Aristodemus,[3]
the father of Eurysthenes and Procles. Moreover, it seems
clear from the discrepancy of one year that Callimachus
and Phanias both used the Agiad list in Herodotus, reckoning back from Leonidas' death in 480, the one giving 34
years each to the two extra generations over the five
centuries, the other 67 to the two. The explanation of the
higher dates for the Fall of Troy and the ' Return ' given
by Eratosthenes and his followers is no doubt that they
made an attempt to reconcile Spartan tradition with Ionian
and to fix a date for the Ionian migration. But in fact the
Spartan and Ionian traditions were not in agreement,[4] and
by introducing the latter Eratosthenes must have introduced a source of error in the earlier part of his scheme of
dating. For dates below the ' Return ' he clearly used
the same criterion as Phanias and Callistratus, namely the
number of generations of Spartan kings.[5]

Little interest would attach to this formal chronology
were it not that, on the one hand, the reckoning of three

[1] For the dates given by these writers, cf. Clinton, F. H. I., pp. 124,
128, 139. The interest of Phanias in the Spartan king-lists was no doubt
due to the work of Charon of Lampsacus on their chronology, which had
the title of πρυτάνεις ἢ ἄρχοντες Λακεδαιμονίων, since Phanias himself
chose the title περὶ πρυτάνεων Ἐρεσίων for his chronological work on his
own native city. The interest of Callimachus may well have arisen on
account of his own family, which was that of the Battiadae of Cyrene,
connected with the Spartan royal house through their metropolis of Thera.

[2] Cf. Herod. II, 142 : γενεαὶ γὰρ τρεῖς ἀνδρῶν ἑκατὸν ἔτεά ἐστι.

[3] This was the purely Spartan tradition ; the literary version made
the twin sons Eurysthenes and Procles the invaders. Cf. Herod. VI, 52 :
Λακεδαιμόνιοι γὰρ ὁμολογέοντες οὐδενὶ ποιητῇ λέγουσι αὐτὸν Ἀριστόδημον
. . . ἀγαγεῖν σφέας ἐπὶ τὴν χώρην τὴν νῦν ἐκτέαται, ἀλλ' οὐ τοὺς Ἀριστοδήμου παῖδας.

[4] This is sufficiently illustrated by the claim of Hecataeus of Miletus
to be descended from a god at his sixteenth ancestor (Herod. II, 143),
for the sixteenth ancestors of his Spartan contemporaries Cleomenes
and Demaratus were Eurysthenes and Procles, sixth in descent from
Heracles. The Genealogiai of Hecataeus are therefore unlikely to have been
the first source of these king-lists, as supposed by E. Meyer, and more
recently by Prakken (Trans. Amer. Philol. Assoc. LXXI, 1940, pp. 460 f.),
both of whom assume a 40-year generation. [5] Cf. Plut. Lycurg. I.

generations to a century turns out to be astonishingly accurate over a long period [1] when examined in the light of irrefutable evidence in historical times ; and that on the other, the actual results derived from the application of this reckoning to the very early period of Greek history are far from unacceptable judged by modern standards of archaeology. With regard to the accuracy of the chronological principle, the well-attested lists of Spartan kings in the period from about 560 to 221 B.C. cover a series of eleven generations in each royal house, an average of just under 31 years to a generation ; [2] a corresponding average for the kings of England from 1066 to 1461 gives just under $30\frac{1}{2}$ years, and for the Stuarts and Hanoverians from 1603 to 1936, $30\frac{1}{4}$ years. All three averages are taken over a period covered by eleven generations ; [3] the number of actual reigns naturally varies in the three cases.

By applying their principle rigidly to early Greek chronology,[4] and using the table of Spartan kings, Phanias and Callimachus as we have seen dated the ' Return of the Heraclidae ', in other words, the Dorian invasion of the Peloponnese, to the middle of the eleventh century B.C. The first signs in the Peloponnese of Geometric pottery, which, by reason of its complete contrast with the pottery which precedes it, may reasonably be supposed to be connected with this migration, are dated by the archaeologists to about 1000 B.C.[5] If we make what appears on later evidence to be a necessary correction, and reckon 30+ years to a generation rather than $33\frac{1}{3}$, the difference on seventeen

[1] But not over a short period. See further below, p. 346.

[2] The date 560 is approximate, but not far from the truth for the accessions of Anaxandridas and Ariston, who had recently won success against Arcadia c. 550 (Herod. I, 67) and continued to reign respectively until c. 520 and rather later. Anaxandridas is mentioned together with the Ephor Cheilon in *Rylands Pap.* 18 as having overthrown the tyranny at Sicyon, which would put the beginning of his reign a few years earlier (*cf.* Busolt, *Gr. Gesch.*[2] I, p. 667, n. 1).

[3] For the sense in which the word ' generation ' is here used, see below, p. 342, n. 5.　　　　[4] In contrast with Eratosthenes. *Cf.* above, p. 335.

[5] *Cf.* Pfuhl, *Meisterwerke Griechischer Zeichnung u. Malerei* (1924), p. 7 : ' um die Jahrtausendwende '. In the Peloponnese it appears later than elsewhere, reflecting perhaps the later arrival of northerners. The great complexity and obscurity of dating Geometric pottery is well revealed by Myres (*Who Were the Greeks ?* pp. 473 ff.) ; but it is no doubt possible to arrive at an approximate date for its beginning by working backwards from proto-Attic, proto-Corinthian, etc.

generations would be as near as possible half a century, resulting in a date very near 1000 B.C. for the invasion.

It seems therefore not at all unlikely that the Spartan king-lists preserve an accurate record of the number of the generations which elapsed from the time of the Dorian invasion, or for that matter, even earlier ; and such a record would be preserved quite automatically if it were the practice for each king to attach to himself the number of his generation in descent from Heracles. We know from the inscriptions of the Roman period that descendants of the royal houses in the reign of Hadrian made use of this practice,[1] and it is extremely unlikely that it would be adopted for the first time at so late a date. And after all it is a custom attested as early as the sixth century B.C. among the aristocracy of other Greek states.[2]

Whether the actual names in so long a list as the Spartan ones could be preserved from a period before the introduction of writing is a different matter, and this leads us back to the question of the relative reliability of the two royal pedigrees, since the names in the Agiad line are credible in every case, whereas two of the Eurypontid names (' Prytanis ' and ' Eunomus ') are most improbable, and the order of the five names following Procles varied in different accounts even as early as the fifth century B.C.[3] ' Eunomus ' is clearly a personification of the *Eunomia* derived from Lycurgus ; and as for ' Prytanis ', he seems most likely to have been invented by the author who gave this title to all the persons in the Spartan royal genealogies who were not ἄρχοντες (*i.e.* kings ?), Charon of Lampsacus in his work Πρυτάνεις ἢ ἄρχοντες Λακεδαιμονίων.[4] The reason for the

---

[1] I.G. V, i, 471, 477, 529, 530, 559, 562, 614, 1174.

[2] *Cf.* Herod. II, 143 (Hecataeus of Miletus).

[3] Simonides (the younger) *ap.* Plut. *Lycurg.* 1 makes Lycurgus the son of Prytanis and brother of Eunomus, thus implying the same order of names as in Pausanias' list ; whereas Herodotus gives the order Prytanis, Polydectes, Eunomus, Charillus. The date of this Simonides, who was supposed by some to be the grandson of the more famous one, is given by Suidas as πρὸ τῶν Πελοποννησιακῶν. His works included three books of Γενεαλογίαι.

[4] *Cf.* F.H.G. I, p. xvi, n. 2. The point of the alternative titles, πρυτάνεις ἢ ἄρχοντες, seems to be that not all the names in the lists were necessarily those of kings ; for example the five names preceding Leotychidas in Herodotus' list (VIII, 131) represent ancestors who did not reign. For this class Charon might appropriately use the word πρυτάνεις (*i.e. principes*).

addition of these two fictitious names was evidently the
desire to make the Eurypontid pedigree the same length
as an already existing Agiad one. This does not mean
that the Agiad list is historically correct throughout, but
rather that before the Eurypontid list was made up Agiad
kings had employed a lyric poet or poets to sing their
praises and the Eurypontid kings had not. On the other
hand, the Spartan belief that Eurysthenes in the line of
the Agiadae was the ' elder ' of Aristodemus' twins [1] certainly
arouses suspicion that this royal house existed before the
other, the double kingship being a later innovation.[2] In
any case, the Eurypontid list, when shorn of the later
accretions, appears to go back to the beginning of the period
which may be regarded as historical, roughly speaking, to
the first half of the eighth century. Theopompus, son of
Nicander, was the hero of the first Messenian War as we
know from Tyrtaeus ; beyond him the only known name
seems to have been Charillus, son of Polydectes, the fetter
war against Tegea being assigned to Charillus, but nothing
at all, even by the inventive imagination of later times,
to his father Polydectes. The generation of Charillus takes
us back (on the reckoning of 30 years to a generation) to
c. 810–780 ; beyond that all is dark, as we should expect
from the fact that this was still about a century or rather
more before the appearance of Terpander and the later
poets associated with Sparta. There could be a true folk-
memory going back as far as Charillus, but no further.

But the same argument applies to the list of Agiadae.
Here the generation of Agesilaus, as corresponding in the
numerical series to that of Charillus, is the first which
comes within the scope of folk-memory. The explanation
of the longer list and absence of impossible names in this
case would therefore seem to be that some lyric poet at a
fairly early period in the history of the art provided a pedigree
for them, no doubt incorporating the names of distinguished
members of the family at the time when the poem was
composed. Appropriate occasion for the singing of such
poems must often have arisen at the common meals of the
Andreia, at least on special occasions, when, as we know

---

[1] Herod VI, 52. 7 (cf. 51).

[2] Additional evidence on this point is cited in Appendix V, pp. 471 f.

from Alcman, poems sung to music were a regular part of the proceedings.[1] An example of a seventh-century lyric poem in honour of one member of the Agiad house, the maiden Agido, is seen in Alcman's *Partheneion*. The pedigrees of noble families from many states which occur in Pindar's Odes are doubtless derived partly from similar poems dating from an earlier period, partly from the information which his noble patrons could themselves give him; but the first impulse to the construction of such pedigrees must have come from the poets, in the absence of a real tradition. The reasons for thinking that in the case of the Spartan Agiadae such a list was first produced by an early poet, presumably in the seventh century B.C., are the early disappearance of poets from the scene (the reasons for which have already been given)[2] and the practical difficulty of incorporating in a single lyric poem a very large number of names each representing a new generation.[3] And finally it may be mentioned that Terpander, according to most accounts the earliest of all the lyric poets, was described by the Spartans as τῶν ἡρωικῶν πράξεων ἐπαινέτην,[4] alluding to his songs commemorating their own national heroes, from which it may be deduced that some poem of the kind, preserved at Sparta, was actually attributed to Terpander. That they would be at pains to preserve such poems seems certain from the very lively interest which was still maintained in their own national heroes of the mythical age in the later fifth century.[5]

[1] *Cf.* Alcman *ap.* Strabo, X, 4. 18 (482): φοίναις δὲ καὶ ἐν θιάσοισιν Ἀνδρείων παρὰ δαιτυμόνεσσι Πρέπει παιᾶνα κατάρχειν. 'Praises of great men' are mentioned as a part of the proceedings which followed the common meals in Crete (Dosiadas *ap.* Athen. IV, 143*d*), and in view of the very close resemblance between these and the Spartan ones the custom may well have been observed in the Spartan Syssitia also from a very early period. The translation of such praises into song can scarcely have begun before the early seventh century. In later times the *Akroama* seems to have become a regular feature at the Syssitia (*cf.* Plut. *Cleom.* 13).

[2] *Cf.* pp. 308 f.

[3] Pindar, *Nem.* VI, 15–40, speaks of six generations of the Bassiadae of Aegina, but mentions only alternate names; the rest of this pedigree can be supplied from Herod. IV, 147, and it seems probable that Pindar had the whole list before him from which he made his selection.

[4] *Cf.* Plut. *Inst. Lac.* 17 (238*c*).

[5] *Cf.* Plato, *Hippias Major*, 285B, f. The vast and varied learning of Hippias of Elis left his Spartan audiences cold, but everything he had to say (even though it was specially learnt up for the occasion) on mythology and genealogy was eagerly absorbed.

Herodotus implies that in his time there were several such poems in existence,[1] and it was doubtless from them that Charon of Lampsacus constructed his lists of kings and other members of the royal house.

(iii) The Spartan king-lists as evidence for the date of Lycurgus

There is little difficulty in demonstrating that the various statements found in Greek authors about the date of Lycurgus' reforms are derived either from the supposed connection with the founding of the Olympic festival in 776, or from chronological calculations based on the Spartan king-lists. The various conflicting accounts from this latter source can all be traced to the use of two different standards of reckoning, the normal Greek one of three generations to a century, and a shorter Spartan one, probably of 27 years to a generation.

Consider first the statement of Eratosthenes and his followers that Lycurgus propounded his laws 108 years before the first Olympiad, i.e. 884 B.C.[2] At three generations to a century, this gives exactly twelve generations before 484 B.C., from which date the original calculation was doubtless made. The significance of 484 B.C. is not at present clear ; it might conceivably represent the date of composition of Charon's πρυτάνεις ἢ ἄρχοντες Λακεδαιμονίων.[3] But the significance of the twelve generations back from that point is obvious ; it takes us to the beginning of the reign of ' Eunomus ' in the table of kings.[4] Two divergences from this tradition of the twelve generations now call for examination ; the Agiad account followed by Herodotus makes Lycurgus the uncle of Leobotas[5] or fourteen generations from c. 484 B.C., while Thucydides puts the reforms a little over four hundred years before 404 B.C.,[6] or in other words 320+ years before 484 B.C.

---

[1] Cf. Herod. VI, 52.   [2] See above, pp. 320, 328, n. 2.

[3] But see further below, pp. 342 f., where reasons are given for supposing 485 B.C. to be a significant date in Spartan chronology. Lycurgus' laws may well have been ascribed to the first year of the new period of 100 years (884) rather than to the exact meeting point of two Spartan ' centuries ' (885).   [4] On the significance of the name ' Eunomus ' cf. above, pp. 337f.

[5] Herod. I, 65.

[6] Thuc. I, 18 : ἔτη γάρ ἐστι μάλιστα τετρακόσια καὶ ὀλίγῳ πλείω ἐς τὴν τελευτὴν τοῦδε τοῦ πολέμου ἀφ' οὗ Λακεδαιμόνιοι τῇ αὐτῇ πολιτείᾳ χρῶνται.

Both these statements seem to be derived from a shorter average length of generation than the common reckoning of three to a century, and both may in fact be seen to be deduced from the same reckoning. Thus fourteen generations, covering 400 years (884–484 B.C.), represents 28–29 years to a generation; twelve generations ('Eunomus' to Demaratus inclusive), covering 320+ years, represents an average of slightly under 27 years. An average of precisely 27 years in the last case would imply that Thucydides (I, 18) was referring to 808 B.C.[1] An average of precisely 27 years in the first case might be arrived at by counting in the reign of Leonidas and reckoning fifteen reigns[2] from 885 to 480 B.C.

There is good reason to think that 27 years to a generation was in fact the Spartan reckoning, at least in the fifth century B.C. and possibly later. There was after all no reason whatever why the Spartans should choose the square of ten as a significant period of chronology, seeing that their whole army and tribal organisation rested in early times on multiples of three and nine,[3] and in view of the fact that in their chronological reckoning they are known to have adopted a cycle of nine years, like the Dorians of Crete. For this is clearly implied by the ceremony of watching the night sky every nine years at Sparta to see whether the deposition of a king was called for,[4] and in Crete by the description in the Odyssey of Minos:

ἐννέωρος βασίλευε Διὸς μεγάλου ὀαριστής.[5]

[1] Cf. preceding note.

[2] There is in fact a considerable difference between 'generation' and 'reign' from the chronological point of view (see further below, p. 342) but the ancients appear frequently to have overlooked this fact. Cf. e.g. Herod. II, 142, where the equation of reigns with γενεαί leads to the conclusion that the first king of Egyptian Thebes began to reign 11,340 (sic) years before the invasion of Sennacherib. The same confusion appears ibid. II, 143 (also relating to Thebes); I, 7 (Lydian chronology).

[3] Cf. pp. 392 f. and Jewish reckoning by squares of seven.

[4] Cf. Plut. Agis, 11, for an attempted revival of the practice in the reign of Agis IV. δι' ἐτῶν ἐννέα in this passage must mean (on the analogy of δι' ἔτους, δι' ἐνιαυτοῦ) 'after the lapse of every nine years', as also in Plut. De Defect. Orac. 21; not 'after every eight years', as sometimes supposed (cf. Roscher, s.v. Apollon, p. 424; Parke, The Delphic Oracle, p. 11).

[5] Od. XIX, 179. The word ἐννέωρος, which obviously cannot here mean 'nine years old', has puzzled the editors, but is satisfactorily explained by the parallel Spartan usage. Possible ethnological analogies are discussed by Frazer, Golden Bough,[3] Part III (The Dying God), pp. 58 f.

But the clearest indication that the early Dorians in general made use of a system of multiples of three and nine in preference to the number ten and multiples of ten is in a sacrificial calendar from Cos,[1] which directs each of the three Dorian tribes Hylleis, Pamphyloi and Dymanes to provide nine oxen, these being for each tribe ' one from each ninth ' (ἐνάτα)[2] (sc. of the φυλή). But a few lines further on, each tribe is directed to supply three extra oxen, one from each χιλιαστύς,[3] in case previous sets of three prove displeasing to the god. It is clear from this that the χιλιαστύς was a third of the tribe and that originally at least it was not a cube of ten but a cube of nine. It may be concluded that early tribal organisation at Sparta was exactly similar from the division by thirds and ninths (representing an early army organisation) which was prescribed in the celebration of the Carnean festival.[4] There are therefore good grounds for thinking that this system of reckoning was characteristic of the early Dorians in general. The notion of a hundred as a basic number may easily have come to the rest of Greece through their monetary system ; but since the Spartans did not introduce any currency until a very late date in their history, the habit of reckoning a hundred drachmae to the mina cannot have influenced them. It is therefore *a priori* probable that for the Spartans the significant longer period in chronology was represented by the square of nine rather than the square of ten, and that for them 81 years stood for three generations (γενεαί), an approximation not so very far from the truth whether applied to generations in the true sense [5] or to the average length of reigns.

Further support for the hypothesis of an 81-year cycle comes from a Spartan inscription of A.D. 163 which proves this year to have been one of special commemoration by

---

[1] Ditt. *Syll.*[3] 1025 ; Paton and Hicks, *Inscriptions of Cos*, 37. The date assigned by Dittenberger is fourth or third century, B.C.

[2] *Ibid.* 1. 6 : βοῦν ἐξ ἐνάτας ἐκάστας ; cf. Paton, *ibid.* p. 84.

[3] *Ibid.* 1. 17.

[4] On the number of soldiers to each tent at the Carnean festival see further p. 392.

[5] Generation, *i.e.* the average length of time by which the last surviving member of each group of members of the family who stand in the same degree of descent to the supposed common ancestor outlives the corresponding last surviving member of the group representing the preceding degree of descent from the common ancestor.

public banquets lasting for nine days, and involving also the revival of the obscure and obviously ancient office of ἀγρέτης.[1] Now this date fits in with the conclusion of one of the regular Spartan nine-year periods for which there is evidence in pre-Roman times,[2] and would also fit into a series of 81-year cycles of which 242 B.C. would mark the end of one. This was the year chosen by Agis IV, who had already been reigning for several years, to propound his scheme for the thorough revival of the traditional Lycurgan constitution. On the same hypothesis 485 B.C. would be included in the series, and reason has already been given for thinking that this was the date from which the Spartans reckoned back exactly twelve generations to the beginning of the reign of ' Eunomus ', in other words, to the institution of the Eunomia and the traditional constitution. A final argument in favour of supposing that the Spartans held ' secular ' commemorations of some kind every 81 years is that in the Roman Secular Games, supposedly derived from the Spartan colony of Tarentum,[3] the peculiar significance of three times nine was preserved in the choirs

---

[1] I.G. V, i, 1346 : ἡ ἱερὰ [γερου]σία Γ. Ἰούλιον Ἐπαφρόδειτον ἀγρετεύσαντα τὸ ρϙδ΄ ἔτος καὶ δόντα ἑκάστῳ γέροντι νομῆς δηνάρια δέκα καὶ τὰς ἐννέα οὐχὶ κατὰ τόν νόμον, ἀλλὰ δειπν[ή]σαντα λαμπρῶς καὶ τῇ δεκάτῃ τὴν πόλιν ὅλην, τὸν ἑαυτῆς εὐεργέτην, ἀνέστησεν. ψ(ηφίσματι) γ(ερουσίας). Kolbe is undoubtedly right in preferring to interpret ' the 194th year ' as A.D. 163, dating from 31 B.C., rather than A.D. 48, dating from 146 B.C. The early adoption of emperor worship at Sparta and the partiality of Augustus for the city make it much more likely that the Actian era was introduced and the Macedonian era discarded in 31 B.C. The main claims of Epaphroditus to be honoured with a statue appear to be (1) that he gave the Gerontes 10 denarii each, (2) that he gave a public banquet at his own expense the day after the normal nine days' feast, which was presumably paid for out of state funds. Hesych. s.v. explains ἀγρέτης as ἡγεμών. It is clearly derived from ἀγείρω and so may mean ' assembler ' or ' musterer ', implying an office parallel in this respect to that of the Roman censors, and involving an estimation of the number of Spartan citizens.

[2] Cf. Plut. Agis, 11.

[3] This is not the place to enter into the controversy as to whether the Secular Games were in fact derived from Tarentum, but a strong argument in favour of this (apart from the repetition of the magic number three times nine) is the statement of the Augustan and Severan Acta Ludorum Saecularium that the games were to be celebrated Achivo ritu, i.e. according to the rites of Magna Graecia. Tarentum, though not precisely ' Achaean ' itself, was surrounded by other Greek cities which claimed this origin, and the description was doubtless near enough to the truth to satisfy the Romans at the time when the Secular Games were introduced or remodelled.

of twenty-seven girls and twenty-seven boys [1] who sang hymns to Apollo and Diana and in the offerings of nine each of three different kinds of cake, [2] all of which, be it noted, have Greek names.

The hypothesis of a regularly celebrated 81-year cycle (and if the Spartans had such an institution at all, it is certain from their tenacious and meticulous conservatism that they would observe it consistently and regularly) would clearly make a great difference to our estimate of the reliability of Spartan official chronology, at least in so far as it concerned the most outstanding turning point of all their history, namely, the introduction of the Lycurgan constitution. But before deciding which of the various versions of the date of the reforms is to be preferred, one more variation remains to be noticed.

The writers who follow the tradition represented by list B of the Eurypontid kings [3] put the Lycurgan reforms in the beginning of the tenth generation before that of Cleomenes and Demaratus instead of in the twelfth or fifteenth, namely in the reign of Archelaus in the Agiad line, and in that of Charillus (now supposed to be a contemporary of Archelaus) [4] in the Eurypontid line. [5] It is to be observed that in the later form of the Eurypontid list Charillus has been moved down a generation by means of eliminating Anaxandridas son of Theopompus, [6] and inserting at the upper end ' Soos ' next after Procles. The name Soos suggests misinterpretation of some poet ; [7] it seems to have no early authority. The purpose of moving down Charillus is evidently to bring into line the belief that the reforms occurred at the beginning of the tenth generation from Demaratus with the earlier tradition (found in the list which makes Charillus son of Eunomus, and in Herodotus' story of immediate expansion into Arcadia after the institution of Eunomia) [8] that the reign of Charillus marked

[1] Cf. I.L.S. 5050, l. 147.
[2] Ibid. ll. 115, 117, 139–141. For the libi and pthoes, cf. Athen. 647d ; popana (πόπανα) are frequently mentioned in Greek authors.
[3] Cf. above, p. 334.　　　　[4] Plut. Lycurg. 5.
[5] Arist. Pol. II, 10. 2.　　　　[6] Cf. Paus. IV, 15. 3.
[7] It might for example arise out of some such line as ἐκ σοῦ γὰρ γένος ἐσμέν, ἀτὰρ καὶ παῖδες ἐκείνου (cf. Cleanthes, fr. 537) intended to explain why the descendants of Procles were not called after him Proclidae, but after Eurypon, Eurypontidae.　　　　[8] Cf. above, pp. 330 ff.

the beginning of a new period in the constitution. But how explain the view that the reforms were made at the beginning of the tenth generation reckoning back from Demaratus ? The obvious clue is Thucydides' statement that they occurred a little more than 400 years before 404 B.C., for ten generations back from 480 B.C. at three generations to a century would give 813 B.C. The whole account in fact is produced by juggling with the king-lists at a later date in order to fit in with the statement of Thucydides, and so possesses no independent chronological authority.

If we consider the other three versions which have already been mentioned, two of them may be seen to be ultimately dependent upon the third. Part at least of the basic assumption is that the reforms occurred twelve generations before 485 B.C. ; hence the insertion of the name ' Eunomus ' before the name of Charillus into the Eurypontid list in its earlier (fifth century) form. The date 884 B.C. is produced by translating twelve generations into the common Greek reckoning of three generations to a century. The Agiad tradition recorded by Herodotus, which made Lycurgus uncle of Leobotas, arises out of the translation of 405 years (885–480 B.C.) [1] into fifteen Spartan generations [2] of 27 years each, and is therefore ' third from the truth '.

But Thucydides' version seems to preserve a purely Spartan account, implying a lapse of twelve generations of 27 years each to 485 B.C., an account which is worthy of greater respect not only because it is of respectable antiquity so far as the ' twelve generations ' are concerned, but because it is purely Spartan, uninfluenced by outside literary tradition. For after all no outsider could possibly discover the truth about such a question if it was not known to the Spartans themselves. The claim to consideration of the version preserved by Thucydides is further strengthened by its obvious independence of the king-lists ; for

---

[1] The Agiad claim must first have been made *after* the insertion of the name Eunomus into the Eurypontid list, for at the time of Charon of Lampsacus, the probable author of the list in this form, the Agiadae were much the more influential of the royal houses, and if their claim to Lycurgus had already been established the ' Eunomus ' tradition could never have been attached to the rival royal house.

[2] Counting Leonidas ; *cf.* above, p. 334.

had the ' twelve generations ' been arrived at in the original
Spartan account by counting back kings to the one whose
name was associated with the reforms, the numerous differences of opinion about the name of the king could never
have arisen. No chronology based on the average lengths
of actual reigns can be accurate in detail except by accident,
in view of the wide differences in the length of the various
reigns, and in any case 27 years (not to speak of $33\frac{1}{3}$) is much
too high an average, as may be seen from the lists of historical Spartan kings. But since the Lycurgus-tradition
now being considered did not attach the law-giver to any
particular reign, the ' twelve generations ' in question must
have been purely formal or nominal ones, arrived at, as
we may justifiably suspect, by subdividing four 81-year
periods each into its three magic twenty-sevens. The
hypothesis is not at present capable of absolute proof, but
reasons have already been given for regarding it as a likely
one. And on this basis there could be a real and reliable
tradition at Sparta about the date of the Lycurgan reforms ;
some simple method of recording the passage of years is
known to have been adopted to determine the incidence
of each ninth year, and therefore a machinery was in
existence by which the completion of nine of these periods
could be determined. It was in accordance with the
whole mentality of the Spartan state to cling unshakably
to such a procedure once it had been instituted, and the
parallel custom of observing nine-year periods in Crete
suggests that in Sparta it was of high antiquity. There is
therefore no difficulty whatever in supposing that in 728
B.C. Sparta marked the end of the first period of nine times
nine years from the Lycurgan reforms by special feasts and
other celebrations, and that similar celebrations marked
the years 647, 566, 485 and so on. The celebration of 485
B.C. was destined to have exceptional effect upon later
chronological tradition because this was the one by which
Charon of Lampsacus would be influenced in the composition
of his πρυτάνεις ἢ ἄρχοντες Λακεδαιμονίων. It has been
shown that the resulting non-Spartan chronology is deprived of authority and full of inconsistencies ; the general
conclusion to which this examination of the sources leads is
that there are fairly cogent reasons for dating the Lycurgan

reforms to 809 B.C. But except at the long intervals when they were bidden by the voice of authority to commemorate these reforms, individual Spartans were not likely to have any clear idea of when they took place ; in this way we may explain the reappearance of the true tradition, after a long interval of many and various errors, in 404 B.C. which marked the end of another 81-year period.

CHAPTER X

THE SPARTAN ARMY ORGANISATION
AND THE POPULATION PROBLEM

BOTH from the modern and from the ancient points of view, the Spartan army organisation and the population question are closely bound up together. We have here to deal with two aspects of the same general problem, which neither could in antiquity, nor can at the present time, be considered in isolation from one another. The modern historians in general find in the army organisation of Sparta evidence of a general downward trend of the numbers of Spartan citizens over a long period, and would explain the eventual political collapse in this way.[1] They have the explicit support of Aristotle for their interpretation.

The Spartans themselves, however, consciously sought by various means to guard against the danger of a declining population, and consequent decline in military strength, both by a system of rewards for citizens who had large families, and penalties for those who remained unmarried,[2] and (as the evidence from the Roman period has demonstrated) by the carefully controlled admission of individuals of non-privileged classes to full citizenship.[3] The marriage-laws were also framed with the primary intention of securing the greatest possible number of fertile unions.[4] Whether these precautions entirely failed in their purpose, and if so, why they failed, is still a matter of some general interest even at the present time ; the more so, in that there is no reason to suspect a general decline of population throughout Greece during the period in question. The insignificant town of Phlius, for example, is stated by Xenophon to have

---

[1] Cf. Grundy, *Thucydides and the History of His Age* (1911), pp. 216 f. ; Cavaignac, *Klio* XII (1912), pp. 261 f.

[2] Arist. *Pol.* II, 9. 18 (rewards) ; [Xen.] *Resp. Lac.* IX, 5 ; Plut. *Lycurg.* 15, *De Amore Prolis*, 2 ; Clearchus *ap.* Athen. XIII, 555c (penalties).

[3] Cf. pp. 100 f.   [4] Cf. [Xen.] *Resp. Lac.* I, 7–9.

had a citizen population of at least 5,000 [1] at a time when Sparta, though still mistress of the Peloponnese, had (according to Aristotle) only about 1,000.

There can be no doubt that Aristotle himself believed his figure of 'less than a thousand' to account for the whole of the free citizen population of Sparta as distinct from the Perioikoi and the Helots.[2] Cavaignac supposes him to be referring to his own time, about thirty years after Leuctra,[3] and sees evidence of a further drop in the size of the population from the time of that battle, when the whole number of 'Spartiatae' of military age seems to have been rather more than 1,100.[4] If we accept the view that Aristotle's figure is an approximately correct estimate of the total number of Spartan citizens, and does not refer to an aristocratic section of them only, we must suppose, with Cavaignac, that the Spartan citizens who fought in the battle of Leuctra represented less than one-third of the total hoplite force employed,[5] the rest of the number being made up by Perioikoi. To this interpretation there is the fatal objection that the numbers in Spartan hoplite armies remained in the middle of the fourth century as high as ever,[6] in spite of the fact that those of the Perioikoi who did not openly revolt after Leuctra refused to obey the summons to army service,[7] while the Helots all revolted outright.[8] The alternative is to suppose that Aristotle is mistaken in his interpretation of the meaning of 'Spartiatae',[9] and in fact it seems unlikely, in view of his usual reliance on the works of others for his historical details, that he has

[1] Cf. Xen. Hell. V, iii, 16 : πόλει . . . πλέον τεντακισχιλίων ἀνδρῶν. The number presumably represents the whole population including women and children, not merely the members of the Ecclesia. But there were in addition at least 1,000 Phliasian exiles of military age (Xen. ibid.).

[2] Cf. Pol. II, 9. 16 : τοιγαροῦν δυναμένης τῆς χώρας χιλίους ἱππεῖς τρέφειν καὶ πεντακοσίους καὶ ὁπλίτας τρισμυρίους, οὐδὲ χίλιοι τὸ πλῆθος ἦσαν.

[3] Cf. Klio, XII, p. 271.

[4] I.e. 700 in the four Morae which fought (Xen. Hell. VI, iv, 15), + 350 for the two other πολιτικαὶ μόραι, + c. 100 in the age-classes 55–60, which did not fight (ibid. 17). Cavaignac's proposed total of 1,296 (Klio, ibid.) implies that the 55–60 age-classes formed an impossibly high proportion of the whole (cf. Thuc. V, 64. 3).

[5] Xenophon implies a total hoplite force of 2,304 at Leuctra (4 Morae, each of 16 Enomotiae containing each 36 men ; cf. Hell. VI, iv, 12, 17, with Resp. Lac. XI, 4). Of these 700 were 'Spartiatae' (Hell. VI, iv, 15).

[6] See further below, pp. 352 f.   [7] Cf. Xen. Hell. VI, v, 25, 32 ; VII, ii, 2.

[8] Ibid. VII, ii, 2.   [9] See further, pp. 351 f.

any information independent of that preserved in Xenophon, from whose statements about the numbers at Leuctra his own figure of ' less than a thousand ' could easily be deduced.[1]   But there are grounds for thinking that Aristotle's information on this subject came only indirectly from Xenophon, through Ephorus.[2]

Aristotle cites by way of contrast the alleged figure of 10,000 for the one-time number of the Spartan citizen population, without either giving his authority or appearing to believe in it himself.[3]   But since Plutarch ascribes to Lycurgus' reorganisation the figure of 9,000 citizens,[4] we may suspect that the so-called ' Ten Thousand ' really represented nine χιλιαστύες, these being in fact not cubes of ten, but the cubes of nine found among the Dorians in early times ;[5] in which case the actual figure implied would be 9^4, or 6,561.   This hypothesis finds some support in the fact that both Aristotle and Plutarch in the passages in question give 30,000 as the number of the Perioikoi ; it looks therefore as if Plutarch has preserved the earlier and Aristotle the later version of the same tradition.   It will be demonstrated later that the theoretical total 6,561 (an approximation only) accords remarkably well with the general estimate of the total size of the male citizen population as late as about 400 B.C., as we can deduce it from other figures given by Xenophon,[6] the size of the hoplite field army at the same time being as nearly as possible half this number.[7]   We may well ask whether the 5,000 hoplites mentioned by

[1] I.e. 300 survivors of the battle (700-400), + 350 in the same age-classes for the two πολιτικαὶ μόραι which did not fight, + a few hundreds made up by those of the age-groups 55-60, those below 20 or over 60, and the unfit.

[2] Ephorus is the most likely common source of Pol. II, 9. 15 f., and of Plut. Agis, 5, in both of which the Rhetra of Epitadeus authorising alienation of κλῆροι is assigned as the real cause of the decline in the number of Spartan citizens.   The source in question evidently repeated the figures given by Xenophon for the battle of Leuctra (the ' single blow ' referred to in Pol. II, 9. 16), since Plutarch concludes that ' not more than 700 ' were left (i.e. 700 + 350 + ' oldest ' - 400).

[3] Cf. Pol. II, 9. 17 : εἴτ᾽ ἐστὶν ἀληθῆ ταῦτα εἴτε μή.

[4] Plut. Lycurg. 8.   [5] Cf. above, pp. 341 f.   [6] See below, pp. 354 f.

[7] I.e. 7 Morae (including Sciritae, for whom see below, pp. 375 f., excluding ' Brasideans and Neodamodeis ', who fought at Mantinea in 418 but appear from their absence on later occasions to have been reserve troops) of c. 512 men each when excluding ' oldest and youngest '.   For details of numbers see further below, pp. 384 f., 388 f.

Herodotus[1] as the full complement of the Spartan field army at the time of Xerxes' invasion is not to be explained simply as half the theoretical ' Ten Thousand ', which is so unlikely to have been ten thousand at all.

Whatever may be the truth about the ' Ten Thousand ', modern exponents of the view that the Spartan citizen population rapidly declined prefer to start from the number 5,000 given by Herodotus (accepting it at its face value) and from the same author's quotation of a statement made by the exiled Spartan King Demaratus to Xerxes, that Sparta was ' a city of eight thousand male inhabitants (ἀνδρῶν), all the equals of those who fought at Thermopylae '.[2] The higher figure was doubtless assumed by Herodotus to include those over military age and the unfit ; it is his 5,000 ' Spartiatae ', who must be taken as the basis for comparison with the much smaller number (between three and four thousand) available in 418,[3] of whom a high proportion were apparently not ' Spartiatae ',[4] and the total of 3,456[5] available in 371, of whom as we have seen less than one-third were ' Spartiatae '.

The whole crux of the question lies in the meaning of the term ' Spartiatae '. Herodotus obviously uses it as the widest possible term to denote Spartan citizens as distinct from Perioikoi or Helots.[6] Many other Greek authors adopt the same usage, including Aristotle, in the passage of the *Politics* which has already been referred to.[7] Modern authorities have not unnaturally accepted the term in the same sense.[8]

But there are several difficulties in the way of accepting this as the accurate technical usage. To explain the supposed sudden and permanent drop in numbers in the fifth century (5,000 to c. 1,480 in the 20–60 age-groups between

[1] Herod. IX, 10.   [2] *Ibid.* VII, 234.
[3] *Viz.* seven main regiments of 512 each, and in addition 600 Sciritae, See further below, p. 384.
[4] At Sphacteria in 425, in an apparently representative selection of 292 prisoners, 120 were ' Spartiatae ' (Thuc. IV, 38).
[5] *I.e.* 2,304 in four Morae, + 1,152 for the remaining two Morae.
[6] *Cf.* Herod. VII, 235 ; IX, 19, etc.
[7] *Pol.* II, 9. 17, 18. *Cf.* (Xen.) *Resp. Lac.* V, 2 ; Isocr. *Panath.* 171, 173, 179, etc. ; Diod. XI, 64 ; XV, 90.
[8] *Cf.* Grundy, Cavaignac, *ibid.*

480 and 418 B.C.),[1] much has been made of the earthquake
of 464 B.C.[2] But the detailed accounts of this in Diodorus
and Plutarch contain so many improbable features and fantastic inventions that it is reasonable to suspect gross
exaggeration of the effects of the disaster. More than 20,000
' Lacedaemonians ' are said to have been killed in Sparta
alone ;[3] yet Archidamus is said to have marched out the
Spartan army in time to save it,[4] and the young men exer-
cising in the gymnasium were also saved by running out
in chase of a hare.[5] In these accounts of loss of life, these
later authors appear to assume that Sparta was a considerable city, with crowded streets of houses and many
public buildings, whereas it is clear from Thucydides'
description that in the fifth century the population lived
dispersedly over the countryside, the buildings of Sparta
itself being few and very humble in character.[6] Houses
were probably built either of wood, or of sun-baked brick
with thatched roofs ;[7] that they were more than one
storey high is most improbable. The notion that the
inhabitants were crushed by collapsing walls[8] is anachronistic ; in any case we know that the whole population,
women and children included, prided themselves on their
outdoor life. Later authors doubtless exaggerated the
loss of life in the earthquake in order to account for the
Helot revolt. But no such assumption is necessary ; temporary dislocation of supplies of food and weapons would
encourage the insurgents to seize their chance, even if
Spartan loss of life was inconsiderable.

A greater and indeed fatal difficulty to the view that
the 1,050 ' Spartiatae ' in the army of 371 B.C. represent
almost the total male population is the reappearance of a

---

[1] Assuming that the proportion of ' Spartiatae ' to others at Mantinea
was the same as at Sphacteria (c. 120 : 292 ; cf. Thuc. IV, 38), the total
number of Spartiatae in the six citizen Morae at their full strength (i.e.
age-groups 20–60, including ' oldest and youngest ' to the number of one-
sixth of the total) would be 1,473.   [2] Cf. Cavaignac, ibid. p. 272.
[3] Diod. XI, 63.   [4] Diod. ibid.; Plut. Cim. 16.
[5] Plut. ibid.   [6] Thuc. I, 10.
[7] The use of any tools in roof-building, other than an axe, was forbidden
at Sparta (Plut. Lycurg. 13, De esu carn. 6, Apophth. Lacon. 227B, 285C,
Reg. et Imperat. Apophth. 189E, citing a Rhetra of Lycurgus).   Numerous
roof-tiles of c. 200 B.C. onwards (I.G. V, i. 850 f.) suggest that the rule
was relaxed later.   [8] Cf. Diod. XI, 63.

Spartan army able to defeat the combined forces of Arcadia without loss in 367,[1] after the Helots and Perioikoi had revolted ; nor could Sparta have sent 1,000 hoplites under Agesilaus to Egypt five years later,[2] had the total male citizen population of military age been under 1,000 at the time. Diodorus gives details of the force with which the Spartans defeated the Argives, Thebans, and Sicyonians in 352. Their enemies had at least 11,000 hoplites [3] and 500 cavalry ; the Spartan army defeated them in consequence of superior discipline and quality, even though, including 3,000 Phocians, it was still only half the size of the opposing force. Since about the same time 1,000 Spartan hoplites were fighting in Phocis,[4] this implies a Spartan hoplite army of approximately equal size to that which fought at Mantinea in 418, or existed before the battle of Leuctra in 371. Six Morae of between five and six hundred men each were apparently still in existence.[5]

Yet another difficulty in the way of accepting ' Spartiatae' as the equivalent of ' citizens of Sparta ' in all cases arises from Aristotle's explanation of the great drop in numbers. If, as he says, alienation of the citizen land-lot was the cause, how are we to explain the alleged appearance of Perioikoi in the army in preference to Spartiates ? Surely the trained soldiers of citizen origin, even though landless, would be preferred to Perioikoi, especially in a period when on account of the smallness of her citizen population Sparta had long known that (in Grundy's words) she had ' a wolf by the throat '. It may well be asked what did happen to the Spartans who ceased to be able to pay their contribution to the Syssitia, if their own state repudiated them so utterly as Aristotle would have us suppose. The supposition is in fact impossible. No ancient author goes so far as to say that those soldiers in the πολιτικαὶ μόραι who

---

[1] Cf. Diod. XV, 72.　　　　　　　　[2] Ibid. XV, 92.

[3] 4,000 Thebans + the Argives πανδημεί (ibid. XVI, 39). Argos sent 7,000 men to the battle of Corinth (Xen. Hell. IV, ii. 17).

[4] Diod. XVI, 37.

[5] It is commonly assumed that Xenophon's reference to ' the twelve Lochoi ' after Leuctra (Hell. VII, iv, 20 ; v, 10) implies that the Spartan army was halved in size in consequence of the defeat. On this point see further below, p. 356.

were not ' Spartiatae ' were Perioikoi.[1] The obvious alternative is to suppose that some of them at least were Spartan citizens who had lost their land-lots. Xenophon certainly implies that all were still citizens (πολῖται) of some kind as late as 367 B.C.[2]

In other words, the term ' Spartiatae ' has a technical usage distinct from the popular one. In its more accurate sense, it must denote a class of Spartan citizens with higher privileges than the rest. This is an idea which will cause no surprise in view of the various grades of Spartan society revealed to us by the inscriptions of the Roman period. But there is also a definite instance of the use of the term *Spartiates* in its technical sense in Xenophon's account of the conspiracy of Cinadon (397 B.C.). Asked to count the number of ' Spartiatae ' present in the Agora, the Spartan who eventually gave away the secret replied by counting one of the kings, the five Ephors, the Gerontes, and a few others, making up a total of about forty.[3] The mention of the king and the magistrates, together with an additional number of about 4,000, implies that a meeting of the Apella was in progress, presided over by the Ephors. The spy obviously could not count the 4,000 individually ; this number must represent an approximate figure already known.

This account implies that the ' Spartiatae ' were in general the office-holding class. That a considerable number of them were not in the Agora at the time is indicated by the reference made in the same passage to the hated landowners of the country estates, each surrounded by a hostile crowd of Helots, Inferiors (ὑπομείονες) and Perioikoi. Unless Aristotle's identification of the Spartiatae with the land-holding class is completely mistaken, we must in fact suppose that the great majority of the Spartiatae (using the word in its technical sense) at the time of the conspiracy of Cinadon were absent from Sparta superintending

[1] Little importance can be attached to the statement of Diodorus (XII, 63) that of 300 prisoners taken at Sphacteria, 120 were Spartiatae and 180 σύμμαχοι. The figures are obviously taken from Thuc. IV, 38 (*cf.* above, p. 351, n. 4) substituting the round number 300 for Thucydides' 292, and the assumption that those who were not Spartiatae were allies (not, be it noted, Perioikoi) is evidently due to Ephorus or Diodorus.

[2] *Cf. Hell.* VII, iv, 21 : χαλεπῶς δὲ ἡ τῶν Λακεδαιμονίων πόλις φέρουσα ἐπὶ τῇ πολιορκίᾳ τῶν πολιτῶν (*i.e.* the three Lochoi left to garrison Cromnus).

[3] Xen. *Hell.* III, iii, 5 ; *cf.* Part I, pp. 54 f.

the working of their estates and keeping the subject population under control.   In view of the numbers of the Spartiatae who fought at Leuctra, this would account for rather more than 1,000 men af the age-groups 20–55, in addition to those over fifty-five and the unfit (the last presumably a small number).

But to the 4,000 in the Agora at the time of Cinadon's conspiracy a considerable addition must also be made on account of other male citizens who were not in the technical sense Spartiatae ; for attendance in the Spartan Agora was forbidden to citizens under the age of thirty,[1] and in all probability was also excused to citizens over the age of sixty.[2]   The limitation of citizenship at Athens in 411 to τοῖς δυναμένοις καὶ τοῖς σώμασιν καὶ τοῖς χρήμασι λειτουργεῖν, and who were over thirty years of age, involved a reduction from about 13,000 [3] to 9,000.   This parallel suggests a total male citizen population at Sparta in 397, exclusive of Spartiatae (in the technical sense) of c. 5,000–5,500.   Together with the Spartiatae a total citizen population (of men between 20 and 60) of between 6,000 and 7,000 seems to be indicated.   This leaves a considerable reserve of manpower in addition to those included in the first-line field army.

This assessment of the numbers which, it may be noted, is curiously close to the figure suggested by the nine χιλιαστύες ascribed to Lycurgus, brings no obvious improbabilities in its wake.   It does not ask us to believe that under 1,500 Spartans of military age (the number indicated for the ' Spartiatae ' in 418) continued to hold down a hostile subject population of great size, defeated Athens, founded and governed an overseas empire, engaged in many military expeditions far from home, and imposed their will on Greece.   It does not require us to account for the reduction of the total population by 70 per cent. (assuming Herodotus' ' 5,000 ' to be approximately correct) [4] in the period between 480 and the loss of Sphacteria.   On the positive side, the

---

[1] Plut. *Lycurg.* 25.   [2] *Cf.* above, pp. 18, 136.

[3] This was the number of hoplites (zeugites) in the age-groups 20–50 in 431 (Thuc. II, 13).   It was probably considerably reduced by the plague and by losses in war.   On the other hand, allowance must also be made for zeugites of the 50–60 class, over the age for field service.

[4] *Cf.* above, pp. 350 f.

new figure for Spartan man-power makes it possible to explain how Sparta was able to maintain the hoplite garrisons in the territory of the Perioikoi to which Thucydides and Xenophon occasionally refer ;[1] it also, in particular, enables us to account for Xenophon's statement (otherwise inexplicable) that a Spartan hoplite army of 6,000 fought at Corinth in 394.[2] The probability is that a large proportion of the ' Lacedaemonians ' in question on this occasion were Perioikoi fighting in separate regiments, as at Plataea. But further information is lacking on this point. The new figure for the total male citizen population also explains how a hoplite army of the same size as before could still be raised in the years following the losses at Leuctra, when non-citizen sources could no longer be drawn upon.[3]

It has been generally supposed, however, that Xenophon's allusion to ' the twelve Lochoi ' in the years after 371 [4] implies that the total size of the citizen army was halved in consequence of the defeat. But the name ' Lochos ' was obviously very loosely applied in the Spartan army organisation, being used of the Lochos Skirites of 600 men, of the quarters of Morae (c. 128 men) and of the four regiments [5] of Eirenes, which last, since all the Eirenes together made up not more than two year-classes, must have been a good deal smaller still.[6] Since no direct information has come down to us about the internal organisation of the Spartan army in the period after Leuctra, it may easily be that some purely tactical re-grouping was introduced in order to overcome the deficiencies, especially in the depth of the phalanx, which had revealed themselves at Leuctra. The original quarters of Morae (Lochoi of c. 128) may henceforward have been grouped in pairs to which the name of Lochos was transferred, giving twelve Lochoi altogether. A regiment of precisely this size, variously

---

[1] Thuc. II, 25. 2 (Methone), IV, 53. 2 (Cythera) 55. 1 (in general) ; Xen. Hell. VI, v. 24 (forts on the northern frontier of Laconia). Some at least of these last were Neodamodeis, but it seems unlikely that all the rest were, in view of their doubtful loyalty (cf. ibid. III, iii, 6).

[2] Xen. Hell. IV, ii, 16.   [3] Cf. above, p. 353.

[4] Cf. above, p. 353, n. 5.   [5] Cf. p. 391.

[6] Probably 48 or 56 to a Lochos. See further, p. 391. In the Hellenistic army organisation, the name Lochos appears to have been kept for the single file in depth from front to back of the phalanx, whatever number it contained. Cf. Arr. Tact. V, 4, 5, etc.

named σύνταγμα or ξεναγία, was in fact one of the usual constituents of the typical Hellenistic army.[1] Since all the world was anxious in that period to employ a Spartan as its *condottiere*,[2] a Spartan military unit may easily account for the general name ξεναγία given to the regiment of 256 men.

It is instructive to compare the typical Greek army of later times with the Spartan army as it existed in the late fifth and early fourth centuries B.C. In all other respects than in the existence of the unit of 256, and in the doubling of the depth of the hoplite ranks, the ' old Greek ' army described by Arrian [3] corresponds exactly to the Spartan organisation as Thucydides describes it at the battle of Mantinea, or as the pseudo-Xenophon alludes to it early in the fourth century. Both in Arrian's account and that of the earlier authors, the smallest unit is of 32 men, the next double this size (called ' Fifties ', πεντηκοστύες) ; these again were grouped in pairs, which were in turn grouped in fours to form the large unit of 512 men.[4] But whereas at Mantinea there is no trace of the unit of 256, and the depth of the whole line is eight men, in the arrangement described by Arrian the normal depth of the line is sixteen men,[5] and the ξεναγία of 256 has made its appearance. This change would most easily be produced by combining the various units in pairs for the purpose of forming the battle-line, so that in battle formation the smallest tactical unit would now be the ' Pentekostys ' or double-Enomotia of 64 (drawn up sixteen deep and four on the front) instead of the Enomotia of 32 (eight deep and four on the front), while the place formerly occupied by the Pentekostys would be taken by the regiment of 128, and the place of the twenty-four quarters of Morae (formerly of 128 men each) would be taken by twelve units of 256 men. In the

---

[1] Arr. *Tact.* X, 3.

[2] A selection of these may be found in Front, *Strat.* II, iii.

[3] *Cf.* Arr. *Tact.* XXXII, 2.

[4] *Ibid.* X, 1–5 ; *cf.* Thuc. V, 68. 3 (where the name πεντηκοστύς is mistakenly given to the division of 128 men), (Xen.) *Resp. Lac.* XI, 4 (implying 64 for the πεντηκοστύς, 128 for the Lochos, and 512 for the Mora). The confusion shown in the use of the name ' Lochos ' has already been noted ; see also below, p. 384, n. 6. The name ' Pentekontarchia ' for a regiment of 64 is mentioned by Arrian (*Tact.* XIV, 3) in connection with the organisation of light-armed troops. [5] *Tact.* IX, 6 ; X, 4 ; *cf.* Thuc. V, 68. 3.

course of the fourth century much greater use of cavalry
and peltasts posted on the wings made up for the shortening
of the hoplite-phalanx implied in this doubling process.

One reason, then, for thinking that the ' twelve Lochoi '
alluded to by Xenophon for the period after Leuctra testifies
to the introduction of new double units is that the later
Hellenistic organisation, which is so evidently based upon
the Spartan, can be shown to have possessed this double
unit. Another reason for thinking that it was the Spartan
experience at the battle of Leuctra which led to the change
being made is that the Spartans on that occasion made an
exceptional disposition of their troops, drawing up each
Enomotia in three files instead of the usual four, in the
effort to overcome the disadvantage of their inadequate depth
as compared with the Theban hoplite phalanx of fifty deep.[1]
The enormous depth of the Theban phalanx at Leuctra
apparently did not extend to the whole of their battle-line,
but was intended merely to secure an overwhelmingly
strong block against the Spartans on the right wing ; [2] nor
did this exaggerated depth recommend itself to the Macedonians,[3] any more than to the Greeks, as an arrangement
to be universally adopted. But it seems reasonable to
suppose that the advantages of greater depth (and consequently of greater weight) throughout the hoplite line were
first realised after the Spartan defeat at Leuctra, and that
the Spartans themselves then took the obvious course of
halving the length, and doubling the depth, of their heavy-
armed infantry. Xenophon mentions that Agesilaus, campaigning in Arcadia soon after Leuctra, doubled the depth
of his hoplite phalanx, making it from eighteen to twenty
deep, effecting the deployment just outside a mountain pass.[4]
This result was achieved by dividing the whole marching
column into two halves and drawing up the whole of the
rear, from right to left, behind the first half of the column.
It would have the effect of stationing two separate Enomotiae
one behind another, so that the unity of each file from
front to back would be destroyed. But the unity of the
files in depth (normally sixteen men) was an essential feature

[1] Xen. *Hell.* VI, iv. 12. [2] *Cf.* Arr. *Tact.* XI, 1, 2 ; Xen. *ibid.*
[3] *Cf.* Dar.-Sagl. *s.v. Exercitus*, p. 907.
[4] Xen. *Hell.* VI, v, 18, 19.

of the Hellenistic army based upon the Spartan;[1] this implies that the Spartans soon after Agesilaus' campaign carried out the general reform of doubling the size of all the army units, as already suggested. The expert probably realised at the time when this change was made (as made it surely was) that, if necessary, extra depth and weight could be achieved by posting a second line of light-armed troops behind the hoplites, whose ranks of sixteen deep would permit the missiles of the light-armed to reach the enemy from behind them. This disposition of the forces was adopted on occasion by later Greek armies.[2]

The defeat at Leuctra is easily to be explained without calling in the usual hypothesis of decline in population, for at that time the Spartans had allowed themselves to fall behind their chief military rivals in two important respects : in the inadequate depth of their hoplite line, and in the small size and inefficiency of their cavalry force.[3] Ever since the early campaigns of the Peloponnesian War, the armies of the foremost Greek states had been undergoing a gradual transformation, of which the main feature was the growing use of various categories of more mobile and lightly-armed troops than the heavy-armed hoplite. The typical heavy infantry ($\tau \dot{o}$ $\beta \alpha \rho \dot{u}$ $\delta \pi \lambda \iota \tau \iota \kappa \acute{o} \nu$)[4] of earlier times had several fatal defects ; it was slow in movement on the field of battle, by no means immune when attacked from behind or above by long-range missiles,[5] and totally unsuited to long marches in difficult country.[6] The Spartans were not slow to grasp these facts so far as the hoplite force itself was concerned, and, as will presently be demonstrated, were the first to introduce a new type of hoplite with very little defensive armour, in place of the traditional hoplite with crested bronze helmet, bronze breastplate and bronze greaves. They also made use of light-armed mercenaries, through their Boeotian or Corinthian allies, early in the Peloponnesian War,[7] and both peltasts (javelin men) and

[1] Cf. Arr. Tact. IV, 4-6 ; XII, 2. [2] Ibid. V, 5 ; IX, 1.
[3] Cf. Xen. Hell. VI, iv, 10, 11. [4] Cf. Arr. Tact. III, 5.
[5] As illustrated by the defeat of the Athenian hoplite force in Aetolia 426 B.C. (Thuc. III, 98).
[6] Cf. Grundy, Thucydides and the History of his Age, pp. 243 f.
[7] Cf. Thuc. II, 80 f. (Acarnania, 429 B.C.). That the Chaones, etc., were light-armed is clear from ibid. 81. 8. For the Boeotian light-armed, cf. Thuc. IV, 93. 3 ($\dot{u} \pi \grave{e} \rho$ $\mu \upsilon \rho \acute{\iota} o \upsilon \varsigma$).

cavalry were largely used during the campaigns in Asia Minor early in the fourth century.[1] Both the Boeotians and the Athenians seem to have been before them in employing peltasts in Greece,[2] but the Spartans were already making considerable use of these in the war with Thebes which followed the loss of the Cadmeia in 379.[3] What the Thebans apparently realised before the Spartans was that a more lightly-armed hoplite force did not make possible the solid frontal resistance which had been the important contribution of the older type of hoplite army; through becoming more mobile it had also inevitably become more vulnerable to an efficient body of cavalry and peltasts. Hence the Thebans invented the hoplite phalanx of great depth, and the Spartans realised their mistake too late to save them from disaster. But the ' Twelve Lochoi ', implying the doubling of all units, were already in existence by 367.[4]

The evolution by the Spartans of a new type of hoplite may be deduced partly from archaeological and partly from literary sources. There can be no doubt that over a long period, from the first half of the seventh century to the first half of the fifth, the Spartan army was almost entirely composed of heavy-armed hoplites, a possible exception to this being the Sciritae, who appear from allusions in literary sources to have been more mobile than the rest.[5] The earlier type of Spartan hoplite, then, wore a bronze helmet with cheek-pieces and large crest extending over the top and some distance down the wearer's back. This helmet is represented in the lead figurines of local manufacture from the seventh century onwards (Pl. **7**);[6] it also appears without the crest in a Laconian pottery head of about 625 B.C.[7] At the lower end of the series we find it represented, still in the same form, in the marble statue commonly known as the ' Leonidas ',[8] and in some Spartan bone plaques of approximately the same date.[9] It is possible

---

[1] Cf. Xen. Hell. IV, i, 3 (395 B.C.), Ages. I, 25.
[2] For the Boeotians, cf. Thuc. IV, 93. 3 (at Delium). The great development of the peltast force under the Athenian Iphicrates is well known.
[3] Cf. Xen. Hell. V, iv, 14, 39.
[4] Ibid. VII, iv, 20.   [5] See further below, pp. 375 f.
[6] Cf. also Artemis Orthia, Pl. CLXXXIII, CXCVII, CC, p. 263, Figs. a, b, e, and on the dating, ibid. p. 251.   [7] Ibid. p. 98, Fig. 70e.
[8] B.S.A. XXVI, p. 253 f., Pl. XIX, XX.   [9] Artemis Orthia, Pl. CXIV.

that at the beginning of this long period a horse-hair crest was still in use [1] and that it was later made of feathers ; [2] no other change in the form of the helmet can be detected. The same series of evidence also illustrates the use of metal greaves, a metal corselet,[3] a round metal shield covering the body from the shoulders to the middle of the thighs (*i.e.* about 2 ft. 9 in. diameter) and a thrusting spear. It is precisely the equipment described by Tyrtaeus at the time of the second Messenian War.[4] Evidence for the length and thickness of the sword is scanty, but to judge from one of the lead figurines dating from the later seventh century,[5] it was already at that time much shorter than was normal with Greek hoplites, being not more than half the length of the diameter of the shield. Greek swords of the sixth and fifth centuries were in general almost twice this length, though they tended to become shorter.[6] The shortness of Spartan swords was still proverbial in the late fifth century.[7] But even if allowance is made for the smaller sword, and for the fact that Spartan hoplites apparently did not wear metal thigh-pieces, as some Greek hoplites did in the sixth century B.C.,[8] the early Spartan equipment must still be regarded as inconveniently heavy.[9]

[1] *Cf. ibid.* Pl. CXCI, 5.

[2] As suggested by the form of the crest of the ' Leonidas ' (originally painted) and by the bone plaques (*Artemis Orthia*, Pl. CXIV). *Cf.* also Aristoph. *Acharn.* 585 f.

[3] The ' Leonidas ' is represented naked, but this is obviously due to a sculptors' convention, as in the Aegina pediments.

[4] Cited below, p. 380. The large ' Homeric ' shield extending from shoulders to ankles is referred to in Tyrt. fr. 8, ll. 22 f. (Diehl), and by some scholars is thought to have been still in use in Tyrtaeus' time (*cf.* Lenschau, *Die Entstehung des Spartanischen Staates*, *Klio*, vol. XXX, 1937, pp. 269 f.). But numerous other echoes of Homer in the *Eunomia* (for which see p. 293, n. 7) make it clear that the passage in question must be explained as a literary allusion, and is of no value as contemporary evidence.

[5] *Artemis Orthia*, p. 261*d*. The swords represented on the moulded sixth-century *pithos* from Sparta (Pl. 9) are longer, but, since there are other differences in the equipment, need not be regarded as accurate representations of Spartan weapons.

[6] *Cf.* the Corinthian Amphiaraus-crater (Pfuhl, *Meisterwerke*, Pl. 14), and the Athenian R.F. vases, *ibid.* Pl. 43, 52, 62.

[7] *Cf.* Plut. *Lycurg.* 19 (well adapted for the sword-swallowing trick, but long enough to reach the enemy).

[8] As in the Athenian B.F. amphora (Pfuhl, *ibid.* Pl. 21) and in the Spartan *pithos* (above, n. 5).

[9] Grundy (*op. cit.* p. 244, n.) holds that the helmet at least must have been far heavier than any helmet of the medieval period or later.

In the full hoplite panoply it was clearly impossible to
run,[1] and next to impossible to organise forced marches
over difficult country even with the help of shield-bearers
(ὑπασπισταί).[2] The ' hoplite-races ' were actually run by
men wearing only their greaves, and carrying shield, helmet,
and sword and spear ; the breastplate was apparently not
included.[3] But the later Spartan hoplite actually did run
on the field of battle ; the younger men, up to the age of
thirty or thirty-five, were sometimes ordered to run with
the cavalry in the initial charge.[4] During the Peloponnesian
War and later, supposedly impossible mountain routes
were negotiated by Spartan hoplites with the knowledge
that they would have to fight a battle the next day.[5]

The explanation clearly lies in a much lighter equipment,
and some indications of the changes which had taken place
are given by literary authorities. In the first place, the
bronze helmet had given place at some time before the
campaign of Pylos and Sphacteria to the pointed leather
cap (πῖλος) which was later regarded as characteristically
Spartan,[6] and which appears in all later Spartan representations of their patron heroes, the Dioscuri.[7] In the tall
tangled scrub on the island of Sphacteria this headgear
failed to protect its wearers from the enemy's arrows, which
they could not see coming.[8] But it was obviously designed

[1] On the interpretation of the term δρόμῳ in Herod. VI, 112, cf. Grundy,
The Great Persian War, p. 188, who translates ' at the quick step '. The
possibility is not excluded that Herodotus has used the term anachronis-
tically, thinking of Spartan or Boeotian hoplite equipment in the
Peloponnesian War.

[2] For the use of these by the Spartans, cf. Xen. Hell. IV, v, 14 (near
Corinth, 390 B.C.). On this occasion they were used to pick up the dead
and wounded.   [3] Cf. the early Attic R.F. cup, Pfuhl, op. cit. Pl. 34.

[4] As in Boeotia in 378 (Xen. Hell. V, iv, 40). Cf. ibid. VI, v, 31 (at
Sparta, 369), and for pursuit of peltasts by younger Spartan hoplites,
ibid. IV, v, 14, 16.

[5] Cf. Thuc. V, 58. 4 (418), Xen. Hell. V, iv, 4 (379), ibid. VI, iv, 4
(before Leuctra), VI, iv, 26 (after Leuctra), and on the tactics characteristic of Agesilaus, Xen. Ages. VI, 6, 7.   [6] Cf. Arr. Tact. III, 5.

[7] Cf. Sparta Catalogue, p. 113. No Spartan fourth-century reliefs of
this class appear to have survived. All of the third century B.C and later,
but none of the earlier ones, show the πῖλοι. The representation of Pollux
on a bronze cheek-piece from Dodona, showing the πῖλος, may belong
to the late fourth century B.C. (cf. Carapanos, Dodone (1878), Pl. XV,
p. 187). The only known earlier representations of the πῖλος worn as a
helmet seem to be the Theban stelae discussed below, pp. 364 ff.

[8] Cf. Thuc. IV, 34. 3.

for fighting in the open, where it would doubtless give protection against glancing blows from cutting swords, and could be protected by skilful use of the shield against stray arrows. But as we shall see, the new type of hoplite was not intended to be exposed to direct attack by bowmen. About the rest of his equipment the ancient writers are remarkably inexplicit. The writer of the *Respublica Lacedaemoniorum* mentions nothing but a bronze shield and a dark red tunic.[1] The characteristic short sword has already been mentioned. A description of it, originating in the late fifth century, implies that it was used for stabbing, not for cutting, and its proper name was ἐγχειρίδιον, not μαχαίρα.[2] Athenian swords from about 500 B.C. onwards seem to have been in the strict sense μαχαίραι as opposed to the long straight ξίφος, and used primarily for cutting.[3] There is no direct description of the Spartan spear of the same period, but it may perhaps be inferred from a reference to the throwing of their spears by Theban hoplites in the war against Agesilaus [4] that the Spartan spears had also become lighter. For the Thebans also by this time had lightened the equipment of their hoplites to the extent that they were now able to run.[5] They do not, however, appear to have abandoned the characteristic Boeotian metal helmet, which gave even better protection than other Greek hoplite helmets, since it came well down over the neck and protected the base of the neck as well.[6] And Theban hoplites were still wearing breastplates in 362 B.C. at the battle of Mantinea.[7]

[1] (Xen.) *Resp. Lac.* XI, 3.

[2] *Cf.* Plut. *Lycurg.* 19 : Ἄγις μὲν οὖν ὁ βασιλεύς, σκώπτοντος Ἀττικοῦ τινος τὰς Λακωνικὰς μαχαίρας εἰς τὴν μικρότητα, καὶ λέγοντος ὅτι ῥᾳδίως οἱ θαυματοποιοὶ καταπίνουσιν ἐν τοῖς θεάτροις, ' καὶ μὴν μάλιστα ', εἶπεν, ἡμεῖς ἐφικνούμεθα τοῖς ἐγχειριδίοις τῶν πολεμίων.

[3] *Cf.* Pfuhl, *op. cit.* Pl. 43, 47, 52, 62, 71, 72.

[4] Xen. *Hell.* V, iv, 52 : τὰ δόρατα ἐξηκόντιζον. *Cf.* also Diod. XV, 86, referring to Epaminondas at Mantinea as πρῶτος ἀκοντίσας.

[5] *Cf.* Xen. *Hell.* V, iv, 51 : οἱ Θηβαῖοι . . . ἀπολιπόντες ἔνθα παρατεταγμένοι ἦσαν δρόμῳ ἔθεον . . . ὅμως μέντοι ἐπὶ παραθέοντας αὐτοὺς τῶν πολεμάρχων τινὲς ἐπέδραμον. This obviously refers to actual running not to ' the quick step ' (*cf.* above, p. 362, n. 1).

[6] *Cf.* Xen. *de re eq.* XII, 3 : κράνος γε μὴν κράτιστον εἶναι νομίζομεν τὸ βοιωτιουργές· τοῦτο γὰρ αὖ στεγάζει μάλιστα πάντα τὰ ὑπερέχοντα τοῦ θώρακος, ὁρᾶν δὲ οὐ κωλύει.

[7] *Cf.* Diod. XV, 87 (of Epaminondas, who was leading the Theban hoplites in person).

These differences between the later Spartan and the later Theban hoplite equipment raise an interesting problem in the interpretation of two painted grave-stelae from Thebes, one of which has been dated on grounds of style to the early years of the Peloponnesian War [1] (Pl. **8**). At first glance this comparatively light-armed warrior might seem not to be a hoplite at all ; yet he is certainly not a peltast or ἀκοντιστής, in view of the large size of his shield, the manner in which he is using his spear (for thrusting, not throwing) and the inclusion of a sword in his equipment. The sword is conspicuously short, corresponding to the description of the Spartan ἐγχειρίδιον ; it is also attached in unexpected manner to the top of the inside of the shield, still in its sheath, a point which is of particular interest in view of the order given to his hoplites by the Spartan Clearchus, commanding the remnants of the Ten Thousand. They were to fasten their ἐγχειρίδια underneath their shields when they laid the shields aside to dig a trench,[2] presumably so that they would be instantly available if the shields had to be snatched up in case of a sudden enemy attack. In the meantime the swords would not impede the movements of the soldiers as they dug.

The figure of Mnason wears no breastplate and apparently no greaves ; these last, however, may originally have been represented in paint which has now disappeared, for on the later stele of Rhynchon [3] greaves are indicated in this way. To take the place of body armour, Mnason has only a somewhat voluminous tunic tucked into a belt about his waist. No doubt even the folds would be of some use in entangling the weapons of the enemy when fighting was at close quarters, but the absence of a breastplate,

---

[1] *Cf.* Pfuhl, *op. cit.* p. 55.

[2] Polyaen. *Strat.* II, ii, 9 : παρήγγειλε τὸ ἐγχειρίδιον καθέντας ὑπὸ τὴν ἀσπίδα βαθύτατον ὀρύξαι βόθρον.

[3] Illustrated by Pfuhl, *Malerei u. Zeichnung*, Pl. 634. For this and the similar stele of Saugenes (all from Thebes) see further, *ibid.* §§ 722, 733, 767 ; Vollgraff, B.C.H. XXVI (1902), pp. 554 f., Pl. 7 ; Keramopoulos, Ἐφημερίς, 1920, pp. 1 f. (with illustrations). Pfuhl regards the stele of Mnason as much earlier in date than the other two, which he compares in regard to style with the similar subject on coins of Opus (400 B.C. and after). The style of both the later stelae suggests over-elaborated and decadent copies of a well-known original which might well be the stele of Mnason itself.

especially if the figure represents a Theban soldier, is surprising. So is the helmet, which is the characteristic Laconian πῖλος, here making what seems to be its earliest appearance on the historical stage. The shield, too, is of the Spartan not the Boeotian type. We may well ask whether the painting is intended to represent, not a Boeotian, but a Spartan soldier, perhaps one who fell at Plataea during the Spartan siege, and was buried at Thebes. It happens that the name Mnason, though not exclusively Spartan, is a very common one among Spartans of the upper social class in later times,[1] and if the painting at Thebes represented a Spartan, it would probably be thought unnecessary to commemorate the fact in words when the peculiarity of the military equipment made the origin of the soldier evident to all. There may also have been some explanatory inscription outside an enclosure containing the tomb, as in the case of the late fifth-century Spartan tombs at Athens.[2] That there existed at least one conspicuous grave of a Spartan in Thebes before the Theban invasion of the Peloponnese is implied in an anecdote relating to Epaminondas,[3] and as we have seen, the πῖλος and the peculiar position of the dagger strongly suggest a Spartan. It is true that the hoplites under Clearchus who were ordered to place their daggers in this position were for the most part not Spartans, but Clearchus himself was, and he doubtless practised in the main the principles of Spartan military drill. The size, shape, and recessed rim of Mnason's shield also agree with the evidence of a captured Spartan shield of approximately the same date, found at Athens.[4]

It may perhaps be objected that the picture of Mnason cannot be intended to represent a Spartan, because it shows him wearing a moustache, and the supposedly Lycurgan

---

[1] Cf. I.G. V, i, index, s.v.

[2] Cf. Arch. Anz. 1930, pp. 90 f., Abb. 5 (grave of the Spartans who fell in the fighting at Peiraeus in 404-3 B.C.).

[3] Cf. Front, Strat. I, xii, 5. His soldiers were alarmed because the wind had seized a fillet decorating his spear, and in sepulcrum Lacedaemonii cuiusdam depulerat. The army was setting out from Thebes.

[4] Cf. Hesperia, VI (1937), pp. 347 f. The shield is bronze, slightly oval, and measures 95 × 83 cm. The outer surface bears the inscription Ἀθηναῖοι ἀπὸ Λακεδαιμονίων ἐκ Πύλου. The central portion of the shield has perished, so that it may have been marked originally with the letter Λ mentioned by Eupolis (cf. below, p. 385, n. 5).

injunction μὴ τρέφειν μύστακα [1] is usually interpreted as meaning that the upper lip must be clean-shaven. Indeed, the 'Leonidas' statue has been supposed to represent a Spartan rather than any other Greek warrior because, though bearded, it shows no trace of a moustache.[2] This argument is not in any case a cogent one, since the head of the statue was originally painted,[3] and a short moustache could quite well be represented in paint only, without the aid of sculptural additions.[4] But that moustaches were actually worn by Spartans is proved by several of the characteristic local clay 'warrior'-masks, of sixth-century date, which show a short, carefully clipped triangular moustache.[5] It is therefore probable that μὴ τρέφειν μύστακα was not an absolute prohibition of the moustache, but merely vetoed long and elaborately cultivated moustaches, just as the Argive vow μὴ θρέψειν κόμην [6] meant (as obviously it must have done) 'not to grow the hair long', rather than 'to wear the head shaved'. The Lycurgan injunction in its positive form (κείρεσθαι τὸν μύστακα) [7] admits of exactly the same interpretation as the negative version, as may be seen from Herodotus' alternative version of the Argive action (κατακειράμενοι τὰς κεφαλάς).[8]

It may also be objected that the hair of Mnason on the Theban stele is not conspicuously long, and that the Lycurgan laws obliged all adult male Spartans κομᾶν.[9]

[1] Cf. Plut. de ser. num. vind. 4: ἐν Λακεδαίμονι κηρύττουσιν οἱ ἔφοροι παριόντες εὐθὺς εἰς τὴν ἀρχὴν μὴ τρέφειν μύστακα καὶ πείθεσθαι τοῖς νόμοις ὡς μὴ χαλεποὶ ὦσιν αὐτοῖς. In Cleom. 9, Plutarch cites Aristotle as the source of this passage, quoting it in almost exactly the same words, but giving the injunction about the moustache in the positive form κείρεσθαι τὸν μύστακα. The negative version gives the impression of being the more archaic.   [2] Cf. B.S.A. XXVI, p. 263.   [3] Ibid. p. 254.

[4] Cf. Dar.-Sagl. s.v. Sculptura, pp. 1141 f. It is clear that the feathers of the crest of the 'Leonidas' (cf. above, p. 361, n. 2) must have been indicated by the paint only, for the marble surface is quite flat.

[5] Cf. Artemis Orthia, Pl. LIII, 1 and p. 181. The Laconian II pottery head (ibid. p. 98, Fig. 70e) also clearly shows a moustache.

[6] Cf. Herod. I, 82, tracing the origin of the short hair of the Argives and the long hair of the Spartans, to the Argive defeat at Thyrea.

[7] Cf. above, n. 1.   [8] Herod. loc. cit.

[9] Herod. loc. cit., Resp. Lac. XI, 3, Plut. Lycurg. 22. 1. The last two passages, citing the law more fully, limit its application to those over the age of Epheboi, which suggests that it actually referred to beards and moustaches, rather than to the hair of the head. The length of hair implied in Plutarch's description of the alleged statue of Lysander (Plut. Lys. i) is not clear.

But again it is a question of degree. The hair of the 'Leonidas' statue, in short curls, comes barely to the nape of the neck, exactly as in the picture of Mnason. The popular notion at Athens that the Spartans (who after all were but rarely seen outside their own state) wore enormous shaggy beards and unkempt trailing hair [1] prob ably arose from a natural interpretation of the injunction κομᾶν in the light of the ancient custom of wearing the hair really long, which had formerly been universal among free-born Greeks ; [2] for the Spartans were notoriously old-fashioned. The 'Laconising' students of philosophy then carried what they supposed to be imitation to absurd lengths, [3] and the comic poets in their turn exaggerated the exaggerations of the philosophers.

In view of all these considerations, military and tonsorial, it is proposed to identify the picture of Mnason with a representation of a new type of hoplite, as it were a cross between the hoplite in the strict sense, ὁ ἀκριβὴς καὶ βαρὺς ὁπλίτης in the words of Arrian, [4] and the light-armed soldier. These new troops came into existence at some time between the date of the Leonidas (about 470 B.C.) and the first campaigns of the Peloponnesian War, and on grounds of general probability it may be suggested that they had been but recently invented at the time when the Spartans were clearly anxious to precipitate the Peloponnesian War ; for the element of surprise, which might be lost as time went on, would be an added advantage in the launching of a new form of attack, far more sudden and more de-moralising to the enemy than that which was implied in the coming together of two hoplite lines of the old type. For the new type of hoplite was obviously designed to rush immediately within the enemy's guard, making it impossible for him to use his spear or his cutting sword, or to protect the exposed portions of his person from the short daggers of his assailant. Moreover, the Spartans'

---

[1] Cf. Arist. Lysistr. 1073 f., Plato Comicus, fr. 124 (Kock), Müller (Dorians, II, p. 281) accepts these pictures as more or less accurate.

[2] Cf. Iliad, passim, Thuc. I, 6. 3 (Athenians and other Ionians), Antiochus ap. Strabo, VI, 278 (Spartans).

[3] Cf. Ollier, Le Mirage Spartiate, pp. 181 f.

[4] Cf. Arr. Tact. III, 5 (implying incidentally the existence at one time of a lighter-armed type of hoplite).

lack of body armour would be all the more tempting to the enemy hoplites to engage them on level open ground, where their superior skill had always given them the advantage. It goes without saying that the innovation was confined to the Spartans themselves, and was not extended to the Peloponnesian hoplites in general. Hence there is no difficulty in supposing that it was already in existence during the first Spartan invasions of Attica, even though it has passed unnoticed by Thucydides. If the interpretation here suggested of the stele of Mnason is correct, the new type of hoplite must already have been in existence very early in the Peloponnesian War, and after all we know from Thucydides' reference to their πῖλοι at Sphacteria that these troops were certainly in existence in 425. It must therefore have been exceptionally disappointing to the Spartans that their provocative tactics in Attica failed to tempt Pericles to lead the Athenian hoplites out to battle in force. Had he done so, it is not improbable that the whole Peloponnesian War would have been decided by a single engagement on land.[1]

The Spartans had in fact created (or so all the evidence suggests) a land arm which was comparable in its own sphere to the small and mobile Athenian triremes with their highly trained crews. They could now travel faster over long distances, negotiate the most difficult mountain passes as the Athenian trireme could weather the stormiest sea, and on the level plains they could out-manoeuvre the enemy by their more rapid movement. But like the Athenian fleet, they were more than ever dependent on good generalship to keep them out of places which were tight in the literal sense,[2] and this was probably the main reason for their defeat at Sphacteria.

It is relevant to examine more generally this factor of Spartan generalship, which probably goes far to explain problems which have puzzled the modern historians ; how for example Sparta while still concentrating on the hoplite force

---

[1] As Pericles himself apparently realised. *Cf.* Thuc. I, 141. 6.

[2] The observations of Phormio on the Athenian navy (Thuc. II, 89. 10) might well be applied *mutatis mutandis* to the new type of Spartan hoplites :
τὸν δὲ ἀγῶνα οὐκ ἐν τῷ κόλπῳ ἑκὼν εἶναι ποιήσομαι, οὐδὲ ἐσπλεύσομαι ἐς αὐτόν. ὁρῶ γὰρ ὅτι πρὸς πολλὰς ναῦς ἀνεπιστήμονας ὀλίγαις ναυσὶν ἐμπείροις καὶ ἄμεινον πλεούσαις ἡ στενοχωρία οὐ ξυμφέρει.

of the old cumbrous type could extend her military hegemony over a country like Greece, bristling with easily defensible strong points.[1] Ancient writers have confused the issue by directing excessive attention to the superior training and skill of the Spartan common soldier, as is natural, seeing that even Pericles (who was probably not alone among Greek generals in this) was not above encouraging the amateur troops of Athens, before they went into battle against Spartans, by suggesting that these qualities of the Spartan were more than counterbalanced by their own superior intelligence and adaptability, and by enthusiasm in the cause of free institutions.[2] In other words, the reason why we hear so much about Spartan ἐμπειρία is that other Greeks tended to underestimate its importance ; [3] the even more important factor of generalship escaped public attention altogether, because it lay beyond the mental horizon of the typical citizen-soldier, and the ablest generals refrained from enlarging his field of vision in this matter, knowing that it could lead only to discouragement in battle, and apathy in time of peace.[4]

But it is evident on general grounds that the Spartans won the great majority of the battles which they fought on land, less on account of the superior training and physique of the individual Spartan soldiers, than as the result of good generalship. The superior quality of Spartan troops doubtless counted for more in the early days when Sparta was establishing her supremacy over the Perioikoi, but from that time on Spartan troops formed a small and ever-dwindling proportion of the total number fighting under Spartan command in any battle, so that this factor of superiority in the fighting men themselves must have greatly diminished in importance. Of far greater significance was a long succession of first-rate generals in the two royal houses, men who were able to take every advantage

[1] Cf. Grundy, *Thucydides and the History of his Age*, p. 245.
[2] Cf. Thuc. II, 39. 2.
[3] Cf. Arist. *Pol.* VIII, iv, 4 (the Spartans succeeded through their laborious training simply because for a long period they were the only Greeks who practised it). Aristotle himself shares the usual Greek contempt for Spartan preoccupation with military matters. Cf. *ibid.* VII, 2. 9-13.
[4] Cf. the penetrating observations in (Xen.) *Resp. Lac.* X, 8, τὸ πάντων θαυμαστότατον, ἐπαινοῦσι μὲν πάντες τὰ τοιαῦτα ἐπιτηδεύματα (*i.e.* Lycurgan institutions) μιμεῖσθαι δὲ αὐτὰ οὐδεμία πόλις ἐθέλει.

24

of the terrain and to make the best possible disposition of such various types of troops as they possessed. The genius of Pausanias, for example, can alone explain the Greek victory at Plataea over a much larger Persian army, abundantly provided with the cavalry which the Greeks lacked. Pausanias in the first phase of the battle placed the few archers at his disposal precisely where they could do the most damage to the oncoming Persians, and stationed the great majority of his hoplites where they were unassailable by the Persian cavalry.[1] There is nothing here, nor in the later phases of the same battle, of that fatal disposition, supposedly characteristic of all Greek armies in the fifth century, ' to seek out the fairest level plain that can be found '[2] and make the battle a direct contest of weight against weight. The same adaptability is seen in later Spartan commanders, in particular in Brasidas, Dercyllidas and Agesilaus. So far from attempting to fight the more mobile barbarians and mercenary troops with which they came in contact by the traditional Greek methods, they improvised a new technique and organisation, introducing innovations such as the hollow square formation[3] and the use of cavalry[4] and peltasts. But in Greece itself, so long as Athens was able to keep the barbarians at bay with her fleet, and Sparta was head of a united confederacy on land, there was no need to introduce such innovations. What is more, their introduction would have involved political and financial problems, such as the need for payment of troops, and the dangers inherent in giving military training to the landless class, which were too difficult for Sparta, or her allies in the League, to deal with in the fifth century. South of the isthmus of Corinth, an almost exclusively hoplite army continued (within the framework of the Peloponnesian confederacy) to be the most satisfactory; for campaigns north of the isthmus troops of other categories could if necessary be supplied, for the Boeotian allies of

---

[1] *Cf.* Grundy, *The Great Persian War* (1901), pp. 459 f.

[2] Herod. VII, 9. 2 (a criticism attributed to Mardonius in 481).

[3] *Cf.* Thuc. IV, 125 (ἐς τετράγωνον τάξιν). The absence of a technical term here, as contrasted with *ibid.* VI, 67; VII, 78, suggests a recent innovation at the time when Thucydides revised his history of the Ten Years' War.

[4] *Ibid.* IV, 55. 1: παρὰ τὸ εἰωθὸς ἱππέας τετρακοσίους κατεστήσαντο.

Sparta had both a large army of light-armed troops and a trained cavalry force,[1] and Corinth could bring with her unlimited numbers of light-armed troops from among the barbarians of the north-west.[2] We may well credit the contention of Hippocrates, invading Boeotia in 424, that if the Athenian expedition succeeded and Sparta was deprived of the use of the Boeotian cavalry force, the Spartans would never again be able to invade Attica.[3]

The apparent preoccupation with the hoplite force by Sparta in the fifth century must not therefore be taken as evidence of backwardness in military science. On the contrary, the skilful utilisation of other types of troops by one Spartan commander after another, on occasion, suggests that these generals were well acquainted by tradition and upbringing with the art of war, both in its main principles and in its details. The bare fact that over so long a period the chief generals continued to be the hereditary kings, and that in a predominantly militaristic state, implies that the privileged class from which officers were drawn, at least, had actual instruction on the theoretical side of the art of war, as well as practical military training. It would clearly have been fatal for the Spartans to leave it to chance (as the majority of Greek states had done earlier) whether the heirs to the throne would be efficient generals or not. The obvious dependence of the later Greek manuals of the art of war (τεχναὶ τακτικαί) on Spartan sources [4] is another indication that the military science was well developed in Sparta before its importance was recognised in other Greek states. Later ancient writers on this subject admitted the Spartans to have been the pioneers, as appears very clearly from a passage in Vegetius, which refers to early written treatises on 'the art of battles' by Spartan authors.[5] Indeed, this aspect of the whole matter, far

---

[1] For the Boeotian light-armed, cf. Thuc. IV, 93. 3 (ὑπὲρ μυρίους) ; for the cavalry, ibid. II, 9 (also mentioning Phocian and Locrian cavalry, which were at the disposal of Sparta from 446 onwards), IV, 93.

[2] Cf. above, p. 359, n. 7.   [3] Thuc. IV, 95.   [4] Cf. above, pp. 357 f.

[5] Veget. R.M., III, ad init : Lacedaemoniorum autem praecipua fuit cura bellorum. Primi namque experimenta pugnarum de eventibus colligentes, artem proeliorum scripsisse firmantur usque eo, ut rem militarem, quae virtute sola, vel certe felicitate creditur contineri, ad disciplinam peritiaeque studia revocarint, ac magistros armorum, quos τακτικούς appellaverunt, juventutem suam usum varietatemque pugnandi praeceperint edocere.

more than the specific practices which he actually quotes, fully justifies the remark of the anonymous fourth-century writer on Sparta [1] that only the Spartans were real experts in the art of war, all other Greeks being merely improvisers (αὐτοσχεδιασταί). [2]

Thus, when viewed in its proper perspective, against the whole background of the military organisation of Sparta and her allies, the inner organisation of the πολιτικαὶ μόραι of the Spartans themselves may be seen to have had far too much importance attached to it. The same mistake has been made both in ancient and in modern times, even though Pericles was at pains to point out in his Funeral Speech one of the fallacies implied in it. The Spartans, he says, never fight anywhere by themselves ; they are always surrounded by allies. [3] The innuendo received its justification a few years later at Sphacteria, when as an exception, and through an obvious failure in generalship, the Spartans did fight alone (except for Helots) and were defeated. It seemed to be the explosion of a myth. [4] On the other hand, in the circumstances of time and place which as a rule they were able to choose, the πολιτικαὶ μόραι of Sparta, whether of the old or of the new style, could be used to excellent effect as a solid block wherever the whole hoplite phalanx was likely to be most vulnerable, whether on the right wing as at Plataea, [5] or on the left wing as at Mantinea in 418. [6] Apart from anything else, the exceptional spirit of discipline inculcated by their training from boyhood upwards was calculated to help them to stand firm in what might seem desperate circumstances. [7]

In cases where the enemy was the typical Greek hoplite army, unsupported to any extent by cavalry or light-armed troops, Spartan commanders seem to have been well-versed in the art of placing the opposing army just where they wanted it, namely on the open plain where their own superior discipline would give them an additional advantage. Thus before the battle of Mantinea in 418, when

---

[1] On the question of the authorship of this treatise, usually ascribed to Xenophon, see Appendix VII, (pp. 490 f.   [2] Resp. Lac. XIII, 5.
[3] Cf. Thuc. II, 39. 3.   [4] Cf. Thuc. IV, 40.
[5] Herod. IX, 28.   [6] Thuc. V, 67. 1.
[7] It was this factor which enabled Pausanias to snatch victory from the jaws of defeat at Plataea, cf. Grundy, op. cit. pp. 501 f.

the Argives and their allies took up a strong position of advantage on the hill-side, and failed to be tempted down on to the level ground when the Spartans burnt the crops of their Mantinean allies, the Spartan king carried a pretence of attacking the hill position to the length of advancing within a stone's throw of the enemy, then suddenly wheeling round and retreating out of sight, ostensibly in response to a shout of protest from one of the king's own senior advisers, who cried out that Agis was leading them to disaster.[1] The actual direction and extent of the withdrawal was concealed from the Argives and their allies by a bend in the road [2] just behind where the Spartan camp had been, its site having no doubt been deliberately chosen on this account. They therefore spent a night of quarrelling and indecision, the rank-and-file engaged in reviling their generals for not immediately pursuing a patently fleeing enemy, the Mantineans evidently suspecting (what was indeed the case) that the Spartans were occupied in diverting the water-courses on the Tegean frontier so that they flooded Mantinean territory,[3] the commanders afraid to advance in pursuit for fear of an ambush, and afraid to remain where they were for fear of a revolt. As a result, they next day abandoned their strong position on the hillside without securing any compensating advantage, and drew up in battle formation just short of the hidden way of approach,[4] hoping to catch the Spartans unawares when they came round the bend, if they should decide to return to the attack. Thucydides believes that it was the Spartans who fell into a trap, being forced to deploy in battle formation immediately they rounded the bend.[5] But his informant was doubtless an Argive or Mantinean, anxious to represent the tactics of his own side in the most favourable light.[6] For the Spartan hoplites, of which the Spartan army was mainly composed, on this occasion, were well-trained in

[1] Cf. Thuc. V, 65.

[2] In view of the Argive reluctance to advance beyond the bend, it probably led into a defile. But Thucydides gives no explanation of this point.　　　　　　　　　　　　　　[3] Thuc. loc. cit.

[4] Thuc. V, 65. 6.　　　　　　　　[5] Ibid. 66. 2.

[6] This also appears from the statements (ibid. 72. 1, 2) that the Spartans were caught in some confusion in the act of deploying and that their victory was due not to ἐμπειρία but to ἀνδρεία.

carrying out these sudden manoeuvres ; [1] had it not been
so, the daring right-about face of the previous day would
have been impossible, for the enemy might have attacked
suddenly and caught them in confusion. And on the second
day, why should the Spartans have returned to the site of
their previous camp if they believed their enemy to be still
established in their position of advantage on the hillside ?
Clearly they had already discovered the position of the
enemy by means of their trained scouts, and the whole story
thus reveals the superiority of the Spartan army in four
important respects : superiority in generalship, for the
Spartans planted their enemy exactly where they wanted
him ; superiority in tactical training, for they were able
to carry out complete changes of position suddenly without
falling into confusion ; superiority in discipline, for never
would Spartan commanders have allowed the rank-and-file
to force them into movements which were against their
own better judgment ; and superiority in reconnaissance,
for they were evidently equipped with scouts while the
enemy were not. In spite of a desperate Argive attempt
to attack in a wild rush before the Spartans had finished
deploying,[2] their defeat was a foregone conclusion, especially in view of their numerical inferiority,[3] which had no
doubt also been foreseen by the Spartan commander.

The Spartan reconnaissance service was a part of their
army organisation about which they were naturally extremely secretive, since it would ill have suited their purpose
for other Greek states to have copied it. Apart from a
vague allusion to mounted scouts (οἱ προερευνώμενοι ἱππεῖς)
in the fourth-century treatise on Sparta,[4] there are no
references to this as an essential part of the whole Spartan
army organisation until the third century B.C., when the
real nature of the *Krypteia* was revealed at the time of the
battle of Sellasia.[5] In the time of Plato and Aristotle the

---

[1] *Cf. Resp. Lac.* XI, 8–10, and on the *Λάκων ἐξελιγμός* (a reversing
movement) Arr. *Tact.* 24. 2.   [2] Thuc. V, 70, 72. 1.   [3] *Ibid.* 71. 2.
[4] *Resp. Lac.* XIII, 6. It was presumably a member of this force who
brought to Agesilaus the news of the destruction of the Mora at Lechaeum
(*cf.* Xen. *Hell.* IV, 5. 7).
[5] *Cf.* Plut. *Cleom.* 28. Being unable to discover from a point of vantage
the whereabouts of the enemy's Acarnanian and Illyrian troops, Cleomenes
καλέσας . . . Δαμοτέλη τὸν ἐπὶ τῆς κρυπτείας τεταγμένον, ὁρᾶν ἐκέλευσε
καὶ ζητεῖν ὅπως ἔχει τὰ κατὰ νώτου καὶ κύκλῳ τῆς παρατάξεως.

Krypteia was only known as a system of training for the young men, who were inured to all kinds of physical hardship by being compelled to fend for themselves in exposed country, in all seasons and all weathers.[1] It was also darkly rumoured that they were encouraged to waylay and kill Helots during these expeditions,[2] which may or may not be true. But the interesting point to notice is that outside knowledge of the system stopped short at the preliminary training ; of its real purpose, no outsiders seem to have had the least idea. The Spartans themselves were doubtless very willing to encourage the prevalent belief that a general moral and physical toughening was the only object.

In view of the secrecy which (as its very name implies) surrounded the *Krypteia*, it is only possible to make tentative suggestions as to the way in which the personnel was provided for this branch of the service in time of war. But certain elementary considerations suggest the general lines of the solution. The army scouts must above all be loyal and trustworthy ; consequently in the Spartan army they must be full citizens. But it is always implied by the ancient authorities that all the citizens from twenty to sixty years of age [3] were included in the Morae, and whether the seventh Mora, the *Lochos Skirites*, was composed of full citizens or not is a point not at present very clear.[4] Yet it is hard to see how the hoplites in the six πολιτικαὶ μόραι could be employed as scouts, both on account of the rigid formation of the hoplite ranks, which could not have indefinite numbers of men withdrawn from them for indefinite periods, and on account of the equipment, which, with its red tunics and gleaming shields, would be both conspicuous and inconvenient for army scouts.

There remain then the Sciritae, who were undoubtedly different both in equipment and in organisation from the six πολιτικαὶ μόραι. It is true that they fought as hoplites on the left wing, this place being traditionally reserved for them.[5] But it seems doubtful whether they *all* fought

---

[1] Plato, *Laws*, 633B ; Plut. *Lycurg.* 28.
[2] Arist. *ap.* Plut. *loc. cit.* ; Heracl. Pont. fr. II, 4 (F.H.G. II, p. 210).
[3] See further below, pp. 388 f.
[4] But see further below, pp. 378 f.   [5] *Cf.* Thuc. V, 67. 1.

as hoplites, seeing that *Sciritae* were also used, in co-operation with cavalry, to advance in front of the rest of the hoplite army [1] or to harry the enemy's retreat.[2] It has even been suggested, in view of a passage in Xenophon's *Cyropaedia*, that the Sciritae were themselves cavalry,[3] but this interpretation is excluded for the time of the battle of Mantinea (418) because there were then 600 *Sciritae* [4] and only 400 cavalry,[5] and is excluded for the time of Leuctra (371) because the standing cavalry force had then again disappeared, and a heterogeneous and inefficient body had taken its place [6] which certainly could not have been stationed at the post of honour on the left wing. There remains the possibility that the majority of the *Sciritae* fought as hoplites, while the rest, presumably without the large shield and equipped with longer-range weapons, co-operated with the cavalry. The larger size of the regiment of *Sciritae*, containing 600 men as against the 512 of the πολιτικαὶ μόραι (exclusive of 'oldest and youngest') [7] is in keeping with this hypothesis. It would permit the use of between eighty and ninety men either for co-operation with the cavalry, as indicated above, or on the more secret missions of the *Krypteia*.

But it may well be asked how it was possible for men to co-operate effectively with the cavalry, apparently over considerable distances, if they were not themselves mounted. The answer to the problem may perhaps be seen in an ivory plaque found in Sparta, and in view of its purely occidental character probably made in Sparta, which dates from the end of the seventh century B.C. and represents two warriors on one horse.[8] Both are armed

---

[1] (Xen.) *Resp. Lac.* XIII, 6. [2] Xen. *Hell.* V, iv, 52.

[3] *Cf.* Xen. *Cyrop.* IV, 2. 1 : εὔιπποι δὲ καὶ τότε ἐδόκουν καὶ νῦν δοκοῦσιν εἶναι· διὸ καὶ ἐχρῶντο αὐτοῖς οἱ Ἀσσύριοι ὥσπερ καὶ οἱ Λακεδαιμόνιοι τοῖς Σκιρίταις οὐδὲν φειδόμενοι αὐτῶν οὔτε ἐν πόνοις οὔτ' ἐν κινδύνοις.

[4] Thuc. V, 68. 3.

[5] Thuc. IV, 55. 1 : παρὰ τὸ εἰωθὸς ἱππέας τετρακοσίους κατεστήσαντο καὶ τοξότας.

[6] *Cf.* Xen. *Hell.* VI, iv, 10 f. The horses were provided by the richest citizens, and οἱ τῶν σωμάτων ἀδυνατώτατοι καὶ ἥκιστα φιλότιμοι were detailed on each occasion to ride them, without previous training.

[7] See further below, pp. 387 f., 390.

[8] *Cf. Artemis Orthia*, Pl. CIV, 1 and p. 212, where the subject is described as 'knight and squire'. The plaque in question was found with pottery of Laconian I and II.

with spear and small round shield ; the front rider is seated as far forward as possible, the one behind, who perches precariously with one foot and one knee on the horse's hindquarters, is further remarkable in carrying his shield on his right arm. This was presumably to ensure some protection from enemy attack for both riders both on the right and on the left.[1] The horseman at the back is doubtless an ἀποβάτης, a skilled rider who practised the art of mounting and dismounting with the horse actually in motion, as was also done with moving chariots both in Homeric times and later.[2] A precise parallel to the Spartan plaque is not known among the many later representations of equestrian ἀποβάται, who all appear alone on the horse.[3] But these later representations all suggest the circus *milieu* rather than the vicinity of a battle, and two Etruscan monuments of approximately the same date as the Spartan plaque, the one the famous drawing of the game of Troy on an Etruscan vase,[4] the other the painting in the Grotta Campana at Veii,[5] are both singularly reminiscent of the Spartan plaque in that an animal is shown perching on a horse's back behind its rider. In the first case the resemblance is most striking ; not only is the subject military games on horseback, but the rider is armed with spear and small round shield, and the perching animal is a monkey almost as large as the man, so that we may well suspect either intentional caricature by the artist, or misunderstanding of the design he is following. It therefore seems reasonable to infer from the Spartan plaque that it represents no mere flight of the individual artist's imagination, but a recognised part of the Spartan military organisation of that period. If we suppose that it survived into later times, the peculiar features of the Sciritae would be explained, though it must be borne in mind that at some period in between, the greater part of the *Lochos Skirites* must on this interpretation be supposed to have been transformed into hoplites, just as all or part of the original cavalry force was transformed into the hoplites known as the ' Three Hundred Knights '.[6]

---

[1] *Cf.* Arrian's description of the Roman cavalry games, *Tact.* 37.
[2] *Cf.* Dar.-Sagl. *s.v. Desultor.*   [3] *Ibid.*
[4] *Ibid. s.v. Troiae Ludus*, p. 496, Fig. 7102.
[5] *Cf.* Strong, *Art in Ancient Rome*, vol. I, p. 28, Fig. 30.   [6] *Cf.* Thuc. V, 72. 4.

The name *Sciritae* has been commonly derived, as is natural, from the region called Skiritis in the upper valley of the Eurotas, and the *Lochos Skirites* has accordingly been assumed to have been composed of Perioikoi.[1] A serious objection to this interpretation is that Xenophon (*Hell.* VI, v, 26) speaks of troops from Oion in Skiritis as σύμμαχοι. If to avoid this difficulty it be suggested that the *Lochos Skirites* was composed of σύμμαχοι from Skiritis, there is the difficulty that Thucydides (V, 67. 1) calls them Λακεδαιμόνιοι. The third theoretical possibility is that the corps was composed of Spartan residents in Skiritis. But a strong objection to this is that the army contingents of Spartan citizens were not organised on a local basis at all.[2] It is clear that a new explanation, divorcing the name of the *Lochos Skirites* from the locality Skiritis, would be more satisfactory if it could be found.

And in fact the etymology of the name *Sciritae* itself gives a good indication both of the high antiquity of the force (of which the earliest mention in literary authorities is in Thucydides, referring to his own time) and of the nature of its equipment. It seems clear from its various uses that the root meaning of the word σκῖρος (or σκίρρος, Lat. *scirrus*) is any tough or hard covering,[3] whether a limestone crust over the surface of the earth (whence probably the place-names Skiritis in northern Laconia, the ancient name Skiras for Salamis and the promontory Skiradion on the same island) [4] a coat of gypsum or stucco on statues or buildings, the hard rind on cheese, or an induration of the skin. The cult-name of Athena *Skiras* in Attica has been variously derived in antiquity or in modern times from limestone, gypsum or the place-name Skiras; [5] but none of these explanations carry conviction, and all fail to take

[1] *Cf.* Kahrstedt, *Sparta*, p. 304.
[2] *Ibid.* p. 4, *cf.* above, pp. 317 f..
[3] *Cf.* Liddell and Scott (ed. 8), *s.v.* σκῖρον, σκιρός, σκῖρος.
[4] For the geographical character of these regions, see Neumann-Partsch, *Geographie v. Griechenland.*
[5] *Cf.* Roscher, *s.v. Skiras;* also σκιρρίτης, a worker in stucco. The ancient derivation of the name Skiras from the sunshade carried by the priest of Erechtheus at the *Skirophoria* is evidently due to a mistaken connection with σκία, σκιερός. The name *Skiereia* for an Arcadian festival of Dionysus (Paus. VIII, 23. 1) may possibly be due to the same confusion.

account of what would seem an obvious parallel, the cult-name of Artemis *Skiris*, with priests called *Skiritai*, at Miletus.[1]

An explanation which better accounts for the cases of Athena *Skiras*, Artemis *Skiris*, perhaps for Dionysus *Skiereios*,[2] and the legendary brigand Skiron, and for the Spartan Sciritae, is that all wore or were represented as wearing an animal-skin with the hair left on, this being a typical part of Homeric military equipment, taking the place of a shield,[3] and also of the costume of deities and heroes associated with the chase.[4]   The goat-skin aegis of Athena is a particularly conspicuous example, being worn in her case on account of her character as goddess of war.   Moreover, animal-skins (κώδια) are mentioned as having played some part in the festivals of the *Skirophoria*,[5] and the true explanation may well be that the worshippers wore them on that occasion, like the Ethiopian warriors (κωδιοφόροι) mentioned by Strabo.[6]   It is evident from the fantastic explanations offered by the ancients that the original meaning of the cult-names in question had by their time been lost, but this is less likely to have been the case with the Spartans, whose dialect long preserved many extremely archaic words ; and since the relief on a mid-sixth century pithos found at Sparta (Pl. 9[7]) depicts a foot-soldier, with metal helmet and sword, fighting among the hoplites, but wearing an animal skin in place of both bronze breastplate and shield, there is no need to suppose that the name *Sciritae* descended from Homeric times, if the explanation here being put forward is correct.   The figure in question does not, of course, necessarily represent a Spartan warrior, but the fact that he is using a large stone as a missile strongly suggests that this class of troops was

---

[1] *Cf.* Ditt. *Syll.*[2] 660 (Collitz, *Dialektinschr.* 5498).   Late second century B.C.   [2] *Cf.* above, p. 378, n. 5.

[3] *Cf.* Iliad III, 17 ; X, 334, with Leaf's comments (Vol. I, App. B, § VIII).

[4] Especially of Artemis, Apollo, Dionysus, and Herakles.

[5] *Cf.* Suidas, *s.v.* Διὸς κῴδιον . . . χρῶνται δ᾽ αὐτοῖς οἵ τε Σκιροφορίων τὴν πομπὴν στέλλοντες . . . καὶ ἄλλοι τινές . . . .

[6] Strabo, XVII, ii, 3 (822).

[7] *Cf. Artemis Orthia*, Pl. XV, XVI.   The charioteer also wears an animal skin.   See also the contemporary Laconian vase (hunting scene) assigned by Lane to the ' Hunt Painter ' (B.S.A. XXXIV, Pl. 41*a*).

used by the Spartans at that time, in view of the graphic description of a battle in Tyrtaeus : [1]

ἀλλά τις ἐγγὺς ἰὼν αὐτοσχεδὸν ἔγχεϊ μακρῶι
ἢ ξίφει οὐτάζων δήιον ἄνδρ' ἑλέτω·
καὶ πόδα παρ' ποδὶ θεὶς καὶ ἐπ' ἀσπίδος ἀσπίδ' ἐρείσας
ἐν δὲ λόφον τε λόφωι καὶ κυνέην κυνέηι
καὶ στέρνον στέρνωι πεπλημένος ἀνδρὶ μαχέσθω,
ἢ ξίφεος κώπην ἢ δόρυ μακρὸν ἑλών.
ὑμεῖς δ', ὦ γυμνῆτες, ὑπ' ἀσπίδος ἄλλοθεν ἄλλος
πτώσσοντες μεγάλοις βάλλετε χερμαδίοις,
δούρασί τε ξεστοῖσιν ἀκοντίζοντες ἐς αὐτοὺς
τοῖσι πανόπλοισι πλησίον ἱστάμενοι.

The γυμνῆτες described in the last four lines are to be used in exactly the same way as the skin-clad stone-thrower represented on the pithos, the only point of difference (easily accounted for by the interval of nearly a century between the two pictures), being that the warrior on the Pithos has a short sword in a leather sheath in place of the throwing-spear used by the γυμνῆτες of Tyrtaeus. It may therefore be regarded as probable that the design on the Spartan pithos does in fact represent the same military equipment as was used in the Spartan army of that period, and that it shows the force of Sciritae in an intermediate stage of development on their way to becoming (as far as the majority were concerned) hoplites. The survival of the name Sciritae would imply that they continued to wear their corselets of animal skins even then, and so were less heavily armed and more mobile than the six Morae until the time when these last were transformed in the manner already described. [2] When that change occurred the Sciritae would actually be more protectively equipped than the rest of the hoplites, and their vulnerable position on the left wing, mentioned by Thucydides, may in fact date only from the beginning of this new period in the history of the Spartan army. It is interesting to note that in the fourth century the name used by the Spartans to denote a breastplate was αἰγίς, [3] that is, the animal-skin covering characteristic of the Sciritae. This serves as additional

---

[1] Tyrtaeus, 8. 30 f. (Diehl).   [2] Above, pp. 362 f.
[3] Nymphodorus of Syracuse, fr. 22 (F.H.G. II, p. 381).

confirmation of the contention that the heavy-armed hoplites of the old type had by that time disappeared.

The question of the extent to which light-armed troops were used in Sparta in early times is further complicated by the representations of archers, which are a common type among the Laconian lead figurines (Pl. **7**) in the period before the destruction of the old temple of Orthia (*c.* 600 B.C.) and reappear, apparently after a long interval, in the fifth century.[1] It is tempting to associate this evidence of a revival with the Spartan establishment of a corps of archers ('contrary to their custom', says Thucydides [2]) after the disaster at Sphacteria in 425 B.C. Thucydides does not mention the size of this force, and it does not appear to have been used in any pitched battles later, any more than the force of 400 cavalry which was instituted at the same time. It seems possible that both were employed on garrison duty in the numerous outposts which were then established as a precaution against repetitions of the Pylos affair ; [3] for the experience of the Spartan garrison on Sphacteria must surely have made clear the danger of leaving such outposts of hoplites unsupported by more mobile troops or by longer-range missiles.

Both these later archers and the ones represented by the early lead figurines may be supposed to have been Spartans, rather than allies or Perioikoi, from the mere fact that the dedications in question were made at the shrine of Orthia, for it is quite evident that this cult at Sparta was the exclusive preserve of Spartans. In view of the many grades of Spartan citizens, it cannot have been difficult to find men from the lower grades to serve as light-armed soldiers at any period. But it is obviously impossible to assign precise dates to the earliest strata of the lead figurines, and all that can be said at present is that archers appear to have been used in the seventh century, but probably ceased to be used fairly early in the sixth century. Their

---

[1] *Cf.* A.O. p. 262 (Lead I), 269 (Lead II), 276 (a single type in Lead III and IV, surviving from the previous period). Lead III and IV, both above the sand layer on top of the early temple, cover the period 600–500 B.C. (*ibid.* p. 282). Two new varieties of the archer-type, carrying a new form of bow, appear in Lead V (*ibid.* p. 278). The much freer style of these suggests a date which is possibly as late as the last quarter of the fifth century.   [2] Thuc. IV, 55.   [3] *Ibid.*

unprotected condition, except possibly for a helmet—for they wear no clothes whatever, so far as it is possible to judge from the figurines—suggests that in this early period they were stationed immediately behind a single line of hoplites and each shot from beneath the shelter of a hoplite's shield, as Teucer shot from behind the shield of Ajax.[1] The introduction of a deeper hoplite phalanx would account for their disappearance. The later archers represented in the figurines, with their stronger double-curved horn bow intended to be used at long range,[2] do appear to have been protected by something which covers their head, shoulders and back ;[3] this was probably the σκῖρος already described in connection with the Sciritae. It would permit the use of archers in less close dependence on the hoplites.

Finally it remains to consider the use which the Spartan army made of supernumeraries. In this category must be placed the Helots who are mentioned by Herodotus and by Thucydides, as having played a part at Plataea in the Persian Wars and at Sphacteria in the Peloponnesian War.[4] In view of the constant menace from the Helots, it is highly improbable (in spite of Herodotus' assertion to the contrary)[5] that they were armed on these occasions, even if we allow for very considerable exaggeration in the figure of seven Helots to each Spartan which Herodotus gives for the campaign of Plataea.[6] The author of the *Respublica Lacedaemoniorum* appears in fact to imply that the Helots on campaign were always very carefully prevented from coming near to the arms and equipment.[7] They were

---

[1] *Il.* VIII, 266 f. A late example of the same tactic is seen in the late sixth-century R.F. crater Pfuhl, *Meisterwerke*, Pl. 47. The representation may here be anachronistic, since the passage in the Iliad might easily suggest to the artist his design.

[2] For illustration, *cf.* A.O. CXCVIII, 18, 19 ; for the construction of the bow, H. Balfour, *The Archer's Bow in the Homeric Poems* (Huxley Lecture, 1921), and the description of a composite bow from Gilgit in *Man*, 1932, pp. 160 f.   [3] *Cf.* Pl. 7, nos. 23, 24.

[4] Herod. IX, 10 ; Thuc. IV, 8. 9.   [5] Herod. IX, 29.

[6] Herod. IX, 10, 29. The figure pro bably represents the estimated ratio between the total Helot population and that of the Spartan citizens (See further above, pp. 302 f.). Thuc. IV, 16. 1, implies that only one Helot was attached to each citizen soldier at Sphacteria.

[7] *Cf. Resp. Lac.* XII, 4 : τοὺς δούλους εἴργουσιν ἀπὸ τῶν ὅπλων (referring to the rules observed in the camp).

probably used only to carry the food and other stores,[1] to cook for their masters, and for digging and fencing whenever field forts were constructed, which in an army adopting the general tactics of the Spartan, was very frequently indeed.[2] This branch of the Spartan military organisation, called by the author of the *Respublica* στρατὸς σκευοφορικός, was under its own separate commanders.[3]

Other Greek armies must have employed citizens or metics for these indispensable duties,[4] with the unfortunate effects upon discipline which have been alluded to earlier.[5] It is easy to see that the efficient functioning of the Spartan army on campaign depended in very large measure upon the availability of Helots ; that was why the Athenian occupation of Pylos was so serious a danger, and in the larger historical field, it explains both the rise of Sparta to military supremacy in the Peloponnese, and the collapse which followed the loss of Messenia.

A certain number of citizen auxiliaries must also have been employed as ὑπασπισταί, for it appears that some of these were actually included in the citizen Morae, thus bringing up the number in each from a normal 500+[6] to something like 600.[7] The name ὑπασπισταί implies that this class of men were shield-bearers for the hoplites ;[8] they were also employed in recovering the dead and wounded[9] from the field of battle. A Laconian cup illustrates their use in this capacity as early as the middle of the sixth

[1] *Cf.* Xen. *Hell.* IV, v, 4 : τῶν γὰρ τῇ μόρᾳ φερόντων τὰ σιτία οὐδενὸς πῦρ εἰσενεγκόντος κ.τ.λ. On general grounds it can scarcely be doubted that these were Helots. *Cf.* also Thuc. IV, 26. 5 (use of Helots in blockade-running at Sphacteria), Herod. IX, 80 (transport of spoils).

[2] *Cf.* above, pp. 368 f., and for the character of Spartan field-forts, *Resp. Lac.* XII, 1 ; Xen. *Hell.* VI, iv, 14 (with ditch in front).

[3] *Resp. Lac.* XIII, 4.

[4] *Cf.* Thuc. IV, 90 (Athenians at Delium) ; VI, 98 (Athenians in Syracusan expedition).

[5] *Cf.* pp. 373 f. If citizen soldiers could be so troublesome, it is easy to imagine the difficulties which would arise with free civilians not under military discipline. [6] See below, pp. 384 f.

[7] As at Lechaeum in 390 (Xen. *Hell.* IV, v, 12, 14).

[8] *Cf.* Aesch. *Suppl.* 180 f. :

ὁρῶ κόνιν, ἄναυδον ἄγγελον στρατοῦ

. . . .
ὄχλον δ' ὑπασπιστῆρα καὶ δορυσσόον
λεύσσω ξὺν ἵπποις καμπύλοις τ' ὀχήμασι.

[9] Xen. *loc. cit.*

century B.C. ; [1] it shows a procession of youths, still beardless, and unclothed except for greaves, carrying the dead
warriors (who are all bearded) over their shoulders. They
also carry spears. In view of the Lycurgan regulation
that all above the age of ἥβη should let the hair grow,[2]
the beardless condition of these youths implies that they
were below the age for active service with the hoplites, in
fact, Melleirenes ; for even the Eirenes (above the age of
twenty) [3] were not normally included. To this question
of the distribution of the various age-groups in the hoplite
army as a whole a return will be made presently. It is
involved in the question whether we can accept as reliable
the numbers given as the complement of the various Spartan
military units by Thucydides.

Thucydides claims to have pierced the barrier of secrecy
which surrounded Spartan military matters by deductions
which it was possible to make from the story of eye-
witnesses at the battle of Mantinea. His conclusions may
be given in his own words : [4] ' Seven Lochoi fought exclusive
of the Sciritae, of whom there were six hundred ; in each
Lochos there were four Pentekostyes and in each Pentekostys four Enomotiae. In each Enomotia there were
four in the front rank. In depth they were drawn up
not all alike, but according to the wishes of individual
Lochagoi, though on an average eight deep. Along the
whole line exclusive of the Sciritae there were 448 men
in the front rank.' These data enable the reader immediately to deduce the number of men in the main Spartan
regiments (512) and in their various subdivisions.[5]

But Thucydides appears to have been guilty of arguing
in a circle in this passage. His use of the term *Lochos*
in place of the more correct *Mora* has already been noticed
and need not further detain us here.[6] The suspicious

---

[1] *Cf. Jahrb. Inst.* 1901, Pl. III. Assigned by Lane (B.S.A. XXXIV,
p. 143) to the ' Hunt Painter '. [2] *Cf.* above, p. 366. [3] *Cf.* Chap. III, p. 89.
[4] Thuc. V, 68. [5] For details see above, p. 357.

[6] *Ibid.* n. 3. Thucydides reveals his own confusion about the size
of the Lochos by observing (1) that only a few Spartan troops (ὀλίγοι)
were stationed originally on the extreme right at Mantinea (V, 67. 1),
(2) that the detachment transferred from here to the gap on the left at
the last moment consisted of two Lochoi (V, 71. 3). This implies that
the Lochos was the division of 128, not of 512 men. The existence of the
name *Lochos Skirites* for a regiment of 600 men is doubtless what has led
Thucydides astray.

feature is the total number of men in the front line, which purports to be one of the main data used in determining the total numbers on the Spartan side. This number of men, closely drawn up in hoplite formation, would extend over roughly quarter of a mile,[1] and it is ludicrous to suppose that individual observers on the other side would be able to count the whole number accurately, especially in view of the fact that the Argives and their allies actually advanced in a sudden desperate rush.[2] Nor would it be possible for the Argives to station men at fixed intervals along their own front line to count the numbers in the separate divisions of the enemy front line, if they did not already know either the total numbers in the main enemy contingents or the depth of the line. To estimate the number of the enemy hoplites from the length of the overlapping sections of their own line (for at Mantinea the Spartan forces were outflanked on the left) might seem at first sight possible, but would not in practice be so in so far as the purely Spartan troops were concerned, because other hoplite units drawn from the Arcadian allies were posted on their right wing, and the Sciritae, who were apparently not drawn up the same depth as the rest,[3] held the left. Finally the Spartan commander changed the position of the Sciritae, and brought up fresh Spartan troops from the extreme right wing, while the two armies were in the very act of advancing to the attack.[4] How under these circumstances could the number in the Spartan front line possibly be estimated ? But the mere fact that the Spartans, in spite of their ' policy of secrecy ', made their own troops conspicuous not only by their red tunics, but also by the letter Λ on their shields,[5] should dispose of the idea that they ever made it possible for the enemy (at least in the days of the comparatively shallow phalanx) to count the number of men in their front line.

An additional reason for thinking that Thucydides did not in fact arrive at his conclusions from discovering the

---

[1] *Cf*. Vegetius, III, 15, postulating a frontal space of three feet per man in the Roman army. The size of the Spartan shield (*cf*. above, pp. 361, 365, n. 4) implies about the same spacing in order to leave room for use of the offensive weapons.   [2] Thuc. V, 70, 8.   [3] *Ibid*. 68. 3.   [4] *Ibid*. 71.
[5] *Cf*. Eupolis *ap*. Eustath. *In Il*. I, l. 293. Eupolis was writing at about the time of Mantinea.

number in the Spartan front line is that this number (448) takes no account of the three hundred ' so-called knights ' who were stationed round the king.[1] If these were also stationed eight deep, there should have been an extra 37 or 38 men in the front line, and the total would no longer have been divisible by the number of the Morae and their subdivisions.

On the other hand, it was obviously easy for eye-witnesses to observe the average depth of the Spartan line, and to deduce from this the number in the front line, *once the number and size of the main regiments was known.* Whether Thucydides intended to conceal the fact from his readers or not, it seems impossible to avoid the conclusion that he himself knew these main facts about the Spartan hoplite army before the battle of Mantinea ; and it is easy to guess how he acquired this information, namely from the Spartan prisoners who were taken at Sphacteria. For he tells us himself that the Spartan force which fought on that occasion was composed of detachments drafted in turns from ' all the *Lochoi* ' [2] (more correctly, from all the *Morai*), and he gives away his knowledge of the existence of a regiment composed of 128 men (*i.e.* the quarters of Morae) [3] by saying that there were 420 men in the island when the battle was fought,[4] of whom 292 were taken prisoner. This implies that 128 men (perhaps estimated as two Pentekostyes) [5] were killed. But the number 420, being obviously deduced from the known number of prisoners, fits in so well with the rest of Thucydides' account (in connection with the battle of Mantinea) of the inner organisation of the Spartan main hoplite regiments that it seems safe to accept these figures for the numbers in the various regiments as genuine. For 420 men drawn in equal numbers from each of six Morae would give 70 men from each Mora, and as will presently be shown,[6] this would represent as near as possible two full Enomotiae, exclusive of the age-classes of ' oldest ', from each Mora. The seventh Mora, of ' Brasideans and Neodamodeis ',[7] was not yet in existence at the time of Sphacteria, and

[1] Thuc. V, 72, 4.   [2] Thuc. IV, 8. 7.   [3] *Cf.* above, p. 357.
[4] Thuc. *loc. cit.*   [5] *Cf.* above, p. 357, n. 4.
[6] See further below, pp. 388 f.   [7] Thuc. V, 67. 1 ; *cf* IV, 80.

Thucydides can scarcely have included the Sciritae among the so-called ' Lochoi ' from which the garrison of the island was drawn, in view of the difference in size and organisation (which he constantly stresses) between the Sciritae and the rest. That the 420 were drawn from the six πολιτικαὶ μόραι (as Xenophon calls them) can therefore scarcely be doubted.

All this implies that the information given by Thucydides about the numbers in the Enomotiae and larger units, and about the various ranks of officers, is likely to be correct because it was based on information gleaned from the Spartan prisoners taken at Sphacteria. It is essentially the same information, but in some respects more accurate in detail (for as we have seen Thucydides is confused about the application of the name *Lochos*) which reappears in the *Respublica Lacedaemoniorum* ascribed to Xenophon. The information in question was not, therefore, the fruit of Thucydides' own personal researches, but one of the special prizes won by the victorious Athenians at Sphacteria. It is well known, and was doubtless well realised by the Spartans, that the capture of prisoners will always give the enemy his chance of acquiring knowledge of this kind. Hence the ruthless Spartan order, always obeyed except at Sphacteria, to die rather than be captured.[1]

In 425 B.C., therefore, the Athenians appear to have pierced to no small extent the secrecy which had always enveloped Spartan military matters. In this way they must have learnt not only the names and sizes of the various Spartan hoplite units, but also the fact (mentioned by Thucydides in connection with Mantinea) [2] that the oldest and youngest together were roughly one-sixth of the whole. This piece of information further implies that the 292 prisoners were exhaustively questioned about their ages, as are modern prisoners of war. However reluctant one may be to question the veracity of Thucydides, his own

---

[1] *Cf.* Thuc. IV, 40 : τοὺς γὰρ Λακεδαιμονίους οὔτε λιμῷ οὔτ' ἀνάγκῃ οὐδεμιᾷ ἠξίουν τὰ ὅπλα παραδοῦναι, ἀλλ' ἔχοντας καὶ μαχομένους ὡς ἐδύναντο ἀποθνήσκειν. The famous Spartan apophthegm, ' return either with your shield or on it ', reflects the same principle.

[2] Thuc. V, 64.

account of how the estimate of one-sixth became known will convince no one.[1]

Whether Athenian generals were able to turn this new information to practical account seems doubtful. But it enables the modern investigator to move a little further towards discovering the explanation of the obvious superiority of the Spartan hoplite organisation, over a long period, to that of all other Greek states. For as Cavaignac has rightly pointed out, a necessary condition of efficiency in the hoplite organisation was the homogeneity of the battle-line ; [2] it must have no weak points arising from concentrating too young, or too old, or inadequately trained men in any one position. They must be equally distributed over the whole line. But this implies that they must be equally distributed in the smallest operational unit, which, as appears quite clearly from Xenophon and from the *Respublica Lacedaemoniorum*, was the Enomotia.[3] Each Enomotia extended in depth from the front to the rear of the hoplite phalanx, whatever the precise manner in which it was drawn up. It follows from this that the ' oldest and youngest ' who according to Thucydides were sent home before the battle of Mantinea, were on other occasions included in each Enomotia, in the same proportions (*viz.*, one-sixth of the total number). Thucydides tells us that the Enomotia at Mantinea numbered 32 men,[4] whether including the commanding officer (Enomotarch) or not is not immediately clear. Complete with ' oldest and youngest ' the Enomotia therefore numbered 39 or 40 men.[5] What now immediately strikes us is the close correspondence between this number and the number of the age-classes which in Sparta were called out for active military service ; for the age-limits were ἥβη (that is, the

---

[1] The whole available military force was marched out as far as Orestheum (in southern Arcadia), and one-sixth was then sent home again (Thuc. *loc. cit.*). In view of τὸ κρυπτόν, it is most unlikely that the Spartans would have allowed an enemy spy to observe this fact, if indeed it was a fact.   [2] *Cf. Klio*, XII, pp. 263 f.

[3] *Cf. Resp. Lac.* XI, 4, 8 ; Xen. *Hell.* VI, 4. 12.

[4] *Cf.* above, p. 384.

[5] If 32 men represents $\frac{5}{6}$ of the whole, 39 (actually 38·4) is the least possible total, but 40 is also possible on the assumption that the number 32 excludes the Enomotarch. 41 would be too high a total for the purpose.

attainment of the twentieth birthday) [1] to sixty,[2] comprising altogether forty age-classes (20–59 inclusive).

In view of the importance of securing homogeneity of the phalanx throughout its length, it therefore seems not unlikely that each Enomotia was composed of one man from each separate age-class, according to the outside age-limits which were fixed for each particular campaign. Thus a full levy would imply 40 men (including the Enomotarch) for each Enomotia ; a levy up to οἱ πέντε καὶ τριάκοντα ἀφ᾽ ἥβης,[3] and including the youngest age-groups, would imply 35 men. Such an arrangement would, of course, be impossible without a plentiful supply of reserve troops to take the place of members of the Enomotia who were killed or otherwise became permanent casualties ; but we have seen already that there was no difficulty about this.[4] And the hypothesis works out neatly in detail. For in the first place, the name Enomotia, implying that the members swore a common oath of mutual loyalty, indicates a permanently constituted body such as would be produced in the manner suggested, a new member coming in at the bottom (the age-class of the Eirenes) each year, while the oldest member on attaining the age of sixty went out at the top. But if the Spartan army had been drawn up in a manner similar to the Roman Republican army,[5] the age-groups being graded from front to back of the phalanx in respect to the army as a whole, in a manner differing in detail on each occasion according to the number of age-groups called out, the unity of the separate Enomotiae, which is implied by their very name, would be broken. In order to preserve that unity, the alternative method employed must have been that of sending the same number of additional men to each Enomotia from any new group of age-classes (e.g. those of the 35–39 group) which was called out. But this would only be possible if their exact number was known beforehand, and if it was exactly divisible by the total number of the Enomotiae ; and this could most conveniently be ensured in the manner suggested,

---

[1] Cf. pp. 93 f.
[2] Cf. Agesilaus' claim to exemption from active service, as if an ordinary citizen, ὅτι ὑπὲρ τεττεράκοντα ἀφ᾽ ἥβης εἴη (Xen. Hell. V, iv, 13).
[3] As at Leuctra (Xen. Hell. VI, iv, 17).
[4] Cf. above, pp. 354 f.   [5] Cf. Polyb. VI, 21, 22.

each Enomotia being composed of one man from each single year-class, so that the addition of five (or ten) more year-classes would automatically add five (or ten) more men to each Enomotia. Now, at the battle of Mantinea there were, as Thucydides tells us, thirty-two men to the Enomotia, and both the 'youngest' and the 'oldest' were excluded.[1] It is perfectly clear that by the 'oldest' were meant those in the 55–59 age-group, since those were not called out for the battle of Leuctra, but were called out in the critical situation which resulted from that defeat ;[2] and since there is evidence for a general system of grouping by five year-classes at a time.[3] The Enomotiae at Leuctra were drawn up in three files, and Xenophon says that this resulted in a depth of 'not more than twelve '.[4] This information would be compatible with the supposition that on this occasion there were 35 (ages 20–54) in each Enomotia, including the Enomotarch (i.e. two files of twelve men in each, and eleven in the third file). The extra three men, as compared with the number given by Thucydides for the Enomotiae at Mantinea, would be accounted for by two in the category of 'youngest', i.e. those of 20–21 and 21–22 years old, and the Enomotarch not counted by Thucydides.

It is easy to understand why the two youngest age-groups were not normally used in the hoplite line. At Leuctra there was a special reason for their inclusion, for it was essential to counter the great weight of the Theban attack by making the Spartan line as deep as possible. But in general, young men of twenty and twenty-one would not yet have attained the physical weight which was so necessary a part of hoplite efficiency, neither could their training as hoplites have proceeded very far ; on the other hand, they could usefully be employed on campaign in other ways, for example to ride the horses provided by the richer citizens,[5] or to assist in the *Krypteia*, or to control the Helots and ὑπασπισταί. We do know in fact that the Eirenes, that is, the 20–21 year-class at least, were brigaded separately at the battle of Plataea,[6] and this clearly means

---

[1] *Cf.* above, p. 388. [2] Xen. *Hell.* VI, iv, 17.
[3] *Ibid.* [4] *Ibid.* VI, iv, 12. [5] *Ibid.* VI, iv, 11.
[6] Herod. IX, 85 (the Eirenes buried in a separate tomb at Plataea).

that they were not fighting in the hoplite Morae. Moreover the separation of the two youngest year-classes from the rest, implied by these considerations as to the internal construction of the Enomotiae, clears up another point which has hitherto been doubtful, whether young men were classed as Eirenes at Sparta for one year or two. The existence of the term πρώτειραι at Sparta, meaning οἱ περὶ εἴκοσι ἔτη,[1] implies that there was also a class of second-year Eirenes ;[2] and this interpretation is now seen to fit in with the army arrangements. The four Lochoi (Pitanatai, Limnatai, etc.)[3] of Eirenes would on this sup-position be composed each of half the number in a year-class of the 20–21 and 21–22 age-groups, these being them-selves a carefully picked class, as all the evidence about the Ephebic organisation combines to tell us. To fit in with the general hoplite organisation, the four Lochoi would in fact consist of 48 men each if the Sciritae were excluded from the general arrangement, and of 56 if they were in-cluded.[4] In other words, a ' Lochos ' of Eirenes was about the same size as a Pentekostys of mature hoplites. But the ' Phylae ' of the same names from which these Lochoi were drawn would, of course, be a good deal larger, since they appear to have included in addition at least the Three Hundred Hippeis, and probably others also.[5] Much still remains obscure concerning these secondary Phylae, but all that concerns us immediately is to examine how far the hypothesis of Enomotiae composed of one man from each year-class is consistent with the evidence which has already been elicited about the Ephebic and post-Ephebic gymnastic organisation.

Before leaving the subject of the composition of the Enomotiae, we may perhaps venture a tentative explanation

[1] Cf. p. 89.

[2] The τριτίρενες mentioned in I.G. V, i. 1386 (Thuria in Messenia, C. II B.C.) do not necessarily imply that Spartans were Eirenes for three years, though they do imply that the Messenians, when they became independent, imitated the Spartan Ephebic system in general.   [3] Cf. p. 163.

[4] Each Enomotia ($\frac{1}{16}$ of a Mora) is here assumed to have included, when complete, 2 Eirenes, one from each age-group. Thus, the full number of Eirenes in the six πολιτικαὶ μόραι would be 2 × 96, with another 2 × 16 in the Lochos Skirites if that was also included in the general arrangement. The Mora of Brasideans and Neadamodeis, being of non-citizen origin, would certainly not be included in the same arrangement as the rest.

[5] Cf. pp. 133 f.

of the mysterious ' five Lochoi ' (Edolos, Sinis, Arimas, Ploas, Mesoages) [1] on this basis. If the Scholiast who mentions them was using the word Lochos in the sense which was universal (to judge from Arrian's use of it) [2] in the Hellenistic period, the Lochoi in question may have been the five files of the Enomotia when it was complete, an extra file (composed of the five oldest, the two youngest, and the Enomotarch) being added to the four normal files of eight men.[3] It has already been demonstrated at length that five Lochoi in the sense of main regiments are inconsistent with everything that can be discovered about the Spartan military organisation.

That the smallest operational units can at all periods have been constructed in the way suggested here for the Enomotia is not at all likely, since evidence exists for a subdivision of the main regiments into thirds and ninths which was evidently more primitive than the division into fours and sixteenths, and in fact appears to be connected with the well-known Dorian predilection for the number nine.[4] The tradition of this earlier arrangement was preserved in the celebrations at the Carnean festival at Sparta, which, according to a reliable authority of about 200 B.C., took the form of an imitation of the Spartan military organisation.[5] Nine mess-tents were constructed, each to contain nine men (three from each of three

---

[1] *Cf.* p. 315.　　　　　[2] Arr. *Tact.* V, 4 f.

[3] The names themselves have every appearance of being made-up mnemonics, invented to remind the leader of each group whether, when the Enomotia changed from line of march to battle-line, he was to lead his men to left or right of the centre (Mesoages) and into an odd or an even file. It may be noted that the names Sinis and Ploas have each five letters (suggesting the odd, *i.e.* outermost files) while the names Arimas and Edolos have each six letters, suggesting the two even files on each side of the centre.　　　　　[4] *Cf.* pp. 341 f.

[5] μίμημα στρατιωτικῆς ἀγωγῆς, *cf.* Demetrius of Scepsis *ap.* Athen. IV, 141e. The passage is taken from his commentary on a part of Iliad II, a work praised by Strabo (XIII, 603) for its laborious and careful scholarship. The accuracy of the particular piece of information in question is attested by the curious echo of the Spartan arrangement in the Roman Secular Games, at which there was a choir of 27 boys and 27 girls (*cf.* I.L.S. 5050, l. 147), sacrificial cakes were offered to Apollo in three batches of nine each (*ibid.* ll. 115, 117, 141), and the whole procedure was carried out *Achivo ritu* (*ibid.* l. 90). The probable explanation of the close similarity is Roman borrowing of the Carnean rites from Tarentum. The multiples of three are at all events specifically Dorian. *Cf.* pp. 341 f.

phratriae). This arrangement, whatever its precise significance, implies that a similar army organisation was already in existence at the time of the first institution of the Carnean festival (in the first half of the seventh century B.C.) [1] and for some considerable time afterwards ; otherwise the arrangement in question could not have remained the traditional one at the festival. It implies, as indeed the well-known fragment of Tyrtaeus does also,[2] a close connection of the army organisation in the seventh century with the three Dorian tribes. It further implies that each of the three tribes contained nine Phratriae, the Phratria being the smallest army division, and that an intermediate division existed, composed of three Phratriae and representing one-third of the tribe. It reminds us irresistibly of Nestor's advice to Agamemnon :

κρῖν' ἄνδρας κατὰ φῦλα, κατὰ φρήτρας, Ἀγάμεμνον [3]

and indeed must have been a survival from a very early period, since it finds a close parallel in Dorian Cos,[4] and is even implied by the representation of nine warriors running in three groups which occurs on a late Corinthian vase.[5]

But the triple division throughout does not necessarily mean that the six Morae were not yet in existence in the time of Tyrtaeus, for it is clearly possible that each Phyle supplied two Morae, each being subdivided into thirds and ninths. It does, however, imply a much smaller total number of hoplites than existed in the fifth century ; for the smallest unit of all is likely, in view of the attachment to a subdivision by threes throughout, to have consisted of 27 men (doubtless the τριακάδες referred to by Herodotus),[6] so that the intermediate regiment would consist of 81 men and the largest of 243. This is rather less than half the number in the fifty-century Morae. The Sciritae and other light-armed units which certainly existed at the time of

[1] Cf. Sosibius Laco, fr. 3 (F.H.G. II, p. 625) giving the date 676 B.C.
[2] Cf. Tyrtaeus, fr. I, 12 (Diehl).

χωρὶς Πάμφυλοί τε καὶ Ὑλλεῖς ἠδ[ὲ Δυμᾶνες]
ἀνδροφόνους μελίας χερσὶν ἀν[ασχόμενοι].

[3] Iliad II, 362.   [4] Cf. p. 409.
[5] Cf. Payne, Necrocorinthia, p. 325, no. 1390.
[6] Herod. I, 65 (ascribing them, on the authority of the Spartans themselves, to Lycurgus).

the second Messenian War were probably left out of
account altogether in that part of the Carnean celebrations which the Hellenistic author describes, since at that
time, at all events, they cannot have possessed full citizen
rights.[1]

The question of how the transition was effected from
a semi-feudal army organisation based on the three Dorian
tribes and embodying a division by threes throughout,
to an organisation based on a division by fours and independent both of the Dorian tribes and of local divisions,
is one which must be of the greatest interest to the historian
of Sparta. A general explanation which suggests itself,
in view of the evidence for a gradual increase in the size
and importance of the hoplite phalanx at the expense of
the light-armed and cavalry,[2] is that at some period, probably
towards the end of the seventh century,[3] the total number
of the hoplites was doubled and the depth of the hoplite
line doubled also, so that it now had six men in the file,
from front to rear, instead of the three implied by the
arrangements at the Carnea.[4] There would now be 486
men in each main regiment, and the size of the subdivisions
would be correspondingly doubled ; it would in fact be
a change closely parallel to that which seems to have been
made after Leuctra, but in the earlier instance, the frontal
length of the phalanx would remain as before. The change
would call into existence a unit of 54 men (a double Phratria,
and therefore including two officers) which could well be
the origin of the name *Pentekostys*, ' Fifty ', so oddly
attached in later times to the unit of 64 or more. The

[1] *Cf.* above, pp. 380 f.

[2] *Cf.* pp. 375 f. (Sciritae and Hippeis), p. 381 (archers).

[3] In view of the disappearance of archers (*cf.* p. 381) about that time
and in view of the possibility of providing additional land for hoplite
citizen-soldiers after the second Messenian War. It should be observed
that doubling the number of hoplites would not involve doubling the
number of citizen κλῆροι, since it is clear that those who had fought as
Hippeis in the primitive Spartan army were later transformed into hoplites.
The number of new κλῆροι added at the end of the second Messenian War
was probably under 1,000 (*cf.* above, p. 296).

[4] Pausanias' statement (IV, xi, 1) that already in the first Messenian
War the Spartans were using the deep hoplite phalanx (ἐτάσσοντο βαθείᾳ
τε ὡς οὔπω πρότερον καὶ πυκνῇ τῇ φάλαγγι) merits no more serious attention
than the rest of his account of the Messenian Wars. It conflicts with
the description of the Spartan army in Tyrtaeus (*cf.* above, p. 380).

second main change, from the organisation by thirds to the organisation by fourths, must have occurred at some time during the Pentekontaetia, for it involved the abandonment of the three Dorian tribes as the basis of the army organisation, and these were undoubtedly still in existence in the years immediately following the invasion of Xerxes.[1] It may further be argued from the ignorance of the Spartan fourfold division which seems to have persisted until the Athenian capture of Spartan prisoners at Sphacteria, that the change came after 462 B.C., when the Athenians had had direct contact with the Spartan army at Ithome. The period in which the change could most easily be made without attracting attention was in the long interval of Spartan quiescence between 446 and 431.

The main features of this change must be supposed to have been a further increase in the depth of the line, from six to eight men, the introduction of the Enomotia based wholly on age-classes (taking the place of the earlier Phratria) ; the increase in the size of all hoplite units (probably by increasing the length of the period of active service) and the substitution of a new division throughout by fours (made necessary by the new depth of the line) in place of the earlier division by threes. In place of a normal 27, the smallest unit now contained a normal 32, and in exceptional circumstances 40. This result could be obtained without upsetting the existing economic basis of society, by calling upon thirteen more age-classes than before, or eleven more exclusive of the two age-classes of Eirenes, who had not been included in the earlier hoplite arrangement.[2]

---

[1] In addition to the evidence of Pindar, *Pyth.* I, 62 f. (*cf.* above, p. 314), there is that of the Delphic column which is in the form of three entwined snakes, undoubtedly symbolising a predominantly Dorian army under Spartan leadership, as appears from the oracle cited by Herod. VI, 77 (δεινὸς ὄφις τριέλικτος ἀπώλετο δουρὶ δαμασθείς). For the metaphor of a snake applied to a marching army, *cf.* also Soph. *Ant.* 124 (ἀντιπάλῳ δυσχείρωμα δράκοντι). The Spartan army in Tyrtaeus' time was drawn up with the three Dorian tribes in separate blocks forming the two wings and the centre (*cf.* above, p. 393, n. 2). It is clear from Tyrt. fr. 7 (Diehl) that the three tribes were not in separate ranks from back to front, since the arrangement in depth was based on age-groups. If the three tribes also marched in parallel or approximately parallel columns, their winding course over the countryside would easily suggest the resemblance to three snakes. [2] *Cf.* above, pp. 390 f.

This would mean that the new age-limit of sixty years succeeded to an earlier limit of forty-nine.[1]

The introduction of the lighter hoplite equipment, which independent evidence dates to about the same period,[2] may actually have come at the same time as the change in internal organisation ; in any case it must be closely connected with it, for the introduction of lighter-armed hoplites would necessitate a deeper phalanx in order to compensate for the lack of weight, and the calling-up of men of the older age-classes would make it desirable to lighten the burden of equipment which hoplites had hitherto been called upon to carry. In whatever order these changes were carried out, whether they were effected at precisely the same time or not, it seems clear that the Spartans confronted the Athenian empire at the beginning of the Peloponnesian War with a completely new army, preserving all the advantages of the old system but much better adapted to the character of the country in which the fighting had to be done.

The earlier main changes in army organisation imply also political changes which fall outside the scope of this chapter. These will be considered in a more general survey of the evidence bearing upon the early history of Sparta in its various aspects.

[1] The description of the Spartan army in Tyrtaeus, fr. 7 (Diehl), at first sight implies the inclusion of old men at that time (κεῖσθαι πρόσθε νέων ἄνδρα παλαιότερον | ἤδη λευκὸν ἔχοντα κάρη πολιόν τε γένειον) ; but the interpretation to be placed upon it depends upon the age at which the poet wrote it, and the rest of the same fragment (extolling the beauty of youthful warriors even in death) suggests that the poet was himself young at the time. [2] Cf. above, pp. 367 f.

CHAPTER XI

THE MAIN STAGES IN THE DEVELOPMENT OF THE CONSTITUTION

§ 1. *General Conclusions from Earlier Chapters.*

The attempt to reconstruct in its chronological outlines the development of the Spartan city-state constitution has been left until last because all the preceding chapters have a bearing upon this most obscure subject. The theories which will be put forward in the present chapter are based, as far as possible, not only on the ancient evidence in general, but on the fresh information upon various aspects of Sparta which (as we may venture to hope) has been contributed by the rest of this work.

It will be well to begin by summarising the main positive conclusions which have emerged from the preceding chapters on the earlier Sparta. The investigation of similarities between Sparta and Crete (Chapter VI) established the feudal character of the earliest social organisation, and taken in conjunction with the study of the late survivals which form the subject of the first part of this work, enabled us to realise that selective devices invented in feudal times were preserved into much later times as a means of keeping up the numbers of a privileged citizen body. The collection of the evidence about the conquest of Laconia and Messenia (Chapter VIII) led to the conclusion that a homogeneous Dorian civilisation established before the Spartan conquest, determined in advance the lines of social and economic organisation under Spartan rule in these regions also. A semi-feudal civilisation resulted, and only a comparatively small part of either region was taken over directly by the Spartans as citizen land-lots (κλῆροι). The chapter on the traditions concerning Lycurgus (Chapter IX) exposed the worthlessness of the Spartan King-lists for dating purposes when applied in detail to short periods, and revealed the faked character of the Eurypontid list. At the same time we found that the peculiar Spartan system of chronology has its value for dating purposes when applied to long periods, and in particular leads to the conclusion that the Spartans themselves believed the reforms which they ascribed to Lycurgus to have been introduced in the year which we call 809 B.C. It also appeared likely that they had some justification for this belief, based upon some simple device for marking the passage of the years.

In Chapter X we followed the gradual transformation of the Spartan army from one consisting mainly of light-armed and cavalry, appropriate to a state organised on a feudal basis, to an army composed almost exclusively of hoplites, appropriate to the organisation of a fully developed unified state. This transformation was still far from complete in the first half of the seventh century, at the beginning of the second Messenian War.

In the present chapter an attempt will be made to utilise these general conclusions in reconstructing, in its main outlines, the probable development from the feudal to the ' totalitarian' state. That this development was in some respects slow and gradual, notably in the case of the internal organisation of the army, is evident. But at some early stage there must have occurred a sudden (or comparatively sudden) fundamental change ; for it is clear that the systematic scheme of conquest which brought the whole of formerly free Laconia under Spartan domination could not have been embarked upon by a feudally organised state.

The main changes which may be safely assumed to have occurred before the conquest of southern Laconia as far as the two promontories, and before the conquest of the eastern coast-towns of Messenia, are, first the transformation of the army, which must have been brought under close central control ; secondly, the development of a new system of land tenure (the distribution of the first citizen κλῆροι) controlled by the state ; thirdly, and connected with this, a transformation of the Syssitia, bringing them for the first time under state control and so reacting automatically upon the character of the army.

A fourth main change is perhaps less certainly attested than the others which have been mentioned, namely the creation of the double kingship.[1] But the doubts which

[1] Cf. Chap. IX, p. 338.

have been cast in an earlier section upon the existence of Eurypontid kings earlier than about 800 B.C., together with the evidence of cults for the great antiquity of the Agiad royal line (Appendix V), would fit in well with the hypothesis that the double kingship was introduced in connection with an early reorganisation of the army, perhaps in connection with a change which doubled its previous size.[1]

§ 2. The Relation of the Spartan Kingship to the Homeric Monarchy.

A strong argument in favour of supposing the double kingship at Sparta to have arisen at a comparatively late date is the close resemblance between the powers of each Spartan king, regarded in isolation from the other, and those of the Homeric kings. Yet nowhere in the Homeric poems have we any hint of dual kingship, or of kingship in commission ; even if it be true that the Homeric king was only *primus inter pares*,[2] yet the other βασιλῆες (twelve in the island of the Phaeacians),[3] with whom he shared his power, were very far below him in dignity and authority, and in fact may be seen to have enjoyed the title of βασιλεῖς only by courtesy, and because the single ruling βασιλεύς chose to summon them to his councils. In a society in which (taking Greece as a whole) there was a whole hierarchy of βασιλεῖς it was obviously difficult to draw a clear line of division. In very early times every noble was in some sense a βασιλεύς ; the impression given by the Homeric poems in this respect entirely agrees with the picture of the feudal age to which the present investigation has led us in the case of Sparta and the Cretan towns. Yet even in Homer that phase is disappearing ; and even though the lesser βασιλεῖς in each separate kingdom may be referred to as σκηπτοῦχοι,[4] the sceptre being the symbol of authority of their immediate overlord,[5] their constant identification

---

[1] See further below, pp. 421 f., 424.
[2] *Cf.* Schoemann, *Antiquitates Iuris Publici Graecorum* (1838), pp. 62 f.
[3] *Od.* VIII, 390.   [4] *Cf. Od.* VIII, 41, 47.
[5] *Od.* II, 37; cf. *Il.* XVIII, 505 ; XXVIII, 568. The σκῆπτρον of Agamemnon comes to him direct from Zeus (*Il.* II, 101 f.) ; an oath sworn upon it is the most solemn one conceivable. In *Il.* I, 234 f. the royal σκῆπτρον in general stands for the symbol of justice. See further below, p. 410.

with the members of the deliberative Council of the king,[1] and in some cases more specifically with the Gerontes,[2] means that they must be regarded as the origin, not of the βασιλεύς of historical times, but of the Gerontes. It may incidentally be observed that this conclusion entirely explains the limitation of membership of the Gerusia at Sparta (until the time of Cleomenes III) to members of certain aristocratic families only. The leading part which the single Homeric king, upon whom all the lesser βασιλεῖς (the βουληφόροι ἄνδρες) were directly dependent, himself played in these councils [3] also explains the position of the Spartan kings (apart from their collegiality) with regard to the Gerusia.[4]

It is, however, to the single overlord of the lesser βασιλῆες (so-called) that each Spartan king must be directly compared. The Spartan king, like the Homeric king, is god-descended,[5] and god-protected ; [6] his rule is strictly hereditary ; [7] he enjoys the revenues of hereditary estates (τεμένη) set apart for him by the common consent of his people.[8] The Spartan king, like his Homeric prototype, also enjoys the right to definite gifts and prerogatives at regular intervals and for

---

[1] Cf. Od. VI, 54 ; Il. X, 414.   [2] Il. II, 53 f. ; cf. 79, 85 f.

[3] The epithet βουληφόρος in Homer is applied equally to the single βασιλεύς (even to Agamemnon himself. Cf. Il. II, 24) and to his councillors (cf. Il. VII, 126 ; X, 414). The single βασιλεύς presides himself over the council of lesser βασιλῆες (Gerontes) and initiates the discussion (cf. Il. II, 55 f.).

[4] As clearly indicated both in the archaic Rhetra examined below, pp. 415 f., and by Tyrtaeus, fr. 3a (Diehl)

ἄρχειν μὲν βουλῆς θεοτιμήτους βασιλῆας
οἷσι μέλει Σπάρτης ἱμερόεσσα πόλις.

[5] I.e. from Herakles. The belief that the Spartan kings were more than mortal still persisted in the fifth and fourth centuries (cf. Thuc. V, 16. 2, [Xen.] Resp. Lac. XV, 2. 7). The Homeric epithet διογενεῖς was intended to be interpreted literally. Cf. Il. IX, 106 (Agamemnon), IV, 489 (Ajax).

[6] θεοτιμητός ; cf. the passage of Tyrtaeus cited above, n. 4, and Il. II, 196 f., which may have inspired the epithet.

[7] For the Homeric kings cf. Od. I, 387 ; Il. II, 46 etc. An instance of the royal power being shared with a son-in-law with obvious intention of its transmission to the daughter's son occurs in Il. VI, 191 f. (referring, however, to Lycia). But to the Greek mind, inheritance through an ἐπίκληρος was never regarded as involving a departure from strict hereditary succession.

[8] For the τεμένη of the Spartan kings, cf. p. 286, note 2 ; for those of Homeric kings, Od. VI, 293, XI, 185 ; Il. VI, 194 ; XII, 313 ; XX, 184.

special occasions,[1] as for example a double share at all the meals in the Syssitia to assist him in entertaining guests, a sucking pig from every litter to provide him with the material for sacrifices. The corresponding obligations, to perform certain sacrifices for the people, especially on campaign,[2] and to entertain the nobles and distinguished strangers at banquets [3] were also a well-recognised part of the functions of every Homeric king. In the judicial sphere, the powers of the Spartan kings had been reduced by the fifth century B.C. to a mere shadow of what they had been formerly,[4] but still showed some survivals of the pre-eminent right of the Homeric monarch to dispense justice.[5] But in the purely military sphere the Spartan king still enjoyed, even in the fourth century B.C., a complete authority [6] which can best be compared to the *imperium militiae* of the Roman consul. In this respect his powers seem to have suffered scarcely any diminution since the Homeric period, although it is clear that the principle of dual control on campaigns, for so long as it lasted,[7] must have imposed a very considerable limitation.

As in Rome, so in Sparta the theoretical conflict between the recognised supremacy of each war-leader (in the military sphere) and the principle of complete equality between two colleagues was only solved for practical purposes by ceasing to send out both colleagues in command of the same army.

[1] For the perquisites of Spartan kings, cf. Herod VI, 56, 57 ; [Xen.] *Resp. Lac.* XV, 1 ; for those of Homeric kings (δῶρα, δωτῖναι), *Il.* IX, 155 ; XII, 310 ; XVII, 225, and Hesiod's epithet βασιλῆες δωροφάγοι (*Works and Days*, 38, 264). Schoemann (*ibid.* p. 65) interprets as compulsory presents from subjects the ῥητὰ γέρατα referred to by Thuc. I, 13 (ἐπὶ ῥητοῖς γέρασι πατρικαὶ βασιλεῖαι). This view receives support from Herodotus' use of the term γέρεα in VI, 56, to denote the privileges of the Spartan kings.
[2] Aristotle remarks of the early kings in general that they performed the sacrifices ὅσαι μὴ ἱερατικαί only (*Pol.* III, 14. 12 ; cf. VI, 8. 20). This is true both of the Homeric kings (cf. Schoemann, *ibid.* p. 63) and of the Spartan ones (cf. (Xen.) *Resp. Lac.* XIII, 2f.). For other aspects of the Spartan kings as intermediaries with the gods see further below, p. 407.
[3] Cf. [Xen.] *Resp. Lac.* XV, 4 ; Plut. *Cleom.* 13, and for the Homeric kings, *Od.* VII, 49, 189 f. ; VIII, 41 ; XIII, 8 ; *Il.* IV, 259, etc.
[4] See further below, p. 406.
[5] As indicated by the epithets δικασπόλοι and θεμιστοπόλοι (*Il.* I, 238 ; *Od.* XI, 186, etc.) ; cf. also Arist. *Pol.* III, 14. 14.
[6] Cf. [Xen.] *Resp. Lac.* XIII, 10, 11. In the fourth century the far greater extent of their authority in the military than in the civil sphere leads Aristotle to regard the Spartan kingship as a life-generalship (στρατηγία τις ἀΐδιος ; cf. *Pol.* III, 14. 4, etc.).   [7] See below, p. 407.

But if in the case of Rome the theoretical conflict arises out of the attempt to preserve unchanged the character of the early kingship in the person of two annual magistrates, even more clearly must this have been the case in Sparta, where the powers of the kings were not nearly so far limited as those of even the earliest Roman consuls, but continue to be life-long and hereditary for so long as the kingship itself persists.

There are therefore four good reasons for believing that the double kingship at Sparta developed comparatively late out of the Homeric monarchy ; the parallel between Spartan kings and Roman consuls in the military sphere, the many close resemblances in their minor functions and attributes between Spartan kings and Homeric βασιλεῖς in general, the survival at Cos of the title of μόναρχος,[1] implying a single king, in a state where a large number of characteristically Dorian institutions survived, and lastly, the faked character of the early generations of the Eurypontid kinglist at Sparta. The transformation of the monarchy into a ' diarchy ' would obviously mark a very significant stage in the development of the Spartan constitution. To the question whether this change is to be connected with the ' Lycurgan ' reforms a return will be made later.[2]

§ 3. *The History of the Ephorate.*

Whether Herodotus is right in ascribing the introduction of the ephors to the Lycurgan reforms,[3] or whether the tradition is correct which ascribes this innovation to Theopompus at the end of the eighth century B.C.[4] are questions which cannot be answered without more exhaustive inquiry into the nature of the office itself. Both from the tradition that the Spartan sage Chilon altered the existing powers of the ephors in the first half of the sixth century,[5] and from the extremely wide powers enjoyed by the ephors in later times, it is evident that this office suffered many transformations ; and no plausible guess can be made about the date of its origin until some attempt has been made to reveal

---

[1] *Cf.* Paton and Hicks, *Inscriptions of Cos* (1891), Index III, s.v.
[2] *Cf.* below, p. 421.   [3] Herod. I, 65. See further below, p. 419.
[4] *Cf.* p. 405, n. 4.   [5] *Ibid.*

the character of the powers attached to it in the early stages of its existence.

The number of the ephors first attracts attention in this connection. For although it has been shown in earlier chapters to be impossible to trace a relation between the number of the ephors in the developed constitution and the number of the tribes of the citizen body,[1] it will be generally admitted that the absence of such a connection is curious, and suggests that five was not the original number of the ephors ; the more so, in that several of the Laconian towns of the Perioikoi had a board of three ephors as their chief magistrates,[2] and that three ephors appear as the chief officials of the *Oba* of Amyclae [3] in purely Spartan territory. Pursuing this line of speculation, we find that two of the five Spartan ephors had functions in time of war which were not shared by the other three, going out with the army on campaign and serving in some capacity as advisers to the king.[4] These ephors are said to have been in an entirely subordinate position, being there less to act as a check upon the king's actions [5] (which indeed might have had fatal military consequences) than to assist him, when called upon by the king himself, to decide any special problems which might arise.[6] It was for the king to decide whether, when, and to what extent he should make use of the services of these advisers ; whereas in their relations with the whole board of ephors in time of peace, the kings in the fifth century B.C. (to which period the evidence for the two campaigning ephors relates) could by no means dictate, but had to accept control themselves.

[1] *Cf.* above, p. 167.　　[2] *Cf.* above, p. 283.　　[3] *Cf.* above, p. 165.
[4] Xen. *Hell.* II, iv, 36 : ὥσπερ γὰρ νομίζεται σὺν βασιλεῖ δύο τῶν ἐφόρων συστρατεύεσθαι κ.τ.λ. According to Solari (*Ricerche Spartane*, 1907, pp. 153 f.) this occasion (the siege of Athens in 403) marks the last or nearly the last appearance of the two ephors in question ; they were in his view supplanted by 30 σύμβουλοι in 400/399. They are, however, mentioned as if still existing in *Resp. Lac.* XIII, 5, but it is possible that the author is here guilty of an anachronism. Their presence at Plataea is implied by Herod. IX, 76, and with Agis in 418 by Thuc. V, 60. 1 (ἑνὶ ἀνδρὶ κοινώσας τῶν ἐν τέλει.　　[5] As suggested by Solari, *ibid.* p. 160.
[6] *Cf. Resp. Lac.* XIII, 5 : πάρεισι δὲ καὶ τῶν ἐφόρων δύο, οἳ πολυπραγμονοῦσι μὲν οὐδέν, ἢν μὴ ὁ βασιλεὺς προσκαλῇ· ὁρῶντες δὲ ὅτι ποιεῖ ἕκαστος πάντας σωφρονίζουσιν, ὡς τὸ εἰκός. The author appears to suppose that these ephors on campaign had the general supervisory powers which the ephors normally possessed over Spartan citizens. It is clear that he does not mean that they supervised the kings.

It seems therefore not improbable that these two ephors mark the survival of a much earlier stage in the development of the magistracy, and as a rule it may be supposed that the king in command of the expedition would not make use of them to confirm any important decision affecting the interests of the whole state. Thus Pausanias in 403, when he received overtures of peace from the Athenians, first communicated them to the two ephors present with the army, but these passed them on to the home government, who sent out a commission of fifteen Spartans to arrange the terms of peace.[1] But on an earlier occasion, when Agis in 418 made use of one of his two advisory ephors to conclude a four-months' truce with Argos instead of continuing the campaign,[2] ' the Spartans ' (i.e. the ephors and Gerusia) on his return introduced a new law making it necessary for any Spartan commander in future to be accompanied on campaign by ten special advisers (σύμβουλοι).[3] Agis may have been reviving a traditional power of the king on campaign which had become a dead letter ; the two ephors who still continued to be sent on campaigns after the introduction of the σύμβουλοι represent a mere archaic survival, and must be supposed to have been present only in a formal capacity.[4]

If the sending of two ephors on campaigns was indeed a survival from a much earlier period, an explanation which at first sight suggests itself is that in some way they represented the two Dorian tribes which were not represented by the king himself, namely, the *Pamphyloi* and *Dymanes*, for both kings were alike attached to the tribe *Hylleis*, claiming direct descent from Hyllus himself.[5] But further speculation on this point is best postponed until other survivals from early times among the powers of the ephors have been included in our consideration.

Obvious instances of such survivals are the ephors' right of watching the night sky at intervals of nine years for some sign that the conduct of the kings was displeasing to the gods,[6] and the custom of sending them to the oracular

---

[1] Xen. *Hell.* II, iv, 36 f. [2] Thuc. V, 60. [3] *Ibid.* 63.
[4] As the author of the *Resp. Lac.* implies, *cf.* above, p. 403, n. 6.
[5] *Cf.* Herod. VII, 204 ; VIII, 131.
[6] Plut. *Agis.* 11. If an ephor made a declaration to this effect, the king indicated by the portent was temporarily deposed until the advice of an oracle could be obtained.

shrine of Pasiphaë at Thalamae in Messenia, there to receive the instructions of the goddess in a dream for the guidance of their city.[1] As being the nearest oracular shrine to Sparta, Thalamae might easily be used for this purpose by Spartan ephors even before the first Messenian War, but whatever view may be taken about this, the custom clearly indicates that in the earliest period of the existence of the office the ephors possessed the right of divination, and were credited with the power to interpret the will of the gods to their fellow-Spartans. Another indication of the same thing is that it rested with the ephors alone to decide when an intercalary month should be inserted.[2]

These obviously archaic features in the ephors' powers throw doubt on the explanation of their origin propounded by Cleomenes III—that they first came into existence to assist the kings in jurisdiction, during their frequent absences from Sparta at the time of the first Messenian War.[3] The tradition to which Cleomenes was referring, that King Theopompus ' mingled the ephors with the kings '[4] was evidently a matter of dispute among the Spartans themselves, since others maintained that it was the ephor Chilon in the sixth century who first ' yoked the kings and ephors together,'[5] and Cleomenes himself had no better argument to bring forward than the custom of the kings to refuse the ephors' summons twice before obeying it at the third time.[6] It seems more likely that there was some archaic magical significance in the triple summons, and that it had no special connection with the judicial powers of the ephors, to which

[1] Cf. Part I, p. 59, n. 2, and in addition to the authorities there cited, Cic. de Div. I, 43, 96 : atque etiam, qui praeerant Lacedaemoniis non contenti vigilantibus curis in Pasiphaae fano, quod est in agro propter urbem, somniandi causa incubabant, quia vera quietis oracula ducebant. Cicero is wrong in supposing that the shrine was near Sparta, as is proved by the record of an ephor's dream in the temple at Messenian Thalamae in I.G. V, 1, 1317 (cited earlier, p. 140).

[2] Plut. Agis. 16.   [3] Plut. Cleom. 10.

[4] Cf. Plut. ad principem ineruditum, 2 : ὅς (Theopompus) πρῶτος ἐν Σπάρτῃ τοῖς βασιλεύουσι καταμίξας τοὺς ἐφόρους κ.τ.λ. The phrase seems to have been taken from some well-known early source, in view of the similar expression used by Cleomenes III of the kings and Gerontes (Plut. Cleom. 10 : ἔφη γὰρ ὑπὸ τοῦ Λυκούργου τοῖς βασιλεῦσι συμμιχθῆναι τοὺς γέροντας) and in view of the variation of it recorded in connection with Chilon, who πρῶτος εἰσηγήσατο ἐφόρους τοῖς βασιλεῦσι παραζευγνύναι (Diog. Laert. I, 3, 1).   [5] Cf. preceding note.   [6] Plut. Cleom. 10.

Cleomenes was referring. It seems *a priori* probable that it was only at a comparatively late date in the development of the Spartan ' mixed constitution ' that the ephors first acquired the right of sitting with the kings to dispense justice, a right which had resulted by Herodotus' time in depriving the kings of the power of hearing any cases alone, with the exception of those relating to the disposal of heiresses in marriage and one or two other minor matters.[1] But an early tradition that Theopompus first ' mixed ' or ' yoked ' the ephors with the kings could provide no evidence for the date when the ephorate was first instituted. The indications that it was in origin a Dorian rather than a purely Spartan office,[2] and the peculiar archaic survivals already referred to, combine to suggest that it came into existence long before the ephors began to encroach on the judicial powers of the kings. A more likely interpretation of the tradition about their ' yoking ' would be that Theopompus first admitted them as assessors when he dispensed justice, and Chilon first extended their scope in this capacity, or perhaps first made their presence compulsory.

It seems at all events clear, if there is any value in this Spartan tradition at all, that any *independent* jurisdiction on the part of the ephors, and consequently all their jurisdiction in cases arising out of private contracts, had its origin later than the time of Chilon. The jurisdiction in συμβολαῖαι δίκαι to which Aristotle refers [3] would not seem likely to have arisen at all until the introduction of normal currency about 400 B.C. enabled individual trade to develop ; it seems possible that the ephors acquired independent jurisdiction earlier than this in cases arising out of private family law, since already by the time of Herodotus the jurisdiction of the king in this sphere was very narrowly limited.[4] The ephors in fact appear to have encroached gradually upon the jurisdiction of the king in affairs of private law, while the Gerusia encroached upon it in the sphere of criminal law.[5] This does nothing to show that

---

[1] *Cf.* Herod. VI, 57 : δικάζειν δὲ μούνους τοὺς βασιλῆας τοσάδε μοῦνα, πατρούχου τε παρθένου πέρι . . . καὶ ὁδῶν δημοσιέων πέρι, καὶ ἤν τις θετὸν παῖδα ποιέεσθαι ἐθέλῃ.   [2] *Cf.* p. 283.   [3] *Cf.* above, p. 210, n. 4.
[4] *Cf.* Herod. VI, 57 (cases concerning heiresses).
[5] *Cf.* above, p. 210, n. 4.

the *original* function of the ephors was in the sphere of jurisdiction.

Pursuing further the question of the earlier powers of the ephors, we may note that whereas it was the function of the ephors to receive and bring back to Sparta the oracles of Pasiphaë, it was the kings who were the depositaries of all oracles.[1] And when it was the oracle at Delphi which required to be consulted, two Πύθιοι for each king, chosen by the kings themselves, were sent.[2] These facts suggest a very close connection between the ephors and the kings in the earliest times, for there seems to be a parallel between the sending of ephors to Thalamae and the sending of Πύθιοι to Delphi (doubtless at a later stage in the development of the Spartan state, when the ephors had become indispensable as magistrates and could not be spared for long periods of absence). The kings themselves must have possessed in early times very considerable powers in the matter of interpreting the will of the gods, for they still retained such powers to a notable extent in the early fourth century when on campaigns.[3] According to Cicero (who is right about the ephors and their consultation of the oracle at Thalamae)[4] each king had one assessor to act as his augur,[5] but of this personage there is no sign among the various officials attached to the kings in the fifth century and later,[6] unless we are to interpret in this light the two ephors sent on campaign, who appear to have nothing else to do. It may be objected to this that there were two ephors on the occasions when the number is mentioned, and only one king. But until trouble resulted from the practice late in the sixth century, two kings seem to have been normally sent, each presumably commanding half the army.[7] It was doubtless a mere survival of ancient practice which

---

[1] Herod. VI, 57.　　　　　　　　[2] *Ibid. cf. Resp. Lac.* XV, 5.
[3] Cf. *Resp. Lac.* XIII, 2 f., and for their priestly powers in general, *ibid.* XV, 5 : ὡς μήποτε ἀπορῆσαι βασιλεὺς ἱερῶν ἤν τι δεηθῇ θεοῖς συμβουλεύσασθαι; Arist. *Pol.* III, 14. 3 : τὰ πρὸς τοὺς θεοὺς ἀποδέδοται τοῖς βασιλεῦσιν.
[4] Cf. above, p. 405, n. 1.　　　　[5] *De Div.* I, 43. 95.
[6] These were, in addition to the Πύθιοι already mentioned, τρεῖς ἄνδρες τῶν ὁμοίων (*Resp. Lac.* XIII, 1) and πυρφόρος (*ibid.* XIII, 2).
[7] Cf. Herod. V, 75 ; Paus. IV, 7. 7. According to Pausanias, Polydorus in the first Messenian War is said to have commanded the left wing, Theopompus the right. This tradition is apocryphal, designed to throw lustre on the Eurypontid king, but the double command is attested later.

led the Spartans to continue to send two ephors even in the later period when only one king was in command.

The belief that each king originally had a deputy is further strengthened by the fact that in later times most, if not all the colleges of Spartan magistrates had σύναρχοι attached to them, with the rôle of assessors.[1] The observations which have been made above as to the ephors' ancient powers of divination do not, of course, imply that these were the *only* powers possessed by the ephors in early times, any more than the survival of priestly functions in the case of the kings implies that these were their only original powers. Rather does the survival of deputies to the kings in one sphere suggest that originally they had deputies whose authority approximated much more nearly to their own, and this is the suggestion which is now put forward as to the origin of the ephorate.[2] In particular, the ephors attached especially to the kings may well have had the duty of selecting the citizens for army service ; for the early meaning of ἐφορᾶν ' to choose out ' is attested by Homeric usage,[3] and if this was the original meaning of the ephors' title, it would explain the powers which they enjoyed in this respect in much later times, when it was for them to proclaim the imminence of a campaign (φρουρὰν φαίνειν), and to decide which age-classes should be called out for the purpose.[4] The very oddness of the expression ' to proclaim a defence ', applied to every military expedition whether inside the Peloponnese or not,[5] implies that this particular power of the ephors was not acquired late, but goes back to a period when all Sparta's wars were on her own Laconian frontiers, in other words, to the time before the annexation of Messenia. It was only natural that in

[1] For references, see I.G. V, i, index IV, 3 *s.v.* See further, pp. 143 f., 166.

[2] The theory of Solari (*op. cit.* pp. 153 f.) that what he regards as ' royal ' elements in the powers of the ephors (levying of troops, dealings with foreign powers, etc.) only developed in the fifth century (suggested chronological development *ibid.* p. 175) is vitiated by being based wholly on literary evidence belonging to the period with which he deals, and mentioning the relevant information only by accident. Too much stress is laid throughout on the *argumentum ex silentio.*

[3] *Cf. Od.* II, 294 ; *Il.* IX, 167.

[4] *Cf.* Xen. *Hell.* III, ii, 23, 25 ; V, iv, 13, 47 ; VI, iv, 17.

[5] *E.g.* against Thebes (*ibid.* V, iv, 13, 47).

later times the title of ephor should be assumed to mean what it appeared to mean in view of the current meaning of the word, namely ' supervisors ' and that it should result eventually in the ephors' powers being almost wholly restricted to the moral sphere.[1]

But we still require an explanation of the number of the ephors. If only two kings, why five ephors, not two ? The explanation which naturally suggests itself is that the other three were originally attached to the three φυλοβασιλεῖς of the Hylleis, Pamphyloi and Dymanes. These officials are not directly attested in Sparta, but must none the less have existed at one time for a variety of reasons. In the first place, three βασιλεῖς attached to the three Dorian tribes existed in Dorian Cos ;[2] in the second place, φυλοβασιλεῖς existed in early times not only in Athens but in many other Greek states ;[3] and in the third place, the separate functioning of the three Dorian tribes in the seventh-century army organisation[4] implies that βασιλεῖς attached to the separate tribes were required, at that period at least, in Sparta. In historical times the functions of these βασιλεῖς (as they are called *tout simplement* elsewhere than at Athens) were purely religious, but it must not be assumed from later survivals that this was always the case. The identity of name with the βασιλεύς of the whole state, whose chief functions in early times are shown by the evidence of Homer to have been military rather than religious, implies that the βασιλεῖς of the early Phylae were each the leaders of their tribe (Hylleis, or whatever it might be) on the field of battle. Each of these would also need his deputy to call out the men of the tribe and to assist in the taking of omens, and these deputies, it may be suggested, were the origin of the other three Spartan ephors.

It may be objected against this theory that the Homeric poems provide no clear evidence that the Homeric kings in general, who in other respects seem so closely similar to the Spartan ones, had deputies of the kind suggested. To this it may be replied that the Homeric kings cannot possibly

[1] *Cf.* pp. 157 f. [2] Paton and Hicks, *op. cit.* no. 37, l. 21.
[3] *Cf.* Arist. *Pol.* VI, 8. 20 (1322B), assigning only priestly functions to the βασιλεῖς, but speaking of his own times. [4] *Cf.* pp. 392 f.

have performed unaided all the multifarious tasks for which
the sole ruler was responsible, and that the tasks in question
are unlikely to have been delegated by the king to individual
members of the aristocracy in turn, for fear of inviting
encroachment upon his own powers. Nor would any epic
poet be likely to bring into the forefront in his poem administrative details of this sort. But in fact we do find
hints of the existence of deputies to the kings in the κήρυκες
(one occupying a position of special trust in each case) [1]
who are sent by the king to summon the *Laos* that he may
address them,[2] to summon the council of lesser βασιλεῖς,[3]
to marshal the Laos at a public trial,[4] and to summon
the chiefs to battle.[5] All these functions of the κῆρυξ
could well give rise to the corresponding powers of the
Spartan ephors. But further, although the Homeric poems
provide indications that the κήρυκες in general are in process of being degraded to a lower position in society than
they had formerly occupied,[6] there are also clear indications
of a stage when they actually were the deputies of the
kings, with the right to bear the royal sceptre, and through
this symbol of authority even to confer upon individuals
the right to speak either among the Gerontes or in the
assembly of the people.[7] The high social position and the
hereditary privileges enjoyed by the Genos of the *Kerykes*
at Athens remained to attest the distinguished position
originally held by the κήρυκες in Homeric times.

The peculiarly Spartan procedure on the occasion of a
meeting of the public assembly in the fifth and fourth
centuries seems to be a direct survival from the Homeric
arrangements which have just been described, and thus
goes far to support the explanation of the ephors' powers,
namely, their derivation from the Homeric κήρυκες, which
is now being put forward. One king or both, the whole
Gerusia in a body, and the ephors, all attended the meetings

---

[1] *Cf. Il.* II, 184 (the κῆρυξ of Odysseus, who follows him on campaign) ;
XVII, 322 f. (of Aeneas) ; *Od.* VIII, 8 (of Alcinous).

[2] *Il.* II, 96 f.   [3] *Od.* VIII, 11 f. ; *Il.* II, 50 f.

[4] *Il.* XVIII, 503 f.   [5] *Il.* II, 442 f.

[6] *Cf. eg. Il.* I, 321 : τώ οἱ ἔσαν κήρυκε καὶ ὀτρηρὼ θεράποντε (of the two
heralds of Agamemnon, sent to fetch Briseis from Achilles).

[7] *Cf. Il.* XVIII, 503 f. (the κῆρυξ hands the σκῆπτρον to each councillor
about to speak) ; *Od.* II, 36 f. (similar procedure in the assembly of the
people. The king's sceptre is evidently meant. *Cf. Il.* XXIII, 567).

of the Apella; and in the public debate which preceded the vote, kings, Gerontes and ephors, but not any member of the Apella itself, were competent to speak.[1] An ephor presided, and was responsible for putting the question at issue to the Apella for its final decision,[2] just as the Homeric κῆρυξ had been. Moreover it rested with the ephors to summon the Gerusia when any ῥήτρα was to be proposed to the Apella, and to lay the projected ῥήτρα before the Gerontes first.[3] There is no precise parallel to this in Homer, but the same procedure may be inferred from the part played by a κῆρυξ in criminal trials held before the Gerusia.[4] To this last there is a precise parallel in later Sparta, when the ephors were competent to summon the Gerusia to hold a trial, and presided over it.[5] It also rested with the ephors to summon the Apella,[6] as it had been the function of the Homeric κῆρυξ to summon the Laos. In all these cases it is probable that the ephors had only acquired the right of acting independently of a king after the once unlimited powers of the kingship had been considerably diminished.

It may be thought an objection to the theory here put forward that Aristotle describes the Spartan ephors as οἱ τυχόντες and ἐκ τοῦ δήμου πάντες.[7] The Homeric κήρυκες were obviously important and well-born personages, at least in origin, whereas Aristotle gives the impression that ephors were not only elected by the common people, but also exclusively from among their number, like the Roman tribunes. This, however, is a misleading impression; it is true that all without distinction were eligible for office, at least in Aristotle's time and later,[8] but members of the highest aristocracy are also recorded to have held it.[9]

[1] Cf. Thuc. I, 79, 3, with 85 ad fin. A parallel to this instance (432 B.C.) is provided by Xenophon's account of the conspiracy of Cinadon in 397 (Hell. III, iii, 5. The occasion is clearly a meeting of the Apella). See further, Appendix VI, pp. 482 f.

[2] Thuc. I, 87. Cf. Plut. Agis 8 (the Lysander who presided being then ephor, apparently ephor eponymos).

[3] Cf. Plut. Agis 8 : διαπραξάμενος ὁ Ἆγις ἔφορον γένεσθαι τὸν Λύσανδρον, εὐθὺς εἰσέφερε δι' αὐτοῦ ῥήτραν εἰς τοὺς γέροντας, ἧς ἦν κεφάλαια κ.τ.λ.

[4] Cf. Il. XVIII, 503 f.   [5] Cf. Plut. Agis 19 (trial of Agis IV for treason).

[6] Cf. Polyb. IV, 34. 3 : οἱ δ᾽ἔφοροι . . . περὶ μὲν τῶν βασιλέων ἔφασαν μετὰ ταῦτα βουλεύσεσθαι, τῷ δὲ Μαχατᾷ συνεχώρησαν δώσειν τὴν ἐκκλησίαν.

[7] Arist. Pol. II, 9. 19 ; 10. 10 ; cf. 6. 17.

[8] Cf. p. 156.   [9] Cf. p. 156, n. 7.

There is in fact a much closer correspondence between the ephors and the Roman quaestors than between the ephors and the tribunes, even though the ephors possessed the Spartan equivalent of the tribune's right *agere cum senatu*. In the early stages of the development of the quaestorship there were only two quaestors, one directly appointed by each consul and serving as his personal assistant.[1] This clearly implies a still earlier stage when there was only a single quaestor for the king, corresponding to the Homeric κῆρυξ. Later in the Republic the quaestors, like the Spartan ephors, came to be magistrates of the state, democratically elected.[2] In other respects also the quaestors of the early Republic are remarkably similar to the Spartan ephors ; they accompany the consul on campaign,[3] they have the right of holding *contiones*,[4] they enjoy a right of jurisdiction delegated to them by the consuls,[5] they are responsible for the reception of foreign envoys and for their entertainment.[6] The only conspicuous difference is that whereas the number of the quaestors was only gradually raised from two after the transformation of the quaestorship into an elective magistracy, the number of the ephors must be supposed to have been already four at least (one for the single βασιλεύς of primitive times and one each for the three φυλοβασιλεῖς) in the period before the transformation of the ephorate into a magistracy.

It remains to discover if possible how this change, which must evidently be postulated, fits in with the tradition of the Lycurgan reforms.

§ 4. *The Nature of the Lycurgan Reforms.*

Chronological reasons require us to identify the long series of wars which, according to Spartan tradition, immediately followed the Lycurgan reforms,[7] with the first expansion into the southern promontories, beginning about 800 B.C.[8] The reforms themselves are not improbably to

---

[1] *Cf.* Mommsen, *Römisches Staatsrecht*, II[3], pp. 527 f.
[2] Tac. *Ann.* XI, 22.
[3] *Cf.* Mommsen, *ibid.* pp. 548 f.   It is not clear on what grounds Mommsen assumes that the military functions of the quaestors were of later origin than their civil ones.   [4] *Ibid.* I, 200, n. 2.
[5] *Ibid.* I, 164, 195 ; II, 537 f.   [6] *Ibid.* II, 550.
[7] *Cf.* p. 330.   [8] *Cf.* p. 295.

be dated with precision in 809 B.C.,[1] at a time when law-lessness (κακονομία) had been rife in Sparta 'longer than in any other known state '.[2] This tradition, appearing in literary form in the fifth century B.C., implies that the Lycurgan reforms marked the first notable change in the constitutional sphere since the period depicted in the Homeric poems. Had the Spartans themselves, in Herodotus' time or earlier, any definite evidence upon which this belief was founded ? In this section an attempt will be made to answer this question, and also to arrive at an estimate of the probable nature of the ' Lycurgan ' reforms themselves by the process of removing later accretions.

At first sight the ancient sources give little promise of providing reliable information, since the surviving refer-ences in Tyrtaeus are disappointingly vague, merely testi-fying to provision for two kings, a Gerusia and a public assembly, without mention of Lycurgus ; while the account of Herodotus (which purports to reflect the Spartan tradi-tion in his own time) is detailed at the expense of accuracy, and attributes to Lycurgus a good deal that is demonstrably anachronistic. But on further examination both these sources can be shown to go back to an earlier one, which is the oracle-Rhetra quoted and expounded by Aristotle,[3] together with an addition said to have been made by the kings Theopompus and Polydorus at the time of the first Messenian War.

The text of this document, cited at length by Plutarch (*Lycurgus* 6) has inevitably led to much discussion and controversy among modern scholars. Its most recent exponent, Wade-Gery,[4] accepts it as a genuine product of

[1] *Cf.* pp. 346 f.   [2] *Cf.* p. 246.
[3] *ap.* Plut. *Lycurg.* 6. The only direct comment on the Rhetra ascribed by Plutarch to Aristotle is his explanation of the names Babyka and Knakion, but it is evident from the reference in *ibid.* 5 to Aristotle's explanation of the number of the Gerontes, and in *ibid.* 14 to other criticisms by Aris-totle of the Lycurgan reforms (not found in the *Politics*) that Aristotle was his source for the whole account. The story of Theopompus' con-versation with his wife (*ibid.* 6) also appears in Arist. *Pol.* V, 11. 2. Wade-Gery (see following note) is almost certainly right in assuming the whole exposition of the *Rhetra* to be taken from Aristotle. In his *Constitution of Sparta* (F.H.G. II, 127 f.) Aristotle could scarcely avoid such a discussion.
[4] *Cf. Class. Quart.* XXXVII, 62 f. ; XXXVIII (1944), 1 f. (*The Spartan Rhetra in Plutarch, Lycurgus VI*).

Spartan law-giving (rejecting Aristotle's assumption that it is an oracle) but attributes it to the period of the second Messenian War, contemporary with Tyrtaeus' poem *Eunomia*, which includes a close paraphrase of it. According to Wade-Gery, Tyrtaeus himself was the originator of the oracle-story accepted by Aristotle and later authorities ; his purpose was to confer the greater authority of divine origin upon legislation which in fact was purely human and contemporary. Aristotle, on Wade-Gery's view, was led astray in his interpretation both of the prose-document and of Tyrtaeus' poem by his conviction that Lycurgus propounded his laws at the time of the first Olympiad ; Wade-Gery himself of necessity attributes the prose-Rhetra to a date not earlier than the late seventh century, since it implies the complete reorganisation of the Spartan state which Wade-Gery attributes (for reasons fully discussed earlier in this work [1]) to that date.

If it once be admitted (as the present work seeks to maintain) that the ' Lycurgan ' constitution had long existed in the time of Tyrtaeus, Tyrtaeus' alleged motive for inventing an oracle disappears. For a full investigation of this complicated problem the reader is referred to the Appendix on the Lycurgan Rhetra.[2] It will be sufficient here to summarise the conclusions there adopted, in order to clear the ground for a reconstruction of the probable historical development of the constitution.

The most ancient law of the Spartan constitution, known to the Spartans themselves as the Rhetra of Lycurgus, was either a genuine Delphic oracle, or was so worded as to give the impression (even to the most penetrating investigator) of being one. It is much easier to assume that it actually was a Delphic oracle ; that so elaborate a forgery could have been invented at so early a date is extremely improbable. For the prose-Rhetra in question was already regarded as of high antiquity in the time of Tyrtaeus ; the poet himself assigned to a second consultation of the oracle by the kings Theopompus and Polydorus, two generations before his own time, the addition by the god to an original oracle of a clause concerning ' crooked decisions ' of the Demos.

For these reasons, and on account of a striking contrast in linguistic forms between the beginning and end of the whole Rhetra as quoted by Aristotle, it is proposed to distinguish two chronological stages in its development, and to restore the whole text as follows :

I. Διὸς Σελλανίου καὶ 'Αθανᾶς Σελλανίας ἱερὸν ἱδρυσά-μενον, φυλὰς φυλάξαντα καὶ ὠβὰς ὠβάξαντα, τριάκοντα γερου-σίαν σὺν ἀρχαγέταις καταστήσαντα, ὥρας ἐξ ὡρᾶν [1] ἀπελλάζειν μεταξὺ Βαβυκᾶν [2] τε καὶ Κνακιῶνος · οὕτως εἰσφέρειν τε καὶ ἀφίστασθαι.

II. δαμωδᾶν (or δάμῳ τὰν [3]) γορίαν ἦμεν καὶ κράτος · αἰ δὲ σκολιὰν ὁ δᾶμος ἔροιτο,[4] τοὺς πρεσβυγενέας καὶ ἀρχαγέτας ἀποστατῆρας ἦμεν.

A translation of both sections is given in Appendix VI (p. 488).

Part I is to be identified with the oracle supposedly given to Lycurgus. Its language is appropriate to Delphi, but is hardly affected by the broad Doric of the Spartan dialect. Part II is an enactment of purely Spartan origin, though not, as has sometimes been supposed from its name of *Rhetra*, an enactment of the Spartan Demos.[5] The Gerusia and Kings were its real authors, and it preserves in its dialect forms evident signs of its origin. Part I is a Rhetra in the earlier sense of a categorical pronouncement supposed to have been made by an oracle.[6] Part I consists of instructions to a single legislator (*cf.* ἱδρυσάμενον, φυλάξαντα etc.) supposedly Lycurgus ; he is to lay before the Assembly (εἰσφέρειν) the proposals indicated by the god, and then to resign his functions as legislator (ἀφίστασθαι).[7] Part II issues an instruction to kings and Gerontes ; they are to dissolve the Assembly (ἀποστατῆρας ἦμεν, ' to be dissolvers ') in case a ' crooked judgment ' is laid before it, but this is to be without prejudice to the ancient right of ratification (κυροῦν, implied by γορίαν = κυρίαν) [8] belonging to the Assembly. We observe that the meaning of ἀφίστασθαι in Part I of the Rhetra, though preserved in the usage of

---

[1] For the reading see Appendix VI, pp. 486 f.   [2] *Ibid.* pp. 485 f.
[3] A reading adopted after the time of Tyrtaeus. See further Appendix VI, pp. 480 f.   [4] For the reading see below, p. 416.
[5] See further Appendix VI, p. 482.   [6] See further, *ibid.* pp. 475 f., 479 f.
[7] *Ibid.* pp. 483 f.   [8] *Ibid.* pp. 481 f.

other Dorian states,[1] has already been lost at Sparta in
Part II, for the reason that Part I was not generally recognised by the Spartans themselves as an oracle, and ἀφίστασθαι was consequently believed to refer to the disbanding
of the Assembly.[2]

Such, then, in outline, is the probable relation of the
two parts of the Rhetra, Part II being decidedly later in
origin, as shown both by the testimony of Tyrtaeus (who
implies the previous existence of Part I by his paraphrase
of Part II)[3] and by its own internal evidence as indicated
above.[4] Does the form of constitution implied by Part
II give any ground for believing Part II to be actually
contemporary with Tyrtaeus, or for supposing that any
form of democracy was set up by it ? Certain Spartan
reformers or would-be reformers in later times appear to
have taken this view, as is indicated by a spurious version
of Tyrtaeus' poem.[5] The more authentic version of
Tyrtaeus gives no hint of it, and a closer examination of
the meaning of the clause αἰ δὲ σκολιὰν ἔροιτο etc., implies
the very reverse of democracy.

The metaphor of crookedness and straightness appears
several times in Homer in application to the judicial
decisions of kings and judges,[6] and in Hesiod is repeatedly
so used,[7] whereas in later writers (apart from imitators of
Homer or Hesiod) it has a less restricted application to
thoughts and actions generally. The omission of the
noun altogether in Part II of the Rhetra implies that it
was perfectly well known what the word in question was,
and the parallels in Homer, Hesiod, Solon, and fifth-century
writers [8] show that it can only be δίκη. The MSS. reading
ἔροιτο, justly retained by Wade-Gery,[9] also fits in with this

---

[1] See further, Appendix VI, p. 484, n. 1:   [2] Ibid. p. 483.
[3] Ibid. p. 478.   [4] Cf. also below, p. 417.   [5] Cf. Appendix VI, pp. 478 f.
[6] Cf. Il. XVI, 387: οἳ βίηι εἰν ἀγορῆι σκολιὰς κρίνωσι θέμιστας. The
parallels to this line in Hesiod (see following note) are insufficient ground
for Leaf's supposition that it has been interpolated in the text of Homer,
especially in view of the Homeric parallels (accepted by Leaf as genuine)
in Il. XVIII, 508 (ὃς μετὰ τοῖσι δίκην ἰθύντατα εἴποι) and XXIII, 580 (ἰθεῖα
γὰρ ἔσται sc. ἡ δίκη).
[7] Works and Days, 219, 221, 250 ; cf. 9, 36, 225, 230, 263, 264 ; Frag.
217 (δίκη being the word employed throughout).
[8] Solon fr. 3, 36 ; fr. 24. 19 (Diehl) ; Pind. Nem. X, 21, εὐθείᾳ συνάρ-
μοξεν δίκᾳ. This is probably an echo of Homer, as also is Aesch. Eumen.
433.   [9] Cf. Class. Quart. XXXVII, p. 70.

Homeric usage, but on the assumption that it means, or meant originally 'if the Damos should get pronounced to it [1] (a crooked δίκη) '. It was for the Homeric king or his councillors to pronounce (εἰπεῖν) a judicial decision (δίκη) ; [2] the function assigned to the Laos was merely that of shouting assent or dissent.[3] This seems to be exactly the procedure implied by Part II of the Rhetra ; individual Gerontes might propose δίκαι, 'straight' or 'crooked' as the case might be,[4] but if in the opinion of kings and Gerontes (presumably a majority of them) the Assembly gave its assent to a 'crooked judgment ', its decision was immediately to be declared invalid. So far as concerns the right of the Spartan Assembly to shout assent or dissent to a judicial decision, we have a clear survival in the famous case of the decision that Athens had broken the Thirty Years' truce.[5] Since the Assembly at Sparta could not discuss,[6] this proposition had clearly been reached by the Gerontes beforehand, and the ephor Sthenelaidas was their mouthpiece ; in Homeric phraseology, δίκην εἶπε ; the Assembly exercised its traditional privilege (κυροῦν). A similar case is implied by Herodotus' description of the trial of Leotychidas in the early fifth century.[7]

The important point to notice is that the wording of Part II of the Rhetra implies limitation of the Assembly's right of ratification to the *judicial* sphere, and probably to the sphere of criminal jurisdiction only, as apparently in Homer.[8] But in his exposition of the

---

[1] See further Appendix VI, p. 482.

[2] *Cf.* the detailed description of a criminal trial in *Il.* XVIII, 497 f., and esp. 508, ὃς μετὰ τοῖσι δίκην ἰθύντατα εἴποι referring to proposals by individual Gerontes (*cf.* Leaf, *Iliad*, Vol. II, p. 612).

[3] *Ibid.* 502 (ἐπήπυον).

[4] *Ibid.* 508 (cited above, note 2).

[5] Thuc. I, 67 f. Although allies were present and were allowed to speak, Thucydides clearly states that this was an ordinary meeting of the Spartan Assembly (I, 67. 3) and that its purpose was to hear ἐγκλήματα (67. 4). The decision was a purely judicial one (I, 87 : ὅτῳ . . . δοκοῦσι λελύσθαι αἱ σπονδαί) and the vote purely Spartan.

[6] Arist. *Pol.* II, 11. 6 (Sparta contrasted with Carthage in this respect), Plut. *Lycurg.* 6. 6. See further, Appendix VI, p. 482.

[7] Herod. VI, 85.

[8] The trial described at length in *Il.* XVIII, 497 f. (*cf.* above) concerns a murder charge. The similar setting arranged by Menelaus in *Il.* XXIII, 570 f. for his accusation of Antilochus on the charge of cheating in a chariot

Rhetra [1] Tyrtaeus gives it a much wider application, extending to ' deliberations ' (βουλεύειν) in general, resulting not in δίκαι, but in ῥῆτραί, which in this as in later Spartan contexts clearly means ' laws proposed to the Assembly '. This difference of outlook between Tyrtaeus and Part II of the Rhetra (obscured in Plutarch's commentary) [2] enables us to put both parts of the Rhetra in proper chronological perspective ; already by the time of Tyrtaeus the original ' Lycurgan ' constitution has undergone a considerable modification, of which the poet himself is probably not aware. The principle of limiting discussion to kings and Gerontes only, leaving only the right of ratification to the Apella, still remained and was destined to remain permanently, but to its ancient function of εὐθύνα [3] the Assembly has now added the right to ratify the Spartan equivalent of ψηφίσματα. The lapse of a considerable time is implied by this increase in its power, and the tradition may well be correct which ascribes the Rhetra concerning ' crooked decisions ' to Theopompus and Polydorus at the time of the first Messenian War.[4] In this part of the Rhetra defining the constitution there cannot therefore be any question of democratic institutions, in spite of the occurrence of the word δαμώδεις (Tyrtaeus' reading).[5] In fact the clause in question can only mean (as it meant at any later date in Sparta) ' the landholders are to have the right of ratification '. The whole constitution is the very reverse of democratic.

Having thus considered the implications and the probable date of Part II, we are in a better position to discover the meaning of Part I of the Rhetra, which must ante-date it. The provision for meetings of the Assembly (ἀπελλάζειν ὥρας ἐξ ὡρᾶν) cannot possibly imply regular monthly meetings, but at most three times yearly, in spring, summer and winter, or more probably twice only, in spring and

race does not appear to imply a formal public trial (cf. Leaf's note on l. 574). Other Homeric evidence is lacking, which seems to imply that the procedure was rare.

[1] Cf. Appendix VI, p. 477.　　　　　　[2] Plut. Lycurg. 6, 8.

[3] In a wider sense than that used by Arist. Pol. II, 12. 5 ; III, 11. 8, where it refers only to the power of the Solonian ecclesia to bring magistrates to account.

[4] See further, Appendix VI, p. 478.

[5] Ibid. p. 480.

autumn.[1] At that early period the Assembly can have had no more regular work to do than the Homeric Laos, and in fact must have continued to resemble it very closely, though the institution of any regular public assemblies at all doubtless represents a significant new stage of development. This, then, is one of the new reforms for which Lycurgus was by tradition made responsible. The others in some way concern the cults, the Phylae, the Obae, the Gerusia, and the kings, for it is impossible to doubt the evidence both of Aristotle [2] and of Tyrtaeus [3] that by 'Archagetae' the kings are meant.

Unfortunately Tyrtaeus merely implies the existence of Part I of the Rhetra but gives no paraphrase of it, while Aristotle's exposition is of very little help. Phylae and Obae are defined as 'divisions of the population' (μερίδες τοῦ πλήθους) and no attempt is made to explain the number of the Gerontes or whether it was related to these divisions. The definition of ἀπελλάζειν as ἐκκλησιάζειν, on the other hand must certainly be right, and though it may now seem obvious, it does not seem to have been obvious to Herodotus, who apparently thought it referred to the public meals of the citizens (Syssitia).

For it is interesting to observe what must certainly be an attempt made by Herodotus to explain the same document, even though in this case the Rhetra goes further to explain Herodotus than Herodotus to explain the Rhetra. After mentioning that some authorities (though not the Spartans themselves) maintained that the Delphic oracle dictated to Lycurgus his new constitution, Herodotus says [4] μετὰ δὲ, τὰ ἐς πόλεμον ἔχοντα, ἐνωμοτίας καὶ τριηκάδας καὶ συσσίτια, πρὸς δὲ τούτοισι τοὺς ἐφόρους καὶ γέροντας ἔστησε Λυκοῦργος. οὕτω μὲν μεταβαλόντες εὐνομήθησαν.

However wild some of his identifications may be, there can be little doubt that Herodotus is here giving a list of synonyms of the terms used in Part I of the Rhetra, in the order in which they there occur except that for 'Gerusia' and 'Archagetae' he reads (apparently) Ephors and Gerusia,

---

[1] See further Appendix VI, p. 486. The comparable institution in England is the pre-Norman shire-moot, which met only twice yearly (Maitland, *Constitutional History of England*, p. 40).
[2] *Ap.* Plut. *Lycurg.* 6. [3] *Cf.* Appendix VI, p. 477. [4] Herod. I, 65.

in the reverse order. τὰ ἐς πόλεμον ἔχοντα is a plausible explanation of Phylae and Obae, which he further defines (or perhaps his explanation refers only to Obae) as Enomotiae and Triekades. The last name was given to subdivisions of the Phyle at Athens and elsewhere. ' Syssitia ' is then explained by ὡρᾶν ἐξ ὡρᾶν ἀπελλάζειν—a not unplausible assumption on Herodotus' part, since at Delphi ἄπελλαι means the ' appointed feast ' (θοῖναι νόμιμοι) of a Phratria,[1] and Herodotus is quoting the opinion of those who believed the Rhetra to be a Delphic oracle. He presumably explained ὡρᾶν ἐξ ὡρᾶν as referring to the daily meal times. γερουσίαν σὺν ἀρχαγέταις καταστήσαντα leads Herodotus to suppose (as it easily might) that Lycurgus first established the Gerusia ; he is precluded (on the same principle) from identifying the Archagetae with the kings by his belief that the double kingship originated at the time of the return of the Heracleidae.[2] His assertion that Lycurgus established the Ephors, unsupported by any authors except those who have probably taken it direct from Herodotus himself,[3] seems most satisfactorily explained by supposing that Herodotus assumed the Archagetae (' chief leaders ') mentioned in the Rhetra to mean the Ephors. It is to be remembered that in Herodotus' time the Ephors occupied a very important and prominent position indeed, and that it was they who controlled the movements of all foreign visitors to Sparta.[4] Herodotus himself had not failed to notice the apparent superiority of their authority to that of the kings.[5] The part played by the Ephors in summoning the Gerusia and in laying proposals both before the Gerusia and before the Apella [6] might easily lead Herodotus to think the name of Archagetae appropriate to them. But the main interest of Herodotus' paraphrase of the Rhetra is a negative one ; it shows that there is no valid reason for associating the Lycurgan reforms with the origin of the Ephorate, any more than with the origin of the Gerusia. It is on general grounds more likely that the

---

[1] Cf. Wade-Gery, Class. Quart. XXXVII, p. 66, and Appendix VI, pp. 487 f.   [2] Herod. VI, 52.

[3] The earliest of these is [Xen.] Resp. Lac. VIII, 3, a work which is full of Herodotean allusions. For other references cf. Dar.-Sagl. s.v. Ephoroi n. 1.   [4] Cf. Dar. Sagl. s.v. Xenelasia, Herod. III, 148.

[5] Cf. Herod. VI, 82.   [6] Cf. above, p. 411.

Ephorate, being of very early origin,[1] greatly increased in importance during the continued absence of the kings at the time of the first Messenian War.[2]

Herodotus being a completely unreliable guide, we are left to form our own opinion of the general significance of Part I of the Rhetra, apart from the institution of regular assemblies to which reference has already been made.

The direction to set up a Gerusia which, including the kings, shall be thirty in number cannot, in view of the comparatively late date of the reforms and the ubiquitous existence of Homeric councils of Gerontes, refer to the first institution of the Gerusia. The change implied must concern the number only, and in view of the strong reasons for thinking that the double kingship was of comparatively late origin,[3] we may reasonably connect the change in the number of the Gerontes with the addition of a second king. The strong attachment of the Spartans to threes and multiples of three would suggest that previously the Gerusia had consisted (in theory at least) of twenty-seven members, nine from each of the three Dorian tribes ; this hypothesis is strengthened by the persistent identification of the Gerontes in Homer with army leaders, who would obviously be appointed in equal numbers for each of the tribes.[4] The reason for altering the number, even if the addition was the insignificant one here suggested, was probably to destroy the traditional connection between the Gerontes and the divisions of the army, in fact to complete the process which can be partially traced in Homer, and to confine the powers of the Gerusia entirely to the purely civil sphere. For as the Rhetra clearly lays down, the number of the tribes was to remain as before ; φυλὰς φυλάξαντα can have no other meaning,[5] and we know that in fact the three ancient Dorian tribes continued in existence.

On the other hand, the new Gerusia of twenty-eight would gain independence through the institution of a second king, since both kings together could not control the Gerusia as the typical Homeric monarch had done. As for the

---

[1] *Cf.* above, p. 406.   [2] As already maintained (*cf.* pp. 405 f.).
[3] *Cf.* above, p. 402.
[4] For the φυλαί and φρατρίαι as army-units *cf. Il.* II, 362 ; for the 27 Spartan φρατρίαι, above, p. 393 ; for the Homeric identification of Gerontes with army-captains, *Il.* II, 404 f.   [5] *Cf.* Appendix VI, p. 488.

royal power, this was obviously much diminished by being
made collegiate, even though in theory no royal prerogatives
were taken away.   In particular, it was the beginning of
the virtual limitation of the royal power to the military
sphere, since the reforms ushered in a long series of wars
from which neither king could absent himself for jealousy
of the other.[1] The opportunity was thus given for the
eventual development of the Ephorate, whose membership
must automatically have been raised from four to five by
the addition of a second king.[2] This would in itself make
no real difference to their status, but since in spite of the
limitation of the kings (formerly their immediate masters)
to the military sphere the powers of the Ephors continued
to develop on the purely civil side, it may be inferred that
some change in the method of appointment of the Ephors,
probably in connection with the Lycurgan reforms, released
them from the control of the kings (and φυλοβασιλεῖς) and
brought them more directly into connection with the
Gerusia.   Cleomenes III was certainly right in maintaining
that at one time (though surely not so late as he supposes)
the Ephors were directly appointed by the king.[3] All
that we are told about the later method of their appointment is that it was ' childish '.[4] Aristotle, who tells us
this, makes the same remark about the selection of Gerontes,
which was popular election by acclamation.[5] It is possible
that the Ephors were similarly elected,[6] that is, by the
same archaic method, implying an early date for the change,
though epigraphic evidence for the Roman period suggests
co-optation.[7] The two methods may perhaps have been
combined, the formal public election being a mere farce,
as it no doubt was in the case of the Gerontes.   The suggested arrangement would easily explain how in Aristotle's
time poor men came to be selected for the office, whose
poverty made them easily accessible to bribes, and also
how members of the highest aristocracy came to hold it
in an earlier period.

[1] The persistent and unending jealousy between the two Spartan
royal houses is remarked upon by Herodotus (VI, 52 *ad fin.*).
   [2] *Cf.* above, p. 407 f.   [3] Plut. *Cleom.* 10 ; *cf.* above, p. 405.
   [4] Arist. *Pol.* II, 9. 23.   See further, Part I, p. 156.
   [5] *Ibid.* 27 ; *cf.* Plut. *Lycurg.* 26.
   [6] As assumed by Solari, *Ricerche Spartane*, pp. 84 f.   [7] *Cf.* Part I, p. 167.

The intention of the Rhetra with regard to the assembly of citizens has already been indicated.[1] With regard to the times appointed for its regular meetings, whether ὡρᾶν ἐξ ὡρᾶν (' every season ') means twice a year, in summer and winter (as in the case of the assemblies of the Delphic Amphictiony, or later, of the Achaean League) or three times a year, is not clear, and probably was not intended to be clear, so that a gradually increasing number of meetings could be provided for without changing the law. The same observation applies to the very vague indication of the place of meeting ; the point seems to be that it must be somewhere within the limits of the narrow Eurotas valley,[2] and not, as in Homeric times, on any distant battle-field, wherever the βασιλεύς might chance to summon it. Thus the Spartan Apella embarked on its career as a purely civil assembly, divorced from contact with the army, and the way was cleared for military operations in which the commanders would no longer be hampered by the necessity for constant justification of their policy to the assembled Laos.

Finally, the archaic Rhetra implies the adoption of a new policy of unification, though not (as in most Greek states) the actual concentration of the population by συνοικισμός. The selection of a central meeting-place for the Apella implies this, the more so if (as seems likely) the place was not more precisely indicated than ' within the Eurotas valley ' ; so perhaps also does the name ' Archagetae ' given to the kings ; since this was a title usually reserved for the first founders of cities ;[3] but even more significant is the provision for the cults of Zeus Hellanios (Sellanios)[4] and Athena Hellania, in which all inhabitants of Spartan territory who claimed to be Dorians at all might share,[5] whatever their social status.

[1] Cf. above, pp. 416 f.   [2] Cf. Appendix VI, pp. 485 f.
[3] In other cases ἀρχηγέται (where the word is used in its technical sense) seem always to have been of divine or semi-divine origin (cf. Liddell and Scott, s.v.). But since the Spartan kings were regarded as semi-divine, no inconsistency arose in the use of the term in their case.
[4] Cf. Appendix VI, p. 484.
[5] All Dorians claimed to be in a special sense ' sons of Hellen ' (cf. Myres, Who Were the Greeks, pp. 163 f.). A specially Dorian cult is implied by the use of the cult-title in its Dorian form even at Athens (Aristoph. Eq. 1253).

This leads us to a question which is not definitely answered by the Rhetra under discussion, which, it must be remembered, is only one out of several original Lycurgan Rhetrae. Did the Lycurgan reforms involve an extension of the citizenship, and if so, from what class of inhabitants ? The new cults of Hellanios and Hellania certainly seem to imply an extension of citizenship, and the obscure phrase ὠβὰς ὠβάξαντα may perhaps refer to a first distribution of citizen land-lots,[1] creating a new class of citizens whose political status did not depend upon the possession of land acquired by inheritance. We know that such a class of citizens did exist—in fact, they formed the main body of the citizen population—in later Sparta, and that their title to the land from which they derived the means of paying their subscription to the Syssitia [2] depended upon an individual grant to each male child at birth by οἱ πρεσβύτατοι τῶν φυλετῶν [3] (a phrase which must certainly mean the Gerusia), implying that the land so allotted was quite distinct from private land, and reverted to the state on the death of each individual holder. It is also clear that no such system could exist before the creation of the unified non-feudal state which was (as we have seen) the work of the Lycurgan reforms ; and further, there is a persistent tradition that Lycurgus was the originator of the system of citizen land-lots, even though opinions differ as to the number which he actually created. Finally, it is on general grounds probable that the great new programme of conquests was preceded by a considerable increase in the size of the citizen population, which would give the Spartans the initial advantage of a larger army than any state which they would be likely to attack for some time. It may be supposed that a first distribution of κλῆροι (? ὠβαί) was made from land annexed on the conquest of the nearest towns of the Perioikoi (Geronthrae and Helos).

From the political point of view, this hypothesis of a Lycurgan extension of citizenship through distribution of

---

[1] For various later uses of the word ὠβά at Sparta, cf. pp. 164 f. It appears to be applicable to any kind of section or division, and could conveniently be adopted for the citizen land-lots in public land, to distinguish them from the private and inheritable κλῆροι. [2] Cf. p. 245.
[3] Cf. Plut. Lycurg. 16. The grant was made only if the child was considered strong enough to be allowed to survive.

publicly owned land would explain the later distinction between the Privileged Families [1] (the older landed aristocracy, from among whom the Gerontes still continued exclusively to be drawn) and the ὅμοιοι, all with equal shares (implied by their name) in the γῆ πολιτική.[2] From the economic point of view, it would explain the actual existence of wealthy families in a regime of which the general keynote was equality. From the legal point of view, it would explain the co-existence of two distinct forms of land-tenure in Sparta ; for the continued existence of private property in land side-by-side with the citizen-κλῆροι is implied (apart from incidental later references to individual estates) by the Spartan law of inheritance, which seems precisely similar to that which existed in other Greek states.[3]

Finally, the introduction of a new system of land-tenure side-by-side with the old explains how the Spartan state acquired control (as it evidently did) over the Syssitia and over the Agelae, while at the same time both these institutions retained features clearly derived from the feudal period. For the new κλῆροι on public land were doubtless worked in exactly the same way as the ancient inherited κλῆροι by serfs and semi-independent underlings. The life-tenant (to borrow the corresponding English term) could lord it over them, and build up his own Syssitia and Agelae, but his tenure depended on the central authority, which in this way maintained a strong hold over his activities and controlled the newer Syssitia (which would rapidly come to be the majority) in the interests of the State. And when the first public κλῆροι were allotted, presumably at

[1] This name was provisionally given to them in Chap. III. In view of evidence cited later (Chap. X, pp. 353 f.) we may perhaps venture to identify them with the Spartiatae, using this name in its strict technical sense. If so, they presumably took their name from the locality of Sparta itself, the richest part of the Eurotas valley, in which their estates, having been acquired at the time of the first conquest, would be likely to be situated.

[2] The earlier name was apparently ἀρχαία μοῖρα (cf. Arist. fr. 611, Rose) : Πωλεῖν δὲ γῆν Λακεδαιμονίοις αἰσχρὸν νενόμισται· τῆς ἀρχαίας μοίρας οὐδὲ ἔξεστι) used to distinguish it from private land, for which see following note.

[3] Cf. Arist. Pol. II, 9 (1270a) : ὠνεῖσθαι μὲν γάρ ἢ πωλεῖν τὴν ὑπάρχουσαν ἐποίησεν οὐ καλόν, ὀρθῶς ποιήσας, διδόναι δὲ καὶ καταλείπειν ἐξουσίαν ἔδωκε τοῖς βουλομένοις. The disposal of heiresses in marriage at Sparta appears to have followed the common Greek practice with regard to ἐπίκληροι (cf. Herod. VI, 57).

the time of the Lycurgan reforms, the life-tenants can only have been drawn from the uppermost stratum of dependents on the estates of the ' Privileged Families ', so that these must have started under the new regime with their power very much weakened.

The more we consider the implications of the principal reforms among those attributed to Lycurgus, the more probable it seems that there was indeed a single human lawgiver who was responsible for them, either unaided or with the help of Delphi. It is unthinkable that so complicated and ingenious a system grew up by accident, or that the common consent and co-operation of the various elements in a state conspicuous hitherto for κακονομία suddenly evolved a solution for all its troubles. These warring elements may perhaps have consented willingly to be governed by a new body of laws furnished for them by a legislator, after the manner of the Athenians who were later to choose Solon as arbitrator and lawgiver, but it can hardly be supposed that their collaboration went further than this. The existence of a cult of Lycurgus in Herodotus' time and later [1] does not, as has sometimes been strangely supposed, imply that no human Lycurgus existed. The worship of founders (οἰκισταί) with annual sacrifices was common everywhere in the Greek world,[2] and sometimes re-founders were honoured in the same way.[3] None of the three Greek writers who mention the cult of Lycurgus are in the least shaken by it in their belief that Lycurgus was a human person, and they doubtless assumed that he received these honours as founder of the new constitution.[4] Since we have seen reason to think that the foundation of Eunomia was in fact the beginning of the unified state of Sparta, its author had every claim to be honoured as the original and first οἰκιστής. The additional motive of proving divine authority for the Lycurgan constitution may also

---

[1] Cf. Herod. I, 66 : τῷ δὲ Λ. τελευτήσαντι ἱρὸν εἰσάμενοι, σέβονται μεγάλως. Ephorus (ap. Strabo, VIII, 366) mentions in addition annual sacrifices. Cf. also Plut. Lycurg. 31.

[2] Cf. Herod. VI, 38 : καὶ οἱ τελευτήσαντι Χερσονησῖται θύουσι ὡς νόμος οἰκιστῇ, καὶ ἀγῶνα ἱππικόν τε καὶ γυμνικὸν ἐπιστᾶσι ; cf. also I, 168 : (a ktistes) τιμὰς ὑπὸ Τηίων . . . ὡς ἥρως ἔχει.

[3] Cf. Thuc. V, 11 (Brasidas at Amphipolis).

[4] This appears to be the opinion of Ephorus at least (Strabo, loc. cit.).

have tended, in the fifth century B.C., to greater insistence on the cult of Lycurgus himself.[1] Only long after the constitutional unification, with the true origin of the double kingship forgotten, could the notion arise that it was the mythical Eurysthenes and Procles who ought to have received the divine honours as οἰκισταί which were not, in fact, accorded to them.[2] But until the fourth century B.C. at least, it was still Lycurgus to whom the annual sacrifices were offered ; and so far from throwing doubt on the lawgiver's existence, the cult actually tends to confirm it.

There is no need for us to attribute to the time of the Lycurgan reorganisation all the Rhetrae which by ancient authors are assigned to Lycurgus, primitive as some of these may sound.[3] The tendency in Athens to attribute all sixth and even fifth century laws to Solon should suggest caution to the historian of Sparta, and modifications which in actual fact took place even in Sparta are not difficult to explain. The general atmosphere of discipline and obedience imposed on the rank and file of the citizens made it easy for the Gerusia and kings (at least in the period before written codes of law were commonly introduced in Greece) to deceive them into accepting as ' Lycurgan ' Rhetrae which had in fact been invented by themselves. The general principle of permanence on which the constitution worked (as its whole history proves and various anecdotes illustrate) [4] would prevent them from practising this deception frequently or seriously. The gradual introduction of written law codes elsewhere in Greece probably explains what Plutarch says was one of the original Lycurgan Rhetrae— one forbidding written laws.[5] Its origin must in reality be ascribed to about 600 B.C., and its purpose was to safeguard the time-honoured method of introducing modifications in the code, by making it impossible to convict the innovators of deception. Despite changes, a general ' freezing ' process seems to have taken place soon after the great upheaval

---

[1] See further, Appendix VI, p. 476.   [2] Cf. Ephorus (p. 426, n. 1).
[3] Cf. Plut. Lycurg. 13. (The roof must be made only with the axe, the door only with the saw ; war must not be made on the same enemy twice.)
[4] This is the point of the aphorism ascribed to Agesilaus (Plut. Ages. 30) : ὅτι τοὺς νόμους δεῖ σήμερον ἐᾶν καθεύδειν, ἐκ δὲ τῆς σήμερον ἡμέρας κυρίους εἶναι πρὸς τὸ λοιπόν.   [5] Plut. Lycurg. 13.

involved by the first Messenian War and its resulting conquests, to which period belong (according to Aristotle) Theopompus' limitation of the royal power,[1] the limitation by a new oracle-Rhetra of the powers of the Assembly,[2] and (as we learn from Pausanias) the first introduction of the use by the Ephors of the portrait-seal of Polydorus in transacting public business.[3] With the exception of further changes in the powers of the Ephors, and the army reforms effected in the fifth century, few constitutional or social innovations were introduced after that time. The institutions remained in their main outlines primitive and Lycurgan.

A detailed investigation would therefore lead us to concur with the opinion of Aristotle [4] and indeed of all antiquity, and to accept the historical existence of Lycurgus as one of the greatest of all the early Greek lawgivers. For no other Greek system of laws did in fact endure so long, nor was any other so skilfully designed to permit of some measure of development (as in the case of the Ephorate) within a stable framework. That in some cases the later Spartans interpreted his provisions more narrowly than he appears to have intended, insisting on a degree of isolationism incompatible with the cult of Zeus Hellanios, was not the fault of the lawgiver. Only by this means could the ancient organisation in practice be maintained.

---

[1] Arist. *Pol.* V, 11. 2. [2] *Cf.* above, pp. 414 f.

[3] Paus. III, 11. 10 : οἱ τὰς ἀρχὰς ἔχοντες ὁπόσα δεῖ σημαίνεσθαι τοῦ Πολυδώρου σημαίνονται τῇ εἰκόνι. In view of their functions, this must always have applied primarily to the Ephors, and exclusively to them in the early period to which the origin of the custom is ascribed.

[4] *Ap.* Plut. *Lycurg.* 31. 3.

AGIS IV AND THE REDISTRIBUTION OF THE PUBLIC LAND

It has been shown (Chap. I, pp. 16 f.) that the redistribution of land to citizens of the hoplite class under the schemes of Agis IV and Cleomenes III represented an intention to return to an ancient arrangement. This gives increased significance to a passage in which Plutarch (*Agis*, 8) gives the boundaries of the land which Agis proposed to distribute to the full citizens, all outside it being left for Perioikoi : τῆς δὲ γῆς ἀναδασθείσης τὴν μὲν ἀπὸ τοῦ κατὰ Πελλήνην χαράδρου πρὸς τὸ Ταΰγετον καὶ Μαλέαν καὶ Σελασίαν κλήρους γένεσθαι τετρακισχιλίους πεντακοσίους τὴν δ'ἔξω μυρίους πεντακισχιλίους, καὶ ταυτὴν μὲν τοῖς ὅπλα φέρειν δυναμένοις τῶν περιοίκων μερισθῆναι, τὴν δὲ ἐντὸς αὐτοῖς Σπαρτιάταις.

The position of Pellana seems fixed with certainty about 2¾ miles W. of Vourlia, on the east bank of the Eurotas,[1] and due west of Sellasia which has been located about 1½ miles east of Vourlia.[2] It seems therefore not unlikely that these two points are chosen to fix the southern boundary, being exactly on a line running east and west. If we now suppose the order of the last two names in the passage cited above (which is quite unintelligible as it stands) to have become transposed, the interpretation which suggests itself is that Pellana was chosen as the middle of the southern boundary, which was to extend as far due west as Taygetus in one direction, and as far due east as Sellasia in the other (ἀπὸ τοῦ κατὰ Πελλήνην χαράδρου πρὸς τὸ Ταΰγετον καὶ Σελασίαν). The western boundary would be clearly marked by the Taygetus range throughout its length, for since it was distribution of agricultural land which was in question, the range itself was obviously excluded. It is evident that the remaining fixed point, Malea, cannot be the promontory of that name towards Cythera ; but on the supposition that it refers to the other Malea in the north of Laconia, near Leuctrum on the Spartan-Argive frontier,[3] the meaning of the whole passage becomes clear. The Malea in question must fix the north-east angle of the territory marked out for division, the northern boundary running due west to the north end of the Taygetus range, and the eastern boundary running in a straight line from Malea

---

[1] J.H.S. XV, pp. 45 f. and Pl. I, *ibid*.

[2] *Ibid*. pp. 58 f. and Pl. I.

[3] In Xen. *Hell*. VI, v, 24, Λεῦκτρον ὑπὲρ τῆς Μαλεάτιδος is mentioned as a Spartan border fort guarding one of the approaches into Laconia from Mantinea and Tegea. In Thuc. V, 54. 1, Λεῦκτρα is mentioned on the frontier between Sparta and Argos (*cf. ibid*. 55. 3, referring to an attempt made soon afterwards to cross the same frontier at Caryae). Although in V, 54. 1, Thucydides further describes Λεῦκτρα as πρὸς τὸ Λύκαιον, he clearly cannot mean that it was *near* Mt. Lykaion ; he may mean that it was the most westerly point of the frontier between Sparta and Argos, ' at the end towards Mt. Lykaion '. The combined evidence of Thucydides and Xenophon would locate Leuctrum near the route from Tegea to Sparta. For the latitude, see p. 70. Malea (*cf.* Xen. *loc. cit.*) must therefore be placed near and somewhat to the south of this point,

to Sellasia. This delimitation would be adequately expressed, at least for those who knew the country and something about the proposed scheme already, by the words ἀπὸ τοῦ κατὰ Πελλήνην χαράδρου πρὸς τὸ Ταΰγετον καὶ Σελασίαν καὶ Μαλέαν. The transposition of the last two words in Plutarch's text as it stands makes nonsense of the whole scheme.

Although the position of Malea cannot be exactly located,[1] it can be fixed within sufficiently narrow limits to give a fairly accurate picture of the area included in Agis' scheme for redistribution. The area in question would be a quadrilateral with sloping sides, approximately 10 by 15 sq.-miles. Divided among 4,500 citizens, this would give to each an allocation of 21–22 acres, rather less than the average for the less wealthy class of peasant proprietors in modern Greece (taken as a whole) for the period between the two Great Wars,[2] but strikingly close to the amount of land which would be required to produce the 82 × 2 (Aeginetan) medimnoi of barley which fixed the size of the ancient Spartan κλῆροι.[3]

---

[1] Cf. preceding note. [2] Cf. Admiralty Handbook, p. 99.
[3] Sources quoted in Busolt-Swoboda, Griech. Staatskunde, II, p. 641 (assuming Helots to have occupied one-half of each κλῆρος). Duncker's estimate of the size of the κλῆρος on this basis is 9½–10 hectares (23½–25 acres); cf. Sitzb. Berl. Akad. Wiss. 1881, p. 149.

THE CHRONOLOGY OF THE CLEOMENIC WAR

§ 1. *The Strategiae of Aratus*

THE account of the Cleomenic War (pp. 9 f.) is based upon the reconstruction of the Strategiae of Aratus set out below. It will be observed that it departs from the assumption usually made, on the evidence of Plutarch, *Cleom.* 15, *Arat.* 38, that Aratus was Strategos in alternate years throughout his career in office, except in one year when his son (also called Aratus) took his place.[1] On the other hand, it enables us to retain other statements of Plutarch which are usually rejected as not fitting in with the other conception, namely that Aratus was Strategos for the seventeenth time when he died in office (*Arat.* 53), and for the twelfth time when he was defeated by Cleomenes at Lycaeum (*Arat.* 35, 36). The date of Aratus' death is fixed to the year 215/14 in relation to his difference of opinion with Philip V about Messene (late summer 216, *cf.* Plut. *Arat.* 49 f., Polyb. V, 110, Holleaux in C.A.H. VIII, p. 118), the date of his second Strategia to 243/2 by Polyb. II, 43 (for details see further Clinton, *F.H.* on this year). The years are given according to the Achaean reckoning, the Strategos always entering on office in the second half of May.[2] Further testimonies are cited in the list itself.

(MAY)

244/3	Aratus I	See footnote.[3]
243/2	Aratus II	Polyb. II, 43. Corinth ' freed ' spring 242.
242/1	Aratus III	
241/0	Aratus IV	
240/39	Aratus V	See footnote.[3]
239/8	Aratus VI	
238/7	Aratus VII	
237/6	Dioetas	Polyaen. II, 36, *cf.* Beloch, *ibid.* p. 224.
236/5	Aratus VIII	Strategia implied by Plut. *Arat.* 30. On the number, see footnote.[3]
235/4	Lydiadas I	
234/3	Aratus IX	
233/2	Lydiadas II	Plut. *Arat.* 30.
232/1	Aratus X	
231/0	Lydiadas III	

---

[1] *Cf.* Beloch, *Gr. Gesch.* IV,[2] 2, p. 225. The proposed new reconstruction seems adequately to fulfil Plutarch's general observation about alternate Strategiae by making Aratus Strategos invariably in alternate years 236–226 and 223–219 (223–215 if Plutarch confused him with the younger Aratus).

[2] *Cf.* Beloch, *ibid.* pp. 220 f. (on the evidence of Polybius). The same view is taken by Boethius, *Der Argivische Kalender* (*Upsala Universitets Arskrift*, 1922), pp. 14 f.

[3] These successive Strategiae are deduced (1) from the fixed date of Aratus II ; (2) from the fixed date of Aratus XII (*q.v.*), which is preceded by a known number of alternate Strategiae, for which see details in list above.

(MAY)

230/29 Aratus XI	(In alternate year, *cf.* Plut. *Cleom.* 15, *Arat.* 38.)
229/8 Aristomachus	Plut. *Arat.* 35 (the year before Aratus XII).
228/7 Aratus XII [1]	
227/6 Aegialeus	I.G. IV, 926 = Ditt. *Syll.*[2] 471 ; *cf.* Beloch, *ibid.* p. 224.[2] Lull in Cleomenic War implied by Plut. *Arat.* 37 *fin.*
226/5 Aratus XIII	Plut. *Cleom.* 15, *cf.* 14.
225/4 Hyperbatas	Plut. *Cleom.* 14, *cf.* Polybius II, 51 (Dyme).[3]
224/3 Timoxenus I	Plut. *Arat.* 38 (*cf. Cleom.* 15).
223/2 Aratus XIV	(Transferred from even to odd series of years by refusal of office in 224/3). Aratus *aet.* 53.[4]
222/1 Timoxenus II	Polyb. II, 53. 2 ; *cf.* Tarn, C.A.H. VII, p. 863.
221/0 Aratus XV	Plut. *Arat.* 46, 47 (at time of Antigonus' death),[5] *cf.* Polyb. IV, 19, 26.
220/19 Timoxenus III ⎫	Plut. *Arat.* 47.
219/18 Aratus XVI ⎬	Plut. *ibid.*, Polyb. IV, 76 (*cf.* IV, 5, 68).[6]
218/17 Eperatus	Plut. *Arat.* 48, Polyb. IV, 82 (instead of Timoxenus), *cf.* V, 1, IV, 67.
217/16 Aratus the Younger	See footnote.[7]

[1] The date of Aratus' twelfth Strategia follows from the number of other Strategoi recorded between it and Aratus' death, in his seventeenth Strategia, in 215/14. See the beginning of this Appendix.

[2] The Strategia of Aegialeus must fall within the period 243–224 (Beloch, *ibid.*). The year 227/6 is the only one for which other names cannot be found. Hyperbatas must be assigned to 225/4, not 227/6, since he was followed not by Aratus but by Timoxenus (Plut. *Arat.* 38).

[3] Pausanias (II, 9. 2, VII, 7. 3) who says Aratus was Strategos at the time of the Achaean defeat at Dyme, has evidently been misled by the account of Plut. *ibid.*, implying that Aratus was really responsible, though not Strategos at the time.

[4] *Cf.* Plut. *Arat.* 41 : 'τριάκοντα μὲν ἔτη καὶ τρία πεπολιτευμένος ἐν τοῖς Ἀχαιοῖς', probably cited *verbatim* from Aratus' *Commentaries*, seems to refer to the length of time since he attained citizen rights, presumably at the age of twenty, since he was born in 276 or 275 (*cf.* Beloch, *ibid.* pp. 228 f.). In *Cleom.* 16 (ἔτη τρία καὶ τριάκοντα πρωτεύοντος αὐτοῦ) Plutarch seems to misunderstand the original statement.

[5] The date of Antigonus' death is fixed with certainty to the autumn of 221 B.C. (Beloch, *ibid.* p. 113).

[6] Both these Strategiae are mistakenly transferred by Polyb. IV, 15 (*cf.* IV, 5, 6), to the years 222/1 and 221/0 (the last two years of the 139th Olympiad). They must be assigned as in the list above on account of Polyb. IV, 6 (*cf.* 5), which places them after the death of Antigonus, on which see note [5] above.

[7] Polybius is confused about the dating of this Strategia, as is natural when Aratus, Eperatus and Aratus the younger were all Strategoi about the same time. In IV, 37 he says that the younger Aratus came into office during the year of the Aetolian Strategos Scopas, when Hannibal was beginning the siege of Saguntum, *i.e.* in 219. But from the passages cited under this year (in list above) it appears that the *elder* Aratus was Strategos then. Similarly, in V, 1 Polybius says that Eperatus (here

(MAY)

216/15 Timoxenus IV   Polyb. V, 106. Philip and Aratus quarrel at Messene (midsummer), cf. Polyb. V, 110, Plut. *Arat.* 51.

215/14 Aratus XVII.   Dies in office (Plut. *Arat.* 53). ? Poisoned by order of Philip (cf. *ibid.* 52).

§ 2. *The restored Chronology of the War*

The date of Aratus' twelfth Strategia being fixed as 228/7, it follows that Cleomenes' defeat of Aristomachus at Pallantium near Tegea occurred shortly before the change of Strategos of May 228 (cf. Plut. *Arat.* 35), the defeat of Aratus at Lycaeum soon after his election in that year (cf. *ibid.* 36), and the joint defeat of Aratus and Lydiades near Megalopolis, towards the end of the same summer (Plut. *loc. cit., cf. Cleom.* 6). This last was followed immediately by the constitutional reforms at Sparta (Plut. *Cleom.* 7), *i.e.* autumn 228. The meeting of the Achaean League at Aegium, at which it was decided not to vote any more public funds for the continuation of the war, but to throw the whole responsibility on Aratus personally (Plut. *Arat.* 37, ad fin.), was probably the one held soon after the autumn equinox of 228 (for the times of year at which the meetings were held, cf. C.A.H. VII, p. 737).

Hostilities were only reopened in the Strategia of Hyperbatas (cf. list above, p. 432). *i.e.* 225/4 (*ibid.* n. 3), with Cleomenes' threat to Pherae and capture of Langon (Plut. *Cleom.* 14). Plutarch, who here dates the attack on Pherae ὀλίγῳ ὕστερον the constitutional reforms at Sparta, is confused in his chronology, since a lull in the war is implied both by Plutarch himself in another passage (*Arat.* 37, referred to above) and by the restored sequence of Achaean Strategoi. The capture of Langon was probably autumn 225, at all events before the Achaean elections, held in midwinter (cf. C.A.H. VII, p. 736), at which Aratus refused to stand in spite of it being his normal turn (Plut. *Cleom.* 15).

The year 224 seems to have been wholly occupied with peace negotiations, which broke down twice, the first time through the illness of Cleomenes which coincided with a meeting of the Achaean ἐκκλησία at Lerna (Plut. *Cleom.* 15), the second time when Cleomenes was on the point of attending a second meeting (called σύλλογος by Plut. *ibid.* 17) at Argos. The two regular meetings of the League are perhaps implied (spring and autumn 224). A new declaration of war was then sent by Cleomenes to Aegium (Plut. *Cleom.* 17, citing Aratus) presumably to reach the spring meeting of the League (223). In any case Cleomenes' immediate attacks on Pellene and Pheneus (Plut. *ibid.*) must fall in spring 223 to fit in with his seizure of Argos at the time of the Nemean festival (*ibid.*) which took place in ' uneven ' years of the modern reckoning (Dar.-Sagl. *s.v.* Nemea, Busolt, *Griech. Gesch.* I², p. 668, n. 3) (*i.e.* July 223). Somewhat later Corinth fell to Cleomenes (Plut. *Arat.* 40, Polyb. II, 52. Polybius mentions that it was in a Strategia of Aratus). Cleomenes then besieged Sicyon (Plut. *Arat.* 41). During the progress of the siege a meeting of the Achaean League at Aegium (*i.e.* autumn 223) decided to offer Corinth to Antigonus in return for his assistance (Polyb. II, 52). Cleomenes then raised the siege of Sicyon and began building strong fortifications across the Isthmus (Polyb. *loc. cit.*), *i.e.* winter 223/2. The appearance

---

dated to 218/17) succeeded Aratus the younger, when Dorimachus was Aetolian Strategos. The explanation is probably ante-dating by two years, as in the case of Timoxenus III and Aratus XVI (see note 6).

28

of Antigonus and his army at Pagae (Plut. *Arat.* 43. *Cf.* Polyb. II, 52, *ad fin.*) must belong to spring 222 ; the Achaeans soon afterwards recovered Argos μετὰ Τιμοξένου τοῦ στρατηγοῦ (Polyb. II, 53, *init.*, *cf.* Plut. *Cleom.* 20, *Arat.* 44), *i.e.* after May 222. Antigonus then occupied Corinth (Plut. *Cleom.* 21), where he still was in the winter (as shown by the anecdote related in Plut. *Arat.* 43, and assigned to χρόνοις ὕστερον in relation to his first arrival at Pagae). Plut. *Cleom.* 22 also implies an interval in the fighting, during which Cleomenes sent his mother and children as hostages to Ptolemy.

Antigonus' occupation of Tegea, Orchomenus and Mantinea, followed by the final battle at Sellasia, must therefore belong to spring or summer 221. From Polyb. II, 70. 4, it follows that the battle was over before the Nemean festival. The assumption that the battle took place after the harvest, deduced from Plut. *Cleom.* 26 by Beloch (*Griech. Gesch.* IV², 2, p. 220) and Tarn (C.A.H. VII, p. 863) is not justified,[1] since Plutarch's story, in this passage, of how Cleomenes' troops destroyed the growing corn in the territory of Argos is taken from Polyb. II, 64 (as Plut. *ibid.* 25 shows by citing Polybius by name), and Polybius refers the affair to the spring (ἅμα τῷ τὴν ἐαρίνην ὥραν ἐνίστασθαι) and the battle of Sellasia to the *beginning* of summer (*cf.* II, 65 : τοῦ δὲ θέρους ἐνισταμένου καὶ συνελθόντων τῶν Μακεδόνων καὶ τῶν Ἀχαιῶν ἐκ τῆς χειμασίας).

Supposing the battle to have occurred in May 221, a long enough interval remains for Cleomenes' negotiations in Egypt with Euergetes before the latter's death in the autumn of that year (exact time unknown). This removes the obstacle felt by Beloch (*ibid.* pp. 219 f.) and Tarn (C.A.H. VII, p. 863) to dating the battle in 221. The year 221 is to be preferred to 222, among other reasons, on account of the occurrence of a Nemean festival before Antigonus' return to Macedonia (Polyb. II, 70. 4). The festival was perhaps held somewhat earlier in the summer than usual to permit of his presence. Other instances of variation in the month when this festival was held are cited by Busolt, *Gr. Gesch.* I², p. 668, n. 3.

It thus appears that all the evidence, without exception, points to 221 as the year of Sellasia and of the precipitate flight of Cleomenes to Egypt, where he died about 2½ years later (Polyb. IV, 35). The election of new kings at Sparta, σχεδὸν ἤδη τρεῖς ἐνιαυτοὺς μετὰ τὴν Κλεομένους ἔκπτωσιν (*ibid.*), therefore occurred in the winter of 219/18.

---

[1] There seems to be some misunderstanding of Plutarch's words (*ibid.*) τὸν σῖτον οὐ κείρων, ὥσπερ οἱ λοιποί, δρεπάναις καὶ μαχαίραις ἀλλὰ κόπτων ξύλοις μεγάλοις, κ.τ.λ. The words ὥσπερ οἱ λοιποί must mean ' as invaders normally do ' ; they cannot mean that the Argives were then actually harvesting their corn. If it had been ripe, the obvious course for the invaders would have been to burn it ; wooden staves at that stage would no longer have the destructive effect desired.

THE LACEDAEMONIAN LEAGUE AND THE LEAGUE OF FREE LACONIANS

THERE is some doubt about the date when the League of Free Laconians [1] (Ἐλευθερολάκωνες) came into existence, for Pausanias says that it was founded by Augustus,[2] but Strabo tells us that the Eleutherolaconians 'received a sort of constitution when the Romans were joined by the Perioikoi, at the time when Sparta was under a tyrant '.[3] The natural inference from Strabo's statement would be that the Laconian towns formed a free league of their own during the tyranny of Nabis at Sparta, at the time when the maritime towns were put by Rome under the protection of the Achaean League, that is, in 195 B.C.[4] It would be rash to reject the evidence of Strabo in favour of that of a much later writer when an event ascribed to Strabo's own time is under consideration, and in fact a few inscriptions have been preserved, which testify to the existence of a 'Lacedaemonian League' (κοινὸν τῶν Λακεδαιμονίων) before the reign of Augustus.[5] Since there are also several inscriptions of the Principate which refer to a 'League of Free Laconians' (κοινὸν τῶν Ἐλευθερολακώνων),[6] but none which refer to a κοινὸν τῶν Λακεδαιμονίων, it has been supposed that Augustus was responsible mainly for a change of name,[7] which may go far to explain the statement of Pausanias.

On the other hand, it must be admitted that Augustus made very considerable changes in the pre-existing League (κοινὸν τῶν Λακεδαιμονίων), changes perhaps so considerable as to provide a complete justification for Pausanias' statement. Of the eighteen towns which Pausanias enumerates [8] as belonging to the Eleutherolaconian League in his time, three (Alagonia, Gerenia and Leuctra) were formerly in Messenia and were only incorporated in Laconia by Augustus.[9]

In addition, Augustus made Pherae in Messenia (not mentioned in Pausanias' list) a member of the Eleutherolaconian League,[10] there being some justification for this, in view of the fact that it had once been a town of Perioikoi.[11] There is also reason to think that Zarax and Prasiae, which

---

[1] Cf. p. 56.

[2] Paus. III, 21. 6 : . . . τῶν Ἐλευθερολακώνων, οὓς βασιλεὺς Αὔγουστος δουλείας ἀφῆκε Λακεδαιμονίων τῶν ἐν Σπάρτῃ κατηκόους ὄντας.

[3] Strabo, VIII, 366 : συνέβη δὲ καὶ τοὺς Ἐλευθερολάκωνας λαβεῖν τινα τάξιν πολιτείας, ἐπειδὴ Ῥωμαίοις προσέθεντο πρῶτοι οἱ περίοικοι, τυραννουμένης τῆς Σπάρτης.

[4] Cf. pp. 35 f.

[5] I.G. V, i, 1226, 1227 (Proxenia-decrees passed by the κοινόν).

[6] I.G. V, i, 1161, 1167, 1177, 1243.

[7] Le Bas-Foucart, Voyage archéologique, II (1874–1876), 111 ; Dittenberger, Syll.³ II, 748, n. 3.   [8] Cf. p. 56.

[9] Paus. IV, 1. 1.   The boundary of Messenia had formerly been the river Pamisus ; Augustus fixed the river Choerius further north as the boundary, so as to include in Laconia the three towns mentioned above. Cf. also I.G. V, i, 1431, l. 38.

[10] Cf. p. 58, n. 3.   [11] Nepos, Conon, I, 1.

both appear in Pausanias' list of Free Laconian towns, had not been members of the κοινὸν τῶν Λακεδαιμονίων, since they were included in Argive territory in the second century B.C.[1]

But apart from changes in the composition of the pre-existing Lacedaemonian League, Augustus must have made some change in its status when he changed its name, for an inscription set up at Gytheum speaks of Augustus and Tiberius as the restorers of her ancient liberties to that city.[2] Strabo's description of the same town as the 'arsenal of Sparta,[3] may be an anachronism explained by borrowing from an earlier author,[4] but in any case it tends to confirm Pausanias' statement that the 'Free Laconians' of the Principate had been actually subject to Sparta before Augustus made them independent.[5] That the previous subjection was by no means complete is clear from the fact that the towns in question had enjoyed their own laws and constitutions before the reign of Augustus ;[6] but since when the Laconian towns were made independent of Nabis they were put under the protection of the Achaean League,[7] it is possible that when the Achaean League was dissolved in 146 B.C. they were put under the protection, and to some extent under the control, of Sparta.

Such evidence as there is for the organisation of the κοινὸν τῶν Λακεδαιμονίων (the league which existed before the reign of Augustus) supports the hypothesis that it was controlled to some extent by Sparta. The League had two cult-centres, the temple of Poseidon at Taenarum and the temple of Apollo Hyperteleates in the hills north-east of Asopus. Proxenia-decrees were set up by the members of the League at both these temples in the same period, as we know from inscriptions of the earlier part of the first century B.C.[8] The inscriptions from the temple of Apollo

---

[1] Artemidorus ap. Strabo, VIII, 5. 8 (368), says that Epidaurus Limera was the last of the Laconian towns on the east coast, all north of that being Argive. Artemidorus wrote at the end of the second century B.C., but the same division of territory existed more than a century earlier (cf. p. 21). Some of the towns north of Zarax were recovered for the Spartans by Lycurgus in 219 B.C. (Polyb. IV, 36), but it would appear from this citation from Artemidorus that the Romans in 195 gave back to Argos the formerly Laconian territory which the Argives had acquired after Sellasia.

[2] I.G. V, i, 1160 : Σεβασ]τοῦ Κάισαρος [υἱὸν] ἡ πόλις ἀποκαταστήσαντα μετὰ τοῦ πατ[ρὸς] τὴν ἀρχαίαν ἐλευθερίαν ; cf. also Kornemann, Neue Dokumente (1929), p. 8, l. 8.

[3] τὸ τῆς Σπάρτης ἐπίνειον (Strabo, VIII, 343, 363).

[4] Perhaps from Artemidorus (c. 100 B.C.), cf. above, n. 1.

[5] Cf. p. 435, n. 2.

[6] E.g. from I.G. V, i, 1146 (Proxenia-decree of Gytheum, c. 70 B.C.).

[7] Livy, XXXV, 13.

[8] I.G. V, i, 1226, is a Proxenia-decree set up by the κοινὸν τῶν Λακεδαιμονίων at the temple of Poseidon at Taenarum. Since part of its introductory formula (καὶ κατὰ κοινὸν καὶ κατ'ἰδίαν τοῖς ἐντυγχάνουσιν σπουδῆς καὶ φιλοτιμίας οὐθὲν ἐλλείπων) closely corresponds to that of V, i, 1146 (ll. 3 f.), a Proxenia-decree of Gytheum dated about 70 B.C., and has no parallel in the numerous other Proxenia-decrees from Laconia, there seems good reason for ascribing no. 1226, like no. 1146, to about 70 B.C. That the temple at Taenarum was a cult-centre of the League before the reign of Augustus is also proved by the copy of a Proxenia-decree set up there by Hippola (I.G. V, i, 1336, dated before Gerenia was a member : cf.

Hyperteleates show that Spartans, as well as citizens of Asopus, Epidaurus Limera, and Cotyrta could hold the chief priesthood or minor offices at this shrine.[1] It is clear, therefore, that Sparta herself was a member of this league, although she was not a member of the Eleutherolaconian League founded by Augustus. This indeed is what we should expect in a league called τὸ κοινὸν τῶν Λακεδαιμονίων.

A coin in the British Museum [2] seems to show that in the second half of the first century B.C. Sparta was more than an ordinary member of this league, but not the independent head of it, since although at this time a *libera civitas*,[3] she recognised the higher authority of Rome. On the obverse of this coin is the inscription *ΡΩΜΑ*, on the reverse, *ΚΟΙ ΛΑΚΕ ΚΥΠΑΡΙϹϹΙΑ* (κοινὸν Λακεδαιμονίων Κυπαρίσσια)[4] and the letters *ΤΙ Κ̂Α*. The British Museum editors are probably right in referring the inscription on the reverse to a festival called τὰ κυπαρίσσια, common to all the members of the Lacedaemonian League ; there are many other examples of coins struck for festivals, with similar inscriptions.[5] The reverse type clearly represents Artemis (the goddess wears short chiton and endromides, with quiver at shoulder, and in her right hand holds a cypress branch) ; Head therefore supposes Κυπαρισσία to be an epithet of Artemis here, although Pausanias says that at Asopus it was an epithet of Athena.[6] Head's view is confirmed by an inscription from the shrine of Apollo Hyperteleates, which as we have seen was one of the centres of the κοινὸν τῶν Λακεδαιμονίων, in which Ἀγροτέρα Κυφαρισσία is mentioned as a goddess associated with the cult.[7] Ἀγροτέρα is a well-known epithet of Artemis. Kolbe therefore can scarcely be right in supposing *Kyparissia* on the coin to be the name of the town in Laconia by which it was struck :[8] it seems certain that the coin was issued for a festival

---

p. 435, n. 9). One of the many Proxenia-decrees set up by towns in the League at the temple of Apollo Hyperteleates (I.G. V, i, 965) refers to Biadas as Strategos of the League. The date of Biadas is known from the Gytheum inscription I.G. V, i, 1146, to be 73/2 B.C. Kolbe denies that both refer to the same man, but since there can be no doubt that in no. 965 οἱ ἔφοροι οἱ ἐν τῶι μετὰ Βιάδαν ἐνιαυτῶι refers to a Strategos of the League (*cf.* the formula of no. 932) there seems no ground for supposing that different persons are meant. For other Proxenia-decrees set up at the temple of Apollo Hyperteleates, see I.G. V, i, 931, 932 (by Epidaurus Limera), 961–966 (by Cotyrta), 976 (? by Cotyrta. Compare the formula of nos. 964 and 965), 975 (by an unnamed state).

[1] I.G. V, i, 1014–1016.
[2] B.M.C. *Pelop.* p. 128, no. 68 (Pl. XXV, 9) ; Head, H.N.[2], 435.
[3] See above, p. 2, n. 1.
[4] For the formula, *cf.* κοινὸν Θράκων Ἀλεξανδρεῖα (Philippopolis) (Eckhel, Vol. IV, p. 433).
[5] *Cf.* B.M.C. *Pelop.* p. 148, no. 153, p. 152. no. 170 (*NEMEIA*, within wreath) ; p. 158, no. 28 (*ΑϹΚΛΗΠΕΙΑ*, within wreath), *cf.* also Eckhel, IV, p. 433.
[6] Paus. III, 22. 9, *cf.* Steph. Byz. *s.v.* Κυπαρισσία. The Laconian Artemis and the Laconian Athena may well have descended from a common origin and were in consequence easily confused. This was certainly the case with Artemis Orthia at Sparta ; *cf.* pp. 253 f.
[7] I.G. V, i, 977.
[8] *Ibid.*, introd. pp. xiv, ll. 106 f. Kolbe supposes Kyparissia to be the earlier name of Asopus, relying on Strabo, VIII, 5. 1, 2 (363, 364) and

of Artemis held by the members of the Lacedaemonian League at the shrine of Apollo Hyperteleates.

As to the state by which the coin was struck, the British Museum editors are certainly right in ascribing it to Sparta.[1] Both the types, and the letters *TI K͡A* on the reverse (as will be seen presently), support this interpretation. On the coins of Sparta a figure of Artemis the huntress is a fairly common reverse type :[2] on the obverse of a whole series of Spartan coins we find the head of the youthful Apollo, facing right and bound with taenia,[3] which is represented on the obverse of the Lacedaemonian League coin. The explanation given by the British Museum editors, that the young male head here represents the Demos of Rome, is understandable in view of the inscription but is none the less purely fanciful. Apollo, on the other hand, is the constant companion of his sister Artemis : they are represented on the two sides of several coins of Sparta ;[4] they were worshipped together at the shrine of Apollo Hyperteleates.

Finally, the letters *TI K͡A* on the reverse of the League coin support the view that it was issued by Sparta, because they find a parallel in the numerous series of Spartan monogram coins which belong to the pre-Imperial period.[5] There is no evidence for Kolbe's suggestion[6] that *TI* on the League coin stands for Timokrates, Strategos of the Lacedaemonian League in 72-1 B.C., and this interpretation leaves the monogram *K͡A* unexplained. The alternative explanation given above is supported by the fact that a group of the Spartan monogram coins of the late Roman Republic[7] bear a head of Apollo very similar to that on the League coin, and there is reason also to think that the Spartan coins bearing the reverse type of the standing Artemis are of about the same period as the ' monogram coins '.[8] Thus we have not only a reason for attributing the League coin to the Spartan mint, but an indication of its date. As a negative test of this conclusion it may be mentioned that no coinage at all is known to have been issued by any of the individual towns of Laconia other than Sparta before the late second or the early third century A.D., long after they had become ' Free Laconian ', when Gytheum, Las, Asopus and Boeae all issued coins.

There exist, however, some coins issued under the auspices of the Achaean League which may well be Lacedaemonian League coins, since they bear on the reverse (in addition to the Λ denoting the Achaean League) the monogram Λ͡Λ, and the caps of the Dioscuri, surmounted by stars, which are found on the silver coins of the second century B.C. and on

---

Pausanias' reference (*cf.* above, n.) to a temple of Athena Kyparissia on the acropolis of Asopus. But Kyparissia was in ancient times (and still is) a very common place-name in the Peloponnese.

[1] It seems possible that Sparta also issued coins for the festivals of the Dioscuri at the League centre of Taenarum ; *cf.* pp. 152 f.

[2] *Cf.* B.M.C. *Pelop.* p. 126, nos. 56–60.

[3] *Ibid.*, p. 123, nos. 22 f.

[4] *Ibid.* p. 125, nos. 48–50, p. 126, nos. 56, 57.

[5] *Cf. ibid.* pp. 122 f.   [6] I.G. V, i, p. xiv, ll. 110 f.

[7] I hope to publish a paper on the dating of these coins when the national collections again become available.

[8] This type occurs on the reverse of the coins inscribed *EΦOPΩN* and *ΓEPONTΩN*, for the date of which *cf.* above, p. 155, n. 7.

later coins of Sparta.[1] With regard to the monogram $\text{\AA}$, it may be supposed that the letters $\wedge\!\!\text{A}$ (written separately on the coins of Sparta herself) are conceived to be exactly superimposed, and that the stroke is made through both to show that two letters are intended, not one. It may be suggested that these coins belong to the period 188–146 B.C., during which Sparta was enrolled as a member of the Achaean League,[2] for Sparta could not be a member of the Lacedaemonian League, which included the maritime cities put under the protection of the Achaean League by Rome in 195 B.C., before she herself became a member of the Achaean League ; and as mentioned above, the device of the caps of the Dioscuri surmounted by stars indicates that the coins in question were issued by Sparta.

It seems, therefore, not unlikely that the Lacedaemonian League was finally constituted, with the inclusion of Sparta, in 188 B.C. This is not inconsistent with Strabo's statement that the Laconian towns received a sort of constitution ' when Sparta was under a tyrant ',[3] for some sort of constitution must already have been given to them when they were freed from Sparta and put under Achaean control in 195 B.C. The view commonly held, that the Lacedaemonian League was founded only in 146 B.C.,[4] rejects the evidence both of Strabo and Pausanias.[5] On the explanation given above, both are now seen to be right, though it is evident that Strabo used the name ' Eleutherolakones ', given only in the reign of Augustus when the Lacedaemonian towns were separated from Sparta, instead of the earlier ' League of the Lacedaemonians '.

It remains to consider the stages by which the Eleutherolaconian League came to be composed of the eighteen towns included in Pausanias' list. Some confusion has been caused by Pausanias' statement that there were originally twenty-four towns in this League, but in his own time only eighteen.[6] He has also been interpreted to mean that the other six towns had been absorbed by Sparta since the time of Augustus, but this is not a necessary interpretation of his words,[7] and in any case cannot (as will presently be shown) represent the facts. As to the date at which there were twenty-four towns in the League, it seems impossible to suppose that this was so before Augustus included in it the Messenian

---

[1] B.M.C. *Pelop.* pp. 7 f., nos. 78–86. For the caps of the Dioscuri surmounted by stars on coins of Sparta, *cf. op. cit.* p. 122, nos. 6–13, which are silver coins of the same period and of the same weight as the silver Achaean League coin under discussion, and with a very similar obverse type ; also *op. cit.* p. 126, nos. 58–60 (copper coins of Timaristos) ; also *op. cit.* p. 128, no. 72 (coin of Lakon). The heads of the Dioscuri, or the Dioscuri standing, are very common types on the copper coins of Sparta (*cf. op. cit.* p. 124, nos. 35–40, pp. 125 f., nos. 51–5, p. 127, nos. 62, 66, p. 129, no. 73, p. 131, no. 85), but there would have been no room for them on the Achaean League silver coins.

[2] *Cf.* above, pp. 49 f.   [3] *Cf.* above, p. 435.
[4] *Cf.* Swoboda, *Klio*, XII (1912), 22, 34 ; I.G. V, i, introd. xiv, ll. 106 f.

[5] *Cf.* above, p. 435.   [6] Paus. III, 21. 7.
[7] This view is taken by Tillyard (B.S.A. XII, 1906, p. 465, l. 8). But Pausanias may mean merely that the towns which he mentions later as being in Laconia, and which are not in his list of the eighteen Free Laconian towns, are to be understood to belong to Sparta. See further below.

towns of Gerenia, Alagonia, Leuctra, and Pherae,[1] because there were not enough towns [2] in Laconia itself at this period to make up so large a number. A possible explanation is that for a short time at the beginning of the reign of Augustus an augmented Lacedaemonian League continued to exist, of which Sparta was still a member and to which the Messenian territory had been added. This would account for the six extra towns in the period before Cythera and Cardamyle were given to Sparta ; [3] namely, in addition to the two just mentioned, Sparta herself, Pherae [4] in Messenia, and the two towns Hippola and Cotyrta, which are both known from inscriptions to have belonged to the Lacedaemonian League as autonomous πόλεις in the first century B.C.,[5] but which are no more heard of during the Principate. Pausanias says that Hippola was in ruins in his time, and it may have been incorporated in the new city (Kainepolis) built near the site of the ancient Taenarum.[6] From its position it seems not unlikely that Cotyrta was included in the territory of Boeae. But in any case both lay outside the boundaries of Spartan territory under the Principate, and cannot have been absorbed by Sparta. Asine on the west side of the Messenian Gulf, though still a Perioikid town in the time of Thucydides, had belonged to Messenia consistently since an award of Philip in 338 B.C., and so does not come into consideration here.[7] The disappearance of Sparta herself from the League is, of course, accounted for by the separation of the Laconian towns from Sparta and the formation of the new Eleutherolaconian League. This happened rather late in the reign of Augustus, for the Gytheum inscription already cited associates Tiberius with Augustus in its grateful recognition of the restoration of liberty.[8] This suggests the time when Tiberius was associated with Augustus in the government of the provinces, that is from some time during the last two or three years of the reign of Augustus, possibly as late as A.D. 13.[9] Long before this, in 21 B.C., Augustus had reduced the number of the twenty-four towns of the Lacedaemonian League by giving Cythera to Sparta.[10] It is natural to suppose, though we have no proof of this, that Cardamyle was given to Sparta, together with Thuria in Messenia, which had never been incorporated in the Lacedaemonian League [11] at the time of the liberation of the Laconian

---

[1] Cf above, pp. 435 f.

[2] That is, πόλεις large enough to have their own constitution and laws, such as those which made grants of Proxenia in the first century B.C. (cf. above, p. 436, n. 8). Strabo and Pausanias occasionally refer under the name of πόλεις to places in Laconia, such as Helos, which were supposed to have been flourishing cities in the pre-Dorian period, but which had since decayed into mere villages or had disappeared altogether, or to places which, though they continued to exist, were too small to be included in the Eleutherolaconian League as independent members. Psamathus is an example of the second class (cf. Strabo, VIII, 363).

[3] Cf. above, p. 56.   [4] Cf. above, p. 58, n. 5.

[5] For Cotyrta, see I.G. V, i, 961–966, and cf. p. 436, n. 8. For Hippola, see I.G. V, i, 1336. The date of this inscription must be earlier than Augustus' incorporation of Gerenia in the Lacedaemonian League, since Gerenia is evidently not a member (she sets up her copy of the decree in the local temple of Machaon), but Hippola is a member, since she sets up her copy in the temple of Poseidon at Taenarum (cf. above, p. 436, n. 8).

[6] Cf. Paus. III, 25.9.   [7] Reff. in I.G. V, i, p. 273.

[8] Cf. above, p. 436, n. 2.   [9] Cf. C.A.H. X, p. 158.

[10] Cf. p. 56, n. 4.   [11] Ibid.

towns and the creation of the new Eleutherolaconian League, by way of compensation to Sparta for the loss of prestige and practical advantages which she might be thought to suffer through this change. Since Cardamyle had already been taken from Messenia—the town lay in the territory between the river Pamisus and the river Choerius, which Augustus had added to Laconia [1]—and was a comparatively recent acquisition to the Lacedaemonian League, little hardship can have been caused when Augustus gave Sparta this new port in exchange for Gytheum.[2] As for Pherae, its absence from Pausanias' list of Eleutherolaconian towns is doubtless to be explained by supposing that it was given back to Messenia in exchange for Thuria, when Thuria was given to Sparta, but there is no direct evidence about this.[3] Thus the total was reduced to eighteen, though Cythera and Cardamyle were the only towns of those which had once been members of the Lacedaemonian League which were absorbed by Sparta.

---

[1] Cf. above, p. 435, n. 9.　　　　　　[2] Cf. above, pp. 56 f.
[3] Pherae was again in Messenia in Pausanias' time (IV, 1. 4).

TABLES OF SPARTAN OFFICIALS AND AGOGIC CLASSES

§ 1

BOAGOI AND 'PATRONS' OF KASENS

Names of those actually called *Boagos* in the inscriptions are in italics; those who have Synepheboi are marked with an asterisk. The dates, where given, are in accordance with those assigned in the list of Patronomoi (Appendix IV, § 8). The references to I.G. throughout this Appendix are to I.G. V, 1. For the meaning of the sign < see below, p. 452.

Name of 'Patron'	Evidence	Indications of Date
1. Agathok̥[les]	B.S.A. XXVII p. 217, E 31	His Kasen Nomodeiktes *c.* 126/7 (*cf.* Appendix IV, 3 A, No. 32)
2. Agis Κλεάνδρου	I.G. 281	His Kasen victor in Agelae *c.* 82/3 (*cf.* Appendix IV, 3B, No. 4, n. 4). Probably son of Patronomos Kleandros (*c.* 84/5)
3. Agis, Pomponius	I.G. 71	His Kasen Nomophylax *c.* 160/1 (*cf. ibid.* No. 16) son of Alkastos II (No. 7 below) *cf.* I.G. 494. Patronomos *c.* 172/3
4. Agesilaos Νεόλα	I.G. 278	His Kasen victor in Agelae *c.* 60–5 (for date of the Patronomos Eukleidas *cf.* Appendix IV, 3 B, note 4, No. 7). Probably son of No. 60 below, and brother of No. 61
5. *Alkandridas* ̕Αλκανδρίδα	I.G. 78	Nomophylax ἐπὶ Με[νεκλέους]. If rightly restored, A.D. 97/8
6. Alkastos (I)	B.S.A. XXVI, p. 166, B 8	His Kasen in Gerusia for fifth time *c.* 100 (*cf.* Appendix IV, 3A, No. 9)
7. Alkastos (II) (C. Pomponius)	I.G. 290 (*cf. ibid.* 35, 37, etc., for Roman name)	His Kasen victor in Agelae *c.* 90/1 (*cf.* Appendix IV, 3 B, No. 12). Patronomos *c.* 139/40. Father of No. 3 above and of No. 12 below
8. A̠n̠s̠e̠[tos]	I.G. 266	His Kasen victor in Agelae *c.* 60–5 (*cf.* Appendix IV, § 3B, No. 1 and n. 4, *ibid.*)
9. Antipater	B.S.A. XXVI, p. 165, B 1 (γ)	His Kasens Ephors *c.* 85/6 and 87/8 *cf.* Appendix IV, § 3A, Nos. 1, 14. Not identical with C. Julius Antipater Λυσικράτους of I.G. 663, who must be a generation later (see Kolbe's note, *ibid.*)

Name of ' Patron '	Evidence	Indications of Date
10. Aphthonetos Σωզις. ράτους (Marcus Valerius Ulpianus)	I.G. 323	Dedication as Boagos c. 170. Either nephew or grandson of M. Ulpius Aphthonetos, Patronomos c. 132/3 (for his Roman names cf. I.G. 104, 286), who in turn was probably son of M. Ulpius So[. . .], Geron. c. 88/9 (I.G. 105)
11. Archiadas	I.G. 331 (cf. 473)	Dedication as Boagos c. 60–5. Father of Dameas 'Αρχιάδα, Geron c. 95/6 (B.S.A. XXVI, p. 170, E2, under C. Jul. Agesilaos), and of Neolas 'A., Nomophylax c. 98/9 (ibid. p. 166, B7) ; father-in-law (cf. I.G. 473) of Sokrates 'Αρείονος who with his brother Julius Arion was official at the shrine of Damoia c. 99/100 (under Jul. Charixenos I, cf. I.G. 1314)
12. Aristeas 'Αλκάστου, C. Pomponius	I.G. 495	Title of Boagos mentioned before his various offices. Procurator (?) of Pius [ἐπίτροπος Αὐτοκράτο]ρο[ς .] 'Αντωνείνου, son of No. 7 above
13. Aristeus *	I.G. 47	His Synephebos a Πανέλλην, then in Gerusia some year after 128. Cf. Appendix IV, 6, No. 10
14. Aristokrates I, Δαμάρους (L. Volussenus, ' pattron ' with No. 22 (L. Volussenus Damares)	B.S.A. XXVI, p. 170, E2 ; p. 172, E9 ; cf. I.G. 477 for full name	His Kasen Bidyos and Geron c. 90/1 and 95/6. Appendix IV, 3 A, No. 33. Probably father of the Patronomos of c. 112/13
15. Aristokrates II ('Αριστοκράτους), L. Volussenus	I.G. 82	His Kasen Nomophylax c. 117/18 (Appendix IV, 3 A, No. 7). Aristokrates < Ephor about 120, I.G. 203 (cf. B.S.A. XXVI, p. 192. Probably Patronomos of c. 112/13
16. Aristokrates * Δαμαινέτου, M. Aurelius	I.G. 653a	?ἀπὸ 'Ηρακλέος μη', ἀπὸ Διοσκούρων μδ' (I.G. 529, 530). Brother of Lysippos Δ., Patronomos c. 180 (cf. I.G. 680, n., 531, n., and see further, Appendix IV,

Name of 'Patron'	Evidence	Indications of Date
16. *Cont.*		3 A, n. 4). Victor as Boagos probably *c.* 165–70, with Ti. Claud, Eiranion
17. Aristoteles * Μηνοφάνηρ (*sic*), Pompeius	I.G. 303	His Synephebos victor in Agelae under Claud. Abaskantos (*c.* 190). Probably son of No. 55 below
18. *Aristoteles* Σπαρτιατίκου (Ti. Claud.)	I.G. 527	Contemporary with No. 16 (*cf.* Kolbe, *ibid.*). Probably son of Patronomos of *c.* 145/6, and nephew of Patronomos of *c.* 148/9
19. Atticus (Herodes) (Ti. Claud.)	B.S.A. XXVI, p. 168, C 7	His Kasen in Gerusia *c.* 120. Patronomos *c.* 134/5, father of the Sophist (*cf.* No. 20 below)
20. Atticus * II Ἡρώδου (Ti. Claud.)	I.G. 45	His Synephebos holds offices (including that of Geron) *c.* 152–5. To be identified with the Sophist (consul 143. *Cf.* P.I.R.² II, p. 175, no. 802 ; lived *c.* 100–176) not with his son, as assumed, I.G. *ibid.* (n.). Son of No. 19 above
21. Brasidas (Ti. Claud.)	I.G. 161	Probably the Patronomos of *c.* 157/8 (*cf.* Appendix IV, 3 A, No. 13, n. 2)
22. Damares (L. Volussenus)	B.S.A. XXVI, p. 170, E2	'Patron' with (L. Volussenus) Aristokrates I, No. 14. For his Roman name *cf.* I.G. 477, 581. His Kasen in Gerusia *c.* 95/6 (*cf.* Appendix IV, § 3 A, No. 35)
23. Damares* Βροὐτου, P. Memm.	I.G. 39 (*cf.* 38)	His Synephebos secretary of Gerusia *c.* 162/3, Ephor *c.* 173/4. Another Synephebos ἱεροθύτης *c.* 142/3. The 'Patron' probably the Patronomos Damares of *c.* 144/5
24. *Damion Βέλλωνος*	I.G. 89	Nomophylax about the same time as the Patronomate of Longinus, 155/6 in Appendix IV, § 8. *Cf.* Appendix IV, § 3A, n. 4
25. *Damokles Δαμο-* κλέους τοῦ καὶ Φιλοκράτους	I.G. 32B, 60	In Gerusia under Hadrian's Patronomate, Ephor *c.* 127/8
26. Damokrates I	I.G. 270	His Kasen victor in Agelae, first century A.D. (*cf.* Appendix IV, § 3B, No. 5, n. 4)

Name of 'Patron'	Evidence	Indications of Date
27. Damokrates II Εὐδοκίμου	I.G. 64	Ephor under Eudamidas c. 146/7. Father of No. 36 below
28. Damokrates III * Διοκλέους	I.G. 293 (cf. 493)	Dedicates for victory in Agelae under Cl. Sejanus, c. 149/50
29. Damokratidas * Ἀλκανδρίδου, P. Aelius	I.G. 554	Probably the Patronomos of c. A.D. 180
30. Damainetos (? Θεοξένου), Sex. Pomp.	I.G. 324 (cf. 168)	Dedicates as Boagos. Probably second half of second century (cf. Kolbe on I.G. 168)
31. Damoneikidas	B.S.A. XXVI, p. 164, A5	His Kasen Geron c. 112/13
32. Deximachos P. Memm.	Ibid. p. 167, C 3 ; p. 190	Nomophylax c. 85/6. Probably Patronomos c. 90/1
33. Eiranion * Ὑγείνου, Ti. Claud.	I.G. 653 a	Boagos with M. Aurelius Aristokrates (above, No. 16)
34. Enymantiadas	I.G. 280, 97	His Kasen victor in Agelae c. 82/3, two others Gerontes c. 120 (Appendix IV, 3A, No. 8, ibid. B, No. 9)
35. Eudamos	I.G. 296	May be identical either with the Patronomos Eudamos I (c. 60–5) or Eudamos II (c. 141/2). But cf. Appendix IV, § 3A, n. 4, No. 6, where reasons are given for preferring Eudamos II ; if so, his Kasen won in the Agelae c. 110
36. Eudokimos Δαμοκράτους ὁ καὶ Ἀριστείδας	I.G. 289	Son of No. 27 above, wins as Boagos in year of Alkastos (c. 139/40) with No. 37 below
37. Eudokimos Εὐδοκίμου	I.G. 289	Cousin of preceding (cf. Kolbe, n.) and victor with him
38. Eurykles (Λάκωνος), C. Julius	I.G. 103, B.S.A. XXVI, p. 168, C 6, 7	His Kasens in Gerusia c. A.D. 120 (cf. Appendix IV, § 3A, Nos. 5, 6, 22), the 'patron' is therefore C. Julius Eurykles Herklanos Λάκωνος (cf. pp. 189 f.), Patronomos c. 117/18
38a. Eurykles,* Julius	I.G. 287	His Synephebos wins in Agelae in year of Cl. Atticus (c. 134/5), great-nephew of preceding, cf. pp. 201 f., 202, n. 3
39. Gorgippos,* Ὀνασικράτους, Sex. Pompeius	I.G. 653b	Not the son of S. P. Onasikrates of I.G. 129, but a later descendant. The

Name of 'Patron'	Evidence	Indications of Date
39. Cont.		victory belongs to the early third century ; cf. Appendix V, p. 471
40. Iamos	I.G. 298	His Kasen wins in Agelae under Pratoneikos c. 101/2. 'Patron' with Teisamenos and Kritodamos, q.v.
41. Kallikrates Καλλι-κράτους	I.G. 64, 69	Nomophylax under Eudamidas c. 146/7, Ephor under Cascellius Aristoteles c. 162/3, Patronomos c. 160/1, nephew of Aristokles II (Patronomos c. 133/34), grandson of Aristokles I (Patronomos c. 107/8)
42. Kallikrates 'Ρούφου	I.G. 64	Nomophylax with preceding, nephew or grandson of Patronomos of c. 100 (cf. Appendix IV, § 8, note A)
43. Kleandros Καλλισ-τράτου, ὁ καὶ Μῆνις	I.G. 307, 601	Wins as Boagos under Gor-gippos Γοργίππου c. 190 ; cf. Kolbe, ad I.G. 307
44. Kleodamos (? son of Kleodamos, Patronomos c. 93/4)	I.G. 102, 61	His Kasen in Gerusia c. 130/1. (Appendix IV, § 3A, No. 4) ; another was Ephor c. 132/3, under Aphthonetos
45. Kleombrotos	B.S.A. XXVI, p. 165, B1, γ	His Kasen Ephor under Aristodamos (c. 87/8)
46. Kratesikles Στρά-τωνος, ὁ καὶ Στράτων	I.G. 273	Wins as Boagos in παιδικὸς ἀγών under P. Memmius Theokles (c. 89/90)
47. Kritodamos	I.G. 298	His Kasen wins in Agelae c. 101/2, cf. No. 40 above, and Appendix IV, § 3 B, No. 3.
48. Lakr[ines] *'Αριστο-τέλους	I.G. 286 + Add. 1510	His Synephebos wins under M. Ulpius Aphthonetos, c. 132/3
49. Leilochos	A.O. 2 (cf. I.G. 256, Deilochos)	Uncertain date, cf. Appendix IV, § 3 B, n. 4 (No. 10)
50. Leonteus	I.G. 257 (cf. A.O. 7)	Metrical inscription εἰσαρίθ-μοις ἔπεσι. Unlikely to be earlier than c. 150 (Wood-ward)
51. Longinus * Δαμά-ρους (P. Memmius)	I.G. 548, 89	His father's name shows him to belong to the P. Memmii, (the ligatured letters ΠoΜ in I.G. 89 should be so inter-preted ; not Pomponius, cf. ibid. 91). On the date of I.G. 89, cf. Appendix IV, § 3A, n. 4. Probably son

Name of 'Patron'	Evidence	Indications of Date
51. Cont.		of Patronomos of c. 144/5, himself the Patronomos of c. 155/6
52. Lysimachos	I.G. 68, 69, 70	'Patron' with Mnason (No. 56), His Kasen Nomophylax c. 148/9, Ephor. c. 162/3, in office with Nos. 41, 42 above
53. Lysippos Φιλοχαρείνου	I.G. 85	Nomophylax under Memm. Spartiatikos, c. 91/2, Patronomos c. 111/12. ? Grandfather of No. 73 below
54. Menekles	I.G. 277, B.S.A. XXVI, p. 170, E2	His Kasen in Gerusia c. 95/6 ; probably himself the Patronomos of 97/8
55. Menophanes, Sex. Pompeius	I.G. 325	([βοαγό]ρ restored). Probably father of No. 17 above (cf. Kolbe's stemma, I.G. 303)
56. Mnason	I.G. 68, 69, 70	'Patron' with Lysimachus (No. 52 above, q.v.) ; in the generation following Lysimachus Μνάσωνος (Geron c. 110, I.G. 99). Probably brother of his fellow-'Patron'; for further relationships see below, § 2 (p. 451).
57. Mnason Εὖ[. . .]	I.G. 322	Dedication to Orthia as Boagos, ? second century A.D.
58. Mnas[?istratos] Καλλικρ [. . .]	I.G. 319	Dedication to Orthia as Boagos ἐπὶ 'Ιουλίω . . . (lettering of earlier type than preceding) ; for name cf. I.G. 270
59. Nedymos Γαίου	I.G. 71	His Kasen Ephor c. 160/1
60. Neolas I (?Νεόλα)	I.G. 95	His Kasen in Gerusia in year of Menalkidas (see Appendix IV, § 3, n. 4, No. 1 for evidence of date)
61. Neolas II Νεόλα	B.S.A. XXVII, p. 221, E35	His Kasen Bidyos in year of Kleandros, c. 84/5 ; in view of the dates, the 'Patron' is probably brother of No. 4 above
62. Nikandridas I Νικανδρίδα	B.S.A. XXVII, p. 237, No. 20	σύναρχος of the Patronomos C. Jul. Antipater, c. 109/10
63. Nikandridas (? Νικανδρίδα) P. Aelius	I.G. 69, 70	Ephor under Cascellius Aristoteles c. 162/3
64. Nikandros Νεικοκράτους	I.G. 89	Nomophylax c. A.D. 155 (with Damion Βέλλωνος, No. 24 above)

Name of 'Patron'	Evidence	Indications of Date
65. *Nikephoros* '*Aριστο-βούλου*	I.G. 69, 71 ; B.S.A. XXVI, p. 171, E7	Nomophylax under Cascellius Aristoteles *c.* 162/3
66. [*Nikephoros* ?] *Kαλλικράτους*, Marcus Aurelius	I.G. 692 (*cf.* 568)	Dedicates a new *Stoa*, late C 2
67. *Nikippidas*	I.G. 71 (*cf.* 299)	His Kasen Ephor *c.* 160/1 (*ἐπὶ Kαλλικράτους* <). (Perhaps grandson of Patronomos Nikippidas of *c.* 102/3)
68. *Onasikleidas* *Φιλο-στράτου*	I.G. 36	Nomophylax under Kallikrates '*Pούφου* (*cf.* Appendix IV, § 8, note A) *c.* A.D. 100. Father or uncle of the Patronomos of same name, *c.* 138/9, *cf.* Appendix IV, 7, No. 14
69. *Pasikles* *Kαλλικράτους*	I.G. 69, B.S.A. XXVI, p. 171, E7	Nomophylax with No. 65 above and No. 70 below, *c.* 162/3
70. *Perikles* (Pompeius or Pomponius)	B.S.A. *ibid.*, I.G. 71*b*	Nomophylax with preceding. For Roman name, *cf.* B.S.A. *ibid.* p. 197
71. *Phileros*	I.G. 65, 65*a*, 115 (*cf.* B.S.A. XXVI, p. 201 (β)	His Kasen Ephor under Damokles <, *c.* 131/2
72. *Philippos*, Marcus Aurelius	I.G. 551	High-priest of the emperors in reign of Caracalla
73. *Philochareinos* *Λυσίππου*, C. Julius	I.G. 292, 294	Dedicates to Orthia as Boagos in years of Sejanus, and of Biadas, *c.* 149, A.D. 150. ? Grandson of No. 53 above
74. *Polyxenos* *Πολυξένου*	I.G. 62	Ephor under Atticus, *c.* 134/5
75. *Pratolaos Bρασίδου*, Ti. Claud.	I.G. 472 (*cf.* 663)	His Synephebos wins the wrestling-match of the *ἀγέ-νειοι* in Patronomate of C. Jul. Antipater *c.* 109/10
76. *Prateas Tυράν*[*νου*], Marcus Aurelius	I.G. 314	Dedicates to Orthia as Boagos in Patronomate of the son of No. 43 above, *c.* A.D. 250 (latest of the series)
77. [*Prato*]neikos	I.G. 66	His Kasen Ephor *c.* 139/40, just before *Θεὸς Λυκοῦργος τὸ β'* (*cf.* Appendix IV, § 8, under year 140/1, and B.S.A. XXVI, p. 186 (B9), dating Neikasippos *Eὐημέ-ρου* as Nomophylax to Patronomate of Meniskos (*c.* 135/6) not that of Hadrian)

Name of ' Patron '	Evidence	Indications of Date
78. Seidektas *	I.G. 59, 66, 114	His Synepheboi Nomophylakes under Meniskos (cf. B.S.A. ibid., correcting restoration of I.G. 59), one is Ephor under Lycurgus (cf. No. 77 above). His Kasen Geron about the same time (I.G. 114) ? Patronomos of c. 124/5
78a. Seimedes (C. Julius ?)	I.G. 101, B.S.A. XXVI, p. 164, A 3–4, p. 168, B5	Two of his Kasens in Gerusia c. 112/3, another (for the fourth time) c. 114/15 (cf. Appendix IV, 3A, Nos. 12, 20, 23). Probably brother of Patronomos Polyeuktos (cf. B.S.A. ibid. p. 166, B4γ, referring to a nephew, Ephor c. 131/2 (Ti. Claud. Seimedes of I.G. 152 is a generation too late)
79. Soixiteles, Εὐδάμου (Sex. Pomp.)	I.G. 99 (cf. 137)	His Kasen Bidyos in year of Lampis c. 121/2. For his Roman name cf. I.G. 559 (he and a later Eudamos both ἀρχιερεῖς διὰ βίου κατὰ γένος of Dioscuri etc.)
80. Sosikrates Πολυεύκτου, Ti. Claud.	I.G. 283	Dedication to Orthia as Boagos in year of Lysikrates, c. 96/7
80a. [? So]sikrates	I.G. 89	Perhaps identical with Patronomos of c. 167/8. Cf. Appendix IV, § 3A, No. 15, note
81. Spartiates Σπαρτιάτου, Mar. Aur.	I.G. 539	Patronomos c. 225. ? Inscription of same date as I.G. 538. For the Paulinus there mentioned, cf. P.I.R., sv. Paulinus 125, Nonius 92
82. Spartiatikos (? P. Memm.)	I.G. 65 (cf. B.S.A. XXVI, p. 201, 2β)	His Kasen Nomophylax c. 131/2, after c. 20 years in office. The ' Patron ' may be identical with Patronomos of c. 145/6
83. Spartiatikos Δαμάρου, P. Memm.	I.G. 312	Dedicates to Orthia as Boagos ἐπὶ πατρονόμω Θεῷ Λυκούργω τὸ ια', with Ti. Claud. Brasidas Βρασίδα as substitute. Nephew rather than brother of P. M. Pratolaos Δαμάρους, substitute- Patronomos for Θεὸς Λυκοῦργος

29

Name of ' Patron '	Evidence	Indications of Date
83. Cont.		τὸ δ' (cf. I.G . 541, 542). Victory as Boagos c. A.D. 200
84. Teisamenos	I.G. 103, 298 ; B.S.A. XXVI, p. 168, C7 (β)	Referred to as Boagos, I.G. 258. His Kasens in the Gerusia c. 125 (cf. Appendix IV, § 3A, nn. 1 and 5). One successful in Agelae c. 101/2. Cf. above under Iamos (No. 40) who was his brother (Appendix IV, § 5, n. 1)
85. Theophrastos Θεοκλυμένου, C. Jul.	B.S.A. XXVII, p. 228	Agoranomos at Hadrian's first visit (124/5), Patronomos c. 136/7
86. Timomenes	I.G. 109	Patronomos c. 156/7 (cf. Appendix IV, § 8, under this year)
87. Tyndares	I.G. 60	Shares the Kasen Kleon < with Teisamenos (No. 84)
88. Zeuxippos, ὁ καὶ Κλέανδρος Φιλομούσου, M. Aur.	I.G. 305	Dedicates as Boagos to Orthia, late second century (cf. A.O. p. 331) Priest of Tyndaridae. Descendant of No. 87 above. Cf. I.G. 111, Ζευξίππος Τυνδάρους, son of No. 87

§ 2

RELATED BOAGOI AND 'PATRONS'

Many of the persons in the list of Boagoi and 'Patrons' (Appendix IV, § 1) may immediately be seen from consideration of their names and dates to have been closely related to one another. Thus we find in Nos. 26, 27, 36 and 37 three generations of the same family represented—father, son and grandson and a cousin of the last. Neither in this instance nor in any of the others presently to be cited does there seem to have been any social distinction between those who were Boagoi and those who merely had Kasens ; both are frequently found represented in the same family. A similar instance is that of No. 60, father of Nos. 61 and 4, another is that of No. 7, father of Nos. 3 and 12. No. 19 is the father of No. 20 ; No. 55 is the father of No. 17 ; No. 53 is the father of No. 73 ; No. 14 is the father of No. 15 ; No. 38 is probably great-uncle of No. 39. Pairs of brothers are found in Nos. 22 and 14, Nos. 40 and 84.

Where the Greek names in these lists are in themselves of too common occurrence at Sparta to permit us to assume relationship, relationship may not infrequently be deduced from possession of the same hereditary priesthoods (see further Appendix V, which enables us to detect relationship between the various Sex. Pompeii mentioned in these lists, and between the various Ti. Claudii). Nos. 87 and 88 are a case in point.

Finally, a test of relationship appears in common possession not only of the same Roman *praenomina* and *nomina*, but also of the same Roman *cognomen*, used as the first name in place of a Greek one. Thus, the names *C. Julius* and *Pollio* are shared by persons in this list with the name of Kallikrates (Nos. 41 and 42 ; *cf.* in I.G. 64 Kallikrates 'Ρούφου, *ibid.* 97 C. Julius Pollion 'Ρούφου, a generation later than Kallikrates 'P.) and by persons with the name of Mnason and Lysimachos (Nos. 52 and 56, the latter son of Jul. Lysippos Μνάσωνος, Patronomos *c.* 127/8 ; *cf.* Lysippos Πολλίωνος, Geron in I.G. 95 ἐπὶ Μεναλκίδα). On the origin of the Roman names in this particular family, see further, Appendix IV, § 3B, n. 4.

A strikingly large number of the persons whose names occur in these lists held the office of Patronomos (Nos. 3, 4, 7, 15, 19, 21, 23, 29, 32, 35, 38, ? 41, 53, 54, 78, 80, 81, 83, 85, 86). In addition, No. 62 held office as σύναρχος of a Patronomos ; sons of Patronomoi are found in Nos. 12, 18, 20, 51, ? 56, ? 67 ; fathers of Patronomoi in Nos. 6, 14, ? 68 ; No. 16 is brother of a Patronomos ; Nos. 18, 41, 42 are nephews of Patronomoi.

§ 3

LIST OF KASENS

A. (Office-holders)

(On the dates, where no Patronomos is given, see notes below, p. 455 f. The dates assigned are those in the list of Patronomoi (Appendix IV, § 8). The sign < used in the inscriptions indicates that the father's name is the same as that of the son.)

Name of Kasen	Office held	Name of 'Patron'	Name of Patronomos	Date(Approx.)	Evidence
1. Ti. Claud. Agathokles <	Ephor	Antipater	Nikokrates	85/6	B.S.A. XXVI, p. 167, C3
2. Agathokles Ἀγαθοκλέους	Bidyos	Soixiteles	C. Julius Lampis (I)	121/2	I.G. 99, 137
3. Antiochos Ἀντιόχου	Geron	Zeuxippos	C. Julius Philokleidas	120/1	I.G. 97
4. [- - -] <	Geron	Kleodamos	Ti. Claud. Aristoboulos	130/1	I.G. 102
5. Aristomenes Ἀριστομένους	Geron	}Eurykles	?	See note 1	I.G. 103
6. [. . . .] <	Geron				I.G. 82
7. Archippos [- - -]	Nomophylax	Aristokrates	P. Aelius Dionysios	118/19	I.G. 97, 20B
8. Chaleinos Χαλείνου	Geron	Enymantiadas	C. Julius Philokleidas	120/1	B.S.A. XXVI,
9. Chares <	All offices except Patronomos	Alkastos	Kallikrates Ῥούφου	100/1	p. 166, B8
10. Chryseros <	Geron	Timomenes	Timomenes	156/7	I.G. 109
11. Damakion <	Ephor	Phileros	Damokles Δαμοκλέους	131/2	I.G. 65, 115, cf. B.S.A. XXVI, p. 201, β
12. Damarchos <	Geron	Seimedes	L. Volussenus Aristokrates	112/3	B.S.A. XXVI, p. 164, A3–5
13. Dekmos (sic) <	?	Brasidas	?	See note 2	I.G. 161
14. Diokles <	Ephor	Antipater	Aristodamos	87/8	B.S.A. XXVI, p. 165, B1, γ
15. Eudaimon <	? Ephor	[So]sikrates	?	See note 3	I.G. 89
16. Euporos <	Nomophylax	Pomponius Agis	Kallikrates < τοῦ Ἀριστοκλέους	160/1	I.G. 71

Name of Kasen	Office held	Name of 'Patron'	Name of Patronomos	Date (Approx.)	Evidence
17. Hierokles Ἱεροκλέους	Geron	Atticus (not Enymantiadas. Cf. App. IV, § 8, n. B)	C. Julius Philokleidas	120/1	I.G. 97, B.S.A. XXVI, p. 168, C7
18. Kleodamos ∨	Bidyos	Neolas II (see under this name in Appendix IV, § 1)	C. Jul. Kleandros	84/5	B.S.A. XXVII, p. 221, E35
18b. Kleomachos ∨	Nomophylax	Pomponius Longinus	?	See note 4	I.G. 89
19. Kleon ∨	Geron and γραμματεὺς βουλῆς	Teisamenos and Tyndares	?	See note 5	I.G. 60, 99; B.S.A. XXVI, p. 168, C7 (β)
20. Kleonymos ∨	Geron	Seimedes	L. Volussenus Aristokrates	112/13	B.S.A. ibid. p. 164, A4
21. Nikandros ∨	Ephor	Nedymos Γαΐου	Kallikrates < τοῦ Ἀριστοκλέους ?	160/1	I.G. 71
22. Neikippos ∨	Geron	Eurykles	?	c. A.D. 120 (in office with Chaleinos < q.v.)	B.S.A. XXVI p. 168, C6/7
23. Neikokrates I ∨	Geron	Seimedes	P. Memmius Pratolaos Δεξιμάχου	114/15 (cf. Nos. 12 and 20 above)	I.G. 101 (Cf. B.S.A. ibid. p. 168, B5)
24. Neikokrates II ∨	Nomophylax	Neikippidas	Kallikrates < τοῦ Ἀριστοκλέους	160/61	I.G. 71
25. Neon ∨	Ephor	Damares	Claud. Aristoteles	148/9	I.G. 68
26. Onesion ∨	Geron	Damoneikidas		112/13	Ibid. p. 164
27. Philippos I ∨	Ephor	Kleombrotos	L. Volussenus Aristokrates Aristodamos	87/8	Ibid. p. 165, B1, γ
27b. Philippos II ∨	Geron	Seidektas	? (cf. App. IV, § 1, No. 78)	(with Diokles <)	I.G. 114

Name of Kasen	Office held	Name of 'Patron'	Name of Patronomos	Date (Approx.)	Evidence
28. Philokles <	Ephor	Mnason and Lysimachos	Cas(cellius) Aristoteles	162/3	I.G. 69 (B.S.A. *ibid.* p. 197 for name of Patronomos)
29. Philonidas Φιλωνίδα	Nomophylax	Mnason and Lysimachos	?	cf. No. 28	I.G. 68, B.S.A. XXIX, p. 22
30. Quintus <	Geron	Menekles	C. Julius Agesilaos	95/6	B.S.A. XXVI, p. 170, E2
31. Sosibios < 32. Sosidamos <	Geron Nomodeiktes	Teisamenos Agathok[les]	?	See note 1 126/7 (cf. note 6)	I.G. 103 B.S.A. XXVII, pp. 217 f.
33. Sosikrates Ἐπαφροδείτου	Nomophylax (also various other offices, I.G. 65)	Spartiatikos	Damokles II	131/2 (with No. 11 above)	I.G. 65, cf. B.S.A. XXVI, p. 201, β
34. Stephanos <	Geron	Neolas (I. See under this name in Appendix IV, § 1)	Menalkidas	c. 60–5 (cf. Appendix IV, § 3 B, n. 4, Nos. 1 and 7)	I.G. 95
35. Theogenes Θεογένους	Bidyos and Geron	Aristokrates and Damares	{Deximachos Πρατόλα {C. Julius Agesilaos	{90/1 {95/6	B.S.A. *ibid.* pp. 170, E2, 172, E9

Notes to pp. 452–454.

[1] From I.G. 103, a list of Gerontes lacking the name of the Patronomos, it appears that these two Kasens of Eurykles were in the Gerusia with a Kasen of Kleon and Tyndares who must have been Geron in the decade 120–130 (see n. 5 below). The Kasen assigned in I.G. 103 to ' Gaius Lysippus ' has been omitted in view of the new reading provided by Woodward (B.S.A. XXVII, p. 219, E32).

[2] The ' Patron ' is probably the Patronomos of *c.* 157/8 ; *cf.* Kolbe on I.G. 161.

[3] The ' Patron ' is approximately contemporary with Longinus (I.G. 89), and so perhaps identical with the Patronomos of *c.* 167/68 (Jul. Sosikrates II). On the date of I.G. 89 see n. 4 below.

[4] I.G. 89 belongs to the period of the Patronomoi Cossaeus and Longinus (*cf.* Kolbe, *ibid.*) whose years are apparently *c.* 152/3 and 155/6. Kolbe's argument for dating another contemporary, Sex. Pompeius Onasikrates (I.G. 129), about 20 years later than this is not cogent. Although an Eudamos Ὀνασικράτους appears as μζ' ἀπὸ Διοσκούρων in I.G. 559, we do not know that he was son of Onasikrates (*cf.* I.G. 129) ; the father cannot in fact be two generations later than M. Aurelius Aristokrates, μδ' ἀπὸ Διοσκούρων, for whom see Appendix IV, § 1, No. 16 (*fl. c.* 180). Cossaeus is fixed by I.G. 45 to approximately the same period as Nikias (for whom see Appendix IV, 8, under the year 142/3). It is in fact evident that the reckoning by generations differed in different families ; Eurykles Herklanos was τριακοστὸς καὶ ἕκτος ἀπὸ Διοσκούρων (I.G. 971, *cf.* 1172), and that the Sex. Pomp. Eudamos in question was actually eleven generations later than Eurykles is unthinkable.

[5] The Kasen Kleon < shared by Tyndares and Teisamenos was in the Gerusia with Hierokles < (B.S.A. XXVI, p. 168, C7) who was also in the Gerusia in the year of Philokleidas *c.* 120/21 (*cf.* list above, No. 17). Kleon < was also secretary of the Gerusia *c.* 127/8 under Lysippos Μνάσωνος (I.G. 60). The date assigned to C7 (B.S.A. *ibid.* p. 192) is therefore about fifteen years too early.

[6] The reasons for supposing the Patronomos in question to be Jul. Charixenos I rather than Jul. Charixenos II given by Woodward (B.S.A. XXVII, pp. 217 f.) cannot be reconciled with Sosidamos' tenure of office as Nomodeiktes under Aristokrates, Philokleidas and Damokles (*ibid.* p. 218). The restoration of E32 (*ibid.*) l. 5 must either be [ἐπὶ Φλαβίου Χαρι] ξένου (*cf.* Appendix IV, §8, assigned to *c.* 119/20, the year before Philokleidas) or this list of Nomophylakes must be supposed to have been engraved later than its duplicates (I.G. 51, 52) and after the Patronomate of C. Jul. Charixenos II.

§ 3 LIST OF KASENS (cont.)

B. Victors in the παιδικὸς ἀγών

(For the dates of these victories, see footnote 4 at the end of this list.
Reproductions of lettering will be found in A.O.   References to I.G. are
in all cases to Vol. V, i.)

Kasen	'Patron'	Evidence
1. Aristokṛ[ates 'Αρι]στọδ[άμου]	Ans[etos]	A.O. 15, cf. I.G. 266
2. [Mar. Aur.] Agaṭhopo[us]	[?] Φι[?] [1]	A.O. 63
3. Charixenos [2] Δαμοκρατίδα	⎰Kritodamos ⎱ Teisamenos ⎰ Iamos	A.O. 35, I.G. 298
4. Damion 'Ανθεστίου Φιλοκράτους	Agis Κλεάνδρου	A.O., 34, I.G. 281
5. Herakleidas Πακωνίου	Damokrates	A.O. 20, I.G. 270
6. Nikagoras Σωσιδάμου	Eudamos	A.O. 41, I.G. 296
7. Philokrates [3] Φιλοκλέους	Agesilaos Νεόλα	A.O. 27, I.G. 278
8. Primus Νηρέως	Menekles	A.O. 25, I.G. 277
9. Thrasyboulos Καλλικράτους	Enymantiadas	A.O. 29, I.G. 280
10. Xenokles 'Αριστοκρίτου	Leilochos	A.O. 2, I,G, 256
11. - -] Δαματρίου	?	A.O. 84, I.G. 334
12. (Name lost.) Victor in Patronomate of a Deximachos	A[lka]ṣtọs	A.O. 37, I.G. 290

[1] The restoration of Philetos as the name of the ' patron ' (A.O. loc.
cit.) is inadmissible for the very reason that the Kasen had a brother of
this name (cf. n. 2 below).

[2] Probably not connected with the Patronomoi Fl. Charixenos and
Jul. Charixenos (cf. Appendix IV, § 8, years 99/100, 119/20, 126/7) since
these belong to the ' Privileged Families '.

[3] Probably identical with [M.] Antistius Philokrates, father of No. 4
above, and with M. Antistius Philokrates Φιλοκλέους in B.S.A. XXVI,
p. 170, E2 (a list of Gerontes of the year of C. Jul. Agesilaos), who is not
there called Kasen ; if so, an exception to the general rule that Kasens
who obtained office required to be adopted and given a new name. Note
that in this case the name of the Patronomos is the same as that of the
' patron ' of the Kasen in office ; this may indicate that some special
dispensation from the general rule was made in favour of the Kasen or
Kasens of the Patronomos of the year.

[4] With regard to the dates of these victories, nine out of the twelve
fall in the period from late Nero to some time in the reign of Trajan.
No. 10 appears to be much earlier, and is dated by Kolbe and Woodward
on grounds of lettering, in the absence of other indications, to the first
century B.C. or possibly earlier.   No. 2 belongs (from evidence of names)
to the late second century A.D.   For No. 11 there is no indication of date.
The rest permit of closer dating from the names of the Patronomoi in
whose years the victories were won.

No. 1 (ἐπὶ [Μενα]λκίδ[ᾳ] has been dated to the first century B.C. by
Kolbe and Woodward, on account of connection of the names of Gerontes
ἐπὶ Μεναλκίδᾳ (I.G. 95) with those in the Tainarioi-inscriptions.   These
must, however, be dated not long before A.D. 10 (cf. p. 153, n. 1) ; and
since I.G. 95 contains the name of Lysippos Πολλίωνος among the Gerontes
in the year of Menalkidas, it can scarcely have been inscribed earlier than
A.D. 55–60 for the following reasons.   The name Pollio at Sparta, in view

of its association there with the *praenomen* and *nomen* C. Julius (*cf.* Appendix IV, § 2) is likely to have been acquired either from Julius Caesar or from Augustus, and in view of the known historical circumstances, more probably from Augustus. In view of its association with the name of ʽΡοῦφος (Appendix IV, § 2, *ibid.*) it is likely to have been acquired through the influence of C. Asinius Pollio, the celebrated historian, jurist and collector of Greek statuary (*cf.* P.I.R.² I, 1241). For although C. Asinnius Leonidas and his brother Rufus at Sparta (I.G. 551) may have derived their names from a much later C. Asinius, they serve to illustrate the use of the *cognomen* Rufus among the Roman C. Asinii. C. Asinius Pollio the historian may well have visited Sparta with Augustus in 21 B.C. ; his refusal to accompany him to the Actium campaign had been coupled with the promise to become *praeda victoris* (P.I.R. *ibid.*). In that case a C. Julius Pollio cannot have been born earlier than 20 B.C., his son little earlier than *c.* A.D. 10. Lysippos Πολλίωνος of I.G. 95 would therefore be Geron *c.* A.D. 55–60.

But further, a contemporary of Lysippos Πολλίωνος in the Gerusia under Menalkidas is a Kasen of Neolas (I.G. 95). In view of the relationship of the ʽ Patrons ʼ Agesilaos Νεόλα (Appendix IV, § 1, No. 4), Neolas II Νεόλα (*ibid.* No. 61) whose Kasens win victories in the Agelae *c.* A.D. 60–65 and appear in office *c.* 84/5, the father of both ʽ Patrons ʼ is likely to be identical with the ʽ Patron ʼ of the Kasen of Neolas in I.G. 95. The Patronomate of Menalkidas must therefore be dated *c.* A.D. 60–5.

The victory of *No.* 3 falls in the Patronomate of Pratoneikos (*cf.* Appendix IV, § 8, under the year 101/2) ; that of *No.* 4 in the Patronomate of Lakon III, which falls about the same time as that of Kleandros (*cf.* A.O. p. 315, No. 34), for whose date *cf.* Appendix IV, § 8, under the year 84/5. The ʽ second Patronomate of Lakon (I.G. 480) may well refer to the same year as A.O. 34, in view of his earlier substitute-Patronomate (I.G. 280). The victory in question must fall at least twenty years later than that of *No.* 7 below, who was apparently his father. The victory of *No.* 5 falls in the Patronomate of Mnasistratos, of whom there is no indication among the Patronomoi after *c.* A.D. 82 (*cf.* Appendix IV, § 8). Paconius, the father of the Kasen, bears a Roman name of which there are no known Roman holders before the first century A.D. The victory is therefore likely to have fallen towards the end of Nero's reign or in the earlier Flavian period. In view of the general aristocratic character of the ʽ Patron ʼ class, Eudamos, the ʽ Patron ʼ of *No.* 6 is likely to have been one of the two Patronomoi of that name. Eudamos II, *c.* 141/2 (*cf.* Appendix IV, § 8), is more likely than Eudamos I, *c.* 60–5 Patronomos in No. 8 below since the lettering of No. 6 is very definitely later in character than that of Nos. 8 and 7 below, whereas if Eudamos I were the ʽ patron ʼ in No. 6, the lettering should appear about 30 years earlier than that of Nos. 7 and 8. The victory of *No.* 7 falls in the Patronomate of Eukleidas, for whom there is no evidence in the period after *c.* 82 (*cf.* Appendix IV, § 8). The victor is in the Gerusia τὸ β' (by special dispensation without changing his name, *cf.* above, n. 3) in the year of C. Julius Agesilaos (? his ʽ Patron ʼ) *c.* 95/6. The date of the victory is likely to be 30–5 years earlier than this, *cf.* also above, No. 4. *No.* 8 is probably Kasen to the Patronomos of A.D. 97/8 (*cf.* Appendix IV, § 8), another Kasen of Menekles was in the Gerusia *c.* 95/96 (IV, § 3A, No. 30), implying approximately the same date for the two victories of Primus, under Sosinikos and Eudamos I, as for No. 7 above. The victory of *No.* 9 falls in the Patronomate of Lakon III acting for Lakon II, *i.e. c.* A.D. 75 (*cf.* p. 191, n. 2). For *No.* 10 see the beginning of this note. *No.* 12 wins his victory in the Patronomate of Deximachos, for which *cf.* Appendix IV, § 8, under the year 90/91.

§ 4

Groups of Kasens Attached to the same 'Patron'

(The name of a magistracy attached to a name indicates that the Kasen may be found in Appendix IV, § 3 A; '*παιδ. ἀγ.*' attached to the name indicates that it may be found, *ibid.*, section B.)

Kasen	Office, etc.	'Patron'
1. Ti. Claud. Agathokles <	Eph.	}Antipater
Diokles *Διοκλέους*	Eph.	
2. Archippos . . .	Nomoph.	}Aristokrates
Theogenes *Θεογένους*	Bid.	
3. Chaleinos *Χαλείνου*	Ger.	}Enymantiadas
Thrasyboulos *Καλλικράτους*	*παιδ. ἀγ.*	
(For Hierokles < see Appendix IV, § 8, Note B)		
4. . . . . < (*cf.* I.G. 103)	Ger.	⎱Eurykles (Patronomos
Aristomenes *Ἀριστομένους*	Ger.	⎰ of second century
Neikippos *Νεικίππου*	Ger.	A.D.)
5. Kleon *Κλέωνος*	Bid.	⎱
Sosibios *Σωσιβίου*	Ger.	⎰Teisamenos
Charixenos *Δαμοκρατίδα*	*παιδ. ἀγ.*	
6. Kleodamos *Κλεοδάμου*	Bid.	}Neolas
Stephanos *Στεφάνου*	Ger.	
7. Quintus <	Ger.	}Menekles
Primus *Νηρέως*	*παιδ. ἀγ.*	
8. Damarchos *Δαμάρχου*	Ger.	⎱
Kleonymos *Κλεωνύμου*	Ger.	⎰Seimedes
Neikokrates *Νεικοκράτους*	Ger.	

§ 5

Associated "Patrons"

(*a*) *Groups of 'Patrons' attached to the same Kasen or Kasens* (For detailed evidence, see Appendix IV, § 1, 3A and B)

'Patron'	Kasen
1. Kritodamos	⎫
Teisamenos [1]	⎬Charixenos *Δαμοκρατίδα*
Iamos	⎭
2. Teisamenos	}Kleon *Κλέωνος*
Tyndares	
3. Neikippidas	}Neikokrates *Νεικοκράτους*
Seimedes	
4. Aristokrates [2]	}Theogenes *Θεογένους*
Damares [3]	
5. Mnason	⎱Philonidas *Φιλωνίδα*
Lysimachos	⎰Philokles *Φιλοκλέους*

---

[1] For two other Kasens attached to Teisamenos, see above, § 4, No. 5. Teisamenos and Iamos were apparently brothers (see below, § 6, note 1).
[2] For another Kasen attached to Aristokrates, see § 4, No. 2.
[3] For another Kasen attached to Damares, see App. IV, § 3A, No. 25. (Neon *Νέωνος* who also appears as *συνέφηβος Δαμάρους* below, § 6, No. 9.)

(b) *Pairs of Boagoi attached to the same Synephebos.*

<table>
<tr><th colspan="2">Boagoi</th><th>Synephebos</th></tr>
<tr><td colspan="2">1. Teisamenos
υ υ – (? Iamos) [1]</td><td>} (Name not preserved)</td></tr>
<tr><td>2. M. Aurelius Aristokrates</td><td>Δαμαινέτου</td><td>} M. Aur. Euarestos Ζωίλου</td></tr>
<tr><td>Ti. Claud. Eiranion</td><td>'Υγείνου</td><td>} (Appendix IV, § 6, No. 12)</td></tr>
</table>

[1] *Cf.* I.G. 258, with the new reading discussed above, p. 106.

§ 6

LIST OF SYNEPHEBOI

(For the dates when they were in the Agelae, see footnote 8 at the end of this list.)

A. *Synepheboi whose names connect them with the Privileged Families* [1]

(a) *Dedicators in the* παιδικὸς ἀγών

Synephebos	Boagos	Evidence
1. M. Ulp. Aristokrates Καλλικράτους	Jul. Eurykles	I.G. 287
2. Kallikrates Εὐρυκράτους	?	I.G. 259
3. Neikephoros Στεφάνου	Pompeius Aristoteles Μηνοφάνους	I.G. 303

(b) *In lists of Magistrates*

4. Klearchos Εὐδάμου 5. Korinthas Νεικηφόρου 5a. ? Agathokles Ξενοκράτους	P. Memm. Deximachos Attikos Damares	B.S.A. XXVI, p. 167, C3 (β) I.G. 45 B.S.A. *ibid.* p. 202e (wrongly restored as Kasen)

B. *Synepheboi with names of the type of Kasen-list A* [2]

6. Eutychos < 7. Dion <	Damares Bruti P. Memm. Deximachos	I.G. 39 B.S.A. *ibid.* p. 167, C3 (β)
8. Hymnos < (ὁ καὶ Μαρ. Αὐρ. Κλεώ- νυμος)[3]	Sex. Pomp. Gorgippos 'Ονασικράτους	I.G. 653, 653 b.
9. Neon < 10. Spendon < 11. [. . .]es < [4]	Memm. Damares Aristeus Seidektas	I.G. 38 (*cf.* 68) I.G. 47 I.G. 66 (*cf.* 59)

C. The rest [5]

12.	M. Aur. Euarestos Zωίλου	{ M. Aur. Aristokrates { Ti. Claud. Eiranion	I.G. 653a
13.	Lykeinos Στι[- -]	?	I.G. 44
14.	Nikokrates Νικομήδους	P. Memm. Deximachos	B.S.A. ibid.
15.	Neikostratos Διονυσίου	Longinus Δαμάρους [6]	I.G. 548 (cf. 89)
16.	Pasikrates Φιλοστράτου	P. Memm. Deximachos	B.S.A. ibid.
17.	Ti. Claud. Sophron	P. Ael. Damokratidas 'Αλκανδρίδα	I.G. 554
18.	[C. Avidius Agathangelos] [7]	Ti. Claud. Pratolaos Βρασίδα	I.G. 472

---

[1] See Appendix IV, § 1 (Boagoi and Patrons of Kasens).

[2] The sign <, indicating that the father's name was the same as the son's, is here adopted for convenience. In most cases the father's name is given in full in this group of inscriptions. All these names with the exception of No. 8 (a βωμονείκης) occur in the lists of magistrates, the magistracies represented being Geron, Nomophylax, Ephor, σύνδικος καὶ δαμοσιομάστης, and lower offices (not Patronomos). The same applies to Nos. 4 and 5 above, and to those in Section C.

[3] In I.G. 653 this Synephebos is referred to as τὸν εὐγενέστατον.

[4] The inclusion of two Synepheboi of Seidektas in I.G. 59 (neither name preserved) is probably due to a mistake, since the full complement of Nomophylakes is accounted for with only one Synephebos included.

[5] No. 12 is honoured as βωμονείκης, the rest commemorated as office-holders.

[6] Longinus also has a Kasen (Kleomachos <, cf. Appendix IV, § 3A, No. 18a).

[7] Not actually called συνέφηβος, but called Πιτανάτης and honoured ἀνδρείας . . . χάριν, and the expense of the statue is met by his Boagos.

[8] The dates when the Synepheboi in the foregoing list were in the Agelae may in most cases be deduced from the names of their Boagoi (cf. Appendix IV, § 1). In general they cover the same period as the Kasens in Appendix IV, § 3B (cf. ibid. n. 4), but in this case there is no example earlier than the Flavian period. Nos. 4, 7, 14, 16 are contemporary (cf. B.S.A. XXVI, p. 167, C3, β, all Nomophylakes c. 90-91) and must have been in the Agelae towards the end of Nero's reign. No. 11 belongs to c. A.D. 90-95 (in the Agelae; this also applies to the rest of the dates here mentioned); Nos. 5, 13 and 18 are about fifteen years later; Nos. 6 and 9 (both Synepheboi of Damares, the Patronomos of c. 144/5, cf. Appendix IV, § 1, No. 23) belong to about A.D. 120, Nos. 1 and 15 some ten years later; No. 17 belongs to about A.D. 155, No. 8 to c. 170, the Boagos of the victor (who describes himself as Mar. Aur.,) being evidently the son of the Onasikrates of I.G. V, i, 129, q.v. The latest of the series appears to be No. 3, but the date of the Patronomos Claudius Abaskantos under whom the victory was won, is uncertain (cf. Appendix IV, § 8, last section).

§ 7

DEDICATORS IN THE παιδικὸς ἀγών WHO ARE NEITHER BOAGOI, NOR
KASENS, NOR SYNEPHEBOI [1]

(For dates of victories, see note 5 at the end of this section.)

Dedicator	Patronomos	Evidence
1. Alkimos [Σωκλεί]δου	Ξ[ενόκλ]ης	A.O. 14
2. Arexippos [2]	?	A.O. 1
3. Aristokrates 'Αριστίωνος	Damippos 'Αβολήτου	A.O. 12
4. Glykon 'Ερμογένους	?	A.O. 39
5. Damippos 'Αβολήτου	Sidamos	A.O. 11
6. Damokleidas Χαλέα	Alkippos	A.O. 32
7. Lach[ares] [3] 'Ηρακλανοῦ	[- -]mos	A.O. 10
8. Lachares Λαχάρεος	(Three Patronomoi, names fragmentary)	A.O. 16
9. Lysikrates Χαριξένου	Aristokles	A.O. 26
10. Neikephoros⎰ οἱ Νεικηφόρου	Sosineikos	A.O. 55
10a. ?		
11. Neikokrates Θεογένους	Lichas	A.O. 28
12. Nikippos Καλλικρατίδα	Pratolas	A.O. 17
13. Xenokles Ξενοκλέος	Euetes	A.O. 19
14. Onasikleidas Φιλοστράτου [4]	?	A.O. 31
15. Pratiadas 'Αρίστωνος	?	A.O. 18
16. Sion Δαμίππου	Tịmarchus and Polyd[am]as	A.O. 13
17. Timokrates 'Επινικίδα	Aristoteles	A.O. 4
18. Philetos Φιλήτου	Gorgippos Γοργίππου	A.O. 62
19. Philonikos Φιλονίκου	?	A.O. 21
20. Philostratos Πασικλέος	?	A.O. 22
21. C. Jul. Charixenos Λυσικράτους	Sikleidas	A.O. 30

[1] All the inscriptions in this group are sufficiently well preserved to
make it certain that none of the titles *Boagoi*, etc., was originally included
in the form of dedication.

[2] Φωρθείαι τάδ' 'Αρ[ή]ξιππος νικῶν ἀνέσηκε
ἐν συνόδοις παίδων πᾶhιν hορῆν φανερά.
The use of the Laconian dialect, combined with the retention of the
letter H for the aspirate, indicates an early date. Wilamowitz suggests
fourth century B.C. The stele contains sockets for four sickles, and possibly
belongs to a period when dedications on account of victories in the παιδικὸς
ἀγών were only made in exceptional cases.

[3] Lachares son of Heraklanos is supposed by Woodward (*cf.* Kolbe
ad I.G. V, i, 94, 265) to be the father of C. Julius Eurykles I, who fought
at Actium. But the absence of the Roman *praenomen* and *nomen*, cited
in support of this view by Kolbe (*ibid.*), has no significance, since very many
later Spartan possessors of Roman names are recorded in the inscriptions
without them. In actual fact the name Heraklanos, by its Latin termination, in itself implies the possession of Roman citizenship, which can
hardly be supposed to have been conferred upon the grandfather of
Eurykles I. It also appears likely from an Athenian inscription (Ditt.
Syll.[3] 786) that the grandfather of Eurykles I was called Eurykles. An
alternative explanation of the name Heraklanos which avoids this difficulty, and which explains the possession of the additional name Heraklanos
by C. Julius Eurykles, the Patronomos of the earlier second century A.D., has

already been given (p. 199 f). The epigraphical indications are contained in I.G. V, i, 210 (one of the lists of the *Tainarioi*, of the early years of the first century A.D. ; *cf.* p. 153, n. 1) and *ibid.* 94, a list of Gerontes which includes the name of Lachares 'Ηρακλανοῦ. It seems likely from comparison of the names that the *Tainarioi* inscriptions are a generation earlier than No. 94 (*cf.* Euangelos 'Αρηξίππου in 94, Arexippos Δαμοκράτεος in 210, Lykomedes 'Αράτου in 94, Aratos Δεξικράτεος in 211) ; but admittedly it is difficult to decide from the names alone whether the chronological relation of the two is reversed (*e.g.* from the name Agesinikos Λαχάρεος in 210, compared with Lachares 'Ηρακλανοῦ in 94 and Timagoras Λαιστρατίδα in 212, Laistratos Λαιστράτου in 94). This point, however, is settled by the difficulty which would arise in regard to the name *Heraklanos*, if it were supposed to belong to two generations earlier than the *Tainarioi* inscriptions.

It therefore seems likely that Lachares 'Ηρακλανοῦ belongs to the late first century B.C. and the earlier first century A.D., and we may suggest about the end of the first century B.C. for his victory in the παιδικὸς ἀγών, about A.D. 30 for his membership of the Gerusia (*cf.* the genealogical tree, p. 204).

⁴ No. 14 became a Boagos later ; *cf.* Appendix IV, § 1, No. 68.

⁵ The victories dateable by the year of the Patronomos or by clear prosopographical indications are as follows. *No.* 4 is son of the Patronomos of *c.* 116/17, *No.* 9 wins under Aristokles about 107/8, *No.* 12 wins under Pratolas *c.* 113/14. These three are therefore approximately contemporary. Only two (*No.* 10 and *No.* 18) are later than these, and apparently belong to the late second century (*cf.* I.G. 307, note, and for the Patronomoi concerned, Appendix IV, § 8, last section). *No.* 14 seems to belong to *c.* A.D. 70 (*cf.* above, n. 4). The rest are all apparently earlier, to judge from the general character of the lettering, than the group which falls in Trajan's reign, and Woodward has attempted to arrange them all (with the exception of *No.* 6 which exists only in a fifteenth-century copy) in chronological order starting from *No.* 7, which he believes to be the earliest on grounds of lettering, and to record the victory in the boys' contests of the father of C. Julius Eurykles I. Reasons against this have already been discussed (above, n. 3), and the victory in question must now be assigned to the last years of the first century B.C., not to *c.* 60 B.C. This implies that the remaining victors in the series belong to the first three-quarters of the first century A.D. rather than to the last half of the first century B.C. ; that at least two generations are recorded appears from the two pairs of names, Lachares 'Ηρακλανοῦ and Lachares Λαχάρεος, Damippos 'Αβολήτου and Sion Δαμίππου, and from the appearance of Damippos as victor in *No.* 5 and Patronomos in No. 8, Woodward believes the lettering of No. 5 (victor Damippos 'Αβολήτου) to be exactly contemporary with that of *No.* 7, and so restores [Sidam]os as the name of the Patronomos in the second case. But it is not possible in the case of the Spartan inscriptions to lay much stress on lettering, as may be seen from the wide difference of lettering in inscriptions which are demonstrably contemporary, as in the *Tainarioi*- inscriptions (*cf. Sparta Catalogue*, nos. 205, 206) and in two inscriptions dated to the year of the second century Patronomos Sejanus (*Sparta Catalogue*, no. 787 ; A.O. p. 233, no. 50). The majority of Patronomoi mentioned in the present list must therefore remain undated until further evidence about them comes to light. It is clear both from the general character of the lettering in the inscriptions concerned, and from the completeness with which the names of Patronomoi after *c.* A.D. 75 are known (*cf.* Appendix IV, § 8) that they belong to the period before this.

§ 8

CHRONOLOGICAL LIST OF PATRONOMOI

(From Nero to Septimius Severus)

This list includes only names of persons who are actually called Patronomos (ἐπὶ πατρονόμου τοῦ δεῖνος) in the inscriptions ; no persons to whom others were Kasen are included on that account (*cf.* p. 101), and no Patronomoi other than the Eponymos of the year. The dating is from autumn to autumn, since the Spartan civil year began at the first new moon after the autumnal equinox (Dar.-Sagl. *s.v. Ephoroi; cf.* Thuc. V, 36). The dates are exact only in a few cases (mentioned in the notes) ; the order of the Patronomoi themselves, deduced from comparison of many inscriptions recording individual careers, determines the date within fairly close limits for the greater part of the second century. In view of the great number of names preserved, it has been found necessary to transfer to the Flavian or Antonine periods many names which Kolbe and Woodward assign to the reigns of Trajan and Hadrian.

The names of Patronomoi belonging to the period before Nero do not permit us to trace any direct chronological sequence, nor is even the approximate period to which they belong at all certain (*cf.* Appendix IV, § 7, n. 3, on the names associated with the lists of *Tainarioi*). The same observation applies to the Patronomoi of the third century, and in a lesser degree, also to the group assigned to ' late second century ' at the end of the list.

(i) *Patronomoi from Nero to Domitian*

(*The number I or II attached to the name indicates that there are two Patronomoi of the same name in this list.*)

c.	
60–5	Menalkidas ⎫ Eukleidas ⎪ Sosinikos I ⎬ See Appendix IV, § 3B, n. 4, Nos. 1, 7, 8. Eudamos I ⎭
70	Sikleidas with Ti. Claud. Harmoneikos as substitute I.G. 275 (*c.* 30 years before C. Jul. Charixenos, for whom see below, under year 99/100).
75	Lakon III (acting for Lakon II. I.G. 280 (*cf.* p. 191, n. 2, and the family tree, p. 204.

(ii) *Reign of Domitian* (precise order uncertain)

c.	
82/3	Lakon III (τὸ β'. I.G. 480). For the date, *cf.* Appendix IV, § 3B, n. 4, No. 4.
83/4	Eukletos. B.S.A. XXVI, p. 166, B4, a.
84/5	Kleandros. *Ibid.* p. 197, E5, *cf.* Appendix IV, *ibid.* (near in date to Lakon III).
85/6	Deximachos ὁ καὶ Νεικοκράτης (= Neikokrates ; *ibid.* p. 163, A9 ; 165, B1 (β)).
86/7	Dion I. I.G. 31 (between Kleandros and Theokles). See also under 147/8 (Dion II, perhaps a grandson).
87/8	Aristodamos. B.S.A. XXVI, p. 161, 183, near in date to Deximachos ὁ καὶ Νεικοκράτης.

c.

88/9   Damokles I *Φιλοκράτους*. I.G. 36 (before Perikles. For Damokles II see below, under year 131/2).

89/90   P. Memm. Theokles I.G. 31 (after Kleandros and Dion).

90/1   P. Memm. Deximachos I, *cf.* B.S.A. *ibid.* p. 164, 175 (A.D. ' 95–100 '). Probably the Patronomos of I.G. 290, and father of the Patronomoi Pratolaos and Seidektas below.

91/2   P. Memm. Spartiatikos I. I.G. 85, (*cf.* B.S.A. *ibid.* p. 190, assigned to reign of Trajan and assumed to have been Ti. Claud. But *cf.* Appendix IV, § 1, No. 53).

92/3   Lysimachos. B.S.A. *ibid.* p. 185, B5 (assigned to between Damokles and Perikles).

93/4   Kleodamos. *Ibid.* p. 165, B2, 183 (near in date to Lysikrates and to Kallikrates *'Ρούφου*. See under years 96/7, 100/1).

94/5   Gorgippidas. *Ibid.* p. 171, E4. Menekles (*cf.* 97/8) Ephor in his year.

95/6   C. Jul. Agesilaos. *Ibid.* p. 161, 195. Agonothetes in year of Menekles (97/8).

96/7   C. Jul. Lysikrates. *Ibid.* p. 166, B6. Nomophylax under Kleodamos (*cf.* above, year 93/4). A son of Ti. Claud. Polyeuktos wins in his year (I.G. 283). Probably a brother of C. Jul. Charixenos (victor in Agelae *ἐπὶ Σικλείδα*. *Cf.* I.G. 275 ; Patronomos *c.* 99/100. See below.)

c.   (iii) *Nerva to Marcus Aurelius*

97/8   Menekles. Fixed date, *cf.* I.G. 667. First celebration of *τὰ μέγιστα Σεβάστεια Νερουανίδεια*.

98/9   Cl. Perikles. (After Damokles, I.G. 36, before Pratoneikos, I.G. 42).

99/100   C. Jul. Charixenos I (B.S.A. XXVI, p. 172, E12, XXVII, p. 219, L4 ; after Deximachos, before Mnason, *cf.* I.G. 1314, lists of different dates, Patronomoi being widely spaced). Victor in *παιδικὸς ἀγών* under Sikleidas (App. IV, § 7, No. 21).

100/1   Kallikrates *'Ρούφου*. See chronological note A.

101/2   Pratoneikos. Between Perikles and Damoneikidas (I.G. 40, 42). An Ephor in year of Cl. Brasidas may be his grandson (B.S.A. XXVII, p. 226).

102/3   Neikippidas. Between Perikles and Pasikrates II (I.G. 41).

103/4   Damoneikidas. Between Pratoneikos and Polyeuktos (I.G. 40 ; B.S.A. XXVI, p. 163, A9). His name or that of Neikippidas should be restored in I.G. 33 in place of [*Κληνικ*]*ίδα*.[1]

104/5   Lykourgos (*θεός*. See below under 140/1). *Cf.* B.S.A. XXVI, p. 164, 175, A3–5 (there assigned to early C 2).

105/6   Polyeuktos. After Pratoneikos and Damoneikidas, before Aristokles, Antipater and Pius (I.G. 40, B.S.A. XXVI, p. 163, A9).

106/7   Mnason. Between Charixenos and Straton (B.S.A. XXVI, p. 172, E12).

107/8   Aristokles I (B.S.A. XXVI, p. 163, A9), *cf.* App. IV, § 7, No. 9.

108/9   Jul. Sosikrates I. Between Polyeuktos and Pasikrates (I.G. 40).

109/10   Antipater. Between Aristokles and Pius (B.S.A., XXVI, p. 163, A9). Perhaps son of C. Jul. Lysikrates, *cf.* B.S.A., XXVII, p. 237, No. 20.

---

[1] On Klenikidas, see Note E at end of list.

c.

110/11   Straton. Between Mnason and Pasikrates (B.S.A. XXVI, p. 172, E12).

111/12   Lysippos Φιλοχαρείνου. Before Pius (I.G. 32B). Sosikrates Ἐπαφροδίτου, διαβέτης (an office held early in career) under Lysippos, is Nomophylax under Damokles II, *c.* 131/32. Probably the grandfather of Philochareinos, son of Lysippos, Boagos in the years of Sejanus and Biadas.

112/13   L. Volussenus Aristokrates. Before Pratolas and Dionysius (I.G. 32B) ; should perhaps be restored in B.S.A. XXVI, p. 202, *e.* At least five years after Lycurgus (*ibid.* p. 164). For relation to other Patronomoi *cf.* B.S.A. XXVII, p. 218. Not identical with the Voluss[enus Aristokrates] of I.G. 68.

113/14   P. Memm. Pius. Before Hermogenes (I.G. 65), before Eurykles (I.G. 32B).

114/15   Pratolas (P. Memmius Pratolas II ?). I.G. 32B, between Aristo-krates and Dionysios.

115/16   Pasikrates II. After Neikippidas (I.G. 41), after Mnason and Straton (B.S.A. XXVI, p. 172 E12), before Seidektas (I.G. 32A).

116/17   Hermogenes. After Pius (I.G. 65), before Hadrian's first [1] visit (B.S.A. XXVI, p. 165, A12). [Γλύ]κωνος (I.G. 284, *cf.* 329).

117/18   Eurykles Herklanos.[2] After Pius (I.G. 32B) and Mnason (I.G. 44).

118/19   P. Ael. Dionysios. Before Hadrian's first visit (I.G. 32), after Hadrian's accession in view of his Roman name (I.G. 82).

119/20   Fl. Charixenos. After Eurykles, I.G. 34.

120/21   C. Jul. Philokleidas. See Note B at end of list.

121/22   C. Jul. Lampis I. Shortly before Hadrian and near in date to Jul. Charixenos II (I.G. 33), *cf. ibid.* 137.

122/23   Kleon ?[3] (B.S.A. XXVI, p. 165, A12). After Eurykles (I.G. 44, ΚΛ . Ι[—]). Before a Spartan embassy to Hadrian at Nikopolis (B.S.A. *ibid.*) perhaps asking him to visit Sparta.

123/24   Hadrian. Before Lysippos (I.G. 32B), *cf.* below, 127/8 (B.S.A. XXVI, p. 170, D3, is not completely chronological).

124/25   Seidektas. At Hadrian's first visit (I.G. 32A).

125/26   Seipompos. Between Seidektas and Seiteimos (I.G. 32B).

126/27   Jul. Charixenos II. Between Seidektas and Seiteimos (I.G. 32A), hence restoration in B.S.A. XXVII, p. 218, E32, is untenable.

127/28   Jul. Lysippos Μνασῶνος. After Seipompos, before Aristoboulos (I.G. 34). Earlier than names in years 129/30–136/37, *q.v.*

128/29   Seiteimos. At Hadrian's second visit (I.G. 32A).

129/30   Neikephoros ⎫
130/31   Aristoboulos ⎪
131/32   Damokles II ⎪
132/33   (M. Ulp.) Aphthonetos ⎬ See note C at end of list. The Damokles
133/34   Aristokles II ⎪ in question appears in I.G. 105, 138.
134/35   Attikos ⎪
135/36   Meniskos ⎪
136/37   Theophrastos ⎭

---

[1] There is no room for his name between Hadrian's two visits.

[2] See Chap. V, pp. 188 f. To be distinguished from the Eurykles of I.G. 287 who is about a generation later.

[3] The date suggested here assumes that the first two offices mentioned in B.S.A. *ibid.* are not in chronological order. The office of Geron is in fact usually held after that of διαβέτης.

c.

137/38 Aristoneikidas. Between Attikos and Alkastos (I.G. 32A).

138/39 Onasikleidas. Between Aristoboulos and Eudamos II (B.S.A. XXVI, p. 163, A9).

139/40 Alkastos. After Aristoneikidas (I.G. 32) ; Nomophylax under Meniskos (I.G. 59 corrected by B.S.A. XXVI, p. 166, B9) ; same career includes Pasikrates II (*c.* 115/16).

140/41 Lykourgos θεός (*i.e.* τὸ β′, *cf.* I.G. 45). After Onasikleidas (B.S.A. XXVI, p. 168, C5) ; before Nikias and Damares (*ibid.* p. 200, 2*a*, with note, p. 203).

141/42 C. Jul. Eudamos II. (I.G. 63.) After Onasikleidas (B.S.A. *ibid.* p. 163, A9 ; same career includes Deximachos ὁ καὶ Νεικοκράτης and Pratoneikos (see under 90/1 and 101/2)).

142/43 Nikias. Between Lykourgos and Damares (B.S.A. *ibid.* p. 200, No. 2*a*).

143/44 Deximachos. After Onasikleidas (B.S.A. *ibid.* p. 166, B9, *cf.* p. 189).

144/45 P. Memm. Damares (I.G. 1314) (Thalamae). Latest of these lists connected with the worship of Damoia. Lettering indicates celebrations at long intervals. Probably identical with P. Memm. Damares I (I.G. p. 117).

145/46 Spartiatikos II. Earlier than Eudamidas, Sejanus, Charax, (I.G. 71).

146/47 Eudamidas. Between Spartiatikos and Sejanus (I.G. 71). After Lykourgos, Nikias, and Damares (B.S.A. XXVI, p. 200, no. 2*a*).

147/48 [Di]on (the younger). (Fixed date.) I.G. 87 gives termination of name, *ibid.* 446 gives the date. The restoration Dion (Woodward, B.S.A. XV, p. 61) is preferable to Areton or Mnason (Kolbe *ad* I.G. 87) both on account of the space to be filled on the stone, and on account of the date (*cf.* under years 106/7, 161/2).

148/49 Claud. Aristoteles. Before Biadas (I.G. 71, B.S.A. XXVI, p. 165, A12).

149/50 Sejanus ⎱ See Note D at end of list.
150/51 Biadas ⎰

151/52 Charax. After Sejanus and Biadas, before Cascellius Aristoteles (I.G. 71).

152/53 Cossaeus. (*Cf.* I.G. 45) ; before Panthales and Longinus.

153/54 Marcus (Νεικηφόρου ? *cf.* I.G. 111, 59). Before Timomenes, after the νεωτερισμός, I.G. 44 (*cf.* below, Note D. The letters read by Fourmont after the name possibly represent ἐπιστάτης, or some other office.)

154/55 Jul. Panthales. After Cossaeus and Lykourgos (I.G. 45).

155/56 Longinus. After Panthales. Probably son of Damares (I.G. 548), *cf.* Appendix IV, § 3A, n. 4.

156/57 Timomenes. After the νεωτερισμός and Marcus, *cf.* under year 153/54, near in date to Claud. Aristoteles (I.G. 109). [L.] Volussenus [Aristokrates ?], who took his place as Patronomos, I.G. 295, cannot be identical with the Patronomos of that name in Trajan's reign (see above, year 112/13). I.G. 44, thus interpreted, implies a long but not impossibly long career

		Brasidas is after Panthales (I.G. 46).
c.		Order fixed by I.G. 46, B.S.A. XXVII,
157/58	Brasidas	p. 226. ' The year of Brasidas will
158/59	Jul. Agathokles	fall in the decade 160–70, or perhaps
159/60	M. Aristokrates *Φίρμου*	late in the previous one ' (Woodward,
		ibid).

160/61   Kallikrates < *τοῦ 'Αριστοκλέους*. I.G. 71 seems to indicate the year before Areton for Kallikrates.

161/62   M. Aur. Areton. I.G. 71, *cf. ibid*. 529.

162/63   Cascellius Aristoteles. I.G. 71, with Roman name corrected by B.S.A. XXVI, p. 197. Year after Areton (I.G. 71, l. 35).

163/64   Kleonymos *Κλεωνύμου*. B.S.A. XXVI, p. 210 (Cleon seems to be wrongly restored *ibid*. p. 208, No. 6).

164/65   ? Lampis II. B.S.A. XXVII, p. 240   ? Son of Patronomos Lampis I (before Hadrian).

165/66   Lysikrates. Between Kleonymos and Titianos (B.S.A. XXVI, p. 208. 6, *cf*. note on Kleonymos above).

166/67   Titianos. Between Lysikrates and Jul. Sosikrates (B.S.A. *ibid*.).

167/68   Jul. Sosikrates II. *Cf*. note on Titianos.

168/69   Agetoridas. Between Titianos and Xenarchidas (I.G. 39).

169/70   Sokrates. Exact date unknown (*cf*. I.G. 144 ; B.S.A. XXVII, p. 234). Inserted here to allow interval between Agetoridas and Xenarchidas.

170/71   Xenarchidas. After Agetoridas (I.G. 39).

171/72   P. Aelius Damokratidas. Soon after Sokrates (I.G. 144).

172/73   Agis. After Agetoridas (implied by his *cursus* in I.G. 71).

173/74   Nedymos. After Xenarchidas (I.G. 39).

c. 180   P. Aelius Alkandridas *Δαμοκρατίδα, cf*. Woodward, A.O. p. 331.

Late Second Century (*Order Uncertain*)

Lysippos *Δαμαινέτου*. I.G. 680. Near in date to Agetoridas (above), *cf. ibid*. 531 with Kolbe's note.

Mar. Aur. Sosineikos II, *Νεικάρωνος*. I.G. 301, *cf. ibid*. 567 (about 30 years later one of his Kasens calls himself Aur. Nikephoros).

Gorgippos *Γοργίππου*. I.G. 307.

? Claudius Abaskantos. I.G. 303.

Θεὸς *Λυκοῦργος* III-XI. *Cf*. Appendix IV, § 1, No. 83 ; I.G. 130.

§ 9

CHRONOLOGICAL NOTES TO § 8

A. *Kallikrates 'Ρούφου*. (See p. 464, under 100–1).

In spite of arguments adduced by Woodward (B.S.A. XXVI, p. 186) in favour of dating the Patronomos of this name about the middle of the second century, the reasons given by Kolbe for placing him near in date to C. Jul. Lysikrates and to Kleodamos (*q.v.* in list above) still hold the field ; *cf*. I.G. 53, also *ibid*. 36, which indicates that he preceded Lysippos *Μνασῶνος*. Of the two more recently discovered inscriptions cited in support of a later date by Woodward, one, B.S.A. XXVI, p. 166, B8, raises in itself no difficulty against Kolbe's earlier interpretation of his chronological affinities, while B.S.A. *ibid*. p. 169, C9, dated to the year of Biadas, about A.D. 150, need not be contemporary with it, since Chares <, Geron for the third time in that year, and not called *Kasen*, need not be identical with Chares <, Kasen of Alkastos, and πρεσβὺς συναρχίας in the Patronomate of Kallikrates ῾Ρούφου, Nor is it necessary to identify Kallikrates ῾Ρούφου, Nomophylax under Eudamidas (I.G. 64) about A.D. 146/7 with the Patronomos of the same name. Both he and the Chares < of B.S.A. *ibid.* C9, may be nephews or grandsons of their namesakes about fifty years earlier. Alternation of two names in succeeding generations of Spartan families is too common to require comment. For evidence of it in this case, *cf.* I.G. 64, 69.

Note B (See p. 465, under 120–1).

The Patronomate of C. Jul. Philokleidas is assigned to about A.D. 100 by Kolbe (*cf.* I.G. V, i, 97). But among the Gerontes in his year one (Hierokles <) is Kasen to Atticus (not Enymantiadas, *cf.* Woodward's convincing restoration in B.S.A. XXVI, p. 192, restored from *ibid.* p. 168, C7), and among the Gerontes of a year very close to that of Philokleidas and containing many of the same names (B.S.A. *ibid.* C6) is a Kasen of Eurykles. This implies a date for the Patronomate of Philokleidas not far removed from those of Eurykles (*c.* 117/8) and of Atticus (*c.* 134/5). Although the Gerontes of the year of Philokleidas include Aristokles Καλλικράτους and Aristokles Καλλικράτους 'the younger' (? cousins) one of whom is certainly the grandfather of Kallikrates Καλλικράτους τοῦ ᾿Αριστοκλέους, Patronomos *c.* 161 (*q.v.*), this is not inconsistent with a date about A.D. 120 for Philokleidas. *Cf.* also Appendix IV, § 3, A, Note 5.

Note C (See p. 465).

The order of the eight names in group 129/30–136/7

(a) With regard to the names :

Aristokles is not later than 135/6, *i.e.* at least two years earlier than he was sent on embassy to L. Aelius Caesar (= L. Ceionius Commodus Verus) who died in 138 (*cf.* I.G.V. i, 37, n.).

Atticus is not later than 136/7, because his son succeeded him in the life-priesthood of the Emperors at Athens before the death of Hadrian in June 138 (P.I.R.[2] II, p. 175. Ti Claudius Atticus Herodes).

Aphthonetos and *Aristoboulos* are both before Atticus and after Seitimos, I.G. V, i, 32a. For Aphthonetos, see also I.G. V, i, 104, 286, B.S.A. XXVI, p. 200 (γ) (M. Ulpius).

Lysippos Μνάσωνος, (I.G. 34), is earlier than Aristoboulos and later than Seipompos.

Theophrastos is also Patronomos before the death of Atticus. (B.S.A. XXVII, p. 228, which is obviously in chronological order). He did not hold his Patronomate on account of Atticus (*i.e.* combining it with offices of ἵππαρχος and Κυθηροδίκας), but on his own account, as appears from B.S.A. XXVI, p. 166 f. B9, and C5.

Neikephoros and *Meniskos* are earlier than Theophrastos and after Seitimos (B.S.A. XXVI, p. 166, B9 ; *cf.* C5).

Damokles is after Neikephoros (I.G. 65, with B.S.A. XXVI, p. 203) and before Aristokles (I.G. 37).

This accounts for nine names, but only eight are needed ; one must therefore be moved back before Seitimos. The reason for supposing Lysippos to be the earliest and to be moved back appears from arguments which fix the chronological order, *cf.* below, (b).

(b) With regard to the order :

Meniskos appears to be not earlier than 135/6, because his office falls in a year in which reference is made to a son of Hadrian (*cf.* Woodward, B.S.A. XXVI, p. 189). But 136/7 is the last year of the series, and Meniskos is before Theophrastos. Therefore the last two names are (7) Meniskos, (8) Theophrastos. Theophrastos must have been $Kυθηροδίκας$ on behalf of Atticus, combining this with the office of $ἵππαρχος$ on his own account in 137/8, the year of Atticus' death.

Aphthonetos held office shortly before Theophrastos (*cf.* Woodward, B.S.A. XXVII, p. 229), but before Atticus (I.G. V, i, 32A). It is therefore reasonable to suppose that Aphthonetos held office in or about 133/4 and Atticus in 134/5.

This leaves Lysippos, Aristoboulos, Neikephoros, Damokles and Aristokles, of whom Lysippos precedes Neikephoros, Damokles and Aristokles (I.G. 37, 65), as well as Aristoboulos who in turn precedes Aphthonetos (I.G. 34, with B.S.A. XXVI, p. 203, β).

Therefore Lysippos must be excluded from the group and put between Seipompos and Seitimos.

Of the rest, at least one year intervened between Damokles and Aristokles (*cf.* I.G. V, i, 37), and Neikephoros preceded Damokles (I.G. V, i, 65 ; B.S.A. XXVI, p. 201 (β) ; so also did Aristoboulos precede him (*cf.* I.G. V, i, 32B). This implies (1) Neikephoros, (2) Aristoboulos, (3) Damokles, (4) Aphthonetos, (5) Aristokles, (6) Atticus (these last two perhaps in reverse order), (7) Meniskos, (8) Theophrastos.

Note D (See p. 466, under 149/50, 150/51).

For these two years identical lists of Gerontes are extant, and Philochareinos, son of Lysippos, appears as Boagos under both Patronomoi (references above, pp. 97 f.). The hypothesis that internal disturbances prevented the elections from being held in the second year of the two is supported by the reference to $νεωτερισμός$ before the Patronomate of Marcus ($Νεικηφόρου$?), *c.* 153/4 in list above. Woodward (B.S.A. XXVII, pp. 235 f.) suggests a possible connection with a revolt about the middle of the reign of Pius, referred to in the *Vita Pii*, 5, and in Lucian *de Morte Peregrini*, 19, *init.* This hypothesis now seems to be confirmed by the probable date of Sejanus and Biadas, arrived at on the basis of the recorded order of Patronomoi only. Further corroboration may perhaps be seen in the remarkable series of Spartan dedications $Ζανὶ Ἐλευθερίωι Ἀντωνείνωι Σωτῆρι,$ apparently by individuals in private houses (I.G. 407–445), especially in view of the embassy to Pius mentioned in I.G. 37.

That the year of Biadas was the later of the two is indicated by the numbers attached to the year of office of individual Gerontes. Philoumenos $Σωτηρίδα$ is recorded as holding office $τὸ δεύτερον$ under Biadas, but no number is given to him under Sejanus. Chares, the $πρεσβύς$ under Biadas, is holding office as Geron for the third time, once more than Philoumenos. This implies that he held office for the second time under Sejanus, though his name is actually missing from the list.

Note E (see p. 464, under year 103–4).

The Patronomos Klen[ikidas ?] is known to us from I.G. V, i, 359, and the name appears in full in one of the lists of *Tainarioi* (*ibid.* 210, l. 31) and in a list of Agoranomoi in the year of Pasikles (*ibid.* 126). His name is restored as Patronomos in *ibid.* 33 before Lampis and Hadrian, but there is no other evidence for a Patronomos of the name in question, nor for that of Pasikles, in this period. It seems probable that both Klen[ikidas], or Klen[ikos] (*cf.* I.G. 211, also a list of *Tainarioi*), and Pasikles were Patronomoi of about the same time as the lists of *Tainarioi* (for which see p. 153, n. 1), and that the name of [Nikipp]idas or of [Damoneik]idas (*cf.* the list of Patronomoi, under years 102/3 and 103/4) should be restored in place of [Klenik]idas in I.G. 33. A rather long interval between the offices of Hipparch and Geron, if we place the former *c.* 102/3 or 103/4 and the latter (in the year of Lampis) *c*, 121/2 (see list of Patronomoi under this year) creates no difficulty for this interpretation; it is only to be expected in view of the nature of the two offices.

THE HEREDITARY PRIESTHOODS

§ 1

The accompanying table of the Ti. Claudii (below) from the ate first to early third centuries is reconstructed on the basis of the inscriptions, the numbers under each name referring to I.G. V, i, where the full evidence of relationships may be found. In general the table follows Kolbe's tree (*ibid.* p. 131), but with some differences which affect the whole question of dating. In general, Kolbe's dates appear to be too late (see further below, § 2, notes 2, 4, 5 and 6), and additional evidence of marriage has now been incorporated in the case of Pomponia Kallistoneike II (*ibid.*, n. 7) which provides us with further information upon the way in which the hereditary Spartan priesthoods passed from one holder to another. The priesthoods of the emperor-cult have been treated separately (*cf.* Chap. V) and do not here come into consideration.

HEREDITARY PRIESTHOODS AMONG THE TI. CLAUDII

(Priests and priestesses in italics) [1]

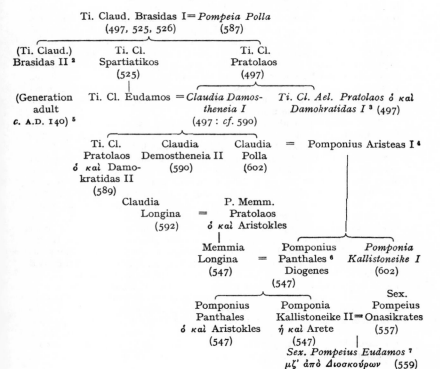

Although few holders of hereditary priesthoods appear in this table, see number of cults which they represent is very extensive, and indicates the concentration of almost all the Spartan cults for which there is evidence at all in the hands of two or three closely related families. A single family of Ti. Claudii had the lion's share. Thus we learn from G.I. V, i, 497 that Ti. Claud. Ael. Pratolaos ὁ καὶ Δαμοκρατίδας was hereditary priest (ἱερεὺς κατὰ γένος) of Karneios Boiketas, Karneios Dromaios, Poseidon Domateitas, Herakles Genarchas, Kore and Temenios ἐν τῷ ῾Ελει and of the other deities associated with these in their various temples (τῶν συγκαθειδρυμένων θεῶν ἐν τοῖς προγεγραμμένοις ἱεροῖς). The sister of the same Pratolaos was hereditary priestess of exactly the same gods and goddesses (mentioned in the same order, I.G. V, i, 589, cf. 608). Since in the first century A.D. a certain Ti. Claud. Onasippos describes himself as descendant of Krios (i.e. priest of Karneios Boiketas, cf. Paus. III, 13. 3), Megatas and Skopelos (V, i, 488), and since the office of μάντις of Skopelos was also hereditary (V, i, 60, 259) we may conclude that this last mentioned office also belonged by right of birth to the same family of Ti. Claudii.

Three points as to the manner in which the priesthoods passed call for attention. The priesthood could be held by a minor (V, i, 259 refers to a συνέφηβος, winner in the contest μῶα, who was priest of Apollo τετράχειρ and also μάντις ἀπὸ Σκοπέλου), which implies that it was not necessary for the priest to be married. The priestess in the case referred to above (V, i, 589) was not the wife but the sister of the priest. Thirdly, the father of this particular priest and priestess was apparently still alive when they held their priestly office (V, i, 497. The same is perhaps implied by V, i, 259, but the evidence here is not clear). These peculiarities imply that the priesthoods in question were not directly hereditary, passing immediately from father to son, but passed to the next generation in which there was both a brother and sister to hold office at the same time. But in any case the appointment of the sister, not the wife, of the priest as priestess of the same cults is a very striking example of insistence on inheritance through the male line only.

This example is rendered all the more striking by instances of precisely the opposite principle in the case of other Spartan cults. Thus the office of hereditary priestess of Apollo Hyakinthios was held by Pompeia Polla, the wife of Ti. Cl. Brasidas I (see the tree of the Ti. Claudii), and at another time by one Memmia Xenokratia (V, i, 586). Since it is abundantly evident from the Spartan inscriptions that in Sparta the Roman *nomen* passed exclusively in the male line in the case of daughters as well as in the case of sons, Pompeia Polla and Memmia Xenokratia cannot belong to the same family in the male line of descent. Similarly, in the case of the hereditary priesthood of the Dioscuri and of a number of other deities, including Orthia, the priestess at one time is Pomponia Kallistoneike I (see the table), in the next generation but one Sex. Pompeius Eudamos holds the priesthood (cf. below, § 2, n. 6), and it may be supposed that in the interval it had been held by Pomponia Kallistoneike II, the niece of the first bearer of this name. In both the recorded cases a long list of deities is given rivalling that of the priesthoods held by Ti. Claudii ; and it is particularly interesting to observe, in view of the evidence for the Minoan origin of the cult of Artemis Orthia (cf. Chap. VII) that this goddess is among the number (V, i, 602). A long list of deities is mentioned in the case of the hereditary priest Eudamos (V, i, 559) : Zeus, the Dioscuri, Poseidon Asphalios, Athena Chalkioikos, Athena Poliachos and the deities associated with her, Tyche Sopatros, Artemis Patriotis, Demeter and Kore ἐν Φρουρίῳ, Sostratias ἐν Ἐγείλοις, Aphrodite Ourania, Tyche Toichagetas, Hermes Ouranios, Dionysos, Demeter and Kore ἐν Δικτύνῃ (another trace of Minoan influence appears here), Mnemosyne, the Muses; the list is incomplete. None of the cults coincide with those associated with the Ti. Claudii. The list of cults mentioned in connection with Pomponia Kallistoneike is much shorter, but coincides with this in the case of the Dioscuri and Artemis Patriotis; Aphrodite Enoplios is also probably to be identified with Aphrodite Ourania in V, i, 559.

Thus it appears that while one family monopolised a large number of priesthoods which passed in the male line, another family, equally distinguished in the second century A.D. (since it intermarried with the first) monopolised a large number of other priesthoods which passed in the female line. This points to the fusion of two distinct elements among the Spartan nobility. It is not to be supposed, however, that at this late date the principle of descent in the female line had any validity whatever apart from determining the succession of the priesthoods. Further, we have a hint of ultimate origin in the case of the ' family ' (in this peculiar sense) which monopolised the hereditary priesthoods which passed in the female line. Sex. Pomp. Eudamos was also hereditary celebrant of the Leonidean Games (V, i, 559), implying a close connection with the royal house of the Agiadae, and evidence has been cited above (p. 268, n. 1) for the view that the Agiadae had some special connection with the cult of Artemis Orthia, one of the cults which may be seen to have passed to a succession of priests in the female line. This point has a bearing upon the question of the relative antiquity of the two royal houses (see further above, pp. 337 f.), especially in view of the inclusion of the cult of Herakles Genarchas (' originator of the Genos ', and surely implying a worship closely connected with one of the royal houses) among those which passed by descent in the male line (cf. above, p. 472). It would appear then that the system of succession to priesthoods in the male line came in later, and was specially connected not with the Agiad but with the Eurypontid house, to which this particular family of Ti. Claudii must therefore be supposed to belong. Survival of members of the Eurypontid house as late as the second century B.C. is attested by evidence already cited (p. 27, n. 3).

§ 2. *Notes on the tree of the Ti. Claudii and related families* (above, p. 471)

1 Priests of the emperors are not included, and only those holders of Spartan priesthoods are indicated whose priesthoods are directly attested by the inscriptions. Ti. Claud. Brasidas I and one of his sons may have held hereditary priesthoods, but the evidence is uncertain (cf. above, p. 472).
2 Ti. Claud. Brasidas II can hardly be (as Kolbe supposes) the father of the Brasidas, who was Patronomos on account of Lycurgus τὸ ια' (V, i, 312). The date of this Patronomate is shortly before A.D. 200 (cf. Appendix IV, § 8, p. 467), whereas a member of the next generation following Brasidas II was Patronomos c. 139/40 (cf. Appendix IV, § 8, for this and following references to Patronomates, and n. 4 below).
3 The alternative *nomen* and Greek name of this Pratolaos connect him with P. Ael. Damokratidas (Patronomos c. 171/2) by whom both he and his sister's son Pratolaos (already perhaps his own adopted son, to

judge from the name) were adopted. This indicates that the eldest Pratolaos, *i.e.* the first mentioned on Table, p. 471, belonged to the generation before P. Aelius Damokratidas.

⁴ Kolbe supposes Claudia Polla to have married Pomponius Aristeas II (grandson of his namesake). Pomp. Aristeas I, son of Pomp. Alkastos I (Patronomos *c.* 139/40) and brother of Pomp. Agis (Patronomos *c.* 172/3), is suggested in place of Aristeas II as fitting in with the chronological indications mentioned in note 3 above.

⁵ For this indication of chronology, *cf.* notes 3 and 4 above.

⁶ The *floruit* of Pomponius Panthales Diogenes (which determines that of his sister the priestess Kallistoneike I) depends upon that of his πένθερος (father-in-law, brother-in-law, or son-in-law ; *cf.* Liddell and Scott, *s.v.*) P. Memm. Pratolaos ὁ καὶ Aristokles (V, i, 547) who married Claud. Longina (*ibid.* 547, 592), daughter of Claud. Aristoteles (*ibid.* 592), presumably the Patronomos of *c.* 148/9, since Pratolaos ὁ καὶ Aristokles was himself Patronomos on behalf of Lycurgus τὸ δ' (*i.e. c.* 190. See Appendix IV, § 8, p. 467 ; *cf.* also his contemporary M. Aur. Alkisthenes Εὐελπίστου (V, i, 547), Patronomos on behalf of Lycurgus τὸ έ in V, i, 683). Probably, therefore, the Patronomos in question was father of Memmia Longina, and father-in-law (as supposed by Kolbe) of Pomponius Panthales Diogenes.

⁷ The generation of Sex. Pompeius Eudamos is fixed as μζ' ἀπὸ Διοσκούρων, therefore five generations later than P. Memm. Deximachus (*cf.* V, i, 537), Nomophylax under his namesake *c.* 85 (Appendix IV, i, No. 32) and three generations later than M. Aur. Aristokrates Δαμαινέτου (V, i, 529) who was a contemporary of Cascellius Aristoteles, the Patronomos of *c.* 162/3 (*ibid.* 531 indicates Casc. Aristoteles rather than Claud. Aristoteles as the contemporary). Sex. Pomp. Eudamos therefore held his hereditary priesthood about A.D. 240 or a little later, and was of the right age to be the son of the niece of the priestess Pomponia Kallistoneike I, for whose date see note 6 above. Her marriage to Onasikrates is presumed in order to account for the inheritance of the priesthoods by his son Pompeius Eudamos, whose name Eudamos is also found in the family of Pomponia Kallistoneike (*cf.* p. 471).

DELPHI AND THE RHETRA OF LYCURGUS

§ 1. *The Reliability of the ' Oracle' Tradition.*

That the main outlines of the Lycurgan constitution were delivered to the law-giver by an oracle from Delphi was believed by no less critical an authority than Aristotle.[1] The poet Tyrtaeus either believed or professed to believe the same ; in either case he expected the majority of his fellow-citizens to believe it, for otherwise his own profession of belief would have been without point. We touch here upon a fundamental assumption of early Greek political thought, that in the Polis the authority of Law (*Nomos*) must be supreme (and this surely was why Tyrtaeus called his poem *Eunomia*) and that Nomos derives its binding power from divine sanction. The origins of the saying *Nomos Basileus,* originally ' The King is the Law ', not ' Law is King ', are lost in antiquity,[2] but it certainly goes back to the time when the king, being the only source of the law of the state, was universally recognised to be a descendant of the gods and vessel of divine authority. Such was the immemorial tradition which formed the background of constitution-making in the post-feudal age of Greece.

This being so, it would be the natural impulse of a lawgiver or leading persons in the state, when the authority of the king began to break down, to seek some alternative form of divine authority for a new constitution.[3] For such authority what more natural source could be found than an oracle of wide repute among the Greeks in general, and particularly likely to secure acceptance in another Dorian state, attached as much as Delphi itself to the worship of Apollo ?

About 550 B.C., when its monarchy was growing weak, Dorian Cyrene adopted a similar course, and was advised to seek a legislator from Mantinea, which advice was followed.[4] At that time therefore, the authorities at Delphi knew something about Greek constitutions and were in a position to judge what type (in this case a federal one [5]) would be likely to suit Cyrene. Moreover the Cyreneans confidently expected them to know.

---

[1] *Cf.* above, p. 413, n. 3.

[2] See further Jaeger, *Paideia I* (1939), p. 106, n. 2.

[3] This seemed a natural and wise course to the author of the *Resp. Lac.* in the early fourth century. *Cf.* (Xen.) *Resp. Lac.* 8. 5 (Lycurgus and leading Spartans seek authority for the proposed new code of laws from Apollo at Delphi). Similarly, in Plato's description of an imaginary and very ancient constitution (*Critias,* 119 C) the source of the laws is made out to be ' letters of Poseidon '.

[4] *Herod.* IV, 161.

[5] The five villages which at that time composed the Mantinean state evidently inspired Demonax' arrangement at Cyrene of three separate political divisions corresponding to three distinct ethnographic strata of the population (*Herod. ibid.*). Aristotle (*Pol.* VI, 4. 4, 5) praises the ancient limited democracy of Mantinea. All this goes to illustrate the wisdom and experience of Delphi in constitutional matters in the middle of the sixth century.

How long a period of experience is implied before such a stage of confidence is reached ? To this question it is obvious that no definite answer can be given, but the Odyssey already implies that the Delphic oracle had a wide reputation throughout Greece by representing Agamemnon as consulting it,[1] and on general grounds it is likely that consultation of the oracle on the subject of constitutions began earlier than consultation about colonisation, which by its nature implies a much more extensive knowledge of the ancient world than does advice (to Greeks only) on constitutions. But the part played by the oracle in the foundation of Naxos in Sicily in (or very near to) 735 B.C. is well-attested [2] and convincingly dated,[3] and this distant colony certainly cannot have been the first to be guided by Apollo Archagetes. Consultation of the oracle about constitutions can therefore easily go back to the age of the break-up of the monarchies in Greece, in the ninth century B.C. or thereabouts. At all events there is no inherent improbability, in the consultation of the oracle about a new constitution for Sparta about seventy years before the known consultation of it by the Chalcidians about the foundation of Naxos, and this (shortly before 800 B.C.) is the date proposed in the present work for the Lycurgan reforms.

Thus two distinct lines of reasoning, both independent of Sparta, would lead us to regard the Spartan oracle-story as true, on the one hand the attitude of the Greeks in general to *Nomos*, on the other the history of the Delphic oracle. The probability is further strengthened by the prominence of Sparta in the Delphic Amphictyony in historical times, and by the title of $Πύθιοι$ borne by the two officials permanently attached to each Spartan king.[4]

But it may be asked how, if the tradition which Tyrtaeus recorded about the Lycurgan oracle was true, the Spartans in Herodotus' time came to deny the connection and to maintain that Lycurgus brought his laws straight from Crete ? [5] The answer to this is not difficult to find. In the first place, knowledge of Cretan similarities had by this time tended to undermine the theory of Delphic origin, and it was no doubt to meet this difficulty that a later Delphic oracle was sought, supporting the theory that Lycurgus himself was a god.[6] In the second place, Delphi at the time of Herodotus' travels in Greece was no longer trusted by Sparta, because the pro-Athenian Phocians, instead of the Delphians themselves, were in control of the shrine.[7] Moreover, the oracle had earlier brought itself into disrepute with Sparta for giving bad advice at the time of Cleomenes' war with Argos.[8] The authority of the Lycurgan laws was now safeguarded by stressing the divine origin and the cult of Lycurgus, and the theory of the original oracle was conveniently forgotten in Sparta, though not permanently lost to students of Tyrtaeus.

There is therefore nothing *a priori* unlikely, but on the contrary a general probability, that the original constitution of Lycurgan Sparta really was a Delphic oracle as Aristotle believed. Whether the document on which

---

[1] *Od.* VIII, 79 f.
[2] *Cf.* Parke, *The Delphic Oracle* (1939), p. 69.
[3] *Cf.* Clinton, F. H., I, p. 164. The date is accepted by archaeologists.
[4] (Xen.) *Resp. Lac.* XV, 5 (Dindorf).
[5] *Herod.* I, 65.
[6] Cited by Herod, *ibid.* *Cf.* Plut. *Lycurg.* 5.
[7] *Cf.* Parke, *op. cit.* p. 199 f. (from *c.* 457-446 B.C.).
[8] Herod. VI, 80 (*cf.* 76 init.).

he commented was rightly identified by him as this oracle, is another question which cannot finally be answered without detailed examination of its contents, but even a cursory view reveals the authentic oracular flavour of Delphi in the instruction to the inquirer (after setting up certain cults) ' from season to season to hold Apollo's gatherings between the pelicans and the haunt of wild goats.[1]

§ 2. *The text of the Lycurgan Rhetra and its Interpretation.*

The text of the Rhetra in the surviving MSS. of Plutarch, *Lycurgus* 6 (the only evidence preserved) reads as follows : [2] Διὸς Συλλανίου καὶ 'Αθανᾶς Συλλανίας ἱερὸν ἱδρυσάμενος,[3] φυλὰς φυλάξαντα καὶ ὠβὰς ὠβάξαντα τριάκοντα γερουσίαν σὺν ἀρχαγέταις καταστήσαντα, ὥρας ἐξ ὥρας ἀπελλάζειν μεταξὺ Βαβύκας τε καὶ Κνακιῶνος· οὕτως εἰσφέρειν τε καὶ ἀφίστασθαι· †γαμωδανγοριανημην καὶ κράτος.

The enactment which Aristotle regarded as a later addition,[4] but which Wade-Gery [5] assumes to be contemporary with the rest, reads : αἰ δὲ σκολιὰν ὁ δᾶμος ἔροιτο, τοὺς πρεσβυγενέας καὶ ἀρχαγέτας ἀποστατῆρας ἦμεν.

Aristotle's exposition of the whole document is as follows. He assumes that it provides for a Gerusia of twenty-eight,[6] not counting the Archagetae, whom he explains as the two kings ; he further supposes that Babyka and Knakion are mentioned in order to fix the place of meeting of the Spartan Ecclesia, Knakion being identified as a river and Babyka as a bridge. The addendum about a ' crooked decision ' is said to mean that the Gerusia and kings shall have the final power of ratifying, or rejecting by dissolving the meeting, any decision taken by the Ecclesia on a motion brought before it. Such decisions are assumed by Aristotle to be general, not only judicial,[7] in character. The main document is called a *Rhetra*, but at the same time is said to be a Delphic oracle, the words of Tyrtaeus [8] being cited in support of this interpretation :

Φοίβου ἀκούσαντες Πυθωνόθεν οἴκαδ' ἔνεικαν
μαντείας τε θεοῦ καὶ τελέεντ' ἔπεα·
ἄρχειν μὲν βουλῆς θεοτιμήτους βασιλῆας
οἷσι μέλει Σπάρτης ἱμερόεσσα πόλις,
πρεσβύτας τε γέροντας, ἔπειτα δὲ δημότας ἄνδρας
εὐθείαις ῥήτραις ἀνταπαμειβομένους.

---

[1] See further below, pp. 485 f., and for the indication of place by the fauna, *cf.* the Delphic oracles referring to Ephesus and to the colonisation of Ozolian Locris, Byzantium and Tarentum (Parke, *op. cit.* pp. 60 f., 78).

[2] MSS. variants and emendations in Plutarch, *Vitae*, ed. Lindskog and Ziegler, Vol. III, fasc. II (1926). Wade-Gery (*Class. Quart.* XXXVIII, p. 116), consistently with his belief that the document is an enactment of the Spartan Apella, restores Dorian forms throughout, and for the last clause reads δάμῳ δ'ἀν⟨τα⟩γορίαν ἦμεν καὶ κράτος, or (*ibid.* p. 8, n. 3, following in part Blumenthal) δαμώδ⟨ων⟩ ἀν⟨τα⟩γορίαν, the feminine noun being deduced from ἀνταργορεύειν, ' contradict '.

[3] See further below, p. 480.

[4] *Cf.* p. 413.

[5] *Class. Quart.* XXXVII, pp. 62 f. ; XXXVIII, pp. 4 f., 115 f.

[6] *Cf.* Aristotle *ap.* Plut. *Lycurg.* 5 f., and for the general grounds for regarding Aristotle as the source of the exposition, Chap. XI, p. 413, n. 1.

[7] But *cf.* Chap. XI, pp. 416 f.

[8] Frag. 3*b* (Diehl).

At this point it may be noted that Tyrtaeus' poem *Eunomia* is cited by Aristotle in the *Politics* as his source of information about a *stasis* which occurred in Sparta at the time of the first Messenian War,[1] and is therefore likely to be his source for information about the addition made to the original oracle by the kings of that period, Theopompus and Poly-dorus.[2] This implies that Aristotle regarded these two kings, rather than Lycurgus and his associates, as some have maintained,[3] as the subject of ἔνεικαν in Tyrtaeus' time, and that he supposed the passage in question to illustrate not the whole history of the oracle-Rhetra, but only the meaning of the addition made to it by the intervention of Theopompus and Polydorus.

On further examination of the prose-Rhetra, it does in fact appear that the substance of Tyrtaeus' lines, as quoted by Plutarch (Aristotle) is contained in the second half, beginning after εἰσφέρειν τε καὶ ἀφίστασθαι. Of this second half, the πρεσβυγενεῖς reappear in Tyrtaeus as the Gerontes, the Archagetae as the kings, † γαμωδανγοριανημην he presumably heard (for we must remember that the Rhetra was orally transmitted) as δαμωδᾶν (not δάμῳ τάν ; see further below) κυρίαν ἤμην,[4] since he speaks of δημόται ἄνδρες ; the last-named are to ' respond to straight Rhetrae ', implying an interpretation of αἱ δὲ σκολιὰν ὁ δᾶμος κ.τ.λ. It is also significant that Tyrtaeus introduces this information as giving the substance of the ' concluding words ' (τελέεντ' ἔπεα) of the oracle, thus implying that he also knew of the existence of a first half (Διὸς Συλλανίου etc.).

A longer version of Tyrtaeus' lines which appears in Diodorus[5] has rightly been regarded with suspicion. To arguments already advanced by others in support of this view[6] may be added the comment that a new addition (μυθεῖσθαι δὲ τὰ καλὰ καὶ ἔρδειν πάντα δίκαια) goes over the same ground again, and provides in addition to the first explanation (εὐθείαις ῥήτραις ἀνταπαμειβομένους) a *second* explanation of αἱ δὲ σκολιὰν ὁ δᾶμος κ.τ.λ.—the general sense being ' the Gerontes and kings are to address to the people only fair and just proposals '. That the author has not in the least understood the prose-Rhetra is also seen in his failure to account for the corollary to αἱ δὲ σκολιὰν ὁ δᾶμος ἔροιτο, namely τοὺς πρεσβυγένεας καὶ ἀρχαγέτας κ.τ.λ. ; though an indication that the Rhetra

---

[1] Arist. *Pol.* V, 7. 4.

[2] Arist. *ap.* Plut. *Lycurg.* 6. *Cf.* also Arist. *ibid.* 7, on the wisdom of Theopompus in permitting reduction in the powers of the kings.

[3] *Cf. Class. Quart.* XXXVIII, p. 5.

[4] On this reading see further below, pp. 481 f.

[5] Diod. VII, 13 (= Tyrt. fr. 3a (Diehl). MS. variations are given by Wade-Gery, *C.Q.* XXXVIII, p. 3). The two initial lines of Tyrtaeus, fr. 3b, are here remodelled and the whole passage reads as follows :

⟨ὧδε⟩ γὰρ ἀργυρότοξος ἄναξ ἑκάεργος Ἀπόλλων
χρυσοκόμης ἔχρη πίονος ἐξ ἀδύτου·
'ἄρχειν μὲν βουλῆς θεοτιμήτους βασιλῆας
οἷσι μέλει Σπάρτης ἱμερόεσσα πόλις,
πρεσβυγενεῖς τε γέροντας, ἔπειτα δὲ δημότας ἄνδρας
εὐθείαις ῥήτραις ἀνταπαμειβομένους·
μυθεῖσθαι δὲ τὰ καλὰ καὶ ἔρδειν πάντα δίκαια,
μηδέ τι βουλεύειν τῇδε πόλει ⟨σκολιόν ?⟩·
δήμου δὲ πλήθει νίκην καὶ κάρτος ἔπεσθαι'.
Φοῖβος γὰρ περὶ τῶν ὧδ' ἀνέφηνε πόλει

[6] *Cf. C.Q.* XXXVIII, pp. 3 f.

was so read by the author appears in his substitution of πρεσβυγενεῖs for Tyrtaeus' πρεσβύταs.

The palpable intention of the new (clearly later) version is to make the traditional constitution appear democratic on the basis of a version of the prose-Rhetra δάμῳ τὰν κυρίαν ἦμεν (MSS. γαμωδανγοριανημην) καὶ κράτοs [1] and to assign the origin of it unmistakably to a Delphic oracle by eliminating Tyrtaeus' oblique reference in his first couplet (ἔνεικαν) to the kings Theopompus and Polydorus. E. Meyer was not improbably right in ascribing the poem to a forger of the early fourth century, perhaps the exiled king Pausanias himself.[2]

Thus we have before us two rival metrical versions, not indeed of the whole Rhetra upon which Aristotle commented, but of its second half, the crux of the whole issue lying in the, at present obscure, MSS. reading γαμωδανγοριανημην καὶ κράτοs. The character of the post-Tyrtaean poem, as well as reasons already adduced for thinking that the Spartan Ecclesia in early post-feudal times was limited to *judicial* decisions,[3] together suggest a strong suspicion that the words καὶ κράτοs (cf. καὶ κάρτοs ἔπεσθαι in the late poem) are a late addition made not long before Aristotle's commentary. The phrase which immediately precedes them is best considered in relation to the text of the document as a whole, for we notice at once that all the MSS. of Plutarch are here singularly unanimous, and that the crucial phrase itself, senseless though it must have appeared to a scribe, is identical in all the surviving MSS. with the insignificant exception of ιμην for ημην at the end in one MS.[4]

Further consideration of the peculiarities of the whole text as preserved leads to the conclusion that Aristotle took pains to transcribe the Rhetra exactly as it was communicated to him, as Xenophon did in the famous case of the intercepted Spartan dispatch from Cyzicus.[5] It is not, however, precisely what we might have expected from a genuine law of the Spartan constitution, since the use of Dorian forms is not consistent throughout, and it might be urged that Dorian Delphi no less than Dorian Sparta would have made use of these forms. But the distinction made a century ago by Ahrens still holds after the discovery of many more inscriptions ; the Doric of Delphi and indeed of northern and central Greece generally is far less broad than that of the Peloponnese, and the Laconian dialect seems to be broadest of all.[6] In view of the purely

---

[1] Resulting in the poet's line δήμου δὲ πλήθει νίκην καὶ κάρτος ἔπεσθαι. For discussion of the MSS. reading see further below, pp. 480 f.

[2] Wade-Gery in *C.Q.* XXXVIII, p. 5, notes 4 and 5, accepts Meyer's general thesis, but objects that Pausanias' pamphlet was entitled κατὰ τῶν Λυκούργου νόμων, and was not therefore intended as a reinstatement of Lycurgus. This objection would be met by supposing Pausanias' title to refer to the ' Lycurgan ' laws as administered in his own time. He may have maintained in his tract that they were contrary to the original instructions of the oracle.

[3] *Cf.* Chap. XI, pp. 416 f.

[4] For the text and variants *cf.* above, p. 477.

[5] Xen. *Hell.* I, i, 23 : ἔρρει τὰ κᾶλα. Μίνδαρος ἀπεσσύα. πεινῶντι τὦνδρες· ἀπορίομες τί χρὴ δρᾶν.

[6] *Cf.* H. L. Ahrens, *De Dialecto Dorica* (1843), pp. 403 f. Ahrens concludes (p. 411) from the Amphicytonic decree of 380/79 B.C. (C.I.G. 1688, Ditt. *Syll.*³ 145) that until this time the Delphic dialect was broader than that of the rest of northern Greece, and from somewhat later inscriptions that it soon afterwards came into conformity with the rest.

Spartan origin which now seems to be indicated for the second half of the Rhetra [1] we should expect broad Doric in this part of it, but not in the first half, if a Delphic oracle was in fact responsible for that. On the other hand, the supposition that the whole document is a genuine Rhetra or Rhetrae (a part of the Spartan constitution) entails the further supposition that it was preserved by *oral* tradition only, the official publication of the laws in writing being forbidden by one of the Rhetrae themselves.[2] This would inevitably lead to contamination of any part of the document which was not in the broad Doric of Laconia by some at least of the Laconian forms of pronunciation, the original grammatical forms remaining otherwise unchanged.

This is what we should expect, and this is what we find in fact. For to consider the language of the first part of the document first, the ξ in ὠβάξαντα might well be part of an original pronouncement from Delphi, for not only is it in accordance with universal Dorian usage in the case of verbs ending in -ζω,[3] but the parallel of φυλάξαντα would almost inevitably suggest it here, and the resulting jingle would be in keeping with the language of other Delphic oracles. But the final letter of ἱδρυσάμενος (in all MSS.) where it obviously stands for ν, is broad archaic Doric,[4] a well-attested sound-change, which has probably produced in this document, in addition, ὥρας ἐξ ὥρας in place of ὡρᾶν ἐξ ὡρᾶν [5] and Βαβύκας in place of Βαβυκᾶν.[6] On the other hand the terminal ν in γερουσίαν (as well as the non-Doric form of the word itself) has been retained, perhaps because the following word is σύν, and the combination νς, which other Greeks found exceptionally difficult, was preserved and even inserted in archaic broad Doric.[7] The termination of Συλλανίου, the participles ἱδρυσάμενο(ν) and καταστήσαντα and the infinitives ἀπελλάζειν, εἰσφέρειν, ἀφίστασθαι are normal Greek, in contrast with the purely Doric ἤμην [8] of the next clause and ἤμεν of the addendum. So far then the document seems to be in essence and apart from the ' contaminations ' an example of the ' milder Doric ' characteristic of Greece north of the isthmus.

We now come to the chief linguistic crux, the letters γαμωδανγοριανημην. This puzzle requires historical as well as linguistic arguments to solve it. As a guide towards the separation of the first word from the rest, we have, on the one hand, Tyrtaeus' δημότας ἄνδρας,[9] and on the other, the name *Neodamodeis* given in later times to an inferior (new) class of citizens.[10] This implies that δαμώδεις (the form γαμώδεις will be discussed presently) [11] in normal Spartan usage meant ' citizens ', and that at all events until interested critics set to work on the rest of the Rhetra, the word δαμωδᾶν (the normal Doric genitive plural of nouns ending in -ης) was thought to be what the Rhetra contained at this point. The word δημόται in the passage of Tyrtaeus would then be merely a ' de-Doricised ' version of

---

But in view of the many legends which imply early changes of political control at Delphi, it is unnecessary to suppose that Delphians (rather than, *e.g.* Phocians) were in charge of the oracle at the early period indicated for the Rhetra.

[1] *Cf.* above, pp. 478 f.   [2] *Cf.* Chap. XI, p. 427.
[3] Ahrens, *op. cit.* p. 89.
[4] *Ibid.* pp. 86 f. The known examples all apply to the final letter only.   [5] See further below, p. 486.
[6] See further below, p. 485.   [7] Ahrens, *op. cit.* p. 104.
[8] See further below, p. 481.   [9] *Cf.* above, p. 477.
[10] *Cf.* Chap. I, pp. 39 f.   [11] Below, p. 482.

δαμώδεις,[1] for Tyrtaeus does not write in Doric. It was characteristic of Laconian Doric to broaden all the vowels,[2] and although the interchange of τ and δ is usually the other way round, the well-attested and apparently invariable form *Neodamodeis* serves to corroborate the example of Doric τ to δ (τῆδες for τῆτες) cited by the ancient grammarians.[3] But it is evident that the same interested critics who in the early fourth century B.C. sought to make the Rhetra appear democratic regarded -δᾶν here as the article referring to a feminine noun which they read or paraphrased as νίκη (implying the decision of the majority).[4]

What actually follows (δ) αμωδᾶν in the MSS. is γορίαν, which the ordinary criteria of the Spartan dialect enable us to identify as κυρίαν (noun or adjective). The change from κ to γ before a vowel is attested by an Attic vase-inscription of the early fifth-century [5] as well as by later inscriptions from Rhodes and from the Argolid,[6] but apart from its frequent occurrence before γ or δ [7] it is not otherwise recorded in the Spartan dialect except in the names Knageus and Artemis Knagia,[8] corresponding to Artemis Knakeatis and Knakalesia in Arcadia, and the mountain Knakalos and Knakadion in Laconia and Arcadia.[9] All these names are connected with the wild goat (Dor. κνακίας and kindred forms).[10] The same sound-change occurs in Latin derivations from Dorian Greek (*e.g.* Agrigentum from Akragas, *gubernator* from κυβερνάτης, in this last instance again preceding υ) so that it may have been more common in early times among the Dorian Greeks than the scanty surviving evidence would suggest.

The change of υ to ου is a common Spartan phenomenon ; [11] we thus get γο(υ)ριαν [12] for κυρίαν (the parallel of σκολιάν in the next clause suggesting that it should be interpreted as an adjective rather than a noun). For historical reasons and in view of the evidence of Homer and Hesiod, the noun to be supplied is clearly δίκη.[13]

The letters ημην which follow are a normal Doric form of εἶναι,[14] and the remaining words of the clause (καὶ κράτος) explain themselves, but are not improbably to be regarded as an interpolation in the original document.[15] Thus the whole clause δαμωδᾶν γορίαν ἤμην may stand

---

[1] *Cf.* Hesych, *s.v.*   [2] *Cf.* Ahrens, *op. cit.* p. 171.

[3] *Ap.* Eustath, 1648, 40.   *Cf.* Ahrens, p. 84.

[4] *Cf.* above, p. 479, n. 1.

[5] *Cf.* Ἀσωποδώρω ἐ λέγυθος (original inscription painted before baking) on a vase made and painted by Douris (Beazley, *Proc. of British Academy*, 1944, p. 40). A vase by Exekias has *heγτορ* for Hector (*ibid.* n. 1) but this change has probably been influenced by the following τ.

[6] *S.G.D.I.* 3. 1. 3380, 4327*a* (Agasigratis, Agestima) ; Ditt. *Syll.*³ 724, 1. 1, (Βρυγινδάριος for Βρικινδάριος at Camirus).

[7] *S.G.D.I.* 4. 4. p. 711.

[8] Paus. III, 18. 4. This goddess had a temple between Sparta and Amyclae.

[9] Paus. III, 24. 6 ; VIII, 23. 3, 4 ; 53. 11.

[10] *Cf.* Roscher, *s.v.* Artemis, p. 565.

[11] Ahrens, *op. cit.* pp. 124 f., 416. *Cf.* also Κονοουρεῖς (I.G. V, i, 480, etc.).

[12] In this case the substitution of υ for ου must be explained by the hypothesis of a written version, the transcription in question being normal in archaic Spartan inscriptions, as in those of other states.

[13] *Cf.* Chap. XI, pp. 416 f.   [14] *Cf.* S.G.D.I. 4952, 4998, etc.

[15] *Cf.* above, p. 479.

as normal Laconian Greek, the only change required from the MSS. being in the initial γ (γαμωδᾶν).

According to the ancient grammarians the Spartans said δᾶ for γᾶ,[1] a statement doubted by modern authorities, since it appears to have no support except possibly from the name *Damater*.[2] The ancient grammarians need not be supposed to be right in order to explain the form γαμωδᾶν; it is enough to conclude from their statement that there was a popular belief to this effect, which might easily arise from this very document. γαμωδᾶν would then naturally be substituted in a technical exposition, as was that of Aristotle, for what was really δαμωδᾶν.

In the next clause (αἱ δὲ σκολιὰν ὁ δᾶμος ἔροιτο) it cannot be denied that ἔροιτο is a possible Laconian dialect form of ἕλοιτο, since dropping of the aspirate is common in Spartan inscriptions[3] and the substitution of ρ for λ (though usually the change is the other way round)[4] occurs in a Doric inscription from Corinth.[5] But there are no actual Spartan examples of the change from λ to ρ, and the MSS. do not indicate that aspirates were otherwise dropped in this particular document. Moreover ἔροιτο as it stands is a possible grammatical form (Fut. Mid. Opt. from εἴρω) and easily explains itself by Homeric usage, which indicates the meaning ' if the Damos should cause to be told to it ' or merely ' should have told to it ;[6] σκολιὰν (sc. δίκην) then being, according to a normal construction with the Middle voice, that which is told. This interpretation, although it implies a meaning very closely akin to ' should ask '[7] does not necessarily imply that the Damos had the right of discussion, or any power of initiation in the matter at all ; and here it is necessary to digress from the exposition of linguistic points in order to consider the historical reasons which require us to reject the otherwise tempting explanation put forward by Wade-Gery, who concludes from ἔροιτο here, from Tyrtaeus' εὐθείαις 'ρήτραις ἀνταπαμειβομένους, and from historical references to discussion before the Spartan ecclesia, that the Damos itself had the right of discussion.[8] This conviction leads him to propose the emendation δάμῳ δ' ἀν⟨τα⟩γορίαν (an otherwise unknown noun assumed from ἀνταγορεύω) where we have seen reason to read δαμωδᾶν γορίαν, following the MSS. exactly.

Wade-Gery believes that the recorded instances of individual speeches before the Spartan Assembly are sufficiently conclusive to justify the rejection of the plain statement in Plutarch (almost certainly based on Aristotle)[9] that the Assembly could not discuss, and he attempts to explain otherwise what appears to be an equally plain statement to the same effect in Aristotle's *Politics*.[10] But the instances of individual speeches are easily to be explained as survivals of Homeric practice, of which there have been shown to be many others in Sparta ;[11] kings or Gerontes (and so later, in Sparta, kings, Gerontes or Ephors) are represented in Homer as holding debates *among themselves* in the presence of the assembled people, but by the withholding of the royal symbol of authority (σκῆπτρον) members of the Laos are deprived of any part in the

[1] Ahrens, *op. cit.* p. 80.   [2] *Ibid.*
[3] *S.G.D.I.* 4. 4, p. 708 (*e.g.* ἀμέρα, ὁρίξω, υἱός).   [4] Ahrens, p. 86.
[5] *S.G.D.I. ibid.* p. 386.   [6] *Cf.* L.-S. *s.v.* εἴρω.
[7] As in Attic usage of ἐροῦμαι.
[8] *Cf. Class Quart.* XXXVII, pp. 70 f. ; XXXVIII, pp. 6 f.
[9] Plut. *Lycurg.* 6. 6 (*cf.* Chap. XI, p. 413, n. 3).   [10] *Pol.* II, 11. 5, 6.
[11] *Cf.* Chap. XI, pp. 399 f. ; 410 f.

discussion.[1] Their rôle is merely to listen, and to approve what is decided in their presence, and in Homer no instance of disapproval is recorded. Aristotle implies the same of Sparta when he says of Carthage (*Pol.* II, 11. 6) : οὐ διακοῦσαι μόνον ἀποδιδόασι τῷ δήμῳ τὰ δόξαντα τοῖς ἄρχουσιν, ἀλλὰ κύριοι (οἱ δημόται) κρίνειν εἰσὶ καὶ . . . ἀντειπεῖν. This, he says, did not happen in Sparta. In view of these indications, we must conclude that a σκολιά (δίκη) [2] though theoretically an *unjust* decision, was in fact whatever did *not* seem good to the ἄρχοντες (kings and Gerusia) but was applauded by the Damos in response to a speech by an individual magistrate,[3] presumably an Ephor. The object of the Rhetra of Theopompus and Polydorus was to deal with this problem by the simple expedient of authorising kings and Gerusia to ' be removers ' (ἀποστατῆρας ἦμεν) of the Assembly, that is, as Plutarch (Aristotle) explained, to disband it (διαλύειν) [4] without any decision having been taken on the business in hand. Thus the second part of the Rhetra provides the earliest indication (an appreciable time before Tyrtaeus) of growing influence of individual magistrates (certainly Ephors) where before the authority of kings and Gerusia had been unchallenged.

The highly peculiar locution ἀποστατῆρας ἦμεν (the noun being otherwise unknown and formed only by analogy) was evidently chosen for the same reason as the word ἀρχαγέτας, to link up the addition to the Rhetra with the first part, in which occur (as well as ἀρχαγέταις) the words οὕτως εἰσφέρειν τε καὶ ἀφίστασθαι, now (by the authors of the addendum) interpreted to mean ' to introduce motions and to dissolve the Assembly '. It may or may not be fanciful to discern a close parallel here to the Roman *Senatus consulta per relationem discessionemque facere,*[5] as between the ἔροιτο of the Rhetra and the *rogationes* laid before the Roman Assembly. This might conceivably throw light on the interpretation of the Rhetra current at Sparta when Roman ambassadors were sent to Greece in the middle of the fifth century B.C., and if so, the interpretation of ἀφίστασθαι has by this time changed once more and refers to the division in the voting. That the interpretation implied by ἀποστατῆρας ἦμεν already marks a change from the intention of the original legislator becomes clear if one asks, *who* was to dissolve the Assembly according to Part I of the Rhetra ? The majority of scholars at the present time would probably reply ' the Damos ', but this has been shown to be historically

---

[1] The debate before the Laos of Ithaca (*Od.* II, 35–257) is particularly instructive. See further Chap. XI, p. 410.

[2] In Tyrtaeus, ῥήτρα. But *cf.* Chap. XI, pp. 416 f.

[3] There is no attested case of any speaker in the Spartan Ecclesia other than an official. *Cf.* the evidence collected in *Class. Quart.* XXXVIII, p. 8. In view of the Homeric parallels, I cannot agree with Wade-Gery (*ibid.*) that this feature of the evidence is fortuitous.

[4] The explanation given (*cf.* Plut. *Lycurg.* 6. 8, τοῦτ' ἔστι μὴ κυροῦν, ἀλλ' ὅλως ἀφίστασθαι καὶ διαλύειν τὸν δῆμον) implies that its author could not decide whether ἀποστατῆρας had an intransitive or a causal meaning. Modern scholars appear all to have adopted the first alternative, as if the noun was equivalent to ἀποστατεῖς. The other alternative seems preferable both on account of the existence of ἀποστάτης as well as ἀποστατήρ-ηρος, and in view of the causal sense usually implied by the termination τήρ-τῆρος (*e.g.* δηλητήρ, λωβητήρ, ἐλατήρ, δαμαντήρ, παυστήρ, σωτήρ, στατήρ, the last being presumably the weight which causes the balance to stand still). All the examples given are words occurring in early literature.

[5] *Lex de Imperio Vespasiani* (*I.L.S.* 244), l. 5.

without foundation and improbable. The Spartan authors of the addendum to the Rhetra would no doubt have answered ' the kings and Gerusia ', but the text of Part I of the Rhetra shows that a single author (καταστήσαντα etc.) was in question. A simple explanation is possible on the assumption (supported by other considerations presently to be enumerated) that many points in Part I had already become obscure when Part II of the Rhetra was added. In Part I οὕτως εἰσφέρειν τε καὶ ἀφίστασθαι may be taken to relate to the inquirer of the oracle, who is instructed (after setting up cults, etc.) ' thus to propose and immediately to resign office ' (a common technical meaning of ἀφίστασθαι [1]). But although this may have been the underlying meaning, the superficial one, in keeping with the usual obscurity of oracular responses, would be simply ' to go away '.

Both the meaning and the antiquity of Part I of the Rhetra will reveal themselves more clearly after a closer investigation of the proper names and other obscure phrases.

1. Συλλάνιος, Συλλανία.

Σελλάννου occurs as an indication of place, and most probably represents a temple, in an inscription of Epidaurus (Argolid) of the third century B.C.[2] On the analogy of the identity of the words Σέλλοι, Ἕλλοι and σέλλα, ἑλλά [3] and other philological evidence for a general dropping of the initial Σ of Greek words in very early times in favour of a simple aspirate, Σελλάννου would therefore seem to represent an extremely archaic form of Hellanion. Cults of a goddess Hellania as well as that of the much more common Zeus Hellanios are attested by inscriptions.[4] But our text has Συλλάνιος; and the MSS. tradition has been shown to be otherwise so good that the hypothesis of a mere mistake here is unconvincing. No evidence for a dialect change from ε to υ is cited by the standard works on the subject, but the following examples seem to justify the assumption that it sometimes occurred. The Cretan cult name Velchanos [5] reappears in Rome as Vulcanus; the Greek Hermes reappears in Etruria as Turms. In Crete the name Ὑρτακινίων (on coins) [6] appears to be connected with the tribal and other names Ἐρταίων etc.[7] With these clues before us we may perhaps venture an interpretation of two Spartan inscriptions, the first in very archaic lettering, written from right to left, containing the name Ὑρμυνία,[8] the other, of much later date, mentioning the festival Σύρμαια [9] in a list of athletic contests. It is tempting to connect Ὑρμυνία with the gens Herminia, supposedly of Etruscan origin in early Rome, but mentioned only by authors whose evidence is derived ultimately from early Greek written sources.[10] Hesychius (s.v.) brings us no nearer to the origin of the festival Σύρμαια by deriving the name from the cakes

---

[1] Cf. Ditt. Syll.[3] 241 A, 5 (Delphi, IVth century B.C.) 527. 105 Dreros, IIIrd century).

[2] S.G.D.I. 3025.   [3] Hesych. s.v. Ἑλλά.

[4] For Hellania at Cyzicus, cf. C.I.G. 3670.

[5] Cf. S.G.D.I. 4. 4, pp. 1173, 1203; no. 5114.

[6] Ibid. no. 5055.   [7] Ibid. 4. 4, p. 1180.

[8] I.G. V, i, 824 (restored as Ὑρμι[ν]αί[α], but the letters νι appear to be ligatured, and the name complete as it stands).

[9] Ibid. 222. The context leaves it uncertain whether a feminine noun or a neut. pl. is meant.

[10] References in Smith, Dict. Biogr. s.v.

given as prizes ; here surely we have both a survival of the prehistoric initial Σ before a vowel, and the substitution of υ for ε which occurs in *Turms*, and in that case Σύρμαια must be archaic Doric for ῾Ερμεια.[1] Athletic festivals of Hermes are very common throughout the Greek world,[2] and we know from Pindar, though from no other inscriptions, that Sparta also had its ῾Ερμεια.[3]

It may therefore be concluded that Συλλάνιος stands for *Hellanios*, that the initial Σ is not specifically Spartan but is a mark of high antiquity, and that the υ, being a mark of the broadest Doric to judge from the Etruscan cult names with their Dorian-Greek affinities, is in this instance a Spartan corruption rather than a part of the original document.

2. μεταξὺ Βαβύκας τε καὶ Κνακιῶνος.

It appears from Plutarch's exposition, and also from glosses in Hesychius attempting to explain Βαβύκας[4] that the Spartans themselves in Aristotle's time no longer knew what localities were referred to under these names. Aristotle said that Βαβύκα (or some similar form)[5] was a bridge and Knakion a river ; by the Spartans themselves the river Oinous, a tributary of the Eurotas which joins it from the east a few miles north of Sparta, was thought to be the river in question, but the Spartan explanation of Βαβύκας seems to have disappeared from the MSS. of Plutarch.[6] ' A torrent ' and ' a city ' appear to have been alternative explanations.[7]

From the form of the word Κνακιῶνος we may conclude that it meant (in origin at least) something more than a mere place-name. The masculine termination -ών always appears to connote the place in which the object or creature indicated by the rest of the word is to be found, as in ἀνδρών, ἱππών, ἀμπελών and many other examples.[8] This connects Κνακιών with Dor. κνακίας, the wild goat, which was certainly common in the mountains of Laconia, as we know from the cults and place-names already referred to.[9] But from the scattered distribution of the names in question, it is clear that no one definite locality can have been intended by Κνακιών. ' The place of wild goats ' would more appropriately refer to all the mountains which enclosed the Eurotas valley on north, east and west.

This interpretation gives us at once the probable explanation of Βαβύκας, or rather of Βαβυκᾶν, the terminal -ς of the text as preserved being easily explained on the analogy of ἱδρυσάμενος for ἱδρυσάμενον.[10]

---

[1] According to Kuhn and others, the name Hermes is connected with Sanskr. *sar*—(cf. P.-W. *s.v. Hermes*, p. 738).

[2] Roscher *s.v. Hermes*, p. 2369.

[3] Pind. *Nem.* X, 53 (97). [4] See following note.

[5] There are no MSS. variations in the form Βαβύκας in Plut. *Lycurg.* 6, but in Plut. *Pelop.* 17, where Sparta is referred to as ' the place between Babyka(?) and Knakion ', two of the best MSS. have Βαβύκτας (which recurs in Hesych. *s.v.* Βαβύκτα· γέφυρα), and another Βαβύτας. Hesychius' gloss Βαβύη(?)· χείμαρρος, οἱ δὲ πόλις suggests yet another tradition.

[6] It has been suggested by Wade-Gery (*Class. Quart.* XXXVII, p. 63, n. 1, that Babyka-and-Knakion together were later identified as the river Oinous.

[7] See note 5 above.

[8] γυναικών, βοών, μελισσών, ὀρνιθών, ἐλαιών, μηλών, συκών, φηγών, πιτυών, δενδρών, μυλών, οἰνών, etc.

[9] *Cf.* above, p. 481. [10] *Cf.* above, p. 480.

Βαβυκώς means a pelican according to Hesychius ; [1] if we suppose it to be contracted from βαβύκαος, Βαβυκᾶν would be a normal Dor. gen. pl. of this, and the whole phrase would mean ' between the pelicans and the wild goats ', that is, in the area shut in by mountains on three sides and by the marshy flats (Helos) haunted by pelicans [2] on the south. Such a periphrasis might well issue from the Delphic oracle ; too precise an indication of the locality was not in keeping with its utterances in general, and the pelican is in fact commonly found in southern as well as in northern Greece.[3]

3. ὥρας ἐξ ὥρας (ὡρᾶν ἐξ ὡρᾶν).

Wade-Gery has shown [4] that there is no reason for emending the genitive in this phrase as it occurs in the MSS. A genitive expressing time within which events occur is common in Greek, and whether the singular or the plural is here the right reading, the meaning must be ' in one season after another '. The meaning of ὡρά is, of course, very vague, and it would be in keeping with the character of many Delphic oracles if it were deliberately framed to be vague in this case, to allow for the gradual introduction of more frequent Assemblies if experience proved this necessary. An annual meeting is hardly likely to have been intended at any time, since even Homeric Assemblies were summoned both to approve decisions of war and to ratify the conclusion of peace, and these two decisions, under normal conditions of Greek warfare, were likely to be made at different times of the year. Our Rhetra also implies popular approval of verdicts in criminal trials,[5] and this in turn implies Assemblies more frequent than annual. Since Homer and Hesiod distinguish only three ὥραι in the year,[6] the earliest instance of division into four seasons occurring in Alcman, the *original* meaning of the phrase ὥρας ἐξ ὥρας (or ὡρᾶν ἐξ ὡρᾶν) in the oracle, in view of its early date, was probably ' one Assembly in each season, in spring, summer and winter '. Our evidence for later Spartan practice in this matter is insufficient to conclude that regular monthly meetings were ever introduced ; the words of the scholiast on Thucydides I, 67. 3 (τὸν εἰωθότα λέγει ξύλλογον ὅτι ἐν πανσελήνῳ ἐγίγνετο ἀεί) do not justify this conclusion, but merely indicate that whenever the regular meetings were held, they were held at the full moon—not necessarily at *every* full moon. The ' usual meeting ' here referred to by Thucydides took place in the early summer ; [7] the Assembly for the election of magistrates took place in the early autumn.[8] ' Unusual ' (or irregular) meetings in the fifth century are also implied by Thucydides' phrase ξύλλογον τὸν εἰωθότα and by general probability. Wade-Gery has suggested, with reserve, that the name μεγάλαι ἀπέλλαι which occurs in inscriptions of Gytheum implies a main assembly at Sparta once a year, with ' lesser Apellae ' in the other months [9] but in the view

---

[1] Hesych. *s.v.* βαβυκώς· πελεκὰν ; βαβυκάνες· πελεκάνες (*cf.* Schmidt's edition, p. 286, l. 70, note).

[2] The pelicans of Ravenna, feeding in the mud-flats, are mentioned by Martial (XI, 21).

[3] *Cf.* D'Arcy Thompson, *A Glossary of Greek Birds* (1895), p. 135.

[4] *Class. Quart.* XXXVII, p. 67, n. 2.

[5] *Cf.* pp. 416 f.   [6] *Cf.* Liddell and Scott, *s.v.*

[7] *Cf.* Thuc. I, 67. 3, with I, 87 and with I, 125. 3 (' less than a year ' elapsed between the decision of the allied assembly which immediately followed that of Sparta, and the invasion of Attica in May 431).

[8] *Cf.* Thuc. V, 36.   [9] *Cf. Class. Quart.* XXXVII, p. 67.

of the present writer the distinction between ' greater ' and ' lesser ' Assemblies is more likely to lie in their different composition.[1] As a restoration of the original text of the document, the plural (ὡρᾶν ἐξ ὡρᾶν) seems preferable to the singular, not only on account of the Spartan tendency to substitute σ for ν of which another instance occurs in the same text,[2] but because the similar phrase ὡραῖς ἐξ ὡρᾶν occurs in the metrical inscription of Isyllus from Epidaurus,[3] instituting a religious procession. Even though the correspondence of phrase is not quite exact, Isyllus may well have been influenced by knowledge of the Spartan Rhetra, since he actually refers at the end of his poem to ' the oracles of Phoebus which Lycurgus sought and established for his city ',[4] and prescribes a prayer for εὐνομία [5] immediately before his use of the words ὡραῖς ἐξ ὡρᾶν. He apparently supposes the expression to mean ' for ever and ever ', rather than ' annually ' or ' in each season,' but in view of the late date,[6] this idea provides no indication of the original meaning.

4. ἀπελλάζειν.

The analogy of φυλάξαντα and ὠβάξαντα in the same document, from φυλή and ὠβή respectively, makes it virtually certain that ἀπελλάζειν is derived from the noun ἄπελλα, which occurs (always in the plural) in late inscriptions from Gytheum,[7] at Sparta itself according to Hesychius, and outside Laconia only (so far as is at present known) at Delphi, in the inscription which preserves the constitution of the Phratria of the Labyadae.[8] It is significant that in the last case ἀπέλλαι does not mean ' an assembly ' (in the same inscription always called ἁλία) but the annual festival (probably extending over more than one day, since ἀπέλλαι occurs only in the plural) at which the offerings called ἀπελλαῖα were made by all members of the Phratria.[9] The analogy of the other θοιναί νόμιμοι of the same Phratria ('Ηραῖα, Λάφρια, 'Ηράκλεια etc.) [10] clearly shows that ἀπέλλαι and ἀπελλαῖα are derived from the normal Delphic form of the name Apollo ('Απέλλων). There is nothing to prove that the festival in question was held in the month Apellaios, which may have been named from the god independently of the festival of the Phratria.

The essential point to notice about the ἀπέλλαι of the Labyadae is that (unlike the other sacred festivals of the Phratria) they were the occasion for a general gathering of all its members for the purpose of paying their subscription, fines being levied upon ordinary members for non-compliance with this rule, and upon officials of the Phratria who received the offerings at any other time of year.[11] It is also important to bear in mind the high antiquity in Greece of gentile associations of this kind, and the strong probability that Phratriae such as that of the Labyadae, with the same cult-festivals, already existed at Delphi at the time when Sparta first acquired a constitution.

In view of these considerations, considering also the peculiar characteristics of Delphic oracles and the general arguments already adduced in favour of supposing that Sparta derived her earliest constitution from Delphi, we may conclude that the occurrence of ἀπέλλαι only in Laconia and at Delphi (and there in a different sense) is not fortuitous, but is

---

[1] Cf. p. 154 of the present work.   [2] Cf. above, p. 480.
[3] I.G. IV², fasc. i, 128.   [4] Ibid. ll. 70 f.
[5] Ibid. l. 24.   [6] c. 280 B.C.   [7] I.G. V, i, 1144, 1146.
[8] Inscr. Iur. Gr. 2 sér. (1904) XXVIII (c. 400 B.C.).
[9] Ibid. (A), ll. 31 f.   [10] Ibid. (D), ll. 2 f.   [11] Ibid. (A), ll. 44 f.

explained by the direct derivation of the one from the other. There may, of course, have existed ἀπέλλαι in other north-Greek Phratriae outside Delphi, but without the intervention of an oracle the application of the term to a general assembly of citizens would not have suggested itself in the Peloponnese. ἀπελλάζειν will therefore mean ' to hold Apollo's gatherings ', that is, ' to hold meetings of *all* the citizens '. The addition of ὡρᾶν ἐξ ὡρᾶν in the oracle doubtless meant (as already suggested) that the Assemblies in question were not to be annual like the ἀπέλλαι of the Delphic Phratriae, but held ' in each season '.

§3. *Conclusion.*

To conclude the examination of the text of the oracle-Rhetra, a reconstruction of its two distinct parts, in what appears from the foregoing analysis to have been its earliest form (with Spartan corruptions removed) is set out below, with translation appended. Letters which involve departure from the MSS. tradition are enclosed in brackets, and for the justification of these changes the reader is referred to the preceding detailed discussion.

I. Διὸς Σ(ε)λλανίου καὶ ᾿Αθανᾶς Σ(ε)λλανίας ἱερὸν ἱδρυσάμενο(ν), φυλὰς φυλάξαντα καὶ ὠβάς ὠβάξαντα, τριάκοντα γερουσίαν σὺν ἀρχαγέταις καταστήσαντα, ὡρᾶ(ν) ἐξ ὡρᾶ(ν) ἀπελλάζειν μεταξὺ Βαβυκᾶ(ν) τε καὶ Κνακιῶνος· οὕτως εἰσφέρειν τε καὶ ἀφίστασθαι.

II. (δ)αμωδᾶν (κυ)ρίαν ἤμην [καὶ κράτος]·[1] αἰ δὲ σκολιὰν ὁ δᾶμος ἔροιτο, τ(ὼ)s[2] πρεσβυγενέας καὶ ἀρχαγέτας ἀποστατῆρας ἤμεν.[3]

Translation.

I. ' Set up (*sc.* O Spartan) a temple of Zeus of the Hellenes and one of Athena of the Hellenes. Keep in tribes the tribes, divide the divisions, set up a Gerusia of thirty with the Leaders, hold Apollo's gatherings season after season between the pelicans and the place of wild goats. Thus propose and depart.'

II. ' Confirming to belong to the citizens, but if they should get said to them a crooked decision, the Elders and the Leaders to be dissolvers.'

It remains to answer a possible objection to the theory that the original Rhetra of the Spartan constitution was a Delphic oracle, and the first addition to it an invention of two kings who also professed to have oracular authority behind them. Wade-Gery has recently maintained [4] the view that the word Rhetra, when it does not mean a treaty between two parties, means ' an enactment of the Demos ', or on occasion ' a proposal laid before the Demos ', and regards these meanings as compatible with one another but not with the sense of ' oracle '. But the three meanings about which the evidence [5] leaves no doubt are already sufficiently different to make

---

[1] A fourth-century interpolation. *Cf.* above, p. 479.

[2] MSS. τούς. τώς has been restored here as being more in keeping with the broad Laconian Doric of the rest of this clause.

[3] Or perhaps ἤμην, as in the previous sentence. The Spartan use of the same letter for both ε and η would easily lead to the adoption of the more common Doric form ἤμεν in the MSS.

[4] *Cf. Class. Quart.* XXXVIII, pp. 6 f.

[5] Collected by Wade-Gery, *ibid.*

it impossible to exclude from consideration an oracle which became a law, and in fact it seems as dangerous to dogmatise about the precise meaning of *rhetra* as about the precise meaning of *lex*.[1] Regarded in the light of their derivation from verbs meaning ' to say ' or (more formally) ' to utter ', the words *rhetra* and *lex* are in fact strikingly similar in their use. It is evidently the fact and not the source of the utterance which determines the use of both terms. Generally speaking, the word *rhetra* seems to be used as equivalent to ' law ' in English and with almost as great variation of meaning. An oracle incorporated in the law of the constitution, being originally regarded as an utterance of the god, would most appropriately be so called.

---

[1] Which may mean an enactment of a popular assembly, an enactment of commissioners in virtue of such a law (*lex data*), a private contract, judicial procedure in general, an ancient formula of consecration (*cf. I.L.S.* 112), or any generally accepted rule.

APPENDIX VII

THE AUTHORSHIP OF THE *LACEDAEMONIORUM RESPUBLICA* ASCRIBED TO XENOPHON

IT might perhaps have been expected that in a critical study of Spartan institutions, and especially in an account of military institutions, more attention would have been paid to the *Constitution of Sparta* ascribed to Xenophon [1] than has been assigned to it in the present work. In this Appendix it is proposed to set forth as briefly as possible the general reasons why the treatise has not been more extensively used as evidence in the preceding study, and to indicate more fully some of the reasons for not accepting the attribution to Xenophon, in spite of the many *prima facie* grounds for doing so.

In the first place, the purpose of the author is clearly didactic rather than critical.[2] A brief chapter of political criticism of Sparta in the author's own time is indeed included,[3] but has only a rhetorical connection with the rest of the work, which consists of an unbroken flow of praise of an obviously idealised Sparta. We may suspect that it emanated from that school of philo-Laconian philosophers (many of them pseudo-philosophers) whose existence at Athens has been very fully demonstrated by Ollier,[4] being a somewhat later example of that *genre* to which the Λακεδαιμονίων Πολιτεία of Critias also belonged.[5]

The work has, in general, been accepted with greater respect than it otherwise merits, on the assumption that the historian Xenophon was its author. But the correctness of the attribution to Xenophon is still by no means settled. The testimony of ancient authors on the matter is not unanimous, and is relatively late ; [6] but even were it completely

---

[1] The attribution to Xenophon is accepted by Bazin, *La République des Lacédémoniens de Xénophon* (1885), by Pierleoni in his edition of the text (Berlin, 1905), and more recently by Ollier (*Xénophon : La République des Lacédémoniens*, text, translation, introduction and commentary, Lyon, 1934).

[2] Ollier (*Le Mirage Spartiate*, 1933, p. 392) rejects this interpretation on the ground that it is incompatible with the attribution of the work to Xenophon, but positive evidence in favour of it will be found in my paper 'The Date and Authorship of the *Respublica Lacedaemoniorum* (Manchester Univ. Press, 1948) ascribed to Xenophon ' in which I argue that the whole work, including the displaced chapter, was written in 395 B.C. (possibly by Antisthenes the Socratic), and that this chapter originally formed the beginning, not the end, of the treatise.

[3] This chapter which appears in all collated MSS. as the penultimate one (XIV) has been displaced from its original position. Ollier (*République des Lacédémoniens*, Introd. p. xvii) suggests that it was written in 378 B.C. by Xenophon as an epilogue, not for publication but to relieve his own feelings of indignation at the policy then being pursued by Sparta.

[4] *Cf.* Ollier, *Le Mirage Spartiate*, pp. 195 f.

[5] See below, p. 494.

[6] *Cf.* Ollier, *Rép. Lacéd.* pp. viii f. Demetrius of Magnesia (first century B.C.) who appears to have denied the authenticity of the treatise, is the earliest of the authors concerned.

united, the verdict of Hellenistic critics would not necessarily prove the attribution to be correct, as may be seen from the example of the *Old Oligarch*, the attribution of which to Xenophon is quite certainly false. Internal evidence of date, style and coincidence of views with those in undoubtedly genuine writings of the same author provides better criteria. In this particular case the indications of date agree well enough with the assumption that Xenophon wrote the treatise, though at an earlier date than the rest of his works. Those who are experts in the matter of style, again, appear to be generally agreed that, so far as this criterion is concerned, the *Respublica* may be the work of Xenophon ; but it is perhaps permissible to suspect that their conclusion has also been influenced on the one hand by the testimony of ancient writers to its authorship, on the other by the indications that the *Respublica* was written a great deal earlier (even on the assumption that it was written after 395) [1] than any of the undoubtedly authentic works of Xenophon. In such a case absolute coincidence of style could not be expected.

With regard to the coincidence of ideas, Ollier writes as follows : ' jamais ouvrage ne porta mieux que celui-là (the *Respublica*) la signature de son auteur. Aucune des idées exprimées qui ne se trouve en parfait accord avec tout ce que l'on sait par ailleurs des idées de Xénophon.' [2] But there is a certain exaggeration here. Ollier himself points to two examples of contradiction ; the scorn for all other armies but the Spartan expressed in the *Respublica* contrasts with the preference for the Athenian organisation expressed in several works of Xenophon, and the admiration which the author of the *Respublica* finds for the system by which the Spartan boys were expected to steal their food is contradicted by the disapproval of Xenophon for this arrangement in the *Anabasis* and the *Cyropaedia*.[3] To these two examples others may be added. In the *Respublica* we read that Lycurgus, thinking of his young bride, πανὺ καλῶς ἦλθε πεπαιδευμένη· ὅπερ μέγιστον ἔμοιγε δοκεῖ παίδευμα καὶ ἀνδρὶ καὶ γυναικί.[8] But in the treatise on Sparta, the normal Greek practice of allowing boys and girls to eat as much as they like is condemned,[9] and Lycurgus' system of semi-starvation is applauded. Again, the wife of Ischomachus was married to him at the age of fourteen,[10] but in the *Respublica* Lycurgus' regulation of the age of

---

[1] *Cf.* above, p. 490, n. 2. [2] *Ibid.* p. viii. [3] *Ibid.* p. xxxiii.
[4] *Resp. Lac.* I, 3, 4. [5] Xen. *Oecon.* VI, 12–17.
[6] *Ibid.* VII, 30–36 ; *cf.* also *ibid.* VII, 6: οὐ γὰρ ἀγαπητόν σοι δοκεῖ εἶναι εἰ μόνον ἦλθεν ἐπισταμένη ἔρια παραλαβοῦσα ἱμάτιον ἀποδεῖξαι ;
[7] *Ibid.* X, 10, 11. [8] *Ibid.* VII, 6.
[9] *Resp. Lac.* II, 1 : ⟨οἱ μὲν ἄλλοι Ἕλληνες⟩ σίτου γε μὴν αὐτοῖς γαστέρα μέτρον νομίζουσι, κ.τ.λ.
[10] Xen. *Oecon.* VII, 5.

marriage, which is to take place for women ἐν ἀκμαῖς τῶν σωμάτων,[1] is approved. The *Respublica* approves Lycurgus' ban on money-making,[2] but in the *Oeconomicus* money-making is accepted as a natural and proper aim for the citizen.[3] Finally, Plutarch quotes from Xenophon a much more liberal opinion with regard to wine-drinking than that professed by the author of the *Respublica Lacedaemoniorum*.[4]

These differences of view are not in themselves sufficiently serious to invalidate the opinion that Xenophon wrote the treatise on Sparta. They are such as might easily develop in the course of a long life, and on the supposition that the treatise on Sparta was written by Xenophon when he was a young man, and was on that account, perhaps, more ready to believe in the desirability of state interference in all the details of private life. As we see from Plato's *Republic*, the teaching of Socrates would be likely to influence enthusiastic young disciples in this direction ; it obviously had this effect upon Critias, leader of the extreme pro-Spartan party among the Thirty, and himself the author of an extravagantly eulogistic Λακεδαιμονίων Πολιτεία.[5]

But there are also contradictions in historical outlook between the treatise under consideration and works which can with certainty be attributed to Xenophon, and here the explanation is by no means so simple. For example, we have the statement of Polybius that Ephorus, Xenophon, Callisthenes and Plato, ' the most learned of the ancient writers ', stressed the resemblance between the constitution of the Cretan towns and that of Sparta.[6] In the *Respublica Lacedaemoniorum*, on the other hand, as Ollier points out, the complete originality of Spartan institutions and their independence of models is a point made at the outset.[7] Convinced as he is of the authenticity of the *Respublica* ascribed to Xenophon, Ollier is forced to conclude that Polybius must have been the victim of confusion in this matter, perhaps because he was relying wholly on memory.[8] But this particular error would not be one which we should naturally attribute to so accomplished a historian as Polybius ; and it is clear that a critic unhampered by previous conceptions about the correctness of the attribution to Xenophon might draw quite a different conclusion from the contradiction in question, namely that Xenophon did indeed write a *Constitution of Sparta*, but that the treatise under consideration (in spite of the testimony of some ancient critics) is not the one. There is, however, yet another possibility which would leave the question of authorship still hanging in the balance. Xenophon may indeed be the author of the *Constitution of Sparta* which now passes under his name, and he may later have changed his mind about the supposed originality of Lycurgan institutions after reading the observations of Ephorus or of Plato on the subject, enshrining his later view in some work which has not been preserved.

But what is to be said about a fundamental difference of outlook between the *Respublica* and works of Xenophon which have actually been preserved ? It can be shown that the *Respublica* is not, as has

---

[1] *Resp. Lac.* I, 6. An indication of the precise meaning may be seen in Plato's fixing of the minimum age of marriage (ἀκμή) for a woman at about twenty years (*Rep.* V, 460 E), while Aristotle fixes it at about eighteen (Pol. VII, 16. 9, 1335a).

[2] *Resp. Lac.* VII. [3] Xen. *Oecon.* XI, 9, 10 ; XX, 26–29.

[4] *Resp. Lac.* V, 4 ; *cf.* Plut. *Ages.* 29.

[5] *Cf.* F.H.G. II, p. 68, and see further below, p. 494, n. 2.

[6] Polyb. VI, 45. 1. [7] *Resp. Lac.* I, 2. [8] Ollier, *op. cit.* p. x.

been suggested, a work of propaganda in favour of Sparta,[1] but rather a eulogy of Sparta in the past combined with an attack on Sparta in the present, and that the date of composition was 395 B.C.[2] But in both the *Hellenica* and in his life of Agesilaus, Xenophon appears as the consistent admirer of Sparta, even after the latest conceivable date for the misplaced chapter of the *Respublica*. In neither of these works does he give any hint of the development of corruption at Sparta or of ceasing to obey the laws, but rather implies that the Spartans were in these respects faithful to their ancient traditions until the battle of Mantinea itself.[3] He also continues to speak of them in both works as the real saviours of Greece in the past, and potentially (from the Persians) in the future.[4]

An explanation not very creditable to Xenophon does certainly suggest itself ; he may have felt less free to express his real views after he had received a grant of land near Olympia from the Spartans,[5] and had permanently settled there (about 392 B.C.), than he felt in 395. He mentions near the end of the *Hellenica* that Elis, to whose territory his estate again belonged at the time when he was writing,[6] was still allied with Sparta at the battle of Mantinea,[7] so that he may never have felt himself free to express his real political opinions. That he was ignorant of the criticisms of Sparta and the Spartans which during this period were being made by others is not credible ; indeed he mentions in his account of the conspiracy of Cinadon the hatred felt for the Spartiates by the Perioikoi and others.[8]

It remains to consider whether the treatise itself contains any positive indications that Xenophon is likely to have been its author. It was, of course, quite natural that Alexandrian scholars should identify it with the Λακεδαιμονίων Πολιτεία of Xenophon. Here is a work written in Attic Greek, by a writer who, in the first place, faithfully reproduces a great many of the ideas of Socrates.[9] Xenophon was a pupil of Socrates, and proves beyond a doubt the extent of his debt to his teacher in the *Memorabilia*, *Apology* and *Cyropaedia*. The last-named work, indeed, is a treatise on education in the manly virtues which might easily be regarded as an expansion and modification of the *Respublica Lacedaemoniorum*.[10] Further, here is a work written (on internal evidence) during the life-time of Xenophon, which, though professing to be an account of the laws of Lycurgus in general, devotes three unusually long chapters out of a total of fifteen to a detailed description of

---

[1] *Cf.* Ollier, *op. cit.* pp. xxi f. [2] *Cf.* above, p. 490, n. 2.
[3] *Cf. Ages.* VII, 2 f. ; *Hell.* VI, v, 42.
[4] *Cf. Ages.* VII, 7 ; *Hell.* VI, v, 43, 48, *ad fin.*
[5] *Anab.* V, iii, 7. [6] *Cf.* Paus. V, 6. 6.
[7] *Hell.* VII, v, 18. [8] *Ibid.* III, iii, 6.
[9] Contemporary evidence for the philo-Laconism of Socrates in general is cited by Ollier, *Le Mirage Spartiate*, pp. 210 f. In particular, *cf.* also Xen. *Memor.* IV, iv, 15, attributing to Socrates warm approval of the Spartan view of the importance of obedience to magistrates which recurs in *Resp. Lac.* VIII, 2.
[10] In the sense that the *Respublica Lacedaemoniorum* is primarily concerned with educational theory in general, rather than with Sparta in particular (see further my work cited above, p. 490, n. 2), while the *Cyropaedia* is clearly a theory of education acceptable to Greeks rather than a historical account of the education of Cyrus. The *Cyropaedia* is a full-length study remarkable for character drawing : the *Respublica* might conceivably be regarded as a skeleton outline written as a preliminary sketch.

contemporary (or allegedly contemporary) [1] Spartan military organisation. The close association of Xenophon with the Spartan army in Asia Minor is made known by his own literary works. Two more chapters in the *Respublica* are devoted to a eulogy of the Spartan kingship—and Xenophon was the close personal friend of Agesilaus, whose biography he has written. No other pupil of Socrates can have appeared to ancient critics so likely as Xenophon to have had an intimate knowledge of Spartan military organisation, with the possible exception of Critias, who was also pro-Spartan, also served as a general, and also wrote a Λακεδαιμονίων Πολιτεία. But enough has been preserved of the treatise in question by Critias to show that the work we are here considering is not the *Constitution* written by him.[2] In any case, consideration of internal evidence of date would show that the treatise which has been preserved in full was written after the death of Critias. This must also have been evident to the ancient critics, who not unnaturally came to the conclusion that the work in question was by Xenophon.

As to the ' Socratic ' character of the treatise, this might equally well be explained by supposing Socrates himself to be the common source both of the undoubtedly authentic works of Xenophon and of the *Respublica Lacedaemoniorum* attributed to him. This explanation would also explain the close coincidence of ideas between the authentic works and this one, a coincidence which has been supposed by modern critics to be in itself almost sufficient to prove that Xenophon wrote the *Respublica*.[3]

Does the military knowledge displayed by the author of the treatise in fact make it likely that Xenophon was the author ? Many reasons make it difficult to believe this. In the first place, it is to be observed that except for a cursory reference to mercenary levies,[4] the treatise is wholly concerned with the citizen army (πολιτικαὶ μόραι) [5] as distinct from Peloponnesian allies and Perioikoi, who are nowhere mentioned. But the only Spartan army with which Xenophon was familiar, at least before 395 B.C. when the treatise seems to have been written, was the army in Asia Minor, in which the only rank-and-file troops from Laconia itself were enfranchised Helots (Neodamodeis),[6] and the only Spartan officers, apart from the commander-in-chief, thirty of the ὅμοιοι who were sent out as the military advisers and subordinates of Agesilaus.[7] There

---

[1] Actually the account seems to be less up-to-date than it professes to be. See further below, pp. 495 f.

[2] *Cf.* F.H.G. II, p. 68 : Κριτίας γράφει· "Ἄρχομαι δέ τοι ἀπὸ γενετῆς ἀνθρώπου, πῶς ἂν βέλτιστος τὸ σῶμα γένοιτο καὶ ἰσχυρότατος, εἰ ὁ φυτεύων γυμνάζοιτο καὶ ἐσθίοι ἐρρωμένως καὶ ταλαιπωροίη τὸ σῶμα, καὶ ἡ μήτηρ τοῦ παιδίου τοῦ μέλλοντος ἔσεσθαι ἰσχύοι τὸ σῶμα καὶ γυμνάζοιτο. This passage (composed at all events before the death of Critias in 403) is clearly the source of several passages in the *Resp. Lac.* (I, 3 ; II, 1, 5, 6 ; V, 3, 8, 9). In the same works Critias described a difficult dancing step which Spartan boys were trained to execute (F.H.G. *ibid.*) ; the author of the extant *Resp. Lac.* may well be referring to this in V, 9 : ὁμοίως τε γὰρ ἀπό τε τῶν σκελῶν καὶ ἀπὸ χειρῶν καὶ ἀπὸ τραχήλου γυμνάζονται.

[3] *Cf.* above, pp. 491 f.

[4] *Resp. Lac.* XIII, 4 mentions ξένων στρατίαρχοι. The use of ξένοι as night guards is also alluded to, *ibid.* XII, 3.

[5] *Ibid.* XI, 4 ; cf. Xen. *Hell.* V, iv, 41 (πολιτικὸν στράτευμα contrasted with σύμμαχοι).

[6] Xen. *Hell.* III, i, 4 (1000) ; III, 2 (2000 sent with Agesilaus).

[7] *Ibid.* III, iv, 2, 20.

was a very high proportion of mercenaries,[1] including the remnants of the Ten Thousand. Other Greek states in the Peloponnese furnished altogether about 10,000 men,[2] a number so large compared with the usual levies from this source at this period that it seems probable that a high proportion of these were also mercenaries.[3] Peltasts armed with javelins [4] were much more in evidence than hoplites,[5] the great need in Asia Minor being an army of attack, not an army of defence. For the same reason continual efforts were made to increase the number of cavalry.[6]

Xenophon himself had the poorest opinion of all sections of this army with the exception of the veterans of the Ten Thousand.[7] Discipline seems to have been entirely lacking ; when Dercyllidas attempted to introduce the stately ritual of sacrifice before a battle,[8] the Peloponnesians were impressed but the Asiatic allies seized the opportunity to run away.[9] Other mass desertions are recorded by Xenophon.[10] Dercyllidas appears to have been better able to prevent his army from plundering their own allies than previous commanders-in-chief had been.[11] But even he had trouble with discipline among the Spartan army commanders,[12] and in general an uphill fight. The Greeks appropriately nicknamed him Sisyphus.[13]

No army, in short, could have been more different from the πολιτικαί μόραι described by the author of the *Respublica*. General composition, distribution of commands, military equipment, morale and discipline, and as a consequence of all the rest, tactics, must have been entirely different.

In the case of tactics, the adoption of two-by-two formation on a route march [14] indicates a fundamental change. According to the author of the *Respublica*, the Spartan citizen army under similar circumstances still marched in threes ; [15] this was a legacy from at least a century earlier.[16] The Spartan army in Asia Minor, when threatened with attack, adopted the hollow square formation [17] (πλαίσιον, πλινθίον) which had been first

---

[1] Taxiarchs and Lochagoi were in command of the infantry (*ibid*. III, i, 28 ; ii, 16) ; and these names seem to have been used elsewhere by Xenophon exclusively of commanders of mercenary troops (*cf. ibid*. IV, ii, 5 ; VI, ii, 18) except when he is referring explicitly to the πολιτικὸν στράτευμα of Sparta.

[2] About 4,000 under Thibron (*ibid*. III, i, 4), another 6,000 under Agesilaus (III, iv, 2).

[3] *Cf. ibid*. V, ii, 20 (proposal to supply another 10,000).

[4] *Cf. ibid*. III, ii, 4.   [5] *Ibid*. IV, iii, 15.

[6] *Ibid*. III, iv, 15. The high proportion of cavalry in the later campaigns is indicated by the fact that out of five Spartiates appointed to command the main sections of the whole army, two were assigned to the cavalry (*ibid*. III, iv, 20).

[7] *Cf. ibid*. III, ii, 18.   [8] *Cf. Resp. Lac.* XIII, 8.

[9] Xen. *Hell.* III, ii, 17.

[10] *Ibid*. IV, i, 22, 26–28 (under Agesilaus).

[11] *Ibid*. III, ii, 6, 7.   [12] *Cf. ibid*. III, i, 28.

[13] *Ibid*. III, i, 8.   [14] *Ibid*. III, i, 22.   [15] *Resp. Lac.* XI, 4.

[16] The ' triple snake ' of Herodotus VI, 77, and the three combined snakes of the Delphic column, both refer to armies under Spartan command, and must certainly refer to marching formation.

[17] *Cf. Hell. Oxyr.* VI, 3 ; VII, 2, and for the general character and purpose of the πλινθίον, Arrian, *Tact.* 29. 8, 30. 2.

used (as it would appear) by Brasidas in Thrace,[1] and was later copied by the Athenians in Sicily,[2] and by the Persians.[3] Of this formation there is no hint whatever in the detailed account of Spartan army drill in the *Respublica*.

Thus, while the Spartan army which Xenophon knew in Asia Minor was inferior in discipline and training, it was in many respects more up-to-date than the Spartan citizen army described in the *Respublica*. The new tendency was for greater weight and a more compact formation in the centre, and for greater mobility on the wings by the use of peltasts and cavalry, than the Spartans adopted at this time in Greece. Xenophon himself ridicules the Spartan cavalry force of the period, as used by them in Greece.[4] The richest citizens furnished the horses, and any further equipment which might to the individual seem suitable, and the least fit and able citizens were detailed to ride them, as need arose and without previous training. This description may be brought into connection with the τριακόσιοι ἱππεῖς καλούμενοι,[5] who fought as hoplites in the later fifth century, but were doubtless still required, as in earlier times, to furnish horses for the state. Xenophon's strictures imply that the small trained cavalry force instituted in a crisis in 424[6] had only a short-lived existence.

Could the real Xenophon give unqualified approval (as the author of the *Respublica* always does) to an army which was in many respects outmoded, and which he himself condemns so heartily in respect of the absurd organisation of the cavalry ? Or could the real Xenophon, supposing him to be the author of the *Respublica*, write in the following terms of the Spartan cavalry force : ' Lycurgus made six Morai both of cavalry and of hoplites, and each of these citizen Morai had one Polemarch, four Lochagoi, eight commanders of Fifties, sixteen Enomotarchai ' ?[7] This passage, implying a cavalry force equal in size and parallel in organisation to the hoplite one, neither agrees with the information just cited from Xenophon, nor corresponds to reality (so far as can be ascertained) at any period in Spartan history. But even more striking is the ignorance of the hoplite arrangements which the author of this passage reveals by following it to its logical conclusion. He assumes the ' six Morai both of cavalry and of hoplites ' to mean not six of each, but three of each, as appears quite incontestably from his account of the transformation from line of march to line of battle.[8] But the real Xenophon knew very well that in the πολιτικὸν στράτευμα

---

[1] *Cf.* Thuc. IV, 125 (ἐς τετράγωνον τάξιν). The absence of a technical term here, as contrasted with Thuc. VI, 67 ; VII, 78, suggests a recent innovation at the time when Thucydides revised his history of the Ten Years' War.

[2] *Ibid.* VI, 67 ; VII, 78.

[3] *Cf.* Xen. *Anab.* I, 8. 9 (of the army of Tissaphernes).

[4] Xen. *Hell.* VI, iv, 11 (referring to 371 B.C.).

[5] Thuc. V, 72. 4 ; *cf. Resp. Lac.* IV, 3.

[6] Thuc. IV, 55. 1 : παρὰ τὸ εἰωθὸς ἱππέας τετρακοσίους κατεστήσαντο.

[7] *Resp. Lac.* XI, 4 : μόρας μὲν διεῖλεν ἓξ καὶ ἱππέων καὶ ὁπλιτῶν κ.τ.λ.

[8] *Cf. Resp. Lac.* XIII, 6 : ἦν δέ ποτε μάχην οἴωνται ἔσεσθαι, λαβὼν τὸ ἄγημα τῆς πρώτης μόρας ὁ βασιλεὺς ἄγει στρέψας ἐπὶ δόρυ, ἔστ' ἂν γένηται ἐν μέσῳ δυοῖν μόραιν καὶ δυοῖν πολεμάρχοιν, *i.e.* until the Mora which he is leading is flanked on each side by a Polemarch in command of another Mora (*not* until there are two Morai on each side of him, which would imply an army of five Morai, not six). οὓς δὲ δεῖ ἐπὶ τούτοις τετάχθαι no longer applies to the πολιτικαὶ μόραι, as is obvious from the change of command.

there were six Morai of hoplites,[1] and this had been the case in the previous century also.[2] He also reveals complete ignorance about the three hundred ἱππεῖς καλούμενοι, who fought as hoplites, by assuming that they were drawn from the Epheboi under the age of twenty.[3] This confusion is doubtless due to a better knowledge of the Athenian than of the Spartan system of military training.

In his detailed description of tactics, the author of the *Respublica* reveals by many small indications that he is not, as Xenophon was, an expert in such matters. It is incredible, for instance, that the battle order of all the rest of the forces with the exception of the citizen Morai should have been decided by the eldest present among the committee of civilian advisers (οἱ περὶ δαμοσίαν).[4] At the battle of Mantinea this was certainly decided by the king ;[5] in Asia Minor (and probably in Greece also), the Spartan ξεναγοί were responsible.[6] Again, the author of the treatise sneers at professional teachers of the art of war (ὁπλομάχοι) for finding any difficulty in executing the transformation from column of march to battle line in various situations ;[7] for the Spartans, he says, it is all ' perfectly simple ' (εὐπορώτατα ποιοῦσι). After giving various other examples, he cites the case of an unexpected enemy advance on the right hand of the approaching column. All the Spartans have to do in such a case, he says, is ' merely ' to turn each λόχος (a company of 128 men) round ' like a trireme ' to face the enemy.[8] This betrays the mentality of the Athenian trierarch, unable to adapt himself to the complications of infantry manoeuvres. But if by some wheeling movement a company of 128 men, marching three or six abreast,[9] did achieve a new position at right angles to its original one, the depth of the line of battle would be either about forty-three or about twenty-one. Yet at the battle of Leuctra, where the greatest possible depth of line was required to withstand the fifty deep of the Thebans, the Spartans only managed to achieve a depth of twelve ;[10] their more normal arrangement would appear to have been eight.[11] From the account which Xenophon gives of this exceptional arrangement at Leuctra, it is also clear that he thought that the unit employed in the wheeling operation in question was not the Lochos, but the smaller Enomotia.[12] In view of the prevailing uncertainty among

---

[1] *Cf. Hell.* VI, i, 1, together with VI, iv, 17.

[2] *Cf.* Thuc. V, 68. 3 : λόχοι - - - ἑπτὰ ἄνευ Σκιριτῶν includes also the Βρασιδεῖοι (λόχος is here used in place of the more accurate name μόρα).

[3] *Cf.* p. 133.   [4] *Resp. Lac.* XIII, 7.

[5] Thuc. V, 71. 3 ; *cf. ibid.* 66. 3 : βασιλέως γὰρ ἄγοντος ὑπ' ἐκείνου πάντα ἄρχεται.

[6] *Cf.* Xen. *Hell.* IV, ii, 19 ; *cf.* (for the use of ξεναγοί in Greece Thuc. II, 75, 3 ; Xen. *Hell.* V, ii, 7.

[7] *Resp. Lac.* XI, 8.

[8] *Ibid.* XI, 10. Xenophon's use of the same phrase ἀντίπρῳρον ὥσπερ τριήρη in *Hell.* VII, v, 23 is confined to the head-on attack, and implies no turning movement. The phrase itself doubtless occurred in some well-known work on tactics, being used to describe the specially strengthened striking-head (ἔμβολος) of an advancing force.

[9] *Cf. ibid.* XI, 4 : ἐκ δὲ τούτων τῶν μορῶν διὰ παρεγγυήσεως καθίστανται τότε μὲν εἰς ἐνωμοτίας, τότε δὲ εἰς τρεῖς, τότε δὲ εἰς ἕξ. The last two cases refer to the marching column. *Cf.* Xen. *Hell.* VI, iv, 12 : τοὺς μὲν Λακεδαιμονίους ἔφασαν εἰς τρεῖς τὴν ἐνωμοτίαν ἄγειν.

[10] Xen. *Hell.* VI, iv, 12.   [11] *Cf.* Thuc. V, 68. 3.   [12] Xen. *ibid.*

Greek military writers as to whether the Enomotia was identical with the Lochos or a quarter of its size,[1] it seems probable that the author of the *Respublica* has confused two different accounts, and that instead of ascribing the wheeling operation to the Lochos, he should (to be consistent with his own account of the sizes of these various units)[2] have ascribed it to the Enomotia. Such uncertainty does not suggest practical acquaintance with the evolution in question. In point of fact, the description which the author gives of the trireme-like manoeuvre is appropriate enough to the wheeling movement of a much smaller unit in the typical Greek army,[3] also referred to as the Lochos by Arrian, but certainly containing only sixteen men.[4]

The fact seems to be that in his account of the Spartan army drill, the author of the *Respublica* follows the opinion of the military writers who regarded the names λόχος, ἐνωμοτία and στίχος as interchangeable,[5] but fails to observe that their account is not applicable to the Spartan army, in view of its very different organisation and use of military terms[6] as compared with typical Greek hoplite armies. The conclusion which follows is that the author is not a military expert at all, otherwise he would

---

[1] Arrian, *Tact.* 6. 2.

[2] *Resp. Lac.* XI, 4 (four Enomotiai to the Lochos).

[3] *Cf.* Arr. *Tact.* 21. 3 : ἐπιστροφὴ δέ ἐστιν, ἐπειδὰν τὸ πᾶν σύνταγμα πυκνώσαντες κατὰ παραστάτην καὶ ἐπιστάτην καθάπερ ἑνὸς ἀνδρὸς σῶμα ἐπὶ δόρυ ἢ ἐπ' ἀσπίδα ἐγκλίνωμεν, καθάπερ ἐπὶ κέντρῳ τῷ λοχαγῷ παντὸς τοῦ τάγματος περιελιχθέντος, καὶ μεταλαβόντος τόπον μὲν τὸν ἔμπροσθεν, ἐπιφανείαν δὲ τὴν ἐκ δεξιῶν, διαμενόντων ἑκάστῳ τῶν τε ἐπιστατῶν καὶ παραστατῶν. ' The ἐπιστροφή is when we close up the whole unit two by two (lit. ' by odd and even men ', *cf. ibid.* 6. 4, on the arrangement of the Lochos in single file, alternately ἐπιστάτης and πρωτοστάτης), and incline it to right or left as if it were one man, the whole line revolving about the leader of the Lochos as a centre, and taking up the same relative position as before, but facing at right angles to it, each man keeping his original companion on right or left ' (ἐπιστάτης or παραστάτης as the case might be).

[4] For the number in the Lochos referred to in the preceding note, *cf.* Arr. *Tact.* 5. 5 ; 9. 6 ; 10. 1.

[5] *Cf. ibid.* 6. 1 : τὸν δὲ λόχον καὶ στίχον ἤδη τινες ὀνομάζουσιν, οἱ δὲ δεκανίαν, τυχὸν οἷς ἐκ δέκα ὁ λόχος ἦν. ὑπὲρ δὲ τῆς ἐνωμοτίας ἀμφιγνοούμενόν ἐστιν · οἱ μὲν γὰρ ἄλλο ὄνομα τῷ λόχῳ εἶναι τοῦτο, οἱ δὲ τὸ τέταρτον τοῦ λόχου ἐνωμοτίαν καλοῦσιν. Arrian himself uses the terms λόχος and στίχος indiscriminately in his account of the Λάκων ἐξελιγμός (a reversing movement, *cf. ibid.* 24). The author of the *Resp. Lac.* also speaks of the στίχος as performing the ἐξελιγμός (XI, 8) although he has just been speaking of the ἐνωμοτία as the operational unit. Similarly, in *Resp. Lac.* XI, 10 the λόχος suddenly appears as the operational unit, although ἐνωμοτία and στίχος have hitherto been named in that capacity.

[6] The relative sizes of the various Spartan units and the names assigned to them in *Resp. Lac.* XI, 4, have the support of Xenophon and of Thucydides, apart from the latter's mistake in substituting the name *Lochos* for that of *Mora* in the case of the largest unit. The identification of the *Enomotia* as one-sixteenth of the largest unit (32–36 men) appears in all three authors ; in all three the Lochos is at least four times as large ; *cf.* Thuc. V, 67 ; Xen. *Hell.* VII, iv, 20 (12 Lochoi after Leuctra) ; VI, iv, 12 (36 men or less in the Enomotia).

have observed these discrepancies; still less is he an expert on the military organisation of Sparta.

As a final comment on the problem of authorship, it is worth noting that Arrian, who reveals profound admiration for Xenophon as an expert on military matters,[1] either did not know of the existence of this treatise, or knowing of it,[2] did not attribute it to Xenophon. For he says that Xenophon did not specify the size of the Lochos in relation to the Enomotia,[3] whereas the author of the *Respublica* distinctly implies, by his enumeration of the various grades of officers,[4] that there were four Enomotiae to the Lochos. The list of authorities which Arrian claims to have consulted for his work on Tactics is a formidable one, and includes many who dealt only incidentally with the subject.[5] It seems most unlikely that he would have omitted the treatise on Sparta by Xenophon if the work had been generally attributed to Xenophon at that time.[6] The denial of its authenticity by Demetrius of Magnesia [7] in the time of Cicero was evidently still accepted by the critics. On the other hand, the attribution to Xenophon was accepted by Pollux,[8] so that the view which eventually prevailed with the critics seems to have been introduced (or more accurately, revived) in the second half of the second century or a little earlier. Arrian may perhaps have been unaware of the new attribution which was already being made in some quarters.

There are undoubted echoes of the *Respublica Lacedaemoniorum* in authentic works of Xenophon, and also in other fourth century authors; but the investigation of this subject is not appropriate to the present inquiry, which seeks merely to justify the somewhat reserved attitude towards the document in question which has been adopted in the main body of this work.

---

[1] Cf. Ἔκταξις κατὰ Ἀλανῶν, 10 ; *Tact.* 6. 3, 29. 8.

[2] The author may possibly be alluded to in *Tact.* 6. 2 among those writers who regarded the Enomotia as a quarter of the Lochos.

[3] *Tact.* 6. 3 : Ξενοφῶν δὲ πόστον μὲν μέρος τοῦ λόχου ἡ ἐνωμοτία ἐστίν, οὐ διασαφεῖ.

[4] *Resp. Lac.* XI, 4 (four Enomotarchae to each Lochos).

[5] Cf. *Tact.* 1.

[6] The *Tactica* were composed in the twentieth year of Hadrian (*Tact.* 44. 3).

[7] Cf. above, p. 490, n. 6.   [8] *Onomastikon*, VI, 142.

TABLES OF LATER SPARTAN KINGS

AGIADAE[1]

*Generation from
Eurysthenes* [1a]

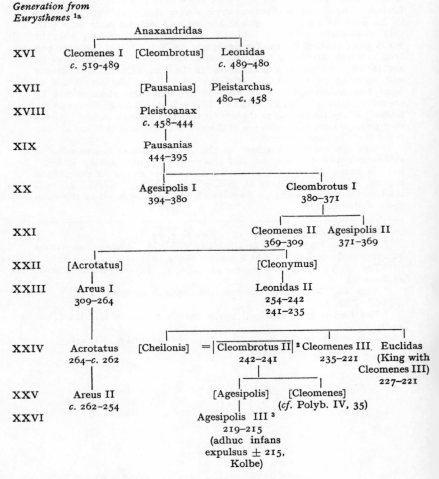

	Anaxandridas		
XVI	Cleomenes I *c.* 519–489	[Cleombrotus]	Leonidas *c.* 489–480
XVII		[Pausanias]	Pleistarchus, 480–*c.* 458
XVIII		Pleistoanax *c.* 458–444	
XIX		Pausanias 444–395	
XX		Agesipolis I 394–380	Cleombrotus I 380–371
XXI			Cleomenes II Agesipolis II 369–309 371–369
XXII	[Acrotatus]		[Cleonymus]
XXIII	Areus I 309–264		Leonidas II 254–242 241–235

XXIV	Acrotatus
	264–*c.* 262
		[Cheilonis] = Cleombrotus II [2]
		242–241
			Cleomenes III Euclidas
			235–221 (King with
			     Cleomenes III)
			     227–221

XXV	Areus II *c.* 262–254	[Agesipolis] [Cleomenes] (*cf.* Polyb. IV, 35)	
XXVI		Agesipolis III [3] 219–215 (adhuc infans expulsus ± 215, Kolbe)	

[1] Names in brackets indicate collaterals who did not reign.

[1a] For earlier generations see the table on p. 334.

[2] A collateral, precise descent unknown.

[3] The thirty-first king of the Agiad line, including Eurysthenes.

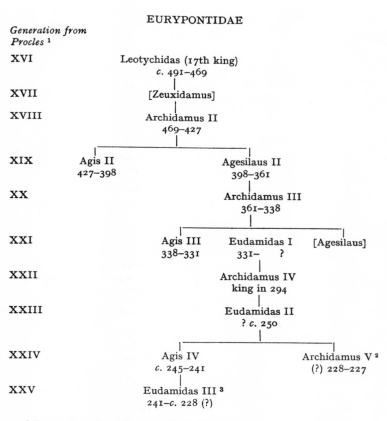

EURYPONTIDAE

Generation from
Procles [1]

XVI   Leotychidas (17th king)
                c. 491–469

XVII   [Zeuxidamus]

XVIII   Archidamus II
                 469–427

XIX   Agis II   Agesilaus II
       427–398   398–361

XX   Archidamus III
                       361–338

XXI   Agis III   Eudamidas I   [Agesilaus]
         338–331   331–   ?

XXII   Archidamus IV
                 king in 294

XXIII   Eudamidas II
                 ? *c.* 250

XXIV   Agis IV   Archidamus V [2]
        c. 245–241   (?) 228–227

XXV   Eudamidas III [3]
        241–*c.* 228 (?)

[1] For earlier generations see the table on p. 334.

[2] Twenty-eighth king of the Eurypontid line, including Procles.

[3] According to Paus. II, 9. 1, II, 10. 6, ' Eurydamidas ', but the names of his ancestors indicate rather ' Eudamidas ', for which see also I.G. V, i, index.

I. SUBJECTS

A

Achaean League, supported by Rome (199), 28, 29 ; gains Sparta (192), 37 ; controls Sparta (192–179), 45 ; gives privileges to Sparta (183), 47 ; attitude to Sparta (182), 49 ; strategoi of (249–215), 431 f.

Acriae, town of Free Laconian League, 56 ; πολιτικὴ χώρα at, 286.

Acrotatus, Spartan King (Agiad), 500.

Aegiae, in Spartan territory under Principate, 57.

Aegytis, location of, 65, 70 ; lost to Sparta after Cleomenes III, 22 ; taken from Sparta by Antigonus Gonatas, 66 ; restored to Sparta *temp.* Polybius, 67.

Aetolians, alliance of Cleomenes III with, 22 ; organise murder of Nabis (192), 37.

Agasicles (Hegesicles), Spartan king (Eurypontid), 330 f., 334.

Agathoergoi, at Sparta, 305, 313.

Age-classes, at Sparta, 86 f. ; in army, 388 f. ; *see also* Agelae.

Agelae (at Sparta), 86 f. ; position of Boagoi in, 116 ; place in Agoge, 95 f. ; come under state control, 425 ; social classes in, 116 ; Plutarch on, 84 ; (in Crete), 85, 219, 220, 222.

Agelaoi (in Crete), 229.

Ager Dentheliatis, *see* Dentheliatis.

Agesilaus I, Spartan King (Agiad), 324, 334, 338.

Agesilaus II, Spartan King (Eurypontid), 353, 358, 359, 363, 493, 494, 501 ; generalship of, 370.

Agesipolis I, Spartan King (Agiad), 500.

Agesipolis II, Spartan King (Agiad), 500.

Agesipolis III, Spartan King (Agiad), 500 ; elected (219–218), 23 ; exiled by tyrant Lycurgus, 25 ; death of, 25.

Agiad Kings, at Sparta, 473 ; list of earlier, 334 ; list never varies, 333 ; list drawn from lyric poet, 338 f. ; celebrated in Alcman's *Partheneion*, 339 ; list of later, 500.

Agis I, Spartan King (Agiad), 334.

Agis II, Spartan King (Eurypontid), 501.

Agis III, Spartan King (Eurypontid), 404, 501.

Agis IV, Spartan King (Eurypontid), 501 ; occupies Pellene, 3 ; economic reforms of, 5 ; gives citizenship to Perioikoi, 5 ; distribution of landlots by, 12, 15, 287 ; revives Lycurgan constitution, 343 ; death of, 3, 8 ; compared with Gracchi by Plutarch, 8.

Agoge, at Sparta, date of introduction, 311 f. ; constitutional importance of, 117 ; foreigners' belief in rigour of, 118 ; educational aspect of, 118 f., 130 ; military character of, after 600, 312 ; in period after Nabis, 46 f., 49 f. ; abolished by Philopoemen, 85 ; restored by Romans, 85 ; Aristotle on, 84 ; Plutarch on, 84 ; ps.-Xenophon on, 84.

Agogic Classes, at Sparta, lists of, 442 f.

Agoranomoi, at Sparta under Principate, 143.

Agrianios, Dorian month name, 277 n.

Alagonia, Perioikic town in Messenia, 298 ; in Free Laconian League, 56, 435, 440.

Alaric, his invasion of Sparta causes abandonment of city, 83.

Alcamenes, Spartan King (Agiad), 334.

503

506   ANCIENT SPARTA

B

Babyka, in Lycurgan Rhetra, 415 ; meaning of, 485 f.
Barbosthenes Mt., in Spartan territory, 70.
Bardounia r., in territory of Thalamae, 59.
βασιλεύς, used of nobles, 399 ; tribal leaders in early states, 409, 412 ; meaning in Homer, 400.
Belbina, on Spartan frontier, 146 ; occupied by Cleomenes III, 9.
Belbinatis, taken from Sparta by Antigonus Gonatas, 66 ; lost to Sparta after Cleomenes III, 22 ; recovered by Sparta (146 B.C.), 67.
Bidyoi (Bideoi), at Sparta, functions of, 137, 158 ; number of, 143.
Boagoi, at Sparta, meaning of title, 95 ; functions of, 96, 98, 116 ; not same age as Agela, 96 ; age of, 95 f. ; annually appointed like magistrates, 97 f. ; relation to Kasens, 105, 451 ; relation of Kasens to, 107 ; relation of Synepheboi to, 107, 108, 459 ; dedicate sickles in παιδικὸς ἀγών, 98 ; alone dedicate after Hadrian, 99 ; drawn from privileged class, 111, 451 ; relation to Patronomoi, 451 ; lists of, 442 f. ; lists of, with Synepheboi, 459 ; Plutarch on nature of, 84.
Boeae, town of Free Laconian League, 56 ; three ephors at, 283 ; cults at, 285 ; coinage of, 438.
Boeotian, Constitution (447–386), 16, 18 ; governor in Sparta after Cleomenes III, 22.
βωμονίκης, meaning of, 131 f., 135 ; in whipping ceremony at Orthia temple, 264.
Brasiae, see Prasiae.
Brasidas, generalship of, 370 ; Helots under, in Thrace, 39
Brasideioi, in Spartan army, 386.

C

Caenepolis, town of Free Laconian League, 56 ; new name for Taenarum, 56.
Callicrates, strategos of Achaean League, 43, 50.
Caphyae, Peloponnesian town, joins Cleomenes III after Dyme, 12.
Cardamyle, Perioikic town in Messenia, 298 ; three ephors at, 283 ; given to Sparta by Augustus, 440 ; remains in Spartan territory under Principate, 56 ; lead mines near, 76 ; site of town moved in early Empire, 58 ; convenient port for shipping animals from Taygetus, 80 ; useless for export of marble, 74.
Carnean festival at Sparta, arrangements at, 342, 392 f.
Carnion, r., sources of, in Aegytis, 65 ; S.W. boundary of Aegytis, 70.
Carthage, treaty with Philip V of Macedon, 25.
Caryae, fortress on N. frontier of Sparta, 69.
Cassandra, cult of, at Amyclae, 258.
Castellani, agricultural class in Laconia in second century B.C., 42 ; Livy's description of, 38 ; in inscription of Aemilius Paullus (in Spain), 38 ; relation to Helots, 38 ; personally free, 39.
Chaeron, Spartan exile, 48, 49 ; attempts revolution at Sparta (181), 48.
Charillus, Spartan King (Eurypontid), 331 f., 334, 338, 344 f.
Cheeses, in whipping ceremony at Orthia temple, 262 f.
χιλιαστύς, at Sparta, size of, 297, 350 ; in Cos, 342.
Chilon, Spartan ephor, extends power of ephorate, 402, 405 f.
Choerius r., on W. frontier of Spartan territory, 60, 62, 63 f. ; upper valley lost by Sparta after Cleomenes III, 22.

H

33

M

Penteleum, joins Cleomenes III, 12.
Perioikoi, at Sparta, 272 f. ; numbers of, 288 ; military contingents from, 288 ; racial origins of, 274, 278 ; relations of, with Sparta, 287 f. ; towns of, on Messenian coast, 288 ; in Messenia, 298 ; in east Messenia before First War, 300 ; pre-Dorian cults in towns of, 285 ; Dorian cults of, 282 f. ; treatment of, by Agis IV, 5, 429 ; towns of, under Achaean League, 21, 37, 41 ; triple ephorate among, 403.
Pharmakoi, relation of to whipping ceremony at Sparta, 264 f. ; scourged at Athens, 260, 265.
φᾶρος, offered to Orthia, 252.
Pheneus (Peloponnesian town), joins Cleomenes III, 12.
Pherae, town of Free Laconian League under Augustus, 435 ; formerly Perioikic, 435.
Phiditia, see under Syssitia.
Philip V, alliance with Carthage, 25 ; invades Laconia (218 B.C.), 24 ; relations of, with Nabis (197 B.C.), 28.
Philokareinos, Boagos in two successive years, 97, 448.
Philopoemen, at battle of Mantinea (207 B.C.), 26 ; relations of, with Messenia (201 B.C.), 30 f. ; enslaves ex-Helots, 40 ; overthrows Spartan constitution *ap.* Livy, 43.
Phlegon (of Tralles), on history of Olympic festival, 321.
Phlius, joins Cleomenes III, 12.
Phloiasios, Dorian month name, 277 n.
Phratriae, at Sparta, in Carnean festival, 392 f. ; in early army, 393.
Phylarchus, source of Plutarch's account of Sparta (*c.* 240 B.C.), 4 ; history of, criticised by Plutarch, 4 ; by Polybius, 4 ; borrows from Ephorus, 6.
Phylae (Dorian), see under Dorians.
Phylae (athletic), at Sparta, nature of, 154, 165, 168, 317 ; number of, 164 f., 168 ; in late period, 162 f. ; see also Limnaeis, Konooureis, Neopolitai, Pitanatai, Mesoa.
Phyllikos, Dorian month name, 277 n.
φυλοβασιλεῖς, relation to army, 409 ; at Sparta, 409 ; at Athens, 409 ; at Cos, 409.
πῖλος, later Spartan helmet, 362 f., 365.
Pitanatai (Phyle), at Sparta, 154, 163 ; (Lochos of), interpretation of, 314 f., 318.
Pithos, moulded, from Sparta, with representation of Skiritai, 379 f. ; illustrated Pl. 9.
Plataea (battle of), Spartan organisation at, 314 ; Eirenes at, 318.
Platanistas, at Sparta, scene of sham fight in Agoge, 118.
Plato, on Sparta, 206 ; imitated by Polybius, 32 ; on importance of dancing in education, 124 f. ; on songs suitable for education, 129 ; resemblance to Sparta of his *Republic*, 129 ; account of ephebic training in his *Laws*, 130 ; on promotion of classes in his *Republic*, 221.
Pleistarchos, Spartan King (Agiad), 500.
Pleistoanax, Spartan King (Agiad), 500.
Pliny (Younger), on Maximus' office in Achaea, 53.
Ploas (lochos), at Sparta, 315, 392.
Plutarch, on Agelae, 84 ; on Agoge, 84 ; on Boagos, 84 ; on economic reforms of Agis IV, 5 ; compares Agis IV and Cleomenes III with Gracchi, 4 ; on changes in Spartan constitution (192–179 B.C.), 46.
Polichna, Perioikic town, recovered from Argos by ' tyrant ' Lycurgus, 24.
Politeuma, at Sparta, *temp.* Cleomenes III, 18 ; of Cyrene, 17 ; Aristotle on, 17.

II. PASSAGES AND INSCRIPTIONS QUOTED.[1]

[1] Only passages and inscriptions from which actual quotations are made are included in this Index.

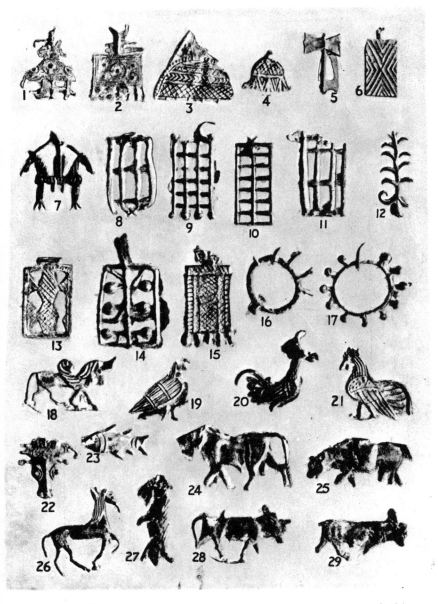

PLATE 2.—Symbols and Attributes of Orthia (*Artemis Orthia.*, Lead II) Scale 2 : 3 (see pp. 250 f.).

PLATE 3.—LEAD FIGURES OF ORTHIA (*Artemis Orthia*, Lead I and II) Scale 2 : 3 (see pp. 250 f., 267).

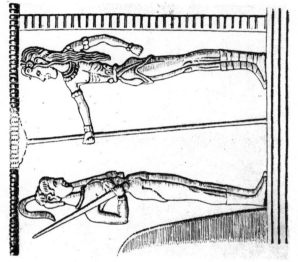

(a) The Minoan Goddess (seal from Cnossos).

(b) "Young Prince" and Officer on Hagia Triada Cup.

PLATE 4.—THE SICKLE AS A CRETAN WEAPON (see pp. 254 f.).

(*a*) Clay Seal from Cnossos.

(*b*) Gold Signet-Ring from near Candia.

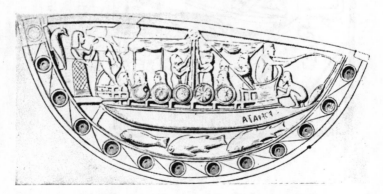

(*c*) Ivory Relief of a Warship from Sanctuary of Orthia,
Sparta.

PLATE 5.—THE CRETAN AND THE SPARTAN GODDESS
(see pp. 256, 266 f.).

PLATE 6.—THE MINOAN GODDESS.
Faience Statuette from Cnossos (see pp. 267 f.).

PLATE 7.—LEAD FIGURES OF SPARTAN WARRIORS.
(Nos. 1-22, Nos. 23-30 Lead V.)   Scale 2 : 3 (see pp. 260 f., 381 f.)

PLATE 8.—PAINTED TOMBSTONE FROM THEBES (see pp, 364 f.).

PLATE 9.—PITHOS WITH COMBAT AND CHARIOT SCENES FROM
SPARTA (see pp. 379 f.).

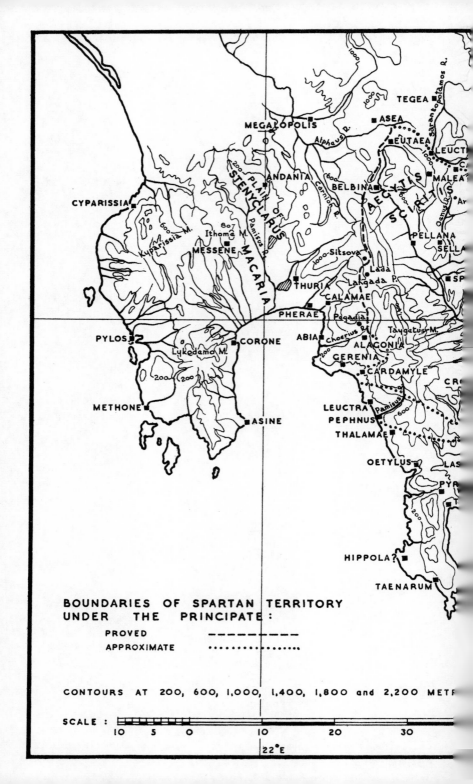

BOUNDARIES OF SPARTAN TERRITORY
UNDER THE PRINCIPATE :
PROVED ———————
APPROXIMATE ················

CONTOURS AT 200, 600, 1,000, 1,400, 1,800 and 2,200 METR

SCALE :

10	5	0	10	20	30

22°E

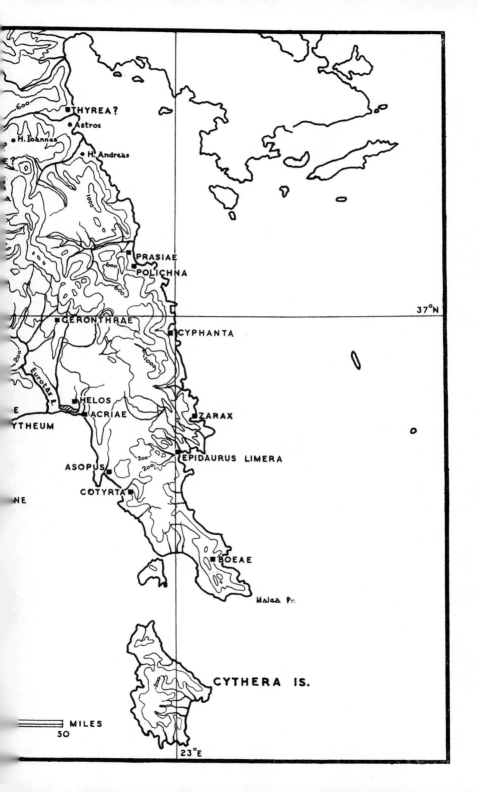

600

THYREA?

● Astros

● H. Ioannes

● H. Andreas

1000

■ PRASIAE
POLICHNA

600

600

37°N

■ GERONTHRAE

■ CYPHANTA

200

Eurotas L.

1000

■ HELOS
■ ACRIAE

YTHEUM

■ ZARAX

ASOPUS ■

200

COTYRTA ■

200

■ EPIDAURUS LIMERA

NE

■ BOEAE

Malea Pr.

CYTHERA IS.

MILES
50

23°E